THE PEREGRINE FALCON

THE
PEREGRINE FALCON

Second Edition

DEREK RATCLIFFE

With illustrations by

DONALD WATSON

T & A D POYSER

London

Text © Derek Ratcliffe, 1980, 1993
Illustrations © Donald Watson, 1980
ISBN 0–85661–060–7

First published, 1980
Second edition in 1993 by T & A D Poyser Ltd
24–28 Oval Road, London NW1 7DX

United States Edition published by
ACADEMIC PRESS INC.
San Diego, CA 92101

A catalogue record for this book
is available from the British Library

Text set in Erhardt
Typeset by Phoenix Photosetting, Chatham
Printed and bound in Great Britain by
Mackays of Chatham, PLC, Chatham, Kent

This book is printed on acid-free paper

ISBN 0–85661–060–7

To my parents

Contents

List of Photographs

COLOUR PLATES　*facing page*

List of Figures

List of Tables

Preface to the First Edition

This is a book mainly about the Peregrine in Great Britain. Its content is drawn from three principal sources: my own experiences of the bird in England, Wales and Scotland beginning in 1945, talk and correspondence with numerous other Peregrine fanciers, and gleanings from a fairly large but scattered literature. Whilst I believe that much of what may be said about the Peregrine in Britain applies also to Ireland, my acquaintance with the bird in that country is slight, and Irish Peregrines are not dealt with in any depth. I have not attempted a detailed review of work on the various races of this almost cosmopolitan species, and only selective reference is made to Peregrines in other parts of the World, mainly as seems relevant to the better understanding of the natural history of the British bird. On certain topics, notably behaviour, the most detailed work has been done on other races of Peregrine, and it has seemed appropriate to make extensive reference to these studies, since they appear to be valid for our subspecies. A whole book would be needed to deal adequately with the Peregrine and falconry, and since I am ill-equipped to handle this topic, it is mentioned largely as an important historical aspect of the bird's relationship with Man.

My field experience with Peregrines is mostly in the breeding season, and in inland haunts. I have seen relatively little of coastal nesting falcons and do not know the bird in southern England or south Wales. My earlier field-work on the species was as a hobby, during holidays and weekends, and although I was able to work virtually full-time on Peregrines during 1961–62, as organiser of the British Trust for Ornithology's national enquiry, and was involved in pesticide studies for some years afterwards, of late my interest has had to be, again, mainly a spare-time concern.

This book naturally emphasises those aspects of Peregrine natural history which have interested me most. It has no pretentions to scientific sophistication and, though some parts are more technical than others, I have tried to present ecological concepts as simply as possible. My intention has been to write the story of the bird in an ever-changing scene to which it has so far adjusted with remarkable success, though this is no longer true in many parts of the World. A great many people have written and spoken of their experiences with Peregrines, and I have tried to build some of this knowledge into the account, not only to reinforce content and accuracy but also in tribute to their contribution. Often, relevant passages are quoted, sometimes at length, to convey the originality and perceptiveness of many references. Some of the comments in older works which so clearly anticipate the erudite findings of modern animal ecology are specially fascinating. A reference which does not relate to the Bibliography can be assumed to indicate a personal verbal or written communication or other unpublished source of information. I have also deliberately resorted in places to what are sometimes termed 'anecdotal observations' in an attempt to infuse some life and leavening into the text when this seems in danger of becoming too heavy with abstract generalisations. While isolated observations run the risk of being misleading when broad principles are needed, they can sometimes give a useful pointer in the right direction.

The need, in the interests of the Peregrine itself, to minimise the use of names of extant nesting places leaves me with the sense that contact with field reality is in danger of being lost at times. If, therefore, I have occasionally broken the rule on this, I hope local Peregrine well-wishers will forgive me and accept that the places named are so well known, or so inaccessible, or so long deserted that further anonymity is pointless. I have generally used the names of the old counties since these are more sensible units than the new. Most of the regional avifaunas and other sources of historical records are based on the old counties, and these relate to the valuable Watsonian vice-county system which has for so long been the standard geographical basis for biological recording in Britain. English names of birds, mammals and plants are used in the text, but species lists with scientific names are provided in the Appendix. There follows a brief mention of the major literature sources. County avifaunas are a fruitful source of information on the species though only some of the recent examples are particularly enlightening over exact numbers or details of distribution.

The book by Francis Heatherley (1913) was a valiant first attempt to depict the Peregrine at the eyrie, and its rearing of the young, and is outstanding for the quality of the photographs taken by Heatherley and his colleagues, especially bearing in mind the limitations of the equipment then available. It is sad but necessary for the record to point out that his text contains serious errors of fact and misinterpretations of observations. Some of the confusion evidently stems from an attempt to merge three seasons' observations into one, but the worst flaw is the evidently mistaken identity of the two sexes and their roles in the care of the young.

One of the best early accounts was by John Walpole-Bond in 1915, and in 1938 this remarkable nest-hunter published in his *History of Sussex Birds* a long synopsis of his experiences with the Peregrine. This essay is written in a colourful style, and is an excellent general account of nesting biology and habits. E. B. Dunlop (1912), H. A. Gilbert (1927), D. Nethersole-Thompson (1931) and B. H. Ryves (1948) contributed interesting essays, and the papers by I. J. Ferguson-Lees (1951, 1957) gave valuable summaries of the data acquired during the first Peregrine surveys of Britain in the early post-war years. The major ornithological works on British birds are an invaluable source of reference material. The classic *Handbook* of 1939 was followed by the superb Bannerman and Lodge volumes, with their captivating specialist essays, and now we have the second volume of *Birds of the Western Palearctic*, by Stanley Cramp and his team and containing a most comprehensive distillation of virtually all major sources of information on the Peregrine in Europe. I have used their terminology for displays and calls for the sake of standardisation.

Two books have recently appeared on the Peregrine in Britain. That by J. A. Baker (1967) is a remarkable work with primarily a literary impact, and tells in somewhat extravagant style the story of Peregrines wintering on the lowlands bordering the Essex coast. The author has assured me of its factual accuracy, and the account of winter prey selection is one of the few available. It is a fascinating book, which Peregrine enthusiasts should read for its originality of approach.

Dick Treleaven (1977) has recently written a delightful book on the Peregrine in the West Country. Packed with fresh and vivid accounts of the bird straight from the field, and skilfully enlivened further by the author's own drawings, it conveys the special magnetism of the bird in its setting on this rugged coastline. The enthusiasm never flags and there are splendid descriptions of hunting tactics against a background of Atlantic breakers surging at great cliffs. I have found it a valuable source of ideas and information.

Treleaven (1980) has also written another extremely useful paper on hunting behaviour, and the detailed observations by Parker (1979) at an eyrie with young are an important source of material on the nestling/fledgling period. A. S. Cooke, A. A. Bell and M. B. Haas have just provided a synthesis of the Monks Wood analytical studies of organochlorine residues in British raptors, including the Peregrine.

On the European continent, the book *Der Wanderfalk* by Wolfgang Fischer (1967) is a valuable and full review of published work on Peregrines in various parts of the World, supplemented by its author's observations on the bird in Germany. The observations on behaviour at the eyrie contained a good deal of new material at the time. The *Handbuch der Vögel Mitteleuropas* by U. N. Glutz von Blotzheim and his colleagues contains important summaries of data on all aspects of continental Peregrines, and the review of status of *Birds of Prey in Europe* by M. Bijleveld (1974) gives details of Peregrine numbers and trends for each country. The symposium on Fennoscandian Peregrines reported in *Pilgrimsfalk*, edited by P. Lindberg (1977), is another up-to-date source of data for this region.

In the North American literature there are five outstanding works. Joe Hickey's 1942 paper in *Auk* on the Peregrine population of the eastern United States is a classic, and suggests that this form was extremely close ecologically to that in Britain. This study gains in importance from the sad fact that this population is now extinct, and it was the earliest published regional survey of a falcon population. Frank Beebe's 1960 account of the race known as Peale's Falcon in the Queen Charlotte archipelago is fascinating as a description of the densest Peregrine population yet known, and portrays a falcon with a food adaptation somewhat different from that of the British bird, living on the sea cliffs and feeding on the myriad seafowl of strange conifer-grown islands in the cool, humid and misty climate of this eastern Pacific region. It is full of interesting observation which its author, an experienced falconer, brings to bear.

Tom Cade (1960) has given a marvellous account of the natural history of both Peregrine and Gyr Falcon in Alaska. Written with appropriate scientific detachment, it is a scholarly and very readable work packed full of information and ecological insight, yet manages to convey the splendour and solitude of this great wilderness, which so dwarfs anything that we have in Britain. This is a study made possible only by hard physical effort and exploration, in the tradition of the old traveller naturalists. The Peregrine is a bird which usually gives up its secrets only to the more energetic kind of field worker, but how especially was this the case in Alaska before 'development' began.

In 1969 there was published the monumental Proceedings of the 1965 Madison Peregrine Conference, the testimony to Joseph Hickey's energy and inspiration in bringing about this great occasion. *Peregrine Falcon Populations: Their biology and decline* is the largest synthesis of information on the species yet available, and its numerous papers collectively afford a mine of information. The important discussions of many topics are also reported in some detail. Wayne Nelson's (1970) unpublished MS thesis on the breeding behaviour of Peregrines on Langara Island in the Queen Charlottes is a most painstaking and detailed account of the bird at the eyrie, and I have made repeated reference to his descriptions of behaviour.

Finally, there is the now large and scattered literature on pesticides and Peregrines, produced by groups of scientists on both sides of the Atlantic. I shall not make specific reference to any one work here, but have indicated some of the key papers at appropriate places, notably in Chapter 13.

Preface to the Second Edition

Two key events in the last decade have required that this book be revised. The first is the continuing increase in Peregrine numbers in Britain and Ireland, and dramatic recovery of many populations elsewhere in the World. The second is the publication of much new information on the biology of the species, both in these islands and in other countries.

Although well aware that they will soon again be out of date, I have up-dated the population figures in the light of the available information. In Britain this has been supplied especially by the third and fourth National Peregrine Surveys of the British Trust for Ornithology in 1981 and 1991. Since the pesticide situation does not appear to have shown any significant changes during the last 13 years, I have left my treatment of it almost unaltered. The most important additions to our knowledge of the Peregrine's natural history in the British Isles have been about population dynamics, movements and nesting adaptations. In the first edition I drew selectively upon overseas information to give a wider geographical perspective on the bird than that of Britain and Ireland alone, and to illuminate certain aspects of the species' biology. It was in no sense an attempt at a book on Peregrines worldwide. While I have made modest revisions to these aspects, the second edition of *The Peregrine Falcon* remains essentially a book about the bird in Britain and Ireland.

Much of the new information worldwide was brought together in the magnificent volume of papers from the second international Peregrine Conference, at Sacramento, California, in November, 1985. The Sacramento proceedings have now provided a book on Peregrines of the World, and for serious enthusiasts everywhere, the new volume, *Peregrine Falcon Populations, their Management and Recovery*, should be required reading.

Acknowledgements

I owe more than I can ever say to the late Ernest Blezard, my informal tutor in natural history, whose knowledge and wisdom were profound and whose love of his native Lakeland and its wildlife was so inspiring. Ernest was the most remarkable naturalist I have ever known and I count it a privilege to have been his friend. He encouraged my youthful enthusiasm but without ever 'talking down' and he had an endearing patience with youngsters eager for knowledge. Later, during innumerable sessions round his fireside and outings in the field, I learned a great deal more from his lore, his craft and his philosophy. He set high standards but never lost humility, and he could see the wood as well as the trees. Ernest was an all-round naturalist but had a specialist knowledge of birds and did remarkable work on their food. His ability to identify feathers presented to him randomly was not the least of his talents, and one which I made free use of over my prey remains. To Dorothy Blezard and Peter, Andrew and Crispin, I express my appreciation for much kindness and friendship over the years.

Desmond Nethersole-Thompson sought me out in Edinburgh to discuss a Dotterel note I had published, but the talk soon turned to Peregrines. It was 1960, when the BTO Peregrine Enquiry was just beginning. Desmond gave me his lists of nesting haunts and also one of contacts likely to help, and he has kept the closest interest in the Peregrine story every since. He has given me much valuable information on the history of the Peregrine in Sussex and the West Country, and on various aspects of breeding biology. Among his many helpful thoughts in discussion and comment on drafts, I am especially indebted to his suggestion that I should weigh a series of old and recent Peregrine eggshells to test my tentative idea that the recent wave of egg-breaking might result from thinner shelled eggs. Without his help also in gaining access to collections with recent eggs, the shell-thinning saga would not have unfolded in such a convincing way. Desmond encouraged me to write this book and he and his wife Maimie have given unflagging support while I worked at the task.

I shall forever be grateful to the British Trust for Ornithology for inviting me in 1960 to organise their Peregrine Enquiry and thereby allowing me to work on Peregrines as my job. The Council, Officers and Members of the Trust have given me unfailing support, and in particular I thank the Ringing and Migration Committee for permission to use the Peregrine ringing data held by the Trust. Chris Mead has most kindly provided analysis of these records and has drawn relevant maps for me to use. Bob Spencer supplied valuable information about weights of birds and patiently dealt with a selection of queries. My co-workers in the field during the 1961–62 and 1971 Enquiries, as employees of the Trust, were K. D. Smith, David Wilson, John Morgan and John E. Davis, who made marathon rounds of eyries in the remote places of Britain with great success.

The Nature Conservancy, my employers, encouraged my participation in this work and I thank Max Nicholson, then Director-General, for his support and keen interest then and ever since. When I moved to the Conservancy's Monks Wood Experimental Station in 1963, the then Director, Kenneth Mellanby, and Derek Ovington, head of the Woodlands Section (in which I worked for a while), allowed me to spend part of my time working on Peregrines within Norman Moore's Toxic Chemical and Wildlife Section. Monks Wood was a most stimulating place to work at and there was a special excitement when the pesticide battle was at its height. I look back with great pleasure on my time there. To Norman Moore, who more than anyone pioneered the field of pesticide/wildlife studies in Britain, I owe a great debt for his encouragement, help and interest in the Peregrine work. Without his years of patient and wearing committee work within the bureaucracy, our boffin efforts would have counted for very little and there would probably be fewer Peregrines flying around this country today. I greatly enjoyed working closely with Ian Prestt, Don Jefferies, Tony Bell and John Parslow, and received much help from Selene Knowles and Margaret Haas. I also thank Jack Dempster, Frank Moriarty and Arnold Cooke for their helpful discussion and information on pesticide problems.

Pesticide work is impossible without the dedicated support of analytical chemists who perform the routine laboratory measurements of tissue and egg residues, and whose part in the conservation of the British Peregrine population is sometimes in danger of being overlooked. For their vital part in the combined effort I express my deep gratitude to the staff in the Laboratory of the Government Chemist, especially J. O'G. Tatton and D. C. Holmes and their colleagues; Neville Morgan, George Hamilton and their colleagues in the East Craigs Laboratory of the Department of Agriculture and Fisheries for Scotland; Colin Walker, Michael French and Paul Freeman of Monks Wood Experimental Station; and Jim Bogan of the Department of Veterinary Pharmacology in the University of Glasgow.

Many people helped me by allowing access to egg collections when I was seeking peregrine eggshells to measure, and I am most grateful to C. J. O. Harrison, I. C. J. Galbraith and M. P. Walters of the British Museum (Natural History), I. Lyster of the Royal Scottish Museum, D. Clarke of the Carlisle Museum and the various owners of private collections who have preferred to remain anonymous. Ian Newton very kindly measured a further large series of Peregrine eggshells, and for making this material available I thank also the Keepers of the National Museum of Wales, The City of Liverpool Museums, The Sheffield Museum and the Glasgow Museum, and a further group of owners of private collections. I am also grateful to John Temple Lang for giving me a copy of his measurements of Irish Peregrine eggs in the National Museum of Ireland.

C. Tyler, Professor of Biochemistry and Physiology in the University of Reading, very kindly measured the thickness of a series of Peregrine and Sparrowhawk eggshells for me and made helpful comments on the eggshell work, and Arnold Cooke has given me invaluable advice and information on eggshells and wildlife/pesticide matters in general.

John Mitchell has generously spent much time in finding, abstracting and copying references on Peregrines for me, and has given many helpful ideas which I have worked into this book. Through the kindness of S. Sloane Chesser, who has the John Walpole-Bond diaries, and Ian Newton, who abstracted the data, I have had the use of this unrivalled series of nesting records of British Peregrines. R. Wayne Nelson has most generously allowed me to quote from his unpublished MS thesis on the behaviour of the Peregrine, and Tom Cade kindly supplied me with a translation of *Der Wanderfalk*. Stanley Cramp, Ken Simmons and Peter Olney have been most helpful in allowing me to use their unpublished material on the Peregrine in the forthcoming *Handbook* Vol. II, and I thank Ken Simmons and M. G. Wilson for giving me a copy of the latter's translation of the Peregrine section from *Handbuch der Vögel Mitteleuropas*. Philip Oswald has given much help over historical reference material in the Cambridge University Library, and has translated the Medieval Latin text of Albertus Magnus. I am grateful to Dorothy Blezard for lending me her late husband's beautifully written and detailed field journals, to Christopher Perrins for allowing me to consult E. B. Dunlop's diaries in the Edward Grey Institute Library, and to the late Marjory Garnett for copies of the Peregrine records of J. F. Peters and J. Coward. Miss M. Lawrie gave me the records made by her father and lent me negatives from his extensive series of Peregrine photographs. J. A. Gibson kindly gave me copies of Dugald Macintyre's articles on Peregrines as well as his own data for the Clyde area. Janet Kear drew my attention to interesting references to Siberian Peregrines. Colin Osman has given helpful discussion on the homing pigeon issue, as well as copies of his writings on this subject.

A very large number of people have helped me in one way or another with information on Peregrines. Those who have contributed directly have been acknowledged in my various papers, but many others whose records have been passed to me by these contacts have remained anonymous. I thank again this legion of informants and regret that personal acknowledgement of every one is not possible here. For invaluable historical Peregrine records of various kinds I am much indebted to the late G. D. Abraham, T. Adam, E. K. Allin, G. Allsop, C. Best, F. C. Best, R. J. Birkett, H. M. S. Blair, D. Brown, R. H. Brown, W. A. Cadman, B. Campbell, R. Chase, W. M. Condry, the late D. Cross, P. R. K. Davis, G. Douglas, P. Douglas, G. Franklin, W. Gibbs, P. Glasier, I. E. Hills, Mrs A. Hughes, D. Humphrey, S. Illis, W. R. Laidler, A. McArthur, R. Newman, D. Nethersole-Thompson, P. J. Panting, the late P. W. Parminter, C. A. Parsons, I. D. Pennie, H. Platt, C. H. Pring, A. Rendall, J. Robson, H. Morrey Salmon, P. W. Sandeman, the late E. S. Steward, R. Stokoe, the late G. W. Temperley, B. A. Tolley, G. Tomkinson, G. Took, C. R. Tubbs, N. Usher, J. Verhees, A. Watson, A. D. Watson, H. Watson, J. E. Wightman, the late K. Williamson, Mrs E. J. Wilson, K. L. Wilson and M. H. Woodford.

Some of the above have also helped with recent Peregrine breeding records, but my special gratitude is due to a dedicated group of helpers whose enthusiasm in the field and in other ways has enabled me to follow the fortunes of the Peregrine through the exciting and anxious times since the population took the unexpected plunge revealed by the BTO enquiry in 1961–62.

Doug Weir has been most generous in supplying me over many years with the data on his Spey Valley Peregrines which he has collected so conscientiously each year in his long-term study of this population. His records along with those collected annually by Adam Watson, David Rose and Graham Simpson on the Deeside and Angus hills to the east, were crucial to the case for pesticide effects on Peregrines, by establishing that a normal falcon population still existed in the area of lowest contamination risk. Roy Dennis and Jonathan Hardey have more recently helped to extend monitoring of the central Highland Peregrines, and during the last few years Roy has organised a Royal Society for the Protection of Birds survey of Peregrines over a large part of the northern Highlands, with help from R. Broad, P. Ellis, D. Peirce, B. Hendy, G. Bates and G. Dickson.

Since 1965 John Mitchell has, with the assistance of John Mason, annually surveyed breeding Peregrines in the south-west Highlands and the outlying foothills to the south. More recently Bob MacMillan, Don MacCaskill and Patrick Stirling-Aird have extended survey north-eastwards from the Trossachs area through much of Perthshire. Mike Gregory has checked eyries in part of southern Argyll for many years, and in 1979, David Fleming made a Peregrine survey of mainland Argyll for the RSPB. Kenneth Graham and Iain Hood have followed the falcons of the Kintyre peninsula during recent years, and Sue King, E. Bignal, I. Hopkins and J. A. Gibson have supplied data for Arran. In Ross-shire and Skye, Dick Balharry followed a widely spread group of eyries. In Orkney, the RSPB officer, Eddie Balfour, sent me an annual report until his death in 1974. Bobby Tulloch of the RSPB also contributed records for Shetland. R. D. Lowe conducted surveys for the RSPB over part of north-east Scotland in 1978–79.

In Galloway Dick Roxburgh has devotedly covered all the inland nesting haunts for many years, and sent me superbly vivid and detailed accounts of his findings. George Carse has checked the eastern Southern Uplands with great dedication and faithfully kept me informed of results. Since 1974 Richard Mearns has conducted a detailed study of the population biology of the Southern Scotland Peregrines under the direction of Ian Newton. This project has involved a detailed ringing and colour ringing programme, and is developing radio-telemetric tracking of Peregrines. It is likely to go far towards filling major gaps in our knowledge of British Peregrines, and I am grateful to its authors for allowing me to mention some preliminary findings.

Jim Birkett has given me the benefit of his unrivalled knowledge of Lakeland Peregrines going back to 1933, and has continued to provide me with records ever since. Geoffrey Horne has systematically monitored the Peregrines of the northern half of Lakeland for many years, and Terry Pickford has lately complemented this by covering the southern half. Both Geoff and Terry have contributed to the colour ringing programme organised by Ian Newton, as well as to the BTO scheme. Geoffrey Fryer and formerly Frank Parr have also provided much valuable information on Lakeland Peregrines. Walter Thompson, the late Bill Robson and Colin Armitstead have been my main sources of data on the falcons of the Yorkshire–Cumbrian Pennines, while Sedbergh School Ornithological Society has provided records from the Howgill Fells for a long period.

In Wales, during recent years, Graham Williams of the RSPB has most valuably collated survey data for all counties and given me a synthesis. I thank all those who have contributed towards his reports, and acknowledge also the information sent to me directly in earlier years by T. A. W. Davis and J. W. Donovan. Dick Treleaven has long been my main source of information on Peregrines of the West Country, and was among the very first to realise that things were amiss with the falcon population after 1955, and to help put the finger on pesticides as the cause. He has eagerly followed the pattern of recovery and, with many other local ornithologists, especially R. Khan, has kept a watchful eye on the fortunes of the Devon and Cornwall Peregrines.

In Northern Ireland, M. Gilbertson, J. S. Furphy, and C. L. McKelvie, have supplied me with information on status, while the RSPB have made available the results of their 1977–79 surveys organised by Dinah Browne in collaboration with Joe Furphy. In the Republic of Ireland John Temple Lang has conducted Peregrine surveys and most kindly kept me informed about the results of these. Besides providing copies of the unpublished reports to the Irish Wildbird Conservancy by himself, D. Norriss and B. Holden, he has also helped me over the section on Ireland in Chapter 4. I am also indebted to Brian Holden for allowing me to see his confidential report on the 1973 survey and his detailed analysis of several years' data for the Irish Wildbird Conservancy.

I thank also the following who have contributed records at various times in recent years: P. J. Dare, R. C. Dickson, L. S. Garrad, J. M. Harrop, P. Hope-Jones and J. Watson. The Royal Society for the Protection of Birds has always been most helpful and anxious to contribute to the study of the Peregrine situation. The former Director, Peter Conder, and the present Director, Ian Prestt, have allowed their staff to contribute in many ways and I express my appreciation of their support and the assistance given by George Waterston, Frank Hamilton, John Hunt, Roger Lovegrove and Peter Robinson, in addition to the officers already named. The recent RSPB campaign of wardening and surveillance of eyries has been a significant factor in the increase in breeding performance in some areas.

Many of the field workers have helped further by taking addled eggs (under licence) for chemical analysis, and the trouble taken by various people to send in dead Peregrines has been invaluable. Data on food have been contributed by E. Blezard, F. Parr, R. Roxburgh, D. Weir, R. Mearns, R. D. Lowe, J. Morgan, K. D. Smith, P. Glasier and J. Hardey. I am also indebted to E. Blezard and A. Allison for identification of prey remains.

Joe Hickey, formerly Professor of Wildlife Ecology in the University of Wisconsin, Madison, has been a tremendous source of encouragement and stimulation for many years and I owe him a deep debt of gratitude for his help and friendship. Tom J. Cade, Professor of Zoology at Cornell University, New York, has been most kind in giving me information, and I have made much use of his lifetime's work on North American Peregrines. I express thanks also to Walter and Sally Spofford, Ithaca, New York; Morlan and Pat Nelson, Boise, Idaho; Clayton M. White, Provo, Utah; James H. Enderson, Colorado Springs, Colorado; Richard Fyfe and Harry Armbruster, Edmonton, Alberta; and Tony Keith and Iola Price, Ottawa, Ontario. All these American and Canadian friends have shown great interest in the Peregrine story over here, besides taking me to see Peregrine haunts in their own marvellous countries.

My field companions over the years have been numerous, but it has been a particular pleasure to be in search of Peregrines with Bill Robinson, Ian Prestt,

Stuart Illis, Jim Birkett, Chris Durell and John Mitchell. I have discussed Peregrines with more people than I can remember, but for their special help with information or with comments on sections of this book I am immensely grateful to Derek Langslow, Art Lance, Ian Prestt, Ian Newton, Don Jefferies, Chris Durell, Arnold Cooke and John Birks. I thank other colleagues in the Nature Conservancy Council for their help and interest in the Peregrine work over the years. The Director, Scotland, J. Morton Boyd, has maintained a keen interest in events, and I thank him and his Regional Officers, J. Grant Roger, Sandy Kerr, Niall Campbell, Mike Matthew and Eddie Idle for their support, and especially in allowing Warden staff to conduct field survey of Peregrines in Scotland. Many other Regional staff in England, Wales and Scotland have also supplied me with information on Peregrines. Tony Colling and Alan Lennox have been most helpful over licencing issues. I am grateful to Shirley Penny and Malcolm Rush for library services, and to Robin Fenton and Peter Wakely for photographic assistance.

To my present employers, the Nature Conservancy Council, I acknowledge facilities, information and other help which has accrued through my official position, though the views expressed in this book are my own and are not to be taken as representing those of the Council.

Donald Watson has gone to great pains to satisfy my fastidious instructions on illustrations, and I thank him for his beautiful paintings and drawings which so well convey the character of the bird and the atmosphere of its country. I am also indebted to the several photographers whose names are acknowledged on the Plates.

An appreciative word is due for the anonymous staff of the Ordnance Survey, without whose dedicated labours in the field we should all be bereft of our most basic tool. I thank them for making field studies possible and for giving enormous pleasure besides. The landowners on whose land I have worked are too numerous to mention individually, and I make collective acknowledgement to their help. The staff of the Forestry Commission have always been most helpful over access and with information on Peregrines on their ground.

It is a special pleasure to thank the kind friends with whom I stayed in the Southern Uplands of Scotland: Will and Mary Murdoch, then of Dregmorn in the Galloway Hills; John and Elizabeth Borthwick, then of Polmoodie in the Moffat Hills, and the late Louisa McGarva of Craigenbay in the Galloway Hills. I have the happiest memories of times spent with them in their lonely homes deep amongst the hills.

My father did everything he could to encourage my youthful enthusiasm for natural history and was always so interested to learn of my exploits in the field. My mother mended socks, washed clothes, made packed lunches and the supper on my return, and worried greatly if I was late, but always supported and encouraged me. I owe so much to their help.

I thank Lynne Simmons for her help in the typing of the final draft and in other ways. Jeannette, my wife, has done the rest of the typing and I am deeply grateful for all her help, not least her enthusiasm and encouragement over the writing of this book.

Further Acknowledgements

The recent Peregrine story in Britain and Ireland is largely the work of an immensely committed group of people who have laboured mightily in the field, and then painstakingly set down their findings for the record. I am even further in the debt of all those Peregrine enthusiasts who have continued to supply me with information, and those who have joined in this data provision since 1979. Without their generous and unflagging help, there would have been little justification for a thorough revision of this book. In particular, I thank again the faithful recorders who have charted the recovery of Peregrine populations since the dark days of the 1960s: Geoff Horne in Cumbria, Dick Roxburgh in Galloway and Ayrshire, George Carse in the eastern Southern Uplands, John Mitchell in Stirling and Dumbartonshire, Patrick Stirling-Aird in Perthshire, Roy Dennis in Highland Region, Adam Watson and Jonathan Hardey in Grampian Region, Graham Williams in Wales, Colin Tubbs on the Isle of Wight, Dick Treleaven in Cornwall and Joe Furphy in Northern Ireland.

I am grateful besides to the following people who have provided information since 1979:

Southern England

Heather Woodland, Steve Jackson, Katherine Hearn and National Trust field staff in Devon and Cornwall; Treleaven Haysom, Granville Pictor and Ronnie Baker in Dorset, W. J. Webber in Somerset, J. Cox in the Isle of Wight, Chris Durell and Bart Atfield in Sussex, and Bryn Green in Kent.

Wales

Iolo Williams has during the last few years collated for the RSPB the records of a large number of observers in the Principality. The county organisers in 1991 were Alastair Moralee, Bob Corran, Duncan Brown, Reg Thorpe, Graham Williams, Peter Davis, Tony Cross, Steve Roberts, Jerry Lewis, Richard Poole, Jack Donovan and Bob Haycock. I thank Adrian Fowles for extracting Peregrine records from the diaries of the late J. H. Salter, and Graham Williams for giving me the records of the late J. H. Howell.

Northern England

Paul Stott, Carl Smith, Paul Marsden and Terry Pickford in Bowland and southern Lakeland; Clive Varty, John Armitage, Malcolm Priestley, Chris Hind and Geoff Carr in Yorkshire; Dave Sharpe in Lancashire; Geoffrey Fryer, Derek Hayward, John Davidson and Bob Buchanan in Lakeland; Terry Wells, Ian Findlay, Paul Burnham, Colin Armitstead, Fred Birkbeck, Ron Baines and John Miles in the northern Pennines; and Brian Little in Northumberland.

Southern Scotland

Richard Mearns in Dumfries and Galloway, South-west Scotland Raptor Study Group in Galloway and Ayr.

Highlands and Islands

Roger Broad in Highland Region, Argyll, Stirling, Dumbarton and Perth; Sandy Payne in Perth; Claire Geddes in Aberdeen; Tayside Raptor Study Group in Perth and Angus; Grampian Raptor Study Group in Kincardine, Aberdeen and Banff; Stuart Rae in Sutherland; Eric Meek in Orkney; and Dave Okill and Peter Ellis in Shetland.

Northern Ireland

Joe Furphy, Dinah Browne, Jim Wells, A. J. Balbi, R. Ellis and C. S. Dawson.

Republic of Ireland

John Wilson, David Norriss, Declan McGrath and Gabriel Noonan.

I am much indebted to various friends for other help and kindnesses. Tom Cade invited me to the second Peregrine Conference in Sacramento in 1985, where I had great discussions with North American and other colleagues. Gordon Court generously presented me with a copy of his MSc thesis detailing his valuable study of a Peregrine population in northern Canada. In New South Wales, Jerry and Penny Olsen most hospitably received my wife, Jeannette, and myself, besides introducing us to Australian Peregrines and giving the benefit of enthusiastic exposition of their studies of this and other birds. John Wilson and David Norris invited me to accompany them on a most enjoyable tour of their Peregrine country in Co. Kerry.

I have had further valuable discussions with Geoff Horne, Dick Roxburgh, Ian Newton, Arnold Cooke, John Mitchell, Ian Prestt and Dick Treleaven. Des Thompson has given me critical comments on some of the revised text, and he and Sue Holt have undertaken statistical analysis of data and prepared some of the graphs.

Chris Mead has most ably analysed the now large body of ringing data for the British Peregrine, and generously contributed an account of the findings on movements and mortality. I thank him and the British Trust for Ornithology for providing this invaluable help. It is especially in this field that substantial new information has accumulated since 1979, but I thank also the actual ringers whose energies, and willingness to risk life and limb on the cliffs, have provided the basic data. My gratitude is due also to John Cooper for his kindness in adding a new section on diseases of the Peregrine.

This new edition depended very much on a comprehensive updating of knowledge of Peregrine status in the United Kingdom. In 1991, the British Trust for Ornithology sponsored the fourth national survey of the Peregrine breeding population, and this was organised by Humphrey Crick. It involved mainly the seeking of the help of the already well-established network of Peregrine monitoring by various key individuals and regional raptor study groups that have been formed in recent years. Regional Representatives of the BTO also contributed as appropriate. I am much indebted to the Trust and Dr Crick for allowing me to use the survey results as the crucial basis for revising the population picture. A separate report to the Trust on the 1991 survey is in preparation, and will acknowledge the help of individual participants. The BTO have also kindly allowed me to reproduce the map of the Peregrine in their *New Atlas of Breeding Birds in Britain and Ireland* (in press).

I am grateful also to Birdlife International, and especially Melanie Heath, for allowing me to use the latest population figures from the European Bird Database (EBD), which they run jointly with the European Bird Census Council.

Although I did not feel that the pesticide story merited further elaboration in this revision, I cannot let the occasion pass without paying some tribute to the work of Jim Bogan who died tragically while on holiday in France. Dr Bogan was one of the small band of chemical analysts whose dedicated efforts in the laboratory provided the factual basis from which restriction and eventual withdrawal of the organochlorine insecticides came about. Without this vital scientific evidence there would have been no recovery of the Peregrine population, and no grounds for a second edition of this book. Jim Bogan was a keen naturalist who laboured long and hard to supply objective data to the conservation cause, and we should salute his contribution to the success story that we now celebrate.

It is sad also to mention the deaths of various friends whose help and/or companionship was acknowledged in the first edition: Desmond Nethersole-Thompson, Stanley Cramp, Bill Robinson, Walter Thompson, John Borthwick, Will Murdoch and David Rose.

Trevor Poyser was enthusiastic about a new edition and, in taking over management of the Poyser imprint, Andy Richford has warmly encouraged me to proceed, while showing great forbearance over the delay in its completion. I greatly appreciate his help and advice and that of Carol Parr, in bringing it into being. Finally, I owe much again to the support and encouragement of my wife, Jeannette.

Introduction: a reminiscence

When, as a small boy, I first became interested in birds, my imagination was fired by the pictures of a fierce-looking and beautiful bird of prey which the books said was rare, nesting only on the most formidable cliffs, and surpassing all other birds in its powers of flight. The descriptions and colour plates of the bird's eggs, said to be regarded by collectors as one of the greatest prizes on account of their exceptional variety and beauty of colouring, was enough to whet the appetite of any bird's-nesting boy. My father borrowed for me from the adults' library other books written by the great field naturalists and photographers of an earlier generation, and the vivid accounts of their experiences in the wild places of Britain conjured up a romantic vision of the Peregrine and its country. The local museum had one of the most skilfully presented exhibitions of birds in the whole country and was a most appealing place. I used to pore over the mounted specimens in their habitat settings, and was especially captivated by the Peregrines – wonderful creatures which had once graced the hill country not far away.

One day, my father took me to see the museum curator who was known to guard in his inner sanctum a magnificent egg collection which he would unlock and show on request. I gazed in fascination at these treasures, but above all at the drawer with its series of clutches of large, rich red eggs, mottled and blotched so variously that hardly two were exactly alike. I marvelled at the prowess of the god-like beings who had so evidently come to terms with my bird, and then the curator, by a casual remark, made it apparent that he was himself one of these supermen who could track down and reach the eyries of the Peregrine Falcon among the Lakeland fells. From then onwards, I knew there would be no rest for me until I too was on intimate terms with this beguiling bird.

During two holidays with my parents in the Lake District, I saw something of the country wherein Peregrines were said to live and nest, but gained little enlightenment. My parents were not fell-goers and our walks were confined to the roads and well-worn lower tracks, whilst I was too young to be allowed off alone. The difficulties and dangers in my future quest seemed, if anything, to increase; there were so many cliffs, and the most likely looking, often viewed through mist and rain, were horribly steep and tall. As I grew older I became more venturesome in the range of exploration around home, and with a friend hunted the farmland and woods, the lonely peat mosses and the great flat expanses of saltmarsh bordering the Solway, in search of birds and their nests. My pocket money went on bus fares and maps, and I invested in Bartholomew's one inch sheet of the Lake District. It was fascinating to pore over this and make plans, and my eagerness to penetrate the fell country finally overcame parental anxieties and objections.

Some pioneering trips to Lakeland, in search of nesting Buzzards, planned largely on the basis of likely-looking woods on the maps, were successful and encouraged me to think of tackling the birds of the crags. During the autumn of that year, 1944, I did some prospecting among the fells, for information about the whereabouts of Peregrines was difficult to come by. The bird books themselves were extremely reticent about naming nesting places, though a few supposedly deserted haunts were mentioned. When, on subsequent visits with specimens to my hero, the curator, I raised the question of Peregrines nesting on particular cliffs, the replies were so guarded as to be discouraging – 'Oh, they have done' or 'they could do'. I took to reading through more general works on the hill country, by mountaineers, walkers and others with no more than a casual interest in birds, and here I began to pick up clues from passing mentions of the mountain birds. A few writers had, however, taken a deeper interest in the fell creatures. I found great inspiration in an essay from the pen of Canon Rawnsley, 'After the Ravens in Skiddaw Forest' – a tale beautifully told in the full and gracious prose of its author's time, but remaining fresh and vivid to this day; it is, to me, one of the gems of Lakeland literature.

My prospecting trips produced at least one certain Raven nesting place, and the following February saw me after the Ravens myself, armed with a couple of sixty foot hemp plough-lines bought at a local ironmonger's. By the end of March I had found three Raven nests with eggs and triumphantly climbed to the easiest of them. The Raven cliffs included one of my main Peregrine hopes mentioned in two of my books, but when April came in I still had not located any falcons. I decided to try first a certain Westmorland crag figured in several books and mentioned by one as a Peregrine haunt. On the 21st of the month, an early train set me off at a country station nearest to my mountain destination, and I could not cover the intervening seven miles fast enough. Mid-day saw me at the crest of the crag facing down the head of a long dale to spacious plains beyond. Following the level crag top, I scanned the ledges below. A Buzzard's skirl was followed by an unfamiliar chattering call, and there high over the dale was what I judged to be a Peregrine tiercel stooping at a pair of these hawks. The Buzzards departed and the falcon planed down to a rock high on the fell above. Much encouraged, I continued to follow the crag edge, peering tensely down each face. At one point a recently killed Fieldfare lay near the edge and when I looked over there was a sudden movement as a blue-grey form flung itself from a ledge and out over the screes below. My gaze turned quickly from the fleeing falcon to the rock below where, on a grassy shelf, lay three beautiful eggs, reddish brown mottled with white.

The intensity of excitement at such moments is perhaps something reserved for youth, but then the young tend to have simple ambitions which can be achieved in a wholly fulfilling way. It was certainly the impetuosity of youth which set me clambering down that sheer wall to reach the eyrie. And there at last was the marvellous bird in life, cruising up and down for me to admire, and filling the dale with its strident chatter. I was at one with the gods and it was a very happy if weary schoolboy who boarded the northward-bound train that day. There have been many red-letter days in my life as a field naturalist, but none to eclipse this one.

This was beginner's luck, but it held. A week later I crept along a ledge in the Lake fells and looked down to a shelf only eight feet below to where an oblivious Peregrine brooded her hatching eggs, and in June I climbed to an old Raven eyrie in which three fine eyasses glared out from amidst a gory shambles of pigeon remains. That autumn and winter I did more prospecting, read more books and bought more maps, over which I pored for hours on end, laying plans for the following spring. When the Easter holidays came I made for pastures new and spent ten days exploring the Galloway hills, which in 1946 were as gloriously wild and untrodden a stretch of upland as any in the British Isles.

By now I had the fever, and have never really shaken it off. During every year since then I have managed to be among Peregrines at nesting time. Each spring saw me roaming the Lakeland fells, but I was drawn even more strongly to the quieter hills of the Southern Uplands, where there was the additional satisfaction of prospecting unknown ground, and working out the distribution of Peregrines and Ravens for myself. In Moffatdale and Galloway I stayed with kindly and hospitable shepherd folk in their lonely homes deep in the Peregrine country, and there spent some of the best days of my life. After long and exhausting treks, I returned each night to marvellous suppers and good talk. There was then a struggle to write up the field notes before sleep finally won. The Southern Uplands had a degree of solitude then, and forestry had only the odd foothold here and there. For some years cars were few, and although the shepherds could be seen assiduously going their rounds, I seldom met anyone else on the hills during my April visits.

Galloway, especially, was a magic country to which I returned every year with renewed enthusiasm. It was then a vast sheep walk, the last grouse moors virtually abandoned, and tourism a thing hardly worth mentioning. Few roads or even recognisable footpaths penetrated the wilderness and some of the Peregrine haunts were only to be reached by long, arduous walks. I well remember the sudden feeling of solitude when the train set me down with my bicycle at the

Adult male Peregrine; northern Sweden (photo: Peter Lindberg)

lonely station on the moors, and I headed along the rough road across the wild and windswept uplands towards the abrupt granite crags that were always my first call. One time I passed an adder coiled in the road, as an indication of the scarcity of traffic in those days. I vividly recollect, on sunny days in April, sitting high on the hills and watching the smoke from innumerable moor fires rising into the still air at almost every point of the compass. The 'reek' from shepherds' fires was then so characteristic a feature of the scene, and the freshly burned moor had a marvellously aromatic smell as one walked over the ground. It was a land of Curlews, and as they rose and sank in graceful display flight, their liquid bubbling calls sounded far and wide over the moorlands. Now and then I slept out in the deserted cottage at Backhill of the Bush, and remember the sense of loneliness as I sat on the doorstep and watched the sun go down behind the Dungeon and Craignaw, where the granite slabs and crags took on a steely blueness as the light faded. In those days it was five miles to the next human being and the nearest road end.

As a research student, I was fortunate to live for three years in the magnificent Peregrine country of Snowdonia, and although my work was to study mountain vegetation, there were four pairs of falcons on my area to provide added attraction. During days off I tracked down most of the other Peregrine haunts in the district, and made periodic forays to the sea cliffs of Anglesey where the bird nested in contrasting habitat. A visit to the wild north-west of Sutherland in 1952 left me with the clear impression that, contrary to my expectations, there were few Peregrines among these rugged hills, and that this was, first and foremost, Golden Eagle country.

The original preoccupation with the excitements of the chase, the hunting down and reaching of nests and the sheer delight of watching and hearing these marvellous creatures, broadened gradually into a curiosity about the influences which ruled their lives. My searches began to have a more purposeful intent, though they still had to be a spare time concern. I became impressed by the apparent constancy in numbers, combined with the regularity in spacing distance between pairs, and began to wonder how this could have come about, and what it meant. Later, I started to write down my ideas and the field data, and eventually made these into a paper. Then, to my great delight, there came the opportunity to work on the Peregrine as a full time job for a couple of years, and soon I found myself involved, with many other people, in what became a cause célèbre in nature conservation: the impact of the organochlorine insecticides on birds of prey. The Peregrine itself has come to symbolise one of the foremost trends of our time – the relentless domination by Man, the supreme competitor, of the rest of the living world.

And so the Peregrine story has become far more complicated than I could ever have foreseen, leading on the one hand to the deep mysteries of the physiology and biochemistry of response to pesticides, and on the other to the battleground where wildlife conservation is matched against the march of progress. My part has been that of a field naturalist trying to understand the population biology of the bird, and to direct the attention of others to more fundamental or technical issues which it was beyond my capacity or inclination to tackle. It would be less than honest of me to pretend that I was motivated other than by a wish to see my beloved bird hold its own, but I have tried hard to keep emotion out of the scientific arguments. These must stand or fall on the collection, presentation and interpretation of facts, free from wishful-thinking or hidden assumptions.

The Peregrine is, in fact, a fascinating subject for scientific study, and my attempts to understand its natural history more closely have given me much stimulation and satisfaction, though there are many deeper aspects which remain as puzzles for others to solve. Beyond this, there has been the immense pleasure of knowing so many other Peregrine enthusiasts. I owe so much to those who taught and encouraged me in my youth, to my many field companions over the years, and to the numerous other helpers and informants who have made it possible to present the Peregrine saga in more detail than would otherwise have been the case. But the greatest enjoyment, all the way through, has been the simple one of seeing these fine birds and learning of their ways in their native haunts – a country endlessly varied and magnetically beautiful.

Mortimer Batten (1923) has summed it all up for me: 'I remember in my childhood seeing or rather recognising my first Peregrine as he glided through immeasurable space among the clouds, and never in all my life can I recall having witnessed anything in Wild Nature which left an impression so indelible and so full of romance as that small black cross against the sky.'

CHAPTER 1

The Peregrine and Man

BEFORE THE RECORD BEGAN

One can but conjecture about the prehistory of the Peregrine in Britain. Geolo-gists and pollen analysts have given us a vision of the country during the Quaternary Ice Age, with its alternating glaciations and warmer interglacial periods, and during the subsequent period of warming climate up to the time when the actual written record began. From about 30,000 to 15,000 years ago, in the middle of the last full-glacial period, the great ice sheets of the Devensian glaciation covered most of Britain west and north of a line from Glamorgan to Teesmouth. In those far-off and inhospitable times, early man was largely banished to more temperate regions, and so much water was locked up as ice that Britain and the continent were joined. There were then widespread scenes of Arctic splendour, with vast snow-fields and glaciers in the mountains, and large areas of fell-field and tundra on adjoining lower ground lying free of ice and snow in summer. Farther away from the ice was evidently a region of steppe.

The vegetation of these snow-free barrens consisted of open communities of herbs and low grasses, dwarf shrubs, mosses and lichens, similar to the types to be seen today close to the limits of permanent snow and ice in northern Europe. There was a prevalence of small Arctic and Alpine plants, such as dwarf birch, mountain avens, saxifrages, sedges and montane willows, which in Britain today linger in small quantity mainly at the higher levels of the Scottish mountains. The steppe country probably had a prevalence of herbaceous and low shrubby vegetation. There may have been scattered bushes and small trees but the forest zone lay far south-eastwards in Europe.

The mammal fauna of this full-glacial period was a most exciting one, as the actual fossil record reveals (Stuart, 1977). Living on the steppes and tundras were large animals including mammoth, woolly rhinoceros, giant deer (Irish elk), bison, lion, spotted hyaena, brown bear, wolf, musk ox, horse, reindeer, red deer and elk. What a superb assortment of wildlife there must have been. We may surmise that the bird fauna contained a comparable northern element. Predators such as the Gyr Falcon, Rough-legged Buzzard, Snowy Owl and Long-tailed Skua doubtless ranged over the desolate landscapes of that earlier Arctic zone in Britain, whilst the wildfowl, wader and passerine breeding populations are likely to have included many northern species which now occur here only as non-breeding visitors. Our remnant trio of truly montane birds, Ptarmigan, Dotterel and Snow Bunting, probably nested widely in the lowlands then, on ground with certain similarities to that now found on the high tops of the Grampians and Cairngorms, where fringe or relict populations of these species survive today. The Peregrine goes far north in the Arctic regions at present, overlapping considerably in breeding range with the Gyr Falcon in Fennoscandia, Siberia, Greenland, Canada and Alaska, and nesting locally on flat bogs and tundras, as well as on steep river banks and cliffs. It is thus quite likely that Peregrines bred widely in England to the south of the ice, even at the height of the last glaciation, and especially if the bird was then less restricted to high cliffs in its nesting.

Around 15,000 years ago, the climate slowly became warmer, causing the onset of a retreat northwards of the ice and permanent snow, and a consequent spread of plants and animals over the ground freed from their embrace. The glaciers lingered last in the mountain systems of Wales, Lakeland, the Southern Uplands and the Scottish Highlands, and at one stage readvanced temporarily. This late-glacial period, which lasted until about 10,000 years ago, was marked by the spread first of those plant and animal communities which had been peri-glacial. A zone of Arctic habitat, with fell-field, tundra and steppe, advanced northwards, westwards and upwards. In the rear of this zone, where conditions were more favourable there was invasion by taller shrubs and small trees, such as juniper, willows and birch, to produce a patchy scrub and open woodland akin to the taiga of the Subarctic. The late-glacial ended with the general establishment of birchwood, as the first phase in development of a woodland climatic climax, and the transition to the post-glacial period.

Even by the onset of the late-glacial period the rich mammal fauna had already dwindled. The mammoth, woolly rhinoceros, and bison were extinct altogether, and some of the other large mammals disappeared from the area of Britain; their demise, it is now believed, may well have been connected with the spread of men of the Early Stone Age. The late-glacial fauna nevertheless retained a strongly northern element, in the form of reindeer, horse, elk, lynx, varying hare, arctic fox, arctic lemming, Norway lemming and northern vole, as Stuart has described.

Juvenile female Peregrine; northern Finland (photo: Peter Lindberg)

The Peregrine was probably around widely during this period, as a characteristic member of the Arctic–Subarctic fauna which achieved fairly early colonisation of land freed by the receding ice. In his review of fossil and sub-fossil bird remains from bone deposits in Britain, Bramwell (1959) mentions frequent finds of Ptarmigan in lowland sites, and the presence of bones of Peregrine and other raptors in cave earths in Somerset and Derbyshire. These deposits were said to be of late-glacial age but were not precisely dated, and Bramwell's interpretation was that they represented, in context with many other remains, a Subarctic and Boreal fauna rather than a truly Arctic one. Such deposits can span a long spread of centuries, so that these finds do not tell us much about the exact conditions under which the Peregrine then lived; only that it is likely to have been continuously present in Britain for a very long time.

The post-glacial epoch began with the Pre-Boreal period, and was one of consolidation of forest cover, with Scots pine following birch over much of the country. As the climate warmed steadily, woodland advanced over all but the wettest ground, and spread up the mountain slopes to fully 750 m in many districts. By the time of the post-glacial climatic optimum (c. 5500 BC), the pollen evidence is of forest climatic climax over most of Britain. Only certain far northern districts, Caithness, Orkney, Shetland and the Outer Hebrides, did not carry significant woodland cover at any time since the end of the last glaciation. Forests of Scots pine and birch were extensive in other parts of northern Scotland, and many glens had large areas of oak, ash, hazel, wych elm, alder, aspen and rowan. In England and Wales the woodlands were mainly of these same broad-leaved trees, but in the south there was locally a good deal of small-leaved lime. Beech and hornbeam did not appear until about 500 BC.

The plant and animal communities belonging to the Arctic environment gradually became restricted and eliminated over large areas by the expansion of scrub and forest, eventually surviving mainly on the upper levels of the highest mountain systems. Some species which were once widespread have totally disappeared from Britain as their habitats dwindled away thus. Forms of the Peregrine breed from the Arctic to the Equator, so that the species is not likely to have suffered the climatic displacement which affected so many birds of the late-glacial fauna. Nevertheless, although the Peregrine nests in trees in limited parts of its European range, it is not really a bird of extensively wooded plains. We shall never know whether the species once occupied a woodland niche in Britain, but it seems much more likely that the period of widespread forest cover did not favour the Peregrine particularly, and that it may well have occurred mainly where there was a good deal of open ground more suited to its hunting. The rocky coasts were probably always a stronghold, and also the more rugged uplands where high cliffs gave a good outlook over the forests. Areas with only scattered growth of trees, and the vicinity of large rivers, lakes and swamplands were probably all favoured. Habitats of these kinds are used freely today by hunting Peregrines through various parts of their Arctic, Subarctic, Boreal and Temperate Zone range. The bird was probably widespread in Britain and Ireland during most of the post-glacial period, but no firm estimate of its numbers can reasonably be made, and the frequency with which the species nested in non-cliff habitats must have had an important influence on population size. Species which appear to compete successfully with the Peregrine, such as the Eagle Owl,

Adult male Peregrine; northern Sweden (photo: Peter Lindberg)

Golden Eagle and perhaps White-tailed Eagle, were probably also widespread then, and may have restricted the numbers of Peregrines in many areas. The population may thus have been rather smaller than in more recent times, but probably numbered a few hundred pairs.

Early Man, of the Middle and Late Stone Age periods, colonised Britain in increasing strength as the ice retreated, but for several thousand years his numbers and way of life were such that he made relatively little impact on the environment. Forest clearance occurred on a modest scale, but the nomadic hunting ways and later shifting cultivation of these early peoples had only minor effects. It was the Bronze Age (1800–500 BC) and even more the Iron Age (500 BC–500 AD), with their more efficient tools and greatly increased demands for timber as metal-smelting fuel, which brought the first real onslaught on our forestlands. Deforestation had become significant in Roman times and it continued to accelerate through later centuries, reaching a peak in the Middle Ages and finally leaving a country largely denuded of its woodlands by 1800.

These changes were probably beneficial to the Peregrine in producing a vast expansion of the kind of open or only partly wooded country which the bird especially favours in its hunting. The actual use of the deforested land for agriculture was not intensive, and the agrarian regimes of the period right up to

World War II gave an abundance of prey species in most districts. Man thus incidentally provided good Peregrine habitat in plenty.

THE AGE OF FALCONRY

There is no telling at just what point Man began to regard the Peregrine as a competitor or an ally. Probably his first thoughts about it were as an item of food, as indeed it is still treated in various parts of the World, by people ranging from Eskimos to Spanish peasants, who regard the unfledged young as good eating. Some of the early hunters are bound to have noticed the prowess of this bird at their own art and to have benefited by retrieving some of its kills for themselves. It may quite early have dawned on them that this skill could be more directly harnessed to their own use, and so the first falconers could have practised their wiles. But we shall never know exactly when this happened. Falconry was known to the ancient Egyptians and the Chinese as early as 2000 BC and it was practised right across the east from Arabia through India to Japan long before the Christian era. It is strange that hawking seems to have been unknown to the Greeks, and E. B. Michell (1900) says, 'Even the later Roman authors refer to the use of trained hawks as an unfamiliar practice, in vogue only amongst some of the barbarian tribes'. Harting (1891) states that falconry was practised in Europe by 300 BC, and the first mention of it in Britain is during the reign of the early Saxon King Ethelbert (860–865 AD).

I cannot do better than quote Michell on the early history of falconry in Britain. 'Before the end of the ninth century it was familiar to the Saxons in England and throughout the west of Europe. Henry the Fowler, who became Emperor in 919, seems to have been so nicknamed on account of his devotion to this form of sport, which was already a favourite with princes and magnates. The Saxon King Ethelbert wrote to the Archbishop of Mayence for hawks able to take cranes. King Harold habitually carried a trained hawk on his fist; and from the time of the Norman Conquest hawking was a sport as highly honoured in the civilised world as hunting. The greatest impulse that was ever given to the sport in western Europe was derived from the returning Crusaders, many of whom had become acquainted with the Oriental falconers and the Asiatic modes of training and flying hawks. Conspicuous amongst such Crusaders was the Emperor Frederick II, who brought back with him some Asiatic hawks and their trainers, and who not only was himself an enthusiastic and accomplished falconer, but even declared that falconry was the noblest of all arts.

'From that time – early in the thirteenth century – for more than four hundred years falconry flourished in Europe, as well as in the East, as a fashionable sport amongst almost all classes. As in the case of hunting and fishing, its attractions as a sport were supplemented by the very material merits it possessed as a means of procuring food. While the prince and the baron valued their falcon-gentle [female Peregrine] for its high pitch and lordly stoop, the yeoman and the burgher set almost equal store on the less aristocratic Goshawk and the plebeian Sparrowhawk as purveyors of wholesome delicacies for the table. Even the serf or villein was not forgotten in the field, and was expected, or at least allowed, to train and carry on his fist the humble but well-bred and graceful Kestrel'.

Juvenile male Peregrine; Sweden (photo: Peter Lindberg)

Some mention is required of the remarkable treatise *De Arte Venandi cum Avibus* by the Emperor Frederick II of Hohenstaufen, which Charles Haskins dated to 1248–50 in original form. We are indebted to Casey A. Wood and F. Marjorie Fyfe for an English translation of this classic work as the *Art of Falconry*. It contains an exposition of the methods of catching, keeping, training and flying of birds of prey for hawking, and many of the methods and devices described are still used as standard practice at the present day, so that the whole account reads as though it were fresh and modern. There are sections on the biology and habits of birds of prey, including anatomy, plumage, behaviour (mainly in relation to training and hunting), food and feeding, health, breeding, migration and comparisons between different species, which are full of perceptive observation and sound interpretation. Frederick had a good deal to say about hawking with Peregrines and clearly recognised that there were at least two forms of the species. He was also experienced at flying Gyr Falcons and knew about their nesting haunts in Norway, Iceland and Greenland.

Fisher (1966) stated that historical records of the Peregrine in Britain appear from the 8th century onwards, and excavations of 9th and 10th century Viking dwellings at Yarlshof in Shetland yielded Peregrine bones (Venables and Venables, 1955). Forrest (1907) said that in Wales the laws of Hywel Dda (c. 940 AD) refer to the head falconer of the King's Court and his entitlement 'to the nestlings and also the nests of the Falcons.' During the reign of the Scottish king, William the Lion (1165–1214), Robert of Avenel, in granting his lands in Eskdale (Dumfries-shire) to the Abbey of Melrose, reserved the right to the eyries of falcons (Ritchie, 1920). Ritchie also noted that 'So long ago as the twelfth century, Giraldus Cambrensis observed that, in spite of the care taken of the breeding places of Falcons and Sparrowhawks in Ireland, their nests did not become more numerous and their numbers did not increase' – a profound observation as we shall see later. Harting (1883) mentions that Henry II sent annually from 1173 for young Pere-grines from the sea cliffs of Pembrokeshire, and that King John obtained falcons from Carrickfergus, Co. Antrim, in 1212–13.

It was in the 13th century that the first precise references to breeding places of the Peregrine appear in the literature. The earliest record of a specific nesting place is Lundy Island in the Bristol Channel, where the falcons from an eyrie were bestowed in 1243 by Henry III 'to his beloved cleric Ade de Eston' (Gurney, 1921). In this Golden Age of falconry it seems to have been common practice for the rentals of estates on which Peregrines bred to include the requirement to supply regularly a given number of young falcons. In England, another early reference to an eyrie is in the tribute of Middleton, near Dent in north-west Yorkshire, during the 13th century, the breeding haunt in question being one still regularly occupied up to the present day. And in the rental of Coldingham, Berwickshire, for the year 1298, there is mention of 'two aeries of Falcons'. This refers to the St Abbs cliffs, a noted haunt of Peregrines right through the 19th century and up to the present.

In a historical review of the subject for Scotland, Ritchie (1920) noted that Alexander III, King of Scots from 1249–86, kept falcons at Forres and at Dunipace in Stirlingshire; and there were falcon eyries near Stirling and also on the summit of the Ochil Hills. In 1343 there are records of eyries on the islands of Coll, Tiree and Colonsay. In 1496 the royal falconers obtained hawks (clearly Peregrines) in the Forest of Atholl, Orkney and Shetland. In 1549, Sir Donald Munro, High Dean of the Isles, mentioned Peregrines on the Treshnish Isles, Argyll and Hirta, St Kilda. Mary, Queen of Scots (1542–67), had falcons from the Abbey Craig near Stirling and the Ochils above Alva.

In England, after the Lundy and Dent records, the next mention of an eyrie appears to be at Freshwater Bay on the Isle of Wight in 1564. This haunt was occupied regularly up to about 1957. In Wales, the famous breeding station on the Great Orme's Head near Llandudno is the earliest record I have seen, dating to the reign of Elizabeth I (1558–1603).

From 1600 onwards, records increase steadily and become too numerous to detail at length: they include celebrated eyries such as Ailsa Craig in the Clyde, Dunnottar Castle (Fowlsheugh) in Kincardineshire, Brean Down at Weston-super-Mare, Beachy Head on the Sussex chalk and Flamborough Head in Yorkshire, all of which are currently occupied. Haunts used regularly up to 1800 but now long deserted include Hunstanton Cliff in Norfolk and Dumbarton Castle Rock near Glasgow. A remarkable older reference is to a list of 25 localities in Orkney where Peregrines bred in 1693, made by the Rev. J. Wallace, who thereby goes down in history as the first man to census a Peregrine population.

Although the records for these earlier years are otherwise extremely sporadic and unsystematic, it is remarkable how many localities appear in print sooner or later, sometimes in rather unlikely sources. This was clearly a bird which continued to excite interest and attention as one of the most spectacular feathered inhabitants of any neighbourhood, long after the Medieval hey-day of falconry had passed. In Scotland, the parish records in both the Old and New Statistical Accounts name many nesting haunts, and right up to the present day this is a bird which often receives casual mention in guide books, travelogues, local literature and so on.

By contrast, there are surprisingly few place-names on maps to indicate the former presence of nesting Peregrines. The Lake District has a score or so of Raven Crags, the majority of them still occupied by that bird to this day. There are also ten Eagle, Erne, Iron or Heron Crags, (the last two names believed also to denote Erne or Sea Eagle), but, to my knowledge, only two so-named Falcon Crags exist. In Wales there are plenty of Craigs or Carregs suffixed with Fran or Cigfran (Raven), and a few named Gwalch (hawk), but hardly any specifically designated Hebog (falcon). In the Highlands, too, there are plenty of rocks labelled Creag an Fhithich (Raven Crag) and Creag na h'Iolaire (Eagle Crag), but only a few named Creag an t'Seabhaig (Falcon Crag). The slightly more frequent name Speireag referred to virtually any hawk, while the fairly common Eun or Eoin (literally 'the bird') denoted especially Eagle or Osprey, but could have included the Peregrine also. In the Scottish Lowlands and Southern Uplands there are only the occasional Hawk Craig and Falcon Craig. Could it have been that in the palmy days of Medieval falconry, the nesting places were so jealously guarded that the local peasantry were discouraged from drawing attention to them by the use of place-names? Whatever the case, it is one of the mysteries of the past.

The first known use of the name *peregrinus* appears to be in the treatise of Frederick II (1248); in the Latin text the most frequent use is in the unqualified form *peregrini* (plur.) but there is reference also to *peregrini falcones*. In the Wood and Fyfe (1943) translation of the work, the Peregrine is said by Frederick to be so-called because of its wandering flights over the sea. Albertus Magnus of Cologne (1206–1280) used the name and gave two reasons for this designation: (1) that it is always wandering from one region to another as if flying through every land; (2) that its nest can never be discovered and the bird is caught in flight far from its place of origin. The name thus seems to have arisen from observation of the bird in districts where it did not breed, and was mainly seen on passage or during winter. Confusion was introduced by the use in Britain of the name 'laner' or 'lanner' for the Peregrine. Crown Jurors in their assessment of Lundy in 1274 referred to the esteemed Peregrine eyrie as 'una ayeria falconum lanerium'. Lanner Falcons were evidently brought back from the Middle East by returning Crusaders, and this may have led to confusion, although the two species were clearly distinguished at that time, at least by the knowledgeable, including Frederick II. The general use of the English name Peregrine is itself a fairly modern usage, coming well after the 16th century, though Turbervile (1575) mentions 'the Haggart Falcon, and why she is called the Peregrine or Haggart.' The name seems originally to have meant simply a falcon of foreign origin. The term falcon was the earlier designation for the Peregrine, but was later reserved for the female alone, while the male was known as the tiercel or tercel, on the grounds that he was smaller than his mate by *une tierce* or one third. In English the word was corrupted to tassel or tassle. The name gentil was introduced as an honorific denoting the elevated status of the Peregrine in the hierarchy of falconry, and it was qualified by addition of falcon or tassel.

And so falconry began to develop its own esoteric language. The young bird in the nest was known as an eyass or eyess, up to two to three weeks old, becoming in turn a ramage hawk, then a brancher. After leaving the nest and up to about mid-September, when it was recognised that a migration began, the young Peregrine was called a soar-hawk. Young birds seen or taken during the first autumn were called passage-hawks or, in French, *pèlerin*, denoting their migrant tendencies at this time of year. French falconers applied the name *antennaire* to juveniles after the turn of the year, and this word appears to connect with the English use of lantiner, lentener or lent-hawk towards the arrival of Lent. The name laner or lanner could have been derived from this root. During the period from fledging to the time of first moult, the young Peregrine was known as a red hawk, from the prevailing warmness of feather coloration.

The timing of the first moult varies between individuals, but usually occurs during the spring of the second year of a Peregrine's life. After this moult, a wild Peregrine is known as a haggard falcon or hawk and described as blue, by reference to the change in plumage of the upper parts from a dark brown to a distinct slaty blue. The bird is now in adult plumage and, although reproductive maturity may be delayed by at least another year, subsequent changes in colour of plumage, the skin of the feet and the bill are too minor to be an accurate guide to age. A haggard falcon can thus be an adult plumaged bird of any age. A bird

Peregrine perched at the stern of a boat at sea: from the facsimile edition of De Arte Venandi cum Avibus, *by Frederick II, Codices Selecti vol. XVI, Academische Druck- u. Verlagsanstalt, Graz*

which has moulted in captivity is described as intermewed. The mews are where falcons moulted, from the French *muer* (to moult), and came to mean the outhouse where the birds were kept.

The species was named *Falco Peregrinus* in the new binomial Linnaean system in 1771 by Marmaduke Tunstall from a specimen taken in Northamptonshire. In my youth I met shepherds in the Southern Uplands who still spoke of the Blue Hawk, but nowadays the name Peregrine is used almost universally in this country. Interestingly, the Americans have totally abandoned their earlier name of Duck Hawk in favour of Peregrine for their particular races of the species. The term falcon is still generally used by falconers to denote the female Peregrine, but the majority of ornithologists do not follow this convention.* Eyass is now a designation for any unfledged Peregrine regardless of state of development. In

*And I have not done so.

falconry the word hawk is sometimes still used loosely for any raptor, but in general usage it has become restricted to the short-winged types (genus *Accipiter*), as distinct from the long-winged true falcons (genus *Falco*).

It is those long wings which have helped to make the Peregrine such a favourite with falconers through the centuries. There was early recognition that the speed, agility and power of this bird on the wing made it one of Nature's supreme hunters. Even more remarkably, perhaps, this aerial prowess was found to be allied to an essential docility of temperament in captivity, giving a subject most amenable to training. It is said that some falconers can, through constant attention and handling, train a wild caught Peregrine in two to three weeks, whereas the normal period is three times as long. When the process is completed, and done well, there can be the most remarkable rapport between bird and trainer. The Peregrine seems to understand exactly what is expected of it and an especially fascinating spectacle is the sight of a well-trained falcon 'waiting on' in the air as its master and his dogs attempt to flush quarry. The bird circles high above, seemingly free to go its own way, yet entirely under control and ready to stoop to the lure and be taken onto the fist if no game can be aroused. It is small wonder, then, that the Peregrine was revered and possession reserved for the most privileged.

There seem always to have been differences of opinion about which raptor should have absolute pride of place in falconry. Some have preferred one or other form of the still larger and more powerful Gyr Falcon, while others have claimed better performance from Lanner or Saker Falcons. Some falconers prefer other smaller subspecies of the Peregrine, such as the Indian Shaheen and the Barbary Falcon of the Middle East. Such comparisons are loaded with subjective preferences and so much depends on training, as well as on the climate and other conditions under which a bird is flown. Each species has presumably evolved the particular mode of hunting and the physiology that give greatest effectiveness under the particular environment, including both the physical conditions and the variety of available prey. Individuals also vary greatly in aptitude and temperament within any species. On the whole, nevertheless, there seems to be a fair consensus among falconers that, all things considered, the typical race of the Peregrine, or any of the subspecies close to it, has the combination of attributes closest to the ideal, and produces the best and most desirable performers on average.

During the Middle Ages, the Peregrine was the sovereign's or the nobleman's hawk, and protected by harsh penalties. For centuries it was mentioned only as an object of esteem, ably assisting man in the chase and deserving only of the greatest admiration and affection for its prized qualities of hunting skill, killing power and courage. Portraits and engravings of Medieval sovereigns, noblemen and their falconers frequently show Peregrine-like hawks sitting on the wrist or the perch, and trained hawks figure in the tapestries (including the Bayeux Tapestry), carvings, earthenware and jewellery. Shakespeare made frequent use of falconry terms, and showed evident familiarity with the sport. The shift in attitude which later became a complete reversal can be ascribed to the invention of gunpowder and the fire-arm, although their impact was delayed. Ritchie (1920) mentions that in 1551 in Scotland, in order to preserve the sport of hawking, killing game with guns was prohibited under pain of death. The fowling

Falconer's Peregrine wearing hood and jesses; captive bred bird, from female Falco peregrinus brookei *crossed with male* F. p. pealei *(photo: R. B. Treleaven)*

piece nevertheless gave its owner a much simpler and more convenient method of taking game and, with this, the realisation that all birds of prey were now competitors for the game. The early shot guns were doubtless soon turned against the former feathered accomplices, and the feud against the raptors began. Michell (1900) has surmised that the unsettled state of Europe at the Reformation with its endless wars made it difficult for falconers to detect or punish those who destroyed their hawks, but he believed that in England the Civil War in the first half of the 17th century struck a great blow against falconry. Not only were many of its practitioners removed from the scene, but the Puritan regime which followed took a censorious and suppressive view of sports in general.

There was something of a revival subsequently, but falconry never regained its former widespread popularity, and during the 1700s it became the more exclusive preserve of a smaller scattering of devotees with the particular inclination to follow this form of recreation. The colourful sportsman Colonel Thornton (1757–1823) of Thornville Royal in Yorkshire was a leading enthusiast and with Lord Orford formed a Hawking Club around 1775; within a few years there were 50–60 members owning, besides other hawks, 32 Peregrines (ap Evans, 1960). Edward Newcome (1810–71) of Hockwold, Norfolk, was a famous Victorian falconer and the last person in England to keep 'Heron-hawks'. In 1891, J. E. Harting, one-time secretary of the Linnaean Society, published his valuable bibliography of falconry containing 378 titles in 19 languages. The 19th century closed with the sport holding its own within a limited but dedicated circle of enthusiasts.

THE AGE OF GAME PRESERVING

The extensive land enclosures of the late 1700s made conditions increasingly difficult for traditional falconry, and as game shooting with the gun became the more fashionable pursuit, so the tide of favour turned strongly against the Peregrine. The great age of game bird preservation now came into being, and special custodians of the rapidly expanding shooting preserves multiplied in numbers. The war against predators as enemies was intensified. In August, 1767, Gilbert White sent Thomas Pennant the corpse of a female Peregrine which he had found nailed up on a barn in the parish of Farringdon; the bird had been shot feeding on its kill of a Rook. And White, in his 57th letter to Daines Barrington (c. 1782), said, 'One of the keepers of Woolmer Forest sent me a Peregrine Falcon, which he shot on the verge of that district as it was devouring a Wood Pigeon'.

The gamekeepers' onslaught on this raptor had begun and it was waged with unremitting vigour throughout the 19th century. Indeed, a perceptible slackening of this warfare did not begin to show until quite recent years, and it is by no means over. Anyone who browses through the literature of the Peregrine cannot fail to be struck by the sickening refrain of ruthless killing which emerges almost as the dominant theme for the species during the whole period from about 1770 until well into the present century. The carnage was greatest on the moorlands of the north and west which had become extensively preserved for Red Grouse, and included any adjoining seacliff haunts, but in the lowlands, any coastal eyries close to Pheasant or Partridge ground suffered similarly.

This was an easy bird to shoot or trap at the eyrie, though it was not nearly so vulnerable to poison as the carrion-feeding predators. The Peregrine's propensity for re-mating rapidly when the partner is killed, its habit of clinging to the ancestral nesting cliffs, and the magnetism of these places for new falcons if both of a previous pair are destroyed, ensured that there was a steady supply of new victims in any one locality, and reduced the chances of broods escaping undetected. The persistence of both persecutor and persecuted was remarkable and led to some sorry tales of slaughter. Nor was the campaign limited to the nesting grounds. Peregrines were destroyed whenever and wherever the keepers came across them and many were killed far from their upland and seacliff breeding haunts.

I have tried to pick out some of the most telling examples from the formidable catalogue of destruction in the literature. The Peregrine figures as a matter of course in the vermin lists of estate records in the north and west and these show that even in Scotland, the war on raptors began quite early. Sue King has extracted records from the Arran Estates Office which list payments for the destruction of 13 'gamehawks' (Peregrines) at 2s. 6d. each and 14 'gamehawks' nests at 10s. 6d. each during 1779–90. At the monetary values then obtaining, such bounty rates must have been a considerable inducement to many people to go hunting. Pearsall (1950) has quoted much more staggering vermin lists, including one from five parishes around Braemar, Aberdeenshire, listing 2590 raptors killed during 1776–86; and the best known inventory from Glen Garry, Inverness-shire, with 98 Peregrines in a total of 1799 raptors destroyed in only four seasons 1837–40. Though it is now suspected that lists were subjected to exaggeration through 'fiddles' on bounty payments, they nevertheless give a clear indication of the indiscriminate and massive slaughter inflicted upon all birds and mammals which could conceivably be regarded as predators of game.

John Harvie-Brown said in 1895, 'About the end of April or beginning of May the Peregrine "crop" commences to be gathered, judging from the numbers annually sent in at that time for preservation to Inverness. From the numbers that are sent in to be stuffed, it is a wonder the bird holds its own as well as it does.' He noted also, 'Many specimens have at different times been killed at the Falls of Glenletterach and especially in 1834–8, when one or two were annually obtained.' The then Duke of Atholl told Harvie-Brown that 33 Peregrines were killed on his estates from 1875–87. Harvie-Brown recorded that in 1884 no less than eight Peregrines were trapped at the same cliff on Loch Hourn, Inverness-shire and H. A. Macpherson said that in 1889 the proprietor of Vaternish in Skye himself killed seven Peregrines from the middle of April to the middle of May, and in the spring of 1891 he destroyed six more on the same ground. Ferguson-Lees (1951) stated, 'At one Scottish eyrie the keeper admitted that he had shot both adult Peregrines in 13 years out of 23 and that he had killed the female alone in five more, while he had always destroyed the young or eggs – yet the cliff continued to be occupied.' In 1962, J. Duthie told me that in earlier years, a keeper in the Lochgoil area of Argyll had killed one or both Peregrines at a breeding haunt in 17 successive years.

Macpherson (1892) quoted a statement dated 1840 to the effect that two keepers of the Earl of Lonsdale in Westmorland had 'Killed, young and old, not less than 18 of this species.' As an example of persecution on the Yorkshire grouse moors, Nelson (1907) reported, 'Mr W. Eagle Clarke visited an eyrie on the north-western fells in 1880. . . . The falcon was shot as she left her nest, which had 4 eggs, she being the sixteenth victim to the gun, all killed from eyries on this fell.' And in Wales, George Bolam (1913) described in Merioneth '. . . an ancient nesting station of the Peregrine' where 'although one or other of the birds are often killed, others always turn up to take their places, if not at once, then certainly before the following season.' Kennedy Orton (1925) noted that there had been a wide importation to the grouse moors and pheasant preserves of North Wales of 'that most efficient of mortals, the Scottish keeper.'

These are the extremes of persecution. By no means all gamekeepers were as assiduous in removing Peregrines from their ground as fast as they came. There have always been some with a regard for their adversary, and even in 1890, H. A. Macpherson quoted a headkeeper on Skye as saying 'The Falcon is a real sportsman; I just grudge him the maintenance of his family.' Some keepers took the moderate view that if they removed a proportion of the Peregrines on their ground, or prevented the rearing of young, the rest could stay. Nevertheless it is clear that in districts where there was significant interest in grouse, or where eyries were close to lowland Pheasant and Partridge ground, nesting Peregrines were seldom tolerated, and the chances of successful nesting at any particular haunt were low. Some managed to survive and rear young in these areas every

year, but survival as a statistic for the population was consistently low. In the Highlands I have been struck by the regularity with which one finds stone hides below the nesting cliffs or, on their summit, specially built cairns to carry traps, as well as the actual remains of gintraps in strategic positions. It is evident that most eyries were marked down for fairly regular destruction as a matter of course.

The first Wild Birds Protection Act was passed in 1880, but the Peregrine was not on the schedule of named species. It was thus not protected from landowners or their servants and authorised agents, so that safeguards for this species were derisory. Further Acts in 1894 and 1896 gave County Councils and then County Borough Councils powers to add to the schedule of listed species and to protect the eggs of named species. Protection at first covered only a close season (the nesting period) but the 1896 Act gave councils the right to apply for orders to protect any bird or area throughout the entire year (Sheail, 1976). The response was somewhat variable but by 1900 the Peregrine evidently received some degree of legal protection in the majority of counties where it nested. For all the good that they did for the Peregrine, these laws might never have existed. Those keepers who knew of them just took no notice, and the chances of prosecution in earlier days were remote. Few people concerned enough to take action ever went around Peregrine haunts, and though there were occasional prosecutions, the weight of public opinion was too slight to have any effect. The new Protection of Birds Act of 1954, which included total protection for the Peregrine and its eggs on a First Schedule of species covered by special penalties, marked the onset of an era of much greater public concern for wildlife conservation in Britain, and the persecution of raptors generally has diminished measurably during the last quarter of a century.

This improvement has not always been through a change of attitude. In some areas, such as the Lake District, it has come about quite simply because the remaining grouse moors have fallen into disuse and the keepers have gone. Sometimes keepers have reached an understanding, usually with due remuneration, that falconers could lift the young from any eyries on their beat and so reduce the drain on their grouse stocks. Yet an increasing number of keepers have come to respect both Peregrines and the law, and many employers give strict instructions that these birds are to be left alone, or even guarded against other human enemies. The drift of the tide of public feeling about bird protection has increasingly influenced the attitudes of game preservers, and there are many estates nowadays where Peregrines find sanctuary. Even so, enlightenment has not yet penetrated to all quarters and there are still also many estates where this and other raptors are treated with as much severity as ever. Douglas Weir knew of the killing of three female Peregrines at the same cliffs on a Morayshire grouse moor in 1971, as they attempted successively to breed or hold territory. Hen Harriers are ruthlessly destroyed on many grouse moors, and the quite illegal use of poisoned egg and meat baits could even be on the increase. Supposedly used against foxes and crows, poison annually accounts for an appreciable part of the total mortality amongst Golden Eagles, Buzzards, Ravens and Red Kites in certain districts, and even Peregrines are more frequent victims than might be expected.

To be fair, the gamekeeper often has a difficult job and one ill-rewarded. If the landowner, shooting tenant or, as so often nowadays, the syndicate are concerned only with the size of the bag, he has to be seen to be doing his utmost to eliminate all possible competitors, and it may be as much as his job is worth to leave alone such obvious predators as Peregrines. Sometimes, though, the employers may be well disposed towards birds of prey, but the keeper knows better and quietly removes them, despite instructions to the contrary. The old attitudes die hard, and the simple logic that a grouse killed by a Peregrine means one less for the shooters is a difficult argument to counter. It is the more remarkable that a hundred years ago, at the height of the game preserving era, Harvie-Brown could write, 'I wish sportsmen would begin to hail the Peregrine as a bird of good omen; as a herald of good sport and an indicator of a well-stocked grouse-moor; as a sanitary commissioner appointed by Nature, looking out for the weakly members of the community, and removing these. . . . Where the grouse are, there will the Peregrines be gathered together; but where the grouse are not, do not blame the Peregrines, but look for much more deeply-rooted causes [bad moor management].' Even today, few grouse preservers would see things this way.

Many gamekeepers are first-rate observers and field naturalists, and some are a mine of information about Peregrines and their ways. Scotland, in particular, has produced a number of discerning writers on wildlife amongst the ranks of the keepers and stalkers, and their changing attitudes to predators show the dawn of enlightenment. Tom Speedy writing in 1920 had little good to say about our bird and a generation later, Dugald Macintyre believed in keeping it under control. It is not until very recent years, and the writings of people such as Lea MacNally and David Imrie, that an unreservedly tolerant and kindly view of such raptors as Peregrines and Golden Eagles appears. There have been many other Peregrine haters who have persecuted the bird in a more desultory fashion. Some farmers and small-holders tend to regard all hawks as potential chicken-takers and in the days when raptors were more generally looked upon as undesirable creatures to have around, there were plenty of people who were glad to destroy any Peregrines they came across.

This country has never suffered to the same extent from the fire-arms mania that afflicts some European countries such as France, Belgium, Spain, Italy, Cyprus and Malta or, even more, the United States, and probably many fewer Peregrines and other raptors are killed here through idle target-practice by trigger-happy vandals. The annual rituals of mass destruction of birds of prey on certain of their well-defined migration routes are among the most horrifying examples of the way in which man has abused the creatures which share his world. They express a primitive and wanton blood-lust hanging over from the dark ages of savagery and totally unworthy of any society calling itself civilised. One former scene of such carnage, Hawk Mountain, Pennsylvania, is now a sanctuary where the public come to admire and learn (Broun, 1948), but nearer home the destruction continues virtually unabated in such places as the Pyrenees and Malta. Peregrines figure as victims in the general slaughter, but probably as only a small proportion of the total.

THE PIGEON FANCIERS

Pigeon fanciers have also developed a long-standing hostility to the Peregrine. Domestic pigeons derived by selective breeding from the wild Rock Dove have probably long provided the Peregrine with an important item of food. Dovecots were widely established from the Middle Ages onwards to augment human food supplies, and fancy breeds of pigeons were later developed for mainly ornamental purposes. Domesticated forms of pigeons constantly revert to the wild, so that a sizeable population of feral pigeons, both urban and rural, has probably existed for a considerable time.

The homing abilities of the pigeon led to breeding for this trait, and so the sport of pigeon-racing developed. It rose to popularity with the advent of the railways which, until recently, provided the most convenient means of transporting 'homers' to the distant release points. Since the mid-19th century, but especially after 1900, pigeon-racing has thus locally provided Peregrines with a source of prey, with the result that the species has in some areas become regarded as an obstacle to the sport. Fanciers are understandably incensed at finding the remains of homers struck down and eaten and especially by the discovery of whole batches of legs with their identifying metal rings in Peregrine eyries containing young. Over the years there has in consequence been a good deal of sporadic destruction of adults, eggs and young in some districts. An oft-quoted method of destroying adult Peregrines is by releasing in the vicinity of the nesting quarters pigeons whose feathers, bodies or legs have been daubed with strychnine or other poison. This is a device probably more talked about than actually used, and, in general, pigeon fanciers seem to have been haphazard and intermittent in their efforts to wage war on this enemy.

My view is that pigeon fanciers have accounted for few Peregrines compared with the gamekeepers. They have rather, by contrast, sought to protect their interests by the proper and constitutional means of trying to persuade the Government to change the law protecting Peregrines so that some degree of control over the species' numbers could be exercised. Colin Osman (1970) has given an interesting account of the attempts by fanciers to have the law amended so that licences could be granted for the removal of certain Peregrines proved to be killing racing pigeons. The first was in 1925 when, after controversy in *The Field*, a deputation petitioned the Home Office and then canvassed for a legal amendment. This was unsuccessful and the matter rested there until 1940 when, under the emergency powers created in this time of war, an Order allowed the destruction of Peregrines in certain districts of Britain and Northern Ireland to reduce the risks of predation on message-carrying pigeons. An account of this officially sanctioned period of Peregrine control is given on pp. 64–66. In 1946 normal protection was restored and, under the new Protection of Birds Act of 1954, the Peregrine was included in a list of rarer breeding birds of the United Kingdom protected by special penalties.

The pigeon fanciers' indignation came to the boil again in the late 1950s, and spilled over once more into public debate, especially in South Wales. There followed a second deputation to the Home Office in 1959, and this led to a Government-sponsored enquiry by the British Trust for Ornithology into the numbers, distribution and feeding habits of the Peregrine in Britain. The results, which became available by the end of 1962, were totally unexpected, showing that the Peregrine population was declining at a headlong rate and was already reduced to a low level in the southern half of Britain. Circumstantial evidence put the finger of blame on the persistent pesticides of agriculture, and the battle for the survival of the Peregrine was on. In the perverse way of things, the fanciers' wishes had come true in a manner quite unforeseen, but their own intervention was most timely in allowing ornithologists to measure the decline while it was at its peak, instead of realising too late what had happened and trying to assemble the facts retrospectively.

Under the circumstances, there was no question of any slackening of legal protection for the Peregrine, but Colin Osman (1963, 1970–71), writing as a balanced spokesman for the pigeon fanciers, saw the problem as having solved itself. The Peregrine had virtually disappeared from the districts where complaints from fanciers had been strongest. The continuing recovery of the Peregrine population is, however, reviving the problem, and there is a great deal of protest in some areas.

THE EGG COLLECTORS

From the 19th century onwards, as if game preservers and other persecutors were not enough to contend with, the Peregrine was also increasingly hounded by egg collectors. This craze began around 1840 as the pastime of leisured Victorian gentlemen and within 30 years had taken a strong hold of the ornithological fraternity as a whole. From about 1870 to 1920, to be an ornithologist was almost synonymous with being an egg collector, though there were a few notable exceptions. As well as being a relatively uncommon bird, the Peregrine also had the misfortune to lay particularly beautiful and variable eggs (see colour plate), so

that these became especially sought as one of the prize items for any collection. Some 'eggers' exercised moderation, but for the collectors of insatiable appetite – and there have been many – the acquisition not just of whole clutches, but of large series of clutches, became an obsessive goal. Some of these people were incapable of keeping their hands off any uncommon eggs which came their way: apart from the desire for possession, there was always the nagging thought that someone else would take anything they left. The net result is that there must, in this country alone, now be thousands of Peregrine clutches lying around on beds of cotton wool.

The earliest clutch I have come across in this country was from the Vale of Cliviger in Lancashire, taken around 1790–1800. Few Peregrine eggs for the period 1850–80 have survived, and the majority in collections were taken during 1900–1960. Most of the serious collectors were professional and business men and others with private means, able to travel around widely at the right time of year, but many of them drew upon the services of more indigent locals who acted variously as field guides, middle men, or actual takers of the coveted eggs. Certain districts were systematically 'farmed' for their Peregrine eggs during the period 1900–1940, and sometimes the competition was keen. A prodigious number of eggs was taken from the south coast of England. John Walpole-Bond saw over 250 eyries with eggs on the Sussex coast from 1904–49, and it would seem likely, by all accounts, that he compulsively looted any he could reach. Now and then other collectors beat him to it, or accounted for eyries off his main round. In Kent there was a good deal of robbery too, though perhaps not on quite the same scale. But in Dorset to the west, things were if anything even worse; the notorious Levi Green made a point of lifting not only all the first clutches but as many of the repeats as possible too. In the British Museum (Natural History) there is, with the data tickets of the Edgar Chance collection, a famous – or infamous – photograph of Green and dealer Arthur Blinn sitting on top of a Dorset cliff with the coils of climbing rope and a pyramid of blown Peregrine eggs. This incredible heap, said to contain 64 eggs, was the year's crop for 1928 taken back to the scene of crime for this bizarre record.

The seacliffs of Devon and Cornwall were plundered a good deal, as were those of Pembrokeshire across the Bristol Channel. Inland in South and Central Wales, the generally relatively accessible eyries were a strong attraction. One pair of collectors, father and son, took 20 clutches from one Breconshire cliff during 1912–38, and 15 clutches from a second haunt in the same county during 1919–35. And other clutches were certainly lifted by other collectors from the same places during these years. Parts of North Wales, both coastal and inland, received a good deal of attention from eggers between the wars.

The Lake District was another of the happy hunting grounds for collectors, and for more than half a century the majority of eyries were raided every year. This area suffered by having, at any one time, several resident collectors, who between them covered most of the territories and left little for the visitors who came from outside Lakeland. Several hundred clutches must have been taken here during 1900–60 and at best only a few pairs managed to rear young in any one year. I have no clear idea of the scale of collecting in southern Scotland before World War II, but this region received considerable punishment during the years 1945–60, and hill eyries generally had a poor record of success. The Peregrines of the Scottish Highlands were evidently not subjected to the same scale of egg robbery as districts farther south. Raiding of eyries here seemed to be of a more sporadic and unsystematic kind, and although some pairs were robbed by keepers, many nests were in remote places or on inaccessible ledges of big cliffs, and these were little disturbed, especially in the deer forest country of the west. In Ireland some districts were egged pretty relentlessly over quite a long period, such as Antrim, Waterford and Wexford, but here, too, many eyries were in sequestered locations or on fearsome precipices and breeding success was probably fairly good overall in most years.

Egging continued to be widespread after 1945, but in the 1950s the collectors' game was often spoiled by a new habit which appeared among the Peregrines in many districts; that of breaking and eating their own eggs. And when the collapse of population in southern Britain occurred, few Peregrines remained to produce eggs there at all. Some of the more reasonable collectors called a truce when the Peregrine was at a low ebb in numbers, but not all of them did so. One of the few pairs which hung on in Wales during the 1960s was robbed for several successive years, as the RSPB discovered when police raided the home of a Midlands collector and examined his eggs and data tickets. The RSPB believe that there is still a large number of collectors active in this country. However, their surveillance of eyries, with the assistance of local people and the police, combined with the greatly increased penalties for wilful disturbance at the nest and the taking of eggs has had a beneficial effect, and the number of robberies nowadays, though still worrying, is much less than before 1960.

It has to be said that, whatever judgement others choose to make about egg collecting, it is the collectors who contributed most to our background knowledge of the breeding habits and distribution of the Peregrine in Britain. I owe much of my own information on the bird, and especially the history of occupation of many breeding places, to collectors. As a boy I was helped and encouraged by men who had collected in a modest way, and later on I received tremendous assistance from many others who were in the bigger league of egging. All of these people were first rate naturalists, highly skilled in field-craft, and some of them had the whole country taped when it came to knowledge of nesting birds. Some were adroit with the pen as well as the egg-drill. The splendid essays on the Peregrine by John Walpole-Bond are testimony to the powers of observation and under-standing which some collectors brought to bear and to the regard that they had for birds as living creatures, as well as producers of coveted eggs. Yet many equally accomplished members of the oological brotherhood left few records beyond arid data tickets with their eggs. Apart from what they told others, their remarkable knowledge sadly died with them. Egg collecting is now placed among the taboos of our society, but it was not always so, and no matter what one's views are on its ethics, this pursuit has its place in the annals of the Peregrine's history.

The urge for collecting mounted specimens or cabinet skins of birds is rather more firmly in the past, and although show cases with stuffed birds are in vogue again as antiques, it is now illegal to sell specially protected species. For the most part, as the quotation on p. 21 suggests, the Peregrines which ended up in the taxidermists' shops were the birds shot and trapped by gamekeepers in their war on predators. Dealers used a wide circle of keepers and other suitably placed agents to supply them with corpses, and the financial inducements sometimes behind such transactions probably caused the total numbers of Peregrines killed to be higher than they would have been without this additional strong incentive. The Peregrine also had to run the gauntlet wherever shooting men were gathered in winter, as on the big estuaries; and in earlier days professional wildfowlers were always on the look out for any rarer bird which the gentlemen bird collectors would dip deeply into their pockets to possess. The private collection of bird specimens is now virtually a thing of the past in this country. Rumour neverthe-less has it that a few unprincipled dealers still find a lucrative market for stuffed birds and cabinet skins overseas, and that there are always enough willing agents to procure a ready supply of Golden Eagles and Peregrines from the deer forests and grouse moors of the north.

THE FALCONERS TODAY

Despite its fall from Medieval grace, falconry has kept going in Britain ever since, though for a long time as a rather select and exclusive pastime. The sport has staged something of a revival in recent years, and has a wide following. It is represented in organised form by the British Falconers' Club which currently has around 600 members. Although legitimate falconry is regulated by a strict licensing system under the Bird Protection Acts, it has in addition an irregular fringe created by those who bend or break the law. During the first part of this century, up to around 1960, there was no particular problem. Falconers obtained the birds they needed without any undue worry arising generally. Peregrines were taken mainly as eyasses, often by arrangements with keepers or other local people, and the numbers involved were never so large as to make bird protectionists as a group sit up and take special notice. Then, at about the time that the demand for Peregrines began to increase, the population of the species crashed. Issue of licences for this raptor immediately ceased, and there was a rapid increase in the illegal taking of and trafficking in young birds, mainly in Scotland, where good numbers of Peregrines still remained.

Falconers are another body of people with tremendous knowledge of the Peregrine as a wild bird, and some of them have helped me greatly with their information about occupation of nesting places, and other aspects of breeding biology. Some supported a total ban on the taking of Peregrines until the species had made a really substantial recovery in numbers, and actively assisted in protection schemes. The lawless fringe, however, continued to tarnish the image of falconry, by creating a black market for Peregrines and other raptors, and drawing in an unsavoury element of petty crooks attracted by the cash. The stories about the prices paid for falcons by wealthy Arabs and West Germans are difficult to pin down to hard facts, but, despite exaggerations, some quite large sums of money have been exchanged for young birds.

By 1977 the problem was beginning to look ominous in terms of the numbers of young Peregrines being lifted annually. In this year the RSPB claimed to have certain knowledge of at least 40 broods of young Peregrines taken illegally, in a population pulling back slowly from the brink of disaster, and still numbering only around an estimated 500 pairs in Britain. In 1978 the Society stepped up its campaign of protection for this species and introduced new and sophisticated techniques for detecting robberies. Several parties were caught red-handed with young birds and successful prosecutions followed. The success of these efforts and the subsequent tightening of the law have had a salutary effect, but have by no means stopped the illicit taking and selling of falcons.

The captive breeding of Peregrines was pioneered in the United States as a desirable and legitimate technique for promoting the re-introduction of the species into the eastern States, where it evidently became totally extinct by 1964. The success of inducing Peregrines to pair, lay eggs and rear young in aviaries was such that captive breeding mushroomed in North America, and many whose interests in the bird were far from altruistic jumped aboard the band-wagon. The craze was not long in spreading to Britain, where there has been no justification for using captive breeding of Peregrines as a conservation tool, but an arguable case for developing it as a means of providing falconers with birds to train. It has been much used by the unscrupulous as a convenient 'cover' for possession of illegally taken eggs and young. It is now a legal requirement for captive birds of prey to be ringed with sealed rings and registered, and any acquisitions or changes of ownership have to be notified. Registered keepers and their premises are liable to inspection without notice. This has reduced the scale of illegal taking from the wild, but some are still prepared to risk the fine of £2000 per bird or egg.

Nowadays the taking of eggs is not always for their shells; captive breeding has demonstrated the value of the incubator for hatching eggs. One of the people successfully prosecuted in 1978 had a clutch of wild-taken Peregrine eggs in an incubator; they were alleged to have been laid in captivity and given by a friend, but there was proof from secret markings that they came from a particular eyrie. In 1990, two Germans were caught in Scotland with nine Peregrine eggs in a portable incubator: they were each fined £6000, had their van and other equipment confiscated, and were then jailed for 90 days for non-payment. Later in 1990, another two Germans were arrested by Customs at Dover for trying to smuggle out 12 Peregrine eggs taken in Scotland and Wales, and received prison sentences of 30 and 15 months.

Since 1945, some use has been made of trained Peregrines to reduce bird-strike hazards to aircraft on military airfields, such as RAF Lossiemouth. Service and civilian falconers have been employed to manage these bird-scaring operations with falcons. The technique had somewhat indifferent success, and has been superseded by more cost-effective methods.

THE ORNITHOLOGISTS

So far, most of the connections between Peregrines and Man have been about human concern to destroy or exploit the bird. No doubt, all the way down the ages there have been folk who admired the Peregrine simply for itself and relished all that it represented, while feeling no great urge to destroy it or to possess it and thereby turn the bird into an extension of themselves. Genuine falconers have a deep affection and respect for their hawks, but a trained raptor is, nevertheless, a possession. It is only in fairly recent years that there has come to be a significant number of people whose particular concern about the Peregrine is to see it living wild and free, and to find pleasure in simply watching and learning about its ways.

Those who live close to Peregrines often have a keen and lively interest in the bird. Hill shepherds usually know of eyries on their ground and can be most informative about the species, while many foresters in falcon country are similarly knowledgeable, and frequently cooperate in wardening and protection schemes. On rocky parts of the coast, fishermen and lighthouse keepers see a good deal of the bird and are often good sources of information. Some rock climbers are aware only of a noisy medium-sized hawk which seems to resent their presence on certain cliffs, but many know and admire the Peregrine as a fellow-denizen of the crags. Pioneer rock climber George D. Abraham, one of the Keswick Brothers, wrote an interesting essay on this and other hill birds many years ago (1919).

The growth of enthusiasm for birds and bird-watching during this century has led something of a revolution in thinking about wild creatures and plants and man's responsibilities towards them. Tansley's concept of 'the heritage of Wild Nature' is now a built-in part of the prevailing attitude, and nature conservation is a public duty which Parliament accepted within the ambit of Government in 1949 by creating the Nature Conservancy. The development of a conservation ethic is reflected in the literature of ornithology, and the way people wrote about birds. It is appropriate here to repeat the much-quoted passage of G. H. Thayer, written in 1904 and expressing eloquently the aesthetic appreciation of wildlife which was once the preserve of poets rather than ornithologists. He characterised the American Peregrine as 'perhaps the most highly specialised and superlatively well-developed flying organism on our planet today, combining in a marvellous degree the highest powers of speed and aerial adroitness with massive, warlike strength. A powerful, wild, majestic, independent bird, living on the choicest of clean, carnal food, plucked fresh from the air or the surface of the waters, rearing its young in the nooks of dangerous mountain cliffs, claiming all the atmosphere

Peregrines in the Galloway Hills

Peregrine on a sea cliff

as its domain, and fearing neither beast that walks nor bird that flies, it is the very embodiment of noble rapacity and lonely freedom.'

Many indeed are the purple passages which this bird has evoked. Together with the eagle, it is one of those creatures which humans invest with powerful symbolism and projections. The raptors bring out the anthropomorphism in us, and the Peregrine does so especially. It figures variously in folklore, as heraldic insignia, trade emblems and names, public house names and signs, and postage stamp designs. This is among the bird artists' favourite subjects but evidently a difficult one, for few of the many paintings and drawings that I have seen have exactly caught the real essence of the living bird. Some are accurate but lifeless, others are vital but flawed. Two of the ones that I liked best were on inn signs, but perhaps their setting mellowed judgement, so that the comparison is unfair. But I am being over-critical. Bird paintings give pleasure to multitudes and they are one of the best expressions of the human affection for and interest in the other inhabitants of this World.

There have been many who have found sufficient reward in just watching Peregrines and cherishing their memories as the best of all kinds of collection. Some have been moved to write of their observations, and their efforts add up to a significant and valuable literature on the bird. Others again have sublimated the collecting instinct into useful channels. In Lakeland, at a time when the Peregrine was being hard-hit by competition among local eggers, Robbie Brown began diligently searching for the few successful eyries, to ring the young and thereby lay the foundations for knowledge of the species' movements and survival rates. The bird photographers, beginning with the pioneer efforts of Francis Heatherley and his colleagues in 1911, sought to capture the glamour and fascination of the living creature and its family life, and to bring these to a wider audience. Photography of birds at the nest has grown so popular that it too has had to come under fairly tight control, especially for the rarer species. Setting up a hide at the Peregrine's eyrie is now allowed only under licence, as indeed is any intentional disturbance of the bird at its nest. Such legal provisions, within the 1954–81 Acts, show how far public opinion has advanced since 1900, when such notions would have been unthinkable.

So many people want to enjoy seeing Peregrines in their nesting haunts nowadays that uncontrolled visiting of eyries could create a serious risk of reducing breeding success. And so, sadly, the age of enlightenment and respect for wildlife also has to be the age of curtailment of personal freedom. It is a price that most people are willing to pay. The scientific enquirer, too, has to tread warily and take heed of public feeling. For another sign of the times is the interest focussed on the Peregrine as a subject for research, not only to help promote conservation measures through an insight into the factors which militate against the species, but also to increase understanding of its fascinating biology. In various parts of the World, studies of Peregrine ecology are rapidly advancing our knowledge of the bird. And they go hand in hand with concern about the predicament of the species in so many places – to the extent that *Falco peregrinus* as a whole is now regarded as at risk on the World scale, and listed in the Washington Convention on International Trade in Endangered Species of Wild Fauna and Flora which was ratified by ten countries and came into operation on 10 July 1975.

MAN THE DOMINANT ANIMAL

Ironically, it is the incidental and not the deliberate actions of man which have had by far the greatest impact on Peregrine populations. At first, his land-use practices, with extensive forest clearance, probably allowed the Peregrine to increase, and the removal of likely competitors such as the Golden and Sea Eagles may have been beneficial to the Peregrine. The domestication of the Rock Dove, first for food and then for sport, has probably more than compensated for any reduction in wild prey. Yet locally, in western Scotland and Ireland, there are indications that intensive management for sheep lowered the carrying capacity of the ground and, by depleting prey populations, reduced the numbers of Peregrines (Chapter 3). Rock climbing and other recreational disturbance have caused the desertion of a small number of Peregrine cliffs, but the creation of new crags in the form of quarries has more than compensated for any recent losses. Buildings and other structures have also increasingly provided breeding places.

By far the most important and most extraordinary of these unforeseen impacts has been the pesticide effect – an episode of such overwhelming importance that I shall devote a chapter to it later. Since so much of the Peregrine's natural history now has to be seen against this background, it is worth summarising the salient points here. The group of persistent synthetic pesticides developed during World War II and in the post-war years became used increasingly, especially in agriculture, and caused widespread though varying contamination of the Peregrine population, through its food supply. The first effects were much increased breeding failure, apparent from around 1950, in England, Wales and southern Scotland. After more toxic compounds were introduced, a sudden and serious decline of breeding population began around 1956 in southern Britain and during the next few years spread rapidly northwards to affect all districts except certain inland parts of the Scottish Highlands. Decline in numbers continued until at least 1963 but, following measures to reduce contamination by the most harmful pesticides, there has been a remarkable recovery in numbers and breeding success in most districts; but a few coastal areas show only marginal improvement or even further deterioration.

The history of the Peregrine and man is thus a paradoxical one of opposing tendencies which shift in balance over the centuries. First there is protection for falconry and then persecution over game. Man by his actions expanded the habitats and enhanced the food supply for the Peregrine, but later had the reverse effect locally. He again turned on it deliberately as a war-time enemy, but followed by increasing protection. And then he unintentionally hit the bird the hardest blow ever, by poisoning its food supply. Man has redressed the balance in this country by consciously counteracting his accidental damage. At the moment we are thus in a positive phase of relationship with the Peregrine again, and conservation is in the ascendant. Who knows what next? My own views are reserved for the last chapter, but we can go on to look at the Peregrine saga with the realisation that, however much the bird may at times seem to epitomise Wild Nature, its whole existence is inextricably linked with human activities.

CHAPTER 2

The Peregrine's country

The bare essentials of the Peregrine's environment are simple: open country over which to hunt, enough food in the form of other birds, and steep rock faces for nesting places. There are, accordingly, few parts of Britain and Ireland in which the species cannot live for at least some of the year, since the first two needs are satisfied almost everywhere. Even now, after a period of extensive re-afforestation locally, there are probably no areas where woodland is so continuous as to exclude the species completely. In winter, Peregrines can appear almost anywhere, but to most people the real Peregrine country is that in which the bird breeds and is most readily and consistently to be seen.

Since most British Peregrines need cliffs for nesting, and eyries on the ground or on buildings still rank as a novelty here, the species is found mainly as a breeding bird on the more precipitous sections of our coastline, or on the rockier mountains and moorlands inland. This is where the bird truly belongs.

I have tried to convey the main character of areas which represent the range of Peregrine breeding terrain to be found in Britain, rather than attempt a

Coastal nesting haunt: 140 m southern England chalk cliffs; Beachy Head, Sussex (photo: D. A. Ratcliffe)

comprehensive survey. Numbers vary according to the availability of suitable cliffs and to the abundance of food, but details of distribution are presented in Chapter 4. It is convenient to divide the areas into the two main groups, coastal and inland, since these are usually separated by wide tracts of lowland farmland in England, Wales and southern Scotland. In the Highlands and Islands, and in western Ireland, the hills run down to the sea in many places, giving complete continuity between the two types of habitat.

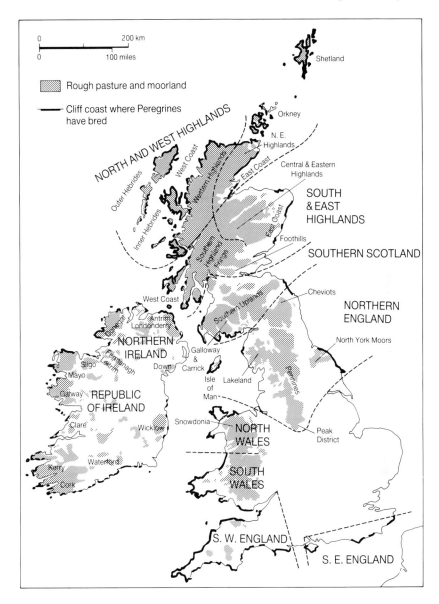

Figure 1. Regions and districts of Britain and Ireland as referred to in the text.

THE COAST

The Peregrine has bred around the British and Irish coasts virtually wherever there were steep cliffs more than 30 m high, and its main absence was from the east coast of England south of Yorkshire (see Fig. 2). The coastal breeding haunts of Peregrines vary greatly in topography and geology, affecting their height, steepness and length. Many faces fall into deep water, but others have a beach below and some are tiered or rise above an undercliff. The other important differences are in the composition of the bird communities on the cliffs, and those of the country adjoining the cliffs, each of which influences the falcon's food supply. The cliff bird communities show a range from those with few if any seabirds to those almost wholly composed of seabirds. The hinterland to the cliffs varies in the amount of cultivated land, from largely arable in the south and east, to an increasing proportion of heath and moorland with distance north and west. Laterally, the cliffs can pass into various other types of coastal habitat.

The south coast of England from Kent to Dorset was once as good a place as anywhere in the country for seeing Peregrines. Some eyries here were in almost urban settings, as on the gleaming white chalk cliffs flanking Dover harbour, and on the outskirts of such holiday resorts as Hastings, Eastbourne and Brighton. Many were in places where people passed frequently along the cliff tops or the shore below, so that casual disturbance was considerable. Yet the eyries themselves were mostly only reachable by the more determined raiders equipped with ropes, and some were in quite formidable situations. Not only are many of the chalk cliffs high, with an overall angle close to the vertical, but they are often faced with projecting horizontal rows of jagged black flints which could easily sever a rope (see page 34). And so the Peregrines lived here mostly unseen by (and safe from) casual passers-by.

Behind these southern cliffs there were in many places tracts of rolling short grass downland which for centuries had been grazed by sheep. There was woodland varying from scattered to extensive, and the broad river valleys between the downlands had rich farmland, which included large areas of permanent grassland, as on Romney Marsh and the Pevensey Levels.

This scene has changed greatly in the last few decades, with ploughing of much of the open downland and conversion to enclosed arable fields, especially of barley. The remaining pieces of downland are mere fragments, mostly on slopes too steep to plough or on cliff edge strips. After myxomatosis and virtual disappearance of rabbits in 1954–55, the remaining chalk grasslands grew tall and lush, and then became scrubbed over by bushes and trees. Agricultural intensification proceeded apace on existing farmland, with widespread grubbing out of hedges and draining of wet meadowland, and Romney Marsh is now quite extensively arable. The whole belt of farmland behind the seacliffs of southern England has been heavily treated with a galaxy of different pesticides.

The south coast seacliffs mostly have rather limited bird populations. Pigeons are quite numerous, breeding in fissures and caves, but the Rock Dove stock is wholly diluted by the various types of domestic forms. Jackdaw colonies are generally distributed, Starlings nest widely, and modest numbers of Herring Gulls breed nowadays. The Kestrel is the only other breeding predator on the cliffs at present. The variety of birds passing along this coast and reaching it as

Coastal nesting haunt: 200 m granite cliffs; Bare Stack, Ailsa Craig, Ayrshire (photo: D. A. Ratcliffe)

landfall or departure during migration times must be considerable, but it would seem that a good deal of hunting by the Peregrines was over the downs, woods and farmland behind, and even Romney and Pevensey grazing marshes would be within reach of some eyries. The falcons of this coast thus had wide scope in their choice of prey. There is little doubt that diversity of bird populations has declined, and perhaps overall numbers, too.

The largely cliff-bound seaboard of Cornwall and Devon in the far south-west of England is a Peregrine stronghold of wilder character. The northern coast is pounded by the Atlantic breakers, which have carved long lines of precipice, mostly falling into deep water and visible from below only by boat. The coast is a more indented one than that of the south-east, and many steep-sided little valleys run down to the shore. There is little calcareous rock and, in this strongly oceanic climate, the soils tend to be relatively acidic and infertile. The farms have less arable land and a prevalence of permanent grassland. There was once a large extent of unenclosed rough pasture and heathland with heather, bracken and gorse at the back of many stretches of cliff, but the war on unproductive land has spread here; and many such areas have been 'reclaimed'. The combination of plough, fertiliser, pesticides and seed-drill have increasingly brought the enclosed land right to the cliff edge, and much of it is now arable. Some areas of heath and rough ground remain, especially in the little deep valleys and steep slopes running down to the sea, but here again myxomatosis and the demise of the rabbit have often been followed by development of dense scrub, especially with gorse and brambles.

The Peregrine shares these south-western cliffs with two other fine predators, the Raven and the Buzzard, which still have strong populations here; but the Chough has entirely vanished from this coast. There are moderate-sized seabird colonies with auks, Kittiwakes and Herring Gulls along the Cornwall and Devon coast, but many seacliffs have mainly feral pigeons and Jackdaws. The bird populations of the rough ground and farmland behind the cliffs are similar to those in south-east England, though on this rather poorer land the total numbers may well be lower.

In some places, especially on the English Channel coast, there are more broken cliffs or merely steep slopes running down to the sea. Sometimes the less precipitous coastal scarps have a good deal of wind-pruned scrub and woodland, and where there are also sizeable rock faces, Peregrines can nest in concealed situations so that their eyries can be quite difficult to locate. Scrub of blackthorn, hazel and tall brambles is difficult to penetrate, and dense scrubby oakwood quite effectively obscures one's view. These habitats add to the woodland element in the local bird fauna.

This south-west corner of England has increasingly become the resort of the holiday-maker and recreation seeker. Many parts of the coast are over-run with humanity in the spring and summer, and footpath walks have been opened up along many cliff-tops which were once little trodden. Where the cliffs are large and steep, this intrusion does not upset the Peregrines, but where they are smaller and less suitable, it has a discouraging effect. A still more significant development is seacliff climbing. In their insatiable search for new cliffs and novel situations, rock climbers have lately latched on to the enormous potential of the coastal precipices all over Britain, and many faces are now criss-crossed with hard routes. This is a very direct disturbance to Peregrines residing on the same cliffs, and could have more damaging effects.

The ecological character of the south-west England seacliffs is repeated at intervals farther north in western Britain. In their plant and bird communities, range of geology and topography, and land-use pattern of the hinterland, the cliff coasts of both South and North Wales, St Bees Head, the Isle of Man and south-west Scotland show an essential similarity to that just depicted. There has been the same advance of agriculture, with loss of uncultivated ground behind the cliffs; so that in most places the fields run up to the cliff edge, and the remaining areas of cliff-top heath and rough grassland are mostly confined to

Coastal nesting haunt: 90 m Old Red Sandstone cliffs with large colonies of Guillemots, Razorbills, Kittiwakes and Fulmars; An Dun, Berriedale, Caithness (photo: D. A. Ratcliffe)

steep and rocky ground. The Peregrine has much the same bird neighbours, and though the Buzzard is absent from some of these coastal districts, the Chough nevertheless persists in several of them. There has been variable invasion by the holiday-maker, but most of these coasts are much less quiet than 30 years ago.

With distance north, the frequency of cliffs with large numbers of seabirds tends to increase. Pembrokeshire has immense colonies of Gannets and Manx Shearwaters on its offshore islands, but in western Britain between Lands End and the south Ayrshire coast, the mixed seafowl colonies are only of moderate size. The abrupt rocky cone of Ailsa Craig in the Firth of Clyde was once the most southerly of the really big mixed seabird stations in western Britain, but its auk population has declined. Even on the rugged western seaboard of the Highlands and Islands there are no major seabird cliffs south of the Outer Hebrides. The precipices of Berneray and Mingulay, the Shiants, the Flannans, and above all, the St Kilda group, have huge numbers of Guillemots, Razorbills, Puffins, Kittiwakes, Fulmars, Shags and Herring Gulls. The north-west coast of Sutherland has two famous seabird breeding haunts on the island of Handa and the Clo Mor precipice just east of Cape Wrath.

In eastern England the great chalk cliffs of Bempton and Buckton in Yorkshire still have large numbers of nesting seabirds, although the huge Guillemotry of former years has declined. In eastern Scotland, St Abbs Head in Berwickshire and the Bass Rock and Isle of May in the Firth of Forth have good mixed seafowl colonies. Farther north there are immense numbers at Fowlsheugh in Kincardineshire, on some of the Aberdeen and Banffshire cliffs, and at intervals along the Caithness cliffs as far as Dunnet Head. The Orkneys have large seabird colonies, with the biggest numbers on the island of Westray and Marwick Head on the mainland. The Shetland group also has large total numbers with the biggest concentrations on Noss, Hermaness, Foula and Fair Isle.

These great cliff seabird stations are among the most important ornithological features of this country, for some of the species are extremely restricted in their European or World distribution, and Britain has significant fractions of their total populations. They are certainly the most spectacular bird haunts in these islands, and among the most fascinating of the places where Peregrines breed. The massed ranks of birds on the ledges, the airborne swarm across the front of the precipice, the tumultuous babel of voices, the stench of guano wafting up from

Coastal nesting haunt: 90 m pre-Cambrian cliffs with few seabirds; near South Stack, Holyhead, Anglesey (photo: D. A. Ratcliffe)

below, and the restless sea surging at the base of the cliffs – all these add up to a vivid and memorable impression of wild Nature on the grand scale. The Gannet colonies are most striking of all, with their clouds of magnificent white birds sailing along the cliffs or stacks and thickly clustered on their faces, against a continuous background of clamour. A Peregrine can seem reduced to insignificance in these great bird cities, and may indeed be difficult to detect, even when on the wing. A careful watch may be necessary to pick up the small, characteristic dark silhouette amidst the wheeling throngs of birds.

At one time it could be confidently assumed that any of the big seabird stations would have at least one pair of nesting Peregrines and some of those occupying longer stretches of cliff or the bigger offshore islands had more than one pair. This is no longer so, and nowadays if Peregrines are present at all in the big seabird colonies, they are seldom birds with an active eyrie. The reasons for this deterioration are discussed in Chapter 4. Over the seabirds themselves, particularly along the North Sea coast, hangs the ever-present threat of catastrophic oil-spills, lately realised through the grounding of the tanker *Braer* in Shetland.

The east coast seacliffs from Ross-shire southwards to Bempton are mostly bordered by rich farmland with a predominance of arable, right up to their edge. The hinterland here is not so very different from that adjoining some of the southern England seacliffs, and the bird populations on which the Peregrines feed are rather similar. But from the Ord of Caithness northwards on the east coast, and from the Mull of Kintyre northwards in western Scotland, most of the seacliffs abut large expanses of uncultivated moorland and sheepwalk. Their bird communities vary much in species diversity and numbers. In some places quite productive grouse moors lie close to the seacliffs, but elsewhere the uncultivated terrain has only sparse bird populations. A most dramatic contrast can be seen in Sutherland, where an especially sterile and birdless moorland behind the Clo Mor ends abruptly at the edge of a huge precipice covered with myriads of seafowl.

Some coastal Peregrines nest within a short flight of lower rocky shores or 'soft' coast habitats such as estuarine flats, salt marshes and sand dunes, which have a greater variety of breeding birds, such as terns, gulls, Oystercatcher, Ringed Plover, and a wide selection of waders and wildfowl on passage. A few nest in places difficult to assign to either the coastal or inland category, such as rocky hills facing the sea but with their cliffs standing back at some distance, or on crags flanking large, sheltered sea lochs.

INLAND

True lowland Peregrine haunts include quarries, the limestone gorges of Cheddar and Avon, a few tree-grown river glens below 150 m, and certain rocky bluffs amidst the plains; but most inland Peregrines belong largely to the northern and western mountains and moorlands which cover nearly one-third of the land surface of Britain. These upland systems vary greatly, but the differences especially important to the Peregrine are geology and glacial history, which determine availability of suitable cliffs; and climate, soils, land-use history and proximity to centres of human population, which affect food supply

*Inland nesting haunt: 90 m Borrowdale Volcanic cliff; Lake District, northern England
(photo: D. A. Ratcliffe)*

The bottom land of the valleys and lower hill slopes has typically been enclosed and improved within upland farms, but there is little arable and the fields are mostly under permanent grass. In steep and rugged areas of hard, acidic rocks, and especially in far western districts where the excessively humid climate has caused a general sourness of soils and tendency to peat formation, there is little farmland at all. In drier districts with lower and more gently contoured uplands, and especially on calcareous rocks, farmland is sometimes extensive amongst the hills and reaches relatively high elevations. The open hill beyond the upper farms is variously used as sheepwalk, cattle range, grouse moor or deer forest, and holds most of the crags where the Peregrines breed.

Within the climatic zone of forest, which descends from at least 600 m in the southern and eastern mountains to 300 m in north-west Sutherland, only remnants of original woodland remain. Clearance for fuel and timber, and to provide land for grazing and cultivation, left the British uplands in a largely deforested state. In North and South Wales, Lakeland and parts of the Highlands, good examples of native woodland remain on the lower hill slopes, but in general there is a prevalence of sub-montane dwarf shrub heaths and grasslands which have replaced forest. The deeper and wetter blanket bogs in many districts are a natural vegetation type, but the shallower and drier peatlands also formerly carried at least some growth of trees.

Over much of upland Britain, the Peregrine thus lives in an environment considerably modified by Man. Only in the Scottish Highlands are there substantial areas well above 600 m representing a montane or Arctic–Alpine zone where human influence is negligible and the habitat thus approaches the truly natural. Britain contrasts markedly with many other parts of the World, where the Peregrine breeds in mountain environments little affected by Man.

The great central and eastern Highland mountain systems are the least modified tract of upland Peregrine country in Britain. This district encompasses the upper catchments of the rivers Dee, Spey and Findhorn to the south-east of the Great Glen, and of the Beauly River to the north-west. It consists of high, glaciated mountains of massive form composed of igneous and metamorphic rocks, with well-developed corries and over-steepened sides, and large summit plateaux reaching 1000–1300 m. The main glens are long with considerable streams, while crags are often large and extensive. The upper levels experience a climate of Arctic severity and solifluction forms are well developed.

This is the country about which Seton Gordon wrote so evocatively and which was, in his youth, a remote and little-trodden wilderness of deer forest and grouse moor. The Aviemore area has been opened up in recent years by tourist developments, but these are localised, and much of the former beauty and wildness still remains. The Cairngorms, in particular, are a magnificent range of high mountains where the naturalist can experience a northern and montane ecosystem still almost intact, and with much of its original richness in wildlife. The Peregrine here belongs to a glamorous bird fauna with a greater variety of northern breeding species than any other upland district of Britain.

The large extent of native woodland is an outstanding feature. Farmland is confined mainly to the valley flats, and the lower slopes of the hills are extensively clothed with woods of Scots pine and birch; fascinating remnants of original forest, and containing many trees of great age. The deforested ground within this sub-montane zone has wide dry moors of ling and bell heather, with other dwarf shrubs such as bilberry, cowberry, crowberry and bearberry, or wetter, peaty ground on which heather is mixed with cross-leaved heath, deer sedge, cotton grasses and bog mosses. Above 750 m there are truly montane communities with dwarf shrubs, grasses, sedges, rushes, mosses, liverworts and lichens in a pattern determined largely by varying duration of snow cover.

The diverse bird fauna is especially rich in waders and predators. The meadows and marshes have Lapwing, Snipe and Redshank; the rivers Oystercatcher, Common Sandpiper and a few Ringed Plover; and the moors Curlew

Inland nesting haunt: 260 m granite cliffs, with eyries at least 915 m above sea level; snowbeds on 8 June 1969, above Loch Avon, Cairngorms, central Highlands (photo: D. A. Ratcliffe)

and Golden Plover, with Dunlin and Greenshank locally. Waterfowl are not numerous, but there are Mallard, Teal, Wigeon, Goosander and Red-breasted Merganser on the lochs and rivers, while swampy loch edges, islands and spongy bogs have modest colonies of Black-headed and Common Gulls in places. The woods, besides their more typical community of widespread lowland birds have a distinctive northern element in the Capercaillie, Black Grouse, Crossbill,

Crested Tit and Siskin. Sparrowhawks and Buzzards are widespread and forest-nesting Ospreys and Goshawks have returned. The lower crags have Kestrels and Jackdaw colonies, but the Raven is sparse in this district. The Hen Harrier, Merlin and Short-eared Owl are thinly but widely spread on the heather moors, while the Golden Eagle nests in trees in open forest as well as on the mountain crags, but hunts mainly over the treeless uplands and shares the Peregrine's domain.

The Red Grouse is usually numerous wherever there is good heather ground and is the most important prey species for the Peregrine here. The Meadow Pipit is the most ubiquitous upland bird and the favourite host of the Cuckoo. Although the Twite is much more local than in earlier times, Skylarks, Wheatears and Ring Ousels are generally distributed over the uplands. These common hill birds nest up to considerable elevations, and overlap with our celebrated trio of exclusively montane species; of which Ptarmigan are widespread and numerous above 750 m, Dotterel are very local and sparse, and Snow Buntings are still decidedly rare.

The Peregrine is a hardy species hereabouts, for although some nesting stations are low in the main glens, and well within the woodland zone, a few are in stark settings high in the mountains and well into the Ptarmigan zone. Although the Peregrine does not reach as high a density in the central and eastern Highlands as in some other mountain districts to the south, it has here a good supply of wild prey species throughout the year, so that dependence on the domestic pigeon is minimal.

Other upland districts have a wild bird fauna which, by comparison, is less diverse through lack of certain habitats, held at lower population levels through habitat limitations, or actually impoverished through habitat degradation.

Since early Victorian times, large expanses of the lower uplands between 150 and 600 m have been maintained as grouse preserves, and these still cover a considerable area, especially in Scotland. Although often lacking woodland and montane habitats, the grouse moors are generally the most productive uplands for birds. They are dominated by ling heather which, as the staple food of the Red Grouse, is carefully managed by rotational burning, to maintain a good proportion of young and nutritious growth. Bilberry replaces heather locally and bracken has often invaded extensively on dry, lower slopes. Where drainage is poor, on broad flats, blanket bogs carry mixtures of cotton grass and heather, often with cloudberry. Apart from the Red Grouse itself, these moors frequently have good populations of waders and passerines. Moreover, they are often located in foothill country of eastern districts, and then pass into extensive areas of fertile farmland with a lowland bird fauna. Marginal land with transitional bird communities also covers quite large areas adjacent to some moors.

The main areas of grouse moor lie along the eastern and southern fringes of the Highlands in a broad belt from Easter Ross to Angus and Perthshire, on the lower parts of the Southern Uplands, in the Cheviots, the Pennines, the Bowland Fells, and North York Moors, and certain of the drier, mainly eastern parts of the Welsh mountains. While these moorlands have a good food supply for Peregrines, they tend to be the least favourable of nesting areas because of the general

Inland nesting haunt: 80 m Borrowdale Volcanic cliff; Lake District, northern England (photo: D. A. Ratcliffe)

scarcity of good crags. The characteristic topography is one of smooth, gently undulating uplands unblemished by outcropping rock. The Peregrine population is thus far less than it might be, given a more suitable terrain. Moreover, the few places which attract the bird are all under gamekeeper surveillance, and the fortunes of Peregrines here depend greatly on the attitudes of these custodians of the moors.

Quite large areas of the Highlands are still managed as deer forest, especially in the higher mountain ranges. The most important single use of the British uplands is, however, as sheepwalk. Some hill districts have been under sheep for several centuries, and this use has increased so that many grouse moors and deer forests also have some sheep. Red deer and sheep, in combination with repeated hill burning, have caused widespread replacement of dwarf shrubs, especially heather, by grasses or their relatives, so that grassland or similar vegetation prevails over large areas. There is dominance of fescue and bent on dry ground, mat grass and heath rush on damper soils, and purple moor grass, deer sedge and cotton grass in still peatier situations. Sometimes bilberry has replaced heather first, but is itself eliminated under heavy grazing, and invasion by bracken is often extensive on dry slopes, representing the most advanced stage of vegetational degradation.

Inland nesting haunt: 90 m granite cliffs, with afforested moorland behind; Galloway Hills, southern Scotland (photo: D. A. Ratcliffe)

The deer forests and sheep walks of the western Highlands and Islands are different from those of the east and centre, and afford an especially sharp contrast with the lower grouse moor country, although heather ground is still quite extensive locally, and there are still a few grouse moors in the west. In Wester Ross, Sutherland and parts of the Hebrides there are large areas of blanket bog or rugged moorland with much exposed bedrock, as glaciated bosses and low outcrops, and a prevalence of stony moraines. Some areas are honeycombed with small to medium-sized lochs. This terrain is extensive below 450 m and often forms a lower platform to the higher peaks and ranges which rise abruptly for up to another 600 m. In places there is some resemblance to a fjord coast, with long, narrow arms of the sea flanked by steep, high mountains; while farther inland the deeply carved main glens often have considerable lochs.

This is a harsh, barren and inhospitable land, ill-fitted for permanent occupation by humans. It is wilderness country by our standards, fascinating and splendid to the visiting naturalist, but heart-breaking to many who have had to wrest a precarious living from its rain-sodden and windswept surface. Agriculture is severely limited by unfavourable climate, so that crofts and farms are confined to the few areas of good soil, mainly on the alluvial flats of the larger glens and in pockets along the coasts. The region is a stronghold of Golden Eagles and Greenshanks, Black-throated and Red-throated Divers, but its bird populations are sparse in the main. Many of the characteristic upland species are present, but on this poor land their numbers are mostly low, as in the case of Red Grouse, Golden Plover, Curlew, Lapwing, Snipe and even Meadow Pipit. Food supply for Peregrines is thus poor, except where they are within reach of productive stretches of coast, and few breed inland in the western Highlands and Islands, in relation to the abundance of good nesting cliffs. For the mountains themselves include the most spectacular ranges in our islands, produced by heavy glaciation in areas of igneous and metamorphic rocks. Magnificent corries and tremendous precipices abound, but they are more often held by Golden Eagles than Peregrines, for the falcons tend to nest here at lower levels, along the flanks of the main glens or on the rugged moorlands, avoiding the cold, high cliffs in the inner recesses of the big hills.

The main sheep hills are in the southern fringes of the Highlands, and from there southwards: the Southern Uplands and Cheviots, the Lakeland fells, much of the Pennines, and the greater part of the Welsh mountains. The common feature of these uplands is that they are predominantly green and grassy. Heathery grouse moors are locally extensive, but where sheep have long been the main interest, heather ground is decidedly patchy and often confined to protected places such as cliff ledges, broken scarps or screes.

The sheep walks vary greatly in topography. They include Lakeland and Snowdonia, two districts of outstanding beauty deriving in part from wealth of scenic variety within a small compass. Both are steep and rugged but compact mountain systems, with prevalence of sharp summits and narrow watersheds, cut by numerous deep valleys and flanked by many fine crags and long slopes of unstable scree. Lakeland is celebrated for its superb cluster of large lakes, while Snowdonia has the highest peaks and the fiercest crags south of the Highlands. Good areas of woodland, with native oak, ash, wych elm, birch and hazel as well as alien conifers, enhance the charm of both districts, but many hillsides are largely treeless.

Mortality among the sheep and lambs in these rugged mountains is often high, and the availability of carrion is the main reason for the good populations of Ravens and Buzzards. Stock Doves are frequent breeders in the lower crags, and Snowdonia has inland nesting Choughs in old quarries and mines, but on the whole, these rocky sheep hills have quite limited bird communities, with poor representation of waders and a general scarcity of grouse. By chance, though, Man has provided a compensatory food supply for the Peregrine, in the form of the domestic pigeon. Throughout much of Britain, but especially from the southern fringes of the Highlands southwards, the Peregrine is largely buffered against shortage of wild prey species by the abundance of this quarry, at least during the spring and summer. Lakeland and Snowdonia are thus enabled to sustain a higher Peregrine breeding density than most other inland districts, and during winter they are within reach of quite productive lowland and coastal hunting grounds.

The western part of the Southern Uplands, in Galloway and Carrick, has an area of rugged hills with numerous crags where Peregrines again reach a high breeding density. This district has something of the character of the western

Inland nesting haunt: 15–46 m granite cliff. Eyrie site on grass ledges half way up vertical face; Galloway, southern Scotland (photo: D. A. Ratcliffe)

Highlands, in physical features, vegetation and fauna, but its special charm is perhaps connected with the variety and contrast of the scene. Desolate, rocky granite moorlands quite quickly give way to green wooded valleys and lush pastures, with lochs and rivers of lowland type. Sparse bird populations on the uplands are offset by a rich and abundant avifauna in the lowlands, and the domestic pigeon is again in good supply. Autumn and winter feeding for the Peregrine is good, for it is a most productive bird haunt at these seasons, with waders and wildfowl especially numerous both inland and on the Solway shore.

The other parts of the Southern Uplands have a characteristic topography of rounded hills, with steep, smooth sides, much dissected by deep, water worn valleys. Cliffs occur in local concentration in the Moffat Hills, but they are otherwise few, small and mainly in stream ravines. This kind of hill landform belongs especially to the softer rocks of the sedimentary formations, and so is also widespread in central and south Wales, where crags are again sparse or absent in many areas but in good number locally. The Pennines have quite big limestone cliffs in a few places, but most of this large expanse of high moorland has only modest and thinly scattered outcrops of this rock, gritstone, shale and whinsill. Bird populations are often larger and more varied on these smoother hills than in the rugged mountains, but Peregrines are fewer, through shortage of nesting places.

Hill sheep farming is in a decline and being steadily replaced by forestry as an alternative land use. During the last 70 years there has been a steady restoration

Inland nesting haunt: 20 m dolerite Whinsill cliff; Pennines, northern England (photo: D. A. Ratcliffe)

of tree-cover over much deforested upland, albeit largely by alien conifers, mainly Sitka spruce, lodgepole pine and larch. Some districts, notably the Southern Uplands and Cheviots, have been transformed by blanket afforestation on a vast scale, obliterating whole areas of moorland along with their characteristic bird fauna. The Raven and Buzzard have declined as the sheepwalks have been planted, but the Peregrine, whose food supply is here largely independent of the new forests, is so far unaffected. These conifer forests also cover large areas of Wales and parts of the Highlands, and foresters press for further expansion of upland afforestation in Scotland. In the remoter parts of the Highlands the Peregrines' food supply could well become affected by such a change, and the impact on wildlife in general is already profound.

Increase in recreation-seeking amongst the hills has taken place over nearly a century but with marked acceleration since 1945. The peace of once secluded districts such as Snowdonia, Lakeland, the Craven Pennines and the Trossachs has been destroyed, at least during the ever-expanding holiday season. There is no disguising the increasingly beaten paths winding over the hillsides, nor the sheer numbers of people in evidence. New long-distance walks, such as the Pennine Way, have opened up once quiet hill country known to few outsiders. The character of the uplands changes by degrees as the pressure of people increases, but what does this growing disturbance mean to the birds?

On the whole it has very little effect. Where large numbers of fell walkers pass close to small cliffs, they create unacceptable intrusion, and the bigger crag-nesting birds then quit. But where the crags are large and the nesting ledges safe, almost any amount of casual disturbance will be endured by birds such as Peregrines and Ravens. Rock climbing has so increased in popularity that in the more accessible districts many Peregrine cliffs are subject to this very direct disturbance, but even this close intrusion has adverse effects only in certain places, again mainly where the crags are small. In districts with many large cliffs the Peregrines usually adapt in one way or another.

Even the remoter parts of the Highlands and Islands are now showing the advent of tourism on a significant scale. There are still large areas of wild country kept as sanctuaries for deer and grouse, but they change gradually. Hydro-electric schemes have degraded the character of many glens, especially through unsightly draw-down zones around the larger lochs. The Landrover has revolutionised travel amongst the hills, and new estate roads have opened up many remote uplands, so that shepherds, keepers and stalkers can cover their beats more rapidly, and idle shooters can be carted up the hill. The new forests are served by networks of roads, and helicopters are used for aerial applications of fertilisers and pesticides. Hill farming, too, has increased in mechanisation, and the improvement of marginal land and reclamation of moorland has been another trend of the times.

The inland haunts of the Peregrine thus lie within a changing environment, but one so extensive that the change overall can only be slow. And although there is great pressure to increase the productivity of such 'waste' lands for economic gain, the natural constraints of adverse physical conditions must place a limit on development. Though lacking the spectacle and excitement of the sheer numbers of seafowl in some coastal stations, the uplands have a bird fauna which gains in interest through the attractions of the setting. The robust crowing of the Red Grouse and the plaintive piping of the Golden Plover epitomise a habitat of appealing rigour to which the Peregrine fittingly belongs. And while a lone Dotterel running silently amidst the solitude of a remote mountain top is the very antithesis of the noisy seabird citadels on the rocky headlands, the experience for the watcher can be just as memorable. Together, the wild rocky coasts and the uplands represent that part of our island least tamed by Man and most likely to endure as wildlife refuge.

OTHER REGIONS OF THE WORLD

Beyond Britain, the Peregrine is again a bird mainly of undeveloped country. In Ireland its haunts cover a range of habitats similar to those in Britain. It is generally distributed on the precipitous coastal sections and well known in the great Irish seabird stations, such as Rathlin Island in Antrim, Horn Head in

Donegal, the Cliffs of Moher in Clare, the Blaskets and Skelligs in Kerry, and the Saltees in Wexford. The main hill massifs of Ireland are scattered round the periphery: the Mountains of Mourne and of Wicklow in the east have some good crags, but the most rugged ranges are in the west, from Donegal to Kerry. As in Britain, the drier and fertile east contrasts with the humid and sterile west, and the difference affects the food value of both coastal and inland areas for Peregrines. The domestic pigeon is again quite freely available in the east, but there are few places where the Red Grouse occurs in any numbers nowadays. The west is a rain-soaked and windswept land with striking similarity to the western Highlands and Islands of Scotland, including notably sparse bird populations, except where seafowl throng the coastal precipices in certain favoured localities. Peregrine distribution and numbers vary accordingly: the east has more food but fewer good nesting cliffs, and the converse is true in the west.

Over the rest of its World range the Peregrine again breeds mainly on rocky coasts or inland crags, but in habitats of widely varying character. As the distribution map in Figure 22 shows, the Peregrine is an almost cosmopolitan species, though absent as a breeder from most of the New World south of Mexico, large desert and equatorial regions of Africa, the Persian Gulf region, south-central Asia, Malaysia, New Zealand, Antarctica and the high Arctic generally. Its breeding range encompasses virtually all the major climatic zones of the World, but the precise distribution of the Peregrine depends either on the occurrence of cliffs or on the degree to which the bird has locally adapted to nesting in other habitats. Basically, it is a cliff-nester the world over, and a large proportion of the populations of all the races of *Falco peregrinus* appears to depend on this kind of physiographic feature.

In the temperate regions of the Old and New Worlds, the Peregrine is mainly a bird of country which has been variably deforested in the interests of agriculture. There are lowland haunts along big river gorges and on precipitous bluffs in a variety of situations, whilst in parts of Europe ruined castles in commanding places are resorted to regularly. The main breeding areas are again in the higher and rockier mountain ranges. The crag-girt valleys of the Alps, the Jura, the Pyrenees, the Carpathians and the fjord country of western Norway are on a grander scale than anything in Britain, and there is usually a general cover of forest within which the upland farms have carved gaps. The Peregrines here belong to the subalpine and forest zones, but they feed also within the alpine zone beyond, and their nesting places often appear against a spectacular background of snow and ice-clad mountains. The great mountains of the Rockies and other North American ranges provide a comparable subalpine/alpine breeding terrain for the Peregrine, with escarpments cut on a similarly massive scale.

In a few regions, notably the Baltic countries and parts of Australia, Peregrines breed in trees, mainly by utilising the vacant nests of other birds but sometimes by using holes, and so have a true niche in forest country, although they still appear to need plenty of open ground for hunting. In Finland and Estonia Peregrines have adapted widely to nesting on hummocks of the great pool-studded bogs forming open enclaves within the Boreal forests, and in the northern regions of both Eurasia and North America the vast spreads of taiga woodland restrict Peregrines in many areas to the open ground along the main rivers where they breed on cliffs and cut banks. The species occurs right across the Arctic regions, but does not penetrate as far north as the Gyr Falcon. Great expanses of tundra are flat or only gently contoured, and Peregrines nest here on the earth banks of rivers or, in Siberia, on the ground. Parts of the western Canadian prairies also become habitable by dint of nesting on river cut banks.

Peregrines have adapted well to nesting in quite dry regions, including limestone karst terrain, steppe and savanna country and semi-desert, and their nesting habitats include the river canyons, dry wadis, exposed buttes and inselbergs representing erosion features of ancient landforms. In the arid regions of the Old World the Peregrine has evolved different, usually browner-plumaged forms which are distinguished by subspecific rank, and in the really arid environments it is replaced by other species – the Lanner Falcon in Africa, the Saker Falcon in southern Asia, and the Prairie Falcon in North America. One of the adaptations of these semi-desert falcons is that they are consistently mammal as well as bird feeders, and this wider choice may give them the advantage over the Peregrine in these harsh climates. In the humid Sub-Tropics and Tropics, Peregrines appear to be rare and dependent on discontinuities in the forest cover.

Peregrines inhabit rocky coasts in all five continents, and, as in Britain, their existence here is mainly related either to the prevailing habitat conditions of the coastal hinterland, or to the seabird populations which give distinction to many seacliffs and rocky islands ranging from the Tropics to the Arctic Ocean. The chalk cliffs of Normandy were once a Peregrine haunt as celebrated as those of Kent and Sussex on the English side of the Channel. The Channel Islands themselves had a number of seacliff haunts resembling some of those in southwest England. Seacliff nesting haunts on the Mediterranean coast have less familiar plants and bird neighbours, such as prickly pear and Osprey, while the nesting places on rocky shores washed by tropical seas vary from the mainly bare headlands of desert regions to scarps set amidst luxuriant forest. Breeding grounds with seabird colonies lie especially in cool northern waters, and the size of some of these concentrations dwarfs even the largest in Britain and Ireland. Peale's Falcon, the race of the Peregrine found in the north-east Pacific islands, is associated especially with the immense throngs of auks and petrels found in the Queen Charlottes and the Aleutians.

As in Britain, Peregrines in other parts of the world appear during winter in many regions where they do not breed. Mostly they would seem to be birds from the far north of both Old and New Worlds, compelled to move southwards by the rigours of the Arctic winter and the departure of their food supply on migration. The result is a passage through country with every habitat between the extremes of dense forest and desert, to take up winter quarters in such places as the oases of the southern Sudan, the swamps of the Florida Everglades, and the tropical islands of the Caribbean Sea.

CHAPTER 3

Population trends in Britain

PRACTICAL PROBLEMS OF COUNTING PEREGRINES

It would be extremely difficult to determine the complete distribution and numbers of the Peregrine in Britain throughout the year. After the breeding season a substantial dispersal from the nesting grounds is apparent since many young birds and some adults vanish from these areas, and there is an autumnal influx of Peregrines into lowland districts where the species does not breed. Juveniles appear to outnumber adults in this dispersal. Besides the breeders and their new progeny, the population contains a further group of adults and sub-adults which formed a non-breeding surplus during the spring and summer. This non-breeding element is difficult to assess at any time, and we do not know if it becomes more widely dispersed during the winter. Even Peregrines which remain in or close to their breeding haunts during the winter become more difficult to locate and follow then. There is also an autumnal influx of migrant Peregrines from continental Europe, mainly Fennoscandia (Chapter 9).

Peregrines can turn up almost anywhere outside the breeding season, and whilst some occupy winter territories, others may remain wanderers unattached to any one place, so that an estimate of winter population size is impracticable.

Counts of Peregrines in known or potential nesting haunts during the breeding season give the only reliable index of population size, though this tells us little about the numbers of non-breeders and so is not a measure of total population. The Peregrine's habit of resorting to traditional nesting cliffs makes it one of the easier species to census and the total breeding population of Britain and Ireland could be counted with a considerable degree of accuracy, given sufficient field effort. Even so, any census is beset with difficulties and pitfalls.

Much depends on the nature of the terrain. If there is only a single cliff within a hill massif, or only a short stretch of rocky coast, it is fairly easy to be sure if Peregrines are present and nesting, or not. The difficulty of locating falcons, or, worse, proving their absence, increases with the number and extent of suitable cliffs, and can be considerable in rugged mountain areas or on extensive coastal precipices. In each territory the known and possible alternative cliffs have to be inspected one by one until the falcons are found, or it becomes clear that they are absent. In some inland areas in good weather it may take several man days of hard searching to establish that a particular territory is vacant.

Some pairs nest late or suffer disturbance and so may be without an occupied eyrie when most other pairs have eggs or young. Before laying time or after loss of eggs, Peregrines will not necessarily be about their nesting cliffs when these are inspected. Cliffs are sometimes held throughout the spring and summer by single Peregrines or by apparently non-breeding pairs; these are also more loosely attached to the nesting cliffs and so are more easily missed than the actual breeders. Moreover, a single bird may have lost its mate and a pair without a nest may have lost eggs or young – yet there may be no way of telling what has happened. If birds have been destroyed or discouraged from nesting before a territory is examined, the place may seem deserted that year, but replacements may also turn up later in the season. It is therefore better not to declare a nesting territory vacant until at least three visits have been made at well-spaced intervals during the breeding season.

These sources of error lead to a tendency to underestimate size of breeding population, but others have the opposite effect. A pair which has lost its clutch may move to a different cliff for a repeat laying and then be reported as an additional pair. Peregrines sometimes frequent one cliff before laying time but nest on another, and a bird may appear at a crag some distance from where its mate is sitting. Pluckings or castings may be left in places far from the eyrie cliffs. Occasionally, a pair will frequent a crag not or only seldom known to be used before, but will then disappear without laying eggs. Some non-breeders may be wanderers visiting various possible nesting areas and leaving traces, but soon moving on.

Egg collecting and gamekeeper persecution once added considerably to the difficulties of counting breeding Peregrines in certain districts, and changes in the Peregrine population caused by pesticides, especially after 1955, greatly complicated the pattern of breeding in most districts. With so many territories apparently vacant or held by non-breeding Peregrines, and with breeding failures so frequent, it became still more difficult than in 'normal' times to census even a local population in any one year.

An estimate of breeding population size based only on actual eyries seen with eggs or young would therefore give a conservative figure. I have preferred to adopt a measure of breeding population which includes all occupations of nesting territories during spring and early summer. Any evidence of the presence of

Peregrines over this period, in a territory where nesting has previously been known, is counted as an occupation. The sight of a bird or the finding of a recent kill are thus considered good enough indication of territory occupation. While this approach could at times lead to an over-estimate of numbers, the only clear line that can be drawn regarding territory occupation is between presence and absence, and I do not believe the errors are serious. When Peregrines are present but do not nest, in a locality where breeding is not previously known, they are counted only as prospecting birds within the non-breeding population.

Population studies are concerned not only with numbers in any one year, but also with fluctuations over a period of years. Learning about breeding population trends in the Peregrine is difficult, because of the lack of good census data for earlier periods. Ideally, a complete census is needed every year, but for the Peregrine, this would be extremely costly to maintain on the Great Britain scale. The national surveys in 1961–62, 1971, 1981 and 1991 attempted full cover, but only the last two came near this goal, and in the other years after 1962, only certain districts were counted annually. Peregrine counting is an activity demanding considerable observer-effort, even to cover a fifth of the total breeding distribution in Britain. If only sample districts can be censused, it is important that they are representative of the whole country, and can thereby provide both a national barometer of trends and an indication of any geographical pattern resulting from significant variations between districts. Preferably, the same selection of territories has to be monitored year after year to give the most reliable results.

Another method of assessing the amount of breeding population fluctuation is based on the probability of finding Peregrines present when a known nesting territory is examined. If a territory is occupied regularly, with no break over a long period, there will be a very good chance of finding the birds in occupation during any one visit. But if a territory is held irregularly, with Peregrines present in only half the years over a long period, there will be only a 50% chance of finding them during a single visit. By adding up the results (presence or absence) for a large number of visits to all or most of the territories in a region, it is possible to calculate an overall figure for the average frequency of territory occupation. When compared with the total number of territories this gives a measure of average population size.

In any kind of sample counts, a tendency to visit territories known to have a history of regular occupation, and to neglect those known to be seldom occupied, could easily cause a marked bias to be built into the results. Many of the older series of records left by Peregrine enthusiasts are of limited value in this context because they mentioned only the presence of birds and not their absence.

In some respects, it is preferable to make a more subjective analysis based on *all* the available information on the history of each territory. In the first edition of this book, I found it useful to adopt a simple classification according to a four-category scale of average frequency of occupation:

Regular   – not known to be absent more than one year in ten.

Irregular   – absent from three to eight years out of ten.

Occasional – present for only two years out of ten or less.

Deserted   – not known to be used since 1930, and where known environmental changes make re-occupation unlikely.

Since 1980, the continuing increases of breeding populations in many districts have made this classification less appropriate: many irregular or occasional territories appear to have become regular, but many new territories have not been held long enough to know what their frequency of use will prove to be.

ESTABLISHING A BASE-LINE OF POPULATION SIZE

The first attempt at an assessment of the total numbers of Peregrines in Britain and Ireland was made by James Ferguson-Lees during 1947–50. Mainly by correspondence with a large number of informants, he established that in Britain and Ireland, excluding the Channel Islands, there were between 570 and 586 Peregrine breeding stations, of which between 480 and 500 were occupied in the three years 1947 to 1949. He estimated that there were probably not less than 100 and not more than 200 further pairs to be found, mainly in Scotland and Ireland. Ferguson-Lees was concerned mainly to evaluate the impact of war-time shooting (1940–45) which he believed had reduced the Peregrine population of England to half its pre-1939 level.

In a re-assessment in 1957, Ferguson-Lees concluded that there had been considerable though incomplete recovery, with numbers still below pre-war level in certain, mainly southern districts. In England he estimated that 85 or possibly 90 pairs out of a pre-war average of 115 were present. For the whole of Britain and Ireland he believed that the current (1957) population could fairly be put at between 650 and 750 breeding pairs, a total probably still 100–200 pairs below the pre-war level.

The origin of the British Trust for Ornithology Peregrine Enquiry in 1961–62 has been mentioned in Chapter 1. This Great Britain census of breeding population, drawing on the help of over 170 observers and organised by myself, established that the Peregrine was in the middle of a catastrophic decline. The Enquiry, and subsequent studies, allowed me to build up a body of background information on distribution and status against which to assess the size of the population in earlier periods, as well as the magnitude of recent changes. I have regarded 1930–39 as a standard period, to provide a base-line in time for assessment of the Peregrine population. Before 1930, information on distribution and numbers is too patchy to give an adequate national picture, while after 1940 there have been major upheavals for the Peregrine, with impact on a scale much greater than any influences during the intervening years.

Our knowledge of breeding distribution in Great Britain has increased steadily, even since 1961–62, when I had records of breeding in 718 different territories after 1930, and estimated that 20–30 additional territories remained to be discovered in Scotland. My estimate for average annual level of breeding population for 1930–39 was then about 650 pairs. Following the 1971 national census, I revised these figures to 805 territories occupied since 1930, up to 50 additional territories still undiscovered, and an average 1930–39 population of at least 700 pairs.

By 1979, I was informed of another 36 occupied Peregrine territories previously unknown to me, and of these only four could be regarded as 'new'. In that year, I also estimated that a further 100 post-1930 territories still remained to be

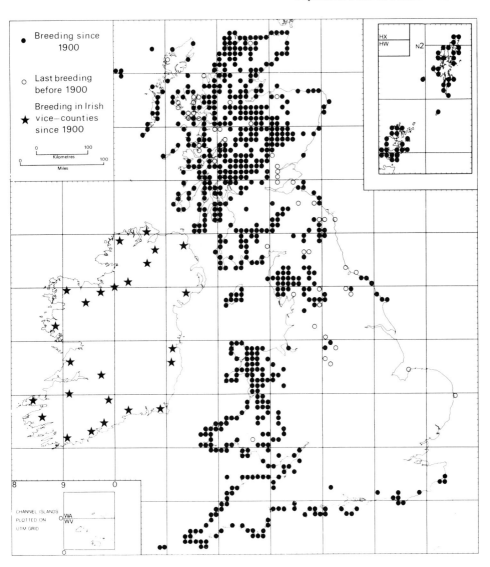

Figure 2. Breeding distribution of the Peregrine in Britain and Ireland during 1900–1960.

NOTES: Symbols show 10 × 10 km grid squares in which the Peregrine has been known to breed, and are probably a good indication of breeding distribution during 1900–1960. This conventional method of mapping does not differentiate between 10 km squares in which there is a single, isolated record of nesting and those in which several pairs have bred regularly.

discovered above the known total of the 1971 survey. These consisted of a mixture, including haunts used perhaps regularly during 1930–39 but deserted during the crash and not yet re-occupied (especially in Cornwall and Wales); those used only occasionally or irregularly because of keeper attentions (grouse moors in the Pennines, North York Moors and eastern Scotland), and a third group which may have remained regularly occupied all the way through (mainly in remote parts of the Highlands and Islands). By making allowance for these additional territories, known and estimated, I suggested that 800 pairs was closer to the true average number of Peregrines nesting in Britain during 1930–39.

By the conclusion of the third national survey, in 1981, another 107 breeding territories had become known, nearly all of them occupied. Of the 107, at least 16 appeared to be completely new territories, in that they were in well-worked areas but had no previous records of breeding: mainly in Wales, northern England and southern Scotland. The remaining 91 represented most of my estimate of 100 unknown additional territories for 1930–39; of these 78 were in the Highlands, while 51 seemed likely to have been regular and 40 irregular in occupation. Yet another reassessment, based on the 1981 census, gave 820 pairs as the best estimate of 1930–39 population for Great Britain (Ratcliffe, 1984). I intend this to be a final figure, which is probably on the conservative side – properly so, rather than an over-estimate. It seems right to draw the line here, and to regard the many additional territories found in the 1991 survey as representing real increase in the Peregrine population over pre-war levels. We shall now never know the precise earlier figures for many areas, and further comment on the matter can be no more than a matter of opinion.

By 1981, older records and recent survey suggested that the Peregrine breeding population of Northern Ireland was around 54 pairs during 1930–39. In the Republic of Ireland, sample surveys in 1981 indicated a total breeding population of at least 225 breeding pairs within an estimated 278 available breeding territories (Norriss and Wilson, 1983). This suggests that the earlier estimate given by John Temple Lang of 180–200 pre-1950 pairs might be revised upwards to 230–250 pairs.

When Britain and Ireland are taken together it thus appears probable that around 1100 pairs of Peregrines annually attempted to nest in this north-west corner of Europe in the period 1930–39. With land surfaces totalling 229,870 and 84,430 sq km, respectively (together totalling 314,300 sq km), this gives a remarkably high density on the World scale, especially when one remembers that there are quite large areas of both countries with no breeding Peregrines at all.

SHORT-TERM BEHAVIOUR OF POPULATION

While I have presented the 1930–39 base-line figures as average population levels, it is proper to enquire what degree of fluctuation there may have been within this or other decades. It is important to know whether there is evidence for past short-term fluctuations in numbers of a kind which characterises some other birds of prey. Only then can we have an accurate perspective on the significance of the irregular population changes that have certainly taken place both before and after this period.

While there was no attempt to make a countrywide census of Peregrine breeding numbers and to monitor trends by field survey until 1961–62 onwards, there is quite good population information from certain areas for earlier periods, sometimes covering a fair spread of years. Mostly these records came from egg collectors, but they are supplemented locally by the observations of Peregrine watchers, falconers, gamekeepers, fishermen and lighthouse keepers. The available information is summarized within the detailed account of distribution on pp. 73–115.

Where adequate data exist, they nearly always point to a relative constancy of Peregrine breeding population, with only small variations between any two consecutive years, at least for the pre-pesticide era. This was, indeed, the feature which impressed me strongly after I had been looking at the species for several seasons. Each nesting place was usually occupied regularly year after year so that, in any one area, no more and no fewer Peregrines were to be found in every successive year. This pattern was confirmed by other Peregrine enthusiasts with whom I spoke. Local residents, in reply to the question about how long and regularly Peregrines had nested in an adjacent locality usually gave the characteristic answer, 'Every year, for as long as I can remember'. The consistent impression was that, whilst not every nesting place was checked every year, whenever a known haunt was examined, it usually held a pair of falcons. However, a relatively small number of territories was known certainly to be held irregularly, with breaks of varying duration in tenancy. Some haunts had runs of occupation only once in a while.

It is noticeable that many writers of county Avifaunas have presented information on Peregrine numbers in such a way as to imply relative constancy of population, as though this were an understood feature. And the older historical references to particular eyries mostly indicated clearly that these were tenanted regularly. This implicit affirmation of population stability is exemplified by selected quotations in the detailed accounts of distribution on pp. 73–115. There is also the shrewd observation of Giraldus Cambrensis from the 12th century, that in Ireland the numbers of Peregrines and eyries did not increase under protection.

The specific information available for each district varies in quality. The best data are from Kent, Sussex, Dorset, parts of South Wales, Snowdonia, Lakeland, the Moffat–Tweedsmuir Hills, Galloway and Carrick. For each of these except Sussex there is reliable evidence that Peregrine breeding populations varied over a period of at least one decade by no more than about 7–8% either side a median level. In Lakeland this degree of constancy was maintained over the whole period 1900–60. In Sussex, fluctuations were sometimes more marked, even between successive years, though the absolute numbers were small: from 8–12 pairs representing 20% either side a median value. Moderate fluctuations were also reported for Devon and Pembrokeshire over a period of a decade or so (see county tallies, Chapter 4). On the whole, though, the high proportion of regularly occupied territories in other counties suggests that their Peregrine populations inclined to constancy rather than otherwise.

I have analysed my own records for two of these districts in the way described on p. 57. In the Southern Uplands of Scotland, in 179 visits to 26 inland Peregrine territories during 1946–60, evidence of occupation was detected on 157 occasions (88%). When all available records for Southern Upland territories were taken for this period, in a total of 228 observations there were 206 occupations (90%) and 22 absences; and 23 out of 29 territories were occupied on every visit. In Lakeland and the northern Pennines, 133 visits to 31 inland territories during 1945–60 gave 114 occupations (86%). All available records for the longer period 1936–60, for 39 territories in this district, show that in 378 observations there were 322 occupations (85%) and 56 absences; and 28 out of 39 territories were occupied on every visit.

There are no good figures from the Highlands and Islands before the 1961–62 census, but from this time until 1978, the Peregrines of the central massifs drained by the Spey and Dee showed an essential constancy in numbers. This segment of the population was virtually unaffected by the general crash, although it showed some fluctuations in breeding success.

While the critical information is thus erratic geographically, it may be said that where the data are adequate to show mode of population behaviour in the short term, they consistently point to a remarkable stability during the period 1900–40. There is an absence of evidence for any fluctuation or cycle in numbers with the kind of time scale found in some other birds (5–10 years). This leads me to argue that for those segments of the British population on which there is little critical information, there is a greater probability that constancy rather than fluctuation was the prevailing mode *during this period*. And since there is no evidence that irregularities in territory occupation between different districts – or even within the same district – were in phase with each other, these minor ups and downs would tend to cancel each other out, giving still greater constancy to the British population as a whole.

In Table 1, the county base-lines of average annual breeding population for 1930–39 are calculated by taking the number of regular pairs, plus half the irregular pairs, but ignoring the occasionals. Where the numbers of pairs in the categories regular, irregular and occasional are not known within a county total, they are estimated by using the average figures of 70, 22 and 8% of total known territories for those counties where there are good data. Apart from Denbighshire, Derbyshire, Yorkshire, Northumberland and Peebleshire, where there were high proportions of irregular and occasional territories, in most counties the average level of breeding population thus works out at about 80% of the known total of territories, excluding deserted ones. Where there are estimates of additional unknown territories, due allowance is made in county totals of breeding pairs.

EARLIER POPULATION TRENDS

While many 20th century Peregrine breeding places are mentioned in the literature as having occupied eyries in much earlier periods, this tells us little about their previous frequency of occupation, and still less about the size of the

Peregrine in a mountain landscape

Series of Peregrine clutches from Britain and Ireland. Edgar Chance Collection, British Museum (Natural History) (photo: D. A. Ratcliffe)

breeding population at any one time. We cannot deduce with any real confidence how many Peregrines bred in Britain during the Middle Ages and in subsequent centuries, and whether or by how much they fluctuated. The only reliable population figures are those produced by the recent enquiries and relating to the past few decades. One way of gauging previous numbers and trends is thus to consider whether there are good reasons for supposing that the Peregrine population during earlier centuries should have been markedly different from that in the recent past. This is necessarily a speculative procedure, but there are a few useful pointers to help.

I believe it is highly unlikely that the Peregrine eyries documented between 1200–1800 were the only ones that existed then. Despite the Mediaeval preoccupation with falconry, it is probable that only a small proportion of extant nesting places in the whole of Britain and Ireland ever became known, or at least sufficiently well known to receive mention by the few chroniclers of the time. Even by the late 19th century, when the literature of British ornithology had reached a considerable volume and included a number of county or regional avifaunas, most ornithological writers of the time give little indication of having an accurate awareness of Peregrine numbers. Up to 1900 the recorded distribution of the species was very patchy, and I believe must have represented much less than the real total. The amount of such information increases with time, but this almost certainly reflects growing interest in birds generally – including a later inclination to count them – and not an increase in falcon population.

Many writers have, indeed, been disposed to assume a reverse trend; that there has been a substantial decline in Peregrine population since the Middle Ages. Ferguson-Lees (1951) pointed out that there is little evidence for this: he found that of 49 eyries noted in the falconry and other literature of the 16th to 19th centuries, 42 were still in use between 1930 and 1939. While some traditional nesting places of earlier centuries have become permanently deserted, the number is not huge, and Ferguson-Lees also commented '. . . there are only 52 cliffs [in Britain and Ireland] known to the writer which once regularly held Peregrines and which became deserted before 1939'. The literature records I have assembled for Britain include only 30 known former territories which were not recorded in use by Peregrines during 1930–80, and at least six of these have since been re-occupied. However, I believe many other territories were deserted before they ever reached the records (see Table 1). I have estimated that during 1800–1930, there were the following losses of territories by desertion: England 60, Wales 49, Scotland 120+.

Most of these haunts were abandoned as the result of human disturbance, formerly involving deliberate persecution as the rule, but latterly more often as the result of recreational or other incidental activities. A few long-deserted nesting cliffs have been rendered untenable through man-made alterations but many remain quite suitable, and have steadily re-tenanted since 1980. A much larger number of new and suitable cliffs has actually been created in the form of stone quarries. A more general decline occurred in the western Highlands and Islands between about 1880 and 1930, seemingly as a response to falling food supply occasioned by indirect human influence, in the form of over-exploitation of carrying capacity of the land (see pp. 295–6). This decline accounted for the desertion of an estimated 100 territories.

I have little information about desertion of nesting places in Ireland, but there is likely to have been a parallel abandonment of low-lying and easily accessible haunts over the same period. Moreover, its strong ecological similarity with the western Highlands suggests that the west of Ireland is also likely to have suffered some decline as a result of reduction in carrying capacity of the land. I venture to suggest that Ireland has lost at least 50 territories permanently since 1800.

A geographically irregular decline thus occurred, mostly during the 19th century, involving the loss of around 265 pairs in Britain and Ireland. If it is a correct assumption that the majority of territories occupied since 1900 were held with similar frequency for at least the previous two centuries, then the earlier hey-day of the Peregrine could be envisaged as an indefinite period preceding 1800, before subsequent decline set in. Since the estimate of the Britain and Ireland breeding population for 1930–39 is 1100 pairs, the addition of 265 lost eyries gives the total of over 1350 pairs as the number of Peregrines which may once have bred in Britain and Ireland.

It is right to question the assumption that, apart from the declines indicated, Peregrine numbers elsewhere in Britain and Ireland have remained at a fairly steady level during the last three centuries. A great deal obviously depends on other evidence for change in food supply, besides that for western Scotland. While the advent and increase of pigeon-racing in the 19th century enhanced the availability of an important prey species, large numbers of dove-cot pigeons were around during an earlier period. It is also quite probable that much Peregrine country may once have had a higher carrying capacity in wild prey than during the past hundred years of intensive exploitation of almost all habitats by Man. Only when the historical perspective is taken sufficiently far back are there ecological grounds for supposing that Peregrines may once have been less numerous. During the time, perhaps as far back as before the Roman era, when most of Britain was forest covered, there was probably less habitat for this bird, and its place may have been taken to some extent by woodland dwelling raptors. The greater extent of open, non-wooded country created by Man during the last 4000 years favours the Peregrine, and the bird may have increased markedly as the great forests of ancient times were destroyed.

My main conclusion is accordingly that the Peregrine population probably did not change markedly in size from, say, the Middle Ages up to about 1800, after which there were slow declines locally. These resulted entirely from human influence, acting directly through persecution and indirectly through a depletion of food supply.

THE WAR-TIME DECLINE

The Peregrine's fondness for domestic pigeons as prey brought it into real disfavour in Britain in war-time, when carrier pigeons were used extensively for carrying military messages and had to be protected against this risk of predation. It has been said that some killing of Peregrines took place in the 1914–18 war, but there is little information on this, and it is the campaign waged in World War II that is of concern here.

Under the war-time emergency defence regulations, the then Secretary of State for Air made on 1 July 1940 the Destruction of Peregrine Falcons Order, 1940, which expired in February 1946, after the war had ended. This Order made it lawful for any properly authorised person to take or destroy Peregrines or their eggs in certain parts of Britain. The particular need for protecting carrier pigeons seems to have been their use by airmen who crash-landed when on sea patrol around the western and north-eastern coasts. In England the Order covered only Cornwall, Devon and coastal areas of the North Riding of Yorkshire, while in Wales it included Pembrokeshire, Caernarvon, Anglesey and coastal Denbighshire. In the west of Scotland it covered all of Buteshire, Argyll, and the islands of Inverness-shire, and in the east, East Lothian and the Forth islands, eastern districts of Ross and Sutherland, all Caithness, Orkney and Shetland.

This seems a rather curious selection of districts. I have been unable to find out whether there were later orders which extended the areas in which Peregrines could legally be killed, but it is certain that some desultory destruction took place on the coast of south-east England, in other parts of Wales and Lakeland. Probably a number of people took it upon themselves or were actually encouraged to kill Peregrines and raid nests without strict legal sanction, and the campaign of persecution evidently began earlier in 1940 than the precise date of the Order.

Ferguson–Lees (1951) stated that, 'As far as it has been possible to ascertain any figures, something under 600 adults and immatures were shot during this period (1940–45), in addition to many eyasses and eggs being destroyed.' That is an average of about 100 birds each year over the 5-year period. The slaughter seems to have been most concentrated and relentless in south-west England, and the Peregrine populations of Cornwall, Devon and Dorset were virtually eliminated, though one pair was said to have escaped in Cornwall. On the coasts of Sussex and Kent some pairs were evidently eradicated but a good many survived. Ferguson-Lees believed that the nesting population in England was reduced to about half its pre-war level, and he knew of 55 pairs still attempting to breed in 1944. Numbers probably fell to about 87% of the 1939 level nationally.

There is little specific information about the impact of Peregrine destruction in Wales or Scotland, and though a good many were killed in each, this evidently caused only local and temporary depletion. In Northern Ireland, A. S. Hughes found that the previous strength of nine pairs on one section of the Antrim coast was reduced to four pairs, but the whole of the Irish Republic was without military persecution of Peregrines. Losses were in general much heavier in coastal areas than inland.

There was another side of the coin, however. As in World War I, the majority of gamekeepers were called up for military service, and in many grouse-preserving districts there was during 1940–45 a general reduction or even cessation in the relentless destruction of this and other raptors which had been so consistent an event previously. In some localities where Peregrines had never had a chance of survival, successions of broods fledged during the war period, and provided some compensation for the heavy losses in some coastal districts.

However repugnant the scale of destruction may have been, it had no permanent effects, for as soon as the campaign ceased in 1946, recovery began in all the depleted districts, as the details on p. 290 show, and the Peregrine was well on the way to restoring its former population level when a new calamity began to overtake it. The effect of synthetic organic pesticides on numbers takes over thenceforth as a much more serious factor in the history of the species.

THE PESTICIDE CRASH

The result of organochlorine pesticide contamination in the Peregrine was a spectacular crash of population with a speed and on a scale seldom found in the vertebrate kingdom except under the onslaught of epidemic disease or the exigencies of collapse in food supply. Decline was continuing at an alarming rate in the districts where Peregrines still survived, when remedial measures arrested and eventually reversed the process. This chapter and the next deal simply with the numerical aspects of the decline and recovery, and the pesticide episode is spelt out more fully in Chapter 13.

The scale of decline can only be measured against a firm base-line of population for the years before 1956, the year when the first unmistakable symptoms of the impending crash appeared. The complication of the local war-time decline, and the possibility that recovery from this was impeded by early pesticide effects, pushes the valid base-line farther back, and I have taken 1930–39 as the key period. The average population for these years is estimated as 85% of the number of territories known to be occupied since 1930 for each region, *and subsequent status is measured by expressing census figures as percentages of this average number.* Tables 2–6 give summary data for counts in 1961, 1962, 1971, 1981 and 1991. The census problems caused by apparently single birds in breeding territories are shown in Table 7: they underline the difficulty of using a single parameter of breeding population size.

Dating the onset of the crash relies on the rather patchy information given on pp. 73–115. In south-east England, recovery from war-time decline was incomplete by 1954–55, and further decrease seems to have begun in 1956. In south-west England, decrease was noticed in 1957–58, and, in Cornwall, reduced breeding success was noted in 1956. On the South Wales coast, decline was apparent first in 1956–57, but in North Wales, although breeding success was poor at inland eyries right through the 1950s, falling population was not observed until after 1957. Northern England had lost a few pairs by 1960, but marked reduction was not obvious until 1961, and no part of Scotland showed evidence of decline until 1961.

By 1961, the Peregrine populations of southern England and the whole of Wales were reduced to a low level, but decrease tended to tail off northwards. In the Highlands, all districts except the central and eastern uplands and the east coast north of the Moray Firth showed some decline. Nationally, numbers were down to 68% of their estimated pre-war level. By 1962, the general pattern of decline was reinforced. In southern England, only six territories remained occupied, and in Wales, the population was down to a quarter of its pre-war level. Numbers in northern England were at just under half the normal level, while in southern Scotland they were just above half. It was noticeable that in Wales, northern England and southern Scotland, the coastal birds had declined appreciably more than those inland. Indeed, the Southern Upland inland Peregrines showed only slight decline, whereas the coastal groups, in Galloway, Ayrshire and Berwickshire, were at only one-fifth normal numbers. In the Highlands, decline was more marked by 1962 in all districts but the two mentioned above, which continued to be normal; where decline had occurred there was no difference in degree between coastal and inland groups. The Great Britain population overall was at 56% of the 1930–39 level (Ratcliffe, 1963).

The crash continued into 1963, when only three territories were reported occupied in southern England, and a sample of Welsh localities gave only 13% occupation. In northern England, southern Scotland and the Highlands, further territory desertions were reported and, although inland areas of the central and eastern Highlands still showed no change, the east coast Peregrines were clearly showing marked decline. During 1963, the national sample of recorded territories included 194 of those examined in 1962, representing an estimated pre-1939 population of 175 pairs. In 1962, 119 (68%) of this sample were occupied, but in 1963 only 93 (53%). Since the fuller census data in 1962 gave 56% occupation nationally, the 1963 sample is corrected by $56 \div 68 \times 53 = 43·6\%$ to give a more realistic comparison between years (Ratcliffe, 1972). If further allowance is made for territories held by apparently single birds (as in Table 7), numbers in 1963 may have been no more than 40% of the pre-war level.

We do not know the annual rate of decline between 1955 and 1961, and it evidently varied geographically (Fig. 19). The Great Britain population was probably around 95% of the 'normal' level in 1955, and in declining to 68% by 1961 the slope of the decline curve is gentler, with an average rate of just over 5% per annum, than between 1961 and 1963, when it accelerated to 12% per annum. The rate was evidently still greater in the worst affected districts (Tables

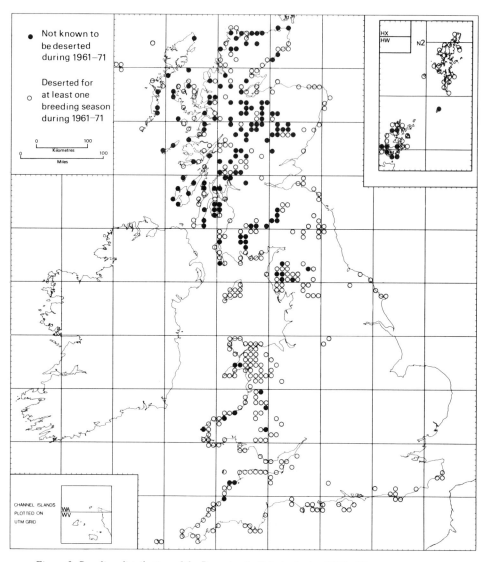

Figure 3. Breeding distribution of the Peregrine in Britain during 1961–71.

NOTES: Records refer only to territories examined during at least two breeding seasons during 1961–71 inclusive. The records do not differentiate between territories deserted for a single year and those deserted over the whole period, nor do they show local recovery during this period; they are presented as a general picture of the geographical bias in severity of pesticide effects.

2 and 3). Although the mean rate of decline during 1955–63 was only 7% per annum, its acceleration, reducing the population from 68% to 44% of normal level in only 2 years, justifies the term 'crash'. Figure 18 suggests that if further decline had continued unchecked at the later rate, extinction of the Peregrine in Britain could have occurred around 1967.

Fortunately, the plunge bottomed at about this point, and by 1964 it appeared that numbers were at least no lower than the 1963 level of 44%. For another 2 years, the sample censuses suggested that the population had stabilised at this much reduced level. There was some degree of flux as regards occupation of particular nesting haunts in depleted districts, with some more territories becoming vacant but others being re-occupied. Sometimes re-occupation and even successful nesting was followed by further desertion or non-breeding, and breeding success generally remained at a reduced level. Minor fluctuations in numbers occurred but were no greater than those found during 1930–39.

THE RECOVERY AND INCREASE

It was not until 1967 that convincing signs of a hoped-for recovery appeared. In that year, in Lakeland and the northern Pennines, there was a net gain of seven reoccupied territories and in four of these young were reared. In general, though, recovery was too slow, and the sample counts too small, to show any marked improvement before 1971. There was a distinct tendency towards improved breeding success in north-west England and the Southern Uplands by 1969, and an impression of fairly widespread though slow filling in of deserted inland haunts in various districts, but little indication of any change in any coastal area before 1971.

The 1971 survey produced the welcome news that the Great Britain population had increased from 44% in the year of lowest ebb, 1963, to an encouraging 54%, with successful breeding up from 16% to 25% (all percentages of pre-war breeding population) (Ratcliffe, 1972). Within this overall improvement, an interesting though disturbing pattern had become apparent. Recovery was almost wholly confined to inland districts, and some coastal areas showed clear evidence of further decline since 1963. Numbers were almost back to normal in inland districts of the northern Highlands, the south-west Highland fringe, the Southern Uplands and north-west England; but they remained very low in the Cheviots, the Yorkshire uplands and Wales. In southern England the Peregrine was evidently still virtually extinct on the Channel coast, but had staged a slight come-back on the Atlantic seaboard of the south-west. Few coastal haunts were occupied on the cliffs facing the Irish Sea, in Wales, the Isle of Man or south-west Scotland. The south-west Highland coastal population was slightly but not significantly higher than in 1962, but on the north-west Highland coast numbers showed a barely significant increase. The most marked change, however, was on the east coast of Britain, where the Peregrine was virtually extinct in former seacliff haunts between Flamborough Head and Inverness, and much reduced since 1962 on the north-east coast of the Highlands from Easter Ross to Shetland.

The 1981 survey showed that recovery was much farther advanced, with numbers nationally at about 90% of their pre-war level. Recolonisation was beginning in the Cheviots and Yorkshire Pennines, while in Wales numbers were well above pre-war baseline inland but somewhat below this level on

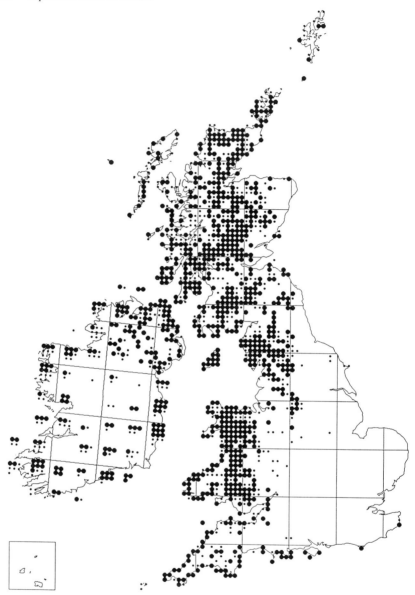

Figure 4. Breeding distribution of the Peregrine in Britain and Ireland during 1988–91.

Reproduced from *The New Atlas of Breeding Birds in Britain and Ireland* (1993) with permission from the British Trust for Ornithology.

NOTES: Symbols show 10 × 10 km grid squares in which Peregrines bred during the recent survey period 1988–91. A large dot refers to a 10 km square with evidence of breeding, a small dot refers to presence during the breeding season but with no stronger evidence of breeding. Records for Ireland are displaced for security reasons. This conventional method of mapping does not show the numbers of pairs breeding in 10 km squares, which vary from 1–8.

the coast. In south-west England, there had been increase to half of this base-line, but most pairs were along the Atlantic coast and there was a rapid fade-out with distance east along the English Channel coast, with continuing absence in Dorset and from there eastwards. In Lakeland and the Northern Pennines, population stood at a startling 173% of 'normal', and the Southern Uplands numbers were only slightly less, though the southern Scottish coast had not shown a full recovery. The Isle of Man population (mainly coastal) was approaching pre-war level. The Highlands and Islands showed a very variable pattern, with numbers just above base-line in south-west coastal districts and the southern inland fringes, markedly increased inland in the central and eastern Grampians, but still low on the east coast from the Moray Firth southwards. North of the Great Glen, numbers were everywhere still below pe-war levels, though the east coast population had almost doubled since 1971, and both the west coast and inland areas showed slight increases. Table 5 gives details for the 1981 situation.

A fourth Britain and Northern Ireland survey was made in 1991, and showed that recovery in many districts had continued to surge forward, to reach a GB total estimated at nearly 1170 pairs with another 95 pairs in Northern Ireland – higher than any time in recorded history, and 145% of the 1930–39 level. The geographical pattern apparent in 1981 has become still more pronounced, with numbers well over twice their previous best from the Southern Uplands through northern England and much of inland Wales. These extraordinary increases have involved many instances of territory doubling or even trebling, as well as the occupation of numerous new and often low-lying inland haunts, especially in quarries but also on man-made structures. Some coastal districts between southern Scotland and Cornwall have shown marked increases but, apart from the Isle of Man, coastal populations have not shown the spectacular rise in numbers of those inland. Recovery is well under way from Dorset to the Isle of Wight, but then peters out eastwards, with only three pairs in Sussex and a single pair in Kent.

In the Highlands, the picture is very mixed. In a broad zone through the southern and eastern edge, from Stirling and Dunbarton through Perth and Angus to Aberdeen and Banff, numbers have roughly doubled. Yet in south-west coastal districts, mainly in Argyll, numbers are no higher than in 1981; and inland in Argyll they are only slightly greater. Inverness-shire was not completely covered, but to the south of the Great Glen numbers seemed to be holding up well; while to the north, through inland districts of Inverness, Ross and Suther-land, they were down on 1981 levels in the west but above them in the east. On the east coast, haunts from the south side of the Moray Firth to the Forth were mostly re-occupied, but from the Black Isle northwards the situation was worse than in 1981. Orkney showed improvement in numbers but breeding success remained poor, while Shetland could muster only 5 single birds. In western coastal districts, of Sutherland, Ross and the Hebrides, numbers were still no greater than in 1981.

This puzzling pattern is set out in more detail in the following chapter, and the possible reasons are discussed later. Overall, the present state of the British Peregrine population represents a most heartening turn around in fortunes from the dark days and gloomy predictions of the early 1960s. Who could ever have imagined that in some districts it would by 1991 outnumber the Raven? It is not often that we are able to celebrate a conservation success, but this one is better than probably any of us had dared to hope. Re-survey of about half the breeding range of Peregrines in the Republic of Ireland in 1991 has given the estimate of a countrywide total of 350–355 occupied breeding territories (Norriss, in press). This represents an increase of at least 23–26% since 1981, and gives the highest known population level for the Republic. With a UK population of 1265 pairs, this suggests that the combined Peregrine breeding population of Britain and Ireland together is now at least 1600 pairs.

CHAPTER 4

Distribution and numbers in Britain

This geographical review aims to summarise the history of the Peregrine as a breeding bird for different parts of the country, giving the earlier records of occurrence and numbers, and sketching the picture of change through the decline period 1956–63, and the subsequent recovery up to 1991. It updates the figures given in the first edition of this book, which went up to 1979. The status of the Peregrine in Britain has proved to be fluid, and the 1991 figures will no doubt also be out-of-date by the time they are published, though I believe not wildly so.

The subdivision of geographical regions used in this treatment follows a mixture of administrative and natural topographic boundaries. Table 1 gives population figures for the old counties, which are also referred to but often subdivided in the text. I chose to use the old counties rather than the new because most of the pre-1975 records are classified accordingly; and I feel supported in this decision by the knowledge that the Boundary Commission is already engaged on a further revision of the counties map. The geographical regions of the present chapter correspond with those of Tables 2–6, except that Eastern England, the Lancashire Lowlands, the Pennines, Lakeland, the Cheviots and the Isle of Man are all lumped under Northern England in the tables. The Midlands appear only in Table 6 because there were no records before 1991.

SOUTH-EAST ENGLAND

The gleaming white chalk cliffs of Kent and Sussex fronting the English Channel were once a great Peregrine stronghold. In Kent the line of precipices extends 19 km from Oldstairs Bay in the east to Folkestone Warren in the west, with a break in their continuity (3 km) only at Dover Harbour, about mid-way along. There are no other nesting places. When N. F. Ticehurst wrote in 1909, seven pairs was the maximum known population, with five reckoned the more normal number. In *The Birds of Kent* (1953), J. M. Harrison refers to G. Mannering's statement in 1936 that six to eight pairs had bred with little variation during the past 40 years. He then quotes G. E. Took: 'Since 1931 I have each year examined nine eyries between Deal and Folkestone. There are none on the far side of Folkestone or Deal, but the nine I know, I believe to have been existent long before I knew them intimately. These nine pairs were *in situ* when war broke out but last year (1946) only five eyries were occupied and obviously four pairs had been shot out of existence by military or RAF orders'. Took found six pairs nesting in 1950 but only five in 1951. Major Took, who affirmed all these figures to me directly, said that five pairs remained up to 1958, but only two in 1961, and by 1962 they had all disappeared. A single pair returned only in 1989, and although they bred successfully then and in the following two years, no others were reported in 1991 (Bryn Green).

The Peregrines of the Sussex coast are the best documented population in Britain, thanks to the Herculean efforts of John Walpole-Bond, who observed them in every year from 1904 to 1949. Walpole-Bond summarised his experience in his monumental *History of Sussex Birds* (1938), but I have had access to his original records. Walpole-Bond found that from eight to 12 pairs of Peregrines attempted to nest annually on the Sussex coast. There were two irregularly used inland nesting places in disused chalk pits on the South Downs and at least two more such habitats where Peregrines were seen at times and could have nested. He believed that only relentless persecution prevented a regular group of inland breeders from becoming established. The records suggest that there were as many as 14 separate coastal nesting territories, but not all of these were occupied in any one year. The population of the chalk coast section between Brighton and Seaford Head varied between three and six pairs, with successive years sometimes showing a difference of up to three pairs either way. Up to 1926, two pairs often nested on Seaford Head, but only occasionally after this time, and the permanent loss of the Rottingdean Head nesting place, through modification of the cliff, eliminated one territory in 1929.

From four to six pairs normally nested on the magnificent 10 km stretch of chalk precipice of the Seven Sisters and Beachy Head between Cuckmere Haven and Eastbourne. In 1910–12 and 1930 Walpole-Bond found six occupied eyries here, and the same number was seen by D. Nethersole-Thompson in 1931, this being the densest concentration of breeding Peregrines reported in Britain or Ireland. The coast is flat and unsuitable for some distance beyond Eastbourne, but a pair nested regularly on the sandstone and clay escarpment between Hastings and Fairlight, and occasionally another pair occupied a low headland between Fairlight Cove and Cliff End.

It would appear at first sight that this population was subject to a relatively large amount of variation, with breeding pairs varying from eight to 12 between successive years. Careful examination of Walpole-Bond's data shows, however, that in many of the years of apparently low numbers not all the nesting territories were visited. From the extraordinary degree of disturbance to which this population was subjected by egg collectors, including not only Walpole-Bond himself but various others besides, it must have been difficult for any one observer to make a totally accurate count of the population in every year. Sometimes pairs moved to different territories for repeat layings, and occasionally there were presumed non-breeding pairs, which may have been only loosely attached to any one territory. Moreover, an error over only one territory is large in relation to such a small population. These factors introduce an element of uncertainty into the data, and make it unjustifiable to place too much meaning on variations in numbers from year to year.

After making allowances for these complications in the records, it would seem that up to 1939, nine pairs was the normal lower level of population. During 1908–12, 1923–26 and 1930–31, peak numbers of ten to 12 pairs were recorded. Most of the variation in numbers related to the Rottingdean–Seaford sector, where most of the eyries were on relatively low cliffs and harried unremittingly every year. While there is an apparent deterioration from 1932 up to 1939, with an upper level of eight to nine pairs in most years, it is difficult to know whether this was real. At least ten territories were occupied in 1936, and at least eight in 1939 (Hastings was not visited and would probably have provided a ninth pair). In 1940, war-time persecution began to reduce this Peregrine population, but decline was only partial. At least six territories were occupied in 1941, seven in 1943 and no less than eight in 1945. Further decline followed slowly, with only five or six pairs in 1954 (Ferguson-Lees, 1957), and then rapidly, as this population was among the first to experience the post-1955 'crash'. By 1961 Peregrines no longer nested anywhere on the Sussex coast, and it was many years before even a single pair re-occupied these old haunts. One pair bred successfully and another held a former nesting place in 1991, but these appeared to be all (C. Durell). A third pair nested successfully in 1992 (B. Atfield).

Hampshire is devoid of cliffs, but the Isle of Wight has some good coastal rocks, and the eyrie at Freshwater Bay was one of those known in Medieval times, there being a record as early as 1564. I have not been able to find any comprehensive historical information on the breeding population of the Peregrine in the Isle of Wight, but have come across records of nesting in five different localities along the south coast, between the Needles and Culver Cliff. Colin Tubbs has supplied me with data for more recent years: he knew of pairs breeding in three of the old territories in 1954 and 1955, and learned from hearsay evidence that a fourth pair bred in the 1940s. Some of the Isle of Wight cliffs are of alternating hard and soft materials, especially sandstone and clay, much given to land-slippage, and the fifth locality may have become unsuitable for Peregrines of late. Tubbs knew of two pairs in 1956, but the species had disappeared from the island by 1960, and there was a long gap before nesting pairs re-appeared in the late 1980s. In 1991, at least three pairs reared young, in ancient breeding stations (J. Cox).

The Channel Islands are probably best considered with south-east England. They held a modest Peregrine breeding population of around ten pairs up to 1940, but this disappeared during the post-1956 'crash' and there has been a dearth of breeding records in recent years. During the spring and summer of 1992, prospecting pairs were seen on Alderney and Sark, but Jersey and Guernsey recorded only winter sightings (N. Milton).

SOUTH-WEST ENGLAND

The coast of Dorset, facing the English Channel, has extensive ranges of high cliff, providing splendid scope for Peregrines, and formerly carried a sizeable population of the bird. The Dorset Peregrines were 'egged' relentlessly during the 1920s and 1930s, yet maintained their numbers remarkably well right up to 1939. The chief egger, Levi Green, had an intimate knowledge of the whole population, but left no records apart from data tickets for numerous clutches now widely spread around collections in Britain. However, Angela Hughes and Don Humphrey knew Green well, and, from his verbal information, provided me with an assessment of the pre-war population. Ray Newman and his father also contributed records. It appears that there were 15 regularly occupied territories, and three others used irregularly or occasionally, during the period 1920–39. In occasional years the numbers could have been as high as 17 pairs. Of these eyries only two, in badly overhung sites at Gad Cliff and Anvil Point, were unassailable by the collectors, and produced young regularly.

Air Ministry destruction, beginning in 1940, evidently hit this Peregrine population severely, but in 1946 at least one pair was breeding. Steady recovery followed and in 1951 Levi Green reported eight occupied territories. In 1953 at least eight pairs were breeding in the ten territories thoroughly checked by Humphrey and Newman. In 1956 at least seven pairs were present in these ten territories, and the eighth, which was displaced by the construction of a new naval establishment up to the cliff edge, may have bred in a new locality. In 1957 only six territories were occupied, and at least two pairs evidently failed to lay. By 1958 the number of occupied territories was down to five, with only two pairs certainly producing eggs, and by 1960, only one pair was left. A single bird was seen in 1961, but the Dorset coast remained devoid of Peregrines for over 20 years. A single pair laid eggs first in 1984, and by 1991 there were nine pairs, eight of which reared young (G. Pictor, T. Haysom, R. Baker).

Devon has two quite separate coasts, both with a considerable frontage of lofty seacliff. That facing the English Channel has a series of bold headlands at intervals along its length, from Beer Head in the east to Plymouth in the west. The northern, Atlantic coast has a more or less continuous rampart of cliff beginning at Marsland Mouth on the Cornish border and stretching round Hartland Point to Westward Ho. There is then a gap with several miles of flat coast around the estuary of the River Taw, but from Morte Bay eastwards an almost unbroken line of cliffs extends beyond the Somerset border. The earlier *Birds of Devon* by D'Urban and Mathew (1895) is extremely vague on the number of eyries then extant, and there seems to be little published information on the Devon Peregrine population of pre-1940 years. In 1931 G. M. Spooner mentioned five eyries in the Plymouth district alone. H. G. Hurrell, in a letter to Michael Blackmore, thought that there were ten eyries between Plymouth and Start Point, and another six between Start Point and the Exe estuary. Other observers reported at least a further five breeding haunts between the Exe and Lyme Regis on the Dorset border. Hurrell believed that there was a peak population in the 1920s, and that numbers were lower both in the 1800s and the 1930s. On the Atlantic coast D. Nethersole-Thompson knew ten pairs during 1927–31, and other records added a further four pairs. The rugged island of

Lundy, 19 km north-west of Hartland Point, had another two pairs in most years up to 1938. It is not clear how many nesting haunts were occupied regularly out of these numbers, but the average pre-1940 Devon population seems likely to have totalled at least 30 pairs.

Apart from an unconfirmed report of a disused quarry nest, there seem to be no earlier records of Peregrines breeding inland in Devon, and the granite tors of Dartmoor have evidently never attracted the species to nest as they have the Raven, at least within historic times.

This was one of the areas most severely dealt with under the Destruction of Peregrine Falcons Order 1940, and local opinion is that the species was all but exterminated during 1940–45. There was fairly rapid recovery after 1945, and by 1955 at least 12 eyries were known to be occupied (Moore, 1969). Decline then set in again, and by 1958 the *Devon Bird Report* noted that although several eyries were known, the species was becoming less plentiful than a few years before. By 1962, only four territories remained occupied, and only one pair reared young. However, at least two pairs remained throughout the worst years of the crash, and both were usually successful. By 1971 there was a slight upturn, with five territories occupied, and at least three, possibly four, pairs successful. Since then, there has been dramatic recovery along the Atlantic coast of Devon, and in 1979 the Peregrine population was close to the pre-war level, of about 15 pairs. The 1991 survey located 20 pairs on the north coast, including Lundy Island, a slight increase on the previous highest level. Although recovery was slower in spreading along the English Channel coast, there were 18 pairs by 1991, perhaps just short of the maximum possible. A startling inland colonisation was also reported, with nine pairs, mainly in quarries (H. Woodland and the National Trust).

Cornwall forms the extremity of the south-west England peninsula and, like Devon, has a rugged seaboard separable into Atlantic and English Channel sections. The Peregrines of the Atlantic coast seem to have been the better known, as far as my limited information goes. This section, beginning at Land's End and stretching for about 85 km to Marsland Mouth, just south of Hartland Point, is precipitous for a large part of its length. From records given me by D. Nethersole-Thompson, G. Garceau and G. Allsop, Peregrines bred in at least 19 different territories along the Atlantic seacliffs of Cornwall during 1927–39, and most of these places appeared to be occupied regularly. By allowing a similar spacing on parts of this coast which were not worked by these observers, I estimate that there could have been up to another four pairs during this period. On the more indented English Channel coast, east of Land's End, some of the cliffs are rather broken and sloping, but there is an extensive frontage of suitable precipice in total. I was given information on only seven pre-war Peregrine haunts here, but a study of the maps suggests that there could have been up to 13 more, depending on the actual nature of the terrain and its suitability as nesting habitat. This is probably the least known section of the English coast, in regard to the former distribution of the species. The Isles of Scilly once had at least two breeding places but, from the large number of islands and islets in this group, it seems likely that knowledge of Peregrine history is extremely patchy. There are no earlier records of inland breeding in Cornwall.

In *Bird Life in Cornwall* (1948) Ryves said that in the years before 1940 there were upwards of a score of tenanted breeding stations in favourable seasons.

R. B. Treleaven knew of exactly 20 eyries in the period 1930–39. Yet in the light of all the breeding records made available to me plus an estimate of additional haunts in 'gaps', I venture to suggest that no one knew more than about half the Peregrine territories in Cornwall, and that the pre-war population was closer to 40 than 20 pairs. The total number of nesting territories is likely to have been at least 45. If this estimate is correct, Cornwall once had a larger Peregrine population than any other county south of the Scottish Highlands, surpassing even Devon and Pembrokeshire, with around 30 pairs each.

Both Ryves and Treleaven believed that Peregrines were virtually exterminated in Cornwall by Air Ministry destruction during 1940–45. G. Garceau nevertheless knew of one pair which escaped on the south coast. In 1946 Ryves watched a single pair return to breed successfully in a shot-out territory, and in 1948 he knew of many old eyries which were re-occupied. By 1955 Treleaven had records of 17 eyries in regular use out of the 20 territories known to him, yet by 1956 he found a decline in breeding success and in each succeeding year the situation worsened. In 1959, with R. Khan, Treleaven found only seven occupied eyries, and only two of them were successful (Treleaven, 1961). By 1962 only a single breeding pair was found in 20 territories. There was no proved nesting again until 1969, when a pair reared three young. In the 1971 census, only three occupied territories were found, and only one of these produced young. In 1979 I was told reliably that Peregrines had spread back along the Atlantic coast of Cornwall from the Devon border, but had not reached much beyond half-way to the Land's End, and none were known on the English Channel coast. Numbers were estimated at about eight pairs. By 1991, there were at least 26 pairs on the north Cornwall coast, with 18 pairs on a section which held 13 pairs in 1930–39. On the south coast, numbers had risen to 13 pairs in 1991, and there was an unprecedented breeding of three pairs in inland locations (R. B. Treleaven, S. Jackson and the National Trust).

In Somerset, the scope for nesting is more limited. E. M. Palmer and D. K. Ballance give fairly detailed information in *The Birds of Somerset* (1968). The main coastal cliffs, continuing eastwards from those of Devonshire, under the northern edge of Exmoor, had two regular pairs, and others irregularly in three places, between 1900–1940. The ancient eyries at Brean Down and Steep Holm were also held regularly during most of this time, but that in the Avon Gorge was used irregularly (1928–34, on the Gloucestershire side in all but 1933), and Sand Point was tenanted only occasionally. Cheddar Gorge had a pair during 1921–24, 1927–28, and perhaps 1929, and there was inland nesting elsewhere in two different disused quarries in the 1930s. The Somerset population seems to have been virtually eliminated during 1940–45, and after the war recovery was incomplete, with pairs known to nest in only four of the former localities. In 1961 only two pairs remained, and by 1962 all the territories were deserted. For some years only sporadic nesting was reported, but in 1978, R. Mearns found most of the coastal territories to be re-occupied. In 1991, five coastal territories were occupied, but four others known to be used in the past were still deserted. Five inland localities were tenanted (W. J. Webber).

In Gloucestershire, the old Wye Valley haunt at Symonds Yat was re-occupied in 1982 and has remained so, and there was a quarry-nesting pair in 1991 (RSPB and R. Purveur). The uplands and valleys of western Monmouthshire belong topographically to the mountain systems of South Wales, and are dealt with under that region.

Elsewhere in the southern counties of England, Wiltshire has claimed breeding Peregrines, on the most celebrated of all man-made nesting stations in this country, Salisbury Cathedral. The known nestings on this fine building are detailed on p. 182, the last appears to have been in the early 1950s. An exceptional instance of ground-nesting occurred in Hampshire in 1928.

SOUTH WALES

South and North Wales are divided by a line from the Dovey estuary to Machynlleth and then the road to Newtown, Welshpool and Shrewsbury. The southern half of Wales has a considerable extent of seacliff, in Glamorgan, Carmarthen, Pembrokeshire and Cardiganshire, the last two counties having especially rugged coastlines, and this was a former stronghold of Peregrines. The coast of Monmouthshire is flat but there was formerly an occasional nesting place on Denny Island.

Birds of Glamorgan (1925) said that there were 'At least three occupied eyries in the eastern half of the county, two being on maritime cliffs and one inland. In the western half there are two more, possibly three, on the coast'. The second *Birds of Glamorgan* (1967) stated that, 'On the Vale coast [between Barry and Porthcawl] there were three eyries of great antiquity', and that, 'In Gower, there were at least three sites of great antiquity on the south coast cliffs . . . and one, used somewhat irregularly, on one of the north coast tors'. This coastal Glamorgan population was maintained at five to seven pairs during the 1920s and 1930s, but was much reduced during 1940–45, and only two pairs were known to nest subsequently, both of them disappearing around 1956. It was not until 1977 that another successful eyrie was known. Even in 1991, there were only four pairs.

The coast of Carmarthenshire is rather short, but there are cliff sections which Col. H. Morrey Salmon knew to hold three breeding places during the 1920s and 1930s, though never more than two pairs in any one year. *A Hand List of the Birds of Carmarthenshire* (1954) reported that there were still two pairs, and one still remained in 1962, but disappeared shortly after. All three were reoccupied in 1991. Topographically, the seacliffs of western Carmarthen may be regarded as part of the Pembrokeshire system. Pembrokeshire has a magnificent coastline, bounded for much of its length by cliffs, and the only large break in their continuity is the deep but low-lying inlet of Milford Haven. The rocky offshore islands of Skokholm, Skomer, Ramsey and Grassholm off the western coast are famous seabird breeding stations, and smaller colonies are scattered along the mainland cliffs. The north coast of Pembrokeshire is especially rugged, and the line of seacliffs stretches north-eastwards right along the Cardiganshire seaboard, reaching with only a few gaps almost to Borth on the Dovey estuary. In 1926, H. A. Gilbert said he knew 12 breeding pairs in Pembrokeshire, but that there were at least double that number. *The Birds of Pembrokeshire* (1949) stated that, 'The maximum number of eyries which could be occupied in one year is probably 35. The average number of occupied eyries pre-World War II was probably 25–28'.

In 1960, the late J. H. Howell gave P. J. Panting a list of 36 localities where he had known Peregrines to nest in Pembrokeshire, but this included some alternative cliffs. It seems likely that at least 30 pairs could nest in the county in a good year, the highest number for any county in Wales. During 1940–45 there was sporadic Air Ministry destruction, but this was incomplete, and in 1947 about 18 pairs were reckoned to be present (Lockley, 1949). Decline followed again from around 1957, and in 1961 only two occupied territories were found. Peregrines hung on in Pembrokeshire right through the worst period of the crash, there being always at least one successful pair, though in 1971 only one pair bred in eight occupied territories. In 1981 there were 21 pairs between the mouth of the Tywi in the south and that of the Teifi in the north, and including the offshore islands. By 1991, 33 coastal territories were occupied, but another six former haunts were still untenanted. The inland Pembrokeshire nesting places had risen from one pre-war location to three in 1991.

Professor J. H. Salter and other correspondents reported eight pairs of Peregrines breeding on the Cardiganshire coast to Col. Morrey Salmon in the 1920s. Another long deserted haunt was reoccupied in 1935, and there is room for a tenth pair. The subsequent history of the bird here closely parallels that of the Pembrokeshire population, and by 1961 only one occupied territory remained. In 1981, nine of the coastal haunts held Peregrines, and in 1991 at least 11 territories were occupied.

Inland in South Wales, the industrial valleys of Glamorgan and Monmouthshire drain southwards from an upland massif which rises farther into the Brecon Beacons and the Brecon–Carmarthen Black Mountains. The exact former population of Peregrines in this district is uncertain, but the Monmouth valleys had two irregular pre-1940 nesting places, one on low-lying woodland cliffs in a picturesque setting away from the coalfield, and the other in disused quarries. There are crags elsewhere which could have held four more pairs in still earlier times. *The Birds of Glamorgan* (1967) said that there were 'at least three [nesting places] on crags in the Rhondda basin, with possibly others or alternative sites in worked-out quarries; and two others inland in the Neath and Tawe watersheds'. This probably gave an average population of at least three or four pairs during the 1920s and 30s. From the distribution of suitable crags, there could once have been up to seven more territories in the Glamorgan coalfield valleys. Two pairs were known up to 1961 but the species had apparently vanished from the district by 1963, and no subsequent nesting was reported until 1979 when three pairs could have laid. Seven territories were occupied in 1981. Recent increase has been substantial and the valleys of Monmouth and Glamorgan had no fewer than 24 territory-holding pairs in 1991.

North of 'the Valleys' are the Old Red Sandstone and limestone hills of Brecon and Carmarthen. *The Birds of Brecknock* (1957), says, 'There are at least eight crags in the county which have held eyries from time to time and in the 1920s–1930s six of them were tenanted regularly, but during the last few years usually only four, occasionally five, have been occupied'. The Brecon Beacons–Western Black Mountains massif held five of these territories, one of them having an alternative crag across the Carmarthenshire border. An occasional sixth territory lay in the western foothills of this massif in Carmarthenshire, and the Brecon Beacons could in pre-war years have held up to four more pairs.

In the eastern Black Mountains, shared between Brecon, Monmouth and Herefordshire, the first two counties each had one regular and one irregular or occasional territory. Bruce Campbell knew all four nesting places to be used in the 1940s. In 1941, two pairs nested only 1·3 km apart on the same long escarpment, but probably there were never more than three in one year, and two seems to have been the more normal complement known to Col. Morrey Salmon and other ornithologists during the 1920s and 1930s. The Brecon sector could once have held an additional pair. An old, unlocalised breeding record for Herefordshire presumably referred to the English sector of the Black Mountains, where there are a few small rocks.

Large but lower tracts of upland stretch away to the north of these mountain systems, in the old counties of Brecon, Carmarthen, Cardigan, Radnor and Montgomery. Apart from four or five small, occasionally or irregularly used rocks in the uplands between Builth Wells and Presteigne, in Radnor, Peregrines were, before 1940, restricted mainly to the western ranges, famous otherwise as the last refuge of the Red Kite in our islands. This was once beautiful, secluded hill country, with deep winding cwms and slopes grown in many places with stretches of hanging oakwood, the nesting haunts of the Red Kites. It is now much violated by reservoir construction and coniferous afforestation, both of them involving a network of roads which cross the high plateaux and effectively destroy the former wildness of the area.

In the hills drained by the headwaters of the Tywi and Irfon, where the old counties of Brecon, Carmarthen and Cardigan meet, there were four pairs of Peregrines breeding regularly in the 1930s (D. Nethersole-Thompson, H. Morrey Salmon). The country west of Rhayader, including the Elan Valley and upper Wye Valley in Radnorshire, had three or possibly four regular pairs which were well known to egg collectors in the 1920s and 1930s. The western and northern parts of this large mountain system draining to Cardigan Bay had five regular pairs with another three localities which were occupied irregularly or occasionally. These upland massifs in the northern part of the region, spread over Carmarthen, Brecon, Radnor, Montgomery and Cardigan, have other crags which may once have held up to 12 more pairs of Peregrines, but where nesting was not reported during 1900–55. The Peregrines of these South Wales districts north of Glamorgan and Monmouth seem to have been relatively free from Air Ministry persecution during 1940–45, and their population was evidently fairly normal in the early 1950s. Yet by 1961 only ten territories out of 33 remained occupied, and by 1962 the number had fallen to seven. In 1971 Peregrines were still present in only seven territories, but in 1981 at least 20 haunts were occupied. By 1991, the number of occupied territories had trebled to an unprecedented 59.

NORTH WALES

Seacliffs are somewhat irregularly distributed in North Wales. The coast of Merioneth is devoid of real cliffs, though the fine crag with its Cormorant colony at the Bird Rock (Craig yr Aderyn) near Towyn was originally coastal. The most extensive seacliffs are those of the Lleyn Peninsula in Caernarvonshire and on

Inland nesting haunt: 245 m rhyolite cliff; Snowdonia, North Wales (photo: D. A. Ratcliffe)

Anglesey, but there are impressive headlands around Llandudno and Conway in northern Caernarvonshire.

Kenneth L. Wilson knew six pairs to nest regularly on the seacliffs of Lleyn during the period 1930–37. A seventh nesting territory not examined by him has had Peregrines in regular occupation during 1966–77, and was probably tenanted also during the 1930s. Nesting was occasional on Bardsey Island, including in the early 1930s. The East St Tudwal's Island was also an occasional nesting place in earlier years.

Forrest (1907) said that five or six pairs usually bred on Anglesey. Five nesting pairs were known to K. L. Wilson and W. P. Dodd in the mid 1930s, and a gamekeeper reported a sixth pair in 1939. At least four pairs were nesting in the early 1950s, but not all the nesting places were thoroughly checked (D. A. Ratcliffe). In 1957 there was an isolated nesting occurrence on the low rock ridge projecting through the sand dunes of Newborough Warren (A. W. Colling). Four pairs were known to nest regularly on the headlands of the north Caernarvonshire coast by W. P. Dodd during the period 1937–59, though they were not all visited every year.

This North Wales coastal population was said to be much reduced by war-time 'control' during 1940–45, and it is unclear whether its post-1945 level matched that of the 1930s, though the four pairs on the north Caernarvonshire coast were certainly present in the early 1950s, all in localities close to large numbers of people. It was evident that things were amiss by 1957–58, though, with pairs dropping out and others not laying, and by 1961, only three occupied territories could be located on the whole of the North Wales coast. They continued at a low level for a long time, but by 1981 there were 13 occupied territories. Anglesey had eight coastal and two inland pairs in 1991, while the Caernarvonshire coast had 13 occupied territories. The Britannia Bridge, shared between the two counties, also had a nesting pair.

The mountains of North Wales contain the most rugged country in the whole of the Principality, and there is particularly good scope here for Peregrines in the availability of suitable crags. In the south-west of this region, the hills lying between the Dovey and Mawddach estuaries include the fine mountain range of Cader Idris, which passes north-eastwards into the Aran range lying between the roads from Mallwyd and Dolgellau to Llanuwchllyn. There are many high crags in the Merioneth part of this area, and the Peregrine population numbered at least six pairs in the 1930s (F. C. Best). A previously unrecorded nesting place was occupied in 1977, and there may have been undiscovered haunts during 1930–39.

Peregrines were formerly little known on the moorlands of the south-east and the Welsh Borders, though there was at least one regular pre-war pair. To the north, and eastwards of the Mallwyd–Bala road lies an extensive tract of mostly rather smooth and rounded uplands, including Lake Vyrnwy and the Berwyn Mountains. This area is divided between the three old counties of Montgomery, Merioneth and Denbigh. There are good crags of slate locally and five regularly occupied territories were known here during the 1930s, with two more irregular places and another used only occasionally. Other rocks could formerly have supported up to four more pairs. North of the road from Barmouth to Bala and Corwen is another wild and little trodden range of uplands. The western sector is formed by the exceptionally rugged massif of the Rhinogs, composed of hard grits of the Harlech Dome. The larger eastern part is a more typical moorland terrain, with extensive tracts of blanket bog, but rising into the higher peaks of the Arenigs. The normal pre-1956 Peregrine population of this area would appear to have been at least seven pairs. Three territories were known to be occupied regularly during the 1920s and 30s (W. P. Dodd, W. M. Congreve). Another was occupied during both of the only two visits made, in 1938 and 1945 (W. P. Dodd), but the remaining three territories were little visited and their history is not known. From vague references to another locality it seems that there may well have been an eighth territory occupied irregularly, and there are other crags which could hold at least two more pairs.

To the north of the road from Portmadoc to Ffestiniog and then Yspytty Ifan lies Snowdonia proper, or Eryri, signifying the land of eagles. It is a district of spectacular heavily glaciated and mainly igneous mountains with a wealth of high crags, and a great popularity amongst mountaineers and hill walkers. Most of the district belongs to Caernarvonshire, but has a northern enclave of Merioneth which includes Blaenau Ffestiniog, and the surrounding massifs of Moelwyn and

Inland nesting haunt: disused slate quarries; Wales (photo: D. A. Ratcliffe)

Manod. This is classic Peregrine country, though it seems never to have been worked by eggers and others in the past to nearly the same extent as Lakeland, a closely comparable district. Perhaps the ferocity of some of the cliffs was a discouragement, when more easily accessible eyries were numerous in other parts of the Principality. Forrest (1907) is rather vague on numbers in Snowdonia, and the only person I have been able to trace who worked the district at all thoroughly and left records is the late W. P. Dodd of Colwyn Bay, who saw eyries in nine different territories during the period 1925–56.

During 1951–53, I independently located Peregrines occupying ten different nesting territories, including five of those known to W. P. Dodd. Another of Dodd's haunts vacant in 1951 had clearly held Peregrines up to around 1948 or so. I subsequently learned of three other pairs in places which I had not visited (Evan Roberts and C. M. Swaine), and there were also rumours of a fourth pair. The probable total number of inland Peregrine territories in Snowdonia during the early 1950s was thus at least 17, of which probably 14 were occupied regularly. In 1956–57, I examined 12 territories in Snowdonia and found all but two occupied, though only four pairs certainly had eggs at the time.

The last inland district with Peregrines in North Wales is in Denbighshire, to the north of the road from Betws y Coed to Llangollen. The larger western part of this district, known as the Denbigh Moors, is an expanse of rather low and undulating, heathery grouse moors, now extensively afforested. This had three or four small crags now and then tenanted, but usually under too vigilant surveillance by gamekeepers to hold Peregrines for long. The eastern part is the limestone range of the Clwydian Hills, with its southern extension of Eglwyseg Mountain above Llangollen, where there was one regularly held territory and two uncertain though probable haunts. Flintshire had only a rumoured quarry nesting place.

There seems to have been little war-time destruction of Peregrines in this district, and in the 10 years after 1945 the population was evidently at its pre-war level. By 1961 the substantial Peregrine population of the North Wales mountains had nevertheless collapsed. I trudged many fruitless miles over my old stamping grounds in Caernarvon and Merioneth, examining 22 territories and finding only eight of them with Peregrines. Other observers added only another three occupations in 11 more territories. Out of the 11 occupied cliffs, only three were known to have nests with eggs. Numbers remained at an extremely low ebb for some years, and when the second Peregrine enquiry was conducted in 1971, only nine occupied inland territories could be found in the whole of North Wales, and only three of these were successful. Since then there has been a remarkable recovery. In 1981 there were 54 territories holding Peregrines in inland areas of North Wales. By 1991, the number had doubled, to 108, not including the two inland pairs on Anglesey. The increase was especially pronounced in the old counties of Denbigh and Montgomery, but the numbers in Merioneth (40) comfortably exceeded those inland in Caernarvonshire (26), previously the Welsh county with the largest inland breeding population. Flintshire had two nesting pairs.

Graham Williams and Iolo Williams, RSPB, have collated the breeding records for Wales for many years and their data have provided information for 1981 and 1991. In 1991, the county organisers were Alastair Moralee, Bob Corran, Duncan Brown, Reg Thorpe, Graham Williams, Peter Davis, Tony Cross, Steve Roberts, Jerry Lewis, Richard Poole, Jack Donovan and Bob Haycock.

EASTERN ENGLAND

The flat coasts of Essex and Suffolk are devoid of possible haunts and the sloping cliffs of Pleistocene sands and boulder clay along the north Norfolk coast have never held Peregrines, though they have breeding Fulmars, and are as suitable as some cut-bank river nesting sites of Peregrines in North America. The eyrie on the ruined tower of Corton Church near Lowestoft in c. 1840, did not persist for long, and the only regular breeding place in East Anglia was on the banded chalk cliff at Hunstanton, Norfolk, overlooking the eastern entrance to the Wash. This was first mentioned as occupied in 1604, and Sir Hamon Le Strange caught 87 Peregrines here in 50 trapping seasons beginning that year, though it is not clear how many were young birds and how many adult. Stevenson (1866) quotes a Mr Hunt as saying in 1815 that 'a nest of the gentil falcon has from time immemorial been found on the Hunstanton cliffs'. The eyrie was finally deserted about 1820 (Harting, 1891). There is a further gap in distribution through the flat coast of Lincolnshire and Holderness in Yorkshire until Flamborough Head in the East Riding is reached. From here the outcropping chalk rises steadily in elevation north-westwards into the magnificent line of vertical precipice reaching 90–125 m and extending at least 8 km at Bempton and Buckton. The Bempton cliffs hold the largest colony of Guillemots and Razorbills in England, and the seabirds were systematically farmed for their eggs by gangs of cragsmen up to 1954.

Nelson (1907) records that in earlier years any broods of young Peregrines which came the way of the 'climmers' were lifted for sale to falconers, so that these people had good reason to keep a look out for the bird. It is therefore perhaps a little surprising – by comparison with the density on the chalk cliffs of Kent and Sussex – to learn that two pairs seems to have been the normal complement of Peregrines on this long line of cliff, with its prolific food supply.

Still farther north-east, the Yorkshire coast between Filey and Redcar has some fine sections of seacliff, including Boulby Cliff near Whitby which, at 200 m, is the highest seacliff in England, though earlier quarrying has modified its form. This is a coast cut in Jurassic rocks, of varying hardness, and some cliff sections are more broken and crumbling than others, and thus of poorer quality for Peregrine sites. Records for this section are probably inadequate but Nelson mentions Huntcliff, near Saltburn, and the cliffs near Scarborough as nesting places, and the Filey cliffs have held falcons. There would seem to be room for at least four more pairs. Subsequent records give a rather indefinite picture for the Yorkshire coast as a whole, but breeding had ceased by 1961 and, although birds have been seen recently, definite nesting records appear to be lacking, even in 1991.

Immediately south of the Scarborough–Redcar coast, the land rises into the dissected upland plateau of the North York Moors, typical grouse moor country but with deeply cut valleys. Crags are rather few, small and scattered, but there are several good faces, and the area would seem well able to hold at least half a dozen breeding pairs of Peregrines. Yet when Nelson wrote in 1907, he referred only to two long deserted haunts at Killingnab Scar and Whitestone Cliff, and to a recent successful eyrie in a secret locality. The history of the bird in this area after 1800 or so seems to have been one of almost incessant persecution by game preservers, and regular breeding has apparently been unknown for a long time, though sporadic nesting attempts continued up to the 1950s. Apart from reported nesting on a tower (since demolished) within the Fylingdales radar complex, I have heard of no breeding attempts on the North York Moors since 1960; if they have occurred, people in the know have kept quiet, and who could blame them? Recent North East Yorkshire survey has been by R. McAndrew, B. and S. Pashby, S. Cochrane and F. Moffat.

Although there are seacliffs, reaching 30 m or so, of Magnesian limestone on the Durham coast, and the volcanic Whinsill in Northumberland, at the Farne Islands, Dunstanburgh, Cullernose, Bamburgh and Holy Island, there seem to be no records of Peregrines nesting here. Bolam (1912) mentions that Peregrines bred regularly on the ruins of Dunstanburgh Castle around 1830–40, but seemingly not on the rocks below. However, the craggy wooded glen of Castle Eden Dene close to the Durham coast was said by Tristam (1905) to be a regular breeding haunt around 1810.

MIDLANDS AND LANCASHIRE LOWLANDS

Apart from a few irregular quarry haunts in the south, inland nesting places in England could previously be assigned to one or other of the main hill districts. During the last decade there has, however, been a growing number of Peregrine breeding records from Midland counties, which cannot be so placed, while western Lancashire has had several that do not belong to either the Pennines or Lake District. Nearly all these breeding records are in quarries or on man-made structures lying below 150 m above sea level. The following details all refer to 1991.

Hereford had one pair breeding on a natural crag, and another prospecting pair here occupied a quarry suitable for nesting (K. Mason). Two pairs nested in quarries in Shropshire (J. Sankey), while in Staffordshire one pair was similarly located, and prospecting Peregrines took up residence in another quarry and on a power station (F. Gribble). In Cheshire one pair bred on a tall chimney and a second on a natural rocky bluff in low-lying country (C. Richards, C. Lythgoe). The lowlands of west Lancashire had five nesting pairs: two were in limestone quarries in the Lancaster area, one on a power station chimney, one on an electricity pylon with a platform, and one on a warehouse overlooking the Mersey in Liverpool (D. Sharpe, D. Owen, B. Townson, A S. Duckels). The total number of proved nestings for this rather artificial geographical area was 12.

THE PENNINES

This long mountain chain forms the largest area of upland in England and extends from Derbyshire and Staffordshire in the south to Cumberland and Northumberland in the north. It is conveniently divided into several different sections, beginning with the Peak District of Derbyshire, Cheshire and South Yorkshire in the south. The history of the Peregrine in this district is obscure. Presumed former nesting places are mentioned vaguely for the narrow, craggy limestone valleys of the Low Peak, but in 1979 there were no breeding records here for well over a hundred years. This area could once have held four pairs. Nesting has recently occurred in at least one quarry. The southwestern extension of the gritstone moorlands of the High Peak into Staffordshire once had a well known eyrie on the crags of the Roaches, now beloved of climbers, and also long deserted by falcons. The higher moorlands and their precipitous 'edges' between Sheffield and Manchester give scope for occupation by at least 11 pairs of Peregrines, at a conservative estimate, but we shall probably never know just how many once bred. There are remarkably few old records of eyries, and game-preserving had virtually extinguished the Peregrine as a regular nester in the Peak District well before 1900. R. A. Frost (1978) believed that there were more or less annual attempts at breeding in one or more of three different localities from 1919 up to 1954 or 1955, but gamekeeper vigilance nearly always ensured failure, usually by shooting of one or both of the pair.

Despite the additional discouragement of almost continual disturbance by rock climbers at many of the bigger gritstone crags in the Peak District National Park, it is gratifying that Peregrines have returned. In 1991, at least seven pairs were in residence, and three broods were reared, in the High Peak (G. Mawson, C. Richards).

The rather dreary second section of the Pennines extends north from Saddleworth Moor through the industrial textile belt where Lancashire and Yorkshire meet, and ends in the north at the valleys of the Aire and Ribble. There are few natural crags here which could ever have held Peregrines, and the only one specifically mentioned is in the Vale of Cliviger, south-east of Burnley, said to be tenanted up to 1820 or later but long abandoned (Mitchell, 1892). Remarkably, after a long absence, six pairs attempted to breed in 1991, including one established on a tall chimney in Darwen since 1989 (D. Bunn). To the north of the lower Ribble valley lies the detached massif of the Forest of Bowland, a dissected moorland plateau divided between Lancashire and Yorkshire. This is one of the least trodden parts of upland England for it has long been grouse moor jealously guarded against human intruders as well as predators. Peregrines received short shrift here after game preservation began, though attempts at nesting occurred in several places, with occasional success up to 1956. Since 1980, numbers have built up and the Bowland area has had attempted nesting in at least 11 different territories. Despite considerable publicity, continuing persecution ensures a poor breeding performance and prevents the regular occupation of some territories. In 1991, nine pairs were certainly located and four broods reared: one nest had a gin trap set next to it. T. Pickford, P. Stott, C. Smith and P. Marsden have contributed the recent records for this area.

North of the Aire lies the Pennine tract of Craven and the Yorkshire Dales, terminating northwards at the Stainmore Gap, and known to geologists as the Askrigg Block. This is a district of fairly frequent limestone scars and gritstone edges, some of them quite lofty, such as the 90 m faces of Malham Cove and Gordale Scar, though parts are gentle moorland terrain with little outcropping rock. The north-west extremity of this Pennine tract marches with Cumbria in the Mallerstang Fells, but I have retained within it the outlying Silurian massifs of the Howgill and Barbon Fells now included in this new county. Nelson, in *The Birds of Yorkshire* (1907), is referring to this Sedbergh area in speaking of four extant eyries in north-west Yorkshire. He mentions also that a pair regularly attempted to nest in Swaledale, but indicated that Peregrines trying to breed at old haunts in the Craven Pennines usually came to an untimely end. The species has a dismal history in this district, for big areas are managed as grouse moor, and most of the suitable nesting places are within easy reach of keepers. In addition to the long deserted nesting haunts at Malham Cove and Kilnsea Crag in Wharfedale, there were at least 13 fairly well scattered localities in this district where Peregrines bred, or tried to do so, during 1900–55. In the least persecuted area, the Howgill–Barbon–Mallerstang Fells, three territories remained regularly occupied, and a fourth irregularly, up to 1960. In the other nine localities nesting was evidently sporadic, though there is a dearth of records to establish the true picture. I believe that occupation of virtually all these places would have been regular if there had been no gamekeeper interference, and that up to ten other lesser crags would also have held Peregrines.

There was a decline even within this small population during 1960–66, but recovery followed and in 1981, 12 pairs nested in this district. By 1991, the total had risen to 19 pairs, though another had dropped out, and one other recently occupied haunt was not visited (C. Armitstead, J. Armitage, C. Hind, M. Priestley).

The most northerly sector of the Pennines, the Alston Block, lies between Stainmore and the Tyne Gap in the old counties of Yorkshire, Westmorland, Cumberland, Durham and Northumberland. Although it contains the highest ground in the whole Pennine Chain (Cross Fell, 894 m), there are relatively few crags suitable for Peregrines, and the catchments of the Tees, Wear and South Tyne are particularly deficient in decent cliffs. Three pairs were known to breed

in the Westmorland–Cumberland part around 1910 (P. W. Parminter, E. Blezard). A fourth pair bred regularly, or tried to do so, in Upper Teesdale, usually
on the Yorkshire side of the river but occasionally in Durham (Nelson, 1907). At
least two former nesting places are mentioned in the older records for Weardale
and there was occasional nesting in either East or West Allendale, but only
isolated occurrences of breeding in the South Tyne catchment.

This large area was predominantly grouse moor, and keeper attention evidently discouraged Peregrines, so that the normal population up to 1960 was only
three to four pairs, confined to the biggest crags (E. Blezard, H. Watson, R. W.
Robson). During 1963–66 only one breeding pair remained, but by 1979 there
were eight pairs, and in 1984 no less than 12. Gamekeeper interference is
suspected in the subsequent disappearance of at least three pairs, but still further
additions in more outlying parts of the area brought numbers up to at least 13
pairs in 1991 (P. Burnham, T. Wells, I. H. Findlay, J. Miles, G. Horne, B. Little,
M. Nattrass).

LAKELAND

I have included within Lakeland all parts of the former counties of Cumberland, Westmorland and Lancashire North of the Sands (or the new county of
Cumbria), except Howgill Fells, Pennines and Border moors. Lakeland is the
main inland stronghold of the Peregrine in England, and all the main fell groups
and dales have breeding places, though density is a little lower on the Skiddaw
Slate hills than on those formed of Borrowdale Volcanic and other igneous rocks,
a difference reflecting the greater availability of good crags on the latter formations. Scope for coastal nesting in the district is very limited, and the great

Inland nesting haunt: 75 m Borrowdale Volcanic cliff set amidst woodland; Lake District, northern England (photo: D. A. Ratcliffe)

majority of nesting places are inland, though some are now in quite low-lying situations.

The earlier works on the birds of the district by Macpherson and Duckworth (1886) and Macpherson (1892) are vague on numbers, but imply that persecution had caused appreciable decline, with extinction a possibility. John Watson of Kendal wrote in 1888 that 'One time and another there have been not less than 17 nesting places of the Peregrine Falcon in the Lake District, about half of which I have visited.' *The Birds of Lakeland* (1943) by E. Blezard and others stated that 'nearly twenty pairs of this distinctive resident annually attempt to rear their young in the Lake counties'. That this figure was an under-estimate emerged from discussions with several ornithologists who between them had a vast experience of the Peregrine in Lakeland. Dr E. S. Steward told me that he or his friends had taken eggs on 23 different cliffs, which he considered to represent 14 separate territories, during the period 1897–1940. The Rev. P. W. Parminter knew at least 11 pairs (including eight unknown to Steward) and the pioneer Keswick rock-climber G. D. Abraham wrote me that he had come across 14 separate pairs; their records referred to approximately the same period.

The diaries of E. B. Dunlop, a fine Lakeland naturalist tragically killed in World War I, give records of Peregrine eyries representing 14 different territories between 1904 and 1913. W. C. Lawrie worked the Buttermere area of Cumberland between 1910 and 1939, and stated in 1925 that there were five eyries within a radius of about six miles. Notes left by J. F. Peters for 1912–22 refer to six breeding pairs, all in Westmorland.

During the 1920s and 30s, several extremely active young men began working the Lakeland eyries more systematically. J. E. Wightman followed 17 pairs from 1926–46, seven of them in Westmorland and two in Furness, Lancashire. The records of J. H. Coward, who operated mainly in the 1930s, mentioned 15 separate territories (June, 1938), and he stated separately that at least 15 pairs bred in central Lakeland in 1934. In 1933, R. J. Birkett began as a youngster to search for and climb to eyries, and went on to develop an unrivalled knowledge of the Lakeland falcons. Jim Birkett, Little Langdale quarryman, veteran all-round naturalist and master cragsman, had personal knowledge of no less than 31 separate territories in the Lake District up to 1960, though he considered that seven of these were used irregularly.

Many more ornithologists besides those mentioned were looking at Lakeland Peregrines during 1900–60. By putting together all the available records I have arrived at what I believe to be a fairly reliable picture of the Lakeland Peregrine population during this period. It is clear that before Jim Birkett made a thorough and systematic search of the district, no one attempted to cover more than about half of the potential nesting places. Even so, the records are sufficient to show that the majority of nesting territories were held regularly throughout the whole period 1900–60, and there is nothing to indicate that the population showed any discernible trend during these 60 years. Average population level for this period can be given as 29 pairs. Only one former haunt was not known to have been used during 1900–60, in the limestone country south of Windermere.

Lakeland was excluded from the Order permitting the killing of Peregrines during World War II and although egg robberies continued to be heavy, only a small number of adults appears to have been destroyed. I began to look at eyries here in 1945, and by 1960 had seen eggs or young in 17 different territories, and pairs likely to be breeding in eight more haunts. Some of these places I visited repeatedly, but others I knew less well. However, Jim Birkett continued to follow the Lakeland Peregrines intensively after 1945, and Frank Parr became another systematic searcher in the mid-1950s. Our combined records make it abundantly clear that although breeding success was poor throughout the 1950s, the numbers of Peregrines were maintained at a normal level in this district up to 1959, when at least 18 pairs or birds were present in 22 territories examined out of the total of 31. One regular pair dropped out mysteriously in

Inland nesting haunt on a third class cliff of only 10 on Carboniferous sandstone, amidst grouse moors; Cheviots, Northumberland (photo: D. A. Ratcliffe)

1958, and in 1960 three 'regulars' were missing, but this could still be regarded as within normal limits of fluctuation, for 18 out of 23 territories were occupied in 1960.

Nevertheless, it was obvious by 1961 that something was amiss with the Lakeland population. In this year, 19 occupied territories were located, but only ten pairs were known to lay eggs, and only three of these reared young. By 1963, levels had dropped to eight territories occupied, four pairs producing eggs, and two broods reared. The Lakeland Peregrines remained at this low ebb until 1967, when there was a slight upturn, with 11 territories tenanted, six pairs with eggs, and five broods reared. Recovery continued steadily thereafter, and by 1979, 33 territories were occupied. The increase has gone on and on, with 48 territories occupied in 1981, 61 in 1985, and an incredible 79 in 1991 (272% of the pre-1960 level).

The gratifying recovery of the Lakeland population has been charted in detail through the dedicated efforts of numerous enthusiasts, notably R. J. Birkett, F. Parr, G. Horne, T. R. Pickford, P. Stott, P. Marsden, C. Smith, J. Davidson, D. Hayward, R. Buchanan and G. Fryer.

THE CHEVIOTS

The Cheviot range of hills extends from the Bewcastle and Gilsland Moors in north-east Cumberland to the Cheviot itself and its foothills in the north-east of Northumberland, and may be regarded as including the outlying lower moorlands of the Simonside Hills and Lorbottle Moors near Rothbury. The Border Line between England and Scotland follows the main watershed, but it is only recently that the Peregrine has been known to nest on the Scottish side, nearly all the suitable crags being in Northumberland.

In 1840, Peregrines were said to nest regularly in the Irthing Gorge at Gilsland, and at two places on the Whinsill crags along the line of the Roman Wall several miles to the eastward. Breeding occurred on the low moorlands east of Chillingham up to around 1820. These pairs evidently dropped out well before 1900, and George Bolam said in 1932 that the Peregrine in Northumberland was 'long banished from all its once well-known lowland eyries, but still maintaining a precarious footing (dependent upon the forbearance of game preservers) amongst the hills, where some half-dozen breeding places are more or less regularly occupied'. His MS notebooks listed five eyries in widely scattered localities in 1929, and a sixth which was occupied in 1920 was possibly not inspected in 1929. At least 16 inland territories have been recorded altogether in the Cheviot range, in the catchments of North Tyne, Rede, Wansbeck, Coquet and Tweed. In byegone days, small outcrops on the moors between Bewcastle and the North Tyne could have held at least three more pairs, while Kyloe Crags in the far north-east of Northumberland are another suitable but unrecorded nesting place.

Several haunts were used in the years after 1945, but some of them irregularly, and the ornithological reports of the Northumberland and Durham Natural History Society up to 1960 suggest that the average population level was less than that given by Bolam. Writing to me about Peregrines and Ravens in 1950, the late George Temperley said that, 'The story of both these birds in Northumberland and Durham is one long tragedy. What with gamekeepers, shepherds, egg collectors and photographers, the breeding of both these birds is very much interfered with.' The addition of rock climbing and pesticides gave still more point to his remarks. During 1960–70, Brian Little knew attempted nesting in five different localities, with birds present at four other crags, but never more than two definite nestings in any one year. Although recovery in Peregrine population was marked elsewhere in Northern England after 1967, numbers in Northumberland appeared to dwindle virtually to nothing during the 1970s.

Recovery was nevertheless well under way by 1981, with four pairs, and had already reached an unprecedented eight pairs by 1984. By 1991, no fewer than 13 pairs were found nesting in Northumberland, well scattered over the county and including areas where there were no historic records of breeding (Brian Little).

ISLE OF MAN

The Isle of Man lies in the northern part of the Irish Sea, equidistant between Lakeland, Galloway and Co. Down, and thus claiming biological affinities with all three. It has a rugged, cliff-girt coast in many places and has long been a noted haunt of Peregrines. The hills of the centre are mostly smooth, but steep locally, and quarrying has added here and there to the few natural crags. Ken Williamson

An ancient inland nesting haunt on a third class cliff of 10 m on Carboniferous sandstone; site on steep face beyond the fall; Cheviots, Northumberland (photo: D. A. Ratcliffe)

worked the Manx Peregrines during the late 1930s, and he gave me a list of 11 coastal territories then occupied, which he believed to be used regularly; while three inland haunts were tenanted perhaps less faithfully.

I do not know how much war-time destruction took place on the Isle of Man, nor the state of the population in the early post-war years. J. N. Keig knew six eyries in 1960, and a pair bred in a seventh locality in 1959 and 1961. By 1962, only four pairs remained and in 1963 all the Manx territories appeared deserted. The 1971 Enquiry revealed only two pairs, which either did not breed or failed after laying, and it was not until 1973 that a successful nesting was again reported: two pairs reared young in that year, and a third pair was seen elsewhere. Dr L. S. Garrad told me that in 1979 there were at least three successful pairs and possibly up to another three unlocated eyries. The situation has since been transformed, and in 1991 at least 18 coastal and two inland territories were occupied, and 12 clutches laid. There were in addition three extra non-breeding pairs and a single bird on the coast. This information is from Dr Pat Cullen, who has coordinated monitoring of Isle of Man Peregrines for many years.

SOUTHERN SCOTLAND

Most of the breeding Peregrines in this region are located in the western half, where suitable cliffs are most frequent, on the coast and inland, though the counties of Dumfries and Renfrew have no seacliffs. There is little historical information about the coastal eyries in Kirkcudbrightshire, but information from E. Blezard, G. Trafford and R. Stokoe suggests that during the early 1950s four pairs bred regularly and two irregularly on the seacliffs of this county. Farther west, Wigtownshire has a longer extent of seacliff, especially on the western side of the long peninsula known as the Rhinns of Galloway. Yet, although Gray (1871) mentions three well known eyries in the county, I have found little in the way of documentary record of Peregrines in the whole county during the present century. Piecing together the records of several observers for the period up to 1960, it seems likely that Wigtown had at least 12 coastal territories, of which perhaps nine were once regular.

Robert Service said in 1903 that about eight to 12 pairs usually nested on the Scottish side of the Solway Firth, but he did not define the area: if he meant from Southerness Point to the Mull of Galloway, then his estimate compares closely with ten pairs as the average tally in more recent years.

Gray stated that five or six pairs bred on the Ayrshire coast, including the well known pair on Ailsa Craig, but implied that the species was declining even in 1871. An ancient nesting place on the Hunterston cliffs was evidently deserted when Paton and Pike wrote *The Birds of Ayrshire* in 1929, but in the 1950s five or six pairs were still nesting on the coastal cliffs of the county (J. Hutchinson, D. Brown and J. Gibson).

The population of the Galloway and Ayrshire coast was severely affected by the great decline; in 1962 only four pairs could be found in 16 territories, and only one of these was successful. Numbers picked up slowly and in 1978 ten out of 17 territories were occupied, eight of them successfully (R. Mearns). However, by 1981, numbers were back to normal, with 21 territories occupied; and by 1991 the total had risen to 32 pairs, the highest ever known (south-west Scotland Raptor Study Group).

Inland, the rocky Galloway and Carrick hills are the chief stronghold of the Peregrine in the Southern Uplands, although there is little scope for nesting inland in Wigtownshire, which is a country of low, gentle moorlands. Earlier information for the Stewartry of Kirkcudbright is scanty, but I have found records of eyries in nine different localities during 1900–25. In 1937 and 1938 R. Laidler, P. S. Day and A. K. Bannister visited six of these same territories and found all of them occupied. During 1946–60, I found 13 different occupied territories among the hills in the western and northern parts of the Stewartry, ten of them held regularly, two irregularly (including one in which the Peregrines were regular up to 1954, but were then displaced by Golden Eagles) and one occasionally. These places included all nine known during 1900–25. Another haunt was found by other observers to be occasionally tenanted, but on visits in 1949 and 1955 I saw no evidence of breeding. There were unlocalised reports of occasional breeding in the south-eastern, Criffel area.

For southern Ayrshire, Paton and Pike stated in 1929 that there were three or four eyries in Carrick (the district south of the R. Doon) and that one pair usually attempted to breed near the eastern border of Kyle. In the 1950s the records of the late Donald Cross and others indicate that four inland territories were occupied regularly and at least another two irregularly or occasionally. Northern Ayrshire had at least one more regular pair, with an alternative site in Renfrewshire.

Farther east in the Southern Uplands the crags and hence Peregrines become more widely scattered. The main breeding areas are in the hills of western Nithsdale, the Lowther Hills between Nith and Annan, and the Moffat–Tweedsmuir range; mostly within Dumfriesshire, but with the last draining also to the Tweed in Peeblesshire. Sir Hugh Gladstone said in 1910 there were from 12–16 nesting places then annually resorted to in Dumfriesshire. Records for the next 40 years are rather inadequate, but in one part of Dumfriesshire I knew four pairs regularly from 1949–60, and in 1960 I located ten nesting pairs in the county. The normal population from 1940 to 1960 was evidently nine to 11 pairs. Gladstone's additional localities were evidently irregularly occupied.

The high hills of southern Peeblesshire which adjoin the Moffat Hills had two regular pairs for at least 60 years, and there were two irregular or occasional territories in this massif, one of them in Selkirkshire.

William Macgillivray (1840) was evidently impressed by the numbers in these Moffat–Tweedsmuir Hills: '. . . it seems to be more abundant in Peeblesshire and the adjoining mountain districts of the counties of Selkirk and Dumfries, than in most parts of Scotland'. Probably Peregrines were no more numerous there than a century later, and he was simply lucky in coming across several pairs.

The Culter Fell range divided between Peeblesshire and Lanarkshire had at least two occasional nesting haunts, one in each county. The rounded, rolling hills of Eskdale, Liddesdale, Ettrick and Teviot which merge eastwards into the Cheviots have a particular scarcity of crags, and I knew of only one nesting place, tenanted irregularly, in this large area. There were occasional nesting attempts in the Pentland Hills, and the Moorfoot Hills south-east of Edinburgh had two other occasional nesting places, one in Peeblesshire and the other in the Mid-lothian catchment. The Lammermuirs forming the eastern extremity of the Southern Uplands in Berwickshire, had at least two old haunts, but neither has been reported occupied since 1900.

Inland nesting haunt: second-class cliff of 21 m in deep ravine of Old Red Sandstone; icicles hanging from the rocks in frosty weather; Southern Uplands, southern Scotland (photo: D. A. Ratcliffe)

The pre- and post-1940 inland population of the Southern Uplands evidently numbered 30–35 pairs and was much less affected by the pesticide 'crash' than that of the coast. Out of 26 territories occupied during 1955–60, only eight were known to be deserted during 1961–65, but non-breeding and breeding failure became prevalent amongst the remaining birds, and in 1962 only one brood was reared. Recovery was apparent by 1966, and in 1971, Dick Roxburgh and George Carse between them found 27 occupied territories. By 1979, 31 territories were occupied, and in 1981 the number had increased to 45 (R. Mearns, R. Roxburgh, G. Carse). Numbers have since 'taken off', with 65 occupied territories in 1985, and the remarkable total of 95 in 1991. Most of the increase has been in the counties of Dumfries, Kirkcudbright and Ayr, but nesting is now regular in Roxburgh, Lanark, Midlothian and Berwick (see Table 1). Increase has been more by the occupation of marginal nesting places, rather than territory 'doubling' (though one former territory now has three pairs), and 16 quarry haunts have been used (R. Roxburgh, G. Carse).

A lowland nesting place on a riverside cliff of the Whitadder, near Berwick, was not occupied after about 1830. It is surprising that Peregrines have not yet been recorded nesting on the rocks of Arthur's Seat, Salisbury Crags or the Castle Rock in Edinburgh, which would seem to be a highly suitable locality, and where Ravens formerly bred. The Peregrine has been seen a good many times in Edinburgh in the winter during this century.

The Berwickshire seacliffs either side of St Abbs Head are an ancient stronghold of Peregrines, and four pairs were recorded by A. Hepburn in 1850. George Bolam in 1912 also reported four pairs, and this number was probably maintained until the 1950s, after which all these coastal territories became deserted. In the Firth of Forth, the Bass Rock was once a regular nesting place (the last known eyrie in 1934), and there was still earlier an eyrie station, possibly alternative to the Bass, on the cliffs below Tantallon Castle on the adjoining mainland coast. The small island of Craigleith to the west has had occasional eyries, and nesting may possibly have occurred on Fidra. From 1987, three pairs have again tried to breed, and in 1991 there was another pair on the Forth islands (G. Carse).

THE SCOTTISH HIGHLANDS AND ISLANDS

This large and mountainous region, with its long stretches of rocky coast, holds and probably always held, the bulk of the British Peregrine population. The documented history of the bird is nevertheless poorest here, and the Highlands and Islands undoubtedly contain the majority of the recent or current nesting places which have escaped record in the Peregrine surveys conducted from 1961 onwards.

The 19th century writers Macgillivray, Gray and Harvie-Brown repeatedly use words such as 'common' and 'numerous' to describe Peregrine numbers in the region, especially in the west. It is impossible now to know what meaning to attach to such terms, but they may always have been used in a relative sense. In districts where it is allowed to breed unmolested, the Peregrine can be a conspicuous bird when the young are in the eyrie, and a journey which chances to pass through several territories could readily give the impression that it is a widespread species, occurring almost wherever there are suitable cliffs. Nowadays, ornithologists tend to be more careful about their designations of numbers, and 'common' is more usually applied to the Kestrel and Sparrowhawk. While there is some evidence for decline, this has to be interpreted with care, for the detailed record is patchy indeed.

The main sources of historical information are the *Vertebrate Fauna of Scotland* series, the inspiration of the great Scottish naturalist J. A. Harvie-Brown, who was the author or joint author of several of these invaluable volumes. These works deal with the large faunal areas into which Harvie-Brown divided Scotland, based on main drainage catchments, e.g. the Moray Basin, the Tay Basin and so on. Harvie-Brown's manuscript diaries and notebooks also provide further details for the period 1860–1910. I have compiled from these and other sources in the literature a list of 115 localities mentioned as Peregrine breeding haunts before 1910. It is, however, a most obviously incomplete list, and population figures for particular districts are tantalisingly few. After 1910 there are only a few local additions to knowledge of Peregrine distribution, and the information available for 1910–60 is extremely thin and patchy. The egg collectors came to the Highlands for other species and concentrated on Peregrines in more accessible regions farther south. Falconers knew a good deal about the bird here but tended to work a particular selection of eyries.

Phillip Glasier gave me details of 54 nesting haunts he knew during the 1950s; Pat Sandeman supplied data on 51 nesting pairs recorded by him during 1947–55; and Adam Watson listed eyries in 30 localities for 1946–60; all three lists referred to localities well scattered over the Highlands and Islands. Several other observers provided lists of 10–25 breeding places for the period 1935–60.

Apart from these more significant contributions, which overlap considerably in the places to which they refer, the picture of distribution from 1910–60 has been built up mainly from scattered records, and the verbal recollections of keepers, stalkers, shepherds and other local residents. *The Birds of Scotland* (Baxter and Rintoul, 1953) gives a useful summary of available information on distribution up to about 1950, but with a bias towards island records.

For most parts of the Highlands and Islands, the only systematic breeding census information is that collected since 1960. Before that date the fragmentary record makes it difficult to judge whether short-term fluctuations in numbers could have occurred, and gives a somewhat unsatisfactory basis for examining the possibility of longer term trends. Ironically, perhaps, the 1961–62 survey took place at a time when numbers were certainly declining, and while subsequent observations have happily charted a substantial recovery, the whole period since 1961 has to be regarded as one of marked instability in the Peregrine population. Strictly, this period cannot be regarded as giving a reliable datum for comparison with earlier periods. Attempts at full surveys were made only in 1961–62, 1971, 1981 and 1991 and only sample censuses were maintained in other years. Because of the unevenness of the record during 1961–91, and the complexity of local differences, I shall not attempt to detail population data for each district over the whole of this period. Instead, I shall make a broad summary of the current position for each region, district by district, drawing on the latest information to give the most up-to-date picture. For convenience, the term *recent* will be used for any territory occupations or actual breeding during 1961–91. Where no date is given for territory occupation it should be assumed that post-1950 records are being discussed.

I have divided the Highlands and Islands into two major regions, along the natural cleavage of the Great Glen Fault from the Firth of Lorne to the Moray Firth. Each region is sub-divided as follows:

Southern and eastern Highlands

1. *Inland fringe*, including all hill ranges south of the Tay in the counties of Perth, Clackmannan, Kinross, Fife, Stirling, Dumbarton and mainland Argyll south of Loch Linnhe.

2. *Inland centre and east*, including all hill ranges in the counties of Perth north of the Tay, Inverness south of the Great Glen, Angus, Kincardine, Aberdeen, Banff, Moray and Nairn.

3. *West coast*, including Buteshire, mainland Argyll and its islands south of the Firth of Lorne.

4. *East coast*, from the South shore of the Moray Firth to the north shore of the Firth of Forth.

Northern and western Highlands

1. *Inland*, including all mainland hill ranges of Argyll north of Loch Linnhe, Inverness north of the Great Glen, Ross-shire, Sutherland and Caithness.

2. *West coast*, from Argyll north of the Firth of Lorne to Sutherland–Caithness march; and both Inner and Outer Hebrides.

3. *East coast*, from Black Isle to Caithness–Sutherland march; and Orkney and Shetland.

SOUTHERN AND EASTERN HIGHLANDS

Inland fringe

Although they lie to the south of the Highland line, the relatively low ranges of hills which interrupt the Central Lowlands of Scotland are treated as outliers of the southern Highland mountain systems. At their western end, the nesting station on the Dumbarton Castle Rock, used in 1764–82, was deserted around 1800 (Montagu, 1813). In the Kilpatrick Hills (Dumbarton), Campsie Fells, Kilsyth and Gargunnock Hills (Stirling) there were four recorded 19th century eyries, and three more during 1920–50. A single pair appeared to be left during the early 1960s, and it was only in 1968 that a second appeared. Even by 1979, only four territories were certainly occupied, but by 1986 the number had increased dramatically to 13, and breeding strength has been maintained at ten to 12 pairs (J. Mitchell, R. A. Broad).

A famous eyrie at the Abbey Craig near Stirling (first record 1496) was said in 1867 to be still occasionally occupied, but is now long deserted. Northwards, the Ochil Hills, shared by Stirling, Clackmannan and Perth, held two pairs in 1960, including the time-honoured eyrie near Alva. There were another five 19th century haunts in the low hills of Kinross, Perth and Fife. This area was little worked during the 1960s, but the dearth of breeding records suggested that few Peregrines remained. Even during the 1970s there were few reports, but at least three pairs were nesting by 1981, and a thorough survey in 1991 showed no less than 12 pairs, some in small and low-lying rocks (P. Stirling-Aird, Tayside Raptor Study Group).

North of the Highland line, the Loch Lomond hills in Dumbarton and Stirling had at least four 19th century nesting places, and four more occupied in the 1930s. To the north and east as far as the road from Tyndrum to Glen Ogle and Strathyre, and then to Port of Menteith and Aberfoyle, is the block of Perthshire containing the high ranges of Ben Lui, the Balquhidder Hills, and the lesser heights around the Trossachs. Up to 1960, ten pairs was evidently the normal breeding complement of this ground. Survey of these two segments was only partial for some years: in 1962, seven out of eight territories were occupied, and in 1971, eight out of ten. In 1981, 24 occupied haunts were known, but a few of these proved irregular, and in 1991 25 territories held only 20 pairs (J. Mitchell, R. A. Broad, D. MacCaskill, P. Stirling-Aird).

In the remainder of eastern Perthshire south of the Tay and east and north of the A84–85 road is the extensive hill country around Loch Earn, Glen Artney, Glen Almond and Strathbraan. These massifs tail off into lower grouse moors towards Callander, Braco, Logiealmond and Dunkeld. Little was known about this ground during the first Peregrine enquiry, but five out of six territories had birds in 1971. By 1981, 14 occupied territories were known, but the number has since reached at least 25, with 22 occupied in 1991 (P. Stirling-Aird).

The rest of the Inland Fringe district is occupied by the larger part of Argyll, a complex area much indented by sea lochs, with high and rugged mountains in the north and large expanses of lower hill and moorland elsewhere. It is now heavily afforested. Earlier information on population is vague, though Harvie-Brown and Buckley (1892) indicated that Peregrines were widespread and in good numbers in the 19th century. Alastair McArthur knew 11 territories (seven regular) during the 1940s and 50s, but few ornithologists worked the district then, and even now it is probably not completely known. In 1962, 16 known breeding haunts were examined, and only 11 were occupied. Little more was known until 1972, when 17 out of 24 territories held Peregrines. Later surveys covered a larger number of breeding places, and indicated something of a pattern in their occupation.

The high mountain country to the north of the Arrochar to Oban road has at least 14 territories. In 1981, only four out of 13 visited had Peregrines, while in 1991, the figure was five out of ten. In the area of Lorne between the Pass of Brander and the Crinan Canal, all of the seven territories visited in 1981 were occupied, and eight of ten in 1991. The Cowal peninsula south of the Arrochar–Loch Fyne road has proved to hold the highest numbers in recent years. In 1981, nine out of ten territories were occupied, and in 1991, 11 out of 13. The long peninsula of Knapdale and Kintyre, south of the Crinan Canal, in the west, has the fewest falcons: there are at least six territories but only three were tenanted in 1991. The overall occupation rate for the whole area was 22 out of 33 (67%) in 1981, and 27 out of 39 (69%) in 1991. This information came mainly from R. A. Broad, S. Petty, M. J. Gregory, D. Fleming and C. J. Thomas.

Inland centre and east

This contains the extensive mountain systems collectively known as the Grampians, which include the highest summits in Britain. Peregrine survey here has latterly been organised into four groupings, and I have taken these as the basis of geographical treatment, as follows:

1. Perthshire between the Tay and the A9 road – Patrick Stirling-Aird and helpers.

2. Perthshire north and east of the A9, and Angus – Tayside Raptor Study Group, coordinator Keith Brockie.

3. Counties of Kincardine, Aberdeen, Banff and part of Moray – Grampian Raptor Study Group, coordinator Jonathan Hardey. Also Adam Watson.

4. Inverness-shire south of the Great Glen, Nairn and part of Moray – Roy Dennis and helpers.

The first area contains the high, green ranges of Breadalbane and Rannoch, beloved of alpine botanists, and the lower massifs which extend northwards to the Inverness march at Loch Ericht and Drumochter. The earlier distribution of Peregrines here was not completely known, and the 1962 survey examined only six territories, of which four were occupied. In 1972, the sample was still small, with six out of eight localities holding Peregrines. By 1981, fuller survey showed 14 out of 16 territories occupied, and in 1986 falcons were located in 19 places with only one territory deserted. This was beginning to suggest a slight increase in population, but the 1991 census produced the surprising result that, of 22 territories visited, only 11 were occupied. Nine of the deserted haunts in 1991 had been occupied in 1986. This situation contrasted markedly with those in the adjoining areas to north and south.

The second area includes the extensive and little-trodden deer forest country of Glen Tilt and the Forest of Atholl, the botanically famous hills at the head of Glens Isla and Clova, and the belt of lower grouse moors between Pitlochry and Glen Esk. This also was incompletely known during the earlier surveys, though the samples suggested a lack of decline. In 1962, all eight of the territories examined held Peregrines, and in 1971 the figure for occupation was 11 out of 13. The 1981 survey produced 25 occupied territories and no desertions, but in 1991 there was a remarkable doubling, with falcons located in 55 proved breeding places, and prospecting birds in several other possible haunts.

The Grampian area contains the Deeside catchment of the high Cairngorm and Lochnagar massifs, and Glens Avon and Don which drain the north-eastern side of the Cairngorms. This fine high montane country holds the most elevated Peregrine nesting places in Britain, but tails off into a broad belt of lower grouse moors forming the eastern and northern foothills. These moorlands are unspectacular, smooth and often gently contoured uplands, where outcropping rocks are mostly small and restricted to the streamsides. The post-1960 picture is similar to that in the previous area. A small sample of eight territories was fully occupied in 1961, and in 1971 10 out of 12 known haunts were tenanted. Increased effort and knowledge of distribution led to the finding of 26 pairs and no desertions in 1981. This total was again doubled in 1991 with a startling 53 occupations of proved breeding places, and prospecting birds in another 10 possible territories.

The fourth area is that part of the administrative Highland Region to the south of the Great Glen. It contains the long Spey valley draining the north side of the Cairngorms, and the Findhorn flowing from the desolate plateau of the Monadh-liath to the north. In the south-west it includes Ben Nevis and the Mamores, and other lofty ranges are the Creag Meagaidh and Ben Alder massifs either side of Loch Laggan. This extensive deer forest and grouse moor country has long been known to hold a considerable Peregrine population, and Harvie-Brown refers to many of the eyries in his writings. Captain Neil Usher and Phillip Glasier gave me information on 18 nesting places used during 1940–60 in the central part.

The 1962 enquiry examined 18 territories and found 16 occupied. Sample surveys during 1963–70 gave 149 occupations in a total of 171 territory examinations (87%) and, in combination with a breeding success of 53% (79 broods in 149 occupations), suggested that this population was little if at all affected by pesticides. The 1971 survey gave a total of 34 out of 37 territories occupied. The Spey–Findhorn Peregrines were monitored for many years by Douglas Weir, who reported that the population in 31 breeding territories stabilised at c. 25 pairs in 1972/75 but fell to 22 pairs in 1976. By 1981, the number of known territories had increased to 47, of which 44 were tenanted. Probably virtually all these 47 territories were pre-1960 haunts, so that the situation was still one of 'normal' population level. Survey in 1991 was incomplete, with 33 territories visited and 26 occupied. Applying this rate of occupation to the known total of 51 territories gives an estimated seven additional pairs, i.e. 40 for the whole area.

West coast

I have included the islands of Buteshire within this area. Arran has five inland territories which, strictly, belong to the Inland Fringe, but for convenience are included here. There are six coastal haunts on Arran, and other islands, Bute itself, Little Cumbrae and Inchmarnock claim another six. The Rev. J. McWilliam said in 1927 that about eight pairs usually nested on Arran, and in 1953 Dr J. A. Gibson gave exactly the same number. In 1962, five out of seven Buteshire territories werre occupied, and in 1971 seven out of nine. The 1981 survey found 13 out of 14 territories to be occupied. Since no data were available for 1991, the 1981 figures have been used as an estimate.

Dugald Macintyre stated in 1960 that the number of Peregrine eyries in the whole Kintyre peninsula (evidently including Knapdale) in southern Argyll remained at 18 year after year, for 30 years and more, to his personal knowledge. In 1962, only six territories were visited, and four held Peregrines; in 1971, eight out of nine were occupied. The 1981 survey examined all 12 known territories and found 11 occupied, while in 1991 Peregrines were present in 13 localities. This suggests that numbers have been at normal level for some time, and that Macintyre's count included the six inland territories mentioned above, as well as the two islands of Sanda and Davarr. The mainland coast of Lorne to the north has only two definite territories, both with an erratic history of occupation since 1960. The chain of small offshore islands, including Lismore, Kerrera, Luing, the Garvellachs, the Lunga group, Scarba, Gigha and Cara, has much apparent scope for Peregrines, but there was little information about them during 1962–81. In 17 visits to known haunts during this period, only nine were positive; and only five pairs were found during incomplete survey in 1991. Recent records for the area are mainly from R. A. Broad, D. Fleming, K. Graham and I. Hood.

The large Inner Hebridean island of Islay is relatively fertile ground with good bird populations to provide a plentiful food supply for Peregrines. It was surveyed in 1961, when six coastal pairs were reported, and there were at least seven in 1971. The number had risen to 10 (one inland) by 1981. The 1991 survey gave 12 coastal and three inland pairs, while two earlier territories were vacant. Although it is difficult now to interpret these figures, the 1991 numbers probably represent a real increase over pre-1960 levels. The sister island of Jura is much more sterile ground, and not a notable Peregrine area: there were few records before 1981 when three pairs were found. In 1991 there were four and a possible fifth. This information is mainly from R. A. Broad, M. Peacock, M. Ogilvie, R. Macdonald, K. D. Smith, D. Weir and D. Fleming. On Colonsay, gamekeeper Malcolm Clark said in 1961 that he had known just one pair annually during a sojourn of 27 years, and a single pair has been known since, up to 1991.

East coast

Pre-1960 distribution here was fairly well known. The Firth of Forth coast in Fife has had an intermittent nesting place on the Isle of May, where the last known breeding was in 1941, and a long deserted one on the low mainland cliffs near Elie. From the Firth of Tay to the south side of the Moray Firth there are good ranges of cliff, though with appreciable gaps in between. In Angus, the cliffs at Red Head and those between Arbroath and Montrose had at least two pairs. In Kincardineshire northwards, the great seabird breeding station of Fowlsheugh had a famous eyrie, while the Stonehaven to Aberdeen coast had two pairs and room for a couple more. The coast from Newburgh to Peterhead in Aberdeen-shire held up to three pairs, but the finest precipices are those on the north coast between Aberdour and Macduff, and lying mainly in Banffshire. Five pairs were regarded as the maximum strength here. Farther west, lower cliff ranges between Banff and Buckie had one pair and scope for two more. From here to Inverness, the otherwise flat coast had just a single nesting place, in Morayshire.

By 1962, only two pairs remained on this east coast, and they disappeared soon after. The area was severely hit by the crash and it was many years before breeding occurred again. The 1971 survey produced only a single bird, but recovery was on the way by 1981, when five pairs were located. In 1991, 15 out of 18 territories were occupied, so that numbers could be said to be back to normal. Adam Watson and Sir Fred Stewart provided most of the earlier information, and the 1991 records came from the Tayside and Grampian Raptor Study Groups.

Summary

The Southern and Eastern Highlands show an extremely varied picture over the last 30 years. The population crash appeared to register slightly in the West Coast and Inland Fringe, but there was fairly early recovery here. The East Coast was seriously affected and took much longer to recover. There were no detect-able effects in the Inland Centre and East. Since then, there has been a divergence, with an approximate doubling of numbers in a broad zone through the eastern half of the region, compared with stability of population or even slight decline in the western half. Islay in the west may also have shown an increase.

First, is the increase over the 1960s and 70s levels a real one, or does it just reflect an increase in field observer effort in a region where the Peregrine population was much less well known than in those farther south? Undoubtedly, until quite recently, there was still a certain number of pre-1960 territories which had been missed in survey. Some may have been deserted for a time during the 1960s, but some were probably occupied all the way through. In the first edition of this book, which gave population data up to 1979, I estimated that another 116 unknown territories remained to be discovered in Scotland. The figure was arrived at largely by examining maps for conspicuous gaps in distribution in areas where there were, or seemed likely to be, suitable nesting places. During the 1981 survey, another 78 previously unreported territories became known in the Highlands. Of these, 46 were probably previously regular haunts which had been missed, but 32 were more likely to be places that had been used occasionally or irregularly before because of persecution.

The apparent doubling of numbers in the eastern part of the region probably represents a combination of all three factors – increased observer effort, reduced gamekeeper persecution, and occupation of completely new territories – with the second two amounting to real population increase. The grand total of 316 occupied territories compares with 227 in 1981 (139%).

NORTHERN AND WESTERN HIGHLANDS

Inland

This district is the mainland of the Highlands north of the Great Glen. There is only a handful of inland eyries in the Islands, and most of these are close to the sea, so that they are included with the coastal groups. The extensive mountain and moorland systems between the line from Loch Linnhe to Inverness and the north coast of Sutherland contain a great deal of wild and inaccessible country, which even now is not fully explored for birds. Many of the western mountains are high and rugged, and even the lower moorlands of Wester Ross and west Sutherland are extremely rocky with numerous crags. There is in many of these areas a great abundance of suitable nesting places for Peregrines. By contrast many of the lower eastern moorlands have rather few good cliffs, and in the Flow Country of east Sutherland and Caithness there are large areas almost devoid of suitable Peregrine rocks.

Probably most of the places where Peregrines nest have been visited in recent years, but the earlier surveys of 1961 and 1971 were clearly incomplete. Ensuring full coverage of western areas is a considerable undertaking, especially in visiting the numerous islands. Even in the east, the recent finding of Peregrines nesting on small outcrops and hidden stream ravines points to the difficulties facing the surveyors in covering all suitable localities. The RSPB, with Roy Dennis and Roger Broad and their helpers, have monitored numbers for a good many years, usually managing to collect information on a substantial proportion of the population annually, and steadily expanding knowledge of distribution. Earlier historical information on the bird remains fragmentary, so that the basis for comparison with recent data is unsatisfactory. Speaking of the western-draining catchments between Mallaig and Cape Wrath in 1904, Harvie-Brown said, 'It is really common over the area', but such a statement is misleading since his own detailed records show the Peregrine to have been thinly distributed at best.

The most southerly part of the district, extending from the Sound of Mull to the line of Loch Morar and Loch Arkaig, has had few breeding pairs of

Peregrines in recent times, yet it covers an area almost as large as the Lake District. In Morvern, two nesting places mentioned by Harvie-Brown were deserted and unknown to a local keeper as Peregrine haunts in 1962, and one was occupied by Golden Eagles. In Ardnamurchan, eagles were nesting on a former falcon crag by the 1930s, and a second cliff where Bruce Campbell saw Peregrines in 1931 was also held by eagles in 1962. Ken Smith made wide enquiries and searches in 1962 through the whole mountainous tract from Lochs Morar and Arkaig to Loch Hourn in 1962, but gathered that Peregrines had been sparse in recent years. He located a single pair in the deer forests of Arisaig and Meoble where Harvie-Brown mentioned four nesting pairs. The whole of inland Inverness-shire north of the Great Glen yielded only eight pairs in 1962, though only 11 nesting haunts were then known. By 1991, there were 24 territories where nesting is known to have occurred since 1960.

Ross-shire is not much mentioned as Peregrine country in the older works, except as part of general statements implying a wide distribution maintained in the face of heavy persecution. Harvie-Brown's MS notes refer to the Fairburn area of Easter Ross as having several pairs, but he identifies only a very few precise localities in the whole county. In the 1962 survey, 22 territories were known, most of them having been tenanted during the previous 10 years. Of these, 16 were visited but only six were occupied. By 1991, the number of inland territories where nesting occurred after 1960 had risen to 42.

In Sutherland, Harvie-Brown and Buckley (1887) mentioned Assynt as having eight inland eyries within a radius of 10 miles. Seven 19th century nesting places are named in the county, and all have been occupied since 1980. In 1960 Thomas Adam gave me a list of 11 inland Peregrine haunts in Sutherland compiled around 1940, and these too have all been occupied in recent years. The 1962 survey had knowledge of 18 territories and examined 13, of which nine were occupied. In 1991, 45 territories were known to have been used in the intervening years. Caithness has very few suitable inland nesting places, and only four had become known up to 1991.

Over the course of the four main surveys, 1961–91, a pattern has emerged which leads me to separate the inland areas into west and east. Breeding density is generally low throughout the west, and has not changed sinced 1961. Western areas also showed clear evidence of decline during the crash, and despite some recovery by 1971–81, were depressed again in 1991. Eastern areas have shown no evidence of decline during the past 30 years, and in some places there appears to have been an increase in numbers.

I have accordingly assigned territories to west or east as follows:

	West	East
Inverness-shire	15	9
Ross-shire	24	17
Sutherland	22	23
Caithness		3
Total	61	52

In the west, only 14 out of 29 territories examined (48%) were occupied by Peregrines in 1962. In 1971, the figures were 29 occupations out of 36

(81%), and in 1981, 29 out of 40 (73%). By 1991, the occupation rate had fallen to 19 out of 45 territories (42%). This contrasts with the east where nine out of nine territories (100%) held Peregrines in 1962, 13 out of 15 (87%) in 1971, 30 out of 33 (91%) in 1981, and 40 out of 43 (93%) in 1991. In the east, at least two territories have been split by extra pairs of Peregrines, and in the Flow Country a traditional Golden Eagle cliff deserted since afforestation of adjoining moorland has been taken over by Peregrines. Prospecting falcons were also seen in 1991 at four places in the east where nesting has not been known previously.

Applying the known rates of occupancy in 1991 gives estimates of an additional eight pairs in the 116 unvisited territories in the west, and eight pairs in nine unvisited territories in the east.

West coast

This may be divided into three areas – the mainland seaboard, the Inner Hebrides and the Outer Hebrides. The mainland coast, beginning on the Morvern peninsula in the south, is rugged and deeply indented by fjord-like sea lochs, but does not have a great extent of sheer seacliff until Sutherland is reached. The coasts of Argyll, Inverness and Wester Ross have thus had only a rather small Peregrine population in recent times, with a total of 18 known territories. It is possible that a few more nesting places remain to be discovered, especially on the inaccessible west coast of Inverness. Sutherland has much more scope for Peregrines, with long lines of almost continuous seacliff fronting much of its coast, and including the huge seabird breeding stations on Handa island and the Clo Mor: 25 post-1940 territories are known here.

In 1962, examination of 27 territories showed only 16 (59%) to be occupied, so that decline appeared to have reached this remote coast, and the position was a shade worse in 1971, with occupation at 16 out of 31 (52%). Subsequent surveys suggest further deterioration, with 17 out of 39 (44%) territories held in 1981, and 11 out of 28 (39%) in 1991. While all these samples are too small to draw far-reaching conclusions, the situation in Sutherland has evidently become worse than to the south. Breeding outcome was unknown for some eyries, but success rate appeared to be generally low in the haunts that remained tenanted.

In the Inner Hebrides, the island of Mull (Argyll), with its satellites Ulva, Gometra, Iona and other islets, has an abundance of suitable Peregrine cliffs, both coastal and inland, yet the history of the species is pretty obscure here. Ken Smith spent nearly 3 weeks searching in 1961, with little success. He reported, 'The story seemed to be the same everywhere. Peregrines used to breed in a number of places on Mull, but have become extremely scarce during the last 20 years or so. A number of old sites were shown to me on the map; these were looked at but without producing anything. I found no difficulty in getting information, and most people were only too willing to tell me about their eagles, etc.' He found a single eyrie with young by hard searching. There was little further information in 1971, when two out four old haunts were occupied. Gradually, other nesting places came to light, and in 1981, seven out of 11 places visited held Peregrines. In 1991, still more thorough survey by Mike Madders showed nine out of 15 known territories to be occupied. It thus appears that decline had reached Mull by 1961, and that there has been appreciable though incomplete recovery in recent years.

To the west of Mull, the island of Tiree has large bird populations, and its rocky headland has been faithfully held by a pair of Peregrines during all four surveys over 1961–91. The adjoining island of Coll is also fairly productive, and Peregrines have been known to nest in four different localities, though never more than two pairs in one year: there were two in 1981, but only one in 1991. The Treshnish Isles closer to Mull had breeding Peregrines before 1960, but there is a dearth of later information.

The Small Isles of Inverness-shire include Rhum, Eigg, Canna and Muck. Despite its large size and rugged nature, and the detailed wildlife studies conducted there since 1957, Rhum is not a noted haunt of Peregrines. Breeding has been sporadic, with a pair in 1961 but none in 1971, possibly two in 1981 but none again in 1991. By contrast, the adjoining and more fertile island of Canna has had two regular and often successful pairs all the way through from 1961 to 1991, this being the number known to Harvie-Brown. Eigg has had one or two pairs and Muck a single pair in times past, but there is a lack of recent records from either.

The Isle of Skye (Inverness-shire) has some of the most spectacular rock scenery in Britain, from the jagged gabbro peaks and ridges of the Black Cuillin to the tremendous vertical basalt precipices of the western coast. It eclipses even Mull in ruggedness. Yet it, too, is nowadays much more a country of Golden Eagles than Peregrines. In 1904, the Rev. H. A. Macpherson gave good details of Peregrine distribution on Skye, gathered from records over the previous 20 years or so. Although he doubted even then that there were as many as five to six pairs in the Cuillin, as one local informant had declared, he named 15 nesting places, of which 14 were coastal. Despite much slaughter of falcons there was no evidence of decline when he wrote.

In 1962, I spent 2 weeks on Skye and, searching during good weather, visited most of these localities and many other suitable-looking cliffs besides. The results were two nesting pairs, two single Peregrines and a 'kill'. A knowledge-able farmer said that a pair had reared young in another locality the year before. It looked as though the crash had by this time further reduced the Skye population which had already suffered from longer term decline. The 1971 survey located Peregrines in five out of 11 territories, but in 1981 there were only six occupations out of 14, and in 1991 only seven out of 15. While there has thus been a slight and slow increase since the crash, the species remains uncommon on Skye. The subsidiary islands of Raasay, Scalpay, South Rona and Soay could once have held several other pairs, but there is a lack of recent information.

The Outer Hebrides have a great extent of seacliff, from Barra Head in the south to the Butt of Lewis, and including several outlying islands or groups noted for their seabirds. Yet, despite the considerable scope for Peregrines here, their history is somewhat vague and uncertain. Gray (1871) said that the species was comparatively common, breeding on every island in the chain and on the higher hills of some. By contrast, Dr J. W. Campbell wrote me in 1961 that nesting Peregrines were few and far between throughout the Outer Hebrides, and appeared to have been so over the previous 60 years. The best areas in recent times have been South Uist, Benbecula and North Uist, where the shell-sand machairs have large nesting populations of wading birds. Peregrines have been found here in at least 13 territories since 1961, though survey has mostly been incomplete. Four pairs were known in 1962, and seven out of ten territories were held in 1971. Occupancy was lower in 1981, with only five out of ten, but a fuller survey in 1991 by T. Dix located ten occupied localities in the 13.

Barra to the south has three territories used since 1960, though records are few (never more than one in any year) and lacking for 1991. Harris to the north has some extremely rugged deer forest country, and Lewis has long stretches of coastal cliff. No more than a single pair of Peregrines has been reported on Harris in any one year since 1961, though Lewis is a little better, with four tenanted haunts in 1981 and three in 1991. Their infertile expanses of rock and peat are terrain much more suited to Golden Eagles than Peregrines.

Among the smaller islands, eyries were known in the late 1800s and first part of the 20th century on the great seacliffs of Berneray, Mingulay, Pabbay and the Shiants, but there have been only a few sporadic records, usually of non-breeding Peregrines, since 1960. Haskeir to the west of North Uist and the Flannans west of Lewis are small rocky islands known as 19th century haunts but with no recent information, and the lonely island of North Rona north-west of Cape Wrath had breeding Peregrines up to 1938, but not in 1958 or subsequently. Some of these places have large seabird colonies, but the most famous of these seafowl stations is the St Kilda group, of four relatively small islands 70 km west of Harris. St Kilda has the biggest colonies of Gannets, Fulmars and Puffins in Britain and was first mentioned as a haunt of Peregrines in 1549. Gray (1871) said several pairs bred on the huge precipices which tower out of the Atlantic to a height of 425 m. The notebook of a falconer, K. Muir, named all four islands as having eyries, evidently in the early 1900s. Eyries were seen on Boreray, Dun and perhaps Soay in 1910, but subsequent records give only two pairs: on Oiseval (on Hirta) and Dun in 1934, on Hirta in 1939, and on unspecified islands in 1950 – though Soay and Boreray were seldom visited after the human evacuation in 1930. Despite much surveillance of St Kilda by ornithologists since 1955, there appear to have been no further breeding records of Peregrines, and only sporadic sightings.

East coast

The coast of Easter Ross from the Black Isle northwards has at least five old Peregrine nesting places, but the shore of Sutherland between the Dornoch Firth and Helmsdale is almost devoid of suitable cliffs. The main falcon stronghold on the east coast of the Northern Highlands has always been in Caithness, where the Old Red Sandstone forms long lines of vertical cliff. Harvie-Brown and Buckley (1887) stated, 'We found several pairs in 1885 nesting in the high cliffs of the north coast', and 'A good many pairs still succeed in bringing off their young on the east coast between Duncansby and the Ord'. These remarks accord with more recent knowledge of 16 territories on the Caithness coast.

The 1962 survey did not manage full coverage of this coast, but found Peregrines occupying all 11 of the territories examined. By 1971, decline was apparent, with only six out of 14 territories holding Peregrines. In 1981, there was evident recovery, with falcons in 17 out of 19 haunts, but breeding success was poor, with only two pairs rearing young. The 1991 survey was incomplete, with only 10 territories examined; six were occupied suggesting a population of 12 pairs for the east coast.

Immediately north of Caithness, the Orkney Isles have a tremendous frontage of sheer cliff cut in the Old Red Sandstone, and support some of the largest colonies of Guillemots and Kittiwakes in the country. Orkney has been famed for its Peregrines over a long period. This was, indeed, the scene of the first Peregrine census in history. In 1693, the Rev. James Wallace listed 25 localities where Peregrines bred in Orkney. I have matched 21 of these against recent territories, two more are probable nesting places not recorded recently, and the remaining two probably refer to recent haunts now known by other names. Wallace's list thus appears to represent a former population of 25 pairs.

Well over two centuries later, George Arthur told Eddie Balfour that he knew of 25 separate pairs in Orkney, and in 1961 Balfour gave me a list of 22 separate territories where he had found Peregrines breeding in 1957–60. Balfour later found seven more territories in areas he had not previously searched, though by then not all were used in any one year. Three more nesting places have recently been found, and at least one old territory has held two pairs, but virtually all the possible nesting places have now been explored. The 20th century population up to 1960 thus seems likely to have been 25–30 pairs. As well as being almost uncanny in its accuracy, the list compiled by Wallace is remarkable in suggesting a constancy of population extending back for over 250 years. The island of Hoy with its huge vertical precipices has 11 territories occurring locally at a higher density than in any other part of Scotland, except perhaps St Kilda in earlier years, and the rest are well scattered over the remainder of the Orkneys, on suitable seacliffs. There are two inland haunts, with an irregular history of occupation. Orkney records were supplied by E. Balfour (up to 1973), C. J. Booth, and most recently by E. Meek.

The 1962 survey showed a still normal population, with 23 territories occupied in the 24 examined. Decline was evident by 1971, with only 14 out of 24 still tenanted. By 1981 there was improved occupancy with Peregrines in 25 out of 31 territories, and in 1991 the position was almost unchanged, at 23 out of 32. In 1991 only 11 pairs in the 23 occupied places were certainly known to lay eggs, and nine reared young.

This geographical scan of the British Peregrine population ends, appropriately, in Shetland, our most northerly land, which reaches latitude 60°50′N, about level with Bergen in Norway. This is another complex archipelago, with a huge total length of highly indented coast, much of it rock-girt. Lofty seacliffs abound, reaching their greatest height (372 m) on Foula, and again carry immense throngs of breeding seafowl in many places. Fair Isle, mid-way between Orkney and Shetland, is usually regarded as part of the latter. Historical Peregrine records are less comprehensive than for Orkney. Saxby (1874) said that many pairs remained to breed and that there were several on Unst. Evans and Buckley (1899) wrote that they were 'distributed pretty commonly' over the Shetland group. The Venables reported in 1955 that they knew of 11 pairs, but from observations covering only a comparatively small part of the total cliff-line of Shetland, which is much longer than that of Orkney.

A statement by Baxter and Rintoul (1953) that Peregrines were said in 1948 to have decreased generally in Shetland is unsupported by detail. Pat Sandeman gave me a list of ten localities where he saw apparently breeding pairs in 1950–53, and I have from various sources compiled a list of 25 territories where Peregrines have bred since 1930. The majority of haunts were said to be occupied regularly, up to 1960, at least. Fair Isle is reported to have held two and sometimes three pairs in the years around 1900, but only one eyrie has been recorded in any year recently. Foula could once have held up to three pairs. Perhaps nobody has ever had an accurate idea of the number of Peregrines that bred in Shetland before 1960, but it seems likely to have exceeded the known total of 25. Indeed, an examination of the maps suggests that there could have been up to 30 additional places where the species nested, even though the known density is lower than on Orkney. Because of the possibility of long-term decline before 1960, I have, however, used the more conservative estimate of 30 pairs as the size of the breeding population during 1900–60.

Numbers appeared to be holding up quite well in 1962, when 12 out of 17 territories were found occupied, but there had been a deterioration by 1971, with Peregrines seen in only five out of 22 old haunts. 1981 gave a slightly better figure, of 12 occupations in 30 territories, but a great effort to cover all possible nesting places in 1991 was rewarded by the finding of single falcons in just five localities. Shetland was the only Scottish county where the species was not known to breed in 1991. The possible reasons for this collapse of population will be discussed in Chapter 13. Shetland survey records have been provided by R. J. Tulloch, J. N. Dymond, J. D. Okill and P. M. Ellis.

Summary

After south-east England, the northern and western Highlands are the only region not showing increase of Peregrine population to above pre-war level. The picture is highly variable, with a marked increase in number of known nesting places in inland districts east of the main north-south watershed, from 39 in 1981 to 52 in 1991. This probably represents a real increase in population, though occupancy has remained the same – 91% in 1981 and 90% in 1991. In the western inland areas very few new nesting haunts became known, and occupancy declined from 73% in 1981 to 42% in 1991. This gives an overall status for all inland districts no better than in 1981.

On both the west and east coast, numbers remain depressed and breeding performance is lower than in any other district of Britain. The east coast has suffered an appreciable deterioration since 1981, and although Orkney has maintained reasonable occupancy, Peregrines are only just hanging on in Shetland.

The grand total of 179 occupied territories compares with 184 in 1981 (97%).

IRELAND

The Peregrines of Northern Ireland are located mainly in five districts: the rugged north-east and north coast of Antrim and Londonderry between Belfast Lough and Lough Foyle, the Mountains of Mourne in Co. Down, the Mountains of Antrim on the basaltic plateau lying behind the coast, the Sperrin Mountains of Londonderry and Tyrone, and the hills of south-west Fermanagh bordering Leitrim. It was only from about 1977 that survey established the full number of Peregrine territories in the region, so that earlier assessments of status and distribution were probably incomplete.

From his post-war enquiry, Ferguson-Lees (1951) said that in 1947–48 certainly 25 and possibly 28 pairs bred, and that this number was almost exactly the same as the pre-1940 population. Breeding again occurred in all of the six counties except Armagh. One stretch of the Antrim coast had its pre-war population reduced from nine to four pairs by 1945 by war-time control, but was in 1949 back to nine to ten pairs. In 1957 Ferguson-Lees mentioned that there were signs of decrease in two or three parts of Northern Ireland.

The region was certainly afflicted by the post-1956 crash, and in 1962 a survey led by Arnold Benington found that in 24 territories, eight were apparently deserted and only eight pairs appeared to be breeding. From 1964–68 surveys gave the following records:

	Territories visited	*Occupied by Peregrines*	*Successful breeding*
1964	16	12 (75%)	3 (19%)
1965	15	11 (73%)	3 (20%)
1966	20	17 (85%)	7 (35%)
1967	27	24 (89%)	?
1968	30	19 (63%)	7 (23%)

These data were collected mainly by Michael Gilbertson, though with assistance from J. W. Greaves during 1966–68. They give higher figures for some categories, especially successful breeding, than those published by Gilbertson (1969) which were restricted to the author's own records. During the years of incomplete survey (especially 1964–66) there may have been a bias in territory occupation through a tendency of observers to visit localities they had known to be occupied previously. Colin McKelvie, helped by other observers, continued and extended this survey during 1970–73, with the following results (McKelvie, 1973):

	Territories visited	*Occupied by Peregrines*	*Successful breeding*
1970	44	31 (70%)	10 (23%)
1971	48	35 (73%)	10 (21%)
1972	48	37 (77%)	13 (27%)
1973	48	42 (88%)	16 (33%)

The records for 1962–73 suggested a situation rather similar to that in southern Scotland, with only moderate decline in actual number of falcons, but much non-breeding and only a low success rate of pairs occupying territories; but a steady improvement in breeding performance from about 1966 onwards.

During 1977–81, annual surveys were coordinated by the Royal Society for the Protection of Birds (Dinah Browne) in consultation with the Conservation Branch of the Department of the Environment for Northern Ireland (J. S. Furphy), and with field help especially from A. J. Balbi, C. S. Dawson, R. Ellis and J. H. Wells. The results were as follows:

	Territories visited	*Occupied by Peregrines*	*Successful breeding*
1977	52	36 (69%)	29 (56%)
1978	52	44 (85%)	26 (50%)
1979	48	43 (90%)	30 (63%)
1980	52	43 (83%)	35 (81%)
1981	64	53 (83%)	28 (53%)

The 1981 survey showed that 19 coastal and 34 inland territories were occupied out of estimated totals of 23 and 41 respectively (Norriss, Wilson and Browne, 1982). The population was regarded as back to normal by 1978–79, with 1981 showing an increase compared with pre-war years, through occupation of quarries and very small inland crags. The figures show that breeding success has also improved markedly since the early 1970s.

The 1991 survey was coordinated by John Milburne in the Environment Service of the Department of the Environment for Northern Ireland, with the help of D. Knight, L. McFaul, J. H. Wells, R. Maybin, C. S. Dawson, J. McEvoy, G. A. W. Hutchinson and H. McCann. It produced the startling finding that there were no less than 99 occupied territories, 74 inland and 25 coastal. In another 14 previously used territories no Peregrines were found, while prospecting birds were seen at three other places not known as nesting haunts. This virtual doubling of the Peregrine population since 1981 goes some way to match events across the Irish Sea in Lakeland and south-west Scotland. At 58 eyries young were reared, so that success rate was fairly good (59%). No fewer than 38 of the nesting places were in quarries, to explain some of the capacity for expansion. Rathlin Island alone had eight pairs – on an area of 1359 ha, with an L-shaped length of 12.5 km and an average width of 1–2 km.

Ussher and Warren (1900) gave an outline of the distribution of the Peregrine over Ireland as a whole, with numbers for certain areas, but their estimates became vague or too low in the districts with the main concentrations. The species has bred regularly in eleven counties in the Republic of Ireland but not in the flat centre and east. The main breeding areas have always been the Wicklow Mountains, the rocky coasts of Wexford and Waterford, and above all the rugged mountains and tremendous ranges of seacliff in the beautiful west of Ireland, from Cork, Kerry, Clare, Galway, Mayo, Sligo and Leitrim to Donegal. Many breeding places here are in remote places and a fair number are on precipitous and uninhabited offshore islands. The possibility of long-term decline in the far west, especially in inland districts, has been mentioned and both John Temple Lang and John Wilson believe that is likely, though there is little direct evidence. Some ornithologists, notably L. W. Montgomery, claimed that there was a slow decline on the south coast during 1930–40.

Ferguson-Lees (1951) was informed by G. R. Humphries and C. J. Carroll that there were at least 163 breeding pairs in the Republic of Ireland, and that there had been no significant change in status between 1939–49. This figure was thought to be probably short of the true total population present in the 1930s. Peregrine surveys in the Republic began in 1966 under the aegis of the Irish Society for the Protection of Birds, and from 1969 onwards under the newly formed Irish Wildbird Conservancy, with John Temple Lang as organiser. Assimilation of previous records gave a total of some 220 breeding localities known in the Republic, though these included some alternative cliffs, and Temple Lang suggested the list represented a pre-1950 breeding population of 180–200 pairs. The complete distribution of the Peregrine in western Ireland is perhaps still not known, though recent surveys have examined much of the ground. Possible long-term desertion of eyries here over a long period, and before 1950, adds to the difficulties of present assessments of possible numbers.

From the published data for 1967–68 (Temple Lang, 1968) and unpublished reports to the Irish Wildbird Conservancy for 1969–73 by J. Temple Lang, D. Norriss and B. Holden, the following results were available:

	Cliffs visited	Occupied by Peregrines	Proved breeding
1967	103	60 (58%)	30 (29%)
1968	126	64 (51%)	22 (17%)
1969	73	46 (63%)	20 (27%)
1970	65	48 (74%)	17 (26%)
1971	88	59 (67%)	21 (24%)
1972	69	44 (64%)	24 (35%)
1973	69	45 (65%)	24 (35%)

Before 1950, the majority of known breeding haunts were occupied regularly, so it was obvious that a substantial decline had occurred in the Republic by 1967, with numbers at least 40% and possibly up to 70% lower than the 'normal' level, since occupied haunts were more likely to be reported than unoccupied ones. Moreover, decline appeared to be continuing into 1968 and decrease in breeding success was even more marked. The onset of decline appeared to be not earlier than 1954, and the last certain year of occupation for 29 closely observed haunts was 1958–59.

John Temple Lang has kindly given me unpublished records which he collected for 1977–79 as follows:

	Cliffs visited	Occupied by Peregrines	Successful breeding
1977	81	66 (81%)	33 (41%)
1978	56	44 (79%)	24 (43%)
1979	89	74 (83%)	35 (39%)

These data suggest that recovery was well on the way by the late 1970s. In 1981, a survey was made by staff of the Forest and Wildlife Service, supported by members of the Irish Wildbird Conservancy (Norriss and Wilson, 1983). Since it was felt impractical to cover the whole of the Republic, survey was limited to intensive coverage of 15 areas chosen as representative of all main Peregrine breeding habitats, and extending to 50% of the breeding range. This gave a basis for estimating total population of the country. The survey located 111 occupied breeding territories, with another four probables, in an estimated total of 136 available territories, an occupancy rate of 83–86%. From a probable total of 278 available territories in the Republic, extrapolation from occupancy of the main habitat types gave an estimate of at least 225 occupied territories overall, with a minimum occupancy of 83%.

Because earlier knowledge of distribution was clearly incomplete, it was not possible to make a reliable comparison with 1930–39 or pre-crash population levels. The total of 278 available territories included some which had evidently been missed in earlier years. In some areas that were previously well worked, numbers had returned to earlier known levels by 1981, with nearly all territories occupied (e.g. Cos Donegal, Waterford and Clare) and it seemed that the population generally could be regarded as close to normal again. In the previously well-known Co. Wicklow a number of new territories had recently been colonised, giving a real increase in density of breeding pairs and, hence, an increase in population. With only 39–41% of occupied territories producing young, breeding success was only moderate, but suffered from the same inclement weather effects that reduced output of young over much of Britain in 1981.

John Wilson has given me summaries of later sample surveys covering representative areas and habitats. These showed that 30–51 (mean 43) territories covered during 1982–87 averaged 94% occupation. The breeding population had continued to expand, with at least 22 new territories established by 1987, within the areas surveyed in 1981. Hutchinson (1989) reported that the Wicklow Mountains alone had at least 27 pairs in 34 known territories in 1986 (G. C. Noonan's records), but McGrath (1987) considered that in Co. Waterford, the number of nesting pairs in 1981–86 was the same as in 1920–45. Population increase has involved pairs taking over smaller and less suitable cliffs, numerous quarries, and 'doubling up' in traditional territories (H. J. Wilson).

A second national survey in 1991 examined about 50% of the breeding range, and located 123 occupied territories (141 when corrected for incomplete coverage). This represents an increase of at least 23–26% since 1981 and, with separate survey of numerous occupied quarries (60–65), leads to an estimate of a total of 350–355 occupied breeding territories (D. Norriss, in press). In the Republic, numbers are thus well above their 1930–39 level. Increase on the coast of County Waterford has occurred since 1986 (D. McGrath), but the main increase has been in quarry occupation in eastern Ireland.

CHAPTER 5

Food and feeding habits

GENERAL ASPECTS OF PREY SELECTION

Although the Peregrine is a specialised predator, in that it feeds almost exclusively on living birds, its prey is drawn from a large part of the avifauna of the country which it inhabits. To this extent, it is a catholic feeder, an adaptation appropriate to one of the most widely distributed bird forms in the World, with races referable to the same species occupying a broad range of habitats from the equatorial to the near-polar regions. The Peregrine is absent only from dense forestland, for it has evolved a build and mode of hunting involving headlong aerial chase and despatch of prey, and so is a bird adapted especially to open country. It is not, however, averse to snatching prey from the tree-tops or from the ground on occasion.

In Britain, the list of bird species known to have been taken as prey totals at least 137 (Table 8) and the further tally of species which *could* be taken would be a long one. Uttendörfer (1952) has listed 210 prey species in Central Europe. It is easier to list species unlikely to be killed by Peregrines here, for these are few and include only the largest forms. The Peregrine is a powerful bird, the female in particular being heavy for its size, with a weight of up to 1350 g; and the manner of its attack gives a capacity for knocking almost any other bird out of the sky. The males, with a maximum weight of only about 800 g, have a much lesser ability for killing large prey.

The biggest species seen to be struck down by a British Peregrine was a Greylag Goose, over the Solway, but the bird fell into the water, and, as the falcon did not follow up the strike, was seen to recover and fly away (Dunlop, 1912). Anything from this size downwards may be presumed at risk and birds as large as Barnacle Geese, Brent Geese, Shelduck, sawbill ducks and Great Black-backed Gulls are certainly killed and eaten on occasions. In Sweden, a Peregrine was seen to kill a male Capercaillie (P. Wennerberg and D. Sjölander) and J. Edvardsson has twice found prey remains of female Capercaillies. A Black-throated Diver was seen to be struck down in flight in Europe (Meinertzhagen, 1959). It is therefore only birds such as swans and eagles which seem to be exempt from predation. There are no records of Cormorant, Shag, Gannet and Great Skua being killed by Peregrines in Britain, but none of these could be ruled out. In Medieval times, trained falcons, often singly but sometimes in 'casts' of two, were flown at Herons and Red Kites as favourite quarry. Sometimes the intention was to force the harassed birds to ground, but quite often they were killed, even by a single falcon. R. B. Treleaven saw a Heron evidently struck down and killed by a Peregrine on the Humber estuary, and P. Wennerberg watched a pair of Peregrines kill a fishing Heron in Sweden. Ravens and Buzzards have occasionally been killed, but the former apparently as a result of redirected attacks during visiting of the Peregrines' eyries by humans.

Virtually all other species are potential prey, for there is no lower size limit, and even Goldcrests and Blue Tits are sometimes eaten. The Peregrine is not only able to kill birds larger and heavier than itself; it can also sometimes carry them. There are at least three records of Blackcock (weight 1250–1400 g, according to age) being carried by female Peregrines (average weight 1140 g). One instance was actually seen in Sutherland by J. Walpole-Bond (per D. Nethersole-Thompson) and the other was a record of remains found on an eyrie on the Bass Rock in the Firth of Forth where the nearest blackgame were 3 miles away on the mainland (Macgillivray, 1840). Montagu (1813) also recorded blackgame ('heath poults') at the eyrie on Dumbarton Rock.

The Peregrine nevertheless feeds mainly on birds of small to medium size, in the weight range 50–500 g, and to the ecologist it is much more important to know the normal type of prey than the exceptional items with a curiosity interest. Prey species are taken mainly according to their availability, and the bulk of the food of any particular breeding pair is drawn from about a dozen of the common bird species in the immediate neighbourhood. The spectrum of prey thus tends broadly to reflect composition of the local bird population at the time and so varies according to habitat and geographical location, and also the time of year. There are considerable differences across the whole country and between the breeding and non-breeding seasons.

There is also an element of selectivity which complicates this simple picture of predation. In Britain the Peregrine is primarily a pigeon killer, and whilst this is largely a matter of availability, it is not entirely so. Individual birds or pairs may also develop a fondness for specific prey items which happen to be in good supply locally, or at a certain time, e.g. a pair on Scottish moorland took to feeding their young especially on Black-headed Gulls from an adjoining loch (R. Roxburgh) while a Shetland pair appeared to be living mainly on Fulmars (K. D. Smith). Puffins are taken in preference to other auks. An individual fondness for Crows, Rooks and Jackdaws has also been reported. Yet, in general, gulls and corvids seem not to be taken in proportion to their abundance. Peregrines in Britain do not, however, show the degree of selectivity for prey reported for certain other races. Peale's Falcon in the Queen Charlotte Islands is said to feed largely on four species of seabird (Beebe, 1960); and Nelson (1970) found that those on Langara Island feed only on Ancient Murrelets. In one area of west Greenland, Burnham and Mattox (1984) reported that 90% of Peregrine prey consisted of four small passerines, with Lapland Buntings amounting to 70%. Yet, on the Yukon River, Alaska, Hunter, Crawford and Ambrose (1988) found that, out of a wide variety of prey, some preferred species (especially waders) were not taken in proportion to their abundance, and were not common in the hunting areas. Hautola and Sulkava (1977) also found that in northern Finland, waders were favourite prey, but they are here probably the most abundant prey group. Factors such as availability, vulnerability, palatability, size and weight of prey, individual variations in hunting ability in Peregrines, and development of specific choice may all play a part in prey selection, but little is known about these complexities.

The study of food by direct observation of Peregrines in the act of killing prey is difficult. Few of the kills made by wild Peregrines are ever witnessed, and a vast amount of time is needed to collect a reasonable sample of observations. By patient watching at eyries, mostly with young, Dick Treleaven has witnessed a total of at least 200 kills. Whilst this is a remarkably good score for observation of wild Peregrine kills in this country, it took very many hours of watching spread over many years. Hide observation at nests with young can give a good deal of information about the kind and amount of prey brought to the eyrie (e.g. Heatherley, 1913; Nelson, 1970; Parker, 1979) and is a valuable way of supplementing more general observations to give a much fuller picture of feeding habits during the fledging period.

Information on food is collected most readily by finding the remains of kills. Peregrines habitually pluck their prey, using their bills to remove a substantial proportion of the feathers, before they begin to feed on the carcase. These pluckings form characteristic litters on the ground, though the feathers often blow around and lie about singly, and their presence may be the first indication that a Peregrine is in the area. Identification of the feathers is often possible in the field, but unrecognisable material can be taken and checked against cabinet skins. Sometimes the wings are left whole and may remain attached by the pectoral girdle, but birds eaten by foxes are often in this state and give the chance of confusion. If the breast-bone can be found, in the larger prey species it usually carries the Peregrine's trademark, in the form of deep V notches, bitten out presumably as the falcon tears the flesh from the breast. There may be other identifiable remains, such as head, mandibles, legs, feet or claws.

The victim may be plucked and eaten where it is struck down, or it may be carried to some other place before receiving attention. Wintering Peregrines in lowland areas sometimes regularly favour a particular perch at which to pluck and eat their prey. More often, though, the remains of kills in autumn and winter can lie almost anywhere within the hunting area, and unless the observer is prepared to watch and search assiduously in the manner described by Baker (1967), few of these will ever be found. The student of Peregrine food relies mainly on the fact that during the breeding season many kills are brought to the nesting cliffs to be plucked and eaten, and that the remains can be found and examined there with comparative ease, though this applies much more to inland haunts than those on

Pluckings of a kill (pigeon); northern England (photo: D. A. Ratcliffe)

seacliffs. Many Peregrines cling to their breeding haunts throughout the autumn and winter, but this is the period when fewest kills are brought to the home cliffs, and adequate records are again more difficult to collect then.

The regurgitated pellets or castings of undigested prey remains which accumulate below the perching, roosting and nesting places of Peregrines also convey a certain amount of information about food, though they are much less useful than the actual pluckings. These castings are composed almost entirely of the body feathers of prey, variably decomposed and pulverised into a greyish, dense, amorphous mass. Sometimes fragments of feathers are recognisable, and there may be other remains such as the claws of grouse, the skin of a pigeon's foot or, occasionally, the fragments of beetle wing-case. Frequently there are the closed metal rings from the legs of homing pigeons, tightly packed in the casting material, but seldom with any traces of bone left. Vegetable remains appear to be usually from the guts and crops of prey, in the form of heather shoots from grouse, grain husks from pigeons and miscellaneous seeds from a variety of passerines. Beetle remains may have a similar origin, or they may be picked up by the incubating bird as they wander over the eyrie ledge, rather than be deliberately sought as food.

FOOD IN THE BREEDING SEASON

As the nesting season approaches, and each pair of Peregrines is to be seen more constantly around its ancestral cliffs, the remains of kills are found with increasing frequency in the vicinity. They become still more frequent as incubation proceeds, and the male brings food to his sitting mate. The plucking places are typically the tops of prominent buttresses or projections of the cliffs, and the actual ledges, though any part of the adjoining ground may be used. Prey is not usually 'feathered' on the eyrie in use before the young have hatched, but old eyries may be so used. After hatching, the remains of prey, both feathers and other parts, often accumulate in the eyrie, for the parents may only partially remove the uneaten debris, especially just prior to fledging. There is a good deal of individual variation in this respect, and some Peregrines appear to make an attempt to keep the eyrie ledge clean by carrying away the picked remains of prey. By the time the young have fledged, the whole vicinity of the eyrie may be liberally strewn with feathers and the ledge itself left thick with bones, though this varies much between one nest and the next, and also with the size of the brood. A successful eyrie is usually marked by numerous litters of kills along the cliffs. Conversely a non-breeding or unsuccessful pair will leave relatively few such remains.

By identifying the feathers from pluckings an estimate can be obtained of the variety and numbers of the prey species, although a certain amount of bias is possible. For instance, the feathers of light coloured birds are more readily seen than those of dark species, and while the pluckings of a domestic pigeon are usually the work of a Peregrine, those of, say, a Red Grouse, could often be attributable to other predators. The same prey item may be plucked in more than one place, so that two or more litters of feathers are produced. At an eyrie with large young and a great litter of remains, it may be difficult to tell how many individuals of the same species are represented, unless very frequent inspections are made or a continuous watch kept. Ian Newton tells me that the feathers at

Sparrowhawk plucking places away from the nest show a greater proportion of small birds than the remains actually on a nest with big young, evidently because smaller species are often swallowed whole after being plucked and so leave no trace on the nest. Another possible source of bias, when dealing with small samples of a population, is the selectivity of certain pairs or individuals for a particular prey species. The six records of domestic chicken and three of Water Vole in Table 8 refer to particular individual Peregrines which had found ready sources of these unusual prey species.

Despite the snags, the examination of prey remains is a reasonable method of assessing the food spectrum at nesting time, and is the basis of Table 8, showing variations in frequency of prey selection between certain regions and habitats. The consistency between the records of different observers in the same region, in the proportions between species and groups represented, also suggests that this is a fairly reliable method for quantitative assessment of the Peregrine's diet. The proportions between the different species become more meaningful when a conversion into actual weights is applied (see notes to Table 8). The table lacks any quantitative analysis of prey for the coast of Wales, the southern counties of England, and Ireland, and only more generalised information is available on food preferences in these regions. The data are spread over the whole breeding season and so give only a broad picture. Migratory species are represented mainly during the early part of the breeding season and pulli of various prey species during the later part, but more detailed studies are needed to illuminate possible changes in predation during this period.

Table 8 shows that in North Wales, Northern England, Southern Scotland and the Highlands, 12 species may be termed 'constants' in the Peregrine's diet, occurring with a frequency of over 80% in the 14 different food lists: they are domestic pigeon/Rock Dove, Red Grouse, Lapwing, Golden Plover, Snipe, Curlew, Redshank, Skylark, Fieldfare, Song Thrush, Blackbird and Starling. These 12 species account for 41% by frequency and 78% by weight of all prey recorded (106 species). Near constants, occurring in over 70% of the lists, are Woodcock, Wood Pigeon, Jackdaw, Redwing, Ring Ouzel, Meadow Pipit and Chaffinch, but these add only another 9% by frequency or 5% by weight to the total prey taken. The remaining 87 species recorded in Table 8 thus amount to only 50% by frequency or 17% by weight of the total 'catch'. Mearns (1983) found that in 3579 prey items collected between late March and July 1975–80, in southern Scotland, 15 species (including ten of the 12 'constants' in Table 8) made up 91·4% of all items by number, and 95% of the diet by weight. The domestic pigeon averaged 69·5% of food by weight.

Table 8 reveals certain differences in prey according to district and main habitat type. The samples are perhaps too small in some instances to attach much statistical significance to comparisons, but there are pointers to certain trends which would be worth closer investigation. Diversity of prey spectrum increases with size of the sample, but only up to a certain point, since the choice in any one district has an upper limit. The interesting feature is that if the data for number of species are plotted against number of individuals killed, there is a distinct tendency for those in columns 10–13 (Scottish Highlands, excluding seabird haunts) to lie on a different line from the rest, representing a higher species diversity throughout compared with districts to the south. This could result

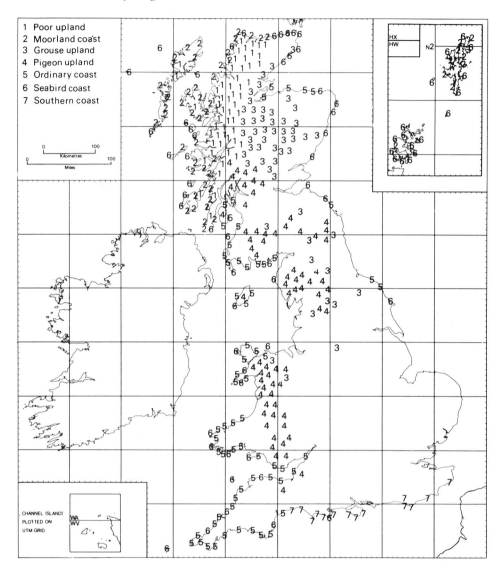

Figure 5. Distribution of different prey habitats in Britain.

NOTES: The seven main prey habitats show the predominant character of the prey spectrum in each area with breeding Peregrines, in approximate order of increasing food value as follows:

1. Poor Upland: sterile moorlands and hills of the western Highlands, with sparse populations of Red Grouse, Ptarmigan, waders and passerines.

2. Moorland coast: seacliff haunts where the moorlands abut the sea, and Peregrines thus prey on both coastal and moorland birds.

3. Grouse upland: prevalence of heather moorland still actively managed for Red Grouse, and often with good populations of waders and passerines. Includes good Ptarmigan mountains in the Highlands.

4. Pigeon upland: mainly sheep walks with sparse to moderate hill bird populations, though sometimes with more productive valleys and adjoining agricultural lowlands. Domestic pigeon is the favourite prey item.

either from a wider choice of prey in the Highlands, or from the lower availability of domestic pigeons, or both. Column 2 is anomalous in this respect in showing an unusually high diversity of prey in Lakeland during 1904–19: it is not significant statistically, and might involve a bias in recording, but it could reflect a slight shift in prey availability. The proportion of domestic pigeons is lower than in most of the other Lakeland records, and while this species was regarded as favourite prey at least as far back as 1900, it may not have been available in quite the same abundance as during later times. Apart from this, there is no evidence of a shift in prey spectrum in Lakeland over a period of several decades.

The outstanding feature is that, over Britain as a whole, wherever they are available, the domestic pigeon or its wild relative, the Rock Dove, are the favourite quarry of the Peregrine. A word on the relationships between these pigeons is appropriate here. The homing pigeon and other domestic breeds have been artificially bred and developed from the Rock Dove, so that all bear the same scientific name *Columba livia*. The homer commonly returns to the wild or becomes urbanised, to give populations of feral pigeons. On rocky coasts, these feral birds take to the cliffs, there to breed with the wild Rock Doves, producing a variety of mongrel forms which may swamp the wild type in the population. On many seacliffs, the true Rock Dove, recognisable by its white rump and two black wing bars, is now quite a rarity. Rex Harper has written an informative piece on feral pigeons in Cornwall in Treleaven (1977).

There is thus a wide range of variation not only in the physical appearance of the individuals of *Columba livia* taken by Peregrines, but also in their status as wholly domesticated, feral or truly wild birds. This latter aspect is highly relevant to the question of predation on homing pigeons to be discussed later. The homing pigeon has long been favourite prey. Bolam, referring to the period 1900–10, remarked on the numbers of legs of homers with rings upon them at eyries in Northumberland and Merioneth. It is highly probable that the advent of pigeon-racing in mid-Victorian times quickly became an important factor in the Peregrine's ecology, and that predation on this bird has been heavy for well over a century.

The Peregrine's preference for domestic pigeons, even when other prey is available in plenty, drew early comment in regard to both coastal and inland breeding stations. Macpherson (1892) noted in 1885 that the St Bees Head Peregrines fed on Stockdoves and pigeons whenever they could get them, and Forrest (1907) mentioned that the Peregrines on the Great Ormes Head in North Wales preferred pigeons, although there are seabird colonies of modest size on both headlands. On Ailsa Craig in the Firth of Clyde, the site of a huge seabird colony, the lighthouse keepers at one time persecuted the Peregrines because of their depredations on the message-carrying homers which were their link with the mainland. In recent years the auks at this locality have declined to

5. Ordinary coast: seacliff haunts backing on to agricultural lowlands, with usually a good deal of arable farmland, variable woodland and locally rough grazing. Feral pigeons important, also Jackdaws and a wide range of lowland birds.

6. Seabird coast: seacliff haunts amongst or close to the larger breeding stations of Guillemots, Razorbills, Puffins, Kittiwakes, Fulmars, Herring Gulls and Manx Shearwaters.

7. Southern coast: seacliff haunts adjoining fertile agricultural lowlands, formerly with much downland and lying on the continental bird migration landfall.

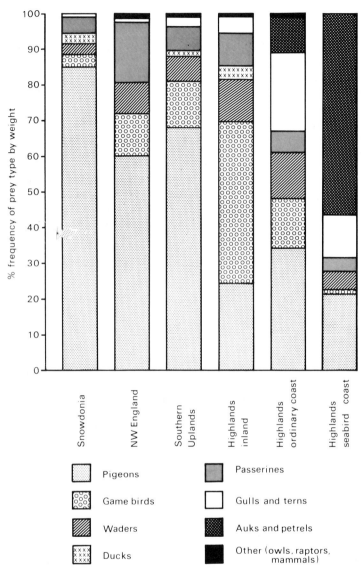

Figure 6. Geographical variation in frequency of main prey types.
NOTES: Data are from Table 8 and refer only to the breeding season.

such an extent that the Peregrines must perforce depend largely on other prey species. Speaking of a Cheviot haunt, Bolam (1912) said, 'although this "eyry" is surrounded by grouse and partridge ground, remains of either of those birds are comparatively rarely to be seen about it, pigeons, both wild and tame, forming by far the greater proportion of the Falcons' food.' Dunlop (Table 8, column 1) found the domestic pigeon to be the principal prey species in Lakeland during 1904–14, even on grouse moors.

Inland eyries

Homing pigeons are freely available to breeding peregrines in inland areas of England, Wales and southern Scotland because so many routes of races or practice flights pass through falcon country. With a population of several million homers in Britain there is thus a fairly constant supply of an ideal prey type which tends to follow a straight course over open ground, giving maximum vulnerability to attack. It has sometimes been alleged that Peregrines situate their eyries close to favourite flight-lines of homing pigeons, the more readily to pick off these victims. In the absence of evidence that there *are* favourite flight-lines, it is difficult to know whether there is any truth in this assertion. My impression in northern England and southern Scotland is that homers travel through all the valleys and across all the watersheds almost at random; and that during spring and summer there are so many of them, especially at the weekends, that a good number must pass quite close to every Peregrine eyrie. Location of eyries is determined primarily by the distribution of good cliffs, and where these are numerous eyries tend to be regularly spaced. It is nevertheless possible that unusually dense clusters of pairs could be associated with particularly high availability of pigeons. In southern Ireland, Norriss (in press) connects the high breeding density of Peregrines on the Waterford seacliffs with the presence of a favourite pigeon racing route along this coast.

Pigeon race days are usually at the weekends, so that this source of food comes mainly in periodic bursts and then tails away in between. The numerous stragglers drifting around the country, and those fully returned to the wild, form a reservoir maintaining the supply of pigeons during the week, between races. Caching of food could also compensate for any mid-week reduction in food supply (see p. 138).

In the total prey inventory for northern England and the Southern Uplands (Table 8), the domestic pigeon forms 41% by frequency and 61% by weight, but this may even be an underestimate. Some of the records for these regions in Table 8 did not always give the numbers of pigeon kills found on each occasion, so that the species is under-represented before 1974. Examination of the more precise records suggests that at many eyries in both regions, domestic pigeon often forms up to 80% of the prey by weight, especially when there are young falcons to feed. In the mountains of Snowdonia the domestic pigeon reaches 70% by frequency and 77% by weight, and these figures could be valid for the Welsh population as a whole.

By contrast, and surprisingly, the Wood Pigeon is taken in rather small numbers. This is a heavier bird than the domestic pigeon, and lives in some numbers within easy reach of many Peregrine eyries, yet for some reason it seems almost to be ignored as food in many districts, at least during the breeding season. While Wood Pigeons may be less exposed to attack than homers, the low frequency of this species in prey records does not seem to be explicable in terms of low predation risk. It may be that homers are so readily available, from their numbers and manner of flight over open country, that they nearly always offer easier targets, and there is no need for the falcon to bother about Wood Pigeons. Out of the eleven observers whose records appear in Table 8, only R. H. Brown found Wood Pigeons to be taken with any frequency. In lists of 241 kills in the Lake District and northern Pennines between March and August, he recorded 91 homing pigeons and 19 Wood Pigeons (Brown, 1929–30, 1934–35). In a large sample (3579 items) of southern Scottish prey, Mearns (1983) found that Wood Pigeons were taken with an overall frequency of only 1·1% by numbers.

Farther north in Scotland, Wood Pigeons have been found to be commonly taken in some areas. In the Grampian Region of the Highlands, Hardey (1981) found a frequency of 3·2% in 895 prey items; while at lowland eyries on Speyside farther west, D. Weir and his colleagues (unpubl.) found a frequency of 17% in 173 items, and only domestic pigeons were more often taken (23%). In Northern Ireland, in 535 prey items from inland, sub-coastal and coastal eyries, McKelvie (1973) found that 55% by frequency were domestic pigeon/Rock Dove, while 7·3% were Wood Pigeon.

In inland districts south of the Highlands, the next most important group of prey species, in terms of numbers taken, is the medium to small passerines, notably the Starling, Blackbird, Fieldfare, Redwing, Song Thrush, Skylark and Meadow Pipit. The last two species are common on the hills, and the others are usually plentiful in the valleys and adjoining lowlands. Fieldfares and Redwings are taken mostly during autumn/winter or in the early spring when they are moving through the hill country in some numbers on migration. There appears to have been a reduction in the numbers of these two species eaten in recent years, and this could correspond to a shift in the migration pattern during the recent run of hard, backward springs. In aggregate, the small to medium passerines amount to 11% by weight of the Peregrine's diet in these districts.

Another important prey group in these more southerly inland districts is the waders, especially the Lapwing, Golden Plover, Snipe and Redshank, forming 8% by weight of the total. These are fairly common breeders in hill country, though the Golden Plover and Redshank are somewhat local. The Golden Plover is confined in its nesting to the uncultivated moorlands but the others nest widely, from the enclosed hill farm pastures to the open sheep walks above. Curlews are often taken when they are numerous in moorland country, and Woodcock appear regularly in small numbers in the prey remains; these may be partly birds which follow open moorland during migration, though breeders 'roding' over open hillside would be vulnerable. In Northern Ireland, McKelvie (1973) reported that waders formed 16% by frequency of Peregrine prey.

The Red Grouse is locally an important prey species in these districts, averaging 13% by weight of the total. Its frequency as a food item obviously varies considerably from one area to another. In some of the sheep walk country of Snowdonia, Lakeland, and the Southern Uplands, grouse are now extremely sparse or even absent, but in other parts of the Pennines, Cheviots and Southern Uplands and, formerly, the Welsh hills, there are flourishing grouse moors with large numbers of this bird. The frequency of grouse remains at eyries thus depends very much on the particular territories being studied.

The variations in prey spectrum according to local differences in habitat can be quite marked. In northern England, the Pennine eyries tend to show high frequency of Red Grouse, Golden Plover, Snipe, Dunlin, Redshank, Curlew and Lapwing, whereas in parts of central Lakeland these species are scarce or absent, and seldom if ever appear among the prey remains. This scarcity of moorland prey leads to an even greater dependence on domestic pigeons for food. The same is evidently true nowadays of certain Galloway eyries situated amidst vast conifer forests which have obliterated the former moorlands and their bird fauna.

Peregrines here must depend largely on birds passing through the area, or living within hunting distance beyond the forests, though they may be able to catch a limited range of species living in these conifer stands. Mearns (1983) found that domestic pigeons formed 73% by weight of breeding season diet on sheepwalk, 64% in predominantly forest habitats, 61% in mixed inland habitats and 57% on grouse moors.

The remaining prey species from the districts mentioned form a long list, but amount to only 7% by weight of the whole spectrum. Collectively they are significant, but individually each species hardly matters, in an ecological sense. Thus, although the total number of prey species in columns 1–9 of Table 8 is 75, only 16 species account for 95% of the total prey catch on a weight basis.

Inland districts of the Scottish Highlands make an interesting comparison with those just described, in regard to variety and proportions of prey species. A greater diversity in Highland prey is apparent from Table 8. Although the total number of records is only about 40% of that for inland districts to the south, the number of species taken is only slightly less, 67 compared with 75. The notable differences in detail are the substantially reduced importance of domestic pigeon (22% by weight) and the greatly increased significance of the Red Grouse which, at 37% by weight is outstandingly the most important individual prey species. The reasons are obvious enough. Many parts of the Highlands are away from the main homer flight routes and there are fewer habitats for feral pigeons inland, whereas nearly all districts have some grouse, and many eastern areas are prolific grouse moors. Nevertheless, in the southern and eastern fringes of the Highlands the domestic pigeon is still quite an important prey item, and even in quite remote wilderness country of the north and west, this bird appears with surprising frequency in remains at inland eyries.

Hardey (1981) analysed 895 prey items representing 47 species at inland eyries in the grouse moor counties of Aberdeen, Kincardine and Banff, during 1974–80. Red Grouse formed 43% by weight of total prey, and varied from 18 to 68% at individual eyries. Domestic pigeon formed 31% by weight overall, and the individual eyrie variations, from 16 to 45%, were mostly inversely related to the proportion of Red Grouse. The importance of pigeons probably reflects proximity to the eastern lowlands and flight routes. Waders were the third most important item, at 9% by weight.

Weir (1977) found that within the Spey Valley catchment in the Highlands, there were differences in prey spectrum according to location of eyries in four separate types of inland habitat, which he distinguished as lowland, upland edge, upland valley and mountain. In the breeding season Red Grouse averaged 42% by weight overall, and varied from 14 to 80% of the catch in individual territories, but were the main prey in mountain territories. Domestic pigeons averaged 24% by weight overall, but varied in proportion according to nearness to farmland.

Ptarmigan are also taken in numbers in the higher mountain massifs with a large extent of montane heath and fell-field. The Oystercatcher is regularly taken, and both Greenshank and Whimbrel fall victim now and then, the latter probably mainly on passage. The Cuckoo appears to figure more frequently in prey remains here than in other districts.

Gamekeeper Tom Speedy, a keen observer of Highland wildlife around the turn of the century, stated: 'Grouse, blackgame, curlews, duck and plover constitute the staple food of Peregrines on inland moors', and he believed that the first two species accounted for over three quarters of all prey. Domestic pigeons were probably little available to Highland Peregrines in those days. Interestingly, another Highland keeper of a later generation, Dugald Macintyre, wrote apropos Kintyre Peregrines, 'On the moor, the principal kills of falcons had been grouse, blackgame, curlew and green and golden plover'. He also said that Cuckoos were frequent victims.

Prey populations (excluding domestic pigeons) in the relatively productive uplands and adjoining valleys of the Central and Southern Highlands probably reach their optimum density and variety for hill districts in Britain, except perhaps for parts of the Pennines in Northern England. By contrast, some of the Western and Northern Highland eyries are situated in barren country where bird populations as a whole are sparse, and the number of species rather small. And when the domestic pigeon is taken into account, the biomass of available prey even in the best parts of the Highlands may well be less than that in inland districts farther south.

Coastal eyries

In the coastal breeding haunts, the variety of prey available to Peregrines can be quite different between one territory and the next, though there are certain broad geographical trends from south to north. Much depends on the proximity of major breeding stations of cliff-nesting seabirds, which are somewhat irregular in distribution (Cramp, Bourne and Saunders, 1974). The presence of estuaries and coastal sand or mud flats within reach of eyries is another important factor. Along the south coast of England, from Kent to Dorset, there are few seabird colonies on the Peregrine cliffs, but most of the eyries here were within close reach of fairly rich arable farmland, downland and woodland, with substantial

and varied bird populations. This coast, especially the eastern sector, is also an important landfall and departure point for migrant birds.

The Peregrines which bred here thus had a wide choice of prey. Walpole-Bond (1938) stated that 'out and away this species' favourite fare in Sussex are carrier and dovecote Pigeons, and then Partridges, both French and English. After these come Jackdaws. But, besides, the following birds have fallen to the Peregrine's prowess in the county: Hooded and Carrion Crows, Rook, Magpie, Jay, Starling, Mistle and Song Thrushes, Fieldfare, Redwing, Blackbird, Ring Ouzel, Finches of several sorts, Buntings (ditto), Pied Wagtail, Skylark, Rock and Meadow Pipits, Wheatear, Stonechat, Cuckoo, Nightjar, Green Woodpecker, Ring, Stock and Turtle Doves, Common and Stone Curlews, Whimbrel, Peewit, Redshank, Oystercatcher, Ringed Plover (once a Little Ringed Plover), Dunlin, Snipe, Woodcock, Coot, Moorhen, Corncrake, Water Rail, Mallard, Teal, Scoter, Wigeon, Heron, Common and Black Terns, Blackheaded Gulls, Kitti-wakes and Herring Gulls, Guillemot, Puffin, Razorbill, Kestrel, Sparrowhawk, Shorteared Owl and domestic fowl. But some of these – notably the last four – are very rarely molested.'

Farther west, in Devon and Cornwall, and on the Welsh coast, the picture changes only a little. Seabird concentrations are still rather few and localised, though there are scattered colonies of auks, and Herring Gulls and Fulmars are generally distributed. Rock Doves or, more commonly, mixed populations of feral pigeons are usually plentiful, and Jackdaw colonies frequent. The land behind the cliffs is possibly somewhat less productive bird habitat than in south-east England, with a higher proportion of grassland or rough heath, but there is still a good choice and abundance of prey species. The same is true of the Isle of Man and the Galloway coast in Scotland. In all these areas, the prey spectrum of Peregrines closely reflects the local conditions, and only at seabird stations does it differ greatly from that at inland eyries in upland districts south of the Highlands. Hill birds, such as Red Grouse and Golden Plover, seldom appear, and there is a higher proportion of coastal and lowland species. *Columba livia* is still the predominant item, but with a larger proportion of Rock Doves and feral pigeons than loft homers, compared with inland districts. In Cornwall, Dick Treleaven estimates that this bird forms 90%, by frequency, of all prey species. However, Francis Heatherley and his colleagues, in their much earlier observations (1910–12) on the Isles of Scilly, found passerines and Puffins to be favourite prey, with very few pigeons taken. At a Pembrokeshire eyrie, Parker (1979) found feral pigeons to be the principal prey. On the southern Scottish coast, Mearns (1983) found the prey spectrum to be identical with that on inland sheepwalks, with domestic pigeon at 69·4% by weight, and few seabirds taken. Collared Doves were a frequent item here, at 6·6% by weight.

Farther north, on the coast of the Scottish Highlands and Islands, there are more marked local differences. This region contains the bulk of the really large concentrations of cliff breeding seafowl in Great Britain, but there are many extensive stretches of seacliff which have few seabirds other than Herring Gulls and Fulmars, e.g. in Kintyre and Sutherland, and on Mull, Skye, South Uist and Lewis. Another important ecological feature is that under the combination of a highly oceanic climate and predominantly hard, acidic rocks, moorland often stretches down to the cliff-tops, and there is little or no farmland, so that hill birds such as Red Grouse, Golden Plover and Ring Ouzel figure in the prey of coastal Peregrines here.

Gray (1871), after mentioning the frequent occurrence of breeding Peregrines in the major colonies of cliff-nesting seabirds in Scotland, said that, 'In these marine haunts the Falcons prey almost exclusively on birds that can be got on the same ledges, Guillemots, Razorbills, Puffins, Kittiwakes, etc.' More recent records indicate that Peregrines breeding in or near the big Scottish seabird colonies usually appear to feed mainly on these four species, together with Rock Doves and Fulmars (Table 8, column 13). Of these seabirds, the Puffin appears to be the favourite prey. In 1890, Grassholm in Pembrokeshire had a huge Puffin colony, and a pair of Peregrines there were said to feed almost exclusively on this bird (J. J. Neale). Tom Speedy recorded that an eyrie on a rocky island in the Outer Hebrides was 'a perfect holocaust of Puffins', and Dugald Macintyre said that a Mull of Kintyre pair fed themselves and their young exclusively on Puffins. Fraser Darling found that the North Rona pair preyed largely on this species, and Philip Glasier found mostly Puffin remains at an eyrie adjoining a northern Scottish grouse moor. In 141 Shetland prey items, Ellis and Okill (in press) recorded Puffins as the most important, followed by Arctic/Common Terns and combined waders, with percentages by weight of 32, 23 and 25, respectively. Ussher (1900) also mentioned that in Irish seabird colonies, Puffins were the favourite prey, but that this varied according to locality.

By contrast, Peregrines inhabiting seacliffs well away from these seafowl colonies take a variety of prey similar to that eaten by inland and upland pairs in the same districts, with a leavening of coastal species such as waders, gulls, terns, Rock Doves/domestic pigeons and, less often, Fulmars (Table 8, column 13). Coastal Peregrines breeding within reach of salt marsh, large shingle beaches, sand dunes and machair have access to a variety of nesting waders such as Lapwing, Redshank, Snipe, Dunlin, Ringed Plover and Oystercatcher and to various species of gull and tern. Ussher said that, in southern Ireland 'Rooks are by far the most usual quarry in Co. Waterford, but small rabbits and Rock Doves are also largely taken. Occasionally the Magpie, Jackdaw, Corncrake, Waterhen, Curlew, Whimbrel, Dunlin or Partridge form the victims, and, in the higher mountains, Grouse.' His observations evidently referred mainly to the coastal eyries of Co. Waterford, where the seacliffs have rather few seabirds.

FOOD OUTSIDE THE BREEDING SEASON

During autumn and winter, many British Peregrines remain in or near their breeding grounds, but the species becomes noticeably more widespread in other parts of Britain, often in quite different types of country (Chapter 2). The food spectrum of the sedentary segment of the breeding population could be expected to change during autumn and winter, with the replacement of summer visitors by species on passage or wintering here, and a reduction in proportion of domestic pigeons, as the homer becomes less available, through restriction to the vicinity of its loft. Limited observations by R. H. Brown and F. Parr on the autumn and winter food of Lakeland Peregrines support this supposition, by showing the Wood Pigeon tending to replace the domestic pigeon as principal prey. In 1961, Parr found that eight out of nine Wood Pigeon kills in his records were made during the months January to April. Similarly, during October to November in 1969 and 1971, large numbers of Wood Pigeons gathered in the Loch Lomond oakwoods, and in both years were followed by a single Peregrine, which was several times seen in pursuit of the pigeons but disappeared when the flocks dispersed. Yet during breeding season observations in several occupied Peregrine territories in the same district during 1965–72, not a single kill of Wood Pigeon was found amongst prey remains (Mitchell, 1973).

In a more recent study in southern Scotland, Mearns (1982) confirmed that small passerines replaced pigeons as the main item of winter diet, but with a difference between inland and coastal birds. In inland territories, 71% of winter pluckings were passerines (45% Redwing and Fieldfare), pigeons 13% and waders 4%. At coastal breeding haunts 48% of winter pluckings were passerines, 30% pigeons and 14% waders.

Peregrines on the coasts and in the hills of England, Wales and southern Scotland probably do a good deal of their hunting over farmland within reach of their home cliffs, and some may range more widely than during the nesting season. Mearns (1982) found that, in southern Scotland, coastal Peregrines appeared to have a more restricted winter range than inland falcons, presumably because food availability was greater on the coast and adjoining lowlands than among the hills. In Lakeland, G. Horne has found that, during the last 10 years, increasing numbers of Peregrines have stayed close to their breeding crags in winter, and these birds have taken greater numbers of gulls and corvids than in the past. Other falcons appear to travel to hunt the adjoining lowlands or even the coasts during the day, but return to their home crags at night.

Individual birds or pairs probably exploit any particularly productive feeding places which they locate, and some may follow the movements of flocks of favoured prey species. The grouse moor falcons are more likely to remain attached to these uplands. Weir (1977) found that in the Spey valley catchment of the Highlands Peregrines fed mainly on passage migrants in spring and autumn, making a particular onslaught on Song Thrushes, Fieldfares and Redwings from late September to early November; but in winter most adults fed largely on Red Grouse or Ptarmigan, there being little else for them to catch.

Peregrines which take up residence on the major estuaries, with their great expanses of saltings and sand or mudflats, naturally tend to prey upon the large flocks of waders, ducks and gulls. We are indebted to J. A. Baker for the only detailed study of the wintering habits of the Peregrine in lowland Britain. His story of infinitely patient watching and searching on the estuaries and arable lands of the Essex coast is told in his highly original book *The Peregrine* (1967), and gives a fascinating picture. Baker supposed that his falcons were visitors from the far north of Europe. He found that his Essex coast Peregrines tended to move between the estuaries and the adjoining farmland behind, and fed even more on the latter. Gulls (17%), waders (16%) and duck (8%) accounted for 41% out of 619 identified kills, whereas pigeons (39%), game birds (5%), corvids (5%), small or medium-sized passerines (5%) and 'others' (5%) accounted for the remaining 59%. Of the pigeon kills, nearly all were of Wood Pigeon (38% of total prey), and Baker found that domestic and feral pigeons were totally ignored – a complete reversal of the situation in most breeding areas. Black-headed Gulls formed the bulk of the gull prey (14%), and Lapwing were the most commonly taken waders (6%). During the exceptionally severe winter of 1962–63, the proportion of Wood Pigeons killed rose to 54% of all recorded prey. As Baker pointed out, duck are killed far less often than is popularly supposed, at least in Britain.

Baker found that in the area under his surveillance, prey was taken in close relation to its abundance and hence availability, so that changes of emphasis were noticeable through the winter. Many gulls and Lapwings, chiefly from ploughed land, were killed in October and November. From December to February, Wood Pigeons were the main prey, especially during hard weather. Predation on Wigeon also increased during cold weather, when the flocks increased. Wood Pigeons were still taken in March, when the killing of gulls and Lapwings increased again, and more duck were killed than in any other month. Game birds, Moorhens, Fieldfares and waders were taken in smaller numbers all through the winter, but in rain or fog, game birds and Moorhens became the principal prey.

Peregrines are often attracted to cities by the large numbers of domestic pigeons and Starlings, and can probably subsist mainly on these species.

UNUSUAL PREY

Although they are an insignificant part of the Peregrine's total diet, some of the unusual prey items have other interest. Peregrines are no respecters of other predators. All five species of British breeding owl have been recorded as killed by them, and in Lakeland, Frank Parr found Long-eared Owls, an uncommon species in the district, taken at two different eyries in 1957. Parr has also found the remains of both Arctic and Long-tailed Skuas in Highland eyries. Several kills of Sparrowhawk have been reported, and a good many more of Kestrel. In Lakeland, both J. F. Peters and R. H. Brown have found the remains of Buzzards at eyries, and H. A. Gilbert flushed a Peregrine feeding on the carcase of a Buzzard in Wales. At a Deeside eyrie, J. Hardey found the fresh pluckings of both Merlin and Kestrel at the same time. It would appear, moreover, that the Peregrine now and then turns cannibal. In 1914, J. F. Peters identified the pluckings of a Peregrine tiercel near a Westmorland eyrie, and in 1971, J. Morgan found the fresh remains of an adult falcon on the top of a Sutherland nesting cliff with young. Then in 1973, in Sutherland and only ten miles from the previous eyrie, A. A. Bell watched a female Peregrine with fledged young eating prey on a ledge of its cliff. He flushed the bird from the remains, which proved to be of another adult female Peregrine. These acts of cannibalism probably resulted from territorial interactions which ended fatally (see also p. 202). Various instances of Peregrines eating their own chicks all evidently involved the prior death of these offspring, as through adverse weather (R. Mearns, G. Horne, R. B. Treleaven).

It may be that some of the attacks on other raptors begin as nest-defending aggression, and that a resulting fatality is then treated by the Peregrine as a normal kill for food. Ravens have been seen to be struck down several times, usually as a result of defensive aggression reinforced by reaction to human intruders, but in Ross-shire R. Balharry has found three instances of this corvid actually being treated as food. In each instance the Raven was evidently a juvenile, judged by the appearance of the bills found in the three eyries; two of these kills were made by the same pair of falcons in different years.

Some observers have been inclined to blame the decline of the Chough on predation by Peregrines. Graham (1852–70) shot a Peregrine which had just taken a Chough on Iona, and Gilbert (1937) recorded finding this species taken as prey three times on the Pembrokeshire coast. Dugald Macintyre, who observed Peregrines over many years on the Kintyre peninsula, one of the few breeding haunts of the Chough in Scotland, said that this species was 'a frequent victim' there. In 1952 I found a kill of Chough at an eyrie near old slate quarries in North Wales which still remain a breeding stronghold of this local corvid. The disappearance of the Chough from south-west England coincided with the 'crash' of the Peregrine population in this district, and it is extremely doubtful if predation by the latter has been a significant factor affecting the status of the Chough anywhere in Britain. The disappearance of the Chough from the coast of south-west England is more likely to be a reflection of the same factors which Jeremy Thomas has found to have caused the extinction there of the large blue butterfly: the great expansion of cultivation over coastal heaths and grasslands, combined with post-myxomatosis changes in vegetation which have led to a great reduction of ant and wild thyme populations in remaining maritime heathland habitats. Choughs eat a great many ants.

The chances of a Peregrine killing a rare breeding bird are small, but instances inevitably happen from time to time. On 1 June 1972, Stuart and Dorothy Illis

found on the summit of a Lakeland fell the fresh pluckings of a Dotterel, evidently taken by a Peregrine nesting in a dale below. And in May 1976 Richard Mearns found the remains of Dotterel killed by Peregrines in at least three different places in the Southern Uplands. These may all have been birds from passing 'trips' but they were victims which could ill be spared, since they were also potential breeders in these districts. The Dotterel has also been recorded as prey in the Grampians (Nethersole-Thompson, 1973). Greenshanks are not infrequently taken on their Highland nesting grounds, especially in the north-west, where they are most numerous. Snow Buntings are sometimes killed in the hills, but are likely to be from the flocks of passage birds rather than from the small population which remains to breed in the Highlands. Weir (1978) stated that Speyside Peregrines preyed selectively on very rare breeding birds such as Wood Sandpiper, Wryneck and Redwing. In 1980 a juvenile Peregrine caused concern by taking 36 Roseate Terns at an important breeding colony at Rhosneigr, Anglesey (G. Williams).

The occasional taking of maritime birds at eyries far inland appears to result from the overland migration of the species concerned. The remains of Common Tern at an eyrie deep in the Pennines; Knot and Sanderling in various places; and Kittiwake and Manx Shearwater (12 kills in 15 years, Weir (1978)) in the Highlands, are explicable in this way, rather than as the result of forays to distant coasts. A Little Auk kill appeared at a mountain Highland eyrie during a 'wreck' of this species, when gales drove many individuals far inland.

The capture, albeit infrequently, of Swift, Swallow, House and Sand Martins, illustrates the combination of speed and agility which hunting Peregrines, especially tiercels, bring into play during the chase. Rob Brown and Geoff Horne have both described to me the unbelievable ease with which they watched Peregrines catching House Martins.

Peregrines have been known to take a miscellaneous assortment of ground prey, notwithstanding their prowess as aerial hunters. Rabbits are the most frequent of such items, and are usually young animals. Many observers, including myself, have found occasional instances of rabbit prey, but Gilbert (1927) reported that several coastal pairs in Pembrokeshire appeared to feed mainly on small rabbits, and Ussher comments on the frequency of this prey item in Co. Waterford. This would be quite understandable in the days when rabbits swarmed on some cliff-tops and rough slopes above the sea, and especially where the populations of coastal birds were rather small. Young hares have been recorded as food, and there are instances of short-tailed field vole, water vole and shrews being eaten. Tyler and Ormerod (1990) reported finding the remains of a fox cub along with nine or more rabbits and hares below a Welsh Peregrine eyrie. Ussher mentions the apparent taking of hedgehogs near an eyrie on the Saltee Islands in southern Ireland. Bats are not recorded as prey in Britain or Ireland, though A. Sprunt found them to be taken frequently by Peregrines in Texas. Very occasionally an individual Peregrine learns to take chickens, and may develop a taste for such easy pickings. Frogs are reported taken and, once, a toad. Walpole-Bond (1938) gives a record of a Sussex Peregrine eating a fish, evidently scooped from a rock pool left at low tide, and Cade (1960) in Alaska actually saw a Peregrine catch a jumping salmonid fish. Weir (1979) has found the remains of a trout, probably *Salmo trutta*, in an Inverness-shire Peregrine eyrie. Snake-eating is not recorded, though in some areas adders lie out on the ledges of cliffs where Peregrines nest, or on the adjoining slopes.

Peregrines are occasionally recorded feeding on carrion. Macgillivray (1840) mentioned one feeding on a dead sheep, and Fischer (1967) reports taking of carrion in Germany. Roy Dennis has in recent years known of instances of Peregrines found dead in the Central Highlands after apparently feeding on poisoned meat baits set down for other predators. Carrion-eating is probably only during winter when severe weather makes live prey harder to find and increases the number of dead birds and other animals lying around, or when a falcon is otherwise finding difficulty in taking prey. Beebe (1960) also mentions North American Peregrines feeding on birds found dead.

FOOD REQUIREMENTS

In most species of raptor, the female is markedly larger than the male, and the difference is especially pronounced in the Peregrine, in which the female is on average about 50% heavier than the male. Some ecologists have supposed that this sexual difference in size is an adaptation which expands the range of prey and perhaps also habitat available to a particular species by allowing females to take larger items while the males concentrate on smaller ones. It may also reduce competition between the sexes.

It has become increasingly accepted that in species such as the Peregrine, size difference between the sexes has some effect on feeding behaviour. The smaller and more agile male is better adapted to taking lesser and more man-oeuvrable prey, whilst the bigger and much heavier female can deal more effectively with birds at the larger end of the size range. While Treleaven (1977), at a number of Devon and Cornwall eyries, found no difference in average size of prey taken by the two sexes, except perhaps in the first week after hatching, Parker (1979) at a Pembrokeshire eyrie found that the male consistently brought in much smaller prey than the female. And at a Lakeland eyrie with young, Martin (1980) observed that, of 37 prey items brought by the male, ten were pigeons and the rest smaller birds; whereas nine out of ten items brought by the female were pigeons. There is, however, a lack of evidence to show whether significant differences in size of prey taken by males and females occur as a general rule, i.e. both widely and throughout the year. Both sexes appear equally adept at killing the pigeons which are their principal food during the breeding season in many districts, and males seem well able to take Red Grouse, the other key prey species.

Females are, however, able to carry prey of any particular size and weight farther and with less fatigue and energy cost than males, and so may have a larger effective feeding range. Weir (1978) found that during courtship, males brought mostly prey items of less than 250 g to the cliffs, but few grouse, though pellet examination revealed they were commonly eating grouse away from the cliffs. He found that in pairs with broods of three or four young the female played a larger role in hunting than if they had only a single youngster, resuming earlier and travelling longer distances on average than the males. The females took mainly large prey including Curlew, Black Grouse, Mallard and Red-breasted Merganser, while their mates tended to switch predation to smaller species near the nest which had remained previously relatively unexploited, e.g. colonies of Black-headed Gulls. Pairs with one or two large young differed in that both sexes continued to hunt mainly grouse and closer to the eyrie. This gives an indication of a size-related division of labour between the sexes when the food demand upon the pair is heavy. In Zimbabwe, Hustler (1983) found that when the female started hunting (as the young grew up), the average size of prey did not increase dramatically, even though she caught prey which the male would have difficulty in carrying.

Possibly the size difference has more effect during the autumn and winter, especially in those instances when the pair parts company and male and female take up separate territories or hunting ranges. Bias in size of prey taken might still confer advantage and thus be subject to selection, if it operated only at certain times or under particular conditions. Nevertheless, while the advantages of such food partitioning seem eminently plausible, they fail to explain why the female is the larger sex. The matter is discussed further on pp. 203–4.

Difference in size of the sexes is reflected even more in food consumption in terms of weight. The experience of falconers with captive Peregrines indicates that the female needs about one third as much food again as a male, on average. Tom Cade has pointed out to me that the female's requirement per unit of body size is somewhat less than the male's because of her overall large body size and thus relatively lower heat loss. Craighead and Craighead (1956) found that the daily food requirements of three captive male North American Peregrines (683 g mean body weight) averaged 104 g during autumn and winter, with a maximum of 147 g. For one male in summer, average body weight 721 g, they found an average food consumption of 83 g and a maximum of 120 g. The average food intake thus varied from 15% of body weight in autumn and winter, to 11·5% in summer. Woodford (1960) gave average daily requirements of raw meat by trained birds of the European Peregrine (very similar to the American sub-species in weight) as 141 g for females and under 113 g for males.

These figures are supported by other falconers. Moreover, Tom Cade has told me that a check based on the weight-specific metabolic rate of birds gives additional confirmation, as follows: 1000 g bird (roughly average female weight) has a standard metabolic rate of about 72 kcal. per day. The calorific equivalent of meat is about 2 kcal. per gram. If the metabolisable energy is about 70% of the total energy intake, the falcon must eat 51·4 g of food just to maintain itself in basal condition. The total daily energy requirement of a bird commonly falls between 2·5 and 3 times the standard metabolism, which gives a range of 129 to 154 g for a 1000 g falcon.

Food requirements are affected not only by environmental conditions, especially ambient temperature, but also by a bird's own activity and expenditure of energy. It may not be strictly correct to assume that the above figures based on captive birds apply equally to wild Peregrines, but the energy requirements of wild falcons probably do not differ markedly from those of trained ones which are flown regularly. They amount to a daily need for a bird of Cuckoo or Mistle Thrush size for males, and of Jay or Golden Plover size for females. Rodriguez (1972) stated that wild Spanish Peregrines required on average one pigeon each per day, but this estimate appears to be at least double that derived from the above calculations.

There is still less information about the food requirements of young Peregrines. These are obviously small at first, but increase rapidly, and during the later stages of growth may be double those of the adults. Weir (1978) found that wild young Peregrines ate 80 g per day soon after hatching and reached a peak demand of 300 g per day at about 33 days. At this point the whole family, with four young, needed an estimated 1550 g per day, and a pair with four large male young brought in over 4000 g of food in two days. These figures include wastage (see below). An estimate of food intake needed by a nestling from hatching to fledging is thus about 7000 g, taking a mean for the sexes. This is more than that needed by an adult (c. 5200 g) over the same period. When the young fledge, they continue for several weeks to eat considerably more than the adults, in building up reserves of fat (T. Cade).

A certain amount of the food eaten by Peregrines is non-utilisable and represents wastage. The castings are composed almost entirely of the feathers of prey, variably decomposed and pulverised, and there are seldom any traces of bone. The frequent presence of homing pigeon closed rings in the castings, tightly packed in a powdery matrix of feather remains, nevertheless shows that bones are often eaten and completely digested away. After being plucked, some of the smaller birds are probably swallowed whole. The breast meat is usually devoured first, though the brains are relished and the male often keeps the head for himself when bringing prey to his mate or young. The biggest bones of larger victims are usually left uneaten, though they are nearly always dismembered. The bill is usually left, and sometimes the intact skull of the largest birds. The alimentary tract is sometimes left uneaten, but castings often contain vegetable remains from the guts and crops of prey in the form of heather shoots from grouse, grain husks from pigeons, and miscellaneous seeds from passerines. For an item of prey completely picked clean, the amount of wastage is therefore estimated at an average of no more than 10%.

Some have alleged that the Peregrine is a wanton killer, at least at times, striking down far more birds than are needed to meet its immediate food requirements, apparently out of a kind of blood-lust. Such profligate killing, of the kind which foxes certainly indulge in on occasion, may occur with the Peregrine, but I believe it to be unusual, and have encountered no instances during my own field experience. Ernest Blezard once found a Pennine nesting place littered with recently killed Fieldfares, but possibly this represented a food store which would be utilised. Under the April conditions at the high elevation (600 m) the dead birds would not decompose readily. Beebe (1960) reported that Peale's Falcons on Langara Island regularly killed in excess of their own needs and those of their broods. Nelson (1970) found that food caches were used regularly on Langara and Fischer (1967) recorded them in Germany, while in Britain, Treleaven (1977) in Cornwall and Parker (1979) in Pembrokeshire both watched pairs which made regular use of food caches while the young were in the eyrie. On Saturday, 7 June 1980, Dick Treleaven saw a female Peregrine on the Cornwall coast kill six pigeons between 09.00 and 15.00 h: one was lost, one used to feed the young, and the other four were cached, after the falcon had partly eaten one herself. This habit, now known in a number of raptor species, would give a rational explanation of apparently wanton killing.

On the whole, the evidence is that Peregrines make the most of each kill, taking two or even more meals from the larger items. Birds at the nesting cliff sometimes return half-eaten prey to a food cache, to utilise for a further meal. Keeper Dugald Macintyre has said that he found it easy to trap Peregrines at the half-eaten remains of larger prey, such as grouse or duck, for the birds would nearly always come back for a second meal. Marjory Garnett was also told by a Lakeland keeper that Peregrines were easily trapped at their own kills. It is, however, likely that some prey is not picked clean, and that the total wastage from kills is around 20% by weight.

All factors considered, it seems that a reasonable estimate of the total annual food catch of a pair of adult Peregrines, measured as weight of birds actually killed, is 116 kg (average of 127 g per day × 365 days × 2 birds × 1·25). A young bird during its first year will need about 47 kg (average of 157 g per day × average life 240 days × 1·25). If the pair rears an average brood of 2·5 young, this will take another 118 kg of prey during the calendar year of its birth. The total prey catch of the Peregrine family during the year, assuming no mortality, would then be 234 kg.

PREDATION LEVEL AND IMPACT

Red Grouse

The question of whether, or how much, the Peregrine affects the populations of its prey species has been debated for a long time, usually with more emotion than reason. At one extreme is the traditional game-preserver's view of such predators as remorseless competitors draining away his potential bag of cherished quarry, in this case, mainly the Red Grouse. At the other is the rosy concept of the Peregrine as Nature's agent of biological health, cleaning away the sick, injured or feeble and so maintaining the quality of the stock. Somewhere in between is the viewpoint of the modern population ecologist, who sees the numbers of predators balanced against and limited by those of their prey, and with the predator drawing often from a 'doomed surplus' which would die from some other cause if this predation were removed.

Which of these views is the correct one? As in so many controversies in science, the truth probably lies in some combination of them all. However much it may be true that predators are limited by the numbers of their prey rather than vice versa, and that the birds taken by Peregrines would have died early anyway, the game preserver has valid reason to feel that the falcon is drawing from a population surplus on which he has the rightful claim. The two are alternative and competing predators. The argument then becomes centred on whether the shooting man can, as a sportsman recognising a fellow hunter, accept the level of Peregrine predation as one which does not too seriously reduce his own bag. No doubt the grouse-preservers will say that their view of the importance of predation varies according to the circumstances. They have been particularly concerned to know whether predation is responsible for long-term declines of Red Grouse numbers on many moors, and whether this is the main cause of the species' failure to recover from low numbers. There are different ways of approaching the problem of measuring predation rates, and several different predators to consider.

Beginning at the Peregrine's end of the business, predation must be influenced by several factors: the abundance of grouse and of alternative prey, the level of Peregrine preference for grouse, breeding performance (and hence food demands), territory size and hunting range. Variations in any of these are likely to cause predation rate to change, and some of them can vary within the same year, as well as between one year and the next. There will also be differences between one pair or moor and the next. It thus seems best to consider a range of possible situations.

Calculations based on Table 8 show that in the major grouse areas of the eastern Highlands, predation on this species averages about 40% by weight of all prey taken by Peregrines during the breeding season. Let us first assume that this figure is roughly true throughout the year, that successful pairs of Peregrines have a mean brood size of 2·5 young, and that they and their offspring remain in the same territories for the rest of the year. The average weight of a Red Grouse is 630 g, so that if each Peregrine family needs 234 kg of food during the year (p. 138), they will take on average 149 grouse. In these districts, maximum density of Peregrines is now one pair to about 4000 ha (40 km^2) (Hudson, 1992), giving a kill of one grouse to every 27 ha annually, assuming predation rate to be constant, irrespective of grouse numbers. Density of grouse on moors in the eastern Highlands usually lies in the range of a pair to 1·5–5·0 ha (with extremes of 1·2–40·0 ha (Nethersole-Thompson and Watson, 1981)). Average breeding success gives the addition of around three young per pair each August (Jenkins *et al.*, 1963), so that grouse numbers are more than doubled during the second half of the year. From these figures, an estimate of predation would be 1·6–5·3% of the grouse population annually on moors in the usual range of stocking density.

In practice, breeding failure, smaller broods and earlier dispersal of young Peregrines would reduce falcon food demands, while larger broods would increase this. In some areas, average territory size is larger, at 10,000 ha or more per falcon pair, which also lowers predation pressure. More precise information is necessary to understand predation at the level of the individual moor or Peregrine territory. Weir (1978) assisted by H. Papke found that in the grouse moor country of the central Highlands the Red Grouse and Ptarmigan (together 'grouse') form about 60% by weight of prey for pairs which hatch, and rather less for those which do not. During the later stages of nestling growth this proportion often falls to 40%, though the actual number of grouse taken may rise because of the increase in total food demand. By August/September when the family moves around and some young begin to disperse, the proportion of grouse drops to 30%; but during winter, when migration is over and so many species have left the uplands, grouse may form up to 80% of the diet. Weir estimated that a Speyside pair of falcons remote from farmland which reared four young would take about 110 Red Grouse and Ptarmigan from courtship to dispersal of their young. Most would be breeding grouse and within 2 km of the nest, covering an area of c. 1200 ha. A 'remote' pair would only rear four young if grouse density was high, say one pair to 4 ha. Under these circumstances possibly 10–15% of the grouse would be taken over the 1200 ha. A pair rearing an average brood closer to farmland with a more varied choice of prey could still take grouse at a level exceeding 5% of population within a 1200 ha area of moor.

Weir's calculations probably give an estimate of predation on grouse at its heaviest, and they involve certain assumptions. Hunting range was not measured by radio telemetry, and even if feeding was mainly within the 1200 ha surrounding the eyrie, such an area is continuous with the larger part of the territory beyond. If predation were especially heavy within this central area, it would be correspondingly light in the outer zone of the Peregrine territory, so that overall impact should be averaged across the whole territory. It is not certain that all grouse taken were breeding, and if surplus grouse were available from the surrounding moor, they would steadily colonise the central area as gaps appeared in the territory-holding population there. If predation on nesting grouse were heavy, the effect on reproductive performance of a population might be considerable. Hudson (1992, Fig. 11.11) has published data showing Peregrine kills of grouse to reach their highest frequency in April and May. In Wales, Bolam (1913) suggested that it is mainly unpaired cocks not holding territories (whose presence he discussed) which are taken by Peregrines in early spring.

The other approach to the predation problem is by focussing on the Red Grouse end of the story. Jenkins *et al.* (1963, 1964) found that in Glen Esk, Angus, annual turnover of adult territorial grouse averaged 60–70%, and mortality of first-year birds was about the same. Losses to all predators were estimated to be only a small part of total mortality (6–20%), and Peregrines were regarded as one of the least important contributions. Predation on non-territorial grouse displaced by the territory-holders was much heavier, and Peregrines probably took more of these individuals – as Bolam surmised. These displaced birds were regarded as likely to have died anyway, from other causes, so that the predators were simply removing a 'doomed surplus'.

More recently, Hudson (1992) has reached different conclusions from his studies of Red Grouse in northern England and the Highlands. He reported that, of grouse found dead on the moor, 34% had been killed by raptors in England and 48% in Scotland, with Peregrines contributing 74 and 64%, respectively, of this predation. It is important to set this against overall mortality from all causes, but Hudson believes that winter loss was the key factor influencing year to year changes in numbers of grouse, at least on low density areas. He claimed that, unexpectedly, Peregrines and other predators appeared to take the same number of grouse irrespective of grouse density. Predators consistently took 2·1 female grouse per square kilometre in winter, with 64% taken by raptors, mainly Peregrines. Similar rates of loss were found for male grouse, though raptors took proportionately more. The implication is that Peregrines take a higher proportion of the grouse population at low than at high densities. It appeared that predators preyed selectively on birds heavily infected with parasites at high grouse densities, but did not show preference for weaker grouse at low densities.

Hudson believes, accordingly, that winter predation is limiting grouse breeding populations in spring – at least at low densities – and that if it were reduced their numbers would increase. The belief no doubt reinforces game-preservers' long-held view that predator pressure should be reduced to an absolute minimum, and its promulgation coincides with a recent resurgence of illegal killing of Peregrines on some grouse moors.

Even visiting Peregrines raise another more difficult issue. It is commonly believed by grouse moor keepers that the mere appearance of certain raptors, especially an eagle or harrier, over a moor will cause the certain ruin of a day's shoot. The grouse rise wildly in droves and fly around fitfully from one area to another, thus becoming impossible to drive systematically over the butts. So, although not a feather on one grouse may be harmed, the intruding raptor is no less detested and persecuted than if it had slain hordes. Peregrines do not seem to cause this problem with grouse, which are safer from this predator if they keep to the ground, but they tend to fall under the cloud of indiscriminate suspicion extended to all birds of prey.

Homing pigeons

Predation on homing pigeons is a rather different issue, for it is not the quantity of birds killed which is most important but the value of some individuals. Some fanciers assume that it is their prize race-winners, leading on the return to the home lofts, which are most at risk to Peregrines. Considerable prestige and financial interest often hang upon the prowess of these star performers, and the loss of a champion homer is no light matter. A pigeon leading a race would be likely to be on its own and thus more at risk than any individual in a flock, but it would seem more likely that the tired and flagging tail-enders to a race would be the more vulnerable to attack. Much will depend on the time of day and the period which has elapsed since a falcon last fed. The frequent presence of rubber race bands in eyries shows that race-homers are taken by Peregrines, and it would be possible, if owners were willing, to study the individual histories of these birds. If predation on the population of a species were a purely random matter, the risks to any particular individual would be very small. There does not appear to be a preference for young birds. Geoff Horne has found from ring dates that about 90% of homers taken were between 1 and 3 years old, with roughly equal proportions between the yearly age classes.

The rank and file of racers are of less concern, and many fanciers them-selves exercise rigorous selection in the breeding of their champions, so that the annual turnover in pigeon population is quite large. The Peregrine is often the scapegoat for the effects of more serious but intractable adversities, especially bad weather, which may cause real havoc among the race flocks. Surreptitious and illegal shooting also accounts for many homers when they stop to feed on farmland. A 10% failure of homers to return from a race is quite normal, and there are occasional 'wrecks' when only a handful of birds reach the home lofts.

While there is thus considerable interest in estimating predation on homing pigeons, it is difficult to do so with any real meaning. Even in districts where the bulk of the pigeons taken are ringed and registered birds, it is difficult to tell how many of these would still have been an asset to their owners after a race had they survived. After every race an unknown proportion of pigeons will either have taken to the wild or become so late in returning home that they are of no further use as racers. In many coastal districts a high proportion of the pigeons taken is from a feral or truly wild stock. Predation on race birds is also limited to the racing season, from mid-April to September.

A crude gross estimate of predation on *Columba livia* can be made, as follows. The data on breeding season prey spectra in Table 8 suggest the proportion of *C. livia* in the food of the British Peregrine population as a whole, could well be around 50% by weight, taking account of all districts. Average daily food consumption is estimated at 127 g per adult bird and 157 g per young bird. The present (1991) British population of Peregrines is estimated at 2378 territory-holding birds, or 1189 pairs with average productivity of 1·25 young per pair (Tables 6 and 19). The number of non-territorial adults is unknown, but to allow for this element it is assumed that there is no mortality of either adults or young during the year (this cannot be so in reality). This gives a total population for the year of 2378 adults plus 1486 young birds (average life 240 days), with a total food requirement of 110,232 kg + 55,992 kg = 166,224 kg. Applying a wastage factor of 20% to prey caught, the total catch would need to be 207,780 kg in the year. Average weight of a domestic pigeon is 425 g, so that at 50% of the total diet, the annual catch would be 224,447 birds. However, these calculations are based on breeding season diet, and homing pigeons become far less available during at least half the year, so that this last figure is likely to be a considerable over-estimate.

In 1979, when the Royal Pigeon Racing Association registered 1,560,000 new homer rings, the estimate of total racing pigeon population was at least five million birds. By 1991, the number of new rings issued annually had risen to 2–2·5 million, and the overall pigeon population could be assumed to have grown accordingly, to at least seven million. At most, using the above over-estimate, the annual Peregrine catch would represent just over 3% of this total, but the real figure is likely to be appreciably lower.

None of these figures gives a proper basis for evaluating damage by Peregrines to homing pigeon interests. For the reasons mentioned, there is in the total pigeon catch a complete range from reliable racers through birds in various stages of reversion to the wild and finally the true wild Rock Dove; yet there is no means of assigning proportions of the catch within this gradient. Gross pre-dation, even if accurately known, would give no clear idea of real losses to the sport as a whole or to any one racing union, while to the individual fancier it is virtually meaningless as a statement of risks. Homer lofts in areas close to Peregrine eyries, or the pigeons following certain flight routes, may suffer greater than average predation, and give rise to especially strong complaints from fanciers. The finding of batches of rings in eyries and, even more, the known or suspected killing of a champion racer arouse natural feelings of anger. A more meaningful picture of real losses could best be gained by a careful study in which time and place of predated ringed pigeons were compared with time and route of race and the individual histories of the birds concerned.

So far, the British Government has been persuaded to remove or reduce legal protection for Peregrines only under the stress of war-time emergency and the creation of risks to humans through predation on carrier pigeons. The war-time campaign against Peregrines as potential killers of message-carrying homers was not without justification. In 1947, Ernest Blezard was sorting through the litter of remains in a Galloway eyrie dating from a brood of a few years before when he found an RAF message container, complete with coded message and still on its special ring. And in 1949, in the Moffat Hills of Dumfriesshire, I found another old war-time eyrie with the special carrier ring, but no message container. Just how many carrier pigeons were taken will never be known, but the risks to these birds were certainly considerable in Peregrine country.

In Sweden, Lindquist (1963) studied Peregrine distribution and habits in relation to complaints of damage by homing pigeon interests. He found that while total losses of pigeons during his investigations amounted to about 5%, the total predation by Peregrines during races could not have exceeded 0·2%, so that the main causes of loss were bad weather, poor quality of pigeons and illegal shooting. He found that the most serious damage resulted from scattering of the flocks by Peregrine attacks, and heaviest losses occurred if this happened soon after release of a flock. The birds apparently suffered disorientation of their homing ability. Lindquist indicated that the study had highly beneficial effects in reducing homer losses through re-locating of some release points and flight routes, though he presented no actual evidence in support of his claims.

The question of damage to racing pigeons without actual physical injury is even more problematical, and comparable with the scaring effect of Golden Eagles and Harriers on grouse moors, though it is equally unquantifiable. And further new problems continue to arise. In South Wales, especially, another variant of pigeon racing is the use of 'tipplers' which are homers trained for endurance flying within the immediate vicinity of the home loft. The birds fly round and round and the one that stays up longest is the winner. When a pair of Peregrines took up residence on the Swansea Post Office tower during the winter of 1978–79 there were complaints of attacks on the local tipplers and, admittedly, there would seem to be a particularly high risk to the pigeons which stay aloft the longest.

G. H. T. Stovin in his book *Breeding Better Pigeons* said that, 'In pursuit of our own hobby and the consequent desire to protect the racing pigeon, I do not personally consider that we have any right to persecute further the Peregrine Falcon.' He spoke of the pleasure which the sight of this bird gave to others and of its relative scarcity, which led him to feel that the Peregrine was but a minor risk to most homers, compared with the adversities of weather and the propensity of many racers for going vagrant. Stovin admonished the fanciers to leave the Peregrine alone and put their own house in order, by improving their breeding techniques to reduce the number of strays, by researching into the racing and homing faculty, and thereby learning to circumvent the bad weather 'smashes' which play such havoc with races. One can only hope that such enlightened views will eventually become widely accepted.

Other species

There remains the possibility that the populations of certain other prey species might be significantly reduced or held down by Peregrine predation. The case of the Chough is discussed on p. 133. Such an effect would seem most likely to occur if Peregrines preyed preferentially on a species but without actually having to depend on that species as a staple item of diet; or in situations where they could move on to other species or other areas when they had exhausted the first one. The predator could then avoid the problem of itself facing starvation and/or competition long before its prey species was eliminated. In Alaska, Cade (1960) found that Peregrines fed on Ptarmigan mainly when these were abundant. In 1952, Ptarmigan occurred at an estimated density of about two per square kilometre around the Colville River. Cade calculated that, with a total food requirement of 54 kg (equivalent of 100 Ptarmigan) during May–August, a Peregrine family which fed on Ptarmigan at the level of 50% or more of their total diet could have removed most of this prey species from many square kilometres around their eyrie. He suggested that such limitation by predators was best regarded in terms of habitat marginality for the prey rather than as predator regulation of the annual turnover in numbers of the prey population, because the falcons hunted only a limited part of the total breeding grounds of Ptarmigan in the district.

Cade remarked that the Peregrine appears to be a good example of Errington's basic hypothesis that vertebrate predators live on the expendable surpluses of their prey populations and do not themselves exert any limiting effect on the annual numbers of prey that remain to breed each spring. In the next section I discuss the belief that Peregrines may, in Harvie-Brown's phrase, act as 'Nature's sanitary commissioners' in selectively removing sub-standard or disadvantaged individuals in prey populations, so that the true predation effect might be substantially less adverse to these species than bare figures might suggest.

HUNTING TECHNIQUES AND PERFORMANCE

The chase

Perhaps more has been written about the Peregrine's manner of taking prey than about any other aspect of its life history, and the references to this subject are so numerous that it is difficult to make an adequate summary. Fascinating detailed accounts have been given by many writers and I recommend especially those by Walpole-Bond (1938), Meinertzhagen (1959), Baker (1967) and Treleaven (1977, 1980a,b).

First and foremost among methods is the legendary stoop, in which the falcon plunges headlong downwards at usually a fairly steep angle, with wings half closed or more, and strikes its victim from above at terrific speed. This is the most spectacular technique, and that which excites the most frequent comment. To use it, the Peregrine, previously on the look-out from either a perch or in flight, usually needs a considerable advantage in height over its intended prey. A soaring bird may already start with this advantage, but one less well placed will climb rapidly, by beating hard on an even course or by circling in big sweeps, often well away from its target, or even flying in the opposite direction. A soaring Peregrine in a strong up-current has a steep and rapid rate of climb. When the required height and position are gained, the bird furls its wings, and accelerating fast, hurtles obliquely downwards at its quarry. After a miss the falcon 'throws up' by directing its flight upwards, usually at about the angle of descent, and using its momentum to carry it high above the level of the quarry, and into position for another stoop. After a strike the Peregrine usually makes a more leisurely descent to retrieve its victim, which has crashed or fluttered to the ground, but will occasionally swing round or stoop again and pick its prey out of the air before it has time to hit the ground.

There are many variations on this theme. The angle of descent is usually between about 30–45° to the horizontal, but it may be steeper or more shallow, and may even be quite vertical. Sometimes the falcon will deliberately stoop wide and hit its victim from below on the 'throw up', or it may make a reversed stoop, shooting up from under its target and again striking it on the upwards thrust, often from an upside down position. The attack may be made from the side, or the falcon may check its stoop at the last second, to seize the prey by its back ('riding it down', Treleaven), or to follow it in level flight, striking from almost any angle, including below. Rodriguez suggested that falcons often strike from below so that they can exploit the 'blind spot' in the quarry's arc of vision. There may be no stoop and the quarry is then simply flown down on equal terms, and when the speeds of pursuer and pursued are more evenly matched, the Peregrine usually 'binds to' the prey, seizing it in mid-air and carrying it off to some suitable place.

The speed achieved by a stooping Peregrine is a favourite topic, but one still not yet satisfactorily resolved by the marvels of modern electronic gadgetry. Estimates vary between the conservative, by those who insist that the impression of great speed is illusory and that the bird hardly exceeds 160 km/h (100 mph); and the extravagant, which assert that 400 km/h (250 mph) is entirely possible. Hantge (1968) timed maximum speeds of 270 km/h (170 mph) at a 30° angle of descent and 350 km/h (220 mph) at 45°. Alerstam (1987) timed three Peregrine stoops by tracking radar and recorded average speeds of about 90 km/h (56 mph), and a maximum of 140 km/h (87 mph), at dive angles between 13° and 64°. These were well below the theoretical terminal speeds, in vertical dive, of up to 270 km/h (168 mph). Alerstam suggested that, by adopting a more moderate stooping speed, raptors may gain in hunting precision. Orton (1975), using theoretical calculations, suggests that a Peregrine stooping with a vertical fall of 1500 m would reach 370–386 km/h (230–240 mph). While he has seen long stoops of this order in display, he believes that more normal strikes at prey reach up to 195–240 km/h (120–150 mph). Measurements of level flight suggest that

The kill by stoop

the bird normally does not exceed 100 km/h (60 mph), but may be capable of faster bursts. Cochrane and Applegate (1986) radio tracked six migrating Peregrines in flapping flight at an average ground speed of only 49 km/h (30 mph).

There has been much dispute as to how the actual kill is made, i.e. with what part of the Peregrine's body. Some writers have asserted that the blow is sometimes made with the wing or breast, because birds have been struck down with no injury other than bruising. These can be dismissed, since such methods would be likely to be as damaging to the striker as the struck. From the frequency with which the falcon rips open the back of the victim or slashes off its head, the talons are clearly often involved in the blow. Peregrines have been shot immediately after making kills, and found to have blood and feathers adhering to their hind talons or to the whole foot. Morlan Nelson in America has filmed in ultra-slow motion a Peregrine preparing to strike, and the bird was clearly seen to lower its feet and extend them forwards, with the toes in a fully open position. Cade (1960) believes, from close observations with trained falcons, that they strike prey with loosely closed feet and that, although the rear talons often protrude back and gash the prey, it is primarily the impact of the blow that knocks the quarry down. This seems the most satisfactory explanation, since the legs fold backwards, and would absorb the force of the impact, which is often considerable. Sometimes the unfortunate quarry seems to dissolve in a cloud of feathers and a loud 'whack' comes down to the watcher on the ground, though Macintyre commented that he had often seen birds killed when it appeared that the falcon had missed, for the speed of strike defeated the human vision. Should the prey

still be alive when the falcon has hold of it, it is usually despatched by a bite at the base of the skull, and the tooth and notch structure on the Peregrine's bill is a suggested adaptation to this need to administer the *coup de grâce*.

There are innumerable variations on the classic stoop, and the technique varies somewhat according to the species attacked, their avoidance actions, and the physical situation. The element of surprise may often help Peregrines to take fast fliers such as many waders or manoeuvrable performers such as the Lapwing, but they also seem endowed with an agility which allows them to catch most prey species in fair flight. The skill needed to take a Swift must be considerable, yet

The kill by binding-to

this bird occasionally appears among prey remains, presumably having fallen to the more agile tiercel. R. H. Brown described to me how a House Martin went into a spiral dive in a vain attempt to escape, but was simply followed down by the Peregrine and gathered in its talons.

By contrast, Peregrines have been seen to beat about low over the ground, rather after the fashion of a harrier, usually when they have driven something into cover, and they will occasionally rake about in long vegetation, such as heather, in trying to catch or flush a hiding bird. Grouse are recorded taken in this way. Wounded birds are sometimes taken on the ground, and sometimes include shooters' crippled quarry. The unfledged young of waders, gamebirds, ducks and gulls are quite frequently caught while running around. Weir (1978) found that in the breeding season 10% of the Red Grouse taken were chicks. Some individuals are evidently adept at catching small rabbits. Dugald Macintyre mentioned a trained tiercel which stooped at and caught young rabbits when being flown at birds. Peregrines occasionally pick prey from water, when they have chased it in, or when it is wounded, and they will also retrieve kills which have fallen into water. Mortimer Batten saw a Peregrine plunge at a Mallard on a hill loch, sending water flying 3·5 m in the air, but the duck escaped by diving. Meinertzhagen and Treleaven have pointed out that coastal nesting Peregrines are mostly careful not to knock their prey into the sea; they either bind to the quarry or withhold the strike until the bird is over the land. Rogers and Leatherwood (1981) watched hunting by an ocean-going Peregrine on board ship: from its perch on the yardarms or crow's nest, in 5 days it made 11 sorties, eight of them successfully, at Leach's Petrels, taking the birds as they pattered across the water. The head and wings were usually removed in the air as the falcon returned to its perch.

Sometimes Peregrines sail around for long periods 'waiting on' high in the air in readiness to deliver their attack when prey approaches, but quite often they sit watching from a cliff-face perch and launch out at the appropriate moment. Treleaven (1980b) on the Cornwall seacliffs found that the latter method ('still hunting') tended to be the more successful (60% kills compared with 40%) and that waiting on was used mainly during bad weather. This writer has given a fascinating account of the species' tactical skill in placing itself to intercept and out-manoeuvre intended victims, sometimes stalking them and timing the final onslaught at an especially favourable point. He believes that surprise is the falcon's most effective weapon. On the Sussex seacliffs, B. Atfield has noted that Peregrines usually hunt from a waiting on position. When hunting in pairs, as they often do during courtship and when the young have fledged, the falcon and tiercel can show remarkable coordination in their combined efforts, and Treleaven describes how one bird may steer the prey into the attack of the other. In hawking, 'casts' of two falcons were often flown at large quarry. In some parts of the World, Peregrines have been seen hunting in groups. Meinertzhagen describes an incident thus, 'In February 1913 on a sheet of water near Meerut I saw eleven Peregrine harrying ducks who were loth to leave the surface. We were there to shoot, the falcons were there to hunt. The ducks were loth to take wing but were forced to do so by beaters. We cooperated in the ducks' discomfiture. It was a beautiful sight seeing the falcons stooping in all directions and paying scant regard to the fusillade. I counted five strikes all over the water and all recovered by the falcons.' The same writer said that on migration, 'The Peregrine appears to feed as he travels.' Tom Cade watched an adult tiercel catch seven bats and eat each one on the wing during 20 minutes of continual flying over the Grand Canyon.

Hunting technique may show some variation between individuals, and it has perforce to be modified during especially unfavourable weather. Baker found that during rain and misty weather, wintering Peregrines in Essex tended to take mainly Moorhens and gamebirds, and during prolonged heavy rain falcons may have some difficulty in catching food at all. High winds and snowfalls may also increase the difficulties of catching prey, though Mortimer Batten recorded a Peregrine striking down a Ptarmigan in a heavy snowstorm. All of these adverse weather conditions may have more effect on the prey, by grounding other birds, rather than on the predator itself. Some kills are made in the dim light of dawn or dusk and Beebe (1960) believed that most of the kills made by Peale's Falcon on Langara were almost nocturnal. He discussed other evidence for believing that Peregrines can see quite well in very dim light. The visual acuity of the birds of prey is legendary, though there are no accurate measurements, and estimates vary from twice to eight times as acute as the average human vision. Perhaps, as usual, the truth lies somewhere between the extremes.

Hunting Peregrines are said to induce a state of near-panic in some birds. Warren in Ireland said, 'The terror shown by the wildfowl on the appearance of a Falcon flying over the sands is extraordinary. Large flocks of Wigeon resting or feeding on the banks immediately take to the water. The Golden Plover and Lapwings rise and keep flying about at an immense height, sometimes for hours. The Curlew and other waders move about from bank to bank, and all the birds become so frightened and restless that there is very little chance of obtaining a shot for the day.' Ussher commented, 'On the decoy-lake at Longneville, near Mallow, far from coasts or mountain cliffs, I have seen a great commotion created among the ducks by its appearance in winter.' Bolam (1912) said, 'The appearance of a Peregrine over the slakes at Holy Island is often a particularly fine sight, as huge flock after flock of all sorts of mud-feeding birds – from Gulls to Dunlins – rise wheeling into the air at its approach.' H. A. Macpherson (1892) said that in earlier days, the Solway punt gunners disliked the wintering Peregrines because they disturbed the Wigeon and made them wild.

The reaction may vary according to the cover available and the options for defensive behaviour. Mortimer Batten witnessed a near stampede amongst wildfowl on a loch when a Peregrine appeared: hundreds rose and flew pell-mell for the rushes and reeds while scores dived. Red Grouse evidently feel safer if they stay on the ground and take cover amongst the heather. Wood Pigeons and domestic pigeons will head for any woody cover and plunge headlong into this to escape pursuit, and coastal Rock Doves and feral pigeons dive into deep caves and crannies. Many people have described the tameness of birds when a hunting falcon is close and sometimes hunted quarry will actually seek human presence, even to the point of allowing themselves to be picked up.

Several writers have commented that other birds seem quickly to recognise a Peregrine's mood, in sensing whether this spells danger or not. During 'safe' times they will take fearful risks which would invite destruction if they had misjudged things. Clearly, much depends on whether the falcon is distracted by other happenings. I have many times seen prey species offer tempting targets to Peregrines during my visits to inland eyrie cliffs, but have seldom seen even a chase under such circumstances. When nesting Peregrines are aware of the approach of human intruders, and certainly when they are actually in the air demonstrating, they seem to lose all interest in prey, though their hostility to other predators, such as Ravens, may be heightened.

Hunting efficiency

An important issue, not only to the mystique of the Peregrine but also to its population biology, is the bird's hunting efficiency. The falcon's command of the air was brought home to me once in North Wales. A nesting pair were in front of their home crags, and a domestic pigeon came into view. The female Peregrine swung out in a wide arc, far from the bird, but across its intended course. The pigeon changed direction, and it became apparent that although the Peregrine was not concerned to close with the alarmed bird, it was shepherding the intended target into a position of greatest vulnerability. The pigeon was manoeuvred at a distance into a course which took it well out from the hillside. The Peregrine then half furled its wings and in a shallow dive streaked after the hapless bird as though it were not moving. At about 10 m behind the victim the falcon braked momentarily, and then shot forward again as if rocket-propelled, right into the pigeon, which seemed to explode in a cloud of feathers, and came fluttering down to the ground. The whole thing was done with a consummate skill which was quite breath-taking, and I was left with the feeling of having watched a master performer, which could do exactly what it liked in the air. The same impression remains after watching some of the dazzling displays of aerobatics during courtship, or sometimes when Ravens on the same nesting cliffs are under attack. Leslie Brown (1976) has given an even more dramatic example of the Peregrine's incredible agility and accuracy in attack, raking his dog along the middle of the back as it stood beside him on the ledge of an African cliff. The precision of control of direction at high speed is almost unbelievable, and is surely one of the greatest wonders of the animal world.

Meinertzhagen (1959) has a relevant passage, in speaking of a pair of Peregrines wintering in the Test Valley in Hampshire, and hunting over flooded land and pools. 'Every evening they harried the duck, preferring Wigeon to Mallard or Teal. Killing was carried out by stoop, always over dry land, and the pair of hawks were amazingly successful, rarely failing at their first attempt. In the still, frosty air we always heard a resounding smack as the hawk struck and then watched the spiral dive to the dead victim lying in the water meadow.' There are also records of male Peregrines which had lost their mates continuing to feed and successfully rear full broods of young on their own; which bespeaks a considerable hunting prowess.

I have selected the above accounts of hunting behaviour as examples which support the romantic view of the Peregrine as an infallible killer which seldom fails once it has prey 'in its sights'. At the other extreme is the conclusion of the Swedish ornithologist G. Rudebeck who, from the observation of a large number of chases of prey by various raptors, concluded that most species had a low efficiency in catching prey. He reported that Peregrines were successful in killing their intended victims in only 19 out of 252 hunts. Rudebeck's view also gains support from the large number of more casually reported instances in which Peregrines have been seen to be unsuccessful during hunts.

The true picture is probably somewhere between these extremes and is much more complicated. An aspect seemingly overlooked by Rudebeck and the 'low efficiency' school is that Peregrines and other raptors have a marked habit of chasing prey without, by all appearances, attempting or intending to strike the pursued bird. A good many writers have described so-called unsuccessful chases in which they said the prey dodged the attack, sometimes repeatedly, as the falcon struck. I have seen several such chases, and each time was quite sure that the Peregrine never really pressed home its attack in earnest. The best demonstration was at a Lakeland crag, one August Saturday, pigeon-race day. Flocks of homers were travelling up the valley and past the crag every few minutes. Each time a party approached, the female Peregrine launched forth, singled out a homer and chased it hither and thither across the hillsides, before losing interest and swinging back into the cliff to await the next flock. No attempt was made to strike a bird and it seemed quite clear that the Peregrine was simply not intent on striking. I also once saw a Peregrine catch a pigeon, then let it go again, only to continue the pursuit, rather in a cat-and-mouse style.

Falconers are well aware of this behaviour, and on the Cornish cliffs Dick Treleaven has learned to predict accurately whether an impending chase will end successfully or not. He distinguishes between high and low-intensity chasing. Whatever the reason may be, Peregrines thus appear to have a well-developed habit of chasing prey without intending to kill it, and this greatly confuses understanding of their hunting efficiency. Probably they benefit by 'keeping their eye in' with constant practice in following the flight behaviour of prey species, or perhaps they are simply unable to resist chasing a tempting target. Possibly these mock chases have some connection with play, now known to be a well developed activity in some mammals. Treleaven also suggests there may be something akin to *joie de vivre*. Whatever the case, this is a trait which appears between meal times. When the Peregrine is hungry and searching for a meal, it is usually a different story. As Treleaven (1977, 1980a,b) has pointed out, the falcon hunting in earnest takes on a more purposeful demeanour the moment it leaves its perch or moves to the attack from a waiting-on position; there is a determined pursuit of prey, and if this dodges the attack or takes cover, the pursuer does not readily give up. He found that in 45 flights initially diagnosed as high intensity hunts, 69% ended in a kill; altogether, 58 hunting flights produced 30 kills (52%). Most hunting flights ending in a kill took only 3–4 minutes, and some lasted little more than 1 minute. At one Cornish coast eyrie, 15 still hunting flights averaged only 58 seconds before a kill was made or the hunt abandoned. At a Lakeland eyrie with young watched by Martin (1980), 49% of 76 hunting trips by the male were successful, but only 29% of those by the female: hunting trips were defined as periods of over 5 minutes spent away from the nesting cliff, and the female's were mostly shorter than her mate's.

The indications are that Peregrines mostly kill their prey early in the morning or in the evening and, except during the short days of winter or when they are feeding young and killing more often, they tend not to be seen at their work by

Female Peregrine in flight; Finland (photo: Jouni Ruuskanen)

humans. When bigger prey is taken, a falcon does not need to kill every day, and a pigeon represents about two days food even for the larger female. There will thus be a probable observer bias towards witnessing low intensity rather than high intensity chases, and the former may well be actually the more frequent. This would exaggerate the apparent inefficiency of hunting. Parker (1979) has taken an intermediate view. He found during observations at a Welsh coastal eyrie that in attacks on pigeons in which the outcome was known, 15% and 17% success were achieved by the female and male respectively. Success was low with flocks whereas single birds were often quite easily caught. Parker was convinced that the falcons were genuinely unable to catch the birds they missed and were not just failing to follow through 'playful' attacks. I have no doubt that Peregrines sometimes fail when they are pressing home an attack, but I have seen sufficient of their powers of flight to believe that genuine misses are much fewer than they might appear.

Nevertheless, hunting ability is likely to vary between individuals, and according to a variety of factors relating to both the quarry and the conditions at the time. While some wild adults at some times appear to be able to take prey at will, a range of circumstances must operate to make the outcome of the average high intensity hunt a good deal less certain.

Variation in hunting performance

The Peregrine's hunting technique gives the impression that it finds food easier to come by than raptors such as Kestrel, Buzzard and the harriers. These species appear to have to work harder in their hunting, and I find it easy to believe that they could at times have some difficulty in catching enough food for their needs. I have more trouble in envisaging the Peregrine finding it hard to satisfy its food requirements, though it would be unique among birds if it never experienced such problems. Bad weather and the disappearance of prey species through migration must create recurrent difficulties for all raptors. An important factor, so familiar to falconers, is the critical weight of a bird of prey. In captivity all species have to be kept carefully within quite narrow limits by regulating their food intake – too much and they will not hunt or come to the lure, too little and they readily go into an irreversible decline, refusing to feed and so setting up a vicious circle of weight loss which soon ends in premature death. This sensitive physiological condition must have some significance in wild Peregrines, and though the species evidently has some capacity for fasting, this is likely to depend greatly on the fat reserves in an individual at the time.

Several writers have pointed out that the most crucial period in a Peregrine's life is when the young birds of the year leave their parents and have to fend for themselves at the approach of winter. They are inexperienced as hunters and their survival depends on their capacity to develop quickly something of the hunting skills of the adults. In many bird species parental abilities, including the providing of food, are known to take up to several years to develop fully, and even one year old Peregrines are usually less capable hunters than fully adult birds. Treleaven (1980a) has noted many unsuccessful hunts by juveniles in the West Country during autumn and winter, and believes that many do not survive the winter. Beebe (1960) and Cade (1960) have surmised that young Peregrines fledged into the harsh environment of the Arctic and Subarctic breeding grounds are especially vulnerable, and that a fair proportion must perish each winter through starvation or related conditions.

This touches upon another interesting subject, the varying physical and even mental endowments of individual Peregrines. These are likely to stem from a combination of genetic and environmental differences. Most falconers believe strongly in the superior qualities of certain individual Peregrines and some go even further in attributing special abilities to the birds from certain eyries, consistently over a long period (e.g. Lundy Island in the Bristol Channel). The literature contains so many references to eyries noted for superior falcons, well scattered over Britain, that there is a temptation to dismiss the whole notion as whimsy handed down from a superstitious age. Dick Treleaven, whose knowledge of the hunting abilities of wild Peregrines is unrivalled, put it to me that this kind of thing should be relegated to the mythology of falconry.

This is not to deny that there may be differences in hunting abilities of trained Peregrines which the knowledgeable can recognise before they have seen the birds fly. Frederick II in his famous treatise on falconry (1250) had a good deal to say about the variations in individual quality in falcons, including Peregrines. Morlan Nelson has described to me the considerable range of performance which trained falcons show between individuals in their flying and hunting

Peregrine carrying prey (cuckoo); Japan (photo: Hisato Okamoto)

prowess, and how this relates to distinctive differences in certain attributes which the knowing falconers can detect. Features such as demeanour, stance and bearing, build, appearance of eye and fine detail of plumage all add up to a picture which the expert can interpret, in much the same way as the knowing horse trainer can pick out the potential winners. Interestingly, the same belief in superior qualities of individual birds is strongly held by pigeon fanciers, who go to great lengths in careful, selective breeding, and insist that champion homers are only to be bred from first class stock. A champion bird is additionally prized as the sire of other potential champions, and there seems to be a great deal of evidence that this view is justified in practice. The homer is obviously being selected for a somewhat artificial quaiity, the ability to win races, but this is also the kind of material on which natural selection must operate.

The special quality of certain individual Peregrines, at least in falconers' terms, thus seems to be an indisputable fact. Some individuals may for various reasons fail to develop their innate hunting ability properly and these will be the birds most prone to elimination under adversity, especially when they are youngsters. Most wild falcons which manage to reach adulthood will, however, be capable hunters. Falconers may be looking at only certain aspects of a bird's performance, and certain falcons may be good at a particular hunting technique while others excel at another. The special quality may be closer to 'trainability' than to intrinsic performance in flying. Moreover, captivity imposes its own artificial environment which may constrain the normal development of a Peregrine's hunting ability, and there are few unbiassed observers who would dispute

Peregrine about to take flight; Japan (photo: Hisato Okamoto)

that the average ability of a trained falcon is appreciably less than that of a wild bird, even though the best trained Peregrines – even immature birds – may achieve a hunting success of over 90% (Treleaven, 1980a). Trained falcons often start their hunts with an advantage, by having quarry flushed beneath them, under favourable conditions.

A possibly relevant factor here is preference shown by some Peregrines for certain prey species, which may lead to specific hunting adaptations. It is generally believed by falconers that a Peregrine trained to take a particular quarry is usually unsuccessful when flown at other quarry, e.g. a falcon trained to Rooks is no good at Red Grouse, and vice versa. Although this is thought to reflect a natural conditioning by early experience of prey species when a young falcon begins to hunt, there is likely again to be a degree of artificiality in this trait, because of the specialisation deliberately imposed by the trainer. The signs are that most wild Peregrines are relatively unspecialised, but there could be a

Flight studies of Peregrines, Japan (photo: Hisato Okamoto)

broader level of specialisation, e.g. a falcon which is accustomed to feeding on seabirds may always tend to seek such prey. Some Peregrines seem to have a strong preference for Puffins but this may not be a fixed adaptation, and it might be mainly a breeding season feature. Peale's Falcon is a highly specialised feeder within a fairly wide possible choice of prey (p. 118), but is unusual in this respect. It is possible that a tendency for Peregrines to vary in development of individual range of food preference, from narrow to wide, might affect their response to training for falconry.

Average hunting ability in the wild population is the more important aspect. Natural selection would be likely to have eliminated too wide variations in such performance. And while Peregrines can give such spectacular shows of hunting skill, there are indications that they do not waste unnecessary energy in pursuit of difficult quarry if easier targets offer themselves. Still hunting may be the favoured method because it conserves energy.

Selection of prey individuals

Some observers have suggested that Peregrines are drawn to attack birds showing particularly conspicuous plumage or feather patterns in flight. That most distinguished of pigeon fanciers, Charles Darwin, speaking of selection for advantageous colouring in animals, said '. . . hawks are guided by eyesight to their prey – so much so, that on parts of the Continent persons are warned not to keep white pigeons, as being most liable to destruction' (*Origin of Species*, Ch. IV). He is likely to have been referring to Peregrines. Geoffrey Horne, from his observations in Lakeland and Scotland, believes that Peregrines tend to select white or pale-coloured pigeons in preference to dark birds. But not enough information exists on the relative frequency of different colour forms within the pigeon populations exposed to predation for this choice to be properly quantified. Light-coloured feathers show up most readily amongst the pluckings of kills and may tend to be over-represented in prey analyses.

Some believe that it is not colour in itself, but individuality in a flock, which draws the attack, i.e. the Peregrine goes for the odd bird out, a dark individual in a light coloured pigeon flock, or vice versa. But the composition of the flocks is usually so mixed, and many of the pigeons are so mongrel in plumage, that it is difficult to obtain meaningful information on this point. Plumage differences are only one expression of individuality, and it may be that Peregrines tend to single out from a flock a bird which differs from the rest in other ways less obvious to the human eye.

Mueller (1971) has shown experimentally that in captive American Kestrels and Broad-winged Hawks, oddity in prey and specific searching image on the part of the raptor were more important in prey selection than conspicuousness of prey. Macintyre (1914, 1960) observed that Peregrines often stooped in feint at pigeon flocks in an attempt to scatter them and split off individuals. He described how a larger feral pigeon joined a flock of Rock Doves which was then attacked by a Peregrine; the flock wheeled sharply with the result that the feral pigeon was thrown out and at once cut down by the falcon. Pigeons scattered by a preliminary stoop usually attempted to re-group, sensing safety in the close-knit flock. Macintyre claimed that pigeons, both wild and feral, living near Peregrines learned to avoid attacks, and said that some experienced birds became so clever in dodging the strike that they could never be killed. Some also learned to evade capture by hugging the cliff face or flying alongside a wall over the moor. Other species have been described as keeping low over the sea for the same reason.

The 'odd-bird out' theory connects with the notion of the Peregrine as an agent of natural selection, weeding out the sub-standard individuals in the prey populations. There are a good many pointers to this as a valid hypothesis, but the only convincing evidence comes from an experiment by a German falconer G. Eutermoser, who flew a trained Peregrine at Rooks and then shot a similar sized sample at random. Of the Rooks killed by the falcon, 40% were not in peak condition (this category included birds markedly in moult, which might not have full powers of flight), whereas in the shot sample, only 23% were so classified. This is not a startling difference, but suggests a tendency to take the sub-standard bird. The ease with which raptors of various species, including Peregrines, are attracted to fluttering tethered pigeons at US hawk-trapping and banding stations suggests that the birds of prey in general will always go for an easy meal. Injured birds are evidently an attraction and Tuck's (1960) observation that Peregrines on Akpatok Island fed largely on injured Guillemots is interesting. This in turn makes it seem likely that birds which have been poisoned by seed dressings might be especially prone to predation during the initial stages of intoxication, whilst they were not capable of flying properly, but yet able to flap about and draw attention.

Occasional feeding on carrion is more likely to be the result of privation or weakened hunting ability rather than recourse to an easy meal. Piracy seems to be only occasional though Meinertzhagen (1959) recorded Peregrines robbing a Kestrel of a vole, a Sparrowhawk of an unidentified bird and a Honey Buzzard of a Bush Chat. The last instance involved triple piracy, in the sequence Sparrowhawk, Merlin, Honey Buzzard, Peregrine.

Hunting range

Another aspect of hunting behaviour concerns the distances travelled in catching prey. Non-breeders and all Peregrines outside the nesting season can and often do travel quite widely to hunt, and follow their food supply if this moves around. Baker (1967) has described the relative mobility and large hunting ranges of Peregrines wintering in Essex. Breeding falcons are tied to their eyries and have a more limited hunting range. At coastal eyries, Peregrines often hunt directly from the eyrie and kill within a few hundred metres (Treleaven, 1977; Beebe, 1960). This is especially so when the breeding place is surrounded by large numbers of seabirds. At inland haunts prey may also be taken close to the eyrie, but the falcons have a less assured food supply at hand and most of their prey is probably taken one kilometre or more away.

There is a widely held belief that Peregrines actually avoid killing prey species nesting close to their eyrie, but this is far from being an invariable rule. The subject is discussed in Chapter 12. Weir (1977, 1978) has given reasons for concluding that central Highland Peregrines took about 70% of their prey within 2 km of their nest cliffs, though females hunted up to 6 km away. Martin (1980), from observing a Lakeland eyrie at the head of a narrow valley for 4 weeks, surmised that these Peregrines (both sexes hunted) had to travel over 4 km before reaching suitable hunting ground where their main prey, pigeons and Starlings, were found. Mead (1969) reported that a ringed (banded) Curlew chick was found more than 13 km away in a Sutherland Peregrine eyrie before it could itself have covered more than a few hundred metres. Glutz *et al.* (1971) quote hunting distances for central European Peregrines of up to 15 km or more from the nest. In a radio telemetry study of a pair of Peregrines at an inland eyrie with young in California, Enderson and Kirven (1983) found that both adults tended to use flight corridors along ridges around the nest cliff. About 47% of the female's flights (139) and at least 65% of the male's (40) were more than 1 km. In 20 cases the pair were tracked to within 3 and 8 km (average 5 km) from the eyrie. Prey was apparently taken fairly uniformly in most directions from the eyrie. Enderson also reported that a radio-tagged female Peregrine in Colorado similarly ranged in all directions from its eyrie, with two flights up to 19 km. Hunter, Crawford and Ambrose (1988) found that most foraging flights on the Yukon River, Alaska, were within 3 km of eyries, but ranged up to 14 km away; and they quote other authors as reporting similar findings. In Idaho, telemetry tracking has shown that Prairie Falcons range at least 24 km from their nesting cliff in search of prey and that hunting ranges overlap widely (Cade and Dague, 1979).

The feeding routine of Peregrines through the breeding cycle is dealt with in Chapter 10.

CHAPTER 6

Nesting habitat

Part of the mystique of the Peregrine derives from its habit of breeding in formidable precipices where its eyries can often be assailed only with great difficulty, and by the daring. As early as 1248–50, Frederick II described in his treatise 'How to reach the eyrie'. . . . 'If, however, the eyrie is built in a fissure of a lofty rock, a man is secured to the end of a rope and descends or is lowered from the rim of the mountain or cliff to the level of the hollow in which the eyrie is built and, entering, lifts the [young] bird from the nest.' And in 1262, Albertus Magnus (1262–80) wrote of a falconer in the Alps who knew nesting places in huge cliffs where the eyries were either totally inaccessible or could be reached only by letting down a man from the top on a rope 'of a hundred paces' or more in length. The favourite technique for nest-storming is evidently over seven centuries old. The Peregrine may originally have evolved the habit of laying its eggs on a steep rock-face to minimise predation by various non-human mammals, but early man could have been a predator for long enough to have been an important influence as well.

Until recently, there were only occasional departures from the crag-nesting adaptation in Britain and Ireland, so that breeding distribution here has been rather strictly limited by the occurrence of suitable cliffs, whether coastal or inland. Not all cliffs are suitable, or some are more suitable than others, and it is interesting to look into the factors which affect the Peregrines' choice and influence fidelity of occupation. For this species, perhaps more than any other of our birds except the Golden Eagle and Raven, is famous for its use of traditional

160

Peregrine eyrie with eggs: sticks from the beginnings of a Raven nest scattered around the scrape; Galloway, southern Scotland (photo: D. A. Ratcliffe)

nesting places, occupied faithfully by generations of birds down the centuries. Such haunts must have special qualities to make them so attractive, at least in the eyes of a Peregrine.

THE NEST SITE

I prefer to use this term for the actual eyrie ledge on which the eggs are laid, and to avoid the more common usage of 'site' as loosely including the cliff itself or even its immediate surroundings. The nest sites themselves are often traditional

Peregrine eyrie with eggs: site on friable Silurian greywackes; the eggs were later destroyed by a rock fall; Dumfriesshire, southern Scotland (photo: D. A. Ratcliffe)

and Peregrines show a distinct preference for eyrie ledges used before, rather than those showing no signs of previous use. While a selection of different sites is typically used on any one cliff over a period of years, certain ledges may be especially favoured by successive occupants, and some have probably been used over hundreds of years. At the two Galloway haunts I visited in 1978, the Peregrines were using the identical scrapes that held the eggs during my first visits to these places, in 1946 and 1947.

The basic need is for a ledge big enough to hold a full brood of up to four large young. The Peregrine makes no nest, but with its feet scratches out a shallow bowl in a soily ledge or appropriates the unused nest of another cliff-nesting bird.

A typical scrape is about 17–22 cm in diameter and 3–5 cm deep; long used sites tend to have wider and deeper nest bowls than those newly formed. A level, vegetated shelf is typically chosen, and a ledge about half a metre long and of similar width will serve, though one of twice this length and slightly wider is better in giving the young more room for exercise when they are big. Nest ledges are up to several metres long, with up to four separate scrapes, and scrapes are sometimes made in large sloping banks on the cliff face, usually on a flatter part.

The vegetation of nest ledges is usually short and, since the majority of sites have been used many times, often much modified from its original state. There are marked differences between inland and coastal localities. While many inland cliffs have ledges covered mainly with ling heather, this plant is soon killed by bird droppings and so has usually been replaced by others on the traditional sites. Occasionally eggs are laid amongst heather in a site not used before or for many years. Shelves grown with bilberry (which may replace heather) are sometimes favoured, and those covered with great woodrush are often used. The vegetation is most typically grassy, though, either with fine-leaved grasses such as sheep's fescue and wavy hair; or with a luxuriant growth of the coarser sweet vernal grass on much-used ledges which have received heavy manuring. Other plants typically found around eyries on acidic cliffs include foxglove, woodsage, ivy, polypody, broad buckler fern, rosebay willow-herb, golden-rod and more locally, wall pennywort. Cliffs formed of basic rock, especially limestone, have a much more varied flora, and on the Breadalbane mountains of Perthshire, including Ben Lawers, some eyries are surrounded by a rich assemblage of Arctic–Alpines.

Many seacliff eyries are on ledges with mostly coastal plants, such as red fescue, sea pink, sea campion, sea plantain, scurvy grass and scentless mayweed. Others are amongst such familiar wayside and woodland plants as bluebell, red campion, great woodrush and sorrel, which often flourish on seacliffs.

Eyrie ledges from which successions of broods have fledged have often become almost devoid of vegetation and denuded down to the bare humus or soil beneath. These much-used ledges, or others immediately below, may have a considerable litter of old decaying bones of past prey, sometimes forming a layer mixed with the soil to a depth of 10 cm or more. On fresh or seldom-used ledges, the scrape may be only in the superficial litter, so that the eggs lie on a soft bed. More often the scrape is in the humus or soil beneath, and though loose material may accumulate to form an insulating layer, the eggs frequently rest on the bare earth, and can become mud-caked during wet weather. Sometimes the scrape contains loose angular gravel and there can be quite sharp projections of larger bedded stones or even bedrock, which would seem to pose a distinct risk of damage to the eggs. The woody roots of shrubs or small trees may also form irregularities in the nest scrape. Larger stones lying loose in the scrape are usually removed, but I have seen a nest in which gravel fragments appeared to have been raked together in the bottom of the scrape and formed a layer under the eggs, in the manner of a Stone Curlew 'nest'.

The Peregrine is not normally regarded as capable of even the most rudimen-tary attempt at nest building, but Nelson (1970) has suggested that debris-raking by the incubating bird may be vestigial nest-repairing activity. Scrapes made in

Peregrine eyrie with eggs in a recently robbed Raven nest; Dumfriesshire, southern Scotland
(photo: D. A. Ratcliffe)

the debris of old nests of other species sometimes leave sticks aligned round the perimeter, but sometimes twigs appear as if deliberately arranged around the edge of the scrape – a tendency still more marked in Merlin nests (see photograph on p. 161). The nests of other species are frequently appropriated, those of the Raven being the favourite choice. My own records of eyries (Table 9) show the frequency of use of nests built by other species, and indicate that about one third of all Peregrine layings are in disused Raven nests, in those parts of the country where Ravens are numerous.

Only ten of these eyries were coastal, and I do not know if the pattern is different for seacliff eyries. The records for North Wales are few, but Graham

Williams has given me additional data on 30 eyries in this district: 17 were on bare ledges, ten in old Raven nests and three on ledges with detectable remains of Raven nests. The adopted Raven eyries range from completely new structures robbed of their eggs only a few weeks earlier, to the last weathered vestiges gradually reduced over the years. When a new Raven nest is used, the eggs usually repose on the intact though often flattened wool lining. Occasionally, the wool lining is scratched out or pulled in a heap to one side, so that the eggs are then laid on the inner lining of moss, grass, litter or small sticks. Old Raven eyries gradually flatten and disintegrate, and Peregrines often scrape out a hollow in the residual debris. Occasionally an unfinished structure is used and the eggs lie on the rather large and hard twigs of the nest basket.

Less often, disused eyries of Buzzard and Golden Eagle are requisitioned, and I once saw a rock nest of a Carrion Crow in Galloway with a Peregrine repeat clutch. John Mitchell found that a Dunbartonshire pair had eggs in a rock nest of Carrion Crow built largely of discarded pieces of fencing wire. On the seacliffs, nests of Jackdaw, Herring Gull and, more rarely, Cormorant and Shag, have been found in use. On Orkney, Eddie Balfour once knew a Peregrine to lay in a seacliff nest of a Heron. In other countries other species' nests are used, including those of Black Stork, White-tailed Eagle, Rough-legged Buzzard and Lammergeyer.

Since cliff-nesting is an adaptation against predation, the value of the nest ledge depends largely on its inaccessibility and, to fulfil its function, it must have a steep fall of rock above and below. Ledges with some degree of overhang are evidently preferred, for they give protection against falling rock or ice, and bad weather as well as predators. The use of old Raven nests is often advantageous in this respect, for these are nearly always built under an overhang, and many are on bare rock ledges, including sloping ones, which Peregrines could not otherwise use. Seacliff eyries are often in much deeper recesses, and both Walpole-Bond (1938) and Nethersole-Thompson (1931) found that on the Sussex chalk cliffs a good many eyries were in quite distinct caves and holes. Now and then hollows between projecting pillars and the cliff face are used.

I have seen very few eyries which were within 6 m of either the top or bottom of big cliffs, but on small rocks the birds have much less choice in placing their eyrie. There appears to be no rule about the position of an eyrie on an inland cliff; but on seacliffs, especially on exposed coasts, they cannot be too near the base because of the storm-surge of waves up the face during on-shore gales, which can place any ledge within 15 m of mean sea level at risk to drenching by salt water. Walpole-Bond (1938) recorded that on the Sussex coast cliffs he saw several eyries only one metre from the cliff top, and the majority were located in the upper third of the precipice, but the majority of chalk cliff eyries were difficult of access without the use of ropes.

In general, fewer eyries on sea cliffs are climbable without ropes than on inland cliffs. This is partly because few seacliffs of less than 30 m in height are ever used by Peregrines. The majority of coastal eyries also have to be approached from above, often without the eyrie being visible, so that the climb cannot be properly assessed before starting. The tops of seacliffs are often loose and dangerous and many have the disconcerting tendency to steepen their angle from the summit downwards. Precipices cut by the sea also tend to be particularly steep and sheer. Their prevailing herbaceous vegetation, though sometimes deceptively lush, is

Peregrine eyrie with eggs: on a broad grassy shelf; Galloway, southern Scotland (photo: D. A. Ratcliffe)

far less dependable for handholds than the tough, woody growths of heather and bilberry so commonly found on inland crags.

Roosting places are also traditional and there are usually several on each nesting cliff. Preferred places are small ledges, knobs and projections on steep bare rock, especially under overhangs, and those in use are revealed by the streaks and splashes of white droppings below, sometimes lying so copiously as to form a conspicuous patch. On more broken and vegetated cliffs the roosting places are often far less obvious. Weather conditions may affect the use of different roosts, but the male typically selects a perch on an adjacent part of the cliff, at some little distance from the eyrie, when his mate is sitting.

THE NESTING CLIFF

The quality of a cliff as nesting habitat for the Peregrine depends largely on the degree of protection it affords to the eggs and young. A cliff must have suitable ledges to hold the eyrie, but only when cliffs are extremely small are they devoid of possible nest ledges, and most rock faces of 10 m or more in height have ledges good enough to hold an eyrie. Even the clean-cut faces of quarries often have ledges and recesses that falcons can use. Many large precipices have suitable ledges vastly in excess of the number ever used. Availability of nest sites *per se* is thus seldom limiting and the attractions of the nesting cliffs tend to be related to other features, especially those affecting the accessibility of the eyrie ledges, though some small faces may be marginal in offering only a very few ledges.

Size, steepness and remoteness of nesting cliff

In general, Peregrines favour the highest and steepest cliffs available. In most districts, both coastal and inland, precipices greater than 150 m high are few, and in the mountains some of the tallest crags lie at too great an elevation climatically. Because of wave surge, few coastal cliffs of less than 30 m are suitable for Peregrines, but inland rocks down to mere boulders are used if nothing better is available. A coastal scarp, mountain side or corrie face consisting of a mass of tiered cliff with no single crag exceeding 30 m will, however, be more attractive than a single rock of this height. Indeed, it is often difficult to know what figure to give for vertical height when there is a broken precipice of this kind. The lateral extent of a cliff is also important, and long escarpments tend to be more favoured than short faces of similar height. Though most cliffs have vertical or over-hanging sections, few in Britain maintain a continuous overall angle of over 80° to the horizontal. Cliffs formed of slate and shale tend to be more broken and sloping than those cut from harder rocks, though granite and gneiss often produce slabby or rounded outcrops. Peregrines naturally seek out the steepest rock faces, but will nest on slabby cliffs of 45–50° if these are high and/or broken by short vertical pitches.

Height and steepness of a nesting cliff have an obvious influence on security of the eyrie ledges and hence on suitability for Peregrines. In general, the birds appear to be attracted to the tallest precipices on the principle of 'the bigger the cliff, the safer the eyrie'. It has been suggested that such preference is also influenced by the likelihood that command of view and still-hunting advantage increase with size of cliff. The nest security factor is, nevertheless, likely to be dominant. Golden Eagles and Ravens show exactly the same preference for the biggest cliffs, yet their hunting and foraging styles are quite different from the Peregrine's, and both are equally adapted to nesting in trees.

Nowadays, with the aid of modern climbing techniques, there must be very few Peregrine eyries which could not be reached, at least by skilled climbers. Were they still occupied, a few of the eyries on the Southern England chalk cliffs could still remain impregnable, from the looseness of the rock and the severity of the overhangs under which they were placed. A considerable number of eyries must nevertheless continue to be quite inaccessible to the ordinary run of mortals bent on intrusion, and the cliff-nesting habit has not in general become any less safe.

In his studies of Peregrines in the Eastern United States, Joe Hickey found that both height of the cliff and remoteness from constant human presence, with their implied influence on security of the eyries, were important in determining suitability and constancy of occupation. He combined these two factors under the term 'cover', and said that the minimum height of rock acceptable to these Peregrines varies inversely with the degree of wilderness to which the cliff or cut-bank is exposed and directly with the degree of human disturbance in the immediate vicinity of the nesting ledge. Hickey proposed a grouping into first, second and third class cliffs according to their size, and the consequent effect of this factor on tenacity of occupation. He found that very large, commanding cliffs were never deserted no matter how much destruction of adults or nest robbery took place (first class). At lesser cliffs, death of one adult did not necessarily cause abandonment of the haunt, but death of both adults could cause desertion for an indefinite period; there was also a greater susceptibility to casual disturbance (second class). At small, low rocks, death of one adult could result in permanent desertion of the cliff by its mate and there was even greater sensitivity to casual disturbance; regularity of occupation of such rocks increased markedly with the degree of wilderness in their location (third class).

Hickey's ideas are broadly applicable to Britain and Ireland also. Most of the inland cliffs regularly occupied in the face of relentless keeper destruction were large precipices. Conversely, most former Peregrine haunts which became completely deserted before 1955 were low-lying and close to roads or houses, and had low cliffs with eyrie ledges much exposed to disturbance. The majority of occasional nesting places were also small crags, where the nest sites were relatively easy to approach. Peregrines evidently respond to the appearance of cliffs according to their conditioning from the effects of human disturbance on survival and breeding performance. Large cliffs may not protect them from being killed, but they increase the chances that one or both birds and their nest will escape destruction. Small cliffs greatly increase the vulnerability of nests to robbing, and the ease with which humans can surprise the birds at close quarters. When the situation of the eyrie also increases the frequency of disturbance, the risk of breeding failure is magnified further.

There is a marked tendency for Peregrines nesting in small cliffs to be less successful in breeding, or even surviving, than those resorting to large crags. And the closer that these small rocks are to human dwellings or vehicular access, the greater is the likelihood that damaging disturbance will occur. Over a long period, human presence has come to spell danger, and natural selection has led the birds to minimise their exposure to it. The tendency to nest in the largest and safest cliffs, and to ignore the small and unsafe ones could have become fixed in the population through its obvious survival value. This could explain why some small cliffs have remained deserted for quite long periods, even though they are visited by Peregrines at times.

It is clear, from the remains of kills, that most deserted Peregrine haunts are visited at intervals by falcons which do not stay and, indeed, adult Peregrines without a territory are probably prospecting potential nesting grounds in the hills and on rocky coasts for much of the year. There is likely to be a range of individual responsiveness to the attractions of a possible nesting cliff, some birds being readily stimulated to stay, take up territory and seek a mate, whilst others will simply pass on until they find a vacant rock with much stronger attractions. A rather unsuitable vacant haunt, such as a small rock or enclosed ravine will thus be attractive only to a minority of Peregrines, and reoccupation will then depend on the fairly small chance of one of these 'tolerant' individuals happening to come across such a place. Perhaps, too, both of the pair would have to be capable of accepting a site which is on the limits of the suitable, and this would increase still further the chances of such a place remaining vacant. Hickey has inferred that pairing in the Peregrine may be based on the selection of a nesting territory, with females responding to males in possession, rather than on sexual selection directly. He stated that females often desert second-class cliffs where males show a tendency to remain. Attractions of a cliff, in terms of good ledges for courtship displays, may also operate through the psychological conditioning of the birds during the development of pair integrating behaviour.

Occupation of a new or deserted haunt can involve full breeding in the first year, though it may take several years, during which the place is held first by a single bird and then by a pair. There is a tendency for the process to become slower with decreasing quality of cliff, and some third-class cliffs may be held by single birds for several years and then become deserted again without breeding having occurred.

In Britain, there appear to be quite marked regional differences in the attractions of nesting cliffs, depending on the quality of those available. In the Lake District and North Wales, where inland cliffs of 60–100 m in height are numerous, few rocks of less than 30 m are used by Peregrines, and such places have the status of third-class cliffs. Yet in areas where big cliffs are scarcer, such as the Pennines, Cheviots, Southern Uplands, parts of Wales and some Irish mountains there are many crags of only 10–20 m which have the status of first class cliffs. In Lakeland the failure of Peregrines to nest on certain lower crags left gaps in regularity of distribution; yet crags of similar size in less rugged districts within a distance of 40–80 km were occupied annually. It is as though a high standard of acceptability has been set in Lakeland, with prospective nesters foregoing the opportunity of breeding, rather than accept sub-standard cliffs. And in Galloway, where some pairs nest regularly in 15–20 m cliffs, two broken escarpments of some 100 m were only occasionally used, though they are ideally located for regular nesting: the difference is that the smaller, regularly occupied crags all offer at least one good, safe nesting site, whereas the broken cliffs do not.

Some of these ideas need re-examination in the light of events stemming from the recent expansion of Peregrine population. The increase in numbers has involved not only the occupation of many more first- and second-class cliffs, but also an apparent relaxation in the limits of the acceptable at the bottom end of the scale. During the last 10 years, there has been a marked increase in the use of third-class cliffs, and many of these are now held regularly. Nesting on man-made structures is increasing rapidly, and the same could be true of ground-nesting. The trend is evidently partly a response to the increasing recruitment pressure under the favourable balance between output and mortality, but must also involve some degree of adjustment to human disturbances.

When the nesting cliffs are high and the eyrie ledges inaccessible except to skilled cragsmen, Peregrines have always tolerated any amount of casual disturbance. The pre-war occupation of the Sussex and Kent chalk cliffs is a good example. People constantly passed along the top or bottom of many of these, but on the 40–150 m vertical faces the eyries could only be reached with ropes if at all, and the birds were undeterred. Walpole-Bond (1938) and others have described south-coast eyries on sections of cliff down which rubbish was regularly dumped, and one clutch had a piece of cardboard resting alongside. The increasingly frequent nesting in working quarries and on town buildings is now the clearest evidence that, when the eyries are not visited and their owners remain unmolested, Peregrines become completely indifferent to human presence. Ironically, beyond a certain level, the proximity of people becomes a safety factor in itself – if the birds are in too public a place, there is a much reduced chance that any individual will attempt to interfere with them. The crucial point is the degree to which Peregrines learn that human beings no longer spell danger, and may even spell advantage. This changed conditioning is likely to be promoted by the now frequent success of birds nesting in places close to people.

Rock climbing is, however, creating an increasing problem through incidental disturbance. The proximity of climbers to the nests, and the length of time they spend on the cliffs, can be a serious interference with nesting activities. Climbing in Lakeland long ago displaced Peregrines from two large crags; the birds found alternative crags, but in both instances these were smaller faces with less secure sites. With the great increase in climbing since 1945, many inland Peregrine cliffs in districts such as Lakeland and Snowdonia are now climbed regularly, and the same is true of numerous seacliff haunts in various regions. The effects are variable. If climbing begins before the falcons have eggs, they may simply move to an alternative cliff to nest, but if it begins afterwards, they may either desert or attempt to carry on. The timing of the Easter holiday can be relevant to this point. During recent years there have been many instances of Peregrines deserting their eggs or losing their young through chilling because of rock-climbing. Occasionally, clutches have been trodden upon, perhaps inadvertently. Yet there have also been numerous instances of Peregrines rearing young on cliffs where they were disturbed by climbers a good deal. Much depends on the particular circumstances, especially the point in the breeding cycle when disturbance occurs, the frequency of climbing, the closeness of the routes to the eyrie and the size of the cliff. Some individuals also appear more tolerant to such activity, and others may well learn to accept it. Yet a few are so held by the attractions of the biggest cliffs that they will continue to risk nesting there even when smaller but quite suitable alternatives occur quite close at hand.

It is only the larger cliffs which can successfully accommodate both Peregrines and climbers. The failure of falcons to nest recently on many of the former breeding places in the Peak District, Cheviots and elsewhere is because the outcrops here are simply too small and the disturbance level to the birds is inevitably too high. Climbers are often quite noisy, and their constant presence within a short distance of all the possible nest and roost sites is just too much for the falcons to stand. There is not room for both at the same time, and there may be no undisturbed alternative rocks where the falcons can go. While Peregrines are showing some capacity to adapt to climbing disturbance, the scope for such adjustment is necessarily limited, and a good deal will depend on how far the climbers themselves are prepared to regulate their activities to give the birds a reasonable chance of breeding successfully in the localities concerned.

The question of disturbance, and its effects on continuity of occupation of a territory, are dealt with in more detail in Chapter 10.

Aspect, altitude and position

For Peregrines, the aspect of a cliff appears in Britain and Ireland to have no effect on its suitability as a nesting place. When there is a wide choice of aspect, as sometimes occurs between the various alternative rocks within an inland territory, no preference is shown. The aspect of seacliff eyries necessarily corresponds mainly to the geography of the coastlines, e.g. along the south coast of England, breeding places necessarily show a preponderance of southerly aspect. While Table 12 might suggest a degree of selection for aspect in inland districts, I believe it more probably again reflects a non-random orientation of suitable cliffs in some regions. In some mountain districts there is a prevalence of suitable crags facing between north and east, evidently as a result of more intensive glacial action on these shaded aspects. In countries with greater extremes of climate there is some evidence of aspect preferences. For instance, in the hot, dry conditions of some arid zones, Peregrines appear to prefer a shaded aspect and a recessed nest cavity which reduce desiccation and heat stress, especially for the young. Conversely, under the frigid climate of the Arctic there is some indication of preference for sun-exposed aspects, presumably for their greater warmth.

Altitude is not a relevant factor at coastal nesting stations, but assumes some importance inland. Until recently, rather few pairs nested below 200 m in inland areas to the south of Scotland, because inland cliffs lying below this altitude tend to be rather small and close to roads and dwellings, with the vulnerability to deliberate disturbance which this usually implies. This is much less true of northern Scotland, where large areas of wilderness country lie below 200 m. During the last 20 years there has been a decided increase in low altitude inland nesting, associated with overflow of population from 'saturated' traditional haunts, and the growing adaptation to sites on third-class cliffs, quarries and buildings (Table 10). Many pairs now nest below 200 m inland in England and Wales, as well as Scotland.

The Peregrine has a fairly distinct upper limit to breeding in Britain, where few nesting cliffs lie above 640 m. This evidently reflects climatic harshness at the higher altitudes, not only involving frequent mist and rain, but even more the low temperatures expressed in severity of frost and duration of snow cover. When a wide choice is available, Peregrines usually avoid the high-lying cliffs where conditions can be truly Arctic at nesting time. This explains why some of the largest and most spectacular mountain cliffs in Britain are without Peregrines, such as the upper precipices of Ben Nevis, Creag Meagaidh, Beinn Eighe, Scafell and Snowdon. Falcons breed in all these massifs, but on lesser faces at lower altitudes. Strangely, though, the most elevated nesting haunt known in our islands is at about 1050 m on fierce crags in the Cairngorms area, in a bleak and Arctic setting more appropriate to the Gyr Falcon (Claire Geddes). A second breeding station in this area is almost as high. Conditions here are frigid indeed at normal nesting time in an average year, and it is hardly surprising that the occupying pairs tend to lay later than most. Another high-lying haunt which must test the hardiness of this adaptable bird is at 825 m on the Ben Lawers range, another massif holding a good deal of late snow. These are nevertheless exceptions, evidently resulting from an absence of suitable crags at lower levels within the territories.

There is a tendency for the average elevation of eyries to be less in the northern Highlands than to the south of the Great Glen, and this accords with the general altitudinal depression of life zones of plants and animals in a north-westerly direction within the Highlands (Table 10). In the uplands, the Peregrine is thus no more than a sub-montane species. It is not so much a true mountain bird as a wide-spectrum predator whose breeding requirements are especially well satisfied in mountainous country. In other countries with warmer climate, the Peregrine nests up to much greater elevations than in Britain, reaching 3,050 m in North America (Bond, 1946). Altitude is a relative factor and Peregrines have to nest below the level at which extent of snow-cover and frequency/intensity of frost are limiting at the nesting time in any region. Extremes of cold can prove fatal to young as well as to eggs (Chapman, 1924).

The position of the nesting cliff varies less in coastal than in inland situations. Many seacliff haunts fall into deep water, but some have an undercliff or storm beach below. A few are on bluffs overlooking the sea, but standing well back, at the crest of an intervening slope. The great coastal Irish escarpments of Slieve

League in Donegal and Croaghaun on Achill Island are virtually mountains cut away on one side by the sea. Many types of position are acceptable to Peregrines inland, from deep corries remote in the mountains to rocks overlooking cultivated valleys, plains, large lakes or rivers. Many are in virtually treeless situations, but the species is equally at home on tree-grown faces situated in the midst of forest, provided the nesting ledges and look-out posts are not too hidden by trees.

A commanding outlook is evidently preferred, but most large crags provide this anyway, as do much lower faces high up on long slopes. The smaller and narrower shut-in ravines, where the view is somewhat restricted are less favoured. Of 708 inland nesting haunts recorded in 1979, only 38 were in stream ravines or gorges, and of these only 12 were occupied regularly. By 1991, under the growing competition for preferred nesting situations, at least 121 out of 1145 recorded inland haunts (including alternatives) were in stream ravines, many of them small and shut-in. While most of the additional ravines have been too recently occupied to judge regularity of occupation, at least 87 were occupied in 1991. Most of these stream ravines are in gently contoured moorland country where frontal crags are scarce, and 42 are in the Southern Uplands. The photograph on p. 97 shows a particularly secluded Peregrine nesting place in a weird chasm, deeply carved by a small stream into the rounded hills of the Scottish Borders. In such places the sentinel bird usually selects a look-out stance to give an unrestricted view since the nest ledges may be rather hidden. Big river gorges with a wider outlook are evidently attractive, and now include several examples in lowland, wooded country.

Tors are not favoured nesting places, at least nowadays, for there are rather few with rocks of sufficient size and such places also have a fascination for human beings, who create too much disturbance. Breeding seems to be unknown on the Dartmoor tors, even in their quieter days, when several pairs of Ravens built their nests on these granite summits, but may well have occurred in more ancient times. There was one such nesting place on a rock-crowned hill amongst the grouse moors of the eastern Highlands, but this has been deserted in recent years, evidently because it became too much a place of pilgrimage for week-end hikers.

Quarries are man-made cliffs that provide much the same features and attractions for Peregrines as natural cliffs. Many command a wide outlook, though some are more akin to huge holes in the ground, and provide little view over the surrounding land. The faces tend to be sheer and clean-cut, and can be up to 100 m high, though the majority are around 10–35 m. They usually have ledges which in disused quarries may eventually develop a cover of vegetation and shallow soil, but even fresh-cut ledges may have enough fine material for Peregrines to scrape a nest hollow. Some have Ravens whose old nests provide additional scope. In 1979 there were at least 25 known quarry nesting places of Peregrines in Britain, though few were in regular use. By 1991, the number had risen to at least 139, of which 121 were occupied that year. Although a few quarry haunts are alternatives to natural cliffs, the majority are in places where breeding would otherwise be inhibited by lack of suitable rocks. With around a tenth of our Peregrine population now nesting in quarries, these man-made excavations have substantially boosted total numbers. Northern Ireland also had no less than 38 pairs occupying quarries in 1991. In the Republic of Ireland, Norriss (in press) reported 60–65 quarry resting pairs in 1991, and a survey of 48 quarries in eastern Ireland in 1991–92 found 44% occupied by Peregrines (Moore *et al.* 1992).

Many of these quarry haunts are in low-lying situations, close to public roads and dwellings. Even more remarkably, many of them are still being worked, and the falcons ignore the continuous disturbance, including frequent rock-blasting, which appears to cause them no more concern than thunder. One pair which actually lost their eggs when their ledge was blasted away simply moved to another part of the quarry and repeated there. These quarry nests have a good success rate, and some in worked sites are especially safe as the quarry managers and workers ensure their protection. The list includes two pairs nesting in opencast coal workings, and another couple in old mine excavations. Yet another two pairs have nested for some years on the scarped slopes of old industrial waste tips.

In recent years, several people have reported success in creating or restoring nest ledges for Peregrines on small and only marginally suitable rocks. This has induced hitherto reluctant pairs to nest on new outcrops, to continue nesting where the only safe site had slipped away, and to move from 'walk-in' ledges to others more difficult to reach (G. Horne, R. Roxburgh, G. Carse).

The photographs in Chapters 2 to 4 illustrate some of the different types of nesting cliff favoured by Peregrines in Britain.

USE OF ALTERNATIVE SITES AND CLIFFS

The use of alternative nest ledges and cliffs is a variable matter in which there are no set rules, and the numbers used in any one territory depend very much on the choice available. Some small inland cliffs offer a very limited choice of movement between different ledges, whereas many seacliffs provide almost endless scope for change of site. Most pairs of Peregrines have at least four different ledges used as alternatives on the same cliff, and some have many more. A single ledge can have up to four separate scrapes. John Mitchell has given me details of an inland Stirlingshire haunt in which eight different ledges were used in the nine seasons 1965–73, though one of these involved a repeat clutch. A ninth ledge was used in 1978. Forrest said that in one North Wales coastal haunt 'there are at least a dozen spots that have been occupied as eyries in successive years'. By contrast, on an inland Galloway cliff for which I have details of 27 eyries during 1947–78, only four different sites were used, with 11, ten, five and one nests; but the longest run of successive eyries in the same site was only three. An analysis of my own records shows that for 23 territories in northern England and southern Scotland in which five or more eyries were seen (totalling 185 eyries with an average of eight eyries per territory), 100 different ledges and 40 different crags were used. Thus, for every eight eyries seen per territory, the number of different ledges averaged just over four and the number of crags just under two.

An alternative cliff can at times be difficult to define. Many inland corrie haunts or long lines of crag have several quite distinct faces used by the falcons over a period, but all belonging to the same escarpment. The term is most readily applicable in those nesting territories where the birds resort to a selection of separate rocks, each of which lies within a different catchment. On rocky coasts the term is equally applicable to separate headlands with no suitable ground between, but on long, continuous lines of seacliff the idea breaks down, for there may be up to several pairs of Peregrines breeding on what is topographically a single precipice.

The largest number of alternative inland nesting cliffs I have known to be used in one territory is nine, in an area of Galloway with many scattered small crags. In one Lakeland territory at least seven different crags, most of them quite large, are known to have been used, and in a second, up to six. Knowledge of the use of both alternative ledges and cliffs depends very much on the length of the observation period. The longer the number of years a particular territory is watched, the greater will be the chances of finding changes in preference, given that a choice between different ledges and cliffs is available. For instance, in Lakeland and the Southern Uplands, where I have fairly full data over a long period, the average number of alternative crags per territory is 2·5; whereas for all other inland districts, where my data are much less adequate, the average appears to be only 1·5. The pattern in any territory can change completely between one decade and the next, or it may remain more or less the same.

Much depends on the terrain. If there is only one good cliff in a territory, the occupying pair are perforce limited to movement between different parts of the same precipice. If there is a wide choice of suitable rocks, the birds tend to move about a good deal over a period of several decades. Figure 16 gives some idea of the variations to be found in a single district. From 1959 to 1960, during the population crash, Jim Birkett found that one Lakeland pair moved 12 km for a repeat laying, but this was to a crag in an adjoining territory which had become vacant. In several inland districts, a spread of 5·0–6·5 km between the alternatives in one territory is not unusual, but the average is much less: 2·7 km in the Southern Uplands (28 territories); 2·4 km in northern England (40 territories); and 2·1 km in North Wales (24 territories). The smaller spread in North Wales probably reflects the shorter observation period for this district, compared with the other two. The recent 'doubling up' in many territories under population increase has reduced the scope for use of alternative cliffs in districts such as Snowdonia, Lakeland and the Southern Uplands.

The use of alternatives, both ledges and crags, appears to depend on individual caprice of the birds as well as external factors. Peregrines which lose their first clutch nearly always lay their repeat on a different ledge, and there is some tendency to choose an alternative crag. On the other hand, Geoff Horne and I find, from examination of our records, that there is no pattern of alternative site use between different years according to success or failure. Pairs which succeed are as likely to move to a different site the following year, and those which fail are as likely to use the same site, as the other way round.

Nesting cliffs and ledges evidently have a clear identity over a long period for the Peregrines themselves. This is not simply a matter of continuity of occupation for, when a long-deserted territory is re-occupied, the new birds often resort to the same selection of cliffs and ledges as their long-dead predecessors. Good cliffs have obvious attractions for any Peregrine, and favoured eyrie ledges are also often distinctive, with a rather bare or green, grassy appearance, and scrapes which may last for years. There is characteristically a persistent green staining on the bare rock below eyries and perches, produced by the growth of tiny algae where a wash of nutrients from the droppings seeps down the face. This green-ness lasts for up to 10 years after the last occupation by Peregrines (or Ravens, which produce exactly the same effect) but gradually disappears. The same roosting or look-out perches and plucking places are also frequently used over a long period and seem to have comparable permanence of identity. These recognisable features may actually help to draw prospecting Peregrines to vacant breeding cliffs. The presence of breeding Ravens, with their usual selection of old eyries, may also be something of an attraction.

ADAPTATION TO OTHER KINDS OF NESTING PLACE

Although Peregrines in Britain and Ireland have always been regarded as cliff-nesters, occasional departures from this habit have long been known. Nesting on the broken, rocky banks of moorland streams occurred here and there, but was usually unsuccessful and so seldom persisted for long. There was the lack of fidelity typical of third class cliffs under disturbance. As an example, Ernest Blezard saw such an eyrie in a remote valley of the Langholm Hills, Dumfriesshire, in 1923, but the keeper had already shot the female from her eggs and nesting was never proved at this place again.

Peregrines with good cliffs will occasionally leave the safer ledges for some spot which can be easily reached by humans without climbing. In so doing they may gain from the greater difficulty of locating the eyrie, as a result of its unexpected position. Raymond Laidler accidentally came on an eyrie in heather on one of several sloping ledges of a Galloway cliff whilst going from one known nest site to another. By chance I came across an old and evidently successful eyrie similarly placed on the heathery slope of a tiered cliff in Arran, and in Ayrshire Will Murdoch saw a nest in woodrush at the foot of a projecting rock on a steep heather slope. At one Cumberland haunt the falcons sometimes used a scrape on the heathery crest of a crag buttress, as an alternative to less accessible sites lower down.

Eyries to which a human could easily walk were recorded a number of times on small, uninhabited, rocky islands off the Scottish coast. Seton Gordon visited such an eyrie on a Hebridean island, and said he could have caught the sitting falcon in its recess on a rocky slope. Ussher said that in Ireland, 'In rare cases, as

Ground nesting Peregrine with small young: Finland (photo: Seppo Saari)

on marine islands, the eyrie can be approached on foot. Two gentlemen and two
ladies landed on such an island, and seeing a Peregrine hatching, set out to reach
the spot by different routes. The ladies got to it first'. F. C. R. Jourdain mentions
a Peregrine with eggs in deep heather on an islet off the Welsh coast where there
were no cliffs and the eyrie was only 15 m above sea-level. Rocky islands in the
larger lakes seem not to be recorded as nesting habitat in Britain, but are perhaps
too much visited by fishermen and mammal predators.

Gilbert and Brook (1931) mention an eyrie on a mere rocky slope on the
Pembrokeshire coast, but the site was so protected by impenetrable thickets of
bramble as to be almost unreachable. It is interesting that Orkney, which lacks
most British mammalian predators and is celebrated for its numbers of ground-
nesting birds of prey, including the Kestrel, has also had ground-nesting Peregrines. Groundwater (1974) quotes from a letter from a Mr Moar in 1961, stating
that some years previously a pair of Peregrines nested 'in the Harray peat hill' for
several seasons, evidently in long heather. An eyass was rescued from the site
during a great moor fire one year. Buckley and Harvie-Brown also quote, 'On 5
June 1886 Mr Halcro told Mr Fortescue that he saw a Peregrine fly out from
some long heather on the steep south-west side of Waulkmill Bay, but on
reaching the spot he found only the beginning of a nest.'

The most remarkable record of ground-nesting in Britain was made in 1928 by W. J. Ashford, who was shown a Peregrine nest in 'a shallow depression in the short scrubby heather at the base of a stump of a small Scots pine, standing on a dry part of a flat, boggy and unfrequented heather common in west Hampshire.' The eggs had been taken by the boy who found the nest so that the attempt failed. The record was confirmed by two independent sources, and Ashford revealed (in litt. to J. H. Salter) that the locality was Parley Common. *The Handbook of British Bird* (1939) states that ground nesting took place in this locality in two successive years, but I have found no second record. Peregrines have occasionally been found nesting on sand dunes in the Netherlands, as is the habit of Merlins locally in Britain. The nearest approach to sand dune nesting in this country was in 1957, when a pair laid four eggs in a 'walk-in' site on the low outcropping rock-ridge crossing the Newborough Dunes on Anglesey. The clutch was eventually deserted after being incubated well beyond full term (A. W. Colling).

From 1975, there has been a remarkable increase in Peregrine use of 'walk-in' nest sites on broken outcrops and rocky banks, and at least ten instances of genuine ground nesting. Most of these are in gently contoured moorland areas with few if any good crags, and in places remote from human disturbance. Such nest sites are mostly readily accessible to foxes and other mammal predators, but a few are on steep slopes covered with long heather, bilberry or gorse, where access is not easy. Success rate is not high, but even some of the ground nests have fledged young. In one little-trodden upland area of Northern Ireland, J. H. Wells reported in 1979 that several pairs of Peregrines were nesting regularly, and with a surprisingly good success rate, on very small rocks with extremely accessible eyries.

An intriguing ground nest was found by Dick Roxburgh in southern Ayrshire in 1983. It was in a newly afforested area of low moorland, where a landslip on a moderately steep slope above a small stream had left an exposed face of peat and glacial till. The nest with three eggs was amongst rushes on flat ground above and at the very edge of this small scarp – 'a Curlew type site', as the finder put it. The young hatched but disappeared. In 1983 also, a pair of Peregrines reared three young in an old Hen Harrier nest amongst long heather on a fairly steep slope of Deeside moors, Aberdeenshire (J. Parkin). And in 1984, two young were fledged from a nest on a bilberry knoll on a steepish moorland slope in the Blair Atholl area of Perthshire (A. Payne). These appeared to be once-off nestings, but two pairs in different parts of the Southern Uplands have used the same ground sites at least twice. One, in south-east Ayrshire, used a sheep-track terraced moraine bank above a stream in 1987 and 1988, and was successful the second time (R. Roxburgh). Another, in the Pentland Hills near Edinburgh, laid in a hollow under a 2 m outcrop on the steep side of a small gill in 1987 and 1989, but failed both times (G. Carse and A. Averis). Other genuine ground nests were reported from the Berwyn Mountains in north Wales in 1990 and 1991 (I. Williams), Galloway in 1990 (V. Fleming), and east Sutherland in 1990 (R. Dennis).

The Hampshire ground nest was evidently the nearest counterpart here to the Peregrine's habit of nesting on the hummocks of the great bogs forming open areas within the Boreal and Subarctic forests of north-eastern Europe (see pp. 177 and 179). According to Linkola and Suominen (1969), about half the former Finland population (totalling around 1000 pairs) bred on the dry ridges

Site of ground eyrie with young on a dry mound of bog; Ledum palustre *and* Betula nana *around nest (photo: Seppo Saari)*

and hummocks separating the multitudes of large pools on the surfaces of these aapa mires raised bogs, and this was also the favourite nesting habitat in Estonia (Kumari, 1974). John Wolley also took several Peregrine clutches in 1848 from hillocks in bogs in Enontekis Lappmark and East Bothnia (Finland). Similar patterned pool and hummock bogs occur widely, though on a smaller scale, in western and northern Scotland, and are represented as far south as the New Forest in southern England; but, with the above exception, Peregrines have never been known to nest on them. On the mainland of Britain, foxes may be a strong inhibition to ground-nesting, as well as humans, though I am told that the Finnish bog eyries were potentially exposed to fox predation too. Kumari said that in Estonia most eyries were in situations hardly accessible to man, in the middle of the swampiest hollows, amongst a maze of bog pools, or on islets of very large pools. Eggs were often laid at the foot of stunted pines or birches which are sparsely scattered over the bogs.

Regular ground nesting in dry habitats seems to be most frequent in Siberia, where mounds on the tundras are often favoured (Dementiev, 1951). Haviland (1926) in her description of the Yenisei tundras said, 'Peregrine Falcons and Rough-legged Buzzards choose the ancestral site; and as cliffs and trees are not available, they build their eyries on the summits of low mudhills'. Commensal nesting associations between Peregrines and geese or other birds are frequent in these situations, and may give increased protection against foxes to the falcons as well as the other species (Chapter 12). Siberian Peregrines nest in a wide range of habitats from almost flat tundra to typical sheer cliffs. Seebohm (1880) described an intermediate type on the Petchora River, where two eyries were on grassy mounds mid-way up steep mud cliffs fronting the river delta. The 'cut-banks' of large rivers flowing through recent sedimentary, fluvio-glacial or loessic deposits are in fact a frequent Peregrine breeding habitat in North America and northern Eurasia, but are virtually lacking in Britain. The nearest parallel is the sand bank of a river in Co. Tyrone, Northern Ireland, where a pair possibly attempted to nest in 1991 (J. Milburne).

These earth cliffs are usually steepest at the top, and tail off into a bank of declining angle. Richard Fyfe and Harry Armbruster showed me many examples along the Bow River in southern Alberta, where Peregrines once nested but only Prairie Falcons remained during my visit, in 1973. Some examples had a 'cliff' of only about 6 m high, but so protected by their crumbly nature and steep bank below that ropes were still needed to reach the eyries. The scrapes were on natural ledges and hollows which tended to fall away through rapid erosion of the unstable faces, and my Canadian friends simply descended on a rope to excavate new ones with a shovel! These were soon taken over by the Prairie Falcons, and by providing nest sites on cut-banks where previously there were none, they were able actually to increase the breeding population. British Peregrines on the whole nest on stable cliffs where rock-falls are infrequent, but on the chalk cliffs of southern England many eyries were on extremely friable rock prone to sudden disintegration, and slaty crags in the hills of Wales and the Southern Uplands are also subject to rock-falls.

Some older works refer to tree-nesting by Peregrines in Britain and Ireland before 1800, but the records are unacceptable. The chances of confusion with the Goshawk are too great and the application of the local name 'Gled' or 'Glead' to both Peregrine and Kite makes it possible that some supposed records referred to the last species. It was not until 1983 that a fully authenticated tree-nesting by Peregrines occurred in these islands. The site was an old Raven nest in open Scots pine growth on heathery moorland, but the four eggs failed to hatch. In 1985, another clutch of four eggs was laid in the identical nest, though evidently by a new female, but this clutch also failed. The finder has wished to remain anonymous to protect the location of the site (Ratcliffe, 1984b). Another Peregrine tree nest was found in 1984 in central Wales, also in an old Raven eyrie in an isolated clump of Scots pines in marginal uplands. This nest, far distant from the other site, successfully produced two fledged young (I. Williams). In both localities, the tree nests appeared to be alternatives to more usually favoured cliff sites. Despite the increase in Peregrine population and saturation of good cliffs, and despite rumours of other occurrences, these remain the only verified instances of tree-nesting here of which I am aware. The departure has not yet become a habit, though it could still do so.

In the Baltic region of Europe, before the recent decline, many pairs of Peregrines bred in the disused tree nests of Crows, Ravens, Herons, Ospreys, Black Storks, Goshawks, Red Kites, Buzzards and Sea Eagles. Some even

became adapted to old shooting platforms and willow baskets placed in trees to provide nest sites. Tree-nesting was especially prevalent in north-east Germany, Poland, Estonia, Latvia and Lithuania, but also occurred in Sweden and Finland. Fischer (1967) has given a detailed account of the tree-nesting habit in Germany and believes that it is a secondary condition after man thinned the forests and created open hunting areas. He states that the forest in the immediate vicinity of the nest often has a 'cliff-like' appearance, and that the Peregrines prefer residual tree stands or thinned mature stands at the edge of clearings and cut-over sites, as well as small stands of high trees surrounded by young trees. An open approach route to the eyrie is a necessity, though a 'camouflaged' eyrie is preferred. Pine trees held 90–95% of eyries, the rest being in oak, beech and larch. Tree-nesting falcons use alternative sites, usually within a 1 km radius, though sometimes over a much larger area, and several traditional territories with a history of regular occupation of up to 60 years were known.

Tree-nesting, sometimes in old nests of Wedge-tailed Eagles and often in those of Ravens, is regular in Australia (D. Dickinson in Hickey, 1969; P. and J. Olsen) and tree-hole nesting has been known there for a long time, in hollow branches and trunks of eucalyptus trees (J. N. McGilp). In Victoria, Australia, 33 out of 95 nest sites were in trees, 17 in hollows and 16 in stick nests of other species (Pruett-Jones, White and Devine, 1981). Tree-hole nesting occurred sporadically in lowland, mainly eastern parts of the United States where there were no cliffs, but never became a firmly-established habit. These hole sites were mostly in cavities in large, wind-shattered trees (Hickey and Anderson, 1969). Six tree eyries were found within a linear distance of about 25 km on wooded islands off the coast of British Columbia: four were in Bald Eagle nests and the other two suspected to be in tree holes (Campbell, Paul and Rodway, 1978).

The final and particularly interesting category of nesting sites is that consisting of various man-made constructions. In Britain, the most celebrated example is

Salisbury Cathedral in Wiltshire, which has at various times been used as a breeding place by Peregrines. This fine building, rising to 123 m above a large area of plain otherwise devoid of nesting sites, has been tenanted only irregularly and the fully authenticated nestings I have been able to trace were as follows:

1864 or 65 – Young reared. Anon
1879 – Eggs laid. Anon
1880 – A pair evidently nesting. Rev. O. Pickard – Cambridge
1896 – 2 young taken for falconry. R. Meinertzhagen
1929 – Breeding reported. Anon
1932–34 – Bred for several years and reared broods in each of these 3. A. Horder
1951, 52 or 53 – Two young flew in one of these years. P. Glasier

In some other years, breeding Kestrels have erroneously been reported as Peregrines.

Other building nests known in this country are:

Corton church tower (ruins), Norfolk, c. 1840. Lubbock
Dunstanburgh Castle (ruins), Northumberland, regular c. 1830–40. G. Bolam
Tay Bridge, Fifeshire side, attempted nesting 1908; possible nesting 1918. H. Boase
Sinclair Castle (ruins), Caithness 1927. R. Meinertzhagen
Llanelly copper works chimney stack, Glamorgan pre-1920. H. M. Salmon
Menai Straits Britannia Bridge, Caerns – Anglesey c. 1945–46, 1989–91. RSPB
Disused railway viaduct, Cumbria, 1984, 1986–88, twice successful. R. Baines.
Tower in Fylingdales radar complex, east Yorkshire, c. 1987. P. Dodsworth
Tall chimney of India Mill, Darwen, Lancashire, 1989–91, twice successful. D. Bunn
Electricity pylon, Avon, c. 1990. B. Lancastle
Post Officer Tower, Swansea, Glamorgan, 1990, successful. I. Williams
Electricity pylon, Lancashire, 1991, successful. B. Townson
Power station chimney, Lancashire, 1991, successful. D. Owen
Tall factory chimney, Cheshire/Lancashire, 1991. C. Richards
Warehouse above the Mersey, Liverpool, Lancashire, 1991. A. S. Duckels
Motorway bridge, central Scottish Lowlands, 1991, successful. K. Brockie
Liverpool cathedral, Lancashire, 1992, successful. T. Pickford
Tower in BP petrochemical complex, Grangemouth, Firth of Forth, 1992, successful. D. Dick

There have also been at least four building nests in Ireland:

Belfast gas works, 1980s. J. Furphy.
Shipyard crane, Belfast, 1984. J. H. Wells
Londonderry church, 1980s. J. Furphy.
Dublin city gasometer, in provided nest tray, 1992, successful. Irish Wildbird Conservancy

I have not been able to verify the more doubtful reports of nesting on St Paul's Cathedral in London and Exeter Cathedral in Devon. It was believed, though never proved, that Peregrines may well have attempted to breed on one of the tall reactor chimneys at Windscale, Cumbria, during 1961–62.

On the European continent there are a good many records of eyries on buildings, especially ruined castles and towers in Spain and Germany, some of which have had a fairly long history of occupation; and nests on tall buildings in Nairobi, Philadelphia and New York are recorded (Hickey, 1969, for a full list).

Fischer (1967) records that desert Peregrines breed on the Egyptian pyramids. None of these building breeding haunts has been as fully documented as the famous skyscraper eyrie on the Sun Life Building in Montreal, which was occupied from 1936 to 1952 without a break (Hall, 1955). One problem for Peregrines seeking these artificial sites is the usual absence of a ledge with a covering of soft material in which a scrape for the eggs could be made. On the Sun Life Building, the Peregrines at first attempted to lay in a rain ledge from which the eggs rolled off. They fairly quickly took to a shallow sand and gravel filled box placed on a ledge for them to lay in. Successful breeding took place that year (1940), and continued until 1947, after which egg breaking and dis-appearance set in, until the birds vanished in 1953, in the great population crash which led to the extinction of the Peregrine in eastern North America to the south of Labrador and northern Quebec.

Nearly 40 years later, Peregrines are now breeding on buildings in many parts of North America, as a result of habituation to these artificial sites through the massive captive breeding programmes there.

Nesting on buildings is certainly on the increase in Britain and Ireland, in parallel with the recent expansion of population. During the last 10 years there have been many records of Peregrines apparently prospecting other city buildings and structures in various parts of the country. Birds or pairs have taken up residence but then eventually faded out without nesting. The food supply in these places is often good, albeit mainly feral pigeons and Starlings, and the problem is most likely to be failure to find possible sites which could hold the eggs. Many more building nesters might become established if suitable nest trays were provided, as has been done widely in the United States and Canada.

Clearly any more general resort to nesting on the ground, in trees or on buildings, would greatly enhance the Peregrine's potential for increase in population. By allowing expansion within or into districts where the bird is at present limited or excluded by lack of cliffs suitable for nesting, both breeding distribution and overall numbers could become much enlarged. In Britain and Ireland, the recent increase of nesting on third-class cliffs and near-ground sites has already boosted numbers appreciably in certain districts.

Hickey and Anderson (1969) have given an extremely full account of the global range of variation in choice of nesting habitat in the Peregrine, illustrated with a well-chosen series of photographs.

CHAPTER 7

The breeding cycle: pairing and courtship

The British literature on Peregrine behaviour is scanty and I have drawn heavily on the published accounts for other countries. Fischer (1967) has given a good description of behaviour through the breeding cycle in Germany, but the most detailed accounts are for North American Peregrines. Cade (1960) described pair formation, courtship, 'pair-integrating' behaviour and domestic interactions based on observations in Alaska and California. In addition, Joseph Hagar's account in Bent (1938) of certain courtship behaviour in the Peregrine in Massachusetts has become a classic, not only for its accuracy of observation, but also as a beautiful piece of writing. His observations appear to hold good equally for the British Peregrine. Nelson (1970, 1977) has given an extremely detailed account of the breeding behaviour of Peale's Falcon on Langara Island, British Columbia.

Captive breeding projects with Peregrines in North America have given unusual opportunities for observing some aspects of courtship and breeding behaviour very closely, though Wrege and Cade (1977) have emphasised that it would be invalid to assume that the display patterns they have described are the same as those of wild falcons. They stress that the interpretation of behaviour in captivity is dependent on study of the same behaviour in nature, and not vice versa. These Cornell studies found no subspecific differences in courtship behaviour between the three North American and Spanish races of the Peregrine in captivity, so that there are good grounds for believing that the American observations are valid for the British race.

It also has to be said that Peregrines, in common with most birds, show a great deal of variation as individuals, and that nowhere does this individuality show so strongly as in behaviour. Generalisations based on the observation of only a few individual birds therefore have to be treated with great caution too.

THE PAIR-BOND IN WINTER

It is particularly difficult to obtain information on the sexual relationships between Peregrines outside the breeding season, and the pattern may be highly variable. For paired birds there is an apparent continuum of variation in winter between strong fidelity to the nesting haunts and movement to distant new quarters, and this could presumably affect the attachment of partners to each other. There seem to be variations in strength of the pair-bond during winter, even for sedentary pairs, and it is possible that this may be influenced by the degree to which food supply determines whether the pair can subsist together or have to take up separate hunting ranges. The death of a mate and the time at which this occurs is likely to be an important factor. No one knows whether new pairings can take place far from the breeding haunts or whether they occur only through association with an actual or potential nesting location. New pairings are also greatly influenced by the availability of prospective partners in appropriate physiological condition.

In Britain, many Peregrines wintering in non-breeding areas appear to be solitary, though Baker (1967) found that at least some of the falcons he watched in Essex were paired, and other observers have reported wintering pairs in the lowlands. Some pairs which remain throughout autumn and winter in the breeding haunts continue to roost quite close together, and can be seen in company frequently during the day. It appears to be more usual for them to separate to some extent, for single Peregrines are more typically seen about nesting cliffs during autumn and winter. Some observers have claimed that it is more usually the female which holds to the favourite cliff, at least for roosting, whereas others have said that it is normally the male. Sometimes the two will resort to quite separate alternative cliffs within the same territory, and sometimes neither will use known breeding places, but move as a pair or separately to other rocks not far away. Until radio-telemetry provides some answers, it can be only a presumption that separated partners take up different hunting ranges. If one bird dies it can seem that the pair have separated and if both succumb it may appear that they have moved away for a time. The return of an existing pair and the re-establishment of their pair-bond may not be distinguishable from the re-mating of a survivor of the previous breeding pair, or from the establishment of a completely new pair in a deserted territory.

There is thus a varied range of circumstances against which courtship and mating activity develop.

THE PRE-LAYING PERIOD

Cade (1960) has recognised eight distinct phases in the pre-incubation activity of Peregrines: namely, (1) the attraction of mates to each other, (2) mutual roosting on the cliff, (3) cooperative hunting excursions, (4) courtship flights, (5) 'familiarities' on the cliff, (6) courtship feeding, (7) copulation, and (8) nest scraping. This list is in approximate order of appearance as breeding activity develops, though Cade pointed out that some of these categories may develop more or less simultaneously, and all but the first are carried on through most of the pre-incubation period. I have modified and developed this sequence of categories according to later work on behaviour.

PAIRING

Fischer has said that in western and southern Europe courtship in Peregrines may begin during autumn and extend, perhaps with a mid-winter pause, through to the beginning of the breeding season, so that integration of the pair occurs over a long period, of 3 or 4 months. In Britain, some of the activities of courtship have been seen during autumn but they do not become noticeably frequent until winter is on the retreat. By mid or late February, when the first stirrings of the breeding urge usually become apparent in Britain, Peregrines are increasingly to be seen holding to the nesting crags. They may be single birds or pairs when first seen, but as time passes they are more likely to be pairs. From the previous comments, it is clearly impossible to tell – unless the birds are marked in some way – how often this reoccupation of nesting place involves a restoration of the pair-bond between a previous pair, and how often it involves a change of partner or of the pair. The majority of females evidently return to the identical places where they nested the previous year, and limited evidence from re-trapping marked birds suggests that the males have the same tendency (Mearns and Newton, 1984). Hickey (1942) suggested that re-mating of the same individuals in successive years may result mainly from the attraction of the same cliff for two falcons rather than the mutual attraction of the two birds to each other: but both processes could be involved.

Cade (1960) stressed the importance, in the traditional use of nesting places, of the continuity of association between individuals and their established localities, and suggested that desertions of favourite cliffs are likely to reflect breaks in such continuity, as when both of an established pair die simultaneously. I believe that an interplay of factors is probably involved in the regular occupation of certain nesting places: the superior attractions of some cliffs, the attachment of already mated birds to each other, the tendency of an individual falcon that has not previously mated or bred to return to the vicinity of its birthplace in spring and the still more specific homing tendency to the cliff where an individual has already bred or established itself previously.

Cade found that single birds reappearing at nesting haunts were as likely to be females as males, and this is my impression, too. Other writers believe that when the birds are not already paired, it is the male which, in more typical avian fashion, takes up a territory first and then tries to attract a mate by various displays.

Fischer (1967) stated that the male is normally the first partner to arrive in the territory, but admitted that it is often difficult to tell precisely which bird arrives first.

Hagar describes thus the initial stages of courtship for unpaired birds: 'This took place at Mount Sugarloaf on March 16 and involved a male Peregrine that at that date, some three weeks after his return to the mountain, appeared to be still unmated. I had been watching him for more than an hour as he sat quietly on a dead pine above the cliff and during this whole period had heard no call or seen no such animation as is associated with the courting period. Suddenly, at about 9 o'clock, he launched out from his perch and began to sail back and forth along the face of the cliff, repeatedly giving the *wichew* or rusty hinge note (Creaking-call). A moment later I spotted a large female Peregrine coming up the valley from the south, some 200 feet above the mountain. Arriving abreast of the cliff, she began to describe wide circles over the crest, flying very leisurely and seeming to watch the proceedings below her. The tiercel redoubled his cries and flew from one shelf to another, alighting for a moment on each one and then swinging along to the next, with every appearance of the greatest excitement. The falcon, having presently completed three or four circles, now straightened her course to the north, and picking up speed with every stroke of her wings soon disappeared in the haze along North Sugarloaf; the male continued his vain activity, wailing and *wichew*-ing for near a minute after she had passed from sight. He then made a short silent sally out over the valley and finally returned to sit hunched up and quiet on his dead tree for many minutes, before leaving on a hunting expedition behind the mountain. This episode introduces several of the elements of the courtship – the first display, the shelf display, the coaxing *wichew* note – and it remains to elaborate on their use and to mention the food-bringing routine.'

Cade wrote that, 'Either mate seems to be willing to accept any other member of the opposite sex that chances along, but neither is willing to accept any other cliff. An established female will drive off all other females. When one of the established mates arrives at the cliff before the other, it will indulge in promiscuous courtship and mating with stray individuals; but when the other established mate arrives, these interlopers are quickly chased away. In one instance, when an established male was trapped alive early in the pre-incubation period, the established female readily accepted another male; but when some two weeks later the first male was again released at the cliff, it fought hard to drive off the newcomer and finally succeeded in doing so even though weakened by a period of captivity.'

The casual observer visiting the breeding haunts in March usually misses the earliest stage of mate selection and sees the pair already formed. Some established pairs in any case arrive together at their nesting cliffs, and courtship is then a matter of reinforcing the pair-bond. I suspect that re-occupation of a deserted territory, either by a single bird or a pair, can occur in any month of the year, though the normal breeding calendar is always observed. A single bird occupying a breeding cliff may remain unmated for a year or up to several years, and the re-occupation of long-deserted haunts often shows this preliminary period of solitary possession. The reasons are not clear, though Hagar's quoted observation suggests that not every potential passing mate is attracted to stay, even when there is an attractive cliff held by a soliciting owner. I suspect that when the cliffs are unattractive, such disinterest is even more likely. Even when a new pair reoccupies a deserted haunt, breeding may be deferred for at least one year. The state of sexual development of the birds is obviously relevant, but in recent years pesticide effects have greatly complicated the pattern of normal reproduction including, most probably, the initiation of breeding.

Cade found that the first indication of successful pairing or re-establishment of a pair-bond was quiet perching and roosting of the two birds on the same cliff or other favourite perching place, at first well apart, but then closer together and eventually often side by side. This is followed by the development of a fairly well-marked pattern of courtship behaviour both on the wing and when perched on the nesting cliff.

COURTSHIP, HUNTING AND FLIGHT DISPLAY

In wild falcons, the most spectacular courtship activities are on the wing and these appear quite early in the cycle. As Hagar has said, the first business of the day is feeding, and early courtship activities include cooperative hunting between the male and female. Cade found that the two may at first simply hunt over the same range in close proximity, but paying little attention to each other. Soon the pair are actually joining forces in hunting the same bird, coordinating their attacks to counter evasion tactics of the target. The male may make a feint at a flock to try to separate an individual at which the waiting female then stoops with the element of surprise. Hagar found that the female usually made the first stoop when both chased the same bird, and he noted that she usually stayed closer to the home cliff than her mate. She also ate the first bird, whether it was killed by her or brought by the male.

Successful hunts are soon followed by display flights which include some of the most spectacular aerial evolutions performed by any flying creature. Hagar has portrayed this vividly: 'We were hidden in the woods below the south end of the cliff, and the Peregrines were quite unconscious of our presence at the time; again and again the tiercel started well to leeward and came along the cliff against the wind, diving, plunging, saw-toothing, rolling over and over, darting hither and yon like an autumn leaf until finally he would swoop up into the full current of air and be borne off on the gale to do it all over again. At length he tired of this, and, soaring in narrow circles without any movement of his wings other than a constant small adjustment of their planes, he rose to a position 500 ft or so above the mountain north of the cliff. Nosing over suddenly, he flicked his wings rapidly 15 or 20 times and fell like a thunderbolt. Wings half closed now, he shot down past the north end of the cliff, described three successive vertical loop-the-loops across its face, turning completely upside down at the top of each loop, and roared out over our heads with the wind rushing through his wings like ripping canvas. Against the background of the cliff his terrific speed was much more apparent than it would have been in the open sky. The sheer excitement of watching such a performance was tremendous; we felt a strong impulse to stand and cheer.'

The most exhilarating aerobatic flight I have seen took place in front of a lofty granite cliff deep in the Galloway hills. The pair of Peregrines had been circling slowly but suddenly began to chase and stoop at one another with increasing vigour as they built up to a truly dazzling pursuit. First one bird then the other shot down at tremendous speed in front of the crags, 'threw up' and hurtled back to regain its previous height several hundred feet above the base of the stoop. Sometimes the pair almost touched and then they would separate and fly on divergent paths before one suddenly plunged at its mate again. My vantage point was several hundred yards away and at that distance and speed it was difficult to separate the sexes, but the two appeared to be changing sides in this aerial game of 'tag'. Intermittent flashes of white showed against the darker background of rock as the sun caught the birds' breasts. After a time the pace slackened and the pair drifted back into the crag to pitch together on a ledge which proved to have an empty scrape. They displayed to each other on the ledge and then soon took off again to repeat the whole performance.

In North Wales I once saw a male Peregrine repeatedly soar to a good height in a tight spiral and then come sizzling down past his circling mate in a terrific stoop, giving lightning flickers of his wings just before he pulled out of the dive. The aerobatic flights are often either preceded or followed by slow soaring of one or both birds, which may often spiral to a considerable elevation. The Creaking-call is frequently given during the aerobatic and soaring flights.

There are many variations on the general theme, but the accounts by Walpole-Bond (1938) and Treleaven (1977) of display flights in Sussex and Cornwall have much in common with the above descriptions. Simmons (in Cramp and Simmons, 1980) has attempted to categorise the main components of these display flights: High-circling, Undulating flights and Figure-of-eight flights by one bird alone (usually the male); and High-circling and Flight-play by the pair. Flight-rolling is another variant, and Monneret (1974) has described a Z-flight, in which a horizontally-flying bird suddenly swings over, dives diagonally in the opposite direction and then swings back into level flight in its original direction again. Monneret also noted horizontal Figure-of-eight flights in which the falcon almost brushed the cliff face. A Buzzard flight is also recorded in which the bird flies in a straight line with slow, measured wingbeats. Any of these flights may terminate by the bird landing on the cliff, usually at a nest site.

Cade (1960) has pointed out that display flights are only slight modifications of basic hunting movements or territorial aggression. The bird under 'attack' often responds as though to a real threat, by rolling over or flipping up and presenting its talons to the 'attacker'. The two birds may close with each other, chest to chest, and indulge in talon-grappling, and Walpole-Bond and Cade have each seen pairs engage their bills in flight. Fischer (1967) described spiralling flights in which each of the two partners seemed to be trying to rise above the other, as does a falcon during a 'ringing-up' flight at prey. D. Nethersole-Thompson also records a symbolic Food-pass with the male flying towards and calling to the female, which banked and flipped up with talons presented below the male momentarily, before the two separated. Display flights occur increasingly up to the time of egg-laying, but are most likely to be seen by watching at a reasonable distance from the nesting cliff. Courtship is probably the most important element in their function, but they may well have an advertisement and territorial role as well.

COURTSHIP FEEDING

After a while, and usually when Ledge-ceremonies begin to develop, cooperative hunting changes to taking of prey by the male alone, who then presents it to the female. Cade (1960) has described and discussed courtship feeding in the Peregrine at length, and believes that it is closely allied to copulation, which often follows immediately afterwards. He points out that in the falcons, courtship feeding has evolved far beyond the role of a symbolic ritual serving pair-integration to become the means of satisfying virtually the whole of the female's energy needs for much of the breeding period. There is some variation between pairs, but the male continues to supply most or all of the female's food requirements through incubation and at least the first half of the nestling period, so that it is a most important element in the whole pattern of breeding activity. Nelson (1970) has suggested that 'food transfer' is a preferable term to courtship feeding because of the wider significance of the behaviour.

Variations in courtship feeding occur within the same pair, and the pattern may change in time. The male may at first show reluctance to bring food to his mate and may cache it for her to retrieve. She sometimes grabs it from him by force. When courtship feeding has developed properly, the male typically flies to the perched female carrying prey and, as he alights, transfers this from his talons to his beak. He bows slowly up and down before his mate, often with head turned or completely upside down, sometimes advancing with tip-toe walk. The female usually takes the prey from him in her beak, sometimes giving a chittering note, and turns away or flies to another perch to feed. Sometimes the male lands, drops the prey and retreats a few feet while the female advances to take the food; and sometimes he flies past and drops the prey on the female's ledge without alighting.

The male sometimes performs a Pluck-display, feathering the prey, often in sight of the female, in a more exaggerated manner than usual. He may eat some of the prey himself before transferring it. Fischer (1967) found that the tiercel would supply the female with food 'on demand' at least 6 weeks before the eggs were laid, and that he established food caches in recesses of the cliff at that time. Food transfer often took place on the branch of a tree growing from the cliff. In wild Peregrines, the various stages of courtship feeding often involve a good deal of calling between the pair.

Observations of food transfers in captive Peregrines have shown the role of displays in this activity, though some degree of modification may occur, compared with the pattern in wild falcons. Wrege and Cade found that the female encourages her mate to seek food by giving the Vertical Head-low display and a wailing food-call. Either sex may invite a transfer when food is obtained, and the female solicits by the same posture and food-call, interspersed with Creaking-calls. Males summon the females to take food by the Wailing-call as they fly into the cliff and then, after landing, by sharp Creaking-calls and bowing. Male postures alternate between relaxed with head up, and head down in contact with the food. Before transfer the male picks the prey up in his beak and stands vertically. Occasionally there are food transfers from female to male.

Aerial transfers of prey are also made, and at varying distances from the cliff. The female may fly to meet her mate when she sees him approaching with food, or he may call to alert her. Both sexes use both the Wailing-call and the

Cacking-call during the exchanges. To make the Aerial-pass, either the male drops the food item for the female to catch, or she flies up beneath him and rolls over or flips up to take it from his talons. Bill to bill exchanges in the air are occasionally made.

LEDGE DISPLAYS

More specific ritual displays and associated calls are developed during courtship activities on the cliff face where the pair now roost together constantly, and such behaviour becomes centred on a selection of possible eyrie ledges. These ledge displays have been described by Nelson (1970) and Nelson and Campbell (1973) and in still greater detail by Wrege and Cade (1977); though these last authors point out that such activities are probably exaggerated in captive Peregrines, which have so little space for flying. Conversely, the vocalisations of courtship may be reduced, or contexts of particular calls changed, in captive falcons because the birds are permanently in such close proximity that the need for such communication is less. On any occasion when the pair are perched, there is commonly a Head-low Display, given by either sex in response to movement or close proximity of the mate, especially when the other approaches or shows signs of doing so. Its postures include holding the head below the body plane, beak away from the mate and usually towards the ground, and generally sleeked plumage. The sharp Creaking-call is frequently given, and often the Whining-call too. Both calls may be given by either sex.

Wrege and Cade recognised four variants of this display, which is the most

Captive pair of adult Peregrines giving Ledge Ceremony Courtship display (photo: The Peregrine Fund, Cornell University Laboratory of Ornithology)

frequently performed activity of this period. In the Horizontal Head-low Bow the falcon crouches with its body horizontal and head bent at almost 90°, with beak often touching the ground. The Vertical Head-low Bow is less intense, with the body held as in the normal perching position and the head lowered. All degrees of intermediate posture occur, in regard to body and head positions, and there is a variable amount of up-and-down head bowing from vigorous to none. In the Extreme Head-low Bow, which is a still more intense form of the first variant, the bird leans right forward with head low and tail high, in line with the body. These three variants are essentially non-aggressive, but the Agonistic Head-low Bow is mildly aggressive, and given by either sex in agonistic situations; the bill is directed at the mate, head and shoulder feathers sometimes erected, and the Creaking or Chittering-calls may be given.

Individual ledge displays are given by either sex alone on a prospective nest ledge, usually at a scrape. In Male Ledge Display the tiercel approaches the scrape in a horizontal head-low posture, giving the Creaking-call continuously. When sexual motivation is high, a high-stepping or tip-toe gait is used and gives the effect of a side-to-side swagger as the bird walks about the ledge. The bird stands in the scrape, high on its legs and in the head low posture with lowered belly feathers and under tail coverts erected, and engages in bowing and intense scraping motions, calling all the time. After five to ten seconds, the bird pauses and looks towards his mate. Movement by the female usually elicits renewal of intense display and the duration of display depends on her reactions. By comparison, Female Ledge Display is generally less intense, with less distinctive and more variable postures, though the full Creaking-call is given. The approach is usually with head, body and tail held level, though the head may be slightly lowered. The female rotates in the scrape, leaning forward and scratching frequently by vigorous backwards pushing of the feet, and often picking at debris with her beak. She less often pauses to look at her mate, and her behaviour is less easy to distinguish from non-display activity, into which it often lapses.

Mutual Ledge Display (Ledge-ceremony; Simmons, 1980) occurs when the male has enticed the female into joining him on a prospective nesting ledge. It involves simultaneous activity by the pair on the ledge, usually around the scrape, with both birds in horizontal head-low posture and Creaking-calling together. Often the birds face each other across the scrape and bow repeatedly with heads close together, but one may stand in the scrape. There are occasional silent breaks in the performance, followed by renewed activity. At first Ledge-ceremonies are short and either bird soon departs, leaving its mate alone. During longer ceremonies later, mutual billing often occurs, with nibbling between beaks. This involves sideways twisting of the head especially by the female which usually keeps its head very low and beak directed upwards, while the male's bill faces downward. The Creaking-call call dwindles to a quiet 'peeping' and 'chupping'. Billing also occurs in flight and at perches on the nesting cliff. Other familiarities noted by Cade include nibbling by one bird at the toes of the other, mutual preening of the mate's wing coverts and scapulars, and wiping of the bill on the plumage of the other.

Hagar found that the male Peregrine tried increasingly to entice the female to particular ledges where he had made or renewed scrapes. At first she paid little attention, but gradually her interest built up and she would follow her mate to a

Horizontal Head-low Bow (male)   *Extreme Head-low Bow (male)*

Food transfer, male to female

Vertical Head-low Bow (male)   *Upright threat display (female)*

Horizontal, threat display (male)   *Agonistic Head-low Bow (female)*

Ledge displays of the Peregrine, mainly in courtship

shelf where mutual ledge displays then took place. One bird usually left before the other, which stayed to work over the scrape. Then the male began to lose interest in possible nesting ledges as the female's interest increased, and she spent more and more time visiting a wide selection of shelves, scraping in each one. This involves a backward scratching movement with the feet in the vegetation, soil or loose debris on a ledge. The bird leans forward with its tail drooping and its bill often raking in the ledge substratum, and position is shifted periodically, so that there is a rotation which keeps the scrape circular and symmetrical in vertical shape.

The scrape in which the female eventually lays seems often to be quite different from those which were the focus of attention during the earlier stages of courtship. Hagar also found that the intended egg scrape could be changed for a new site if the female was disturbed before laying had begun. The number of different ledges frequented and scrapes made by any pair depend on the scope offered by a particular nesting cliff, and captive pairs necessarily have to make shift with a very limited choice. Cade has pointed out that nest-scraping in the Peregrine has evolved beyond its basic function into an important aspect of courtship behaviour and pair-bonding and that the activity itself is at times arguably a part of ledge displays. The number of good ledges on a cliff may accordingly affect its attractiveness to Peregrines, and by influencing the physiological build-up of breeding activity may be an important factor in renewal of nesting at a deserted cliff.

Monneret (1974) found that 10–15 days before laying, the female begged for food by squatting on the tarsi with feathers fluffed, head hunched in the shoulders, tail spread and wings flexed and held, trembling, slightly away from the body. Cade also found that in wild falcons the females sometimes fluttered their wings like a food-begging young bird. More frequently he noted a slow fluttering glide or 'sandpiper flight' by the female in food encounters, with the bird's wings arched slightly below the plane of the body, the wing tips flickering rapidly and the tail fanned. He interpreted this as flight behaviour derived from the food-begging response of young birds. The female often flies in this manner, giving the Wailing-call, to meet the food-carrying male.

COPULATION

As the actual mating time approaches, the male Peregrine begins to use a Hitched-wing Display, given both flying and standing. The flight version has been termed Slow-landing Display by Nelson (1973) and Slow-flight by Cramp and Simmons (1980), and is performed with wings held high and short wing-beats, mainly from the carpal joint. The legs are held well forward and the tail depressed, producing a slow-motion, bouncing flight, ending with an upward bound and vertical drop to perch. Standing Hitched-wing display occurs for brief periods (up to two seconds) after the male lands, often preparatory to Ledge-display and Ledge-ceremony with the female. The wings are held high against the body to form a deep V-channel along the back; the legs are stiff and the head is bowed. The male may tip-toe along the ledge in this position, and will assume the same posture, for a few seconds at a time, while perched and watching his mate. Both versions of this display are consistently performed by the male immediately before copulation. They are less often used by the female, which responds for a while to male displays nearby with Vertical Head-low Bows and Creaking or Wailing-calls.

The first signs of Mating-ceremony, with either male or female initiating activity by soliciting, appear about eight weeks after the onset of courtship and about three weeks before laying (Wrege and Cade). The female solicits copulation by giving the Whining-call in combination with Head-low postures and raised body feathers, and sometimes engages in rapid up-and-down bowing, in which the spread tail may also figure. She is usually sideways to the male or facing away. This Copulation-soliciting display is maintained for up to 20 seconds. In the male Copulation-soliciting display the tiercel performs either Vertical Head-low Bows or Hitched-wing display, or both together, or bows vigorously, often with a sideways motion, and gives the Chittering-call. He may present his profile when his mate is very close. The male approaches the female in Slow-flight if he is some distance away, but occasionally she flies to him, causing him to fly and then mount (D. M. Bremner). Calling frequently increases with motivation to mount.

If the male shows intention to mount, the female sleeks her body feathers, crouches and leans forward, raising her tail and moving it sideways. The male may fly to the female and mount directly from some little distance or he flutters on to her back after standing near her on the ledge or perch. During copulation the female leans forward at an angle of about 45°, with wings slightly open, and gives a special version of the Wailing-call throughout. The male flaps his wings continuously, keeping an upright posture with neck extended and curved, talons bunched in loosely-clenched feet and legs stiff and gives Chittering and Creaking-calls at intervals. Cloacal contact is achieved by the female raising her tail to one side while the male depresses his tail to the other side. The male departs in Slow-flight after mating, while the female fluffs out her feathers and shakes her body. Walpole-Bond (1938) described apparent and unsuccessful attempts to copulate in the air.

Copulation may follow various courtship activities but females usually begin to solicit for a day or two before males respond by mounting. Copulation sequences are at first often incomplete, but the number of successful matings, their duration and frequency, all increase to a maximum by a week before laying. Later copulations average 8–10 seconds and reach a frequency of three to four or even more per hour. Cade and Wrege found that copulation could occur at any time of day though maximum frequency was during the first hour of light, while Hagar (1938) noted a peak around mid-day. Copulation continues in most pairs until the third egg is laid and occasionally occurs after the clutch is complete. Cade has suggested that since copulatory mounting occurs over a more extended period than is biologically necessary for fertilisation of the eggs, it may itself have become an additional form of courtship display helping to synchronise the seasonal maturation of reproductive physiology of the pair.

THREAT

Although it might at first seem alien to the concept of courtship, threat behaviour by one Peregrine towards its mate is one of the elements of this phase of the

Female Peregrine giving partial Upright-threat display at human intruder; Kenya, Africa (photo: Hussein Adan Isack)

breeding cycle. It represents the extreme expression of actions which, though basically pair-integrating in function, contain distinctly aggressive components. Such behaviour is a reminder that the first instinct of a wild creature is self-preservation and that pairing itself requires considerable adjustments in basic responses before another individual can be treated other than as a rival. Threat behaviour has been described mainly in captive Peregrines, but captivity is likely to produce an artificial enhancement of such interactions compared with the wild situation.

Nelson and Campbell (1973) distinguished two threat displays given by either sex. In Horizontal Threat Display the head, body and tail are all held in the horizontal plane, the beak is directed at the mate and the wings slightly extended, and the head and body feathers erected. Bowing movements sometimes accompany this posture and the Chittering-call may be used. In the still more aggressive Upright Threat Display, the Peregrine stands upright with wings and tail spread from slightly to fully, beak open and most of the body feathers erect. This second display is usually directed only at another species which is perceived as potentially dangerous and is probably the normal response evolved to frighten off predators approaching closely to a Peregrine not in flight. Blows are sometimes exchanged between mates, especially when one flies to the other as if with aggressive intent, but actual harm seldom results. Wrege and Cade (1977) rarely observed aggressive displays and other actions in well-adjusted captive pairs. With new pairs such behaviour sometimes occurred early in the season, but became less frequent as the pair-bond developed.

VARIATIONS IN COURTSHIP BEHAVIOUR

The degree to which particular calls and displays are used, the sequences of particular activities, and their timing within the courtship period can all vary within a broadly recognisable overall pattern. Figure 7, modified from Wrege and Cade (1977) gives an indication of the onset and duration of various displays within the pre-laying and incubation period. Most of the calls and displays of courtship can be given outside the normal courtship period. I have witnessed Ledge-ceremony and Creaking-calling in September on a ledge which was actually used as the eyrie the following year. D. M. Bremner (in Cramp and Simmons, 1980) has seen the first signs of courtship in early January in Scotland, involving different initiatory activity, with the female visiting old nest sites on its own, perching there and occasionally lying down in an old scrape. Fischer (1967) believes that the courtship period is normally spread through autumn and winter, but it is not clear whether this conclusion is based on the observation of consistent behaviour patterns or only on scattered incidents. The onset of courtship is probably much influenced by prevailing weather conditions. At a finer level of variation there are differences in frequency and intensity of displays and calls, and of mate responses to these.

In captive Peregrines, Wrege and Cade found that initial courtship interactions began earlier in each successive year of breeding for at least the first three years. Egg-laying also became earlier but not to the same extent, so that the courtship period lengthened each year. All pairs showed earlier onset of copulation with regard to laying dates. The timing of seasonal development of behaviour evidently stabilises after several years. Timing of courtship initiation, first copulation and egg-laying appeared to increase in synchrony between different pairs with age and breeding experience. The actual timing of the breeding cycle depends mainly on temperature and photoperiod as determined by latitude, and thus varies markedly for the different races of wild Peregrines. In the Cornell breeding studies, temperature and photoperiod were manipulated to synchronise breeding activities within the captive population. Natural selection has evidently geared the timing of breeding to these major environmental factors in such a way as to give the best chances of survival to the young in terms of food availability and favourable climate. Fischer (1967) has pointed out that the highly migratory northern Peregrines have a much shorter period in which to achieve pair-integration before breeding than the sedentary populations, though Cade (1960) found that Alaskan falcons often arrived at their cliffs paired, and courtship activity may begin on the wintering grounds or during migration.

If the first clutch is lost before incubation is more than 7–10 days advanced, Peregrines usually produce a repeat laying about three weeks later. It would seem that the break in the pattern of incubation triggers a return to courtship activities

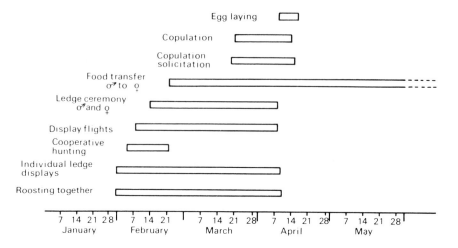

Figure 7. Seasonal development of courtship behaviour in Britain.

NOTES: Data are mostly adapted from Figure 6 of Wrege and Cade (1977), to fit the average laying period for most British Peregrines, begining 8 April. There are wide variations in the timing of the onset of various courtship activities, according to geographical location, individual pairs and, sometimes, weather. The sequence may sometimes be telescoped into a shorter period. Nest-scraping may occur throughout the period of individual ledge displays.

and the renewal of the physiological cycle leading to egg production. If incubation has proceeded beyond about 10 days when the loss occurs, there is a much lower probability that a 'repeat' will be laid, suggesting that the basic physiological cycle of reproduction has gone too far along its downward path for external stimuli to produce a resurgence. Occasional successful repeat layings have been known after first clutches were incubated to full term without hatching and, still more rarely, after loss of a first brood.

The American observers have noted that in both wild and captive Peregrines, the female becomes very lethargic, appearing almost to be ill, shortly before and during egg-laying. This may be a response to the physiological stress of producing eggs, but Nelson suggests that it may help to prevent damage to the maturing eggs and conserve the bird's nutritional reserves for egg formation. Whatever the case, it is dependent on the male's role as food provider.

DOMINANCE RELATIONS WITHIN THE PAIR

Wrege and Cade have divided the displays and calls of Peregrines and other falcons into three groups. The first is essentially non-aggressive, pair-bonding behaviour, and includes aggression-inhibiting, appeasement and approach-eliciting elements. The second group, broadly of precopulatory behaviour, has aggressive components, and the third group is at least partly aggressive. Thus while courtship behaviour serves to integrate the pair towards the primary goal of successful raising of a family, this process has to accommodate the aggressive elements which are so basic a part of behaviour in any bird, and most of all in the birds of prey. The innate aggressiveness still shows through at times, but is checked and countered in various ways which prevent it from obstructing the course of reproduction.

Cade (1960) said, 'Falcons are by nature extremely avaricious and pugnacious over items of food, and much of the interactions between these birds in the non-breeding seasons is concerned with various agonistic types of behaviour relating to the acquisition of food. In some respects it is remarkable that falcons can mate at all, and the performance of the mated male in giving up food to his female represents a striking transition in behaviour.' The fierce temperament of a raptor and its potential for inflicting damage on a mate have probably led to the development of a highly refined behavioural communication system for the conveyance of information about motivation and its intensity between partners. Both sexes are intimidating to each other and have to give anti-aggressive and approach-eliciting signals.

Cade deduced from observations of wild Peregrines that the female is normally dominant over the male. This relationship was especially evident from displacement of the male by the female over rights to food and perches, and during attempts at copulation by the male when his partner was not receptive. In their more detailed studies of captive birds, Wrege and Cade concluded that in Peregrines, Gyr Falcons, Prairie Falcons and Lanner Falcons females were consistently dominant over males. Their evidence was not simply from displacements during conflict situations, but came from detailed measurements of the frequency of aggressive and non-aggressive postures and calls used by each sex within pair relationships. There is an apparent inverse correlation between the degree of overt agonistic behaviour and sexual size difference, both within pairs of the same species and between different species: the larger the size difference the less the aggression, or the greater the frequency of non-aggressive in relation to aggressive behaviour.

Successful breeding evidently requires a fairly delicate balance of responses between the two sexes. With captive pairs, the confined conditions make it important that the female does not constantly intimidate her mate, though in the wild, where the male has more scope for avoidance reactions, exchanges can be more agonistic. In captivity, breeding failures were found to be associated with excessive female dominance, lack of dominance by either sex or, exceptionally, male dominance. While it is evident that successful reproduction is much influenced by the degree of mutual adjustment and overall harmony between the members of any pair, this says little about the ultimate significance of the dominance relationship. It is regarded by some ornithologists as the key to the interpretation of the meaning of reversed sexual size dimorphism in the raptors (see p. 203).

BIGAMY

Bigamous relationships appear to be rare in the Peregrine. In Inverness-shire in 1971, Douglas Weir watched a male Peregrine flying repeatedly between two cliffs 3·5 km apart where different females had clutches of eggs. On one cliff, known to be the favourite haunt, a youngster was reared, but the other bird ended up with a single addled egg. On 20 June 1978, J. H. Wells examined an Antrim coast eyrie from which he had watched three young fledged a week before. By chance, he then found a second brood of two still downy Peregrine chicks on the

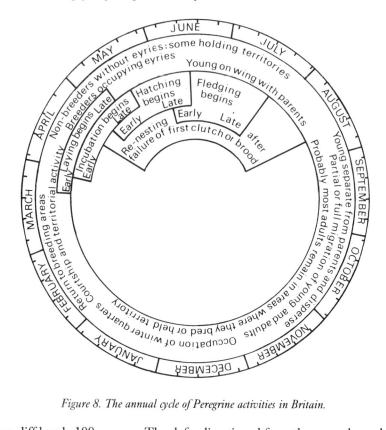

Figure 8. The annual cycle of Peregrine activities in Britain.

same cliff barely 100 m away. The defending tiercel from the second nest later perched on the first eyrie ledge. The second brood did not fly until 2 July. Although the evidence was circumstantial it seems that bigamy would account most successfully for such unusually close nesting. Dick Treleaven observed a bigamous male Peregrine in Cornwall for four successive years 1985–88. The tiercel commuted between the two eyries 1700 m apart, and drove away prospective suitors of the second female. Most clutches of both females failed during this episode. In the United States, Walter Spofford (in Hickey, 1969) watched two females with one male at the same tree-hole eyrie; as one female came off the eggs, the other went onto them. Kearton (1909) was told by a gamekeeper that he shot a female Peregrine from an eyrie and trapped her mate, who escaped leaving a leg behind. The male returned with a new male and female and 'all three occupied the old nesting quarters in the utmost peace.'

TERRITORIAL AND DEFENCE AGGRESSION

As courtship behaviour develops, a pair of Peregrines becomes increasingly aggressive in defending its nesting cliff against other Peregrines. The courtship flights, leisurely soaring around the cliff, and the behaviour termed by Cramp and

Simmons (1980) Eyrie-flyby-and-landing display, may serve the function of territorial activity to warn off other Peregrines. An intruder is usually greeted with Cacking-calls and these often serve to turn it away; a territorial bird may advertise by giving various calls while perched at the nest site. Actual encounters with intruders are infrequent, and occur mainly close to the nesting cliff. If a strange falcon comes too near, the occupant pair will usually together attack the trespasser and if only one of the pair is present at first, its calls often bring the mate to the fray. Either sex may be the more aggressive defender, and this may depend on the stage of the breeding cycle.

Cade (1960) has noted a consistent pattern in these territorial exchanges amongst Alaskan Peregrines. The attacker spirals to gain height and then stoops down at the intruder, which usually flips up on its back to present talons as its adversary closes. Actual blows are seldom struck, but quite often the two falcons grapple with each other's talons and, thus locked together, may fall through the air until they almost hit the ground before breaking apart. Occasionally the intruder is actually thrown to the ground by this contest, and Cade has seen the intruder pinned on its back on the ground by the rightful occupant Peregrine. The territory owners begin by giving a slower version of the Cacking alarm call and sometimes the Wailing-call, but this changes to the Creaking note when the attack becomes more serious, thereby revealing the aggressive content of this call. The attacked bird is usually silent, but may also Creak if a serious fight ensues, and gives a wailing scream 'eeyaik – eeyaik' if the aggressor makes bodily contact. Nelson (1977) and Court (1986) found that territorial interactions were usually accompanied by the Creaking call. Cade observed similar fights with feet-grappling over disputed items of food and at the boundaries of food territories during the non-breeding season, and found that they were directed at other raptors as well.

In a dense but migratory Peregrine breeding population in northern Canada, Court (1986) witnessed a good deal of territorial interaction. The birds competed intensively for nesting territories on their return early in the spring, but competition dropped off as breeding began. Sixty-one interactions were seen in which a cliff occupant flew towards and pursued an intruder, and 93% of these chases were of male by male or female by female. Serious fighting occurred in the immediate vicinity of the nesting cliffs, but then usually developed into a chase. Territory holders were occasionally replaced by new birds before breeding began, but only once was actual displacement witnessed, involving a male. Males were more territorial than females in terms of interaction rate and in pursuing intruders to greater distances, but chases varied much in length and there appeared to be differences in individual aggressiveness.

The same kinds of encounter, with talon grappling, have been observed in Britain, but descriptions of territorial behaviour here have either not specified the stage in the breeding cycle, or have referred mainly to falcons with eggs or young. Since this behaviour seems to be similar throughout the nesting period, I include these further observations here. Walpole-Bond (1938) has described fierce battles, with blows struck, when Peregrines with eyries on the Sussex cliffs attacked and drove off intruding tiercels. Yet, despite the opportunity here for collisions between occupiers and trespassers, because of the close spacing of pairs, interactions of this kind did not seem to be frequent. Fights between Peregrines in the vicinity of the eyrie have been reported in various parts of Britain, but they were at one time rather infrequently

witnessed, and I saw only a few instances myself. Most incidents involved adult intruders, but juveniles were occasionally attacked near the occupied nest. The majority of British Peregrines are resident in the vicinity of their nesting cliffs, so that claims do not have to be staked anew each spring, and this may reduce territorial interaction compared with migratory populations.

Geoff Horne has, however, noted a recent increase in fighting between occupants and intruders around the nest cliffs in winter and early spring in Lakeland, where the Peregrine population has increased so markedly since 1975. He finds an increasing tendency for falcons to stay around first class cliffs during the day, right through the winter, and suggests this is because the pressures of new birds seeking to establish themselves as breeders is now considerable, and puts these good breeding places under particular risk of take-over. Third-class cliffs are much less continuously held outside the breeding season, and would be less attractive to incoming birds.

Only occasionally is serious damage inflicted during territorial fighting, but Hall (1955) noted that persistent fighting between the Sun Life Peregrines and an intruding pair in Montreal ended in the death of one adult male, which was found half eaten on the nesting ledge. On Mallorca, P. Lomax also saw a mortal combat between two Peregrines on the ground, which ended with one killing and beginning to eat the other. It may be that other reported cases of cannibalism (p. 133) also began as territorial squabbles.

It is much more common in Britain for a third bird, of either sex, to appear about an occupied eyrie without eliciting any response from the rightful occupants. Such instances have been noted by numerous observers, and I have seen a good many myself. They have become increasingly frequent during the last 15 years or so, as numbers have built up. Typically, while the owners are circling and often alarm-calling in their usual fashion, one suddenly becomes aware that a third bird has appeared on the scene. The extra bird is seldom seen to come out from the crags; it just drifts into sight, sometimes joining the pair as they cruise around, but often staying away from them and at a greater height. Usually the intruder sooner or later fades out as mysteriously as it came, but occasionally it will remain in the vicinity. No one knows what these third birds represent. They are probably non-breeders hanging around the area, and perhaps actually the previous year's offspring of the same territory; or they could be simply visitors from adjoining territories, especially if they have failed in their own nesting. Against the second possibility, I have seen such extra Peregrines at isolated haunts lying at a considerable distance from the next occupied eyrie. Only rarely are they likely to be genuine triangular matings. Occasionally two extra birds are seen together with an occupying pair.

The more frequently witnessed skirmishes in Britain are with Ravens and Buzzards occupying the same cliffs during the breeding season. These begin during the pre-laying period, but continue for some weeks and are often particularly intense during the egg stage. Pairs of Peregrines vary greatly in their overt hostility to Ravens on the same cliffs, for some will completely ignore these neighbours while others are extremely aggressive, hastening to the attack almost every time the big crows take to the air. Attacks are by repeated stoops, often by both of the pair concentrating on one Raven, and are usually accompanied by a good deal of Cacking-calling. The Ravens' part in these combats is usually defensive, and blows are seldom struck. Similar sparring with Buzzards is frequent and this species is, if anything, even more readily routed than the Raven. Golden Eagles are rather a different proposition though they too are attacked with determination if they approach the Peregrines' home quarters too closely. The aggression of Peregrines towards other predatory birds is perhaps closer to defence of nest-site than to true inter-specific territorial behaviour. I have described it more fully under relationships with other bird species in Chapter 12.

REVERSED SEXUAL SIZE DIMORPHISM

The many attempts to explain why female birds of prey (including owls and skuas as well as raptors) are mostly larger than males, have depended on identifying a presumed advantage (which would have been subject to selection) within the divergent contributions of the sexes to those features special to this group of birds. The special features of the birds of prey are that they are mostly fierce, with the dangerous weapons of hooked beaks and sharp talons, for catching and rending living, often agile prey; and that they are monogamous, with an extended breeding season during which the male provides food for the female and then their highly dependent young. As the evidence provided by Newton (1979) so well shows, *degree* of size dimorphism is explicable as the result of varying selection for food partitioning, with its advantages of widening feeding niche and reduced competition between the sexes. The more extreme degrees, as in the Peregrine, could be regarded as a corollary of exclusive adaptation to bird prey in environments with a wide range of species.

There is no need to seek other explanations for the pronounced sexual size differences in raptors such as the Peregrine. The more taxing problem is rather to explain why, in many birds of prey, where food partitioning is less marked or negligible, there is advantage in the females being only slightly larger than the males or the males only slightly smaller than the females. If a general explanation of reversed size difference between the sexes can be deduced, it provides a platform from which further selection for the separate advantages of food partitioning can then operate.

Various general explanations have been advanced. One group is behavioural, and sees advantages from female dominance, in achieving compatibility between the sexes and maintaining the male in his role of food provider, in birds that are unusually fierce and capable of inflicting damage on each other (Cade, 1960; Amadon, 1975). Others have seen the male's food providing activities as the key, and suggested that his smaller size confers bioenergetic advantage in this role (Schantz and Nilsson, 1980; Cade, 1980). Korpimaki (1986) extends this notion to female selection for smaller, more agile and efficient males, best able to compete with other males for territory, hunt efficiently and provide food adequately. Olsen and Olsen (1987) have suggested that large size is favoured by females competing with each other for the limited resource of a quality male who is a good hunter and holds a good territory.

While the truth may lie within these hypotheses, and possibly in some combination of them, none comes across as a blinding revelation and all seem to have flaws in their arguments. As Newton (1979) has pointed out, some of the advantages for which selection has been supposed (e.g. female dominance) could equally be a consequence of, rather than a reason for, divergent size of the sexes. Perhaps reversed sexual size dimorphism has proved so perplexing because it appears so usually to be considered in isolation from the more frequent state, in which males are larger than females. Preoccupation with the more extreme forms of divergence either way (e.g. bird-feeding raptors versus polygamous gamebirds) has also drawn attention from the fact that the commonest condition is when one sex is only slightly larger than the other, in either direction. In many waders, besides the species with reversed courtship, the females are slightly larger than the males, and some have longer bills. Since the generally accepted view is that sexual selection accounts for the more 'normal' size dimorphism in birds, explanations of the 'reversed' state which involve female choice of mate are the most economical.

Conclusion

There is a good deal more to be learned about Peregrine behaviour in the non-breeding and pre-laying periods: how far consistent patterns can be discerned among the wide range of variation, the significance of variations and their relationship to external conditions, and how all these things relate to success in breeding. The development of breeding behaviour each year includes a delicate process of adjustment between the two sexes through a steady progression of mutually stimulating activities. The smoothness of this sequence is likely to be conditioned by age and experience of the birds, e.g. in the food-transfer behaviour, and such factors may have considerable bearing on the eventual success of the breeding attempt.

CHAPTER 8

The breeding cycle: laying to fledging

THE EGG STAGE

Laying period and timing

When the female Peregrine finally selects a scrape for her clutch, the eggs are laid usually at intervals of about 48 hours, though there may be a longer gap of up to 72 hours especially between the third and fourth eggs. They may be produced at any time in the 24-hour cycle, though the early morning period appears to be the most favourable (Nethersole-Thompson, 1931). Tom Cade tells me that in captive Peregrines the interval between eggs averages 52–62 hours, so that the time of day for laying successive eggs shifts steadily from the time of first laying.

The appearance of the first egg in the nest is the most specific datum in the whole breeding cycle and thus affords the best means of comparing the timing of reproduction between different pairs, places or years. There is some variation in date of first egg between different parts of Britain, as shown in Table 13.

The information on exact date of first egg is disappointingly small, despite the large number of available records of eyries with eggs or young, and especially the number of dated clutches in egg collections. Many observational records could not estimate the state of incubation or the age of young with sufficient precision to make a reliable back-calculation, and the incubation period itself can vary by up to four days. A great many egg collection data tickets do not mention the exact state of incubation of clutches, or do so unreliably; and while the general state of incubation can usually be gauged from the appearance of an egg, this is too imprecise for present purposes. I have therefore relied on those field observations or clutch data where there was good reason to believe that the eggs were fresh; and have then estimated backwards to the date of the first egg by assuming that in half the records the last egg was laid on the date given by the observer/collector, and that in the other half it was laid on the previous day. An interval of 2 days between eggs in the clutch was then allowed, e.g. in a clutch of four eggs dated 8 April the first egg was laid on 1 or 2 April.

The results show that the Peregrines of the south-east coast of England were about a week earlier on average in their laying date compared with birds in the north and west of Britain. Full clutches before the end of March were most frequent here and the earliest British breeding record I have traced was a clutch of three eggs seen by J. Walpole-Bond on the Sussex coast on 23 March 1947. The south-west England falcons were a couple of days behind those in Sussex. Elsewhere there appears to be surprisingly little difference between separate regions. The available data for the Pembrokeshire coast give a laying date about a week later than for the rest of Wales, but as the records come entirely from egg collections with erratic data on state of incubation, this is not a reliable estimate.

Britain has a latitudinal range of only about 11° and this is probably too narrow for there to be marked differences in photoperiodic conditioning of the onset of breeding, as occurs over the much larger range of the Peregrine in North America. Such variations in laying date as occur here are most likely to be the results of temperature differences, either operating directly on the bird or indirectly through the effect on prey. There is a marked decrease in mean temperatures with distance north in Britain and it is to be expected that the Peregrines of the south coast would begin to nest earlier than those farther north. Most of the Sussex coast eyries are close to sea level and in south-facing, sun-exposed situations, in a district where mean monthly temperature for February at average nesting altitude is 41·0°F (5·0°C) (Meteorological Office, 1952). The slightly later date for south-west England corresponds to a February mean of 42·5°F (5·8°C), but the heavier rainfall and generally greater oceanicity of this region may more than cancel out its greater warmth, compared with the south-east. February temperatures are regarded as the most significant, as it is during this month that breeding activity usually begins in Britain.

In more northerly regions there is the additional complication of an altitudinal effect on laying date, operating through the temperature lapse rate of 1°C for every 150 m change in elevation (1°F for every 270 ft). Many of the records for Wales and nearly all those from north-west England, southern Scotland and the central Highlands are from inland eyries at an average elevation of about 400 m. The 15 coastal records for Wales give an average laying date of 5 April compared with 8 April for the 38 inland records. Analysis of all inland records for northern England and southern Scotland combined, 1906–77, is given in Table 14.

It would therefore seem that there is a delay in laying date, on average, of one day for every 122 m increase in altitude within any one region. These comparisons are not statistically valid because of the lack of independence in the data (i.e. some runs of records are from the same females) but they point in a direction which might be expected.

The only part of the Highlands for which I have a usable sample of laying dates is the central and eastern region. Even here the number of records is small, but indicates an average date of 9 April. This is surprising since the region is appreciably colder than the Southern Uplands or Lakeland. While some of the really elevated eyries in the Highlands evidently do not have eggs until quite late, those at average altitudes are only marginally later than in regions much farther south. Derek Langslow has suggested that while photoperiod and/or temperature probably act as the trigger in stimulating onset of breeding activity in the Peregrine, the actual timing of egg-laying may depend more closely on the intensity of courtship behaviour, and that this behavioural conditioning is itself likely to be geared to the timing of the spring increase in availability of prey. The dependence of Peregrines in the central and eastern Highlands on Red Grouse as a principal prey may help to account for the surprisingly early laying date in this cold region, for the Grouse is a hardy resident with a relatively early breeding season itself and is available as food throughout the winter.

Timing of the breeding season has no doubt evolved to match the food demands of the young Peregrines against the seasonal peak in availability of prey in such a way as to give maximum survival on average. The timing of the prey peak has itself evolved similarly in relation to the annual climatic cycle, so that it is likely that the Peregrine is physiologically responsive to the relevant meteorological conditions as proximate factors.

Laying date for the same female is often similar in successive years – Walpole-Bond (1938) said individuals laid 'on almost exactly the same date'. One female in Dumfriesshire which I followed from 1954–60 varied in date of first egg from 3–6 April during seven layings. There may be more variation, though, and a Cumberland falcon laid her first egg on 25 March, 1 April and 6 April in three successive seasons 1945–47. Perhaps a change in male partner may affect onset of laying. At one Galloway haunt which I followed from 1947–77, and which had a good many different females during this period, first egg date in 18 different years varied only between 1 and 9 April, with a mean of 4 April (compared with 8 April for the district as a whole). The breeding crags lie at only 250 m and face due south in a locality not far from the coast, so that favourable local climate might account for the tendency to early nesting here. Even more surprisingly, Walpole-Bond's records show quite marked differences in average laying date between adjacent nesting places on the Sussex coast.

During the period 1905–49, 29 clutches at Seaford Head had an average first egg date of 31 March, while 28 clutches at Newhaven, only 7 km distant, had an average first egg date of 5 April. Tom Cade has found that particular captive pairs are highly consistent in laying dates from year to year, showing a variance of usually less than a week. On the other hand, Mearns and Newton (1988) found a tendency for laying date to become earlier, from 12 to 4 April, as female age increased from 2 to 5+ years in southern Scotland.

Average laying date could be expected to respond to climatic changes involving temperature shifts. Walpole-Bond's Sussex records show a slight shift from an average first egg date of 3 April for 1905–24 (60 clutches) to 31 March for 1925–40 (52 clutches). While it would be unwise to attach too much weight to these figures, such a shift would match the period of greater warmth which reached a peak in the 1930s before suffering a recession after about 1940. During the run of cold, backward springs since 1960, severe night frost has been frequent in many inland haunts during the laying and incubation periods, and recurrent snow-storms often plastered the crag ledges thickly and persistently in the higher-lying localities. There is some indication that laying can be delayed by up to a week or so during exceptionally severe weather in inland districts, as during April 1978, and, even more, during April 1979. G. Horne found that in Lakeland the average date of the first egg during the 1970s was 12 April, but in 1978–79 it was 17 April. Indeed, during this last spring, some of the higher-lying haunts in the Highlands remained snow and ice-bound until so late that some pairs evidently failed to nest at all. Eggs can be lost under such Arctic conditions, but the Peregrine is a hardy bird and once the eggs are laid they are seldom forsaken, however bad the conditions. Although the Raven nests a month earlier in the same crags, the falcon is one of the earliest birds to breed in Britain, especially in the hill country.

The spread of the laying period for 95% of pairs in different districts, based on the data used in compiling Table 13, averages 20 days. If allowance is made for altitudinal differences in upland districts, the period should theoretically be a little less. However, the Sussex coast records give a spread of 20 days, and it seems appropriate to use this as a standard period.

Peregrines which lose their eggs before incubation is more than about 10 days advanced usually produce a repeat clutch. Analysis of 43 re-laying periods, mainly from egg collections, gives a mean interval of 19–20 days to the date of first egg of the repeat clutch, from the day the first clutch was lost. The spread of the repeat interval is, however, quite wide, varying from 18 to 33 days, but with one exceptionally short period of only nine days. I once knew a pair robbed of an incomplete clutch of two eggs on 4 April to have a repeat of three eggs in a different nest on 14 April, but this could have been virtually a continuation of the first laying. D. Nethersole-Thompson has known Peregrines robbed before laying their last egg to deposit this in the same eyrie and proceed with incubation.

Gilbert (1927) and Nethersole-Thompson (1931) give 21 days as the usual period taken by Peregrines to complete a second clutch, while Walpole-Bond (1938) gives 17–24 days. The data I have used, which include 31 of Walpole-Bond's own records, suggest that 24–25 days is the more typical interval taken to complete repeat layings. However, T. Cade has found that with captive

Peregrines the interval between removal of the first clutch and start of the second is 14 days with very little variation.

Not all Peregrines produce repeat layings even when robbed of fresh eggs, but a few will even re-lay a second time if they lose their repeat clutch. The Sussex records of Walpole-Bond and Nethersole-Thompson included at least four instances of Peregrines which laid three clutches in one season, and there have been occasional records from other parts of Britain. One Sussex pair were robbed of their first clutch (c/4) on 19 April 1912, their second (c/3) on 13 May, and had a third (c/2) on 10 June.

In Britain, the great majority of repeat layings are occasioned by human robbery of first clutches, but this factor has probably been less important than other influences during the long time-scale over which the re-laying ability developed. Under 'natural' conditions, clutches are sometimes destroyed by rock or earth falls, especially on the friable cliffs or unstable cut-banks which provide many nest sites in some regions. In colder regions falling ice or cracking of eggs by frost is a hazard, and severe snow blizzards after laying time can result in loss of clutches if there is no thaw soon afterwards. Mammalian predators may occasionally raid eyries in some parts of the world.

The egg

The eggs of the Peregrine are among the most handsome laid by any species of bird. Whilst the prevailing colour is the characteristic red-brown of the genus *Falco*, the range of variation in Peregrine eggs is very large. At first sight, it appears that there are three types of pigmentation. The surface of the fresh egg has variable amounts of bright red-brown markings appearing as a freckled, mottled or blotched layer which can easily be rubbed off when the shell is wet. This non-fast layer of pigment gives a Peregrine egg much of its beauty and richness, and in fresh specimens is often accompanied by a kind of bloom. Beneath the surface markings is a more diffuse and often more continuous 'ground colour' varying from a typical biscuit brown to brick red or to paler shades of pink, fawn, buff and cream. Some eggs also have spots and blotches of darker brown, ashy grey, lilac or even pale purple often referred to as 'shell marks'. Ground-colour and shell marks are each 'fast' colours and can only be removed by chemical treatment or severe abrasion.

Arnold Cooke (unpubl.) has shown that this wide range of coloration in Peregrine eggs is referable to the red-brown pigment-complex, protoporphyrin (related to haemoglobin), and Tyler (1966) pointed out that the apparent colour variations result from differences in the amount of pigment and its vertical distribution within the whole shell layer. Cooke also found smaller amounts of the blue-green pigment (biliverdin) but this is not recognisable as such under superficial examination. The shell consists largely of crystalline calcium carbonate with a distinctive and complex structure and a whitish coloration. The red-brown pigment lies at variable depths within this structure: patches farthest below the surface show as shell marks, while pigment at the surface cuticle appears as ground colour and that lying over the shell cuticle is the superficial layer.

The commonest type of egg has a biscuit brown ground colour, rather lightly and incompletely covered with a mottle of brighter rust-red or red-brown surface markings. Thickening of the surface pigment into a very dark colour, approaching brown-black, is quite common, but such markings are usually small and sparingly present. Some eggs have heavier blotching and marbling on the surface and are especially rich in colour, and occasionally dense pigmentation over the whole shell gives mahogany or tan coloured types. The paler varieties include ginger, salmon-pink and lavender shades. A distinctive type of egg has little or no pigmentation over parts of the shell, giving a pale, sometimes cream or dull white ground, often with well-developed shell marks and a capping of red-brown at either the large or small end. A few eggs are heavily zoned with pigment around their waist, leaving both ends pale. Colour plate IV illustrates some of the main varieties of Peregrine eggs, but it is impossible to do justice to the subject in so short a series.

A few eggs have white surface patches, usually less than a centimetre across and roughly circular. They are devoid of pigment except for a network of fine ridges, and appear as though formed by etching of the shell surface layer with acid. They are usually associated with deposition of small amounts of very thick, dark surface pigment on immediately adjacent parts of the shell. Many eggs are laid with the surface pigment appearing to have been partly or largely rubbed or washed off, often in a vertical, streaky pattern, as though this happened in the bird's own oviduct. Perhaps the surface layer was merely sparse in such eggs. The washy or streaky eggs seem to have been especially common in the Southern Uplands, but I have not otherwise been aware of any regional tendencies in bias towards a particular type of egg. However, Walpole-Bond (1938) commented that Peregrine eggs from the south coast of England were seldom as dark as those from other districts.

Uniformity of appearance within the eggs of the clutch is the exception rather than the rule, and there can be wide variation in the amount of pigment and hence in the colour appearance of the set. Quite often there is one capped egg showing much pale shell in a set of otherwise typical red-brown eggs. A female Peregrine tends to lay a similar clutch in successive years, to the extent that some individuals can be identified with confidence year after year, especially when colour and marking pattern are combined with size and shape of the eggs. However, even repeat layings can sometimes differ markedly from first clutches, being either darker or lighter and either more or less heavily blotched; and there can be a gradual shift in egg type over a period of years, usually towards decreasing pigmentation.

Egg type thus has to be used with great caution as a means of identifying individual birds, especially when the eggs are only of an ordinary type; but when distinctive eggs are involved, it is a reliable guide. A falcon on the coast of Lleyn, North Wales, in the period 1928–35 first laid four normal red-brown eggs. In 1929 and 1930 she laid clutches each with two normal and two white eggs. Thereafter she laid only white eggs, usually only two, but in 1935 three, all infertile (K. L. Wilson and R. Bark-Jones). These white eggs had only a few rather small brown and ashy markings. Single white eggs in otherwise normal clutches have been found occasionally in other areas. White eggs could be produced by premature laying.

The original brightness and richness of the surface coloration in Peregrine eggs disappears fairly rapidly in the nest, especially in wet weather, and changes to a more uniform dull brown, so that in an incomplete or only just completed clutch, the last egg laid is often readily identifiable. Peregrine eggs thus lose their beauty as incubation proceeds. The shell absorbs oil from the brooding bird's feathers and gradually takes on a gloss instead of the original matt texture. During wet weather and in soily scrapes the surface markings may become rubbed off completely, but eggs laid on the wool lining of overhung and sheltered Raven eyries may retain something of their original freshness until well into incubation. Addled eggs which remain after hatching of the rest are usually polished, faded and often quite bleached.

In shape Peregrine eggs are typically between ovate and short ovate, with one end more rounded (larger) than the other, and with some variation towards both elongate and spherical. Shape is usually fairly uniform within the clutch but occasionally a set will have one egg markedly different from the rest. Pyriform eggs occur occasionally, and in the Westmorland Pennines in 1908, P. W. Parminter took an extraordinary clutch of three such pear-shaped eggs, also very handsomely patterned with pale ground and large ashy shell marks.

The measurements of 2253 Peregrine eggs taken in Britain and Ireland gave mean external dimensions of length 51·5 mm and breadth 40·8 mm. Size of egg is highly correlated within the clutch though there is normally some variation and it is rare for all the eggs to be exactly the same size. The average size of eggs in a repeat clutch may be either slightly more or slightly less than in a first clutch, and this also applies to layings by the same bird in successive years. In runs of clutches from six different females over six or more years there was a consistent tendency for average size of egg in each clutch to become smaller with time. The decrease by the end of the run was usually slight, but in one such sequence of eggs from the same female in Breconshire, normal eggs averaging 50·0 × 39·5 mm in 1926 steadily declined to dwarfs of 46·5 × 32·5 mm in 1933.

I have not found any convincing evidence of geographical variations between different regions of Britain and Ireland (see Table 10). Ussher (1900) said, 'After carefully measuring all the Irish eggs available ... I find the average length slightly exceeds 51·0 mm × 40·4 mm; but those from the county of Waterford exceed in size those from Wexford, Tipperary, Cork and Kerry which I have examined. One eyrie in the first-named county contained year after year eggs of such exceptional size as averaged 54·9 × 42·2 mm, the largest attaining the remarkable dimensions of 58·9 × 44·7 mm.' However, ten clutches from Co. Waterford for which I have measurements give a mean egg size of 51·7 × 41·6 mm, not significantly greater than the overall average.

Any egg with length × breadth dimensions (in mm) giving a product greater than 2400 may be regarded as unusually large. British and Irish clutches of exceptionally large mean egg size include:

Breconshire	1950	c/3	55·3 × 44·3 mm
Pembrokeshire	1911	c/2	55·0 × 44·5 mm
Pembrokeshire	1921	c/2	58·0 × 43·0 mm
Dorset	1928	c/4	56·7 × 42·8 mm
Antrim	1940	c/3	55·3 × 43·6 mm
Ireland	1891	c/4	57·0 × 42·1 mm

The female laying the large eggs in Dorset was still present in 1933, when her eggs averaged 54·0 × 43·6 mm.

A length × breadth measurement of less than 1800 can be regarded as an unusually small egg, though there is a rather indeterminate lower limit to egg-size, and runt eggs occur now and then, usually as a single oddment in a normal clutch. I have seen three such dwarfs in eyries, the smallest measuring 32·2 × 27·3 mm. Small clutches include:

Breconshire	1933	c/4	46·5 × 32·5 mm
Radnorshire	1931	c/5	46·5 × 36·8 mm
Dumfriesshire	1949	c/3	45·3 × 37·7 mm
Devon	1914	c/4	45·6 × 38·0 mm
Cumberland	1935	c/3	46·6 × 37·2 mm
Westmorland	1913	c/4	46·0 × 38·5 mm

Fresh Peregrine eggs normally weigh between 40 and 50 g, but lose weight by evaporation quite markedly as incubation proceeds. Twenty fresh eggs (1964–75) measuring an average 51·6 × 40·9 mm had an average weight of 45·5 g, with extremes of 38·5 g and 52·6 g. A clutch of four eggs will thus average 182 g or 16% of average female weight (1140 g).

In the years before 1947, air-dry eggshell weight averaged 3·80 g for British and Irish Peregrines, but from 1947 onwards there was a marked decrease in shell weight in most districts to an average of 3·17 g, except in the central and eastern Highlands where it was 3·72 g. This change did not involve any decrease in size of eggshells and resulted from a reduction in shell thickness. Micrometer measurements and, even more, studies of microscopic structure of Peregrine eggshells have confirmed that the change does indeed involve mainly a decrease in shell thickness and that shell density has not changed appreciably.

When I began to study the eggshell change in 1966 and was faced with the task of measuring a large number of specimens in collections without damaging them, I decided to short-cut the direct measurement of shell thickness. It was obvious that the weight of an eggshell in relation to its size must be some function of shell thickness. Size poses another difficulty, for accurate measurements of surface area or volume are time-consuming to make. The simple product of length × breadth of the shell seemed to give a result with the essential properties of an area measurement, which was what was needed, and when divided into the shell weight it gave a reasonable index of thickness.

$$\text{Eggshell thickness index} = \frac{\text{weight of shell (mg)}}{\text{length (mm)} \times \text{breadth of shell (mm)}}$$

Table 15 gives measurements of eggshell thickness index for different regions of Britain. The overall decrease in shell thickness index for Britain and Ireland during 1947–71 averaged 16·0% below the mean of 1·82, and ranged from 2·2% in the central and eastern Highlands to 20·5% in northern England. Much lower values than these averages have been found in most regions, and the thinnest-shelled clutch was one from inland Wales in 1956, with an index 38% less than the pre-1947 value for the region.

The cause of shell thinning has been established beyond doubt as contamination of the Peregrine's tissues by residues of the persistent organochlorine insecticide DDT or its metabolite DDE. This remarkable phenomenon and its significance are dealt with more fully on pp. 248–250 and in Chapter 13, but Table 15 also shows that in some districts for which eggshell data are available, there has been a distinct recovery in shell thickness since 1971, coincident with decreasing environmental contamination by DDT (Table 30).

Eggshell thinning has now been reported in several races of Peregrine scattered around the world. Peakall and Kiff (1979) have reviewed the evidence, pointing out that in no region does shell thinning pre-date 1947, and have shown that a general correlation exists between thin shells and presence of DDE residues actually in the shell membranes, these amounts reflecting those originally present in the whole eggs and thus in the birds which laid them.

Table 16 shows the decreases in Peregrine shell thickness index found in different regions of the World.

The relationship between DDT/DDE level in the egg (and thus in the parent bird) and the degree of eggshell thinning has been shown to be extremely close in several bird species besides the Peregrine; but it is a logarithmic dose/effect relationship, which means that a small amount of residue produces a relatively marked level of thinning. Newton, Bogan and Haas (1989) found that Peregrine shell indices 10% and 20% below normal were associated with DDE levels of 4·6 and 25·9 ppm. Fox (1979) has used the closeness of this relationship in the Merlin to predict quite accurately from eggshell thickness measurements the level of DDT/DDE contamination of the population in Canada.

While Peregrines occasionally laid single eggs or even whole clutches with abnormally thin shells before 1947, the striking feature of the recent shell thinning has been its all-embracing nature. In many regions, including much of Britain, virtually every egg measured from 1947 onwards has had a thickness index lying within a new and lower band of variation (see Fig. 9). This suggests that the whole population has been affected, except in the central and eastern Highlands, where shell index is not significantly less than before 1947.

Direct measurements of Peregrine eggshell thickness are more difficult to make and are complicated by variations over different parts of the shell, especially between the waist and the poles. Average thickness of the shell with adherent membranes is 0·35 ± 0·005 mm for pre-1947 British eggs (0·28 mm without membranes).

Cooke (1979) has shown by light and electron microscope examination that shell thinning in Peregrine eggs involves roughly proportional decreases in thickness of the outer and thicker palisade layer and the inner and thinner mammillary layer of the shell; suggesting that thin shells result from a decreased rate of deposition. Shell thinning was associated with a proportionately greater decrease in shell strength. Porosity, measured as the rate of passage of water vapour, was lower for the thin shells than for normal shells.

Although eggshell thinning attributable to DDT/DDE contamination has been proved to occur in many species of birds, and a variety of families besides those in the raptors, the precise physiological and biochemical mechanisms involved are still imperfectly understood. Cooke (1973, 1975, 1979) has reviewed the evidence and concludes that the mechanism may vary between different species, but that in the Peregrine a reduction in available shell components in the shell gland during the calcification process is likely to be involved, possibly in response to decreased enzyme activity in the shell gland tissue.

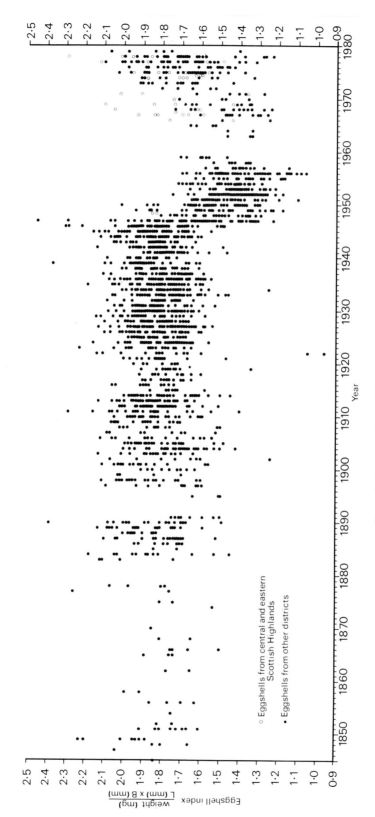

Figure 9. Decrease of eggshell thickness in time.

The Peregrine eggs that I have examined since 1947 have seemed to include fewer of the well blotched and heavily marbled rich red-brown types which commonly appear in collections with older eggs, and there has been a high proportion of the 'washy' or 'streaky' type in which the superficial pigment is largely lacking, or has a rubbed appearance, even in fresh eggs. This is a difficult feature to measure and it can only be stated as a subjective impression, especially since the 'washy' type of egg was fairly common before 1947. One collector with long experience confirmed my feeling, saying that Peregrine eggs he had seen after about 1950 were 'a poor lot'.

The reduced mechanical strength of eggshells resulting from thinning has had a profound effect on the population biology of the Peregrine. Whereas in the years before 1950, broken eggs in Peregrine eyries were an infrequent occurrence (only three were seen in 100 closely observed clutches during 1905–50), since then they have been found commonly in virtually all British breeding districts. I first became aware of this trend in 1951, when I found broken eggs in five out of nine eyries, but one 1949 nest contained a broken egg and it is evident from other records that the increase in egg breaking coincided with the onset of shell thinning, dating from 1947. For the period 1951–66, 163 closely observed clutches included 51 with one or more broken eggs, and another 30 in which one or more eggs disappeared without trace (Ratcliffe, 1970).

Egg-breaking has usually involved egg eating by the parent Peregrines. As well as the direct observational evidence (p. 330), recognisable fragments of Peregrine eggshell occasionally appear in the birds' own castings. Once an egg is damaged it is no longer treated as an egg by a parent, whose instinct is to eat it. Thin-shelled eggs are obviously more easily damaged by the parents than those with normal shells, and as incubation proceeds the risks of damage become considerable. Eggs may be pressed too heavily against each other, or against the bird's feet or body, or against projecting stones or other irregularities in the scrape. I have seen several dented eggs in eyries. Incidence of egg-breaking is closely related to the degree of shell thinning in any district or over a particular period, and many people have argued that it can be explained as a wholly mechanical effect, with egg-eating as a secondary and induced response to damaged shells. There is evidence that in the Heron, egg-breaking can be caused directly by abnormal behaviour not involving eating, and in the Peregrine it is also possible that egg-breaking could sometimes result from disturbed behaviour, with the parent attacking its own eggs before they were damaged. The truth about such events remains an open question, in the absence of any critical evidence.

Eaten eggs are sometimes found away from the nest, and it is evident that many, if not all, of the disappearing eggs (excluding human robberies which are almost invariably of whole clutches) have been removed by the parents without traces being left behind. I have used the term clutch depletion to cover both breakage and disappearance of eggs. Breakage can range from one egg to the whole clutch, and it can occur at any time, from the day of laying almost to the day of hatching. Sometimes the whole clutch is destroyed before incubation can begin but more usually eggs are lost at intervals as incubation proceeds. The amount of depletion within clutches naturally tends to be related to the level of shell thinning. The thinnest post-1947 Peregrine eggshell I have examined had a thickness index 42% less than the pre-1947 mean. It seems that eggs with shells

Dead embryo in thin-shelled Peregrine egg which collapsed at hatching; southern Scotland (photo: R. T. Smith)

thinner than this are unlikely to survive long enough in the nest to be found and measured. Any shell showing thinning greater than 25% has a poor chance of surviving incubation to full term.

The majority of Peregrines known to have lost whole clutches by breakage have evidently not laid second sets of eggs. Some of those which repeated then broke their second clutch too, though the rearing of broods from repeat layings seems to have become more frequent lately. Falcons with depleted clutches continue to incubate remaining eggs, though a rather high proportion of these has proved to be addled, and desertion often occurs after birds have been sitting for some time. Depleted clutches at best can only produce smaller than normal broods.

Eggshell thinning has, in fact, been the main factor contributing to the decrease in productivity of the Peregrine in many parts of Britain since 1947. It has probably accounted for a high proportion of the numerous total breeding failures of pairs which laid eggs, and has led to a marked reduction in average brood size. The contribution of shell thinning to actual population decline has probably varied between different parts of the World. In Britain it seems to have been less important than in North America, where Peregrine decrease is believed to be largely a function of reduced productivity, rather than increased adult mortality. Indeed, Anderson and Hickey (1972) have shown that for a range of North American birds there is a general relationship between population status and degree of eggshell thinning.

The partial recovery of shell thickness in British Peregrine eggs has been matched by a decrease in frequency of clutch depletion; though I do not have precise figures for this decrease, the improvement since 1970 of mean brood size and proportion of pairs rearing young is a good indication of reduced egg loss. Egg-breaking still occurs in most districts, and is likely to remain more frequent than before 1947 unless shell thickness recovers fully to its normal level. It is evident that a Peregrine population showing average eggshell thinning of 20% is inevitably in serious trouble, but the recent British evidence indicates that the critical replacement level of productivity can be exceeded and recovery can take place within populations still showing 6–10% shell thinning.

Clutch size

The majority of Peregrines breeding in Britain lay clutches of three or four eggs (c/3 or c/4). Genuine clutches of two eggs are occasional, but incubated single eggs are likely to represent depleted clutches. Clutches of five eggs occur occasionally, and appear to have become more frequent in recent years: only 22 were recorded in Britain and Ireland up to 1970, but from 1974 to 1988, 25 sets of five (involving 13 different birds) were reported from northern England and southern Scotland alone, at a frequency of about one in every 50 clutches counted (2%). In addition there are four British records of six egg clutches, in Pembrokeshire, Breconshire, Radnor and Argyll. In North America, a Peregrine with a record clutch of seven eggs produced a repeat set with six (Hickey, 1969). Clutches of more than four eggs are, however, hardly frequent enough to be significant in the population biology of the Peregrine. The main interest therefore centres on the exact proportions between 'threes' and 'fours' produced by our Peregrine population.

Egg collectors' Peregrine clutch data contain too much bias to give an accurate measure of average clutch size, or to show reliably whether variations occur geographically or over a period. While a clutch of four eggs was always more prized than a 'three', there was perhaps less tendency to select for bigger clutches than was the case with more common species. Indeed, the main bias lies in the opposite direction. Many collectors coveted Peregrine eggs so much that they took clutches of three or even two fresh eggs without giving the birds a chance to lay more. In some districts competition was keen, and to leave a clutch of three eggs even two or three more days in the hope of a fourth was to risk losing the set to someone else. Many collections therefore contain an unknown number of clutches which were incomplete when taken, so that their data produce a bias towards a lower figure for average clutch size. Only when the data label states that incubation had begun can one be sure that the clutch was complete.

The more reliable information on clutch size comes from eyries which were visited twice to ascertain that incubation had begun, or those where the eggs were obviously well advanced in incubation when first seen. The overall average for the whole of Great Britain up to 1979 , based on reliable data (622 clutches), is 3·63 eggs per clutch (Table 17). The figure based on eggs in collections (663 first clutches) is 3·45 eggs per clutch, this lower value evidently stemming from the bias mentioned. There are no significant differences in clutch size between different districts, or between coastal and inland populations. The only hint of variations which I have noticed is that there seems to be a tendency in certain *years* for clutch size to be lower than normal. This could be an effect of adverse weather, perhaps only locally, but the samples are too small for the differences to be judged significant.

John Walpole-Bond's clutch data for Sussex merit separate examination. Bond's diaries record sizes of 137 first clutches, most of which he evidently took, between 1905–49. The mean clutch size of this sample was 3·50, but many sets of c/3 were fresh when taken and there is a strong possibility that some of them were incomplete, so that this figure may be lower than the true one. If the whole period is divided into 1905–31 and 1932–49, there is a decrease in the proportion of c/4 (from 57% to 37%) and mean clutch size (from 3·55 to 3·37) in time. Desmond Nethersole-Thompson has given me his data on 26 Sussex clutches for 1927–31, with a mean clutch size of 3·69 (73% c/4). Nethersole-Thompson believes that the apparent tendency towards smaller clutches after 1931 was real and matches an incipient decline in the Sussex population. He has also pointed out that there was a tendency towards smaller clutches on the lower stretches of cliff from Rottingdean to Newhaven, compared with the higher precipices from Seaford Head to Beachy Head. For example, 30 clutches from Newhaven were compared with 30 clutches from Seaford Head taken during 1905–49: the Newhaven series averaged 3·17 eggs (33% c/4) and the Seaford Head series 3·53 eggs (53% c/4).

These data are not amenable to significance testing, but they suggest intriguing possibilities for future examination of large data sets, to find out if Peregrine clutch size could vary according to year/weather/food supply, quality of nesting place or territory, age or status of individual birds, or state of the population. The reason why some females lay only three eggs is presumably related to some balance of selective advantage which might be revealed by examining the failure/success rates of different clutch sizes under varying conditions. While clutches commonly became depleted by egg-breaking or unexplained disappearance of eggs in many districts after 1946, the data show that the number of eggs actually laid per clutch maintained the pre-1946 average.

Since the above was written, there has been a distinct tendency for clutch size to fall in all regions of Britain for which there are data (Table 17). The difference is statistically significant for all regions except Wales. The national mean for 1980–91 is 3·43 eggs (1298 clutches). The reason is unclear, but the trend matches recovery and increase in population in most regions.

Any one female tends to lay a clutch of the same size every year, but this is only a tendency and not a rule. John Mitchell found that a female in the south-west Highlands, in 1974–79, laid 5, 5, 4, 4, 5 and 5 eggs. In a marked group of southern Scottish birds, Mearns and Newton (1988) found that 2-year-old females averaged 3·0 eggs per clutch, compared with 3·8 eggs for 3- to 5- or more year-old females. Although it has been surmised by some that clutch size in the Peregrine may decrease in old age, probably most females die before they are overtaken by reproductive senility, and there is little evidence of such an effect in the numerous runs of clutches taken from individual birds. The female which laid the white eggs may have been an example of such an effect, but this may have resulted from some physiological disturbance unrelated to ageing. Tom Cade tells me that his captive breeding Peregrines nearly all lay clutches of four eggs, and that although females eventually stop laying at around 19–20 years, clutch size is not reduced prior to cessation.

There is, however, an undoubted reduction, on average, in number of eggs laid in repeat clutches. For the period up to 1979, the mean for 56 repeat clutches known to be completed is 3·21 eggs, compared with the national first laying mean of 3·63. The 56 clutches consisted of $3 \times c/2$, $38 \times c/3$ and $15 \times c/4$. In 37 instances out of the 56, the size of the first clutch was known and averaged 3·62 eggs ($14 \times c/3$, $23 \times c/4$). The decrease in clutch size is highly significant (Mann–Whitney U test, $n = 93$, $U = 1423·5$, $p < 0·001$). For the later period 1980–91, 58 repeat clutches had a mean of 2·91 eggs, an even bigger decrease from the national first laying mean of 3·43 eggs ($11 \times c/2$, $41 \times c/3$, $6 \times c/4$). In the 37 first layings, where clutch size was known, this averaged 3·46 eggs ($3 \times c/2$, $14 \times c/3$, $20 \times c/4$), again very close to the contemporary national mean, and giving another highly significant difference ($n = 95$, $U = 1557·5$, $p < 0·001$). Third layings are still smaller, four in Sussex known to J. Walpole-Bond and D. Nethersole-Thompson being of only 1, 2, 2, and 2 eggs, though H. Watson saw one of three eggs in northern England.

Incubation

Incubation does not usually begin until the third egg is laid, or sometimes the fourth in a four egg clutch. Captive breeding Peregrines do not begin incubation in earnest until the clutch is complete (T. Cade). Peregrines will sometimes leave single eggs completely unattended for an hour or more but one bird, usually the female, normally stands guard beside an incomplete clutch. The sentinel commonly stands facing outwards, and its conspicuous white breast quickly reveals the location of the eyrie when the watcher scans the cliff. Peregrines with incomplete clutches take wing quite readily, even when undisturbed, and often indulge in flights in the vicinity of the nesting cliffs, circling and soaring in leisurely fashion. Their behaviour depends on weather, and during rain or cold spells they are more inclined to cover the eggs without actually incubating properly. Incomplete clutches are probably covered at night, and certainly during frost. In most of the eyries I have examined, by the time the third egg was laid, it was quite easy to identify the last-laid egg by its appearance, and in a newly completed clutch it is sometimes possible to determine the precise order of laying in this way. The freshest egg still has a characteristic brightness of surface markings and sometimes a bloom on the shell, whereas the others show some degree of dullness through contact with the bird. The loss of the original brightness of colour is most rapid and pronounced in wet weather and in a soily scrape.

The actual incubation period varies between 28 and 33 days. Some of the variation in duration is attributable to difference in ambient temperature according to change in either altitude or weather. Differences in incubation behaviour between individuals and pairs may also play a part and large eggs will tend to take longer to hatch than small eggs.

Incubating Peregrine; Wales (photo: Arthur Brook, Museum of Wales)

Both sexes incubate, though the male takes a minor share. Out of 224 occasions when I flushed a falcon from eggs, it was a male in only 27 instances (12%). This seems to accord with the experience of most other observers in Britain. Nelson (1970) found that on Langara Island only the female incubated at night, and that the proportion of incubation done by each sex during daylight hours depended on the pair concerned and on the stage of incubation. At mid-incubation the male's share was probably from 30 to 50% during the daytime, but decreased towards the end of the incubation period. Cade (1960) found that three male Peregrines he examined in Alaska had traces of brood patches on the abdomen and near the breast, though he believed that females do most of the incubating in this region. Cade also referred to studies of Peregrines in the Yamal Peninsula, USSR, which found that males performed up to a quarter of the incubation duties. Nelson has pointed out that a male Peregrine is only just big enough to cover a clutch of four eggs, and this critical size may be a factor in his share of incubation duties. Macintyre (1914) mentioned an instance in which a tiercel succeeded in hatching out after his mate was shot from eggs within three days of hatching. Cade has found that all captive breeding male Peregrines incubate, but their share varies greatly between individuals, reaching up to a quarter, or even half, of the daytime incubation. None incubated at night.

The male does most of the hunting for the pair during the incubation period. Often the male with food calls the female off and an aerial food pass takes place, as described under Courtship, or he may bring the food to a nearby perch, but seldom to the actual eyrie ledge. The female nearly always takes the prey to a stance away from the eyrie ledge to eat it. Nelson found that his tiercels made most of their kills in twilight before dawn. One male, having finished for the day, took prey from a cache on the cliff to present to the female, up to several times later in the day. The Langara falcons were feeding on Ancient Murrelets, which fly out to sea before dawn, and this hunting is probably exceptional, though in Britain a high proportion of kills is evidently made in the very early morning. While the female is feeding, the male usually takes a turn at incubation, and may stay on the eggs for a while. The female may also leave the eggs to preen or defaecate, or occasionally to hunt on her own, and these absences also allow the male to share incubation. Occasionally, whilst watching a demonstrating pair of Peregrines near the eyrie, I have seen the male return to the eggs while his mate continued to circle and call; but it is usually the female which is the more eager to resume sitting.

Nelson found that the male Peregrine frequently seeks his turn at incubation while the female is still sitting. A tiercel wanting a shift on the eggs would often give the 'waik' call from a perch some distance from but in sight of the eyrie. If his mate continued to sit he might call for some time and eventually fly to the eyrie, usually changing then to 'eechip' calls. A female that had decided to leave would usually rise unhurriedly and give the opposite call to her mate before flying off. The male's turn clearly awaited his partner's pleasure. By contrast, when the female returned to incubate the male would usually depart at once. Occasional reluctance of the male to leave would induce chittering from the female. In Cumbria, Martin (1980) has seen a male Peregrine initiate incubation change-over by landing on the nest ledge and approaching his mate, both birds giving soft 'chuck' calls, after which the female left. This male sometimes continued to incubate after the female had returned, and made her wait for up to 30 minutes.

Nelson (1970) has described Peregrine incubation behaviour in great detail and I have drawn largely on his account. A falcon returning to incubate usually lands on the outer part of the ledge a short distance from the nest scrape, and walks to it. If human intruders are too close the bird may stand watching for some time, though if the weather is adverse it may almost run to the scrape. The bird about to settle stands over the eggs, looking down at them and may rake in with its bill any which have become displaced. The feet are held limply with toes bunched, to avoid the talons damaging the eggs, and are then carefully placed amongst the eggs with a rapid stepping movement. The breast feathers are fluffed out as the falcon lowers itself over the eggs, leaning forward with weight on the toes. There is then a rapid shuffling with the feet, causing a sideways rolling motion, and the bird may partly turn round. This is followed by the fore and aft rocking of the body, evidently bringing the brood patches into more precise contact with the eggs; the chest is then dropped, the back arched, and the falcon finally lowers itself with another shuffle into the level position of normal incubation. The feathers become generally loosened and those of the lower back and the wing coverts are usually erected somewhat (see p. 220).

Incubating falcons may turn at intervals, rising slightly from the eggs to do so, but this depends partly on the space available and the need to maintain watch outwards from the eyrie. The bird periodically moves its eggs with its beak, usually by a backwards pushing and hooking motion which rolls the eggs against the feet, each other, or the slope of the scrape edge. The sitting Peregrine sometimes preens itself, and may partly rise or even leave the eggs for a short while to engage in more vigorous preening and wing stretching. Nelson found that fidgeting with debris on the ledge within reach was a characteristic activity of incubating falcons, and he suggested that the pecking and raking movements might be a vestigial behaviour relating to the nest-repairing activities of species which build stick nests. Many observers have commented that Peregrine eggs do not touch each other in the nest. The female has two brood patches, one at either side of the sternum, which would account for some degree of separation. However, in a deep nest-bowl the eggs inevitably roll together and touch, at least when the bird is not sitting.

Nelson has heard Peregrines 'chuckle' when arriving back at the eggs or when turning them over. Sitting falcons rarely fall asleep during the daytime, though they appear to doze periodically, closing one eye and then the other, and nodding forward with the head, for a few seconds or even up to a minute or two. An incubating bird normally remains watchful, however, and is instantly alert to any disturbance. A passing bird predator may draw the sitter from its eggs to give chase, but reactions vary greatly from one individual to the next, especially in the case of human intruders. Much depends on whether the off-duty partner, usually the tiercel, is on the scene or not. The non-sitter will usually take wing when a human approaches within a critical distance, normally of a few hundred metres. Even if it remains silent, the sitting falcon will nearly always see the mate and will doubtless recognise alarm signals from its manner of flight. Thus alerted, the sitter more readily responds to sight or sound of the disturbers.

Many Peregrines will not leave their eggs if people pass along the foot of the cliff, even when they are clearly visible. A loud noise, such as a handclap, will usually flush the sitter. If the intruders are not visible, the incubating bird usually rises over the eggs on hearing the noise, and on a big ledge may walk to the edge to locate the source of disturbance. Even then it may not fly until a second noise is made. Some Peregrines will stand on their eyrie ledge, calling their alarm 'kek-kek' before taking off. Sitting Peregrines are more likely to fly quickly if viewed from above, provided they have seen the intruder themselves. If an eyrie is viewed from vertically above, the sitter may not spot the watcher until a noise is made. Some bold individuals will continue to sit even with a person looking down at them, especially if the line of sight is oblique. I have known a female stay, watching me quizzically with head inclined, as I waved vigorously from across the gorge where it sat, about 50 m away. Any sound was drowned by a great waterfall plunging down the eyrie cliff, and the popularity of the place with tourists had doubtless accustomed the falcon to people.

The 'tightness' with which a Peregrine sits depends partly on the state of incubation. Some females are difficult to dislodge from eggs when incubation is well advanced, and will not respond to handclaps, especially on big cliffs where the eyrie is some distance away. In earlier days, egg collectors often carried a revolver to fire at the cliff, but even this device has been known to fail to flush seacliff sitters, where the sound of breakers gives a constant background noise. Several instances have been reported in which Peregrines could have been caught by hand when sitting, mostly at eyries in small caves and recesses. A deer stalker told Seton Gordon that he had actually captured a sitting bird in this way. Once, when climbing to a nest from below, I almost put my hand on the sitting bird. Falcons are inclined to sit more tightly on days of high wind when the rush of air up the cliff face masks any extraneous noise. Tight sitting is also more likely if the off-duty bird is away and cannot raise the alarm first.

A Peregrine which leaves its eyrie in its own good time normally does so slowly, removing its feet carefully from the eggs and often standing over or beside them for a short time. Usually, a falcon hearing a noise also rises carefully and walks deliberately to the edge of the ledge before flying, and even though one surprised suddenly at close quarters may appear to leave precipitately, jumping up and scrabbling across the ledge, the feet are usually extricated without scattering or damaging the eggs. Only occasionally are eggs actually kicked out of the scrape.

A Peregrine flushed from eggs by a human will frequently career up and down or circle around in front of or above the nesting cliff, giving the 'cacking' alarm call. If its mate is not already present, the calls may bring it on the scene, and the two then demonstrate against the intruder. In this display the female typically comes closer and calls more than her mate, but occasionally the male is the more demonstrative of the pair. During these activities, the greater size of the female and the higher-pitched voice of her mate are usually apparent as marked sexual differences. The male sometimes disappears after a time, leaving his mate to maintain surveillance of the disturbers. Quite often he is absent for the whole time, but it is rare for a female not to appear if the male is incubating. The presence of the male could be connected with the availability of food. On seacliffs, with large numbers of nesting seabirds and thus a ready supply of food at hand, the male does not need to travel far to hunt. Nelson (1970) found this to be so on Langara. At many inland haunts, by contrast, there may be little prey for some distance and here it is likely that the male will travel much farther afield to hunt and spend more time doing so.

The demonstrativeness of individuals varies greatly. Some keep up an almost continuous cackle as long as a person is anywhere in the vicinity of the eyrie while, at the other extreme, some remain almost or completely silent the whole time. A few bold birds will stay close, within gunshot range, even stooping down to within short range, but others remain a long way off. Occasionally, Peregrines apparently leave the vicinity altogether when their eyrie is visited, but they probably remain watching from a distance. Tom Cade told me that the Peregrines he saw in Spain seemed to have developed the habit of rapid and silent self-effacement when disturbed from their eyries, probably as a defence against human predation, for the young are often sought as food. It is during the bouts of alarm calling that individual variations in voice become most apparent. These are mainly differences in pitch but may produce quite marked variations in sound effects. Some deep-voiced birds produce a hoarse chuckling call while others have an almost gull-like scream. D. Nethersole-Thompson described one falcon as making a noise like the whistle of a Mute Swan's wings, while J. Mitchell likened another's voice to a toy trumpet sound.

Peregrines which have lost their eggs usually behave differently, and their response to humans is then closer to that of birds at the pre-laying stage. If the loss is very recent they may still call a good deal at first, but usually they quieten down and fade out after a while. A robbed pair usually come out from the cliff as someone approaches, or they may float into view after the place has seemed deserted. As the time for a repeat laying approaches, their interest in the nesting place becomes stronger again.

Peregrines with eggs well advanced in incubation are usually eager to return to them after being disturbed. While certain individuals are wary about going back to the eyrie if a human is closer than 500 m, some will return while an intruder is still on the cliff quite close at hand, especially if the weather is cold or wet. Bolder birds may return as soon as the eyrie has been examined and they perceive that the visitor is withdrawing, and I have known a falcon to resume incubation while the rope was still dangling down the face and past its nest ledge.

Peregrines do not readily desert their eggs and seldom do so as a result of people visiting their eyrie ledges. Some can be flushed repeatedly from eggs without harm, though it would be unwise to take this risk. Desertions are usually the result of prolonged disturbance which keeps the bird off the eyrie for several hours, and sometimes happens when rock climbers spend a long time on a route close to the ledge. Even so, there are signs that on big cliffs, as in Lakeland and Snowdonia, Peregrines are adapting to even this degree of intrusion, for broods have been reared lately on several much-climbed crags. Cases have been mentioned in which falcons hard-hit by shot when flushed have returned to their eyrie to die later on the eggs. Peregrine eggs seem also to have a fair resistance to chilling, at least under average British conditions. Kearton (1909) mentioned an instance where a gamekeeper deliberately kept a pair of Peregrines off their eggs for six consecutive hours, but the birds then carried on and reared a brood. Incubated eggs can remain uncovered for at least two hours without harm during normal spring day-time weather, but much depends on ambient temperature and during cold weather fatal chilling can more readily occur. Under the intense frosts which can prevail during the Arctic spring after eggs have been laid, 20 minutes' absence by the sitting bird can bring disaster.

Desertion of eggs, evidently without direct human interference, has been quite frequent during the post-1955 era of pesticide effects. Some of these desertions have involved addled clutches, either complete or depleted, and it would be normal for these to be forsaken eventually when incubated to beyond full term. However, many deserted clutches have been abandoned while at least some of the eggs contained viable embryos, and in these instances it seems likely that there was some physiological disturbance, perhaps affecting behaviour, as a result of sub-lethal pesticide contamination.

There are a good many instances of Peregrine eggs being incubated by a foster-mother after the female parent had been destroyed and the male had rapidly found a new mate. Dugald Macintyre (1960) considered such events quite usual in keepered country where many Peregrines were shot off the nest. Nelson (1970) mentions an instance in which such a happening was followed by loss of the male and re-mating of the second female, so that a pair of foster-parents was left in charge of the eggs. Hickey (1942) referred to an incident in which an intruding female Peregrine actually evicted the rightful owner, and took over her eggs and her mate. Photograph 21 shows a curious event, for the photographer, W. C. Lawrie, believed that both birds at the nest were females, an extra bird having been seen in the vicinity of the eyrie for some time.

In Lakeland, in 1957, I watched a female leave her eggs twice within an hour and join her mate on the wing. On the first occasion the two birds chased each other as if in courtship flight and then disappeared over the hill for ten minutes, after which they returned and the female quickly resumed incubation. The second absence was for only about five minutes, but at both times the eggs were left quite unattended, though it was a warm day. At a Southern Upland eyrie which I watched for several hours in 1963, the female Peregrine incubated irregularly, with prolonged breaks, during which the male made no attempt to take her place. The remaining egg was eventually deserted and proved to have a large embryo which must have died several days before desertion occurred. At an adjoining eyrie in 1968, George Carse watched a female Peregrine, which he had previously seen sitting on four eggs, revert to pre-laying behaviour by performing scraping motions in the eyrie, which proved to have only a single egg remaining. On a ledge below was another egg cracked open and evidently knocked out of the nest. Such events have made me wonder if disturbance of the normal incubation regime could be another effect of contamination of the Peregrine by organochlorine pesticides.

One most curious event in recent years is certainly associated with egg-breaking and disturbance of normal breeding activity. This is the appropriation of Kestrel clutches by Peregrines, which has happened on at least four occasions, all in Scotland and beginning in 1961. In the two instances I encountered, the Peregrines broke their own eggs and then took over the clutches of Kestrels nesting on the same crags. One pair was not revisited, but the other, in the Moffat Hills in 1963, hatched the eggs and successfully reared a brood of four Kestrels, treating them exactly as their true offspring. It was fascinating to see all four young Kestrels intermittently hovering over the hillside near the vacated nest, while the angry Peregrines scolded noisily and stooped repeatedly at me. The same falcon pair again dispossessed a pair of Kestrels of their clutch in 1968, but this time the take-over came to nought (J. Young). In 1975, a Peregrine pair elsewhere in the Southern Uplands took over a Kestrel clutch and reared two young (R. Roxburgh, G. Riddle).

Confrontation between two female Peregrines at an eyrie in an old Buzzard nest; Lake District, northern England (photo: W. C. Lawrie)

In one instance there must have been a substantial gap, of up to a month, between the Peregrines losing their own eggs and taking over the Kestrels', for the latter laid in the falcons' eyrie after the owners had quit the place for a while. The urge to incubate either remained or revived after the Peregrines' own nesting had failed, but such happenings have never been known to follow straightforward robbery, and they appear to be another mysterious effect of organochlorine contamination. Since 1960 it has been quite common for Peregrines to brood on empty scrapes, which sometimes collect a litter of down feathers, and I have flushed females which were still sitting on the broken remains of their eggs.

THE YOUNG STAGE

Hatching

The most detailed observations on hatching are those of Nelson (1970). The chicks begin cheeping before they have begun to break through the shell, though they become more audible once the actual hatch has begun. Starring of the shell is followed by a lapse of more than 72 hours before the chick completely breaks loose. For artificially incubated eggs, 50–55 hours is the usual range in which most eggs hatch after first 'pip', the chick being inactive for most of this time and taking only a few hours for the actual cutting out with its egg-tooth (T. Cade). Experience with Peregrine eggs in incubators and under natural conditions has indicated that maintenance of a critical level of atmospheric humidity is vital to successful hatching. Nelson believes that drying of the shell membranes as they become exposed at the hatch may prevent the chick from rupturing them sufficiently to free itself. He watched one chick die at this stage at a Langara eyrie. It has been suggested that falcons leave their eggs for a short while at dawn to expose them to atmospheric condensation. Nelson noted that although incubating Peregrines are fond of bathing in water, as at other times, he did not see a bird return to incubate with its plumage visibly wet. Peregrines breed in climates with a wide range of atmospheric humidities, and while coastal eyries must in general be exposed to relatively moist air, many of those in inland continental situations are subject to quite arid conditions at nesting time.

Peregrines may move the hatched eggshells about the eyrie ledge, and often nibble at the broken pieces, but they seem not to have any well developed habit of eggshell disposal, either by carrying away or eating the remains. More usually the pieces of shell become trampled into bits by the adults and later the young. Addled eggs are usually left, and may survive after the young have gone as dried and bleached relics, kicked to one side of the eyrie, but they are often broken and trampled to pieces. Peregrine chicks are devoid of cryptic coloration, being covered at birth and until the true feathers grow with a delicate white down. They form a conspicuous white bunch in the open scrape. The extra devices evolved by most birds to protect their small young are unnecessary in this powerful predator which maintains constant vigilance at its eyrie while the young are there.

Although few observations on wild falcons are available, it would appear that hatching of the clutch is fairly well synchronised in Peregrines. Spread of hatching between the first and last eggs does not usually exceed 48 hours, and is often much less. This matches the observation that incubation does not usually begin in earnest until the clutch is completed. There is a contrast with the markedly asynchronous hatching which occurs in other raptors (including some members of the genus *Falco*), many owls and most corvids, and which appears to be an adaptation adjusting brood size when food supply is variable and when the fledging period is long. The tendency to synchronous hatching in the Peregrine suggests that food supply during the nestling period is relatively secure in this species. It is best described as a tendency, for while Enderson *et al.* (1972) found synchronous hatching in three Alaskan eyries, one containing four eggs, another clutch of four eggs gave hatching intervals of 10, 60–72 and 110 hours. Court (1986) has since found a prevalence of asynchronous hatching in a northern Canadian Peregrine population, and an associated 7% brood reduction. While the dead chicks had starved, there were no food shortages to cause this, and the adaptive significance of the habit was unclear.

Several observers have noted that Peregrines, especially the females, become more aggressive at the hatch. Nelson has commented that since this does not happen at the anticipated time of hatch if all the eggs are addled, it appears that sounds or movements from within the egg are responsible for stimulating this increase in defensive behaviour near the nest.

Brooding behaviour with young

Most brooding of the small young is performed by the female, though the male occasionally takes short turns. No attempt is made to share brooding simultaneously. Apart from weaker motivation for brooding, a male has still greater difficulty in covering a full brood of chicks than a clutch of eggs. At a Lakeland eyrie, Martin (1980) saw the tiercel have eight brooding sessions of 20–40 minutes when the chicks (three) were 1–2 days old, but after they were 4 days old he brooded only sporadically and mostly for short periods.

Although Nelson found that the actions of a brooding falcon were essentially similar to those of an incubating bird, there were slight and gradual adjustments appropriate to the change to covering delicate but growing nestlings. Leaning forward and stepping around gradually cease, but shuffling movements become important, evidently to place the feet below the chicks. Rocking stops on hatching and other settling motions are replaced by a gentle lowering of the body onto the nestlings. The adult bird assumes an increasingly elevated brooding position as the chicks grow, and is especially careful with its feet when rising and moving away.

The brooding falcon gently pulls back with the underside of its beak any small chick which moves out of the scrape, rather as it hooks back a displaced egg. Preening of the chicks by the parent involves removal of particles of dirt or food from the down. Sometimes the bird 'chuckles' to the chicks in the same way as to the eggs. Female attentiveness to brooding depends on weather, the number of nestlings and their age. Cold, rain or bright sunshine induce close brooding. The larger the brood the more difficult is it for the parent to cover all the chicks, and this factor is obviously related to the size of the young as well. Brooding will continue longer with a single chick than with a full number, but tends to become increasingly sporadic after about the eighth day. Brooding also continues for longer at night; Nelson found that night brooding of a single chick persisted until

Female Peregrine about to brood, and half-brooding young; Dumfriesshire, southern Scotland
(photos: R. T. Smith)

the 16th day. Parent Peregrines shelter the nestlings from strong sunshine or rain when they are too large to brood but are not yet protected by their own feathers. The sheltering falcon half-spreads its wings and stands close to the scrape with its back towards the sun or rain. It does not go to the young if they are elsewhere on the ledge but provides the shelter if they want it. A. P. Martin found that the mean duration of female brooding decreased up to the 18th day and ceased after the 24th day, with a brood of three young.

Behaviour and growth of the young

Nelson found that on the day of hatching and for several days thereafter, Peregrine chicks respond to creaking calls of an adult by raising their heads, opening and closing their beaks and giving faint 'treble whine' begging calls in reply. Alarm calling of the adults silenced nestlings of 4 days old. The eyes of a newly hatched chick are closed and until about 4 days of age they remain either half open or, as Brown and Amadon (1968) said, 'bleary and unseeing'. Between 4 and 8 days of age a nestling begins to distinguish and react by sight to an adult on the ledge. Very young chicks spend most of their time dozing and sleeping, and huddle together in a single bunch. They give a 'chitter' call when alarmed and have a dark-seeking response which leads them towards the parent or to shade if the parent is away. An uncovered nestling gives a call intermediate between the 'treble whine' and 'chitter' evidently if it becomes too hot or too cold. Chicks nevertheless frequently look out from beneath the brooding falcon.

Nelson noted that preening, scratching, wing/leg stretching and wing-fanning movements by the young began at 8 days, and also the first signs of actions which become marked later, such as ruffling out of feathers and shaking of the body. Locomotion is still extremely limited at this age and confined to an ineffective shuffling motion on the tarsi. Sight is good enough to allow accurate pecking at objects on the ledge. While young Peregrines have a marked instinct to eject excrement away from the scrape, their power of defaecation is slight at first but increases steadily so that at 8 days they have produced a radiating pattern 15–20 cm (6–8 in) beyond the nest scrape edge.

Brown (1976) states that young Peregrines grow a second coat of down at about 10 days. From this age onwards nestlings become more active and strong though the nature of their movements does not change markedly for another week or so. They are brooded less and less during the day and become more vigorous in their movements about the ledge, including backing to squirt their faeces over the edge. Vision develops strongly and the young, when hungry, scream and clamber towards an arrived parent. Most of the day is still spent sleeping, up to about 16 days, but the 'comfort movements' described by Nelson at the 8 day stage become more developed, and include foot nibbling and hitching of the wings into adult position.

The wing and tail quill feathers begin to appear at about 3 weeks old, and wing-flapping becomes more vigorous. The young are now voracious and eagerly watch the return of the parents to feed them. They are brooded little, but still have a marked tendency to huddle together, this being clearly a warmth-conserving adaptation. Eyasses of this age have well developed beaks and powerful feet, with quite large talons. Their response to human intruders changes around this time; instead of lying supine they are alert and frightened,

Female Peregrine at eyrie with small young (photo: Harold Platt)

and begin to give the 'kek-kek' alarm call of the adults. If closely approached they throw themselves on their backs and prepare to lash out with their talons. The developing young nevertheless live together amicably and there are none of the Cain and Abel type battles which are so characteristic of some raptors, notably eagles and buzzards (Brown and Amadon, 1968). This is hardly surprising since such interactions have evolved to reinforce asynchronous hatching as a device for reducing brood-size in certain raptors when food supply is inadequate, but the Peregrine is not normally one of these species (p. 228). Young Peregrines are, by contrast, given to socialisation with each other on the eyrie ledge, right up to the time of flying.

At 4 weeks or so, eyasses may sometimes join their parents in alarm calling instead of falling silent. They are able to follow the flight of the adults and may call for food. The eyasses begin to steal food from the parents and to rend this themselves, though they are still fed for most of the time. Sleeping and dozing still occupy a large part of the day, but a youngster increasingly places its head on its own back during sleep, and huddling between the brood diminishes. The wing and tail feathers are now developing strongly and body feathers begin to appear in lines and patches along the back and breast. Preening becomes a major occupation, and Nelson noted social facilitation by nest-mates, with others following suit

Female Peregrine brooding small young (photo: Harold Platt)

if one youngster began to preen. Feather ruffling with body and head shaking is now marked and increasing time is spent in exercise, notably walking on the feet and wing-flapping. The anal muscles have by now developed a strong ejaculatory capacity, and the young falcons eject their droppings in a liquid stream ('mute') over the brink of the nesting ledge. They present their backs to the edge but are careful not to fall off and have a well-developed sense of the gravitational hazard, though some observers (e.g. Ryves, 1948) believe that eyasses often perish through toppling from their eyrie during defaecation.

Brooding has usually ceased when the young are 3 weeks old and may even do so up to a week earlier. The female spends more time during the day away from the eyrie ledge, though she usually remains fairly close by, often sitting on the cliff for long spells. At night she roosts on the eyrie ledge to guard the young and may do this until they have fledged.

Behaviour of the adults towards human intruders usually changes when the young have hatched, the female in particular becoming noticeably more demonstrative and aggressive. Whereas during incubation the sitting female is often flushed with difficulty, so that the eyrie can easily be missed, both birds frequently take to the air calling while humans are still several hundred metres

distant, and they may come to meet disturbers. Individual differences remain and a few falcons remain undemonstrative or even disappear when disturbed but in general alarm calling is more continuous and sounds louder than during the egg stage, for both sexes become bolder and fly closer to the intruder. Aggression often increases still further as the young grow, and reaches its climax when they are fully developed but still in the eyrie.

In Britain, some individuals with young, usually females, will stoop or fly past extremely close to a person who has reached their eyrie. The rush of a falcon passing within a few metres of one's head is quite alarming, and occasionally a bird will come within striking distance. I have not found an authentic record of anyone being actually touched by an attacking Peregrine in this country, whereas in some parts of the world such as North America and Africa, it is not at all unusual for humans to be struck. Harper Hall lost his hat to the angry Sun Life falcon when standing unprotected on the eyrie ledge of the skyscraper, 100 m above street level. Dogs are often attacked and can become quite terrified, though some remain unconcerned.

Michael Shrubb saw unusual behaviour, akin to distraction display on the ground, accompanied by a wailing call, by a female he flushed at hatching time from an eyrie in a small crag.

Feeding behaviour of parents and young

Nelson found that the male Peregrine was immediately motivated to start bringing food for the young by the sight of newly hatched chicks or signals from the brooding female that hatching had occurred. The tiercel also began regularly to bring food to the eyrie ledge or its vicinity instead of making food transfers to the female at some distance from the nest (but see later). Chicks began feeding on their first day but development of feeding behaviour appeared to involve a learning process in both parent and offspring; in the female of giving up the 'limp-foot' of incubation in order to pin the food, and of presenting morsels

Female Peregrine with young about ten days old; Wales (photo: Harold Platt)

accurately, and in the chick of begging and gaping. A chick learns, on hearing the parental creaking call, to sit up, 'treble whine' call and gape for food. Nelson described a chick Repeated-gaping Display, with the beak opening and shutting repeatedly and accompanied by treble whining. This begging activity stimulates the parent to feed the chick, and in a few days develops into a pecking at the parent's bill.

At first, brooding and feeding are by the female alone but the male later takes a share, though a lesser one, in feeding. Both parents are inclined to encourage the chicks to eat more than they appear to want: at 8–9 days, repeated gaping disappears, for the nestling watches the feeding actions of its parent and reaches up to take food as it is presented. Treble whining increases in volume and is uttered between mouthfuls, but ceases when satiation is reached. Hungry chicks solicit even if the adult arrives without food, but when satiated they remain indifferent. Nelson observed that chicks formed a semi-circle in front of the parent or to one side and all received portions of the prey item. Treleaven (1977) found that each chick was fed in turn until satiated, when it dropped back and was replaced by the next in line. After about 10 days, chicks which called most received the most food.

After the chicks can stand, at 22–23 days, the begging posture becomes more horizontal, though they feed in a normal standing position, and direct themselves

Female Peregrine feeding young about three weeks old (photo: Harold Auger)

at the parent's beak. Nelson first observed regurgitation of castings composed of indigestible remains at 22 days, and wiping of the sides of the beak back and forth against objects occurred at the same age. Signs of self-feeding were noticed at 12 days, but this activity did not begin in earnest until after about 24 days, when nestlings begin assertively to grab at food instead of more passively begging for it.

The prey is often plucked and usually headless when received by the female, the head presumably being eaten by the male, and sometimes the neck as well. If more work is required in plucking and preparing the carcase the female usually flies with it to an adjoining perch before starting this. The adult at the eyrie pins the prey firmly with its powerful feet and soon rips it up, giving the young tiny pieces when they are small, but larger portions as they develop. The parent avoids giving bones, intestines or too many feathers to small young, and picks up and eats any dropped fragments of flesh. The arrival of an adult is the signal for hungry nestlings to crowd forward and attempt to steal any prey from it. A successful chick runs away with its booty and 'mantles' over it to feed, while the adult goes off for more food. If the parent drops the prey, the chicks scramble for it and a tug-of-war often ensues, but once possession is decided, nestlings do not often appear to rob each other.

At 31 days a nestling can rip up a prey item quite well and at 39 days it soon demolishes even intact prey. At this stage prey is usually left intact for the young to deal with, though the parent sometimes breaks it up. There is, however, a considerable overlap between parental and self-feeding, and adults will present young with pieces of torn-up prey until they fledge, especially if nestlings solicit. The food call increases in strength as the young grow, and develops into a wail similar to the parent's; and Cade has heard it carry fully a mile on a calm day. Cade also found that parental creaking calling on arrival with food increased as the young matured. In the second half of the nestling period a youngster consumes quite large amounts of food and its intake eventually exceeds that of an adult of the same sex.

On Langara, Nelson noted that male Peregrines frequently cached food, both when feeding the female during incubation, and when feeding her and the nestlings later. The main prey species is nocturnal and the weather often bad, so that food caches have special value when young have to be fed at frequent and regular intervals. Treleaven (1977) has described food caches at Cornwall and Devon eyries and also believes that they are an adaptation to bad weather when hunting is difficult. Both sexes use these food stores and Parker (1979) recorded at a Pembrokeshire eyrie that 14 out of 78 items brought to the eyrie were from cliff 'larders' while Martin (1980) found that 39% of all prey fed to the young in a Lakeland eyrie was from caches. Half-eaten items are sometimes returned to the cache for a further meal.

The Langara falcons appeared to be assiduous in removing all the larger uneaten remains of prey from the eyrie, notably skeletal parts and whole wings, and Nelson surmised that this action had a sanitary value in reducing the risks of disease. He also noticed that the adult avoided dragging fresh prey about the ledge and lifted items in its beak when moving about. Removal of prey remains seems to vary a good deal between one eyrie and the next, and many in Britain are thickly littered with bones and feathers by the time the young fledge. Treleaven found in Cornwall that eyries were kept scrupulously clean until the young were three weeks old, but after this the remains were allowed to accumulate.

Frequency of feeding visits by the parents obviously depends on the size of the brood, but Nelson concluded that four meals a day per chick was the norm throughout the nestling period. Parker believed that food was brought to the brood four to eight times a day, and Heatherley and his colleagues recorded an average of seven food visits a day. Martin (1980) observed increasing frequency of feeding, from an average of about every 3 hours at chick age 2 days, to just over 1 hour at 14 days, but declining again thereafter (6–11 feeds per day). The last three sets of observations referred to large broods of three and four young. Most observers agree that feeding begins very early in the morning, often before it is light enough for a human to see properly. Martin noted an irregular spread of feeding through the day, with no particular pattern. Parker found that young were nearly twice as likely to be fed during the early morning (05.00–09.00 h GMT) and evening (17.00–21.00) periods than during the middle of the day. He did not see feeding before 05.00 nor after 21.20 h. The Heatherley records show another but less marked bias towards higher frequency of feeding visits during early

Female Peregrine with young about three and a half weeks old; southern Scotland (photo: R. T. Smith)

morning or evening. Heatherley gave a list of times of feeding visits and analysis of these shows that the interval between visits varied from ten minutes to six hours, with an average of about two hours. Intervals of about 5 hours were quite frequent between mid-morning and mid-afternoon. In a list of 51 timed feeds, evidently not all to the complete brood, duration of meal was from 2 to 30 minutes with an average of 11 minutes. Parker recorded that 56 feeds of complete broods varied from 2 to 57 minutes with an overall average of 17 minutes. Martin found that mean length of feed increased from 8 minutes when the young were under 4 days old, to 11 minutes when they were over 18 days old.

Both adults seem to feed mainly on prey separate from that brought in for the young, though they sometimes eat parts of the same item as the nestlings. Although strongly motivated to feed young, males play only a minor part in this role and Nelson, Parker and Martin each noted that they were sometimes driven away by their mates when attempting to do so. This may have been partly the result of the female's inclination to take the food from the male. At Nelson's eyries, male feeding was allowed just after hatching, but not again until the young were 10 days old, after which it became rather frequent. Treleaven also found that until the young were 2 weeks old the food pass between the sexes continued to be more frequent than male delivery of food to the eyrie ledge. Doubtless there is a good deal of variation between pairs in the male feeding contribution.

It is consistently the rule for male Peregrines, in common with most other raptors, to do the bulk of the hunting while the young are in the eyrie, as well as during the egg stage. The contribution by the female to hunting varies, but is usually small, and she spends most of her time near the eyrie, ready to protect the young against predators. Cade stated that when the young are about three weeks old the female begins to hunt actively again and the male takes prey directly to the nestlings. Treleaven saw some hunting by females with young in Devon and Cornwall, and Parker found that although the female spent 90% of her time on the eyrie cliff, she made frequent sallies to chase passing Rock Doves. Martin (1980) noted that a Cumbrian female began to share in the hunting when the young were 16 days old. At an eyrie in Zimbabwe, Hustler (1983) found that the female started to hunt when the chicks were 2 weeks old, but did not move away from the nest cliff. Female participation in hunting may become greater in areas where food is less abundant, or perhaps when bad weather makes the taking of prey more difficult. Heavy rain is especially adverse, and food can run short if it is prolonged, even allowing for use of caches. While the female is disinclined under such conditions to leave the young, she could well add her efforts to her mate's when the weather improves. Weir (1978) found that while females usually resumed hunting about 18 days after hatching, they did so earlier and took a larger share in the hunting when the brood was large than when it was small. The undoubted ability of some tiercels to provide successfully for the large food demands of a full brood is however shown by the several instances in which males have reared young to fledging after their mates had been destroyed.

Fledging

At 4 weeks old the young falcons begin to show the juvenile plumage and become more active, wandering about the ledge. They begin to indulge in frequent wing flapping which helps to shed the down. At 5 weeks they are well feathered and most of the down has been lost, though some adheres patchily to the young birds. The quill feathers are quite strongly developed, though the wings and tail are still short and rounded. By now the young are much more active and restless, and they take advantage of whatever space the eyrie ledge offers. If other adjoining ledges are reachable they will try to get to them by hopping and flapping, and are sometimes in danger of falling down the cliff. The nestlings often separate from each other, unless the eyrie ledge is small and confined.

The sexes are now readily distinguishable if seen together, the females being noticeably larger and with relatively larger feet and talons than the males. Parker (1979) found that females developed more slowly than males, and so retained their down longer. Age at first flight varies from 5 to 6 weeks. Weir (1978) found an average of 40 days in the Central Highlands, with males flying before females. Nelson found that fledging took 43 days on Langara and Cade (in litt.) says that 40–46 days is a normal range in North American Peregrines,

Female Peregrine with young about five weeks old; Wales (photo: Harold Platt)

with males averaging 40–42 days, but captive-bred broods could differ in fledging period by up to a week in both sexes. Factors such as quality and amount of food, number of nestmates and parental attentiveness could affect length of the nestling period in the wild. Parker has given a schedule of first flight for three Pembrokeshire broods in three successive years, of four, four and three young. The spread of departure within each brood was 14–18 June, 16–19 June and 14–20 June, respectively; and in all years the single female in each brood was the last to leave, going three, two and four days after the last male. Flights took place between 06.30 and 20.53 h GMT and there was no bias towards a particular part of the day. Nelson (1970) also found that in one eyrie on Langara the male fledgling flew 2 days before the two females. It seems to be generally believed that this is the normal pattern, though the Heatherley photograph of two males and two females just before flying shows one of the males as the least developed member of the brood.

Nelson did not see any particular action by the parent Peregrines to induce their young to fly, but Parker described how both parents, as they brought in food, repeatedly hovered in front of the young, holding the prey in their lowered feet. Treleaven (1977) believes that the adults may deliberately reduce the food rations at this time, for the young are often quite fat. Generally, the eyasses fly when they are ready and moved by their own instinct. For at least a week before they would naturally fly, young Peregrines are readily frightened into premature flight if the eyrie is visited by a human, sometimes with disastrous results, as at coastal eyries, where a youngster can end up in the sea. If ringing is intended, it should therefore be done before the young become capable of flight, i.e. at 3–4 weeks. The adults will usually find and feed an eyass that has survived a fall to a lower position, but in inland localities, especially, the young bird may then be more vulnerable to predators.

The young falcon about to launch on the world is a most handsome bird, and when the last vestiges of down are shed from the head it has the regal appearance of the adult. The eyes have by now taken on that extraordinary quality of lustrous vitality and intense watchfulness that even the best paintings and still photographs cannot capture, since they freeze the bird into immobility and deny the sense of inner energy. The first flight can be quite strong, but when the youngster has pitched, usually on another part of the cliff, it may remain sitting there for up to several hours. Food calls with the parents are exchanged and wing-shivering motions also help to attract attention, so that each youngster is kept supplied with prey. Flights grow stronger and more frequent within a day or so, but the family normally remains about the cliff for a few days, roosting fairly close around though seldom actually in the eyrie. The old nest shelf usually has a bare look, much trampled, with flattened remains of prey, heavy splattering with white droppings and much down lying about or sticking to vegetation. The cliff top and ledges are freely littered with patches of feathers from the numerous kills.

Treleaven found that each youngster acquired a special feeding area on the cliff where it received food from the adults. By contrast, Parker observed that after a few days the fledged young grouped together to be fed, by either parent. At first this was bill to bill transfer of pieces, but later they were given intact prey to rend, though for 10 days or so after flight it was plucked by the adults. The eyasses often rested by lying prone on ledges, especially during hot afternoons. Treleaven has pointed out that when at rest the young are remarkably well camouflaged. Parker saw billing activities between siblings on ledges. These observers saw very little bickering between youngsters over food. Cade (1960) saw different feeding behaviour in Alaska: adults landed on the cliff with prey and called persistently, whereupon the young flew to them with a 'flutter-glide' and often fought and screamed over the food when more than one arrived at the same time. Nelson also noted that bill to bill feeding often ends with the fledgling snatching the remainder of the food item from the parent. Flutter-gliding by the young is frequent at this stage and appears to be the same flight as used by adult females before egg laying. Nelson regards it as a display, though its significance is still uncertain; he suggests it is derived from wing-shivering and may indicate hunger.

On average, young Peregrines evidently fly about 78 days after the laying of the first egg – 6 days for clutch completion, 30 days for incubation and 42 days for fledging. This would give 20 June as an average fledging date for broods in south-west England, and up to a week or so later in most districts from Wales northwards. There will obviously be considerable variation around these averages, not only from the normal spread of laying dates but also from varying length of laying, incubation and fledging periods. Broods quite commonly fly during the second week of June and sometimes young from first layings are still in the nest in July. The majority of July fledgings are, however, from repeat clutches which are 3 weeks or so later than broods from first clutches.

The young on the wing

Once the young are on the wing, the female Peregrine resumes hunting in earnest, and often joins the male again in cooperative hunts. Increasingly, the fledglings make short flights in pursuit or search of the parents, which in a few days begin to adopt aerial foot-to-foot transfers of prey to their offspring, so that after a week or so this is the normal feeding method. Parker saw youngsters clumsily knock prey from the talons of the adults, which dived to retrieve this before it was lost in the sea. Nevertheless, the young quickly become skilled at taking the food, often turning upside down beneath the parent at the moment of exchange. The adult typically escorts the youngster as the latter carries the prey back to the cliff, and Nelson suggests that this is to decoy away the other youngsters which might harass their sibling holding the food, with the possible result of one or more falling into the sea. This seems to be linked to the motivation of the young to chase parents with or without prey. The fledglings do a good deal of calling to the parents, and the intensity of the treble whine seems to denote the level of hunger.

After about a week the young begin to chase each other a good deal and play 'hunting games' in the air, soaring and circling near the nest cliff and then stooping at each other somewhat in the manner of adults engaging in courtship flight. Frequently one of the mock combatants rolls on its side or back in defensive posture as the other closes with it, and sometimes there is talon grappling. Other bird species in the area, including predators such as Carrion Crows and Buzzards are often 'buzzed' both in the air and at rest. These aerial games have an element of play but serve to develop the power of flight and the fine degree of coordination between sight and muscular response which is so necessary if the young Peregrine is to survive the critical few months when it is alone in the world.

For a time the youngsters indulge in mock attack at a variety of birds without attempting to strike prey, but in a few weeks they begin to attack passing birds in earnest. If these targets are pigeons or other skilful fliers, the young falcons are unsuccessful, for they are simply outpaced and all their meals continue to be provided by the parents, which tend now to stay away from their offspring and even avoid them for part of the day. Treleaven and Parker each found that the youngsters often turned to catching large insects with their feet, and saw attacks on tall herbaceous plants or grass tussocks on the cliff-top. Michael Shrubb watched two juvenile Peregrines taking craneflies from the ground and hawking them in flight. Nelson saw young falcons strike at floats of kelp on the surface of the sea. The contrast in flying ability between the old birds and the young is very striking. Yet the young birds have only a limited time for learning to cope and feed themselves. A male youngster that flew on 12 June was seen to kill a domestic pigeon on 9 August (Nicholson, 1986).

There has been a good deal of debate over the years on the question of whether or how the parents train their eyasses to hunt. The food pass could be regarded as a form of training, for this requires considerable practice before a youngster develops the necessary skill to perform its part with precision. Some observers have described adult Peregrines dropping prey or other objects, such as a clump of vegetation and soil, for the young to catch. Treleaven has described how one

Ground nesting Peregrines feeding young; Finland (photos: Seppo Saari)

adult tiercel on different occasions apparently tried in three ways to help his brood to catch pigeons. He shepherded the quarry close to the youngsters, struck and injured a pigeon so that it fell near them, and finally caught but then released a pigeon deliberately as two eyasses closed in on him. Only on the last occasion were the young successful in making a kill. Treleaven tells me that he has since seen another instance of adults releasing live prey for the young to hunt. Beebe (1960) also believed that adult Peregrines in the Queen Charlottes chased prey species to tire and demoralise them so that the accompanying young had an easier task in catching the quarry. By contrast, Nelson saw no signs of parent Peregrines attempting to teach hunting to their young on Langara, though he suggested that the fledglings may 'learn' more passively by watching the hunting flights of the adults.

Nelson also pointed out that the falconry practice of 'hacking' young Peregrines simply utilises the natural development of flying and hunting abilities in the wild. A young falcon 'at hack' is allowed freedom to wander from its home shed over the neighbouring area, but is provided with food daily. The bird develops its powers of flight and then gradually learns on its own to pursue and catch its own prey, so that it relies less and less on the food provided. Peregrines maintain good condition this way and are ready for training when re-trapped.

As the young grow stronger and more adroit on the wing, they and the parents move increasingly farther away from the home cliff during the day. The family may return there at night to roost, but sometimes they take up temporary residence in another locality some distance away. Broods have been erroneously reported as reared on certain cliffs through this habit of wandering away from their birthplace. It becomes correspondingly difficult to follow relationships between adults and offspring and there are few observations on the manner in which the latter finally achieve independence, or on the timing of this process. The loosening of ties with the parents is probably gradual and spread over several weeks, during which the young birds gradually learn to fend for themselves. Parental feeding of a juvenile has been seen as late as mid-September, fully two months after flying date for even late broods.

The actual time of separation probably varies according to habitat and conditions. Douglas Weir found that in three different breeding haunts in Inverness-shire some young were roosting near or at all three nest sites until well into October. In one locality, two of three eyasses roosted by the nest site while the adults used an alternative haunt, up to mid-October. The young disappeared by the end of October and the adults moved back to the eyrie cliff again. Other observers in Britain have stated that the young leave the nesting place and their parents in August or September. On the other hand, Howard (1920) stated, 'Each year the young can be seen accompanying their parents up to the time when the sexual instinct arises,' which suggests that the families he observed in Donegal stayed together through the winter. Peregrines which depend mainly on breeding seabird colonies for food may move away earlier than those with a good year-round food supply.

It is widely believed that the parent Peregrines finally drive away their young, forcing them to seek pastures new. Numerous references to this supposed habit exist, one as early as 1250. Frederick II said, 'After fledglings have learned to fly and to capture their own prey, the mother bird drives them from the eyrie and out

Brood of eyasses at 4 weeks (photo: Don MacCaskill)

of the locality of their common nest. Were the young ones to hunt with the parents all the birds they require for food would soon leave the neighbourhood and they would find little to eat. Again, when the parents caught anything, one or other of the youngsters would probably lay claim to it. So she drives them away and in addition separates the whole family, each one to fend for himself in new territory' (Wood and Fyfe transl. 1943). And Albertus Magnus (1262) was told by a falconer in the Alps that, '. . . it was the habit of these falcons for the parents, after rearing the young, to drive them out from the place of their habitation because of the scarcity of birds found there, and that the young therefore immediately go down to the plains, in which there are more birds, and fly through the lands, having no settled habitation'. Some experienced contemporary observers believe that the young are driven away, but I have not yet seen any description of actual behaviour which could be thus construed. There is so far a dearth of eyewitness accounts of what happens, and until these are provided it seems to me safer to assume that the young are not actively driven out, but detach themselves from the parents as instinct dictates. On the other hand, Nelson has described how adult falcons will attack other intruding Peregrines, adults or young, during the fledgling period. He noted that food calling and flutter gliding by intruding fledglings did not inhibit attack by the territory owners, and that the young birds were then forced to roll over and present their feet in defence.

The young sometimes stay together as a group for a time, but eventually they part and go separate ways, seeking some place which offers good hunting but is not yet held by another and more dominant falcon. The adults are left in sole possession of their breeding place, but their attachment to it through the winter also depends greatly on local availability of food. Whether or not the early falconers were correct in their belief about the parental evictions of young from the nesting area, it is interesting that they connected this separation with the idea that there was not enough food for the whole family in the one area, and that movements and migration were essentially connected with food supply.

BROOD SIZE

In contrast to the large number of clutch records, there are relatively few records of the numbers of young in Peregrine broods seen before 1947. It is therefore difficult now to discover if there were any significant differences in average fledged brood size between various districts of Britain. The available information is summarised in Table 18 and suggests that, while broods were generally larger on the coast of south-east England, in other districts there was a fairly uniform average of about 2·5 young per brood, a figure which is closely matched in some other parts of the World. Hickey (1969) quotes the following average numbers of young per successful pair: North American Arctic, 2·45 (Cade); southern Canada, 2·60 (Hickey); British Columbia, 2·36 (Beebe); northern Germany, 2·57 (Kleinstäuber); southern Germany, 2·46 (Mebs); and Switzerland, 2·44 (Herren). Only the eastern USA had a markedly higher figure – 3·05 (Hickey) – though around New York the average was 2·50.

The figures for south-east England should, however, be treated with caution. Out of 18 broods, 15 were recorded by J. Walpole-Bond on the Sussex coast, and refer largely to a group of three or four eyries on Beachy Head which were difficult or impossible to reach and had relatively good success in output of young. The remaining five to eight eyries on this coast were subjected to the most relentless robbery for over 50 years, and evidently produced between them only the occasional brood. In this artificial situation it is conceivable that the eyries in the safe sites – in some years only a single one – had a higher output of young than would have been the case in a more normal breeding population. The number of broods of four young is extraordinarily high by usual standards (Table 18). Interestingly, in the Lake District, W. C. Lawrie found that breeding success at one haunt which he followed from 1911 to 1939 was higher than elsewhere, with an average brood size of 3·2 young from 13 successful eyries, including six broods of four eyasses. Lawrie was a bird photographer (Photograph 21) and kept close watch on his favourite Peregrines, with the result that this eyrie had a quite good success rate over a long period, whereas most of the neighbouring pairs lost their eggs regularly to collectors. Again, there could have been a local compensation effect, though how this might operate is obscure.

Juvenile male Peregrine; Sweden (photo: Peter Lindberg)

The data show that broods of two and three young were the most frequent before 1947, with ones infrequent and fours usually in a minority. Larger broods are so infrequent as to have little more than curiosity value. A Mr Tracy stated in *The Zoologist* for 1869 that he once saw six young in a Pembrokeshire nest and Dugald Macintyre claimed to have seen six fully-feathered young in a Kintyre eyrie. Broods of five young have been seen by C. V. Stoney on the Donegal coast in 1929, E. Sidebotham in Sussex in 1935, R. MacMillan in the central Highlands in 1977, R. B. Treleaven in Cornwall in 1980, and the RSPB in Denbighshire in 1990.

With a national average clutch size of 3·63 eggs, an average fledged brood size of 2·57 young represents a normal loss of at least one potential youngster per successful nesting, or almost 30% failure of eggs to produce young. This shortfall results from a combination of eggs failing to hatch, and chicks dying before fledging. Hatching failure in turn is caused by infertility of eggs, death of embryos, breakage and removal of eggs. Before 1947, most hatching failure in clutches which were incubated to full term resulted from infertility and embryonic mortality. Egg breakage was infrequent, and most egg-collecting involved taking the whole clutch. Nestling mortality results from disease and sickness, abnormal development, debility through inadequate parental care (including insufficient food supply), inclement weather, accidents (e.g. rock-falls, falling off eyrie ledge), nestling interaction and predation. Probably the first factor is the most important, though the first four will tend to act together, i.e. bad weather will make it more difficult for the parents to take prey, which may lead to temporary food shortage and/or greater exposure to wet and cold, with final increase in chances of sickness or debility. Probably most nestling mortality occurs within 2 weeks of hatching. Predation is mainly by humans, and it appears that the lifting of only part of the brood was rather more frequent than the partial removal of clutches.

In Galloway, Mearns and Newton (1988) found a slight tendency for brood size to increase with female age up to 5 years. Fyfe (1988) found a falling off in egg viability and chick survival in captive breeding Canadian Peregrines averaging 11 years old.

It is difficult to establish the relative contributions of hatching failure and nestling mortality to the overall reduction in fledged brood size compared with clutch size. Since 1947 the matter has been greatly complicated by pesticidally-induced increases in both kinds of loss, and earlier data are, as usual, inadequate. I have taken pre-1947 records of 22 eyries which were seen with full clutches of eggs, and then again shortly after hatching. The frequency of unhatched eggs recorded in these was 13 out of 79 (16%). This suggests that on average, hatching failure accounts for about half the above loss (the theoretical figure on the assumption of equal failure rate during incubation and the nestling stage would be 15%). The frequency of unhatched eggs is thus quite high, but this seems to be true of the raptors as a whole, compared with groups such as the waders and passerines.

Direct observations on reduction in broods during the nestling period before 1947 are too few to analyse, so that it can only be inferred that this source of loss also has a 15% frequency in relation to clutch size (or 18% of hatched brood size). While asynchronous hatching may sometimes reduce brood size in the Peregrine, and may be more important in certain other parts of the bird's World range, it does not seem to be a major factor accounting for nestling mortality in these islands.

Fledging success is evidently markedly reduced in repeat clutches. In 17 broods from 'repeats' during 1909–41, there were 11 with only single youngsters, and the mean brood size was only 1·65. Addled eggs seemed to form a higher proportion than normal in these repeat layings, though the data are too few to be conclusive. In a later sample of 54 successful nestings from 'repeats' during 1980–91, mean brood size was 1·94 young (16 × Y/1, 26 × Y/2, 11 × Y/3, 1 × Y/4) again well below the contemporary national mean, of 2·31 young.

Some time after 1947, brood size declined in most parts of Britain, but the paucity of records before 1961 makes it difficult to be sure when this trend began. The only region for which any useful information is available, northern England, showed a slight reduction in mean brood size, from the pre-1947 level of 2·60 to 2·32 during 1947–60 (Table 18). But during 1961–70 nearly all regions showed an appreciable and significant drop in mean brood size below the earlier national mean of 2·57 (Table 18). In northern England it declined to 2·02, but in several districts of Scotland it fell to even lower levels. Only in the central Highlands was there no marked reduction below the normal level. These decreases in brood size have been regarded as an integral part of the great malaise which overtook the

Peregrine population, from around 1956, as a result of the rapidly mounting influence of persistent toxic chemicals.

The recovery of the breeding population correlated with decreasing contamination by the organochlorine pesticides has been marked in all regions by an increase in mean brood size (Table 18). In northern England and southern Scotland, mean brood size had returned to normal, pre-pesticide levels by 1979, and only the coastal region of the northern and western Highlands failed to show appreciable improvement. During 1980–85, mean brood size either remained normal or continued to increase towards normality, even in coastal north-west Scotland. Wales was the only region showing a slipping back, but during 1986–91, all regions showed a decline in mean brood size, even though this was marginal in some, and statistically significant only in south-west England and Wales. The recovery in brood size up to 1985 appeared to be another indication of waning pesticide effects, and suggested that mean fledged brood size is a good indicator of population health in the Peregrine, given reasonably sized samples. A high frequency of broods with only a single youngster is a reliable symptom of a population in trouble whereas, conversely, a good proportion of 'threes' and 'fours' is a very healthy sign. The recent decline in mean brood size is puzzling, since there is no obvious reason for it, but it closely matches the reduction in clutch size that has become apparent during the post-1980 population increase.

Reduced brood size after 1947, and especially after 1960, stemmed mainly from:

(a) Increased clutch depletion related to eggshell thinning.
(b) Increased failure of intact eggs to hatch after being incubated to full term.
(c) Increased mortality of nestlings.

Factor (b) could have been a combination of increase in both initial infertility and later embryonic mortality in eggs. Both are physiological effects which have been demonstrated experimentally with certain pesticides, though the second is more likely to result from organochlorine contamination. There appeared to be an unusually high incidence of addled Peregrine eggs, and especially addled whole clutches, during the pesticide episode but the data are not good enough to show this convincingly. Similarly, as regards factor (c), there was evidently a higher death rate among nestlings during the 1960s, and especially in the death of whole broods, a previously unusual event.

Some chick mortality has resulted from adverse spring weather during recent years. This may have simulated pesticide effects or, quite probably, enhanced them, since bad weather must create an additional level of physiological stress for either nestlings or parents when they are carrying an appreciable burden of toxic residues. Severe weather mortality has, however, continued since pesticide problems faded out in many districts. Under the wet and cold May of 1976, eight out of 20 broods hatched in the Southern Uplands perished (R. Mearns, R. Roxburgh, G. Carse). During the arctic spring of 1979, several broods died from related causes in Lakeland (G. Horne, T. Pickford) and probably even more in Wales (G. Williams). The spring of 1981 was another disastrous breeding season, with late April snowfalls and frosts, followed by heavy rainfall and further cold in May. At least 55 pairs in the UK were believed to lose their eggs or young through these harsh conditions, and breeding success of the population was only 49% (Ratcliffe, 1984). Mearns and Newton (1988) regard rain as the most significant adverse weather factor: they found that the percentage of clutches producing young decreased with increasing May rainfall, whereas low temperature appeared unimportant. It is, nevertheless, difficult to dissociate wet and cold conditions in their chill effects on the chicks.

Prolonged rain makes parental taking of prey more difficult, and may induce the female to leave the young unprotected while she joins in the search. Yet even when the female continues to brood, exposed eyries or those below the water trickles that develop during heavy rain may become waterlogged. Several observers report finding sodden broods huddled in saturated nest bowls, or others which had actually died. The finding by Mearns and Newton (1988) that clutches in overhung and recessed nest sites were more successful than those on exposed ledges, evidently relates to shelter from rain.

In the Republic of Ireland, Norriss (in press) has also found that annual productivity variations from 0·8–1·7 young/territorial pair/year) were inversely correlated with spring rainfall, and that the adverse effects of rain were felt most strongly on the smaller cliffs with the most limited choice of sheltered ledges. Norriss also believes that high orographic rainfall limits the actual occupation of some cliffs by Peregrines. In heavy rainfall areas, he finds a tendency for high cliffs facing NW to NE to be vacant, but that low cliffs tend to be ignored whatever their aspect.

BREEDING PERFORMANCE

The term breeding success has been equated with the proportion of territory-holding pairs which rear young, but the best measure of the breeding performance of a population is the combination of this figure with that for average brood size, giving the total number of young reared in relation to the breeding potential. This *productivity* is expressed as an average number of young per pair annually and obviously gives a lower figure than for average brood size, for it has to include the complete nesting failures and non-breeding pairs as well as successful nestings. Since more systematic surveys of British Peregrines began, from 1961 onwards, it has been possible to provide at least some data on productivity, but for earlier periods the basic information is simply too patchy to give any reliable figures. All that can be said is that breeding performance varied widely in different parts of Britain and Ireland.

In certain districts popular with egg collectors, productivity during the whole period 1900–46 was extremely low and probably did not exceed 0·5 young per pair per year: this was probably true for Sussex, Dorset, parts of south and central Wales, and the whole of northern England. Other districts were evidently intermediate in this respect, and probably had an output of around 1·0 young per pair, e.g. Kent, Devon, Cornwall, Pembrokeshire, North Wales, southern Scotland and the southern Highland fringe. Breeding performance was also low in areas much subject to gamekeeper persecution, mainly the grouse moor districts, so that even within the Highlands there was a great deal of variability in output of young from place to place.

It is nevertheless clear that *some* districts must have had good productivity, for the numbers in the unsuccessful districts could not otherwise have been maintained in the manner observed; productivity below 1·0 young per pair per year was probably below the self-sustaining level, and a surplus from elsewhere was needed. I think it likely therefore that the great Peregrine nurseries were in the remoter and more rugged parts of the Scottish Highlands and Islands, and western Ireland, where few Peregrine seekers then penetrated and where many pairs bred in such formidable precipices that the eyries were unassailable anyway. Here, a local productivity of up to 2·0 young per pair was probably the norm. From many of these eyries a steady succession of broods evidently fledged without fail year after year, to compensate for the heavy failure rates in the less successful districts. While the majority of Peregrines tend to return to the vicinity of their birth-place to breed, the ringing recoveries show enough examples of long-distance settlers for compensation effects between widely separated districts to be feasible.

There is, however, unlikely to be any magic figure for productivity necessary to sustain breeding population level. It all depends on mortality rates among adult and sub-adult birds, and these vary geographically and in time. It is also probable that long distance dispersal from more productive areas gave only a partial compensation in providing replacements for areas with poor breeding success, and that the once rather large number of irregular and occasional nesting places in these areas reflected the lack of prospecting Peregrines. Even the denser nesting groups, such as those in Snowdonia and Lakeland, may have been held below their potential level by shortage of recruits. The subject is discussed further in Chapter 11.

It is possible that breeding performance began to decline after 1947, as egg-breaking became a widespread cause of nesting failure, though this is uncertain. In some districts, egg-breaking evidently merely substituted for egg collecting as the major cause of clutch loss. During 1961–70, increase in non-breeding, and reduction in both breeding success and brood size were characteristic of most areas affected by decline in Peregrine numbers, giving a low productivity amongst the survivors: in general, the greater the decline, the poorer the performance of the remaining falcons. Only in the central Highlands was the output of young close to the previous, normal level, and it may even have been higher here than during the earlier part of this century, as a result of a general decrease in gamekeeper persecution.

The low productivity characteristic of Peregrine populations during the pesticide era is compounded from:

(a) Presence of many apparently unpaired birds (Table 7)

(b) Failure of many pairs to lay eggs (Table 2)

Reduced brood size or breeding failure, pp. 247–248

(c) Frequent breaking or unexplained disappearance of eggs (clutch depletion – Chapter 13).

(d) Frequent failure of intact eggs to hatch (infertility and addling – Chapter 13)

(e) Frequent death of the whole or part of a brood in the nest (abnormally high nesting mortality – pp. 248–249).

This appears to be a syndrome of general reproductive pathology caused by the toxic effects of various organochlorine residues in sub-lethal concentrations (Ratcliffe, 1969, 1973). The decrease in incidence of these effects, expressed by a gradual increase in net productivity since 1965–66, is regarded as a reflection of decreasing environmental contamination by these substances. Productivity has shown a marked upturn, in parallel with population recovery, in many districts, and in some it has reached a relatively high level, compared with the pre-1956 period. In southern Scotland, northern England and Wales, breeding is now probably better than at any time in this century. It would scarcely be an exaggeration to say that more young Peregrines were reared in each of these regions every year since 1977 than would fledge in a 10 year period before 1960. This is not only a reflection of falling environmental contamination by persistent toxic chemicals; it is also a tribute to the combined efforts of the Royal Society for the Protection of Birds, dedicated local ornithologists, the Nature Conservancy Council, the Forestry Commission and the police in mounting a protection campaign against the return of the eggers and falcon-lifters.

The spectacular increase in Peregrine numbers in many parts of Britain and Ireland over the last two decades can be taken as evidence that human activity no longer depresses productivity below the level needed for population expansion. There is, nevertheless, much concern about the continuing levels of law-breaking through harassment of nesting Peregrines. The picture is complicated by an unknown incidence of nest failures where direct human interference is not involved, but persecution in some form is probably again the commonest cause of loss since pesticide effects declined to insignificance.

Egg collecting and taking of young Peregrines continued through the period of the crash, and evidently increased again after 1970. In 1977 the RSPB claimed to know of 40 Peregrine eyries robbed of young, but the subsequent legal requirement for captive birds of prey to be registered has evidently had a beneficial effect, along with the acceptance of licensed captive breeding as a legitimate means of supplying Peregrines. The market in illegally acquired falcons has evidently been reduced, though not eliminated. Egg collecting continues and every year many districts report at least some robberies. An unknown proportion of these is taken to hatch in incubators as a means of supplying the illegal trade in captive Peregrines, including that overseas. Yet some of the robberies are certainly for eggshell collectors. The RSPB believe that there are still around 500 eggshell collectors in Britain, and many of the illegal collections uncovered by the Society and the police during the last 20 years or so have held recently taken Peregrine clutches.

There is little doubt that some of the recent increase in Peregrine population is the result of a reduction of persecution by game-preservers, especially on the grouse moors. It is hardly conceivable that the good numbers now breeding in the Pennines and various parts of eastern Scotland could have become established other than through a conscious relaxation of earlier levels of harassment by gamekeepers. This is a welcome trend that deserves our recognition and gratitude. But it is by no means a universal improvement, and there are worrying signs that it is now being reversed. It is always difficult to obtain hard data on this issue, other than on specific cases. I am therefore grateful to George Carse for supplying me with information which, though circumstantial as evidence, points clearly to the adverse effects of gamekeeper interference on Peregrine breeding performance. Mr Carse has for many years monitored the Peregrine population of the eastern half of Southern Scotland. In 13 different inland territories within keepered ground 124 occupations during 1973–92 produced 47 successful nestings (38%); whereas in 17 inland territories in unkeepered areas 177 occupations during 1973–92 produced 100 successful nestings (57%). The difference is significant (G test, $G = 10\cdot1122$, 1 df, $p < 0\cdot01$) and supports the view that keepering causes an increased probability of failure. The sample takes account of the range of attitudes amongst keepers and their employers; in at least two of the keepered territories attitudes were known to be friendly towards Peregrines, but in two others (both on grouse moors in the Moorfoot Hills) not a single successful nesting occurred in nine and 14 occupations.

The Bowland Fells in the western Pennines are another notable grouse moor area with a long history of persecution where local ornithologists and the RSPB have struggled against the odds to stop the killing or nest destruction of both Peregrines and Hen Harriers. Only within the last few years have their efforts had noticeable success (P. Stott, C. Smith, P. Marsden, T. Pickford). The continuing near absence of Peregrines from the North York Moors is also highly suspicious, given the dramatic increase of the species in most other parts of northern England.

As further evidence of recent deliberate persecution, the RSPB/NCC (1991) reported 55 Peregrines in a total of 463 birds of prey (12%) known to be shot or trapped in the UK during 1979–89. The eggs or young in 24 nests were also deliberately destroyed. The indications are that grouse preservers were mainly responsible for this destruction. Given their preference for live bird prey, Peregrines are surprisingly vulnerable to the poison illegally placed in meat baits by game preservers and farmers, mainly to kill foxes and crows. In an analysis of bird deaths from misused poisons during 1968–78, the RSPB (1980) reported four Peregrines; while during 1979–89, no less than ten were recorded in a total of 351 poisoned birds of prey (RSPB/NCC, 1991).

Pigeon fanciers appear increasingly to be taking the law into their own hands. In Wales, the RSPB found that at least 50 nests failed through direct interference in 1992. While some of these were probably robbed by egg collectors or hawk keepers, the shooting of adults at ten eyries, the destruction of eggs or young at another seven, and poisoning of birds at another four, was believed to be the work of fanciers. Many of the losses were in areas where there has been loud clamour for control of Peregrine numbers.

It might be argued that all these forms of direct interference with Peregrine breeding performance are of little consequence nowadays, given the evidence for continuing increase across much of the country. Even so, they could easily get out of hand if bird protection vigilance were to be relaxed.

CHAPTER 9

Movements and migrations

Some of the earliest references to the Peregrine are about its habit of moving from place to place. The Vatican Library has an illustrated manuscript copy of the treatise on the art of falconry by the Emperor Frederick II (1247) in which one picture shows a clearly recognisable Peregrine sitting on the stern of a sailing boat (see p. 17), and the work contains references to the migratory habits of the species. Over seven centuries later, Tuck (1970) speaks of 'the numerous instances of Peregrine Falcons remaining on ships for days on end identified in all the principal oceans of the world, often far out at sea.' The bird is a great traveller, but its transoceanic journeys remain largely a mystery, in that the places of origin and destination are usually uncertain. Voous (1961) has given records of Peregrines on the Atlantic Ocean, and mentions an instance of the species boarding a ship 1300 km west of Africa, staying for two days, and departing while still 1100 km from the nearest point of South America. Rogers and Leatherwood (1981) recorded a Peregrine and an Osprey spending 5 days together, plying between two vessels in mid-Pacific, 2600 km west of Costa Rica.

The original Latin name *peregrinus* or *fugitivus* describes the wandering nature of the species, and has been translated into various European equivalents: passagier, pelgrim, slechtvalk (Dutch); dreckfalke, wanderfalke (German); passager, pèlerin (French); peregrino, pelegrin, halcon comun (Spanish); pellegrino, peregrino (Italian); pilgrimsfalk (Swedish). In some parts of Europe, notably the lowlands where most of the early falconers and chroniclers evidently lived, the Peregrine is known only as a visitor, and mainly during autumn–winter. This is true of much of southern and eastern England, the Netherlands, Denmark, and the plains of western Germany, France and Belgium. The species is, in fact, a migrant to a degree determined by the behaviour of its prey populations. Where these are wholly or largely migrants, the Peregrine has to be likewise, and where its food supply is sedentary, it moves about much less.

OUTSIDE BRITAIN

It follows that the Peregrines with the most marked migratory tendencies are those which breed in the highest latitudes, whilst those from the Temperate Zone to the Equator may move about or stay put according to more local conditions. Hickey and Anderson (1969) have summarised the migratory tendencies of the different subspecies of the Peregrine as follows: 'Migratory behaviour in the Peregrine is importantly restricted to the five more northern races. Within at least four of these subspecies, there presumably exists a continuum of behaviour, individuals in the more southerly latitudes being non-migratory, those in the north moving considerable distances. These latitudinal gradients are in turn strongly modified by the climatic amelioration produced by the oceans on the north-west sides of North America and Eurasia. As a result, migratory behaviour in the Peregrine also tends to increase as one goes east on each of these two continents.' Kuyt (1967) reported that a Peregrine banded in the Northwest Territories of Canada was recovered roughly 14,500 km away in Argentina, only just over 4 months later.

Frederick II noted that the main southwards migration of Peregrines through southern Europe was during September and October, though the time of passage varied according to latitude and climate of the country of origin. The spring return movement was more irregular because mortality and capture had reduced their numbers. Fischer (1967) indicates that the Barbary Falcon of North Africa, Arabia and southern Central Asia is largely sedentary whereas the Red-naped

Shaheen of the southern Altai and western Gobi migrates during winter. In Europe north of the Baltic the Peregrine population appears to be mostly migratory, following its prey populations each autumn as these move southwards to escape the rigours of the Boreal and Arctic winter. The autumn/winter recovery of falcons ringed in Finland and Sweden shows the movement to be largely south-westwards, with the majority found in a broad zone from Denmark and the Baltic Islands through northern Germany, the Netherlands, Belgium, northern and western France into Spain (Linkola and Suominen, 1969; Saurola, 1977; Lindberg, 1977). Migration of Norwegian Peregrines is also south-westwards into the same regions, but some falcons winter along the coast of Norway up to 67° North (Schej, 1977).

Harting (1883) describes how it was customary in his day for British falconers to visit Holland during October to obtain Peregrines caught on migration at the regular trapping stations, which used the time-honoured methods of decoying and netting wild falcons. He indicated that there was a parallel movement of Peregrines into eastern England but commented that nobody seemed to have realised their value if taken alive for sale to falconers, and that it was left for the game-preservers to thin their ranks quite rapidly. There appears to be no counterpart in Europe to the highly concentrated migration route of Peregrines through the eastern United States, at such localities as Hawk Mountain, Pennsylvania, which nowadays gives such rewarding opportunities for banding-studies of the species' movements and survival rates.

I regard various supposed records of North American Peregrines in Britain, based on sight records of especially dark individuals, as unreliable and suggest that only records based on banded birds should be allowed. Apart from the considerable plumage variations, light can play such tricks in field observations.

The status of Peregrine populations during the organochlorine pesticide era has been related in part to winter distribution. In regions remote from heavy pesticide use, populations which are largely sedentary and sustained by adequate winter food supply have been little affected if at all, whereas those which have to migrate because of seasonal food shortage have sometimes been seriously affected. The collapse of the Fennoscandian falcon population is attributable to its winter movement to the agricultural regions of Europe south of the Baltic, where pesticide use is considerable. The symptoms of lowered productivity and incipient decline in Alaska and Arctic Canada have been connected both with movement to winter quarters in croplands of Central America and northern South America, and to the contamination of the migrant prey populations before these move back to their northern breeding grounds. By contrast, the relatively sedentary Peale's Falcon in the north-east Pacific coastal regions has maintained its numbers well. Apparent decline in the Siberian Peregrine population could also be explained similarly by exposure to pesticide contamination on migration south to wintering regions in the Middle East and North Africa.

WITHIN BRITAIN

Mead (1973) suggested that Fennoscandian Peregrines are probably responsible for a majority of the lowland winter sightings in Britain. While this view is reasonable from the pattern of ringing recoveries reported below, so few young have been reared in Norway and Sweden during recent years that this element can hardly have been a significant addition to our winter population. Indeed, it is interesting that the Peregrine became quite an uncommon bird in the lowlands of Britain during the mid-1960s when the breeding population reached its lowest level, and winter sightings in non-breeding areas have steadily increased as the number of nesters has climbed back towards normal. Peregrines now appear quite frequently during autumn and winter in many English counties, and in the lowlands of Wales and Scotland, and they are quite regular visitors to some localities with a good food supply.

Peregrines have always been known to become more widely distributed during the autumn and winter in areas where they do not breed, especially lowland and flat coastal country. The species is then liable to turn up almost anywhere, but tends to favour certain types of country, such as estuaries and their adjoining hinterland, and the vicinity of lakes and reservoirs, where its prey becomes concentrated at this time of year. Even the larger cities, with their big populations of pigeons and Starlings, are sometimes a draw, and there are records of Peregrines taking up residence during the winter on St Paul's Cathedral in London, and tall buildings in other cities. Trees appear to be more favoured as plucking and roosting places at this time of year, but man-made structures are often used when advantageously located. The map in the Winter Atlas (Lack, 1986) showed winter distribution to be similar to that in the breeding season, but with more eastern and lowland records. Many lowland districts of England nevertheless had a dearth of sightings, and the Peregrine appeared to be extremely patchy and sparse in winter occurrence outside its breeding areas.

It has long been remarked that the majority of autumn and winter visiting Peregrines in non-breeding areas are juveniles, and this observation is expressed in the old falconer's name of 'passage hawk' for any falcon in immature plumage. This fact in itself would tend to support the idea that many of these wanderers are home-bred birds. Since the evidence is that most Peregrines, old and young, leave Fennoscandia at the approach of winter (Cramp and Simmons, 1980), if all the birds appearing then in lowland Britain were from that region, one would expect a more nearly equal ratio of old to young. In Britain, on the other hand, it is known that many – perhaps most – adults stay in their breeding territories all the year round, and the young falcons are the birds which move out. The observations quoted from Frederick II and Albertus Magnus on such movement are relevant here (Chapter 8).

It is the recently fledged eyasses which, when parted from their parents and siblings, have to find a place of their own and are likely to be wanderers when autumn sets in. Some take up territories where there are vacancies amongst the hills or on the seacliffs, but probably many of them make their way down to the low country or the 'soft' coasts where food is easier to find at this time of year. Young birds reared in Britain may thus be partial migrants, with a tendency to seek good feeding grounds during autumn and winter, and then in spring to move back to the rocky coasts and mountains in search of vacant breeding places. Peregrines tend to disappear from the lowlands around March and few are to be seen there during the summer, except where there are cliffs not far away. Non-breeders without a nesting territory may be prone to wander widely at any time of the year, seeking suitable places to colonise. Ian Newton tells me that since 1975 there has been a noticeable increase in the number of Peregrines seen during spring and summer in the lowlands of Dumfries and Galloway, and that birds appear to be roaming the farmlands virtually all the time. Mearns (1984) reported that at Caerlaverock, on the Scottish Solway, winter sightings of Peregrines increased markedly from 1974 to 1980. They were nearly all of juvenile birds, whose numbers correlated closely with previous season breeding success in adjoining districts, and which disappeared again during spring and summer.

The extent to which adult Peregrines holding breeding territories in Britain migrate after the breeding season and their distribution during autumn and winter depends largely on availability of food. In those breeding areas where small to medium sized birds remain numerous throughout the winter, the established pairs mostly appear to stay as residents for the whole year round. The pair sometimes separate and roost in different cliffs, and it seems that either the male or the female may then hold to the favourite breeding rock, but many pairs evidently stay together through the winter. Upland Peregrines evidently hunt farther afield in winter than during the breeding season, for prey becomes noticeably less abundant and they may be absent from their nesting cliffs for periods. The ancestral crags or another rock in the vicinity may still be used for roosting, but the foraging birds are often not there during the day, and return only in the evening. Some pairs seem to leave their nesting quarters during the winter and move to another locality only a few miles away, where they roost on a rock unknown as a breeding place. During heavy snow and hard frost, falcons frequently appear to leave the hills, presumably to take up temporary residence in adjacent lowlands, and even the seacliffs may be deserted during heavy snow. Mountain cliffs are sometimes left in stormy weather for the shelter of a wood nearby.

Mearns (1983) found that the majority of both inland and coastal nesting places in southern Scotland showed signs of recent Peregrine presence in winter. Pairs or single falcons were seen at about half the inland territories and at about a third of the coastal territories. More single females than single males were seen. No first-year Peregrines were seen in breeding haunts during winter, and all first-year birds found dead, from August to February, were on low ground. Most winter sightings on low ground away from nesting places were also of juveniles. Geoff Horne has also found that most pairs of Lakeland Peregrines cling faithfully to their breeding crags throughout the winter.

It is in the interests of a territory-holding Peregrine to stay in the breeding quarters all the year round, unless winter weather or lack of food actually threaten survival. A falcon which deserts its 'claim' could easily find on return that its place had been taken in the interval by another bird. In many areas, prospecting Peregrines are probably ready to fill gaps quite rapidly, especially when first-class cliffs fall vacant, or when a single bird is already in possession and ready to accept a new mate. It is evidently the rule for the same individual female, identifiable by egg-type, voice and behaviour, to return to the same territory to breed in each successive year. This trait was well-known to egg-collectors. Females with distinctive eggs were, however, occasionally known to change territories.

Observations showing presence in winter of Peregrines at breeding places in most coastal and inland districts south of the Scottish Highlands suggest that this southern sector of the population is relatively sedentary, behaving in the manner described. Within the Highlands there is evidently more winter mobility, but with marked variations from place to place. There is, however, a shortage of information about the winter whereabouts and movements of the resident, established breeding population of Peregrines, and no accurate picture can be drawn at present. When one considers the probable shortage in winter food supply for some of our northern British Peregrines, it could be expected that there would be a partial and limited migration of the species within this country, involving a dispersal of adults and juveniles.

In northern Scotland coastal haunts, Peregrines which in spring and summer depend largely on the big seabird breeding colonies must suffer a drastic reduction in food supply when these colonies disperse and take to the open sea at the end of summer. These rocky coasts have few large estuaries to hold good winter populations of waders and wildfowl, and the species remaining are chiefly Herring Gulls and Fulmars. The barren moorlands of the adjoining interior are even less productive, for most of the breeding birds are there only for a few months, and during the winter the sparse population of Red Grouse and a few duck are virtually all that remain for Peregrines to feed on. The Winter Atlas (Lack, 1986) supports the view that many of the adult falcons in the north and west of the Highlands and in the Islands therefore have to move to better hunting grounds when their food supply dwindles away. The more fertile Orkneys have many more winter records than the barren Shetlands. There is no information to show where the mobile birds go – whether they sojourn in the nearest fertile lowlands in Scotland, or whether they travel much farther south, to the farmlands and estuaries of England. Possibly they do both.

By contrast, in the Central Highlands, with its generally much denser populations of Red Grouse and Ptarmigan and its more fertile straths, many pairs of Peregrines cling to their breeding areas throughout the year. Much depends on local conditions. For instance, Douglas Weir tells me that the well-known pair at Aviemore are present throughout the winter, whereas at one of the most Arctic of all British nesting haunts, above Loch Avon in the high Cairngorms, the Peregrines clearly move to lower ground during the latter part of the year.

Clayton White (1969) has discussed the tendency of Peregrines – as with many other bird species – to return to the vicinity of their birthplace in seeking a breeding haunt. He believes that this could explain not only the traditional and regular occupation of many cliffs, but also the tendency for persistence of local groups of Peregrines with distinctive plumage patterns and other morphological characteristics. This concept of genetic continuity could also account for persistence of local ecological or physiological adaptations, and may be relevant to the strange phenomenon of the localities renowned amongst falconers over long periods for the quality of their Peregrines. Migrant Peregrines head back to their place of origin during March and April, and even within the apparently self-contained British population there is probably a parallel tendency to re-trace more local movements. It is only the hard evidence derived from precise records of marked individuals which can confirm and fill in details of the picture of movements deduced from general observation.

Chris Mead has kindly provided the following analysis of the British Trust for Ornithology ringing recovery data for the Peregrine in Britain and Ireland.

PEREGRINE RINGING RETURNS AFFECTING BRITAIN AND IRELAND

By C. J. Mead, British Trust for Ornithology

INTRODUCTION

The last 15 years have seen an enormous increase in ringing of the species by Peregrine enthusiasts, as the population has increased, and then surpassed its pre-war level. It was only as recently as 1976 that the annual total passed 100 (139) and that the grand total passed 500 – about six Peregrines in every 10,000 birds of all species ringed in Britain. From 1977 to 1990 a further 3921 Peregrines were ringed – about 36 in every 10,000 birds. This recent surge of activity has greatly expanded the data-base on which our knowledge of movements and longevity depends.

Almost all these marked Peregrines have been ringed as nestlings, with only 66 ringed when full-grown: decade totals are given in Table 20. A few of these full-grown birds were ringed after being found injured and kept in care, but the majority were caught and marked as breeding birds in the study by Mearns and Newton (1984) in southern Scotland, giving a marked regional bias. The patchy distribution of Peregrine ringers also produces a somewhat uneven spread of marking of nestlings within the British and Irish population as a whole, and there is still little information for some of the remoter districts in the far north and west of both countries.

Very few ringed Peregrines are ever recovered alive and in full health, more than 5 km from the ringing location. All ten of such 'controls' on the national file for Peregrine were of birds caught at the nest during the South-west Scottish study (Mearns and Newton, 1984). Their study also produced more than 100 retraps of marked individuals. Otherwise, each recovery has depended on a member of the public reporting the bird, usually after death, but sometimes still alive though sick or injured. It has been assumed that even when Peregrines have been released after care they died as a result of the initial event which led to their recovery. The only three apparently independent records of such birds showed that they had all died within 3 weeks of release.

For many Peregrine ring returns no information is given on the means of recovery. Cause of death or injury reported for Peregrine ringing recoveries is so open to bias that no statistically valid figures for proportions of the different categories can be drawn. All that can be said is that the most frequently reported causes include shooting and trapping, deliberate poisoning (evidently now more common than pesticide deaths), traffic accidents, collision with wires and other objects, intra-specific fighting, and Fulmar-oiling. Protected birds recovered through illegal killing are typically reported as 'found dead' if, indeed, they are reported at all. Dates may be inaccurate, especially through the sometimes lengthy delays in returning rings found, and birds with rings may not be found until long after death. These complications account for slight differences in totals for birds used in the following analysis and presented in the tables.

MOVEMENTS FROM ABROAD

There have been 13 recoveries in Britain and Ireland of Peregrines ringed abroad – all in Scandinavia, and all but two ringed as nestlings. Birds from other countries may reach us too but ringing of Peregrines elsewhere may have been insufficient to give

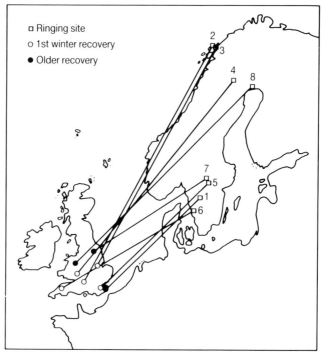

Figure 10. Movements of ringed Peregrines from Scandinavia to Britain. Pre-pesticide period 1935–51.

Number	Sex	Ringing date	Recovery date	Age when found
1	F	5 Jun 35	18 Jan 37	2+
2		5 Jul 38	4 Nov 38	0
3		9 Jul 43	2 Dec 43	0
4		1 Jul 45	22 Feb 46	0
5		20 Jun 46	6 Dec 46	0
6		16 Jun 46	30 Jan 47	0
7		20 Jun 46	11 Nov 47	1
8		6 Jul 47	28 Nov 51	4

NOTE: Age is in years, to the nearest whole year.

much chance of recovery here. Figure 10 shows the eight recoveries reported before the pesticide era and Figure 11 the five since 1980. There was a dearth of recoveries between 1952 and 1982, when the Scandinavian population was at its lowest ebb.

The earliest monthly date recorded for an immigrant Peregrine is 22 October and the latest (accurately dated) 22 February (the May bird was not fresh when found, but it was also in a possible breeding area). Most of the recoveries have been in lowland areas in the southern half of England and Wales, where conflict between the visitors and resident, territorial birds would be least likely. Although seven of these birds were found in their first winter there were three 2 year olds and two full adults. The pattern of recoveries indicates that the direct flight over the North Sea is not a problem for this species. It is presumed that surviving Scandinavian falcons, with their strong migratory urges, will tend to return to their home areas as spring approaches.

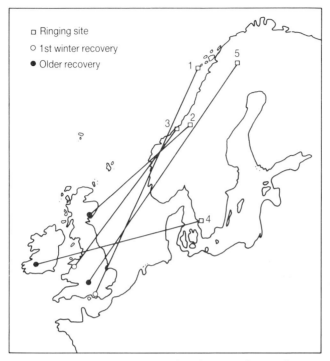

Figure 11. Movements of ringed Peregrines from Scandinavia to Britain. Post-pesticide period 1983–91.

Number	Sex	Ringing date	Recovery date	Age when found
1		4 Jul 82	5 Jan 83	0
2		5 Jul 82	20 May 86	3*
3	F	28 Jun 83	29 Dec 83	0
4	M	19 Jul 88	22 Oct 89	1
5	M	10 Jul 89	17 Jan 91	1

NOTE: * = Not fresh when found or delay in reporting.

MOVEMENTS OF BRITISH AND IRISH RINGED BIRDS

As one of the most powerful flying machines within the bird world, any Peregrine is capable of moving long distances over a short period. That most British and Irish birds do not travel long distances is clear from the ringing records. Only 25 movements of more than 200 km from the natal ringing site have so far been reported in 358 recoveries [7%], and all these are plotted on the maps in Figures 12–15 for four main ringing areas. Month of recovery and age at finding are shown in Table 21.

While the British and Irish populations are clearly interchangeable, the ringing evidence suggests that, taken as a whole, they are remarkably self-contained and subject to only local migration. Only one movement outside these islands is so far recorded – a bird ringed in Northern Ireland which was recovered in Portugal

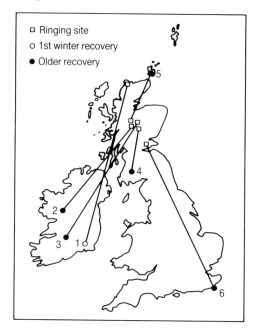

Figure 12. Movements of ringed Peregrines beyond 200 km from ringing sites in the Highlands.

Number	Sex	Ringing date	Recovery date	Age when found
1		27 Jun 50	23 Jan 51	0
2		12 Jun 75	5 May 76	0
3		2 Jun 76	8 Apr 77	0
4		17 Jun 77	21 Mar 79	1*
5	F	31 May 81	17 Oct 83	2
6		22 May 86	9 Dec 89	3*

NOTE: * = Not fresh when found or delay in reporting.

during the September of its second year. Despite the seeming opportunities for cross-Channel exchange, there are as yet no other recoveries of British or Irish ringed Peregrines on mainland Europe, and no birds ringed south of the Baltic have been found here.

Of the 358 recoveries, 177 (49%) were within 50 km of ringing site, 90 (25%) were at 50–99 km, and 66 (18%) at 100–199 km. First year Peregrines had on average travelled shorter distances from their birthplace than older birds (Table 22). Although the numbers marked are still small, no Peregrine ringed as an adult has yet been recovered as far as 200 km from the ringing site; and there is a lack of information about winter movements of established breeders. The finding of a Peregrine of any age during the period August to February is not evidence that it would (had it lived) have been around the same area when the next breeding season came in. Adults recovered in suitable breeding areas during the nesting season may well have been resident or actually nesting there, but only a few recoveries – other than in the Mearns and Newton study – were certainly of breeding Peregrines. While the majority of breeders have probably settled within

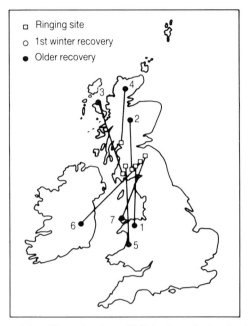

Figure 13. Movements of ringed Peregrines beyond 200 km from ringing sites in southern Scotland.

Number	Sex	Ringing date	Recovery date	Age when found
1		14 Jun 73	3 May 88	14
2	F	1 Jun 75	8 Aug 87	12
3	F	1 Jun 77	24 Aug 79	2
4		8 Jun 78	20 Oct 86	8*
5	M	19 Jun 79	30 Sep 84	5*
6	M	4 Jun 80	3 Dec 81	1
7	F	16 Jun 80	10 Aug 86	6

NOTE: * = Not fresh when found or delay in reporting.

the district where they were reared, there are instances proving that long distance breeding dispersal sometimes occurs. One bird ringed as a nestling in Lakeland in 1923 was found dead below the eyrie in an adjoining territory only 8 km away the following spring, while its sibling was recovered in spring 1925 at an eyrie in Perthshire 224 km north-west. There have been at least two other records of northern England Peregrines being found in later years at eyries in the Scottish Highlands and the Isle of Man, at distances of 243 km and 120 km.

Table 22 shows that, overall, females are more likely to have moved farther than males at any time of the year ($\chi^2 = 13.98$, $p < 0.001$). Of older birds recovered between January and June, only one of 25 males had travelled 100 km or more but 16 of 30 females had done so ($\chi^2 = 15.55$, $p < 0.001$). Evidently males tend to seek to breed closer to their natal area than do females. The data in Table 23 do not show any significant differences in dispersal distance between the main geographical regions.

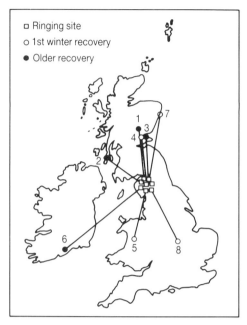

Figure 14. Movements of ringed Peregrines beyond 200 km from ringing sites in Lakeland.

Number	Sex	Ringing date	Recovery date	Age when found
1		29 May 23	1 May 25	1
2		9 Jun 38	20 Apr 42	3
3		5 Jul 49	11 Aug 50	1
4		1 Jun 79	19 Dec 79	0
5	F	1 Jun 80	8 Jan 85	4
6		19 Jun 85	3 Dec 85	0
7		20 Jun 89	11 Dec 89	0
8		8 Jun 90	18 Nov 90	0*

NOTE: * = Not fresh when found or delay in reporting.

The ringing recoveries have been examined for possible trends in direction of dispersal, but no significant differences in orientation have been found, whatever the distance. Peregrines in the more central regions such as northern England and southern Scotland appear to disperse randomly in direction. Given the lack of overseas migration, those in the far north of Scotland, west of Ireland or south of England could be expected to follow the main land masses, and thus to show some degree of orientation accordingly; but the recoveries from these regions are too few to confirm this.

Mearns and Newton (1984), in their southern Scotland study, found 39 ringed Peregrines (24 males, 15 females) among the breeders caught at nesting cliffs. The females had dispersed farther than the males from birthplace on average: median distances were 68 and 20 km, respectively, with maxima of 185 and 75 km. Movements were in any direction from the hatch site, and 11 of the ringed breeders came from districts well beyond southern Scotland – Lakeland (seven),

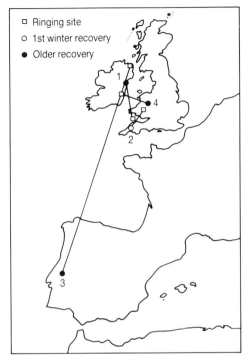

Figure 15. Movements of ringed Peregrines beyond 200 km from ringing sites in Wales, south-west England and Ireland.

Number	Sex	Ringing date	Recovery date	Age when found
1		31 May 53	17 Mar 58	4
2		18 May 80	30 Jan 81	0
3		8 Jun 80	10 Sep 81	1
4	F	2 Jun 84	26 Apr 89	4

the Highlands (three) and Northern Ireland (one). Fifteen birds ringed as nestlings were handled more than once in later life: 11 caught in the same territory each time had travelled a mean distance of 55 km from birthplace, while four had moved mean distances of 64 km to their first nesting place, and then 21 km to another. Taking all breeders that were recaptured in a later year (whether originally ringed or not), 61 of 68 females had stayed on the same territory and seven had moved to a different territory; while all of six males were on the same territory. Mearns and Newton concluded that Peregrines in southern Scotland tended to make their longest movements during their first year of life, but that having established as breeders, they remained in the same general area thereafter, showing considerable fidelity to their chosen territories.

While the great increase in ringing of Peregrines during recent years has considerably expanded our knowledge of movements, a good deal more remains to be learned, especially about the winter distribution of the birds occupying areas where food supply must become poor at this time of year. Until more Peregrines have been ringed in northern Scotland, it will remain a matter for conjecture that some of them possibly move to more productive hunting grounds in winter. The difficulty is that in some places – Shetland above all – so few Peregrines remain that there is little chance of ringing the numbers needed to throw light on these mysteries.

CHAPTER 10

Breeding density and territory

GEOGRAPHICAL DIFFERENCES IN BREEDING DENSITY

Breeding density of Peregrines is measured as the number of pairs nesting per unit area inland or per unit length of coastline, but the actual measurements pose difficulties. Many Peregrine territories contain several different nesting cliffs, used over a period. Unless one cliff is especially favoured, the geometric centre of a cluster is best used as the definitive location. Fluctuations in population stemming from the irregular or occasional use of certain territories give corresponding variations in breeding density. Linear measurements of density along a coastline are straightforward, as the distance from one pair to the next in a series, but they are the least satisfactory, in that they take no account of the *area* which each pair may require.

Area measurements give problems except on islands which are utilised wholly as hunting range and are beyond hunting distance from other land. Few British islands would qualify under these criteria. The average area occupied by each pair in an inland population can be measured by dividing the total extent by its number of pairs, but the problem is first to draw an outer limit to the whole breeding area when there are no boundaries on the ground and the extent to which the Peregrines range outwards is unknown. Since breeding pairs tend to space themselves out evenly, the average distance between each pair and its

267

nearest neighbour (avoiding counting the same distance twice) gives a linear measure of spacing similar to that for coastal populations. Average nearest neighbour distance can then be used to define a hypothetical outer limit to the area occupied by an inland population on the assumption that, if one could create suitable nesting places beyond the outermost pairs and these became occupied, the same degree of average spacing would continue to apply. Since spacing represents a repulsion effect between two adjacent pairs, the influence of one pair extends to half this distance. The intersecting outer segments of circles with this radius, drawn around the outermost nesting pairs, provide a boundary to the whole breeding area.

In practice there is a complication because spacing is not completely even, and closest neighbour distances thus under-estimate the true average spacing between pairs. It would be preferable to measure spacing as the distance from each pair to all its neighbours, but this introduces further practical difficulties. The perimeter of the breeding area is therefore defined by assuming that the outermost pairs exert an influence outwards which is equal to the whole of the average nearest neighbour distance, thereby allowing for the inherent under-estimate.

The process is demonstrated more easily in Figure 16 which shows the regular spacing pattern of Peregrine nesting places in one inland district, not named for obvious reasons. The tendency to even spacing is a rather remarkable feature, repeated again and again in different districts. When suitable cliffs are unevenly distributed, the regularity of the eyrie spacing pattern breaks down. A local concentration of cliffs in an area where they are otherwise sparsely distributed sometimes produces an unusually close clustering of pairs, up to the number of three or four. The species appears to adjust to the irregular scatter of cliffs by relaxing its normal spacing demands. Unusually close nesting also occurs now and then in districts where there is no shortage of good cliffs, but it seldom involves more than two pairs, and may occasionally result from bigamous pairings. Several examples of close nesting are on rather small offshore islands; these and some dense clusters are detailed in Table 24.

Applying these for measuring breeding density to both coastal and inland areas where nesting Peregrines are fairly evenly spaced gives results summarised in Table 25. These show that density varied quite widely across Britain up to 1979, and that 12 out of the 17 listed districts had experienced an increase in density up to 1991. In the Lake District, Snowdonia and Galloway – Carrick, previously regarded as at maximum breeding saturation, density was doubled, to mean levels of 4·7, 3·9 and 3·7 pairs/$100\,km^2$. Within each of these districts are denser than usual clusters of pairs, with that in the Lake District averaging 8·5 pairs/$100\,km^2$ – the highest known density inland in Britain (Table 24). Rathlin Island, off the coast of Co. Antrim, holds the present record of density for Britain and Ireland, with an incredible eight pairs in an area of only 13·59 km^2.

Table 25 excludes districts where availability of suitable nesting cliffs is likely to be a limiting factor, though drawing boundaries here is necessarily a subjective procedure. How can one be sure when suitable cliffs are present in excess of the established population? On long, continuous stretches of high seacliff the answer is self-evident: such places offer scope for huge numbers of Peregrines to breed. In many rugged districts the number of first-class but unoccupied crags is large

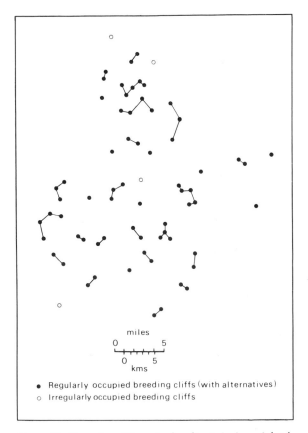

Figure 16. Dispersion of Peregrine breeding pairs in an inland region of Britain 1945–60.

too. Where there are gaps which break the even-ness of spacing between adjacent pairs, corresponding to absences of good cliffs, it is usually a fair presumption that this topographic limitation is at work. And wherever, in areas with evenly dispersed pairs, many territories contain well-spaced alternative nesting cliffs, it is also clear that some other factor is holding numbers down. The actual increase in breeding density within several districts since 1979 is a further confirmation that numbers here were not limited by availability of suitable cliffs.

Even so, this is a tricky topic, especially since the notion of 'suitable nesting cliff' has had to be modified over the last decade or so (Chapter 6). There have been increases in both breeding numbers and density in many areas where it had previously appeared that lack of good cliffs was a major limitation. In parts of Wales, the Pennines, Cheviots, Southern Uplands and eastern Highlands, increases over previous numbers have involved adaptation to small and relatively unsuitable cliffs. Many quite low-lying quarries have also been occupied. This constraint has thus become less important for the size of the Peregrine population as a whole. Breeding density nevertheless remains much lower in

many moorland districts than in adjacent rugged mountain country (e.g. the Pennines compared with the Lake District), and breeding Peregrines are still few or absent in some upland areas where cliffs are scarce (e.g. south-west England, Wigtownshire and Caithness).

The difficulty of knowing at precisely what point these aspects of habitat hold down Peregrine numbers should not, however, divert attention from the conclusion that the upper limits to breeding density appear to be set by the birds' own behavioural interactions with each other; and that these upper limits vary both geographically and in time.

TERRITORIAL BEHAVIOUR AND ITS INFLUENCE ON BREEDING DENSITY

The next step is to consider how not only the regularity of breeding dispersion, but also the actual spacing distances are determined. Many writers have assumed territorial behaviour in the Peregrine from the regular way in which breeding pairs usually space themselves apart. Forrest's (1907) account of the bird in North Wales began by quoting the Rev. Robert Williams from his *History of Aberconwy* (1835) :'This beautiful and noble bird annually breeds in the rocks of Llandudno and Rhiwleden; the birds are so jealous of each other that only one pair will be found to nest in the same rock'. Harvie-Brown quoted a similar passage from the *Black Book of Kincardineshire* (1879): 'Fowlsheugh is noted for being the breeding place of the Peregrine Falcon, of which each season a pair have their nest in the rock, and never more, in accordance with the maxim, adopted by these birds "to suffer no brother near their throne"; and if one of the pair happens in any one year to be killed, it is observed that its place never fails to be supplied next year'.

Eliot Howard, in his famous book *Territory in Bird Life*, had the following to say: 'That the Raven and certain birds of prey exert an influence over the particular area which they inhabit has long been known, and it has been recognised more especially in the case of the Peregrine Falcon, possibly because the bird lives in a wild and attractive country, and, forcing itself under the notice of naturalists, has thus had a larger share of attention devoted to its habitats. Moreover, when a species is represented by comparatively few individuals, and each pair occupies a comparatively large tract of country, it is a simple matter to trace the movements and analyse the behaviour of the birds. There is a rocky headland in the north-west of Co. Donegal comprising some seven miles or so of cliffs, where three pairs of Falcons and two pairs of Ravens have nested for many years. Each year the different pairs have been more or less successful in rearing their young; each year the young can be seen accompanying their parents up to the time when the sexual instinct arises; and yet the actual number of pairs is on the whole remarkably constant, and there is no perceptible increase. It seems as if the numbers of three and two respectively were the maximum the headland could maintain. But this is no exceptional case; it represents fairly the conditions which obtain as a rule amongst those species, granting, of course, a certain amount of variation in the size of each territory determined by the exigencies of diverse circumstances'. Howard's reasoning evidently rested on inference. He noted that the situation he described for the Peregrine and Raven showed suggestive similarities to that in the more familiar birds whose territorial activities he observed so painstakingly, and he drew the parallel.

Observable territorial behaviour in the Peregrine, including actual fighting, is described in Chapter 7, with the comment that such interactions are less commonly witnessed than one might expect, especially in areas where pairs are close together. Tom Cade has found Alaskan Peregrines to be very variable in their territorial aggressiveness. Some individuals were consistently much more pugnacious than others, attacking other Peregrines farther out from the eyrie, but the behaviour of the same bird could vary greatly from one day to the next. Much seemed to depend on the phase of the breeding cycle, weather, time of day, the behaviour of an intruding Peregrine, and the momentary state of the resident falcon. Cade regards the nesting cliff as the centre of a large home range which includes much hunting ground that is not defended in the usual territorial sense. He found that there was always a minimum radius around the eyrie, perhaps of only 100 m, which was vigorously defended at all times by nearly all Peregrines. Beyond this minimum distance, territorial attacks occurred in unpredictable patterns because many factors other than simple 'ownership' of a plot of terrain influence the agonistic behaviour of Peregrines. Frequency of attacks tended to decrease with distance from the eyrie, but could occur up to 1·6 km, and thus within the hunting domain, over items of prey or favourite perches and plucking stations. Peregrine territory could thus be regarded as a series of threshold perimeters around the eyrie, with the intrusion stimulus required for attack increasing as the radius from the centre increases. Cade found that within the hunting domain, which was shared with other Peregrines, favourite perches may form the locus of other small isolated units of defended or, more properly, disputed ground. Here, dominance relations are probably important in determining what individual occupies what perch at what time, since no one bird is present at all times to defend these isolated units.

This interpretation would seem equally applicable to British Peregrines. The increasingly frequent evidence for overt territorial aggression close to the eyrie is sufficient to explain why Peregrines are seldom to be found nesting closer together than 0·5 km, and so could account for the maximum densities found in Britain. But it is not a satisfactory explanation of the more usual minimum distance of 2·5 km between pairs in many districts, and still less of the average spacing of 8·6 km found in inland parts of northern Scotland. Most Peregrines seem to spread their eyries out more widely than their more obvious defence activities would lead one to expect. Many species of bird mark their territories by means of advertisement displays, especially combinations of flight and song, to which other individuals respond by avoidance reactions. For some, actual fighting plays only a minor part in the establishment of a territory. The same may well be true of Peregrines which, as well as showing various types of display flight during the courtship period, could give out more subtle signals amounting to territorial advertisement as they fly around the area containing their eyrie. Niko Tinbergen told me that he watched Hobbies from adjoining territories approach to within a few hundred metres of each other and then drift apart again. Although there were no obvious signals, and certainly no attacks, he gained the impression that these were territorial encounters. While it is seldom that neighbouring eyries are in sight of each other, when the occupant birds rise over their own cliffs they must often become visible to adjoining pairs.

A mutual intolerance and repulsion based on advertisement/avoidance behaviour falls within the general concept of territorial behaviour, and I believe justifies the use of the term *nesting territory* as the area apparently occupied by each pair. Some birds of prey, such as Common Buzzards, Short-eared Owls and Kestrels, have much more readily definable territories, with boundaries which are patrolled and defended. Patient observation allows all the encounters between neighbours to be plotted on a map, so that the area occupied by each pair in relation to the others can gradually be worked out (e.g. Craighead and Craighead, 1956; Lockie, 1955; Picozzi and Weir, 1974; Pettifor, 1983; and Village, 1990). Nelson (1977) found that in the dense population on Langara Island, British Columbia, Peregrines chased intruders to boundaries, and flew display flights outward to, and along, territorial boundaries that were approximately midway between neighbouring nest cliffs. On the whole, though, Peregrines do not show readily observable territorial boundary defence, and in another region of northern Canada, Court (1986) could not identify contiguous boundaries between neighbouring territories, despite witnessing much territorial interaction and chasing. In Britain, as in Alaska (Cade, 1960), the hunting ranges of neighbouring pairs are likely to overlap considerably.

Despite the lack of evidence for defence of exclusive areas, or boundaries, I regard regular spacing, whether considered as one- or two-dimensional, as a territorial phenomenon. For inland populations, the average area measurements of density thus amount to an average measure of nesting territory size. As used here, 'nesting territory' only expresses a concept and provides a convenient designation for the nesting area of a pair of Peregrines, according to the way in which falcons *appear* to apportion a breeding district into roughly equal shares through their spacing behaviour, when suitable cliffs are plentiful. Although I have spoken of irregular, occasional and deserted territories, a territory is impermanent and ceases to exist when no birds are present.

The recovery of the Peregrine population since 1965 gives further food for thought on the spacing process. For a time, it seemed that new pairs were filling the gaps up to the level of the earlier stable ceiling in numbers, at which point the previous control mechanisms restored the same 'saturation' limits as before. Yet, in districts between the east-central Highlands and south-west England, numbers have increased well beyond this level. In the areas of highest density (Tables 24 and 25), the increase has slowed, but not yet stopped, and the final ceiling in numbers is anyone's guess. As breeding density has doubled, the tendency to even spacing of pairs has been maintained. The highest inland densities, in Lakeland, Snowdonia and Galloway, have also remained remarkably similar. While differences between pre-1979 and 1991 median nearest neighbour distances were highly significant for all three regions ($p < 0.002$), none of the differences in variances of nearest neighbour distances was statistically significant ($p > 0.05$). This suggests strongly that, while territories are now much smaller, territoriality still continues to operate. Close nesting (less than 2 km apart) has become more frequent, and additional pairs have 'squeezed in' even where density was at its highest known level.

The increase in population and density has not extended to all regions. It is less marked in most coastal areas of south-west England and tends to fade with distance north and west in the Highlands fringe. In coastal areas of the northern Highlands and Islands, there is either no change or decline, and the decrease in Shetland has been spectacular. Yet increase has shown in the interior of the northern Highlands (Table 25). In some years there appear to be higher numbers in parts of Sutherland, but these are subject to fluctuation.

In districts where population has grown to a higher level than that previously known, the increase has variably affected breeding density. Some pairs have established beyond the edge of the previous population, or in gaps within it, thereby increasing the area occupied but without increasing density. But many additional pairs have squeezed themselves in, as it were, between established pairs, thereby reducing spacing distance and, hence, territory size.

In many cases, the extra places occupied have no previous history of nesting, though some of these may be old haunts which simply escaped the record; this would be especially likely at third class cliffs where persecution soon ended earlier breeding attempts. Many of the numerous quarry haunts are undoubtedly quite new, however. Some cliffs now regularly tenanted were known as earlier breeding places, but only in the irregular, occasional or deserted categories. Quite often, also, the extra pairs have taken over cliffs which were previously used as alternative nesting places of the long-established pairs, so that territories have, in effect, become split. Besides this 'doubling', there are even some instances of 'trebling' with three pairs occupying the selection of cliffs formerly held by a single pair.

In Lakeland and the northern Pennines, only eight occupied territories were known in 1966. By 1979, 47 territories had become occupied, of which only seven had no previous records of Peregrine occupation (the first of the seven in 1973). There was one 'double', with two pairs occupying cliffs previously used as alternatives by a single pair. By 1991, 97 territories were known, of which 53 were additional, including 14 doubles and three 'trebles' (three pairs in a previously single territory).

In inland areas of southern Scotland, 22 occupied territories were known in 1966, and 32 in 1979, of which none was extra or double. By 1991, 97 territories had become occupied, of which 48 were additional, including ten doubles and four trebles.

In most districts, the cliffs that remained occupied through the crash were mostly first-class, though many first-class cliffs were also deserted. During the recovery, old, regular (pre-crash) and first-class haunts have been occupied preferentially, and most of the new nesting places are either third-class cliffs or quarries which, by definition, are usually close to human presence.

In the Southern Uplands, two cliffs only 2·5 km apart were regularly held by separate pairs of Peregrines up to 1960; but during 1965–89 were occupied by only one pair, which used the two cliffs as alternatives, thereby merging two territories into one. The next adjoining territory had a 'doubling' in 1985, and a 'trebling' in 1988, but it was not until 1990 that the merged territory was again divided between two pairs. The same happened in two quite widely separated areas of Lakeland for several years, but each area is now shared by two pairs instead of one. A possible explanation is that some pairs or individuals are more aggressive than others, and better able to prevent territorial encroachment; but that the increasing pressure from new birds gradually over-rides this resistance, except where there are unusually aggressive occupants. The eventually successful contenders for living space are thus likely to be more dominant birds which can, as it were, force their entry against opposition. When falcons are not constrained by the presence of near neighbours, they tend to use alternative cliffs farther apart than in high density areas. Particularly territorial individuals will also eventually die, and be replaced by more normal birds.

The present situation is that, in the general recovery of Peregrine numbers, territorial behaviour is again holding the breeding population in some areas at much the same level as before the crash; but that in other areas there has been a relaxation of spacing responses, to the point where a doubling of breeding density has occurred. Is it likely that, although locally weakened, territorialism is now beginning to hold the population at a new and higher level? This depends on our being able to observe whether density reaches a new ceiling over a reasonable period, especially in those areas where suitable nesting places are still in excess.

This section has tried to establish that, when suitable nesting places are present in excess, territorial interaction is the main factor limiting breeding density in the Peregrine. Hostility towards intruders not only maintains the distances between neighbours but also prevents prospective additional settlers from staking claims in the intervening spaces. The existence of a surplus of potential breeders which is prevented from nesting by the established breeders is crucial to this hypothesis, but the evidence for such a surplus is presented in the next Chapter.

BREEDING DENSITY AND FOOD SUPPLY

Peregrines range widely from the eyrie and it seems highly unlikely that any pair confines its hunting to the presumed territory centred on the nest, even though

Grouse moor country in the Southern Uplands, Scotland; moorland birds (prey) are abundant but suitable nesting places are scarce (photo: D. A. Ratcliffe)

the bulk of the prey may be taken much closer to the eyrie. The bird is a powerful flier, and with a speed in level flight of 100 km/h, a hunting range overlapping those of neighbouring pairs and even overflying the farther limits of adjoining territories seems inevitable. Whatever function territorial behaviour may serve in the Peregrine, it can hardly involve a staking out of an exclusive area in which a pair can find sufficient food for themselves and their young. Yet the striking feature is that breeding density does show a connection with food supply, but on a wider scale, correlating broadly with major geographical variations in overall prey populations.

There are no actual figures of prey populations or densities for the various Peregrine breeding districts, and my statement that Peregrine nesting density varies geographically in parallel with food supply is based on subjective assessments. The highest density up to 1939 was on the rocky sections of the coast of Kent, Sussex and Dorset, where the seacliffs had a good supply of feral pigeons and Jackdaws, and backed into a hinterland with extensive downland, farmland and woods. This Channel coast was also a major landfall and point of departure for migrating birds. The localisation of cliffs may have produced a concentration effect in places, as on Beachy Head, with its dense cluster of Peregrines which were able to radiate out over a wide range of country. Farther west, in Somerset, Devon and Cornwall, the coastal cliffs bound a hinterland likely to have a lower carrying capacity for bird populations than that of the more eastern areas.

Coastal and inland Peregrine districts of Wales, northern England, southern Scotland and the southern fringe of the Scottish Highlands have prey populations in which the domestic pigeon figures largely. The high breeding density in the mountains of Snowdonia, Lakeland and Galloway is indeed accountable only in terms of the large numbers of pigeons available as a mainly mobile and seasonal food supply, for the diversity and numbers of wild prey species are so limited. With distance north in the Highlands the domestic pigeon decreases in availability. In the eastern half of the Highlands, the heathery hills usually have an abundance of wild prey, especially grouse and wading birds, but the deer forest and sheep walk country of the west is much poorer in both variety and numbers of birds. The wild tract of country from Morvern in northern Argyll to Sutherland is singularly sterile and sparsely populated by upland birds. The Peregrine here reaches its lowest breeding density in Britain, if one ignores districts where availability of suitable nesting places is limiting. Distribution is not uniform in the inland areas of the northern Highlands, and most of the Peregrines breeding here are within 25 km of the coast, leaving large gaps in occurrence in the interior of Sutherland, Ross-shire and northern Inverness-shire. The mainland of the Highlands north of the Great Glen covers roughly 18,000 km², and within it there are 120 known inland Peregrine territories, giving an overall average of one pair to every 150 km².

The larger islands of the Hebrides are mostly as barren as the western Highland mainland, and inland Peregrines are now extremely few. Even their rugged coasts have only a sparse population of the species. Competition from Golden Eagles may be an additional factor limiting Peregrine breeding density in parts of the Highland and Islands (see Chapter 12).

These remote western and northern districts of the Highlands furnish still further evidence for the dependence of Peregrine breeding density on food supply. For wherever there are large numbers of nesting seabirds, the spacing distance between adjacent pairs of Peregrines is reduced to a level comparable to that of districts to the south of the Highlands. Indeed, in a few places, breeding density was almost as high as that found before 1939 on the coast of Kent, Sussex and Dorset. Up to 1962, the island of Hoy in Orkney had a remarkably dense Peregrine population, and around 1900–10, the St Kilda group had at least four pairs. Several quite small islands (all of less than 700 ha) at intervals along the coast of Britain have at times held two pairs of Peregrines – Lundy (regularly), Skomer, Ramsey, Ailsa Craig, Holy Island (Arran), Handa, Noss and Fair Isle (sometimes three pairs) (Table 24). Nearly all these islands were, and still are, tenanted by large colonies of breeding seafowl which provide a great abundance of food for Peregrines, so that the area of land is scarcely relevant. There is also evidence (Nelson, 1990) that island-breeding Peregrines are not necessarily limited to their local food supply, but may commute to prey upon more distant sources.

The same kind of relationship between Peregrine breeding density and abundance of prey has been noted in other parts of the world. The highest density reported for any race of the Peregrine is that given for Peale's Falcon in the Queen Charlotte Islands, off the coast of British Columbia. The falcons of this archipelago feed mainly on the myriads of seabirds, especially alcids and petrels, nesting on certain coastal cliffs; they are, accordingly, coastal breeders and their

Golden Eagle and Greenshank country in the western Highlands, with sparse Peregrine populations; Rannoch Moor, Argyll (photo: D. A. Ratcliffe)

densities have to be measured as linear spacing. Distribution of eyries is extremely patchy on the Queen Charlottes, and closely correlated with the presence of seabird colonies. The highest density was found by Alan Brooks and, later, Frank Beebe on Langara Island at the northern end of the group, where the numbers of nesting Ancient Murrelets and Cassin Auklets were described by the latter as 'astronomical'. Referring to Cloak Bay on Langara in 1952–58, Beebe (1960) said, 'Here in a linear distance of somewhat over a mile, but in less than two square miles [520 ha] of land and sea surface, are concentrated never less than five, usually six and sometimes eight breeding pairs of Peregrines. In this area the spatial requirements of Peregrines are, in comparison with other areas, unbelievably small, and evidence of territorialism and intolerance, if present at all, is not easy to observe'. In one close grouping, up to five pairs could be seen in the air at once yet there was no hostility between pairs despite frequent deep invasion of each other's 'territories'; though Beebe pointed out that none of the closely spaced eyries faced each other, and suggested that the direction in which neighbouring eyries face may be as important as the actual spacing distance. The remaining 11 pairs of falcons were rather more widely spaced, at intervals of 0·8–1·6 km, and flat parts of the 42 km coast of Langara were unoccupied, so that total distribution was irregular.

Clayton White (1975) found that in the Aleutian Island chain, the density of Peale's Falcon was again related to seabird numbers. There was a normal spacing of 7–11 km between pairs and a maximum density of three pairs on a 6·5 km stretch of coast with a large auklet colony. Leslie Tuck (1960) found three pairs of Peregrines nesting at approximately 1·6 km intervals along the 5 km of the southern murre (guillemot) colony on Akpatok Island, Canada. He noted that, 'As far as could be determined, the falcons fed exclusively on murres injured by falling rocks, which they captured from the scree bordering the colony. The Peregrine Falcon was not recorded breeding in the large loomeries at Digges Sound or Cape Hay, where injured birds fell directly into the sea.'

In Alaska, Cade (1960) found that Peregrine breeding density varied enormously. Within the taiga zone of the Yukon basin most pairs nested along the main rivers where there were substantial concentrations of shore-birds (waders) and wildfowl within these large gaps in the forest, and forest birds could also be caught as they crossed these breaks. Within the foothill tundra zone of the Arctic slope, Peregrines are concentrated along the Colville River and its tributaries for, although the falcons can range widely over the tundra for food, suitable nesting places (rocky bluffs and steep banks) lie mostly alongside the rivers. Densities were generally low, but slightly higher on the Colville (average of 9·5 river kilometres and 520 km^2 per pair) than on the Yukon (average of 20 river kilometres and 775 km^2 per pair). White and Cade (1971) noted that on the Colville, density was higher, with 45 pairs averaging one pair per 6 km, below Umiat Mountain, compared with 46 pairs averaging one pair per 13 km above. The highest density was on the linear 2·8 km of Uluksrak Bluff below Umiat which had five pairs spaced almost equally in 1952. In subsequent years no more than three pairs were found on this cliff and since 1973, only two pairs (T. Cade). There is no restriction of nesting habitat in this area and, although the food supply here is good, White and Cade had no evidence that availability of food influences Peregrine density on the Colville.

Fyfe (1969) found that in northern Canada, Peregrine breeding density varied mainly according to availability of good nesting habitat. Densities of one pair to 50 km^2 were usual in areas of optimum habitat e.g. in the region around Bathurst Inlet, while one pair to 260 km^2 was typical of areas with limited nesting habitat. Court (1986) has since reported a dense Peregrine population at Rankin Inlet, on the north-west corner of Hudson's Bay, where a 450 km^2 area of arctic, coastal tundra and offshore islands (including stretches of open sea) held an average of 19 pairs, with mean nearest neighbour spacing of 3·3 km and mean density of one pair to 24 km^2. Unlike other dense maritime populations, there was no strict feeding specialisation on colonial birds, and the Rankin Peregrines fed on a good supply, first, of Ptarmigan and, later, of waders, passerines and small mammals. Much of the Boreal and Arctic region of North America is unsuitable habitat and has only low density (less than one pair per 5000 km^2). On the whole there is rather little evidence to relate breeding density to variations in food supply over this vast region. The extremely low densities reported by Bond (1946) for some arid regions of the western United States could reflect poor food supply or simply a lack of adaptation to desert conditions. In west Greenland, Mattox and Seegar (1988) found a density of one pair to about $100\,km^2$, while near the southern tip of Greenland, Falk and Moller (1988) recorded an average territory size of $240\,km^2$.

In Australia, Peregrines tend to be clumped in groups of more or less regularly spaced pairs in areas of plentiful suitable nesting places and stable food supply, especially along permanent river systems, other water bodies and coastal strips (Olsen and Olsen, 1988). In New South Wales, a cluster of 16 pairs had mean minimum spacing of $3\cdot5\,km$ and mean density of one pair to $28\,km^2$, but over a larger district density was one pair to $154\,km^2$. Over much of Australia, density was much lower, at a pair to $200–750\,km^2$, while barren heathland in south west Tasmania had only one pair to over $3000\,km^2$.

Data on breeding densities in Old World Peregrines have been given by Fischer (1967) and Glutz *et al*. (1971), but the figures quoted for central Europe tend to be maxima rather than averages, and it is not clear how they relate either to breeding habitat limitations or to variations in local food supply. The range of variation seems to be similar to that found in Britain and Ireland. The Normandy coast with about $150\,km$ of very favourable cliffs (the counterpart to those of southern England) had about 40 pairs spaced about every $3\,km$ (Terrasse and Terrasse, 1969). In eastern France, 17 nests averaged one to $160\,km^2$ and 14 pairs along escarpments totalling $72\,km$ in length were $5\,km$ apart on average, the closest spacing being $1\,km$ (Formon, 1969). In some parts of Germany Peregrines breed mainly along the river valleys and so have a somewhat linear distribution. Mebs (1969) found seven pairs along $12\cdot5\,km$ of the Main and nine pairs along $30\,km$ of the lower Neckar. Kleinstäuber (1969) knew eight to ten pairs within $117\,km^2$ of the Saxonian Alps bordering Czechoslovakia and R. Zimmerman recorded average spacing here of $8\cdot5\,km$. Tree-nesting populations in North Germany locally reached moderately high density, e.g. four pairs in $210\,km^2$ (Brüll).

In Spain, Heredia *et al*. (1988) give average minimum spacing of $4\cdot9–20\cdot3\,km$, with significant differences according to geological formation. Gibraltar is reported to have a group of five pairs of Peregrines breeding within an area of c. $400\,ha$ – another example of a local concentration effect through nesting habitat restriction (J. C. Finlayson per P. Tate).

In Siberia, Peregrine densities evidently vary a good deal. Glutz *et al*. (1971) state that high densities with spacing of $3–5\,km$ on the Yamal peninsula (Dementiev) were associated with plentiful food supply. In other regions, such as the Timanskaya tundra, south Novaya Zemlya, Waigach Island and the lower Lena River, average spacing of $10–20\,km$ seems to be usual and on the upper Lena it is wider at $30–40\,km$. Doubtless the same situation obtains as in Arctic North America.

It does not follow that when food supply and cliff habitat are favourable, Peregrines will be found in good numbers. Indeed, there are many apparently most suitable areas where the species is quite absent. The Faeroe Islands, with their huge seabird colonies, so close to northern Britain, are a striking example. Cade (1960) has pointed out that, despite extensive coastal cliffs and a superabundance of food, there appears to be a virtual absence of breeding Peregrines from the islands of the Bering Sea lying north of the Aleutian Chain. In France,

J. F. Terrasse told me that the eminently suitable granite cliffs of the Brittany coast were surprisingly devoid of breeding Peregrines.

Even so, within the regions where Peregrines occur, there seems often to be a reasonably good correlation between breeding density and available food supply, and this relationship is maintained in the known instances when food supply has declined. There appears nevertheless to be an upper limit to breeding density. Even in the most massive seabird colonies, Peregrines do not become colonial in the manner of Eleonora's Falcon (see later).

TERRITORIAL BEHAVIOUR AND FOOD SUPPLY

It is not surprising that numbers of Peregrines are greatly influenced by the availability of food, since this is one of the most basic principles of animal ecology. The special interest lies in the process whereby a relationship between numbers of predator and prey is achieved in any one area. In those regions where the Peregrine has shown a general tendency for numbers to remain almost constant, whatever their actual level, this appears to involve an equilibrium.

My reasoning about this equilibrium runs as follows. Breeding density is determined directly (proximately) by strength of territorial interaction (= spacing behaviour). Breeding density also shows a broad numerical match with available food supply, being low where the latter is poor and high where it is good, though there is an upper limit to this density, however prolific the food supply. Although only rather crude observational evidence is available, this relationship appears to be sufficiently consistent between different regions of the World to render it highly improbable that such a feature could have come about by chance. Since territorial behaviour has no purpose in itself, but has evolved to serve some other function, it is tempting to see here a possible mechanism for adjusting breeding population to available food supply. This would not mean that territorial behaviour had no other function in the Peregrine but simply that this was its main purpose. The inference is that the bird must in some way respond to its perception of prey availability so that its intensity of territorial interaction results in a particular spacing distance, on average. The mystery lies in the precise mechanism involved in this response, and the way in which it confers survival value on the Peregrine, since one presumes that this process has evolved through natural selection as one giving the maximum advantage to the individual.

In areas of abundant nesting cliffs, variations in average spacing distance must involve variations in average expression of intolerance between neighbouring pairs of Peregrines. Beebe (1960), referring to Peale's Falcon on the Queen Charlottes, said 'The high density of falcons on Langara ... appears to be nothing more than a very marked contraction of the space requirements normal to the species in response to the easy availability of certain food species present in astronomical numbers and located so close at hand that both sexes can do most of their hunting right from the aerie site.' There is the beginning of an explanation of a possible mechanism here.

Abundance of prey may directly influence the number of hunting contacts between neighbouring Peregrines, and the ease with which food is obtained and hunger satisfied could perhaps affect the behaviour of individuals. When food is

sparse, any individual falcon may have to use a wider foraging range and variety of perches and to spend more time in seeking prey; the chances of competitive interaction between neighbours over the same food item would be increased. Frequency of contacts during hunting or prey-searching flights might affect spacing tolerance between neighbours without any change in intrinsic aggressiveness of the birds. Yet aggressiveness in birds is so dependent on hormonal conditioning, and this in turn is so subject to environmental influences, that change in actual response of individual Peregrines to each other seems quite possible. The exact nature of the spacing adjustment is an enigmatic problem still to be studied in depth.

A behavioural adjustment to perception of prey abundance of the kind inferred would give each individual Peregrine the means of responding to either geographical or time changes in food supply. However it operates, spacing between pairs and hence breeding density is evidently determined by behaviour at the onset of the breeding season. The spectacular courtship displays of this period may also serve a territorial advertisement function in some degree. Evidently, as in some other bird species, territorial behaviour abates once the initial dispersion of breeding pairs has been achieved.

An important effect of this spacing behaviour is to limit the potentiality of the Peregrine for increase within a breeding area. In each year it places a strict ceiling on the number of nesting pairs, and later their young, and thus limits the maximum demand of the particular population on the food supply of the area concerned.

While availability of suitable cliffs and territorial behaviour may separately limit Peregrine breeding density in different areas, they also interact. If Peregrines were colonial like some other members of the genus *Falco*, scarcity of suitable cliffs would be much less important in this respect, for a single good escarpment could hold a considerable number of pairs. Such habitat limitation produces low density only in conjunction with aversion to close nesting. Hickey (1942) was clearly thinking of this interaction in saying, 'Since cliffs are so scarce, territorial jealousy, is, therefore, a factor of considerable importance in restricting the density of nesting Peregrines.' Food supply is also involved. Some of the high densities reported for the Peregrine seem to be the result of both a localisation of habitat *and* the presence of a good food supply. This could be true of the Beachy Head concentration in Britain, the seven mile escarpment with five pairs mentioned by Hickey (1942) in the eastern United States, and the dense clusters of Peale's Falcon in parts of the Queen Charlottes.

This concentration effect is shown by the Prairie Falcon, which breeds in groups of five or six pairs in distances of about 1·5 km on low earth cliffs of the Bow River meandering through the flat Alberta prairies, where the main prey species, Richardson's ground squirrel, is in great abundance. A more extreme example is the great 'colony' of 183–209 pairs of Prairie Falcons and 32–34 pairs of Golden Eagles in the 130 km of the Snake River Canyon, cut through the semi-desert of Idaho, where again ground squirrels and jack rabbits are in tremendous numbers (Morlan Nelson, unpubl., and Olendorff and Kochert, 1977).

At these really high densities, it seems likely that the innate aggressiveness of the big falcons to others of their own kind places an ultimate restriction on the contraction of spacing distance and thus on maximum density. In the Peregrine, 200 m would seem to be around the absolute limit which this intraspecific hostility would allow. The Mediterranean Eleonora's Falcon is, however, an example of a truly colonial falcon which Walter (1979) found breeding at densities as high as 145 pairs per hectare on small islands in the Aegean Sea and off the Atlantic coast of Morocco. The species was nevertheless strictly territorial, defending areas of 60–200 m^2 centred on the nest site. A territory also contained one or more look-out posts, feeding and food-storage areas and sunbathing sites. Contiguous nests were as close as 2 m but more usually averaged 10 m apart. Dispersion could not be explained by territorial behaviour, since territories were originally small and expanded gradually *after* the nest site was selected. Nests were mainly in holes and recesses and spacing tended to be closest when adjacent nest sites were most hidden from each other. Walter concluded that incubating falcons needed a degree of 'visual privacy' from each other, though off-duty partners maintained frequent surveillance of neighbouring territories. The most suitable nesting habitat was thus a rugged topography offering the best selection of caves and crannies separated by projections, ridges and other convexities. Walter found that falcons developed preferred flight corridors to and from their nest sites and that some of the airspace immediately above the site was part of each territory, though he was unable to gauge the vertical height of this influence.

Eleonora's Falcon thus seems to have evolved a social breeding pattern representing the virtual opposite of that in the Peregrine, with extreme contraction of nest spacing. This condition is evidently linked to a special feeding adaptation, for Eleonora's Falcon has a breeding season coinciding with the late summer and autumn migration of birds across the Mediterranean. It is a slightly smaller and more slender falcon than the Peregrine and feeds on the large number of bird species from warbler to dove and quail size which pass its breeding haunts in an almost continuous stream. The colonial habit also seems to be related to the occurrence of suitable nesting terrain, in the form of lofty seacliffs or remote and inaccessible islands where the falcons are relatively safe from human disturbance. Eleonora's Falcon is restricted to the Mediterranean, the Atlantic coast of north-west Africa and the Canary Isles, with Madagascar as its wintering grounds, and has a small World population estimated at less than 4000 birds by Brown and Amadon (1968). This suggests that there are special and extremely localised conditions to which its life-style is matched. The Peregrine's solitary disposition and highly dispersed breeding distribution goes along with an almost world-wide occurrence and a population which, until recently, must have exceeded 100,000 birds.

In closing this chapter, it has to be said that a good deal remains to be learned about spacing behaviour and territory in the Peregrine, though their existence has so long been recognised by perceptive observers. Ritchie, in the same year (1920) that Howard published his ideas on territory in birds, made this remarkable statement, 'Yet even with all the protection afforded them, it is doubtful if hawks did more than remain stationary in numbers in these favoured times [the Middle Ages], for it is well known that each pair reserves for its hunting a patrol area, within which no other pair can breed, and suitable breeding places, especially for Peregrines, are limited in number.' He so nearly had it right, but seemingly fell into the same error as Howard himself, in assuming that territory represented an exclusive feeding area. If the wording were changed to '. . . each pair reserves for itself an area . . .', the sentence would be a neat summary of the way in which territorial behaviour and nesting habitat limit a Peregrine population. It is perhaps more precise to say that while territory/food supply and availability of cliffs either separately or together place a ceiling on the numbers of Peregrines breeding within an area, the first more truly limits *density* while the second determines distribution. Together, these factors restrict total breeding numbers.

CHAPTER 11

Population dynamics and regulation

Earlier chapters have examined the influences that determine Peregrine distribution and abundance. This chapter considers the dynamic nature of Peregrine populations in time: their propensity to increase, decrease or remain stable,
and the underlying reasons. The subject is one fascinating to animal ecologists,
but also of much practical concern to conservationists dealing with the management and maintenance of wildlife populations.

One of the problems in understanding the dynamics of the British Peregrine
population is that it really consists of a number of separate regional populations,
which may vary in their individual dynamics, yet are interlinked in some degree.
The same applies to Ireland, though the degree of interchange revealed by
ringing recoveries suggests that the British and Irish populations are closely
linked. When I first began to study Peregrines it appeared, from the available
information, that relative stability was the most usual state of the British and Irish
populations. Numbers within several districts appeared to fluctuate by no more
than 8% around a mean value over periods of 10 years or more. It is now clear

that major upheavals have disturbed this equilibrium, and population dynamics have to be examined against no less than five different situations in these islands, namely:

1. Stable population as the normal state in many districts, during 1900–55.

2. Population decline through long-term decrease in food supply (western Highlands and Islands, and western Ireland, 1880–1930).

3. Population decline through direct human persecution, and recovery when this ceases (mainly the 1940–45 'control' episode).

4. Population decline through pesticide effects and geographically variable recovery when these were reduced (1947–85).

5. Substantial population increase in certain districts since about 1980.

All aspects of decline are attributable to human intervention, either deliberate or incidental, and are examined mainly in other chapters. Here I want to look at the Peregrine's capacity to resist decrease, from whatever cause, and to recover when these adverse influences ameliorate or disappear. And I wish to consider what holds numbers at a particular level, or allows them to increase during times and under circumstances that are favourable to the bird.

THE ANNUAL BALANCE SHEET IN NUMBERS

All longer term change must begin through events that are part of the annual cycle in numbers, so that we should start by looking at this. A range of factors and mechanisms make adjustments to numbers at different times of the year. During each year there is an inevitable fluctuation, as a new generation of fledged youngsters is added to the population in summer. This temporary increase is then eroded by mortality and, by the following spring, the breeding population is usually not much different from that of the previous year, though some new birds have appeared within it. There is also an additional element of non-breeders which, though far more difficult to measure, is not obviously very different, compared with previous year numbers, either. It therefore seems that roughly as many birds have died – or possibly emigrated – as were added by the previous year's breeding output. We can only infer the details of this total turnover, mainly from ringing recoveries, but death rate is evidently highest amongst the young birds, especially during their first few months of life.

This is the generalised situation in a 'normal', relatively stable population. Yet clearly, and especially in recent years, we are often not dealing with normal populations, but with those in which imbalance between recruitment and mortality leads either to decline or to increase. It is the changes in factors affecting recruitment and mortality that are of such concern to population ecologists, but attaching values to the different components of the equation is usually difficult. When there are adequate data on mortality for a population, the average productivity needed to sustain overall stability in numbers can be calculated. Mebs (1971) has used the equation:

$$f = \frac{2m}{(1 - q)\,(1 - m)}$$

where q = mortality of 0- to 1-year birds, m = mortality of 1- to 6-year birds and f = necessary productivity. Sexual maturity is assumed to be age 2 years for all breeders.

The calculated figure for replacement productivity is useful to set against actual productivity as a guide to the status of any population or segment of it. If the productivity of birds in any region drops appreciably below this critical level for a run of years, there are grounds for supposing that this part of the population may be in trouble. Equally, if critical productivity is well above replacement level, one can look for population increase and/or expansion.

Chris Mead has prepared a life-table from Peregrines recovered under the BTO ringing scheme (Table 27). He points out that the bulk of the ringed sample and recoveries from it are too recent to provide a reliable basis for calculating mortality rates. With successive years after about 1970 there is an increasing probability that further recoveries are yet to be made of ringed birds still at large, so that recovery samples are at present incomplete. Moreover, the data set spans a period of nearly 70 years, during which the population as a whole has been subject to all four major upheavals listed above, involving marked changes in mortality rates.

With these reservations, taking the 46 recoveries during 1923–75 as a reasonably complete sample gives 30% mortality for first-year birds, 25% for second-year birds and about 19% as an annual average for fully adult birds of all ages. This is a much lower first-year mortality than has been calculated for some other large raptors (e.g. 56% for the Common Buzzard by Olsson, 1956). Examination of first year Peregrine recoveries as a proportion of totals ringed (Table 27) suggests that mortality of this age class has varied from about 30 to 40% during each subsequent 5-year period, on the assumption that recovery rates have not fluctuated widely. The recovery rate was 9·8% during 1923–70, but already 12·1% for 1971–80, with more recoveries most probably to come, so that *some* fluctuation is indicated. Applying Mead's figures to the Mebs' formula gives a critical replacement productivity of 0·71 young per territorial pair, and if first-year mortality is increased to 40% the figure is still only 0·83 young. The unknown complication is over the average age at which first breeding occurs. It is the comparative rather than the absolute values, and also the trends, of productivity that are meaningful as indicators of population status (see Table 19).

More precise information on the rate of turnover in Peregrine populations is clearly desirable, but the only direct study to date has been made by Richard Mearns and Ian Newton (1984), by a programme of catching and marking breeding birds at eyries in southern Scotland. During 1977–82, 169 captures were made (139 of females and 30 of males), involving 87 different individuals (64 females and 23 males), mostly in inland territories. Turnover was not wholly due to mortality because, of 68 females recaptured in a later year, seven had moved to a different territory (six recaptured males were all on the same territories). With allowance for known movements, this sample showed an estimated annual mortality of 9% among females, or 11% in both sexes combined. Actual mortality might have been still less, because yet other marked birds could have moved outside the study area and so remained undetected, although still alive.

These are remarkably low figures for mortality, and suggest that in this breeding population, average life expectancy is 10 more years at first breeding. Mearns and Newton point out that, with a 10% annual mortality and no change with age after the second year, about 15% of birds which reached their second year would survive to their 20th year, and about 6% would survive to their 25th. They note that the oldest Peregrine recovered in a ringing scheme was in its 17th year, but that several falconers' birds have lived more than 20 years. The female breeding on the Sun Life building in Montreal was at least 18 years old when she finally disappeared (Hall, 1955). Newton and Mearns (1988) estimated that 44% of the fledglings in their southern Scotland study entered the breeding population, giving an implied mortality of 56% over the mean 2-year pre-breeding period. The study could not provide a figure for first-year mortality, but if the previous higher figure of 40% is assumed, critical replacement productivity is only 0·37 young per territorial pair – an extremely low value.

This low mortality may not be representative of British Peregrines as a whole, even during the same period. After all, it was for an established breeding population, during a time of continuing increase from earlier decline, and referred to relatively sedentary birds nesting mainly at regular haunts, little subject to persecution, and in a district where pesticide problems had declined to insignificance. Average mortality in the same district was certainly higher during the period 1930–55, through the known killing of adults by gamekeepers at some of the same eyries. Even contemporary breeding populations in other parts of Britain might have quite different mortality rates, and the figures tell us nothing about mortality in the non-breeding sector.

Comparison of the Mead data with those given by Mearns and Newton confirms the frequent finding that ringing recoveries of dead birds reported by the public tend to give a higher estimate of mortality than studies of turnover in marked breeding populations. Mortality may well be higher in the non-breeding segment and in some less favourable districts, compared with an established group of breeders in a region where conditions for Peregrines are almost ideal. The randomly reported sample of ringing recoveries seems likely to give the more faithful measure of overall mortality in the British population.

Court (1986) found a maximum mortality rate of 23% annually (females 27%, males 16%) amongst marked breeding Peregrines (evidently all at least 2 years old) in a north Canadian population which was migratory but not believed to be showing noticeably adverse effects of pesticide contamination. There was a high degree of nest site fidelity, with only one of 27 identified females and none of 16 males moving to a different territory. In the sedentary population in the Queen Charlotte Islands of British Columbia, Nelson (1988, 1990) found an even higher breeding adult turnover of 32% annually (females 37%, males 26%), but with a difference according to brood size. Peregrine parents that reared three or four nestlings disappeared from one year to the next at the rate of 43%, compared with only 23% for birds that reared no young or one or two young. In no instance did Nelson find a known adult at another eyrie.

The Mearns and Newton study threw interesting light on other aspects of population dynamics. Of 16 handled and ringed females, two were first breeding at 1 year old, 13 at age 2, and one at age 3. Of six ringed males caught, four were breeding at age 2 years, one at age 3, and one at age 4 or 5. Yearling birds were recognisable whether caught or not, from their brown or transitional moult plumage. In a total of 398 territories seen with pairs during 1974–82, 19 pairs (5%) had a yearling female. There was much annual variation, from none in 1974, 1976 and 1977, to five in 1980 and eight in 1981. Of the 19 yearlings, at least seven laid eggs, but only one reared young. Only one yearling male was found paired on a territory (to an adult), which again suggested that males usually began breeding at a later age than females.

These findings support the more general experience in Britain, that in any year a small proportion of breeding territories is held by pairs in which one bird is a yearling, usually the female; and that yearlings tend not to lay eggs, and are seldom successful if they do. Of four yearlings caught, only one had a brood patch, though all 19 made scrapes and two incubated dummy eggs given to them late in the season. Other observers have reported occasional successful breeding by yearling Peregrines: Phillip Glasier watched a juvenile female feeding two young at a Perthshire eyrie in 1959, and an immature male was photographed by C. Gugg at a German eyrie with young in 1932 (Hickey, 1969, Plate 8). The appearance of an immature bird in a pair holding territory does not necessarily mean that there are no 2-year-old birds left; some yearlings may have chanced to be more available or more active in filling gaps than older competitors.

Tom Cade (pers. comm.) believes that in North America, wild female Peregrines most frequently come into full breeding condition as 2 year olds, but some not until a year later, while most males do not come into full condition until 3 years old, and some not until 4 or 5 years old. He found that captive birds averaged a year later in reaching this physiological state, with males again a year behind females, but stressed that extrapolation from artificial conditions to the wild state needs caution. There may also be a time-lag between reaching the physiological condition for breeding and actual breeding, even in paired holders of breeding places.

How does this information on turnover relate to the different population situations listed above?

THE PRE-1956 POPULATION

The only statistics we have to judge by are the incomplete population figures and patchy records on brood size. During 1900–55, Peregrines in many areas had apparently stable populations, but breeding performance was consistently low in some (p. 249). It is unclear to what extent the much better breeding output from remote parts of Scotland and Ireland provided a surplus of recruits to maintain numbers in districts where few young were reared. While the ringing evidence shows limited movement on average, and a marked tendency to return to the vicinity of birthplace to breed, there are a enough examples of long-distance movements (and settlers) for compensation effects between widely separated districts to be feasible. On the other hand, it is possible that the low

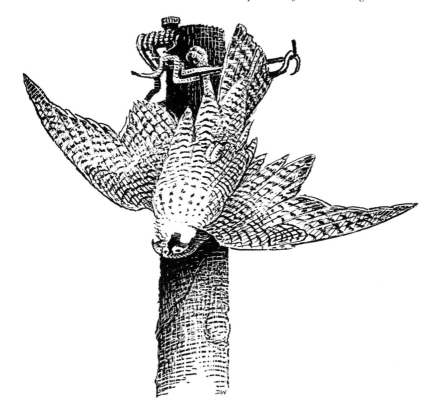

mortality in breeding adults found by Mearns and Newton in southern Scotland during 1977–82 may also once have applied in other districts where persecution was almost entirely confined to taking of eggs and young. With an annual turnover of only 10% amongst territory holders, a population of 50 pairs would need only around ten new recruits a year to remain stable, and this could be provided by a mere handful of successful local eyries annually.

During 1900–39, the main source of mortality was probably destruction of falcons by game preservers. This had a highly irregular geographical pattern, being greatest in the grouse moor areas which lie mostly on the eastern side of the main upland districts. While clearly not heavy enough to disturb the stability of the Peregrine population as a whole, it may have produced a wastage severe enough both to limit the species' capacity for increase through occupation of new or long-lost haunts in marginal habitats, and to achieve regular tenancy of irregular or occasional nesting places. Throughout much of the grouse moor country, mortality of adults and low productivity of survivors were such that more than local replenishments were probably needed to sustain attempted breeding numbers each year. The worst aspect of such destruction is that certain particularly attractive cliffs act as magnets, drawing new birds in rapid succession as the last arrivals are killed off. Such places create a 'sump effect' draining off some of the supply of new Peregrines which would otherwise be available for filling gaps or colonising vacant haunts elsewhere.

The Air Ministry campaign of 1940–45 was the most successful attempt to eliminate a Peregrine population on record. It virtually eradicated the species in Cornwall, Devon, Dorset, Somerset, and severely reduced numbers in several other counties (pp. 64–66). The total impact probably caused reduction of the British breeding population to about 87% of its pre-1940 level. The effect was only local and temporary, however, and its reversal showed well the Peregrine's resilience in staging a come-back, once the organised slaughter stopped. Recovery began to show at once, in 1946. The following records are available:

Cornwall From none to 17 pairs in 20 territories in 10 years (1945–55) Treleaven, 1961).

Dorset From one to eight pairs in ten territories in 6 years (1946–53) (D. Humphrey and R. Newman, letter)

Devon From none to 12 pairs (number of territories unknown) in 10 years (1945–55) (Moore, 1969).

The local rate of recovery is best expressed as the number of pairs recolonising in relation to the number of vacant territories in a given time. If the Cornwall and Dorset figures are expressed this way, they give recovery rates of 0·9 and 1·3 additional occupations (i.e. roughly one pair) per ten vacant territories per year. If all occupations are assumed to be by pairs, then twice these numbers of birds were involved. Since there were probably around 100 vacant territories to be re-occupied, the surplus needed to produce this rate of recovery overall was only about 20 birds per year. This is quite a modest rate of increase. The total population of south-west England was evidently so completely mopped up that recovery here must have *begun* by immigration of recruits from other districts farther away; but once a few pairs were re-established, the recovery would begin to feed on itself, provided these birds were successful. At the time, it was puzzling that full recovery was never achieved. We now know that by 1954–55 other factors were inhibiting the complete restoration of pre-war numbers in at least some of the affected districts, and that the population was beginning to enter a dramatic new phase.

THE POST-1956 POPULATION

The much more serious collapse in Peregrine population during 1956–63 reduced total breeding strength to around 44% of the pre-war level, though this figure included about 20% of apparently unpaired birds. The decline was not synchronised across the country, but proceeded in a wave-like spread from south to north, and its termination was not clear-cut, though in most districts 1964 seemed to be the year when numbers stopped falling. While the British average rate of decrease over the 7 years was only 7% per annum (pre-war population = 100%), it steepened and surged to 40% between 1960 and 1963 (13·3% per annum). In some districts decline was still more rapid; e.g. in northern England, numbers fell by 42% of pre-war level during 1961–63 (21% per annum). Although the 1961–62 Enquiry missed the height of the crash in the worst affected districts, Wales and southern England, similarly rapid rates of decline evidently occurred there too. If decrease is measured as percentage change from one year's level to the next, the rates are still greater. Tables 2–6, and Figs 18 to 20 give the basis for these calculations.

Speed of population decrease such as this must almost certainly have involved substantially increased adult mortality. There is no direct evidence of this, but the case that the crash was caused by the persistent organochlorine insecticides of agriculture is now accepted by the scientific community. Within this case (detailed in Chapter 13), the known effects of dieldrin, aldrin and heptachlor are consistent with much enhanced mortality of Peregrines. These chemicals have an acute lethal toxicity and their widespread use as cereal seed dressings during 1956–62 caused numerous 'kills' of granivorous birds in many parts of Britain. Peregrines were much exposed in many districts to large residue intakes through feeding on heavily contaminated prey, for species such as pigeons appeared less sensitive to these particularly toxic insecticides than the falcon itself, and some individuals could travel large distances from the source of contamination.

Lindberg (1977) examined mortality rates based on ringing recoveries for Peregrine populations in four other countries, and calculated critical productivity values for replacement (i.e. stable population) using Mebs' equation (see Table 26). The values ranged from 1·6 to 2·3 young per territorial pair. Since the four data sets all overlapped the period of international population crash, the high mortality and replacement rates they reveal are unsurprising. And since actual productivity values at the time fell well short of the necessary replacement levels in all four countries, the continuing observed population declines were inevitable. It was a characteristic feature of these declines, in Britain, Ireland and elsewhere, that breeding performance of survivors was generally low, whether measured as mean brood size, proportion of successful pairs, or productivity (p. 250).

During the 1956–63 crash, productivity in the surviving segments of the populations in England, Wales and southern Scotland decreased to very low levels, and probably approached or fell below the critical replacement rate even in the Highlands, except in the central district (Table 19). This trend would accelerate the decline caused by increased mortality. The precise contribution of reduced productivity to the crash is difficult to estimate, but was probably less important than in the collapse of the eastern United States Peregrine population. In North America generally, Peregrine decline is attributed primarily to markedly lowered productivity related especially to eggshell thinning. The interaction was discussed by Young (1969) who pointed out that while 10% rates of increase in mortality, decrease in nesting success and decrease in brood size could each cause population decline, the combination of all three (each at 10%) would produce a theoretical rate of decline approaching that observed in some parts of the United States. The arguments about this issue are discussed in Chapter 13.

The recovery of Peregrine populations and their breeding performance in response to decreasing pesticidal contamination has already been described (Chapters 3, 4 and 8). In Britain, productivity did not show any marked improvement for several years after 1963–64, when mortality had evidently decreased appreciably – since the crash bottomed out then. Probably we shall never know the details of how the recovery in breeding numbers occurred. One possibility is that the recruits first came mainly from the Highlands, and especially the central

district, where most territories had remained occupied and productivity was at
1·32 young per pair through the period of lowest ebb in numbers. This region had
the greatest potential for producing a surplus which could begin to fill gaps
elsewhere, notwithstanding the recent evidence that movements between regions
are more limited than might be supposed. It would need only a few birds to reach
and stay in a depleted area for recovery to begin. Yet it is also possible that even in
districts where a very few pairs remained, a handful of locally bred young each
year could equally give the additional boost needed for this nucleus to start
expanding, provided most of the parents had survived. Most probably a combination of both local and more distant recruits was involved.

We know rather more about the actual rates and geographical patterns of
recovery. Up to the point where pre-1940 population levels were restored, the
following local rates were found:

Southern Scotland From 20 to 27 pairs in 28 territories in 11 years (1965–76)

Northern England From 11 to 30 pairs in 32 territories in 12 years (1965–77)

Wales From 27 to 82 pairs in 118 territories in 8 years (1971–79)

The figures for southern Scotland and northern England do not represent the
total increases because comparison has to be limited to the incomplete list of
territories examined here in 1965. Expressed as occupations per ten vacant
territories per year, the comparative increases are 0·7, 0·7 and 0·75, respectively,
slightly less than the rates of post-1945 recovery given on p. 290. The overall
recovery of the British Peregrine population from an estimated 44% of pre-war
level in 1964 to 54% in 1971 suggests an average rate of increase of about 1·4%
annually (or 2% if 1966 is taken as the base-line for recovery). From 1971 to
1981 the average rate of increase was 3·8% annually (38% overall), and between
1981 and 1991 it increased to 5·3% annually (53% overall). These figures
indicate that recovery 'took off' after 1971, but that the average rate of increase
has not approached that of decline. Such rates of increase represent the addition
to the GB population of 40 pairs in 1981–82 and 53 pairs in 1990–91.

Perhaps the overall rate of increase has not been spectacular, bearing in mind
the low adult mortality in at least one region and the large annual output of young
in various regions. The more remarkable aspect is the continuing increase since
1980 to give an unprecedented *level* of breeding population in Wales, northern
England, southern Scotland and some parts of the Highlands. Increase has gone
on here steadily (Fig. 19), and in several regions numbers are now more than
double the highest levels ever known previously. Yet the overall pattern of
increase has been extremely variable, and falls off both south of Wales and north
of the Great Glen. This must mean that rates of increase have been greater than
average in some regions, and locally approach even the rate of decline at the
height of the crash (Fig. 20).

LIMITATIONS ON BREEDING POPULATIONS

We are obviously looking at a complex geographical picture, in which the
constraints to the upper limits of breeding population are either different in kind

or operate with varying force across the country. The simplest explanation of failure to recover is that the original causes of decline have not disappeared, and that toxic chemical residues of one kind or another continue locally to exert adverse effects. The evidence for this is discussed in Chapter 13. It is possible that Peregrines are especially slow to re-colonise totally deserted districts, such as south-east England, because there are no other birds to act as a stimulus, and all traces of previous occupation have long disappeared. This seems extremely unlikely, nevertheless, for Peregrines re-colonising other districts recently have even taken to a variety of nesting places never known to be used before. The distance from a breeding nucleus may have been another factor, though non-breeding birds certainly appeared in south-east England from the 1970s onwards.

In southern Scotland, northern England and Wales, the recovery took place first in the districts with an abundance of good cliffs which had previously been the great Peregrines strongholds. In northern England, recovery in the Yorkshire Pennines and Cheviots came after numbers were restored in Lakeland, where the nesting crags are mostly much higher than in the other two districts. There was also a clear tendency for recovery of inland populations to precede that of coastal populations. In south-west England there was a westwards advance along the Atlantic coast from Somerset to Land's End, but pairs had begun to reappear on the English Channel coast before this was complete. Recovery in Dorset came later still, with the first proved nesting in 1984.

The increase beyond the 'normal' level of numbers from Scotland to Wales has involved two separate aspects. One is the regular occupation of many new or occasional, and mainly third-class cliffs, especially in areas previously regarded as marginal nesting areas for Peregrines. Many quarries, both used and disused, have been occupied for the first time, but there has also been a marked increase in nesting on, or almost on, the ground, and on buildings; and tree nesting has occurred in two widely separated areas. The second aspect is an increase in breeding density within areas previously regarded as 'saturated' with nesting pairs. In many cases this has involved the splitting of former single territories into two or even three new ones.

There are two possible explanations of this unprecedented increase. The first is that relaxation of persecution, combined with the virtual fade-out of pesticide problems, has led to a massive production of young falcons, with good survival. This in turn has created such a recruitment pressure that territorial resistances from established breeders have been overcome, and previously marginal nesting places have also become more acceptable. Reduced harrying of the birds at these marginal haunts has allowed their regular and often success-ful occupation. Chris Mead has found good evidence from the BTO ringing returns of a decrease in mortality for first-, second- and third-year Peregrines during the last 15 years (Fig. 17, Table 28), and this will have enhanced the pressure of birds seeking breeding territories. The second explanation is that there has been a substantial increase in food supply, notably in the form of increased pigeon racing.

Both explanations could well be true, and exert a combined influence. The first alone could explain the increase within once marginal nesting areas (i.e. expanding *distribution*), but the lack of increase in some Highland districts where

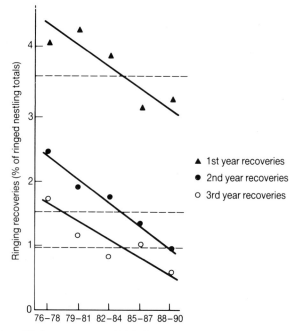

Figure 17. Ringing returns 1976–90. (Figure prepared by C. J. Mead.)

breeding performance has been good suggests that pressure of additional birds alone is not always sufficient to cause enlargement of breeding population. It also seems unlikely that an increase in breeding *density* could have occurred within a corresponding increase in prey availability.

POPULATION STABILITY AND FOOD SUPPLY

The previous relative stability of Peregrine breeding populations, not only in Britain and Ireland, but also in many other regions of the World, contrasts with the tendency of some predators to show large and cyclical fluctuations in numbers. The difference appears to be related to diversity in prey spectrum. Predators which live on a very few main prey species face a greater probability of major ups and downs in this food supply than those which feed on a wide variety of prey. In Britain, Short-eared Owls and Kestrels have long been famous for shadowing the major fluctuations in numbers of short-tailed field voles in upland areas where this rodent is their principal prey. In the northern regions, Snowy Owls, Rough-legged Buzzards and skuas show a similar numerical relationship with the lemmings and voles on which they especially depend. Breeding performance of all these predators is also closely related to prey abundance.

In the agricultural lowlands of England, the Kestrel maintains a more stable population than in the hills, matching the rather more varied and less fluctuating food supply (Snow, 1968). And in inland areas of Alaska, Cade (1960) found that

Gyr Falcons showed quite marked fluctuations in breeding numbers and their success whereas, before pesticide problems arose, Peregrines in this region showed a characteristic population stability. The Gyr Falcons fed on a very limited range of prey, mainly the few resident birds (such as Ptarmigan) and ground mammals, whereas the Peregrines preyed upon the relatively large number of migratory bird species. Interestingly, in the Rankin Inlet of northern Canada, one of the few areas where the species has adapted significantly to feeding on ground mammals, the previously stable Peregrine breeding population increased by 30% during a year of peak lemming and vole numbers (Court, 1986). The percentage of pairs laying eggs, and mean brood size, also increased in the year of peak microtine abundance (1985), leading to a doubling of output of young, compared with the previous four years of Court's study.

In the Scottish Highlands, the Golden Eagle population in many districts has remained almost constant over several decades (Brown and Watson, 1964; Brown, 1976). Golden Eagles take a wide variety of food, both bird and mammal, and eat a good deal of mammal carrion in districts where live, wild prey is in short supply. Their food supply has been stable in many districts, and it is only where obvious decrease has occurred, as through afforestation, that appreciable decline in eagle population has been observed.

Degree of specialisation in prey and proneness to population change in these predatory birds tend to be linked. The wider the choice in number of prey species, the more stable is the predator population, for the less is the likelihood that the total food supply will fluctuate markedly. While any one prey species may well fluctuate in numbers, the more species that are involved, the less is the chance that all will fluctuate simultaneously. If certain prey species decline, the raptor simply shifts attention to those still plentiful, and is thus buffered against the collapse in food supply which so often faces the specialised feeders. The Rankin Inlet Peregrines mentioned above might seem to contradict this point, but they were primarily bird feeders and normally maintained a stable population, so that adaptation to mammal prey simply gave a periodic boost above normal level (Court, 1986).

The manner in which the particular numerical balance between populations of predator and prey is achieved is much more obscure. It is, indeed, one of the still unsolved mysteries of animal ecology, though we can describe some of its observable results. In Chapter 10, I suggested that breeding density and, hence, potential for increase, have become adjusted to geographical differences in food supply, through a gearing of the Peregrine's spacing behaviour to the local availability of prey. A shift in this adjustment would be expected to occur if a change in food supply took place in time, leading to contraction or expansion in breeding density. Territorialism thus becomes a crucial regulatory process for Peregrine populations.

There is some evidence that the western Highlands and Islands suffered a decline in bird populations generally, including Peregrines, from around 1880 to 1930. This region of excessively humid climate and infertile, acidic rocks and soils, was subjected, from about 1820 onwards, to a period of intensive exploitation as grazing land for sheep and red deer, involving repeated burning of the vegetation. It was already a largely deforested country and many ecologists believe that the net result of this extractive land-use, a century or so later, was an extensive degradation of soils and marked lowering of the carrying capacity of the land for animal populations (Darling, 1955; McVean and Lockie, 1969). The best evidence for decrease in Peregrine prey populations is the observation by Mackenzie (1924) that during 1860–1900 substantial declines in Red Grouse, Ptarmigan, Black Grouse, Golden Plover, Snipe, Lapwing, Dunlin and Partridge (and also mountain hares) occurred in Wester Ross. Harvie-Brown (1906) commented on the deterioration of many once productive grouse moors in the western Highlands and Islands, a process which has continued to the point where few grouse moors now remain in this region. Hudson (1992) has also noted the decline of grouse bags to low levels on western Scottish moors from 1900 to 1980. The Peregrine appears to have declined in parallel (see p. 63), but the remaining pairs have maintained their regularity of spacing, i.e. the change has involved increase in territory size and reduction in breeding density. Competition from Golden Eagles could have been involved in this decline, and might thus be an additional controlling factor locally.

Decline is reported from one of the few regions where the Peregrine is a specialised feeder, in coastal British Columbia. Wayne Nelson (1970, 1973, 1977) has studied Peale's Falcon on Langara Island since Beebe (1960) reported very high densities, and found a great reduction; from 16–19 pairs in 1952–58 to only five to seven pairs during 1968–89, coincident with a sharp decline in the alcid populations, especially of the Ancient Murrelet, the principal food species. The alcids are believed to have crashed either as a result of decline in ocean production or through rat predation, or both (Nelson, 1990). Nelson made the interesting observation that, when the Langara Peregrine population declined, paired females at three different haunts prevented adjacent, recently widowed males from obtaining new mates. Nelson termed this behaviour pseudo-polyandry, and suggested that it was the means whereby the females enlarged their territories in response to a serious reduction in the numbers of their prey. A new stability had obtained over at least 20 years at the reduced level of food supply, and Nelson calculated that the numerical balance between each Peregrine pair (needing 1000 prey items annually) and its seabird prey was about 1:50,000.

Apart from the unusual situation in Rankin Inlet, Canada, examples of *increasing* food supply for Peregrines are difficult to find, but we probably have one in Britain recently. It has been said that pigeon racing has grown considerably in popularity here in recent years, and figures issued by the Royal Pigeon Racing Association support this view. The number of rings issued by the Association for young pigeons was 1·54 million in 1977, 1·84 million in 1980 and 2·0–2·5 million in 1991. It is not just a matter of numbers but of availability – duration of racing season, frequency of races, location of race routes, and so on. For example, lorries now transport large numbers of pigeons to release points for races which are often close to Peregrine country. While falcons in areas such as the Lake District manage to find enough wild prey during the winter and early spring, domestic pigeons become especially available to them when the young have hatched.

The very variable geographical pattern of Peregrine status fits quite well with the view that recent increase has depended on expanding food supply as well as on reduced persecution. Increase has ranged from slight to negative in western and northern districts of the Scottish Highlands which are beyond the main pigeon racing routes. Increase has been pronounced in the eastern Highlands and the southern Highland fringe (but not Argyll, in the west): while reduced persecution and greater survey effort account for some of this increase, the homing pigeon is important in falcon diet in these districts and has increased in frequency in the east (p. 127). In Ireland, too, marked increase has been mainly in the east and north-east, close to centres of human population where pigeon racing is popular. Norriss (in press) also connects increase to high density on the Waterford coast, in the south, to ready availability of pigeons.

We are little the wiser about the precise way in which the increase in breeding density operates, as regards the behaviour of the existing territory holders and the newcomers seeking to 'squeeze in'. The increase in density has been gradual, and on the whole, the regularity of spacing between neighbours has been maintained as the distances have contracted. One supposes that either the existing territory holders relax their territorialism, or the incomers become more aggressive or persistent. It may be that when the pressure from new birds passes a certain point, the effort of trying to keep them out incurs too great a cost to the established pairs in terms of their own well-being and breeding performance. It could also be that perception of increased food supply leads to relaxation of territorial demands by the established breeders, through reducing the degree of threat posed by new neighbours to an acceptable level. Yet there are limits to this increased tolerance, and in the Lake District, some further prospective colonists are not managing to breed and thereby reduce existing territory sizes still more (G. Horne). Some new claim stakers have moved in by degrees, as by holding territory for 2 or 3 years before laying eggs.

According to this interpretation, population density should reach a new ceiling, stabilised in balance with the higher level of food supply. But if food supply continues to increase, so will Peregrine breeding density. This is rather different from the wider expansion of population into marginal or new breeding areas, which stems from reduced persecution and relaxation of standards in nest site selection. Such expansion could continue even if there is no further increase in food supply. It involves an increased pressure of birds on vacant areas, but this is created partly by their inability to find space in the areas already saturated with territory holders. Food supply is already sufficient to support a substantial further increase in Peregrines over much of Britain and Ireland, and the point at which numbers eventually level off may well depend on the tolerance of humans.

THE NON-BREEDING ELEMENT OF POPULATION

We are limited in our further understanding of these population processes by ignorance of the true state of the non-breeding sector. Various inferences can be drawn from the life-table data already discussed, but the detailed picture necessary to full insight is simply lacking. Theoretical calculations from the known mortality and productivity rates suggest that the number of non-breeders could be as large as the breeding population. The present high output of young birds and the low mortality of established breeders (at least in some areas) suggest that there is a large wastage of birds which never manage to set up territory and breed. But the 10% sample recovery of ringed birds tells us little about where and how the majority die.

The presence of a non-breeding element during the nesting season is crucial to the view that Peregrine breeding density is limited through spacing behaviour balanced against available food supply. Without such a surplus there would be no need to suppose breeding population to be limited by anything but mortality, and regular dispersion could be just an arrangement which minimises competitive interactions.

The evidence for the existence of this floating element of non-breeders comes largely from the many instances in which the death of one of a non-breeding pair of falcons is followed by the rapid re-mating of the survivor. The literature contains numerous examples of such events in Britain and other parts of the World. Gamekeeper Dugald Macintyre (1960) is especially informative on the point as regards the Kintyre peninsula, where he knew 18 pairs over a long period. A keen observer, though evidently with mixed attitudes towards Peregrines, he records that when a female was shot from the eyrie, the male generally re-mated within 24 hours. He several times saw bereaved males returning with new mates, and knew one tiercel to obtain four adult mates in quick succession. Only once was a new female not in adult plumage. The newcomers usually took over the incubation of eggs or rearing of young, and sometimes replacement was so rapid that the eggs remained viable. As long ago as 1914, Macintyre suggested that this pointed to the existence of a considerable reserve of non-breeding adult and immature falcons, with the perceptive comment that the situation is explicable only on the assumption that the increase of the Peregrine is regulated naturally in a manner not yet understood.

This is the most extreme statement of the case that I have come across, but it was a phenomenon which Macintyre was eminently well-placed for observing, and his essays on Peregrines and their ways have the general ring of truth. Most of the records are less spectacular. For example, in April 1971 Douglas Weir knew of a female shot from eggs on a Morayshire grouse moor. A second female was shot from a new clutch on the same cliff a month later, and a third, brown-plumaged female was killed there in the autumn.

There is no evidence that the new mates come from adjoining eyries. While Peregrines occasionally switch territories, it would seem unlikely that birds with eggs or young would do this, though failed nesters might do so. Most of the rapid replacements are probably by spare, non-breeding birds. Rapid re-mating by no means always follows, and there are plenty of examples in which the surviving bird at an eyrie did not appear with a new partner until the following year. The speed of re-mating would be influenced by the physiological state and motivation of the survivor, as well as by the availability of new birds.

Since the non-breeding element is necessary to fill gaps in the breeding population, if it falls below a certain critical level, the latter must decline too. The continuity in annual occupation of many first class cliffs in the face of heavy losses through persecution, as obtained in grouse moor country, was at one time a general indication that availability of replacements had a healthy edge over mortality, year by year. This was particularly so since most new falcons at eyries were in adult plumage and thus at least 2 years old. The intensive campaign of destruction during 1940–45 succeeded locally in producing a mortality rate which over-rode recruitment by a substantial margin. Local availability of recruits was in any case also virtually eliminated.

Elimination of the non-breeding surplus evidently occurred again locally during the post-1955 crash, when overall mortality and level of breeding failure became so high that the total Britain and Ireland Peregrine population was severely depleted. But the previous existence of the non-breeding element would buffer the breeding population against decrease, and allow the possibility that the decline in total numbers began before 1955, by eroding first the margin of surplus. We shall probably never know the truth about this. The precise balance of numbers may have varied widely between different regions of Britain. Recovery of the depleted (1940–45) south coast population seemed to tail off in the early 1950s before actual decline became apparent, but three long deserted territories in southern Scotland and northern England were reoccupied in 1954, 1956 and 1959, and there were no signs of incipient decline north of Wales until 1960.

Nowadays there is straightforward evidence of a non-breeding population, in the numbers of single Peregrines or pairs which are found each year occupying possible nesting stations, but without attempting to nest. Many of them are adult and the reasons for their failure to breed are unclear. In 1991, at least 11 non-breeding single birds and 46 pairs were seen in places where breeding was previously unknown, or in already occupied territories where double nesting had not previously occurred. There were also 47 apparently single Peregrines and 105 pairs, which did not nest, in known nesting territories, but these were counted in with the breeding population.

STATUS OF NON-BREEDING PEREGRINES

The non-breeding population contains most of the yearling Peregrines, though a small number of these manages to enter the territory-holding sector, and a few actually breed (p. 288). The age structure of the non-breeders is unknown, but is likely to have a younger average than that of the breeders. The majority of the observed non-breeders in Britain during recent years have been paired, and holding a spring/summer territory. There are probably many other single birds, either wandering about or attached to a locality, and widely scattered, both within or around main breeding areas and in country marginal or unsuitable as nesting habitat.

In both the re-occupation of deserted nesting places and the establishment of entirely new ones, non-breeding for up to 2–3 years is quite usual. Sometimes these territories are held first by single Peregrines, but sometimes pairs may fail to produce eggs, especially when one partner is immature. Once pairs have begun to breed (i.e. produce eggs), it is unusual for them to miss a year. Occasionally, single birds or pairs take up station but then disappear, without pairing or breeding. The places where this happens are mostly irregular or occasional haunts, or rocks not known as nesting localities. These Peregrines may have been disturbed or destroyed, or have come from other eyries in the vicinity. It is also possible that some third-class cliffs are only marginally attractive to some Peregrines and fail to stimulate pairing or full breeding activity. Walpole-Bond (1914) mentioned an interesting instance of an apparently sterile female Peregrine which clung to a territory and drove away prospective mates or new pairs. The landowner finally shot this bird and the territory was then occupied by a pair which nested.

It may well be that any Peregrine population normally contains a proportion of pairs which do not nest, and this may vary. Court (1986) found that ten per cent of all territorial pairs in his Rankin Inlet area failed to lay. In Britain, it is always difficult to be sure that pairs without eggs or young have not lost these through human interference. During the pesticide episode the elevated level of non-breeding was clearly an abnormal condition, and it is possible that there is still a residual effect to account for some of the present failures to breed. In the closely monitored Lake District population, 643 territory occupations were recorded during 1982–91; of these, 40 (6·2%) were by pairs which failed to produce eggs and 11 (1·7%) by single birds.

Non-breeding may occur at first when Peregrines are dispossessed by Golden Eagles. In Galloway a nesting haunt taken over by Golden Eagles in 1945 continued to have a non-breeding pair of falcons hanging about its vicinity for several more years. Decreasing food supply has been found to induce a degree of non-breeding in populations of Buzzards (Moore, 1957) and Ravens (Marquiss, Newton and Ratcliffe, 1977), but this situation has not been observed for the Peregrine. Some pairs in the Highlands apparently failed to lay during the Arctic spring weather of 1979, but such an event is probably exceptional.

After 1947, non-breeding became a conspicuous feature of the Peregrine population in virtually all parts of Britain, as a sub-lethal effect of organochlorine pesticides and perhaps other toxic chemicals. Its true incidence is uncertain, since a great many pairs destroyed their own eggs before being checked, and a fair proportion of these were evidently reported as non-breeding. Pesticidally induced non-breeding differs from the normal kind in that many of the affected birds must be presumed to be incapable of breeding, having been rendered sterile. Whether such sterility is somatic or behavioural, or both, is not known. The frequent persistence of non-breeding pairs or individuals in the same territory for several years pointed to permanent damage. The same female in Galloway usually broke her eggs from 1965 to 1978, and then held the territory without laying until 1986, after which she was finally replaced. There are pointers to possible hormonal disturbance which may lead simply to abatement of breeding behaviour, including weakening of the pair-bond. If, as seems possible, non-breeders in the pesticide era held territories and defended them against newcomers, this could have been an additional factor depressing breeding output. While Peregrine populations in most regions have now resumed a normal breeding pattern, the lack of recovery in some coastal districts of northern Scotland has been accompanied by continuation of a good deal of non-breeding.

SEX RATIO

Newton and Mearns (1988) have examined the sex ratio of 133 Peregrine broods with nearly fledged young observed during 1974–82 in southern Scotland: there were 148 males and 167 females, so that the overall ratio did not depart significantly from unity. The sex ratio at the egg stage was examined retrospectively for broods in which all eggs gave rise to large young, and was again close to unity. Brood size had no effect on sex ratio, within the whole sample.

In 218 broods that he ringed in Cumbria between 1979 and 1991, Geoff Horne counted 285 males and 289 females: even closer to unity. Phillip Glasier gave me records of 28 broods seen in the Highlands during 1950–65: they contained 23 males and 35 females. These are the only figures which could possibly lend support to the belief held by some falconers in the past, that the proportion of males in falcon broods was one third, hence the alternative meaning of tiercel (*une tierce* = a third). The sample is, however, too small to show a significant departure from unity in sex ratio.

Hickey (1942) refers to this ancient belief, but the figures he gave for North American Peregrines, of 61 males and 53 females in 114 nestlings seen on ledges, again point to a 1:1 ratio. Hickey felt that sexing nestling Peregrines by size alone has a margin of error as high as 10–20%. Glasier's data were collected during the period when organochlorine pesticide effects on Peregrines were most severe. The average size of his 28 broods (2·04) was less than the earlier average (2·50) for the region, and it is just possible that pesticide effects could have included differential mortality between the sexes. During the 1960s, when many territories appeared to be held by single Peregrines, these were usually females, but it was seldom possible to be certain that the missing mates had actually died. Treleaven (1961) believed that there was an excess of females in the Cornwall population during 1955–60, when the species crashed in this county.

There is so far no evidence to show whether a 1:1 sex ratio is disturbed once Peregrines have fledged. It has been surmised that in districts where gamekeepers destroyed many Peregrines, using the favourite method of shooting them as they flew from the nest, there could have been a tendency for males to outnumber females, since the latter would be more liable to destruction. Since the species is renowned for its habit of rapid re-mating, such an imbalance would only show in the non-breeding population, and is entirely conjectural. Chris Mead finds that of 185 sexed recoveries admitted to his life-table (Table 27), 92 were reported as male and 93 as female; and there is no divergence of ratio with age. The longer average time taken by males to reach sexual maturity nevertheless implies some kind of numerical imbalance between the sexes, and possibly a differential mortality.

CONCLUDING THOUGHTS ON POPULATION DYNAMICS

Before the pesticide episode, Peregrine breeding populations in many – perhaps most – regions of the World showed a general tendency to stability in numbers from year to year. Some process appears to hold numbers of this species to a steady ceiling, without the fluctuations or cycles shown by some predatory birds. Numerical fluctuation *within* each year is inevitable. Even under 'natural' conditions, there is probably a fairly heavy mortality amongst newly fledged young falcons during their first few months of life; and factors bearing especially on an individual's inexperience and uncertain ability to cope, when no longer supported and protected by its parents, must be important in rapidly cutting down the annual increment of juveniles. Variable hunting prowess, predation by large owls and eagles, adverse weather, disease and intra-specific competition must add up to an appreciable level of hazard. And for markedly migratory populations, whose youngsters have to undertake long journeys during their first year of life, the difficulties must be magnified.

Natural mortality appears to be high in the Queen Charlotte Islands, inhabited by the relatively sedentary Peale's Falcon. Beebe (1960) suggested that the young of this race of Peregrine are subject to heavy selection pressure under the harsh winter climate of this north-east Pacific region, when hunting ability, stamina and orientation sense are at a premium. He saw only low numbers of birds in juvenile or transitional plumage each spring and judged that few juveniles survived their first winter. Yet Nelson (1990) concluded from the high rate of turnover in his marked population on Langara that there was a substantial number of non-breeding adults able to provide replacements. Peale's Falcon differs from most races of Peregrine in being a more specialised feeder, and more subject to marked changes in food supply that affects its own numbers (p. 296). Even so, when food supply remains stable, its population appears to be stabilised naturally.

In Britain and Ireland during the last 150 years or more, a substantial part of the Peregrine population has suffered heavy mortality through human persecution. This may well have substituted largely for 'natural' mortality and, with a low breeding output in many districts, probably held the total population below its potential level by reducing the occupation of nesting places – especially the less secure ones – in areas where the food supply is good. Nevertheless, mortality, from whatever causes, was not heavy enough to prevent the Peregrine population from reaching a fairly high breeding density in areas of favourable habitat, and a sizeable population overall, up to 1940 and, in many areas, up to 1955.

Where good nesting cliffs are plentiful, the birds' own territorial behaviour appears to place an upper limit on breeding density, and hence on potential for increase. This territorialism imposes a ceiling on numbers well below the level which food availability could allow directly. As a result, there is never any tendency for the population to outgrow and depress its food supply. Whether food is abundant or scarce, falcon density is in dynamic balance accordingly. A large output of young can possibly create such a pressure on an established breeding population that the previous ceiling in density is raised, but it may simply elevate mortality or emigration. Increase in breeding density seems more likely to be a response to increased food supply, though it must also require an adequacy of recruitment. Conversely, if food supply declines appreciably, then Peregrine numbers thin out through the birds' own reactions.

Growth in population surplus alone is much more likely to lead to modification of site selection responses, with birds becoming more adaptable in choice of a nesting place, and thus more widespread in breeding distribution. It also is conditioned by a second factor – reduced persecution of birds in marginal habitats. The marked increase in use of 'walk-in' sites, genuine ground nests, quarry nests, building nests and the beginning of tree-nesting, evidently reflects this greater adaptability and opens the possibility of a major expansion of range and numbers, by the occupation of areas previously unsuitable for Peregrines. How far this expansion will continue is something we shall watch with great interest. The form of the graph in Figure 18 suggests that, short of some further calamity, the overall increase is set to carry on. This is, however, a matter which moves from the somewhat esoteric field of animal population ecology into that of nature conservation politics, and as such is a topic for discussion in the final Chapter.

Those interested in further discussion of Peregrine population regulation should read the Peregrine volume by Cade *et al.* (1988), especially the papers by Ian Newton and Grainger Hunt. These go on to deal with the more theoretical aspects, including density dependent effects and population models. It remains the case that the nature of the non-breeding sector is especially inscrutable, and that the only population statistic which is both readily collected and immediately meaningful is the annual occupation and success of breeding territories, at least in sample areas. This will have to continue as the main basis for monitoring of Peregrine numbers into the foreseeable future.

CHAPTER 12

Ecological relationships with other birds

OTHER PREDATORS

During the nesting season, various other birds live close to the Peregrine, breeding as neighbours on the same cliffs. The frequent association between Peregrine, Raven and Buzzard is well-known. The Raven is a particularly consistent associate, and at one time there were few Peregrine cliffs in Britain or Ireland which did not have Ravens nesting within a few hundred metres of the falcons. This is less true nowadays, in districts such as the Pennines, Cheviots and Southern Uplands, where Ravens have declined as Peregrines increased. This association is basically because the two species utilise the same types of cliff nesting site, often using the same ledges and eyries in different years. Peregrines frequently take over a disused Raven eyrie, and Ravens sometimes build on a ledge previously used by falcons (see Chapter 6).

Proximity between the two species does not give harmony of relationship. As Ernest Blezard well put it, 'The two are forever in conflict, and when either rises from the crags it is usually the signal for both to display their superb powers of flight in aerial skirmish enlivened by deeply contrasting battle cries.' George Lodge has captured the essence of these encounters in his fine picture in *Territory in Bird Life* (see p. 306). This bickering between the two species often provides memorable scenes of bird flight when the nesting haunts are visited in spring. Though perhaps at times it is a redirected attack, when human intrusion leads to intensified aggression between the two species, such interaction also occurs without this stimulus.

The intensity of these exchanges varies considerably, perhaps according to differences in the aggressiveness of individuals. The Peregrine is usually the aggressor, and the Raven plays a defensive role. Some Peregrines seem to ignore their corvine neighbours, others skirmish briefly and half-heartedly and then break off, and only a minority sustain the attack. The behaviour of the Ravens may also influence the response to them – furtive birds which avoid exposing themselves unnecessarily may elicit less aggression than bold individuals which invite attack by flying in front of the crags. Sometimes the Raven actually begins one of these air battles, and may even seem to win the exchange, but more usually it suffers through such provocation, as the Peregrine returns the hostility, often assisted by its mate. The more aggressive pairs of Peregrines soon drive the Ravens to ground, and may continue to stoop at them there. Yet, while the onslaught may appear relentless or even vicious, these are mostly mock attacks. I have witnessed very many such encounters, but have never once seen one contestant strike the other.

This can happen, but seems to be rare. Bolam (1912) stated that, 'In March 1893, a Peregrine Falcon, no doubt with the intention of herself occupying the site, attacked and killed one of a pair of Ravens that were at the time nesting in Redewater [Northumberland].' Desmond Nethersole-Thompson and Gilbert Garceau on the coast of south-west England in 1930 saw a female Peregrine, flushed by them from its eyrie, strike first a Buzzard and then a Raven which were nesting on the same cliff. The Buzzard was not seriously hurt, but the Raven was mortally wounded. While investigating a Perthshire eyrie, David Wilson saw a female strike down and kill a newly fledged young Raven from an eyrie nearby. Instances in which Ravens were killed and used as food by Peregrines are mentioned on p. 133.

Many writers have described how the Raven attempts to defend itself against attack by rolling over on its back at the crucial moment to present its formidable bill and feet to the closing adversary. This is usually only a gesture, but occasionally the tables are turned. In Ireland, E. F. Clowes recorded how a Raven landed a vicious jab which brought a persecutory tiercel fluttering to the ground. The Peregrine managed to fly feebly away when it was disturbed soon afterwards. S. W. P. Freme recorded that in February 1930 a Peregrine was badly injured by Ravens in a sparring match in South Uist and 'had to be finished off'. Nelson (1907) stated that, 'On the borders of Westmorland [and Yorkshire] in 1881, a remarkable combat took place between a Peregrine and a Raven, in which the black bird was victorious, the Falcon being afterwards picked up dead on a moor.'

The Raven has a special call when under attack by Peregrines – an angry-sounding snarling croak, 'aark–aark–aark' uttered in quick succession on a slightly ascending scale as the falcon hurtles down at it. Quite often the Raven anticipates attack by beginning to give this call half-heartedly before the Peregrine has actually begun its stoop, and I have frequently been made aware of a falcon's presence, before actually seeing the bird, by hearing an anticipatory warning snarl from a Raven.

Peregrine attacking a Raven. Reproduction of the illustration by G. E. Lodge in Territory in Bird Life *(Howard, 1920)*

The Peregrine's aggression towards Ravens may serve to warn these potential predators that they have dangerous neighbours and had better leave the falcon's eggs and young well alone. Yet occasionally the two can nest remarkably close together. Nethersole-Thompson (1931) knew of two instances in which Peregrines and Ravens nested only 5 m apart. I once saw a Lakeland Raven nest with large young only 10 m from a Peregrine's nest with eggs, the two eyries being on either side of a projecting buttress, so that their owners could come and go out of sight of each other. In another instance, Raven and Peregrine eyries with young and eggs, respectively, were only 25 m apart and fully in sight of each other in the same ravine in the Southern Uplands. Probably such close-nesting depends on unusually tolerant behaviour in some individual Peregrines. In both the last two instances there was ample scope for the two species to nest much farther apart, as indeed they usually do at these haunts.

Occupied nests of the two species are more usually at least 100–200 m apart, but much depends on the choice available, and spacing tends to be greater on the longer ranges of cliff which offer more scope for spreading out. Although Ravens nest a month or so before Peregrines, the latter may have marked out an intended nest site by their winter roosting preferences, but perhaps neither species consistently has first choice. I have three times seen deserted clutches of Raven eggs within 10 m of occupied Peregrine eyries, indicating that the Ravens had abandoned their nests because the Peregrines had chosen sites so close.

In moorland areas, some crags are too small to allow Peregrines and Ravens to nest at the same time, because mutual intolerance seldom permits nesting within 50 m of each other. Besides mentioning the actual killing of a Raven by a Peregrine in the Cheviots, George Bolam said that 'Ravens are not infrequently driven from their nesting sites by Falcons. . . . In 1889 a pair were dislodged from a site in Coquetdale which they had occupied for many years, and I believe it is still [1912] held by the falcons.' Abel Chapman (1924) also quoted a note from a Cheviot gamekeeper dated 20 March 1873, 'We have a Peregrine hawk with us at present. The Ravens came to build but he set them off.' And in a subsequent year, another letter stated, 'On 22 May, the Peregrines had laid their eggs in the Raven's nest of last year; and since no Ravens are nesting in the crag this spring, it almost looks as though the falcons had dispossessed their neighbours.'

Ravens are quite often absent from inland Peregrine cliffs on the Highland grouse moors where the big crows are even more vulnerable to persecution than the falcons, because of their susceptibility to poisoned egg and flesh baits, still so widely used by gamekeepers. Yet, while many Peregrine cliffs in the eastern Highlands were without nesting Ravens at the time of my visits, nearly all of them held old Raven nests. Ravens evidently try at intervals to breed on these cliffs, but they do not survive long because of the pressures against them. Their eyries, being solid, durable structures lasting for 15 years or more on sheltered ledges, remain as evidence of these attempts at establishment long after the birds have gone. In the deer forest country of the western Highlands there are also some Peregrine cliffs without Ravens, but in this barren land Ravens are not much more numerous than Peregrines, whereas suitable cliffs abound and there is more scope for the two species to nest apart.

Some ranges of eastern seacliff much favoured by Peregrines before 1956 have no Ravens, notably those of Kent and Sussex, the Yorkshire coast, the Berwickshire coast and the east Highlands coast from Kincardine to the Black Isle. Most of these districts once had breeding Ravens, and the odd pair lingers on the St Abbs coast, but they have been banished otherwise by the combination of persecution and changing agricultural practice. In most of these areas arable land now prevails and the sheep on which Ravens so largely depend for a supply of carrion have either gone or are managed in such a way that mortality is negligible.

The diet of the Peregrine and Raven hardly overlap at all and there is no competition for food, which is perhaps why they are so consistently close neighbours. The Buzzard shares the same food source as the Peregrine to only a slightly greater degree, although it now and then scavenges on the remains left by falcons. Buzzards often breed on the same ranges of cliff as Peregrines, but they are less consistently present than Ravens, and tend to keep a greater distance from the falcons, and to nest in much lesser and more broken rock faces, where their eyries are often quite easy of access. It is thus not surprising that old Buzzard nests tend to be utilised by Peregrines as eyries much less commonly than those of the Raven. Buzzards are subject to the same kind of harassment by Peregrines as are Ravens, but again they are rarely struck, and they sometimes initiate attacks themselves. Buzzards have been recorded as prey only a very few times.

The Golden Eagle is a different case, for in the districts where both occur, mainly in Scotland, this bird and the Peregrine usually give each other a rather wide berth. Unless the range is very extensive, they are seldom to be found nesting on the same cliff at the same time, though they may resort to the same rock in different years, and Peregrines occasionally lay in vacant Eagle eyries. The shortest distance I have known between occupied eyries of the two species is 1 km, but they are usually separated by at least several times this distance. Peter Wormell saw the two nesting only 300 m apart on Mull, but this appears to be exceptional.

Aerial encounters between Peregrines and Golden Eagles are seen occasionally, the falcon being typically the aggressor and appearing usually to have the advantage over its less agile antagonist – but not always. I once watched a female Peregrine stooping at a pair of Golden Eagles in Galloway. The first Eagle merely 'jinked' as the Peregrine flashed past, but when the falcon turned its attention to the second one, this bird immediately furled its wings and followed its tormentor downwards in a steep dive at the same speed. The Peregrine 'threw up' with the Eagle following likewise until both regained their original pitches, whereupon the Peregrine thought better of continuing the exchange and drifted away.

There are, nevertheless, clear indications that the Golden Eagle is dominant when it comes to choice of nesting place. It appears to take precedence, and to exclude the Peregrine from the immediate vicinity of its eyrie. This relationship is inferred from the events connected with the recolonisation of the Galloway Hills by the Golden Eagle. It is doubtful if Golden Eagles were ever totally absent from south-west Scotland during the present century. A pair certainly bred in the hills of southern Ayrshire during 1910–20, and there were sporadic attempts at nesting in the adjoining uplands of the Stewartry between 1900 and 1940. However, the species became more firmly re-established in this district from 1945 onwards. In 1945–51 one pair of Eagles bred alternately on three different cliffs (A, B and C) which had previously belonged to a pair of Peregrines. The

Peregrines bred once on cliff C in the Eagles' absence, but appeared usually to resort to cliff D, some distance away. In 1952 a second pair of Eagles established themselves on cliff C, while the first remained firmly attached to A–B. The Peregrines bred at D until 1954, after which they ceased nesting, and finally disappeared from the territory around 1955.

A third pair of Eagles bred from 1948 onwards in another part of the district, on one or other of two crag ranges 2 km apart. Thse crag ranges were previously used as alternatives by a pair of Peregrines, and the falcons have continued to breed, but always at 2 km from the eagles. During 1962–66 a fourth pair of Eagles became established at yet another Galloway crag which had long been a regular Peregrine haunt, and the Peregrines moved to another rock during this period. In 1967, this last pair of Eagles, evidently inconvenienced in their hunting by the encroachment of extensive conifer forests, moved to another nesting place several miles away on unplanted moorland, where they have remained. The Peregrines returned to the vacated crag in 1970 and have bred there ever since.

The future of the Golden Eagle as a nesting bird in Galloway is now threatened by the blanket afforestation of these hills, which is steadily reducing the available food supply, especially of carrion, as the sheep are removed, but also of wild prey such as grouse, hares and rabbits. Two pairs have already dropped out (from cliffs A–B, and C) and the continued expansion of the forests could so reduce the hunting range of the remaining two pairs as to place their survival in doubt. While the loss of these fine birds is regrettable it is interesting that a pair of Peregrines has begun breeding near cliff C, and a second pair has been seen at cliff B.

In the western Highlands and Islands the apparent decrease in Peregrines during 1880–1930 appears to have been matched by an increase in Golden Eagles. In some cases Golden Eagles have taken over former Peregrine cliffs. The decline in populations of moorland birds which has reduced carrying capacity for the Peregrine has been counter-balanced by an increase in amount of carrion available to Golden Eagles as the major source of food. The combination of local overstocking and reduced carrying capacity of the land has resulted in a generally high mortality of sheep and lambs, and a great deal of red deer carrion is also to be found on the hills. The change in status of the two raptors is evidently a response to the same ecological change, but without necessarily involving an interaction between the Peregrine and Golden Eagle, i.e. it represents replacement rather than displacement of one species by the other, as food supply for the one deteriorated while that for the other improved. However, replacement may sometimes operate in an active way as the one species gains in competitive strength while the other weakens. Moreover, when one looks at the distribution of the two species in the Highlands, the regularity of scatter of the Peregrine so characteristic in more southerly districts is here broken by the presence of numerous pairs of Golden Eagles, and it is tempting to assume that if the Eagles were not there, more falcons would fill the gaps.

The underlying cause of the apparent intolerance between Peregrines and Golden Eagles is uncertain. There could be an element of competition for food, in that both species take birds such as Red and Black Grouse, Ptarmigan, duck, gulls, auks and Fulmars. There is thus an overlap in prey requirements which could become critical in the barren country of the western Highlands, where food is likely to be at a premium for both predators. Meinertzhagen saw a Peregrine robbed of a grouse kill by a Golden Eagle. The Golden Eagle may also represent a direct threat to the Peregrine, or at least to the young, for it is powerful enough to kill a sitting falcon caught unawares and to raid an eyrie containing eyasses. MacNally (1979) found the plucked but uneaten carcase of an adult Peregrine on a feeding perch beside a Ross-shire Golden Eagle eyrie, and the talon punctures with bruised blood darkening indicated it had been killed and not picked up as carrion. However, an angry pair of Peregrines defending their young would be quite capable of striking down a flying Eagle.

Antagonism between Peregrines and Golden Eagles could thus be regarded both as inter-specific territorialism or defence of nest site against a potential predator, whereas hostility towards Ravens more evidently belongs to the second category.

Interestingly, the Raven shows exactly the same avoidance of the vicinity of occupied Golden Eagle eyries, in the location of its own nest, as does the Peregrine. Ravens and Peregrines continue to be closely associated in their nesting haunts in Eagle country, but both of them keep their distance from the bigger predator. Probably four or five pairs of Ravens were displaced by Golden Eagles during the recolonisation of the Galloway Hills by the latter, and the population was actually depleted by this number. Ravens also show a marked overlap with the Golden Eagles in their diet, in drawing so largely on sheep and deer carrion, so that there may be some competition between these two species, especially where the Eagle has to scavenge for carrion a good deal. Moreover, the Eagle certainly does kill Ravens, both old and young, for food on occasion, and the risk of predation may discourage the Raven from showing too neighbourly a disposition, for it does not have the Peregrine's powers of retaliation.

Thesiger (1959) describes how a trained Peregrine in Arabia was stooped at by an unknown species of eagle; the falcon was evidently terrified and in seeking refuge hurled itself at its owner's chest with a thump. On Langara Island, British Columbia, Beebe (1960) found that the numerous Bald Eagles were under frequent attack by the Peregrines, but only occasionally made any attempt at retaliation. There was no evidence of predation by the eagles on the falcons, and although there was an appreciable disturbance factor for Peregrines with eggs or young, no reduction in breeding success appeared to result. On the same island, Nelson (1970) nevertheless noted that Bald Eagles caused considerable annoyance to Peregrines which were feeding young, and suggested that their frequent interruptions could even slow down growth of the nestlings. He saw four unsuccessful attempts by Bald Eagles to pirate food from Peregrines, and noted that when their young were on the wing the falcons were more aggressive to the eagles than to Ravens and other corvids, Yet Deppe (1972) recorded a remarkable instance of pairs of White-tailed Eagles and Peregrines nesting in the same tree at the same time, in Mecklenburg.

Remarkably, in the western United States, the Snake River Canyon in Idaho has a great concentration of Golden Eagles, Prairie Falcons (desert relative of the Peregrine) and other raptors nesting close together on its walls (see p. 282). The two species radiate out over the surrounding sagebrush deserts and overlap considerably in choice of prey, which is extremely limited, with ground squirrels as a major item for both raptors (Morlan Nelson). Nesting habitat is perhaps so localised that normal antagonisms become abated between species as well as within species. In large canyons such as this, Peregrines can occupy territories alongside Prairie Falcons, but the two are evidently sometimes in competition, at least for nesting space. Richard Fyfe described how he watched a male Peregrine, newly returned to a long-deserted cut bank nesting place in Alberta, evict the pair of Prairie Falcons which had been firmly in possession.

Nelson (1969) attributed a decline in peregrines in mountainous regions of the western and north-western United States during the first half of this century to warming climate and reduced precipitation, which resulted in contraction of wetland areas and decline in waterfowl populations that were important prey. Some deserted Peregrine haunts were taken over by Prairie Falcons but although, in contrast to Fyfe's observation, he saw contests with Peregrines won by Prairie Falcons, Nelson believed that the change was species replacement in response to climatic shift. Peregrines retreated upwards and northwards to regain cooler and moister environments, while the Prairie Falcons followed the drier conditions to which they were well adapted. Species interactions could, however, sometimes be involved among the mechanisms of such replacement.

In parts of the Arctic, Peregrines and Gyr Falcons overlap somewhat in distribution though the latter is a more truly northern and montane bird. Cade (1960) has discussed in detail the relationships between the two species in Alaska, especially in regard to possible competition. The two tend to nest well apart and each will attack the other if it approaches too closely. In maritime breeding areas, Peregrines and Gyr Falcons feed on the same selection of bird prey (auks, gulls, ducks, waders) but are more separated in their precise breeding distribution; whereas in inland districts they tend to take different prey (migratory birds for the Peregrine, resident birds and ground mammals for the Gyr) but nest closer together. Cade believes that there is some competition between the two species for nesting areas on cliffs and, more locally, for food. He concluded that the Gyr Falcon is the dominant species, because of its greater size/strength and earlier breeding season, but that the Peregrine is numerically the more successful because of its greater ecological flexibility. These relationships between Alaskan Peregrines and Gyr Falcons are strongly reminiscent of those between Peregrines and Golden Eagles in Britain.

The lesser bird predators tend to avoid the immediate neighbourhood of an occupied Peregrine eyrie. This is true of Kestrels, whose presence at a nesting cliff is often an indication of the Peregrine's absence. Sometimes Kestrels nest within 200 m, but at risk of their lives. They can be quite daring by appearing at a falcon cliff if the Peregrines have no nest and move away elsewhere during the day, and I have seen one fly close past an occupied eyrie while the angry owners demonstrated overhead at my presence. But the danger is considerable and Kestrels are quite frequently taken as prey. The several strange instances of Peregrines taking over and incubating Kestrel clutches seem to reflect abnormal circumstances.

Merlins are often quick to challenge an intruding Peregrine and may some-times seem to give the bigger falcon an uncomfortable time, but they too usually keep well away from an active eyrie when they choose their nest site. In two different areas, Ernest Blezard noted that Merlins moved into Peregrine nest-ing haunts and bred only in years when the Peregrines were completely absent. The Merlin occasionally figures in the remains at an eyrie or plucking station (Table 8).

Donald Watson and Derek Langslow watched Hen Harriers at a winter roost in Galloway react nervously to a pair of Peregrines. Several of the Harriers had pitched into the long grass when the Peregrines appeared and dipped low over the site. The Harriers all at once took wing, drifting some little distance away and showing reluctance to return until the falcons themselves had evidently gone to roost. Cade (1960) watched frequent fighting between Marsh Hawks (North American Hen Harriers) and Peregrines over prey items on their wintering grounds in the coastal marshes of southern California. In Galloway, I watched an adult Peregrine briefly join a circling Osprey over Loch Ken, but there was no reaction between the two birds.

The various species of British owl are all somewhat at risk when they nest too close to Peregrine cliffs, for all five have been recorded as prey. The Short-eared Owl is probably the most vulnerable, nesting widely though sparingly on open moorland and in young forest in Peregrine country and hunting mainly during the day. In Galloway, Barn Owls sometimes have the temerity to take up residence on Peregrine crags. One such bird quickly paid the penalty, its conspicuous white and buff feathers being scattered widely over the slope below a month later, and another pair near a different eyrie had gone by the following year.

Peregrines in Britain do not have to contend with the large and powerful Eagle Owl. This bird and its North American counterpart, the Great Horned Owl, are among the few enemies of the Peregrine apart from Man, and there are a good many records of falcons being killed by them (e.g. Uttendörfer, 1952). In the Peregrine Recovery Program at Cornell, run by Tom Cade and his colleagues, three young Peregrines were artificially fledged to the wild in the famous former nesting place in the nearby Taughannock Gorge. Within weeks two had been killed by Horned Owls, and the other was re-caught to save its life. The Peregrine is only vulnerable at rest, when the Owl can pounce on it unawares. On the wing it is a different matter, and a Peregrine has been seen to strike down and kill a Horned Owl with ease. D. Bramwell (1959–60) has surmised that many of the late-glacial deposits of bird bones in caves in Britain, which include remains of Peregrine (see p. 10), are attributable to predatory birds which lived in these places. He regarded the Eagle Owl as the chief predator, and remarked that bone remains referable to this species indicate a much larger and more powerful bird than the modern form.

PREY SPECIES

The nesting of various prey species in close proximity to occupied Peregrine eyries is also familiar. To begin with a bird which is a potential egg stealer, the Carrion Crow occasionally has its nest very close to that of a Peregrine. In Galloway, a pair of Crows clung to their favourite clump of trees at the foot of a cliff when Peregrines moved in and laid only 200 m away. They were unmolested and actually reared young. In the same district, in two different years, R. Roxburgh saw Carrion Crow nests with young at the foot of a crag where Peregrines had also hatched out. Martin (1980) saw a pair of Lakeland Peregrines with young frequently dive at Carrion Crows nesting on the same cliffs, often locking feet together but evidently without inflicting damage. Passing Crows were also often 'buzzed' but not struck. Crow neighbours are nevertheless somewhat at risk. In 1951 I found a Carrion Crow nest with eggs in a small 8 m rock in the Galloway Hills. A few weeks later, Will Murdoch, shepherd on the ground, found that a Peregrine had laid in this nest after being robbed at another crag. In the vicinity were the pluckings of both the original owners of the nest, and

DW

within the neighbourhood, the remains of other Crow 'kills' were found. This pair of Peregrines were Crow killers. Falconers are said to avoid flying trained Peregrines at Crows, because experience has shown that if the Crow is not cleanly killed and the Peregrine grapples with it on the ground, there is a fair risk that the Crow's mate will come to the attack and injure the falcon. This is, however, perhaps an artificial situation.

Jackdaws commonly nest in small to medium-sized colonies on the hill crags and in old quarries, but they are usually in the lower level faces, and are seldom to be found on favourite Peregrine cliffs. Peregrines occasionally resort to a Jackdaw cliff as an alternative, and then the Jackdaws will usually move out, unless the range is extensive and they can keep their distance. However, there are several inland cliffs which are regularly occupied by Jackdaws and Peregrines. This sharing of the same cliffs is quite frequent on the coast, where, although mentioned by several observers as a favourite prey species, the Jackdaw sometimes nests in very close proximity to Peregrines, even to within a few metres.

In the hills, scattered pairs of Stock Doves seem locally to survive in the crannies of escarpments where falcons breed, and near Inverness I once saw an open rock nest of a Wood Pigeon on a face about 50 m below a Peregrine eyrie. On coastal cliffs, Rock Doves and feral pigeons often breed in caves and clefts quite close to falcons, but Macintyre (1914) and Treleaven (1977) have argued that these birds have become adept at avoiding predation through a combination of experience and selection.

The common small hill birds frequently nest close to Peregrine eyries. Few mountain haunts of the Peregrine are without their Wrens, even in the wildest and bleakest places, and this little bird is commonly to be seen flitting about the elevated crags, especially where these are well vegetated and there is good feeding and shelter. The unlined 'cock' nests are frequent on the crags, and often built under an overhang of the steep rocks favoured by falcons. Nests used for breeding are quite typically lined with the body feathers of victims from the Peregrines' plucking stations, and one nest pulled out by a predator proved to contain the feathers of five different prey species. Bolam (1912) mentioned that in north Wales, a Ring Ouzel reared her young unmolested within 20 m of a Peregrine eyrie, and the cock frequently sang from a projecting rock at less than half the distance. Martin (1980) watched a pair of Ring Ouzels frequently diving at a perched or incubating Peregrine on their shared nesting crags: sometimes the tiercel responded with chase but in a rather half-hearted way. John Mitchell has seen a Twite's nest within a few feet of an eyrie in the Campsie Fells. Meadow Pipits, Wheatears and Stonechats on occasion place their nests in positions which would seem dangerously close to Peregrine eyries. All these passerines can figure as prey, though the furtive flight habits of the Wren make it an infrequent victim.

There is, however, a belief that predators such as the Peregrine do not normally take prey in the immediate vicinity of their breeding place, but prefer to hunt farther afield, so that creatures normally at risk have relative immunity if they keep close enough to their foe. Meinertzhagen (1959), who subscribed strongly to the idea, suggested that too much killing near the nest would draw attention to its whereabouts, and stated that the tendency to avoid killing around

the eyrie ceases when the young are on the wing. This is not very convincing as regards Peregrines because these birds make no attempt to conceal their eyries anyway, and the vicinity so often becomes littered with the remains of kills that the origin of these is irrelevant in this context.

Evidence from other parts of the world sheds more light on this quaint notion of a truce with near neighbours. In some areas it is apparently advantageous for certain other birds to nest in close company with breeding Peregrines, which will tend to keep away other predators such as foxes. A parallel advantage to the Peregrine may be presumed, and the falcon may itself benefit by the extra warning given by its other bird neighbours of the approach of predators. It is perhaps significant that these commensal nesting associations seem to be commonest in the Arctic regions, where many Peregrines nest in easily accessible situations vulnerable to ground predators.

Cade (1960) has given an interesting account of instances in which various bird species appear actually to seek out the vicinity of Peregrine and other bird of prey eyries. In Alaska, he found that wherever a pair of Peregrines had an eyrie, several pairs of Canada Geese were usually nesting on the same cliff, frequently within 50 m; while many stretches of apparently suitable cliff away from falcon eyries were not occupied by nesting geese. Richard Fyfe found that in southern Alberta, where Prairie Falcons and Canada Geese breed in holes and hollows in earth cliffs along the main rivers, the geese which were nesting close to falcons had a higher hatching success than those which did not have this association. Fyfe found that when nesting sites were in short supply, the Canada Geese sometimes took precedence over the Prairie Falcons, but in one large recess he saw the two species incubating only a few feet apart and facing each other.

A parallel nesting association between Siberian Peregrines or other birds of prey and Red-breasted Geese was noted as long ago as 1895 by H. L. Popham on tundras of the Yenisei River. Russian ornithologists have in more recent years found that the Red-breasted Goose typically nests in groups close to the eyrie of a Peregrine, Rough-legged Buzzard or Snowy Owl, or the nest of a Glaucous or Herring Gull, usually within 50–100 m but sometimes much closer. Kretschmar and Leonovich (1967) found that on the Pyasina River in western Taimyr in 1960–62, 19 out of 22 Peregrine eyries (which averaged 7–10 km apart) had colonies of Red-breasted Geese in the immediate vicinity. Naumov (1931) found the same association and noticed that moulting Red-breasts often stayed close to Peregrine nests. Uspenski (1966) reported that all tundra geese nest by birds of prey to some extent, mainly because so few areas are snow-free at the right time, but he considered that, for the Red-breasted Goose, protection against foxes by falcons was a necessary condition for nest-site selection. In addition, Turner (1886) recorded aggregations of Eider Ducks around breeding Peregrines in the Aleutian Islands; and Buturlin (1933) found that in Siberia breeding ducks, waders, pipits and Snow Buntings were concentrated around the eyries of ground-nesting Peregrines.

The idea that the bird of prey finds advantage from such associations in a ready food supply is not supported by observations. Cade found that Colville Peregrines rarely showed any hostility towards their Canada Geese neighbours, and Kretschmar (1965) noted that the Siberian falcons did not attack the Red-breasted Geese, but fed mainly on Asiatic Golden Plover. Buturlin (1933) also observed that birds nesting near peregrines in Siberia walked to and from their nests instead of flying, thereby avoiding attack.

I am not aware of any evidence that nesting birds seek the vicinity of Peregrine eyries in Britain. On the other hand it would be likely in this country that the presence of various neighbours, including Ravens, will help to keep Peregrines warned of approaching enemies, for when its mate is away a sitting Peregrine is easily surprised unawares. The tendency to avoid preying on or driving away close neighbours may thus be similarly developed here. Dementiev (1951) has suggested a further explanation – that this tendency has come about through the instinct to live with the offspring suppressing the instinct to attack prey, within the nesting territory. Perhaps this would apply only to birds on the ground. Several observers have commented that Peregrines seem at times to show no inhibition about taking flying prey close to the nest. Dick Treleaven has seen many kills extremely close to Cornish eyries and people who live near nesting cliffs frequently see Peregrines make successful strikes in the immediate vicinity. Cade also found that Alaskan Peregrines frequently killed prey within 100 m of the eyrie, and Beebe reported similarly from the Queen Charlotte Islands.

Another possibility is that the presence of prey species immediately around the eyrie could represent an assured reserve of food to the Peregrine at a critical time, notably during bad weather, when small chicks are endangered if both parents are compelled to hunt. Or the advantage could be later in the year, when the young have fledged, and are learning to catch prey. In Devon, after several days of bad weather and in fog, I. Waldren saw a tiercel kill a newly fledged Jackdaw near its eyrie; and for the next 2 hours it was continually mobbed by the adult Jackdaws.

Beebe believed that the Peregrines on Langara provided less efficient predators with an abundant supply of food by leaving half-eaten remains scattered around, and it has been suggested elsewhere that scavengers could nest close to Peregrines' eyries for this particular advantage. Buzzards certainly pick up unfinished remains at times in Britain, but this factor is probably unimportant here.

A close association between nesting Peregrines and other birds is usual on the seacliffs, especially where there are large colonies of breeding seafowl. Ussher (1900), referring to Ireland, said, 'When breeding in marine cliffs the Peregrine's eyrie is frequently found in the midst of some great colony of sea-birds. I have seen the Razorbills and Guillemots sitting on their eggs around the recess that contained young Peregrines. In fact no great cliff-bird colony seems to be complete without its pair of Falcons.' I have seen relatively few Peregrine eyries on seacliffs, and most of these were either on cliffs with few seabirds, or on sections of precipice not holding the main seafowl concentrations. My impression is that the falcons prefer to nest on ledges away from the densest throngs of seabirds; but in particularly large and extensive colonies they may have little choice but to take sites thickly surrounded by these neighbours.

In the larger seabird colonies there would seem to be no particular advantage in Peregrines being able to prey on birds immediately around the eyrie, for there is such an abundance of food within easy flight; but the advantages of a commensal nesting association break down here, too, and there is no obvious reason for them to avoid snatching at a bird within close reach. However, from the apparent lack of fear shown by their close neighbours, the 'truce around the nest' appears to hold good on the seacliffs too. Birds sitting on the cliff may be relatively safe, though Gray (1871) said of the Peregrine, 'When located, as is often the case, beside a colony of gulls and Guillemots, it contents itself with plundering the nests of these birds after the young have hatched.' Yet on the whole, these coastal Peregrines evidently take adult birds, struck down in flight and perhaps taken almost randomly from the population. Leslie Tuck (1960) noted that although three pairs of Peregrines breeding on Akpatok Island in northern Canada fed almost exclusively on Guillemots in the huge colony there, these auks nested to within about 3 m of the eyries. He believed that the Peregrines took only Guillemots injured by falling rocks and did not molest the healthy birds.

There could be a counter-risk in Peregrines nesting too close to the larger gulls. However, it would seem that gulls leave the actual eyries severely alone, for there are no reports of even attempts at predation on eggs or young of falcons. D'Urban and Mathew (1898) noted that at least two pairs of Peregrines in Devon bred annually in the midst of Herring Gull colonies, and the great increase in the British Herring Gull population has produced a fairly constant association between the two on the rocky coasts. The large gulls have now and then been seen to rob Peregrines of their prey (Meinertzhagen), but at some risk, since they figure among the list of prey species themselves.

The Peregrine nevertheless has to contend with one quite tough adversary on the seacliffs, the tetchy, oil-spitting Fulmar. During recent years, observers at some of our northern seabird haunts have become increasingly aware that Fulmars cause debility and death amongst quite a wide range of other birds, through squirting their evil-smelling stomach oil over them.

Peregrines are certainly among the victims of this strange hazard. Roy Dennis first mentioned his suspicions about this new problem to me in 1972, by which time he had observed oiling of other large raptors by Fulmars on Fair Isle (Dennis, 1970), and had notes of four possibly oiled Peregrines here and on Orkney. Roger Broad reported in 1974 that on Fair Isle he had records of 28 Fulmar-oiling incidents, covering 20 bird species and including five raptors and two Peregrines.

Fulmar oil has much the same effects in causing clogging of the feathers, with loss of power of flight, heat insulation, and buoyancy on water, as does oil spilled on the sea through human agency. Some birds which escape with only slight oiling may recover, but badly oiled individuals evidently go into a decline from which there is no recovery. Hapless victims already sick or immobile through previous oiling may be caught amongst a group of Fulmars and, spewed upon time and again, become so drenched in the stuff as to succumb rapidly.

The evidence continued to accumulate, and in 1977 Andrew Clarke concluded from careful chemical analysis that the extensive oiling on four dead Peregrines sent to Monks Wood Experimental Station during 1971–75 was indeed likely to be Fulmar oil. Although on exposure to air, light and water, Fulmar oil on plumage loses its characteristic smell and changes colour, it retains distinctive chemical characteristics which clearly separate it from mineral oils. Clarke stated that during 1971–76 there were at least nine recorded instances of Peregrines being fouled with Fulmar stomach oil, and Roy Dennis reported two more cases in 1977. In several instances the oil was so fresh as to be unmistakable. Clarke concluded that oiling by Fulmars appears to be a small but possibly significant cause of mortality in coastal British Peregrines.

This factor thus becomes a possible explanation of the serious decline in the northern and western coastal Peregrine population, and of the current lack of recovery in these areas. There is a quite good geographical correlation between the risk of Fulmar oiling (in terms of distribution and numbers of this bird) and Peregrine breeding status on the coast of northern and western Britain. After spreading out from its original station of St Kilda, the Fulmar has formed large colonies on the big seacliffs which support large concentrations of auks and Kittiwakes, and also breeds in smaller numbers on many cliffs which have few or none of these highly aggregated and localised species. Peregrines were formerly widespread on these seacliffs generally, but reached their highest densities where seafowl, including Fulmars, were most numerous. They are now mostly absent, or showing poor breeding success, at the major seabird colonies, and tend to show better occupation of territories and higher breeding success on the seacliffs with few other birds.

I nevertheless find it difficult to believe that Fulmar-oiling could have been a major factor in the original, post-1955 decline of this sector of the Peregrine population, which was so closely synchronised with the crash over the rest of the country as to be clearly an integral part of it. This decline coincided closely with that in inland districts of the north and west and, as far as coastal localities were concerned, seemed to reflect a general malaise unrelated to potential contact with Fulmars. There are many anomalies historically between the patterns of Fulmar increase and spread, and of Peregrine decline. James Fisher (1952) has given a valuable detailed record of the dates of Fulmar colonisation of new localities. In many of these places, Peregrines continued to breed for long after the Fulmars were present in some numbers. St Kilda was long a noted haunt of Peregrines and Fulmars. Around 1900 when the Fulmar population was probably at least 20,000 pairs, the St Kilda group usually had at least four pairs of Peregrines, and this number was evidently maintained for some years afterwards. On the great precipices of Hoy in Orkney, James Fisher estimated at least 10,000 Fulmar nests, Britain's third largest colony, in 1946, but this coast held one of the highest nesting densities of Peregrines in the country up to 1962 or even later. Peregrines also continued to breed in their usual numbers on the seacliffs of other parts of Orkney, Shetland, Caithness, Sutherland and the Hebrides right up to about 1960, long after these areas had been colonised by Fulmars in large numbers. Douglas Weir also saw five pairs of Peregrines breeding successfully on an island with a huge colony of Fulmars (c. 200,000 pairs) in the Canadian Arctic.

Exposure to Fulmar-oiling is, however, not an all-or-nothing matter, depending on whether or not this bird and Peregrines are present together, but amounts to a statistical risk in which the chances of oiling or serious oiling increase gradually as the opportunities for contact between the two species increase. And the risks could be enhanced not only by an increase in density of Fulmars on a cliff, but by a change either in their behaviour or that of the Peregrines. Fulmars have always had the advantage when not in flight. Peregrines which attempted to occupy or hold nesting ledges, or even perch, within squirting distance of nesting Fulmars would be at constant risk of oiling, and their fledged young would be even more vulnerable, both immediately after leaving the eyrie and for some time before they had mastered their full powers of flight in taking prey. Treleaven (1977) mentions that newly fledged young Peregrines will follow Fulmars, evidently because of their resemblance in flight to the adult falcons. Yet the Fulmar itself is quite commonly taken as prey by Peregrines (see Table 8) and K. D. Smith saw one pair on Shetland which seemed to prefer Fulmars to all other species. Even though flying Fulmars have been seen to eject oil at other birds, they would appear to be extremely vulnerable to Peregrines when on the wing.

If the Fulmar had been an enemy of long standing, through its oiling effect, it would be surprising that the Peregrine had not learned to avoid such a dangerous foe to a much greater degree. Oiling of Peregrines by Fulmars may, in fact, be a rather recent development. The records certainly suggest this, for they are all post-1970, even allowing that a well-established phenomenon may become widely noticed only after someone has first drawn attention to it, so that others then keep a close look-out for such happenings. This would point to a change in the Fulmar's behaviour, with the bird in recent years making increased use of oil-squirting as an aggressive as well as defensive weapon against other birds. Increase in Fulmar density in a particular colony would then enhance the risks to neighbouring species. As numbers have grown, they may have actively competed with Peregrines for nesting ledges where these are in short supply. On the Sussex coast, B. Atfield watched Fulmars occupy ledges in which a pair of Peregrines had previously shown interest.

A final possibility is that oiling of various birds could result more from increased vulnerability attributable to other circumstances. For example, some of the species found oiled on Fair Isle by Broad were tired migrants, and some may have been individuals not in full health. It would be quite likely that a Peregrine which was below par for some reason, notably from a sub-lethal dose of toxic chemical residues, might grapple with a Fulmar on its ledge as apparently easy prey, rather than attempt to strike a flying bird in the usual way. One oiled Peregrine from Shetland had a broken leg and at least two of the four oiled falcons examined by Clarke contained high levels of organochlorine residues, especially PCBs. It has been surmised that Peregrines carrying heavy pollutant loads may show reduced hunting ability. Such an effect would dispose them to tackle prey on the ground, thereby magnifying greatly any normal risks of oiling by Fulmars.

The above was written in 1979. In his study of south-west Scotland Peregrines, Mearns (1983) caught 15 different coastal birds, and four of the 12 females showed moderate Fulmar oiling. Three of these oiled females later reared young, and during the same year none of the three males was oiled. Since this represented a random sample, and in a district with only a moderate Fulmar population, the overall incidence of oiling at 26% was quite high. While Peregrines oiled by Fulmars continue to be reported sporadically, even from as far south as Devon and Cornwall (R. B. Treleaven), the importance of this factor to coastal Peregrine populations remains unclear.

It would seem best to keep an open mind on the intriguing idea that Fulmar oiling may cause significant mortality amongst some coastal Peregrines. This effect could possibly account, at least in part, for the Peregrine's failure to recover its former numbers and breeding success in far northern and western coastal areas. Perhaps, too, it may operate through a secondary action as a final adversity to an already ailing bird. Yet, it has not prevented a massive recovery of Peregrines in most coastal regions south of the northern Highlands and Islands. More detailed observations on the actual interactions between the two species in particular localities are needed, to see if breeding Peregrines are truly vulnerable to this form of oiling. The continued poor showing of Peregrines in northern Scottish coastal areas seems more likely to reflect the lack of improvement in marine pollution than any other cause though Fulmar oiling could be a contributory factor (p. 346). If marine pollution improves markedly in the future, but there is no accompanying increase in territory occupation or successful breeding on the depleted coastal cliffs, then the Fulmar-oiling hypothesis will receive further circumstantial support.

A good many prey species have been recorded mobbing Peregrines on the wing; in particular, they include gulls, corvids, waders and Starlings. Waders seldom mob a falcon outside the breeding season and Starlings only do so when in flocks, but the others will mob at any time of the year and either singly, in pairs, or in flocks. A mobbed Peregrine usually ignores such demonstrations, but is more likely to turn round and attack its tormentors in the breeding season, and when near the eyrie sometimes strikes down an offending bird. Occasionally instances of piracy have been reported, in which Peregrines have lost prey to other predators or scavengers. Beebe (1960) found that a successful kill by a wintering Peregrine (North America, but unlocalised) was the signal for other raptors to converge on the scene, and that the falcon usually yielded its prey to eagles, Buteos and the larger Accipiters.

CHAPTER 13

The Pesticide Story

I had originally intended to keep the pesticide story as a neat compartment in a chapter of its own, but this has not been possible. The effect of the organochlorine pesticides pervades so many aspects of the Peregrine saga from 1947 onwards that omission of comment in the many appropriate places would have led to a strangely disjointed and inadequate treatment. Events integral to the developing theme of unprecedented change in Peregrine population biology are thus dealt with at various places in this book, and few chapters fail to make some reference to pesticide issues. The details of population decline and recovery are given in Chapters 3 and 4; of breeding pathology in Chapters 7 and 8; and of the interplay of mortality and productivity in Chapter 11. The present chapter attempts to knit these aspects and some of their loose ends together, and to set them within a perspective both historical and personal. The full story of pesticides and Peregrines is now vastly larger than one chapter, and I can only try to set out the part that I know.

HOW IT BEGAN

Over the years pigeon fanciers had made desultory complaints and taken sporadic, if illegal, action against Peregrines as a result of predation on homing pigeons, and within 'the fancy' the Peregrine was widely regarded as an enemy. Matters came to a head in 1960, when agitation became fierce in the South Wales mining valleys which were long a stronghold of fanciers. Ivor George of Neath appeared on television to make a vigorous and eloquent protest against the depredations of falcons on the pigeons of the district. This was followed shortly after by a petition to the Home Office requesting the removal of legal protection from the Peregrine, on the grounds that the species was increasing, at least in Wales, and that enormous numbers of homers were being killed annually.

The Home Office, wishing to be sure of the facts on which to judge the issue, asked the Nature Conservancy for information on the status of the Peregrine in Britain, its distribution and food. The Nature Conservancy in turn contracted the necessary survey to the British Trust for Ornithology, and I was invited by the Trust to become organiser. The Peregrine Enquiry was launched in late 1960, though the first few months were spent mainly in setting up the network of observers and contacts, and in tapping all known sources of information about the past distribution and breeding biology of the species. A countrywide appeal was made to all those with an interest in the Peregrine – birdwatchers, falconers, egg collectors, gamekeepers, forestry trappers and rangers – and the response was encouraging. In the spring of 1961 an attempt was made to visit as many as possible of the known nesting territories of the Peregrine in Great Britain, to check on occupation, breeding success and, to a more limited extent, food. In 1962 this census was repeated, and still better national coverage was obtained. The detailed figures which were obtained are given in Chapters 3 and 4.

There had earlier been disquieting reports of apparent decreases in breeding population in the south of England and in parts of Wales, and Treleaven (1961) had drawn particular attention to the severe decline in Cornwall between 1955 and 1960. By the end of June 1961 it was clear that the British Peregrine was in dire trouble. The once flourishing population of southern England had all but disappeared and that of Wales was greatly reduced. In the north of England, numbers were well down on their normal level, and in coastal southern Scotland few falcons remained. In the Scottish Highlands, too, there were local signs of decrease. Breeding success was low amongst the remaining Peregrines and numerous territories were occupied by birds which failed to rear young, or even to lay eggs. Many nesting places were occupied by single Peregrines and over the country as a whole a large number of nesting places once held regularly by Peregrines seemed to be totally deserted, in many cases for the first time ever known.

The picture emerging was thus in marked contrast to that presented by the pigeon fanciers, and by the end of the first year of the Enquiry, the anxiety among nature conservationists was no longer about the homing pigeon issue, but about the apparently headlong decline of the Peregrine population and its causes. The Enquiry continued into 1962 and the results were awaited anxiously. They showed the position to have worsened. In all the main Peregrine districts, occupation of territories and number of successful eyries had each decreased further. For Britain as a whole, occupation of breeding territories was down to about 56% of the average level in 1930–39. Only 21% of territories at the normal level of population produced young; and productivity in many districts was well below the level at which a population could maintain itself.

The picture of continuing and rapid decline was such that the Home Office felt bound at the end of 1962 to maintain the maximum legal protection for the Peregrine. Moreover, since the rate of predation on homing pigeons at the 1962 level of Peregrine population was estimated to be insignificant nationally, even the pigeon fanciers ceased to press their original contention.

HOW IT HAPPENED

The search for causes had begun in 1961 when the first serious symptoms of decline became clear. It was a case of detective work with few clues to follow at first. During the breeding season of 1961, two adult Peregrines were found dead or dying in suggestive circumstances. A tiercel was picked up freshly dead under high tension cables in Cumberland, but the absence of injury suggested that it had been sitting on a cable or pylon and simply collapsed from this perch. A female was found by R. B. Treleaven on the level cliff-top above its eyrie in Cornwall; the bird was still alive, but was in tremors and died next day. These two birds were in excellent condition and the only possibilities for cause of death seemed to be disease or poison, but their bodies were thrown away without being analysed.

While extremist pigeon fanciers might have engaged in local destruction of breeding Peregrines or their eggs and young, it seemed inconceivable that such activities, including the use of strychnine-daubed pigeons, could have been practised on the scale needed to produce the observed decline – certainly not without coming to notice. There was just no evidence of any widespread campaign of persecution against the Peregrine. The recent myxomatosis epidemic and its decimation of the British rabbit population had brought home to many people the impact of disease on a wild animal. Disease in the Peregrine remained a possibility, but there was no evidence whatever for such a cause of decline, either.

Attention quickly focussed on another factor. During the years 1956–60, there had been numerous reports from various arable districts, scattered throughout the country, of large numbers of wild birds found dead on or around fields which had been recently sown, especially with grain. The dead birds included a wide selection of species, often on the same field, ranging from small seed-eating finches, buntings and sparrows to medium-sized types such as Wood Pigeon, Rook, Partridge and Pheasant. It was soon deduced that the birds had died from eating the freshly sown seed, or that left scattered on the soil surface, which had been treated with insecticide and/or fungicide as a protection against crop pests. The incidents were further connected with the increasing use of new insecticides with the proprietary names of aldrin, dieldrin and heptachlor, which had been introduced into agricultural use in Britain around 1955–56 and had rapidly found favour among farmers because of their effectiveness. The connection between these seed dressings and the bird deaths was reinforced by the finding of the same chemicals or their breakdown products in the tissues of corpses which were analysed chemically, and by the observation that many of these birds died with convulsions and tremors, conditions produced experimentally by dosing captive birds with the same pesticides.

Before 1939 only a limited range of chemicals was available to farmers against the crop pests, and it included mainly inorganic compounds, such as those containing arsenic, or naturally occurring plant substances such as derris and pyrethrum. In 1939 D. P. Müller of the Swiss chemical firm of Geigy discovered that a long-known complex synthetic organic molecule of carbon, hydrogen and chlorine had marked insecticidal properties. This compound, dichlor-diphenyl-trichlor-ethane (later to be known as DDT), was manufactured in large quantities in the United States and Britain during the second half of World War II, and undoubtedly contributed to the outcome of that war through maintaining hygiene and preventing epidemics of insect and acarine borne disease, such as malaria and typhus, amongst civilian and military populations. After the end of the war, DDT and another new synthetic organochlorine compound, gammexane (lindane or gamma-BHC), were quickly applied against agricultural pests and disease carriers with great success. Their effectiveness was in some measure due to their persistence, as chemically stable compounds which did not quickly break down after application. Some hitherto intractable scourges of mankind, such as the locust and malarial mosquito, were controlled with dramatic success.

The new age of synthetic chemical pesticides was launched, and the search for still more effective poisons continued apace. A great advantage of DDT was its low toxicity to warm-blooded animals, and especially to Man, though there were clear indications of higher toxicity to certain fish and to domestic cats. The dieldrin (or cyclodiene) family of insecticides represented a further advance. These compounds, though chemically related to DDT and sharing the same quality of persistence, are far more toxic to birds and animals. Treating the seeds of crops, especially cereals, with these insecticides before sowing proved an especially effective way of protecting the growing plants against insect pests, but automatically created a danger for the numerous kinds of seed-eating bird.

There is good evidence that birds were killed by other seed dressings in Britain before 1955–56, but not on such a scale as to attract undue attention (Zuckerman, 1955). The large number of wild bird-seed dressing incidents, and the catastrophic scale of many of these, during the period of ascendancy of dieldrin, aldrin and heptachlor (1958–60), soon gave rise to alarm and complaint. The British Trust for Ornithology and the Royal Society for the Protection of Birds collected the evidence and presented it in two important reports (Cramp and Conder, 1961 ; Cramp, Conder and Ash, 1962). It seemed abundantly clear that these new seed dressings had, for a number of wild bird species, become a serious mortality factor over a substantial part of their British range.

There were, moreover, indications that not only granivorous birds but also their predators were being killed by ingesting the still highly active pesticide residues in the bodies of these prey species. Among the wild bird 'kills' were frequent reports of Sparrowhawks, Kestrels, Tawny Owls, Long-eared Owls, Little Owls and Barn Owls found dead on or near the same fields. And, although the evidence was largely circumstantial, there is little doubt that a sudden, widespread and heavy mortality among foxes during 1959–60, in some mainly arable districts such as East Anglia, was the result of these predators eating dead or dying birds poisoned by the dieldrin insecticides (Taylor and Blackmore, 1961). These indications of secondary poisoning naturally led us to wonder if this was the unknown cause behind the collapse of the Peregrine population. The search for evidence began.

At first sight, there was no very clear connection between Peregrines breeding in hill country relatively remote from arable farmland, and the use of dieldrin-type seed dressings. Yet it was clear that domestic pigeons were frequent victims of dieldrin poisoning on farmland and this was in many hill areas the favourite prey species of the Peregrine. Moreover, experiments with captive birds had established the general principle that any population of any species subjected to dosage with any poison will show a wide range of individual response to that poison. Toxicity of these substances has thus come to be measured as the dose rate required on average to kill half the population during the period of the experiment (median lethal dose or LD 50). And in a field situation the probability is that some birds will be more exposed to pesticide contamination than others. The implications are that in any seed dressing incident the number of birds killed will be only part of the total population, and that many will go away alive but carrying significant amounts of the poison. Some may die soon after, and some may continue to live normally. Not only domestic pigeons, but also many other birds would be likely to move on from farmland where they have absorbed toxic chemicals to non-agricultural districts inhabited by Peregrines. Many of the coastal Peregrines of southern England and some parts of Wales and Scotland also nested on seacliffs abutting arable land where seed dressings would be used widely. The chances of Peregrines picking up these pesticides by feeding on contaminated prey thus seemed to be fairly high in general, but particularly high in certain districts.

The question of whether Peregrines could obtain toxic chemical residues was soon settled. In July 1961 I visited an eyrie in Glen Almond, Perthshire. There were still, at this late date, two heavily incubated and obviously addled eggs, which I removed. One was later broken and the contents lost, but the other was given to my friend and colleague Norman Moore, who sent it to the Laboratory of the Government Chemist for chemical analysis. Our excitement was great when, some weeks later, there came the report that the egg contents contained small amounts of dieldrin, DDE (the biologically derived breakdown product of DDT), heptachlor epoxide, and gamma BHC. The amounts of these chemicals were all well below the levels regarded as lethal for experimental bird species, but their presence proved beyond doubt that a Peregrine breeding in hill country some distance from arable farmland could accumulate a variety of pesticide residues through feeding on contaminated prey. This was also the first time that the egg of a wild bird had been analysed for pesticide residues, and showed the value of this method of assessing contamination levels without having to obtain the birds themselves.

For the time being, the case for connecting causally the 'crash' of the Peregrine population with organochlorine pesticides was flimsy and open to justifiable doubt. Things nevertheless hung together remarkably well to support the hypothesis. If a Peregrine living in uncultivated hills – miles from the nearest probable source of heavy seed dressing use – could pick up readily measurable amounts of four different residues, how much greater must be the chances of contamination for falcons living close to large areas of rich farmland? The pattern of population decline matched very closely that of agricultural land use, and hence seed dressing application. Decrease was greatest in those Peregrine districts where there was most arable farming, or in those closest to the main centres of arable land, but less where there was a prevalence of permanent grassland, and least where there was little or no agriculture at all. The general trend was thus of decreasing severity from south to north, but there were local departures. For instance, along the north-east coast of Scotland from Angus to East Ross, which is bordered inland by a broad belt of rich arable land, nearly all the old eyries were deserted by 1962; yet in the extensive deer forest and grouse moor country drained by the Dee, Spey and Findhorn, and beginning hardly 35 km (20 miles) inland from these coasts, the Peregrine population was virtually normal, with no evidence of significant decline.

There was also a good correlation in dates between seed dressing use and Peregrine decline. The previous population studies of the Peregrine in Britain had pointed to a remarkable degree of stability in numbers as the norm, so that the post-1955 crash was a quite unprecedented event in the history of the species, if the local wartime 'control' during 1940–45 is ignored. Its beginnings, in 1956–58, in southern England and Wales coincided with the introduction and rapidly-increasing use of the dieldrin group of insecticides, while the intensification and northwards spread of decline, from 1959–62, corresponded with the maximum use, in geographical extent and quantity, of these substances. Other insecticides, notably DDT and lindane, were nevertheless implicated, too, as we shall see.

There were/the other symptoms of malaise in the population, apart from disappearance of birds or pairs. Some birds were in solitary possession of their eyries; others which appeared to be unpaired proved to have mates, but their attachment was loose and untypical for the breeding season. Many others were clearly paired, but appeared unable to lay eggs, though some went through the nest-scraping rituals and sometimes brooded long on empty scrapes. Of the pairs which laid eggs, many suffered failure through loss or breakage of the clutch, though with some the loss was partial, and one or two eggs remained. For the pairs rearing young, brood size was on average smaller than in pre-war years, with ones and twos more common in many areas than threes and fours. It seemed that there had developed a gradient of increasing failure, from completely normal breeding to total disappearance and presumed death of a pair. Such a sequence would be entirely consistent with a gradient of pesticidal contamination amongst individuals of a population, producing increasingly adverse effects. Experimental work had demonstrated that contamination of captive birds with levels of these insecticides below the lethal dose could, in fact, induce a range of reproductive pathology leading to lowered output of young. Chance differences in contamination for individuals, combined with variations in individual sensitivity to a particular pesticide residue level, readily accounted for the apparent capriciousness in the pattern of decline in any district. It often happened that certain pairs survived and continued to rear young, while their neighbours dropped out all around, suggesting that some falcons were more resistant than others.

THE TURNING OF THE TIDE

In the face of the strong representations made by nature conservation interests, backed by a large and irrefutable body of evidence on wild bird deaths, the Government's Advisory Committee on Pesticides and other Toxic Chemicals recommended in July of 1961 that a voluntary ban be placed on the use of dieldrin, aldrin and heptachlor for dressing spring-sown cereals. It was judged that birds were much more at risk from spring sowings than from autumn and winter sown grain, but the use of autumn dressings of these chemicals was also restricted to cereals in districts where there was a real danger from wheat bulb fly. The ban came into effect in the following spring of 1962, and in the following months there was clearly a considerable reduction in the number of bird death incidents, compared with the previous few springs. This was a hopeful trend, but what of the Peregrine situation?

As we have seen, there was no response at all in 1962, and numbers continued to plunge, with a worsening situation in the last stronghold, the Highlands. During 1963, a sample census of breeding population was made, by surveying key areas where enthusiastic helpers were checking eyries as a matter of course. The results showed disappointing evidence of a continuing downward trend, with numbers and successful breedings still lower in certain critical areas than in 1962. Single eggs were collected from 13 eyries in northern England, the Southern Uplands, and the Scottish Highlands and all proved to have residues of dieldrin, DDE, lindane and heptachlor epoxide, sometimes in substantial amounts.

Moreover, a Peregrine tiercel was found dead on its eyrie on Lundy Island off the Devon coast in June 1963; its liver proved to have 70 ppm DDE, 4·0 ppm dieldrin, 1·5 ppm heptachlor epoxide and 2·0 ppm BHC. These combined levels were considered by some scientists to approach a lethal dose, and this was the first good evidence to support the view that enhanced adult mortality caused by pesticides was a major factor in the post-1955 population 'crash'. This was news both welcome and depressing.

The 1964 figures were awaited anxiously, and to our great relief, it seemed that numbers had stabilised at around the 1963 level, with the national population at about 44% of the average level for the period 1930–39. This appeared to reflect an improvement in the pesticide situation, following from the restrictions placed on the spring use of the cyclodiene insecticides in 1962. Then, in 1964, the Advisory Committee again reviewed the persistent organochlorine pesticides and recommended further restrictions on the use of aldrin, dieldrin and heptachlor. The autumn and winter dressing of cereals and certain root crops was allowed to continue, though subject to the previous limitations, but a complete withdrawal from use in sheep dips, fertilisers and horticultural pesticide formulations was recommended.

The sample census and collection of a small number of eggs became an annual event. Monitoring of residue levels in other bird species generally showed that these increased restrictions did not significantly affect the amount of dieldrin in the Peregrine's environment until 1967, but from this time onwards, the amounts showed a downward trend in most areas. Although DDT and gamma-BHC were not included in the official restrictions, the use of these substances, as evidenced in residue levels in birds generally, also showed appreciable decline by 1967. Probably this was a response to the generally adverse publicity about the organochlorine insecticides and the widespread pressure to reduce the use of these substances as a whole.

Reflecting these further reductions in exposure to persistent pesticides, the Peregrine population began in 1967 to show an upward trend, with distinct recovery in Lakeland and the northern Pennines. Further indications of increase followed, but before going on to consider these, it is necessary to make an important digression, if the chronological picture of events is to be developed.

A MYSTERY RESOLVED

Late in 1966 the pesticide story took a new turn. I had, for several years before the onset of the Peregrine 'crash', been puzzled by the frequency with which broken eggs occurred in the eyries I examined. My acquaintance with Peregrine eyries began in 1945, and by 1950 I had examined 35 with eggs; only in one, in 1949, was there evidence of egg breakage, and since the egg lay below the eyrie ledge, I was inclined to dismiss the event as a chance accident. Then, in 1951, no less than five out of nine eyries that I examined contained the remains of at least one broken egg. The first of these left me in no doubt as to the cause of breakage. On 10 April I saw a fresh and possibly incomplete clutch of three eggs on a crag in the Thirlmere area of Lakeland. Three days later I revisited the eyrie, an easily accessible one on a ledge viewable from the side of the crag. Thinking that I might have a good view of the sitting falcon, I approached silently. The female was there, but standing over the eggs and apparently pecking at something, which

I presumed to be food. After a while I flushed her and climbed to the eyrie, to find that it was one of her own eggs which she had been eating. Pieces of shell with fresh albumen and yolk lay in the scrape, and there were the comminuted fragments, with dried contents, of a second egg which must have been broken at least a day before. The third egg was intact.

These untoward egg-breakages continued to be frequent. The appearances were usually the same as in the Thirlmere eyrie, but sometimes sucked eggs with gaping holes were found below eyries or on adjacent hillsides, and sometimes eggs simply disappeared one by one without trace. In the absence of any clues to suggest other causes, there was only one possibility to account for egg-breakage or disappearance – that the parent birds themselves were responsible. Other people were finding broken eggs and in 1952, at a Caernarvonshire coastal eyrie, P. Kimber and J. Robson watched a falcon eating its own eggs. In 1957, I thought that these strange happenings were worth recording, and published a note recording egg-breakage or disappearance in 13 out of 59 eyries with eggs seen between 1951 and 1956 (Ratcliffe, 1958). Although parental behaviour seemed to be responsible, there were no obvious clues to account for such actions and the ultimate causes remained unknown.

Egg-breaking and disappearance continued and many instances were noted during the 1961–62 censuses. Since these events were obviously contributing to reduced output of young, it was natural to wonder if they were responsible for the population decline, perhaps through a time lag effect which did not begin to show until the old, established breeding birds began to die off. Yet, decline was so sudden that the proximate cause seemed inevitably to be a rapid demise of a large number of adults, not from old age, but from a much more positive new mortality factor. While reduction in the output of young evidently contributed to the 'crash', and to the lack of subsequent recovery, it appeared a less important factor than enhanced adult mortality. Nevertheless, the egg-breaking phenomenon had become such an integral part of the chain of ill effects associated with population decline that it could be explained as an intermediate response to pesticidal contamination. Since egg-breaking became frequent after the introduction of DDT and lindane, and well before the appearance of the dieldrin group, I was led to wonder if this phenomenon could be a response to one or other of these less toxic pesticides. I set to work to collect the evidence for at least a circumstantial connection between egg-breaking and pesticides, and to consider how parental behaviour might be involved.

A draft paper was circulated to several people for comment in mid-1966. In considering all the possibilities as regards both proximate and ultimate reasons for egg-breaking, I suggested that a decrease in shell thickness could account for increased breakage, but added that there was no obvious evidence for such a change. Two friends, Desmond Nethersole-Thompson and Joe Hickey, both took me up on this point, saying that I could and should put such a hypothesis to the test, or drop it. They suggested obtaining Peregrine eggshells from before and after the onset of the egg-breaking period, and either weighing these or measuring their thickness. So this I decided to do. I had 14 of the shells of the eggs taken for chemical analysis from Scotland and Lakeland in 1963 and 1966, and had access to a few older eggs in a collection which had come into my possession.

I tried the fourteen 1963–66 eggshells first, plus a c/3 taken in 1959, and they gave a spread of weights ranging from 2·60 g to 3·77 g, average 3·21 g. Then I measured two clutches, both of three eggs, from 1945 and 1947, and was excited to find that their weights ranged from 3·20 g to 4·06 g, average 3·59 g. This looked worth pursuing!

However, it was obvious that the weight of an eggshell was strongly influenced by its size, so that it was relative weight which was the crucial parameter. In other words I had to measure the size of the eggshells as well. Reference to the technical books quickly gave formulae for determining volume and surface area of eggs, but these involved tricky measurements such as circumference. Some rapid means of measuring size was obviously needed, and since the eggs I now sought were in collections, it had to be a method which did not entail much risk of damaging any prized specimens! Length and breadth of a shell could be measured in a few seconds with vernier calipers, and when multiplied together gave a result seeming to have the properties of an area measurement, which was what I wanted. I made some elaborate measurements of surface area of some eggs and tested my size index against them: there was a linear 'fit'. I was much encouraged when my learned statistician colleague, John Skellam, thought that this was a reasonably sound pragmatic approach to the problem.

It also followed that, unless shells had become more porous, the decrease in weight was also, in effect, an index of decrease in shell thickness. A little later, Professor C. Tyler of Reading University kindly confirmed that decrease in weight of recent Peregrine eggshells had certainly involved a substantial decrease in thickness.

My next move was to visit the British Museum of Natural History in South Kensington where, through the kindness of Colin Harrison, I worked through the magnificent series of Peregrine clutches in the Edgar Chance collection, assembled in the 1930s, and so composed entirely of 'older' eggs. The weights of 34 clutches gave an average of 3·90 g. It really looked as though the breakthrough had arrived – but how to obtain more of the recent eggs to provide samples adequate for significance testing? Museums had plenty of old specimens, but nearly all recently taken Peregrine eggs were in private and largely illegal collections whose owners were naturally extremely reticent about their activities to anyone outside their own fraternity. I was able to examine one large collection with both older and recent eggs which confirmed the eggshell change, but this was still not enough.

I wrote to Desmond Nethersole-Thompson who was elated to hear that his suggestion about weighing eggs had paid off, and promptly poured his tremendous energy into 'opening the doors of the underworld', as he put it. He wrote to old collector friends on my behalf, and gave me the names and addresses of others not known to him personally. The response was greatly encouraging, for I was invited to examine the collections of all those who were approached. A tour of the country began, with my weighing machine and calipers, and the records grew rapidly as I went through those mahogany drawers with their cherished loot from the wild places of Britain. There was soon no doubt at all that eggshells of the Peregrine taken after 1947 were very significantly thinner, by almost 20% over the country as a whole, than those taken before this year. Although there were a few eggs falling below the normal range of shell thickness in 1946, the critical year appeared to be 1947, with some eggshells normal but a number showing markedly low thickness index values, the average for 36 eggs being 1·65 against 1·84 for older eggs (Fig. 9).

I had thought it worth looking at the eggshells of other species to see if this unexpected change was more general. Sure enough, there proved to be decreased shell thickness in the eggs of Sparrowhawk (17%), Merlin (13%), Golden Eagle (10%), Hobby (5%) and Kestrel (5%) among the raptors, whilst in other bird groups, there was shell thinning in Shag (12%), Rook (5%) and Carrion Crow (5%). Of other species examined, Buzzard, Raven, Guillemot, Razorbill, Kittiwake, Black-headed Gull, Golden Plover and Greenshank showed no evidence of significant change in shell thickness. Among the group showing eggshell thinning, accurate dating of the change was possible only in the Sparrowhawk, and it again appeared to be in 1946–47. In the other species, either the change was too small, or the time sequence of specimens too inadequate over the critical period, or both; all that could be said was that in each of these species, eggshell thinning evidently began not earlier than 1946 and not later than 1952.

Examination of eggshells of Peregrine and Golden Eagle going back to 1850 and of Sparrowhawk to 1890 showed that eggshell thickness had previously been remarkably constant for these species in Britain, and that the marked decrease was a quite unprecedented event. It was natural to see an immediate connection between this new event and the equally unprecedented wave of egg-breaking in all three species which dated from around the same period. The correspondence in time was not exact, though broken Peregrine eggs were noted in 1948 and 1949. Thin-shelled eggs and broken eggs in nests were known occasionally in the Peregrine during the period before 1947, but the complete shift in the range of shell thickness, and the greatly increased frequency of egg-breaking had to be

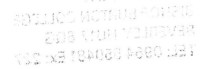

regarded as new events in the biology of the species. The eggshell change itself could hardly be explained other than through some new and extremely pervasive environmental change occurring around 1946–47. The introduction of the new organochlorine insecticides into general use for control of the pests of agricultural and horticultural crops, domestic animals and man was the only change which seemed to fit the circumstances.

It proved possible to date accurately the onset of contamination of British Peregrines by DDT. While DDT did not come into widespread agricultural use until 1948 or 1949, military stockpiles of this insecticide came onto the open market in a veritable flood after the war ended in 1945 and rapidly found a large scale use in domestic, horticultural and veterinary applications. Even in 1946, articles appeared in veterinary journals protesting about the over-lavish use of DDT, which was proving unexpectedly toxic to cats. As early as March 1946 the *Racing Pigeon* magazine carried an advertisement for a DDT formulation suitable for controlling ectoparasites on homers. So the most likely route from a DDT pack to a Peregrine was marvellously simple and direct: the dusted homers carried it straight there on their bodies. So popular did this insecticide become that the potential for contamination of a substantial proportion of the British Peregrine population by 1947 was extremely high.

I had kept homing pigeon rings removed from Peregrine eyries I visited over the years, with notes on the dates and localities. Since the analytical technique by gas-liquid chromatography had proved to be exceedingly sensitive, it seemed worthwhile to examine these rings in case any trace of residues had clung to them. My colleague Michael French analysed these rings. Most gave a blank result, but two showed the presence of minute amounts of DDT and DDE, and the older ring was taken from a Galloway eyrie with young in 1947, the other being from Snowdonia in 1956. This ring was one of the many which had been swallowed along with the pigeon's legs and then regurgitated in castings, and the residues had been in the remains of tissues still adhering to the ring. The presence of both DDT and the metabolite DDE was consistent with the explanation that the Peregrine had eaten a pigeon treated externally with DDT. This was perhaps slender evidence, but David Peakall set the matter beyond doubt by analysing solvent rinsings from a series of British Peregrine clutches taken over the critical period and held in private collections. Three clutches taken in 1933, 1936 and 1946 showed no trace of residues, but a second clutch for 1946 contained traces of DDE. Four out of five clutches taken in 1947 in Sussex, Breconshire and Wigtownshire contained DDE, the blank being from a Dumfriesshire eyrie. And eight further clutches dated 1948–52, from England, Wales and Scotland all contained DDE (Peakall, Reynolds and French, 1976). The detection, after an interval of nearly 30 years, of these tiny amounts of DDE remaining in the shell membranes and traces of the original egg contents demonstrates the great persistence of these compounds.

It is not clear how long Peregrines were exposed to DDT contamination in this way. Whitney, in 1961, listed DDT dusts and sprays as one of the most effective means of controlling ectoparasites of homing pigeons, but I was told that this chemical was eventually withdrawn from use on pigeons because of suspicions of harmful effects. As DDT came into widespread agricultural and horticultural use, from around 1948 onwards, this probably became a major source of contamination for Peregrines, though indirectly, through the eating of birds which had themselves ingested the insecticide.

Publication of the thin eggshell findings in 1967 aroused a great deal of interest and stimulated much further work. It was soon established by Hickey and Anderson (1968) that the Peregrine in the United States had undergone eggshell thinning of the same degree (around 20% on average), dating from exactly the same time (1946–47), and they went on to demonstrate post-war eggshell thinning in no less than 13 species of North American raptor, and in nine species of other bird groups, mainly fish eaters, such as the Brown Pelican. Eggshell thinning has now been shown in Peregrine populations in widely separated regions of the world (see Chapter 8). It is thus a transcontinental phenomenon, and may indeed prove to be global. It has never yet been shown to occur before the introduction of the organochlorine insecticides, and its onset has been correlated with the appearance of these substances in several countries. There is also a general, but not completely consistent, correlation between level of organochlorine contamination, degree of eggshell thinning, and population status, within the range of species concerned. For a variety of raptors, the thinner that eggshells have become, the more likely is the population to be in trouble.

A great deal of careful experimentation has established beyond doubt that the substances pp′DDT and pp′DDE are potent causative agents of eggshell thinning in a variety of captive species, such as the American Kestrel, Mallard, Coturnix Quail, North American Black Duck and North American Ring Dove. Lehner and Egbert (1969) claimed that dieldrin caused slight eggshell thinning in Mallard, but other workers have not found this insecticide to be active in this way. Eggshell thinning has not been shown with lindane, and there is conflicting evidence over whether organomercury compounds have this effect.

It has been shown in several species, including the Peregrine, that the higher the level of contamination of the parent by DDE (usually measured as the DDE content of its eggs), the greater the degree of shell thinning in its eggs. This dose/response relationship is logarithmic, so that even quite low levels of DDE produce appreciable shell thinning. In the British Peregrine, a mean level of 13·6 ppm (wet weight) DDE in eggs corresponded with shell thinning of 21%, on average. Peakall estimated that the amounts of DDE present in the eggshells he analysed from 1946–52 represented contamination levels sufficient to cause the degree of shell thinning found in these early years. In the American Kestrel, Lincer (1975) showed that the correlative relationship between DDE in the egg and eggshell thinning was the same for both an experimentally dosed, captive population and a sample of a wild population. This not only confirms the validity of the experimental testing of this effect, but also suggests that DDE on its own was the main cause of shell thinning in the wild Kestrels.

THE PATTERN OF RECOVERY

In 1969 the Advisory Committee reviewed the now massive accumulation of evidence on the adverse effects of organochlorine insecticides on wildlife, and recommended still further restrictions on the use of the dieldrin group in particular. The annual sample census after 1967 suggested that the trend

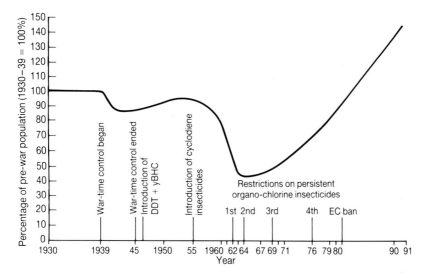

Figure 18. Decline and recovery of Peregrine population in Britain

towards recovery was being maintained in the less strongly depleted districts, in Scotland and northern England. The results of the 1971 national census showed an incipient recovery overall on a national scale, with occupied territories now at 54% of pre-war level, and the number of successful pairs at 25% of the possible total (compared with 44% and 16% in 1963). The recovery was almost entirely in inland districts from the Craven Pennines northwards, and coastal districts either showed only slight improvement or actual deterioration since 1963, as in Orkney and Shetland. In 1971, inland nesting territories in Scotland showed 90% of pre-war occupation level, but coastal territories only 53%. The levels for England and Wales were 45% for inland and 16% for coastal territories.

The third national survey in 1981 covered 93% of known territories in Britain and Northern Ireland, and showed that breeding population stood at 89–92% of the estimated 1930–39 level. Further surveillance suggested that, in total numbers, recovery was virtually complete in Britain by 1985. In Ireland full recovery had occurred in the north by 1981 and extended at least to the south-east by 1985. The fourth UK census, in 1991, revealed that overall numbers had reached around 145% of the pre-war level, so that we are into super-recovery.

The large-scale recovery of British and Irish Peregrine populations has been detailed in Chapters 3 and 4. In Britain it has involved, broadly, a reversal of the geographical/time pattern of decline, with restoration of numbers occurring first in the southern Highland fringe and Southern Uplands, and then, in sequence, northern England, Wales and south-west England.

In Britain the differences, compared with the pre-1956 pattern, are of continuing low numbers and breeding success in the coastal populations of the northern Highlands and Islands, and south-east England, and of slight decline in some inland parts of the Highlands. The increase to unprecedentedly high levels between the east-central Highlands and south-west England has more than

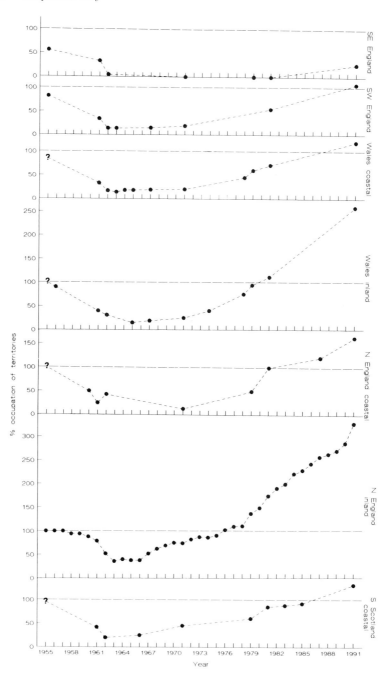

Figure 19. Decline and recovery of Peregrine population in different regions of Britain

NOTES: Records are given only for those years in which adequate samples of territories were visited. Occupation of territories is expressed as a percentage of 1930–39 population level.

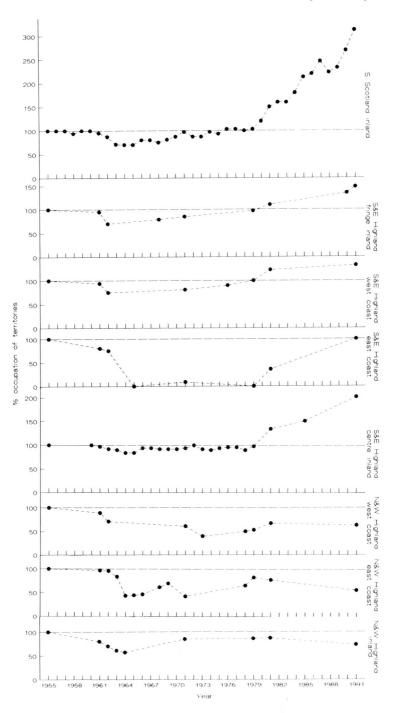

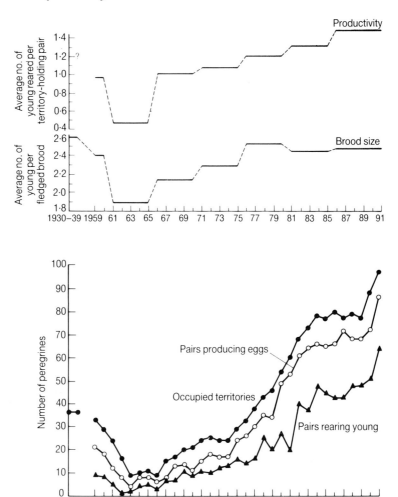

Figure 20. Decline and recovery in different aspects of breeding biology of Peregrines in north-west England

NOTES: Occupied territories, pairs producing eggs and pairs rearing young are all expressed as percentages of the 1930–39 level of population for the sample of territories examined each year.

Brood size and productivity are actual figures, though during the height of the population crash, successful breedings were so few that the records have been expressed as 4-year averages.

Data are for inland eyries in Lakeland and the northern Pennines.

compensated for the lack of recovery elsewhere. The present position confirms predictions made in the 1960s, that eliminating the use of organochlorine pesticides would be followed by restoration of Peregrine population; and that this amounts to final proof that these substances had caused the post-1955 crash.

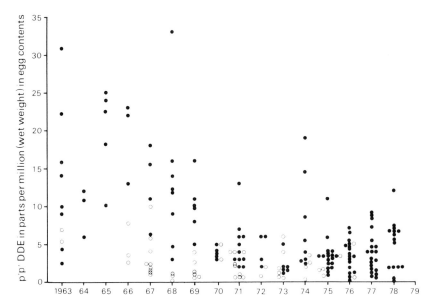

Figure 21. Changes in DDE levels in Peregrine eggs in Britain – ● eggs from N. England, S. Scotland, S. Highland fringe and Wales – ○ eggs from Central and N. W. Highlands

NOTES: Data are from Table 30 but taking means for eggs in the same clutch.

Not only Peregrine numbers, but also other affected aspects of breeding biology have shown recovery. Eggshell thickness and brood size have shown substantial return to normality in most regions (Tables 15 and 18), and the proportion of territorial birds paired and producing eggs has increased. Productivity has also increased, but this parameter is much influenced by more direct forms of human activity, and the increase also reflects the benefits of nest protection.

It appears that over much of Britain and the whole of Ireland, contamination of Peregrines by organochlorine residues has ceased to be a conservation problem. The measures taken to phase out the use of these chemicals, and thereby drastically reduce exposure to their residues, have been successful in allowing the species to recover through its own resilience. We should, however, look at the detailed picture of change and see what can be learned from it. The previously reported analysis of the Peregrine residue monitoring programme conducted by Monks Wood Experimental Station (Cooke, Bell and Haas, 1982) has been updated by Newton, Bogan and Haas (1989), in a re-analysis of all the Peregrine egg residue data for Britain from 1963 to 1986. The following revision of the salient features takes due account of this most recent work. I have judged it not worthwhile to add further to the organochlorine residue data presented in the first edition of this book (Tables 29 and 30, Fig. 20), and there is nothing to suggest that the Peregrine–pesticide story has shown any significant developments since 1989.

During the study period 1963–86, HEOD (dieldrin) residues in Peregrine eggs decreased approximately sixfold in both inland and coastal regions, but showed a slight and unexplained upturn in the central and eastern Highlands between 1980–86. DDE levels fell in parallel in inland regions, but showed a slight tendency to increase again between 1980–86, except in southern Scotland. Decrease in DDE in coastal regions was not significant, but only small samples were available. From 1963, HEOD levels have averaged around one-twentieth those of DDE, though HEOD is by far the more acutely toxic compound. Although residues of heptachlor and lindane were almost constantly present during 1963–66, they had largely disappeared by 1971. Detailed figures are given in Table 30.

While the Peregrine recovery has taken place against a *reduced* level of organochlorine contamination, it has probably been much slower and less complete geographically than if these substances had been entirely and rapidly eliminated. Probably the most important action was the restriction on use of the cyclodiene insecticides, which were regarded as the main agents of the population crash through their acute lethal toxicity. It was the stemming of the tide of enhanced mortality which stopped the decline and allowed recruitment gradually to get on top of death rate. Ironically, the huge effort put into the analysis of organochlorine residues throws little light on this angle – because it began too late. Analytical methods for these chemicals were in their infancy when the crash occurred, and the publicity which later led the public to send dead raptors to Monks Wood had not built up. Few Peregrine corpses were analysed, and several were wasted through ignorance. Moreover, egg analysis is a some-what limited technique, since it looks only at breeding females in presumably reasonable health (i.e. still able to lay eggs), and does not sample the population as a whole.

By the time tissues of dead Peregrines were analysed, the first restrictions on the cyclodienes were in force and the crash was virtually over. Probably for this reason few of these analyses showed HEOD residues high enough to account for death (Table 29). Nevertheless, the records show that some Peregrines, in widely scattered areas, continued to acquire potentially lethal burdens of HEOD up to at least 1974. In 1973, an adult pair were found dead on arable farmland in Stirlingshire, within 5 km of their nesting cliff; their livers contained 17 ($\male$) and 44 ($\female$) ppm of HEOD, by far the highest levels ever reported for this bird in Britain, and almost certainly the cause of their deaths. The only traceable use of dieldrin in the area, but a permitted one, was as a seed dressing on swedes (Bogan and Mitchell, 1973). Annual dieldrin 'kills' of pigeons and other birds continued up to at least 1975 on farmland in the Lothians, as evidence of the risks to Peregrines in eastern Scotland. It is only in the last decade that Peregrines have returned to breed on the seacliffs of this district.

The use of dieldrin as a cereal seed-dressing was finally banned in Britain at the end of 1975. While less formal restrictions were placed on DDT, there was general pressure to phase out all the persistent organochlorines, and this grad-ually took effect. All the 'bans' on the organochlorine pesticides in this country were voluntary, until EC regulations published in 1979 made them mandatory. All remaining agricultural uses of the cyclodiene insecticides were formally discontinued in 1981, and DDT was banned the following year, except for emergency use against cutworms. The residue levels still persisting are believed to represent continuing environmental persistence, especially of DDE in soil

Below: Cliffs of Pembroke coast, Wales, showing heathland, scattered woods and mainly permanent pasture behind (photo: J. K. St Joseph)

(Newtown, Bogan and Haas, 1989). It is staggering that, in a total of 550 eggs from 469 clutches analysed during 1963–86, only one egg, from the central Highlands in 1984, had no detectable DDE; and only 6% of all eggs had no detectable HEOD (Newton, Bogan and Haas, 1989).

While organochlorine-enhanced mortality probably lingered for some years after 1963, at least in some regions, it ceased to be an appreciable statistical risk for most of the remaining British and Irish Peregrine populations. The effect of pesticide residues on breeding performance evidently became the more important factor, by determining the rate and distribution of population recovery. Improvement in the related aspects of breeding impairment followed the decline in DDE contamination, though the first signs of recovery in Peregrine numbers appeared while egg residues were still quite high (mean 15 ppm) and shell thinning pronounced (15–20% below normal). In areas with low mortality of established breeders, a quite small output of young or immigration rate could allow numbers to increase steadily (pp. 291–292). The further recovery in Peregrine numbers was nevertheless associated with substantial decline in all organochlorine residues.

At the second International Peregrine Conference at Sacramento, in 1985, Ian Nisbet caused a stir by suggesting to his North American colleagues that they had exaggerated the role of DDT/DDE and its reproductive effects in causing collapse of their eastern Peregrine population; and that the cyclodiene insecticides had there been the main agents of decline, as was believed to be the case with the British population. Furious debate ensued, and when the conference proceedings eventually appeared 4 years later, there were two papers which not only refuted Nisbet's argument, but concluded that it was the British who were mistaken, and that DDT and its sub-lethal effects had really been the cause of the population crash here, too!

There has been a great deal of argument over the relative contributions of cyclodienes and DDT to the collapse of Peregrine populations in different regions of the World. In North America the prevailing view is that DDT was the primary agent of decline there, through a massive and chronic depression of productivity and probably also enhanced mortality. While dieldrin and other cyclodienes may have contributed, at least locally, the timing and scale of their use suggests that they were far less important than DDT to the main population effect. In discussing the evidence, Risebrough and Peakall (1988) have suggested that in Britain, too, this could also be the truer picture, instead of the converse one that I have presented above. The argument rests on the theoretical considerations discussed on pp. 291 and 299. Though possibly correct for limited areas (mainly south-east England), this view is, I believe, largely refuted by the balance of evidence.

I rest my case for believing that in Britain and Ireland the cyclodiene insecticides were primarily responsible for the population crash on the fact that:

1. Peregrines over much of Britain had endured 10 years of eggshell thinning (1947–56) without showing population decline. Indeed, some populations showed substantial recovery from war-time reduction during this period.

2. The population decline closely followed the introduction of cyclodienes as seed dressings, and spread rapidly as their use expanded.

3. The decline in breeding numbers was so abrupt, especially in the worst affected districts (Fig. 19).

4. Common raptors such as Kestrel and Sparrowhawk certainly figured among the widespread 'kills' of wild birds on farmland in the late 1950s.

5. The population crash halted after the first restrictions on use of the cyclodienes as spring-sown seed dressings in 1962 and 1964. The use of DDT was little affected until the 1969 restrictions.

To prolong this argument further seems rather futile. When a species faces contamination by a cocktail of pollutants, whose toxic effects are different in detail but evidently combinatory, the individual contribution of each pollutant and its effects on population performance will depend on the timing, scale and distribution of exposure to all of them. A complex theoretical model can be constructed from this basic proposition. It is equally obvious that unless there are quantities to put into this model, understanding will progress not one jot further. And since the critical information missing from the past is never likely to be forthcoming, we have run into a brick wall on the events of 1947–63.

Chalk cliffs at Beachy Head, Sussex, showing intensively arable farmland behind (photo: J. K. St Joseph)

Our concern here should be to understand why Peregrines in some regions have not recovered – or not fully – and to know how far toxic chemical problems may still be involved. Although the Dorset coast has shown appreciable recovery since 1985, breeding success here was low up to 1989, when five out of six nests failed mysteriously with no direct interference suspected. This smacked of pesticide problems. Yet in 1991, eight out of nine eyries were successful. It may be that exposure to harmful pollutants in this area is only now falling below the critical level. The extreme slowness of recovery on the coast of Sussex and Kent into 1992 is puzzling and indicates continuing difficulties here. It has been suggested that increased casual disturbance along the nesting cliffs is the problem, but I do not believe this. Even in the 1930s, people constantly passed along the top and bottom of these cliffs, but the eyries were mostly in quite inaccessible situations and the Peregrines were indifferent to the disturbance. For want of any other tenable explanation, continuing pesticide effects have to be the suspect cause of falcon problems here.

The Peregrine cliffs from Dorset to Kent are hard up against rich arable lands which are annually drenched with a galaxy of different pesticides (see above), and must be the area of Britain where the species has been most immediately and heavily exposed to contamination by residues, of both the organochlorines and other pesticides. There was always the worry, back in the 1960s, that insufficient attention was being paid to other kinds of chemical. Events have appeared to confirm that Norman Moore was right to commit most of the very limited Monks Wood resources to study of the persistent organochlorines. There were considerable analytical problems with many other compounds, and for the many non-persistent pesticides there was both the theoretical and practical problem that they could neither cause secondary poisoning nor be detected in tissues.

Organomercury fungicides were regarded as potentially dangerous because of their persistence, and as a probable contributory factor in raptor declines. However, when the restrictions on cyclodienes rapidly brought beneficial results, it seemed that these were the chemicals needing closest attention. Insufficient attention was paid to organomercury residues, and it is only recently that Newton and Haas (1988) have found that they may well be involved in decline of the Merlin in Britain. These substances have always been regarded as heavily implicated in the decline of Peregrines in Sweden, where they were much used as seed dressings, and in the wood processing industry (Lindberg and Odsjö, 1983).

Some non-persistent organophosphorus and organosulphur compounds are directly toxic to birds which ingest them, and under certain circumstances, might have secondary effects on predators feeding on poisoned prey. The totally unexpected effect of the organophosphorus compound carbophenothion on grey geese has served to underline the need for continuing vigilance and the dangers of complacency. In parts of eastern Scotland where this insecticide was used widely, there were several 'kills' of Greylag Geese, involving up to several hundred birds at a time. It appears that, through biochemical chance, this group of birds has a brain cell enzyme which is particularly sensitive to the compound in question, though this was quite unpredictable from toxicological testing on other animals. Although measures were taken to reduce this particular risk, the case well illustrates how, with all reasonable precautions observed, serious hazards to wildlife from pesticides can be expected to arise at intervals, as new chemicals with adverse properties for some species are introduced.

Although the development of resistance to pesticides is theoretically possible in birds, through selection for the genetically more resistant individuals in a population, there is no evidence to show that it has occurred; and in a slow-breeding species such as a raptor it would tend to be a lengthy process at best.

MARINE POLLUTION

The slowness or lack of recovery of the coastal Peregrine population in Shetland, Orkney, Caithness, Sutherland, Wester Ross and the Western Isles is less easily explicable. Peregrines from these districts could winter in lowland country farther south and there become exposed to substantial pesticidal contamination. A more probable explanation is that coastal Peregrines become contaminated by a wide range of marine pollutants, including pesticide residues, but also other chemicals. Pesticides from a variety of sources, including both agricultural and industrial, enter the sea in considerable quantities, and there accumulate via marine food chains, along with other substances of urban/industrial origin, including heavy metals.

In 1966, a Swedish chemist, S. Jensen, drew attention to the potential hazards of another group of persistent organochlorine compounds which had become widespread, cumulative environmental pollutants, the polychlorinated biphenyls (PCBs). These are industrial chemicals, widely used in plastics, lubricants (including oils) and insulating materials, and released into the environment in various ways. While PCBs were used industrially before 1939, they have shown a substantial increase in use during the post-war period, and have proved to be important global pollutants. They accumulate in birds feeding in freshwater and marine habitats.

Chemical analyses carried out in Britain since 1966 have shown Peregrines to be widely contaminated by PCBs, with generally low levels (<10 ppm) in inland birds but quite high levels in some coastal birds (Tables 29 and 30). The PCBs are similar to DDT, and appear to produce similar effects in having a relatively low acute toxicity to birds, but with a range of sub-lethal effects, including reduced breeding performance. Some workers have claimed that they cause slight eggshell thinning in certain species, and there is evidence that they produce increased embryonic and chick mortality in the Sparrowhawk (Newton and Bogan, 1978). Their significance to the Peregrine is not known, though Newton, Bogan and Haas (1989) found no correlation between PCB egg residues and productivity. High levels found in some coastal birds must nevertheless be suspect as an additional hazard which may well amplify the effects of the other persistent pollutants.

Limited analyses of Peregrine eggs from Scottish coastal areas show that they consistently contain higher levels of mercury than those from inland areas, but there is no information about other heavy metals. These substances are among the more important marine pollutants, though their effect on Peregrines is unknown. Coastal Peregrines in areas remote from agriculture can also accumulate quite high levels of DDE and dieldrin. Two northern Scottish coastal Peregrines were found dead in 1971, one at Dunnet Head, Caithness and the other near the Butt of Lewis in the Outer Hebrides. Both proved to be heavily contaminated: the first bird had liver residues of 200 ppm PCBs, 50 ppm DDE, 3·0 ppm dieldrin and 1·6 heptachlor epoxide; while the second had 60 ppm PCBs, 23 ppm DDE and 2·1 ppm dieldrin.

An obvious source of all these residues is the truly maritime birds which feed on both plankton and small fish, and are collectively important Peregrine prey when available: namely gulls, including especially the Kittiwake; terns, petrels, notably the Fulmar; and auks, especially Guillemot, Razorbill and Puffin. It is striking that the coastal areas where the Peregrine is faring best at present are those with fewest rock-breeding seabirds, whereas the areas where it is least successful include those with the major concentrations of such seafowl. Taken as a group, such seabird haunts as Bempton, Bass Rock, Isle of May, Fowlsheugh, Berriedale, Duncansby Head, Dunnet Head, Handa, Clo Mor, North Rona, Flannans, Mingulay, St Kilda, Shiants, Marwick Head, Noup Head (Westray), Noss and Hermaness have an extremely poor record of Peregrine occupancy and success since around 1960. In contrast, the Peregrine has made a marked recovery on some parts of the west coast of Scotland where there are only small numbers of these seabirds, especially in Argyll, Ayrshire and Galloway. It could be that Peregrines frequenting major seabird haunts inevitably build up contamination levels inhibitory to breeding, if not actually lethal. There is a puzzling difference between Orkney and Shetland, both of which are notable for their large seabird breeding colonies. Orkney has maintained a fair level of territory occupation, but with indifferent breeding success: in 1991, there were 22 occupied territories, at least 15 with pairs, of which certainly four and possibly up to nine reared young. Shetland has had few Peregrines and even fewer successful nestings since 1962: in 1991, numbers were down to five single birds. Ellis and Okill (in press), in analysing the Shetland situation, suggest that lack of immigration could have been a problem, once the population was seriously depleted. The only ringed Peregrines recovered there (five) were all reared in Shetland. Further knowledge of food supply, prey spectrum and winter distribution/ movements might perhaps throw light on the difference in Peregrine status between these two island groups.

An additional problem for coastal Peregrines, especially in these northern areas, is that they are considerably at risk from Fulmars breeding on the same seacliffs, through the aggressively defensive habit of these petrels of ejecting stomach oil at other species. The evidence has been discussed in detail in Chapter 12, and I repeat my conclusion here, that while Fulmar oiling has become frequent, and has certainly caused the death of some Peregrines, there is no evidence that it produces mortality serious enough to limit coastal populations. It could, however, as Ellis and Okill suggest, combine with pollutant effects and lack of recruitment to hold down a depressed population. It could also be a secondary factor affecting individuals whose normal vigour and feeding behaviour are impaired by other causes, such as heavy load of toxic pollutants or physical injury.

There is international concern to clean up pollution of the sea, and measures have been taken to stop the deliberate dumping of toxic wastes offshore. Pressure to reduce the amounts of toxic substances, including pesticide residues, in industrial effluent may have had some effect, but PCBs continue to appear widely and often at high levels in the bodies and eggs of seabirds and Peregrines. Despite measures to reduce the environmental release of PCBs in Britain in 1971, levels in Peregrine eggs have increased in some inland areas. They have declined in some more southerly coastal districts of Scotland, but increased in the coastal northern and western Highlands (Newton, Bogan and Haas, 1989). It is still more difficult to control the movement of agricultural toxic chemicals from the land into the waterways, and thence via the main rivers to the sea. If marine pollution is, in fact, a major reason for the present low state of some of our coastal Peregrine populations, it may yet prove to be a particularly intractable obstacle to their full recovery, in view of the foot-dragging on meaningful action to clean up the seas.

OTHER COUNTRIES

The post-1945 status of Peregrine populations in other parts of the World has been extremely varied, from regions where the species disappeared to those where it has remained normal and flourishing. And the position of any population along this gradient has been closely related to the degree of contact with persistent toxic chemicals. The worst affected populations have been those resident, or only partially migrant, in extensive agricultural regions, e.g. the eastern United States and southern Canada. Migratory populations breeding in wilderness country but wintering in agricultural regions and/or feeding on contaminated migrant prey have also been highly vulnerable, e.g. Fennoscandia. Sedentary Peregrine populations in undeveloped country or regions with limited or primitive agriculture with little pesticide use were the least affected, e.g. the Queen Charlotte, Alexander and Aleutian archipelagos, parts of Australia, and probably much of Spain.

Status in Europe up to the mid-1970s was reviewed by Bijleveld (1974), Chancellor (1977), Lindberg (1977) and Cramp and Simmons (1980); but has been updated to the mid-1980s by papers in Cade *et al.* (1988), and by inputs to the European Bird Database of the Birdlife International/European Bird Census Council. Briefly, the picture is as follows:

Norway:
Sharp decline from 500–1000 pairs around 1900 to less than 10 known in 1975. Subsequently a modest recovery to over 50 pairs in 1985 (Lindberg, Schei and Wikman, 1988). 150–200 pairs in 1992 (Gjershaug *et al.*, in press.)

Sweden:
Over 1000 pairs before 1900. Decreased during 1930s through persecution and 350 pairs estimated in 1965, 14 in 1972 and only 4 in 1976 (Lindberg, 1977). Marginal improvement to 10–20 pairs, nearly all in northern Sweden in 1985 (Lindberg, Schei and Wikman, 1988). 25 pairs in 1990 (T. Larsson and L. Risberg *in litt* to EBD 1993, citing Lindberg, 1896).

Finland:
At least 1000 pairs formerly, divided about equally between cliff and ground sites. Declined towards end of 1950s, but more slowly during 1970s. In 1972 a survey showed that only 27% of 139 cliff sites and 36% of 153 bogs were still suitable (Salminen and Wikman, 1977). In 1976, 39 out of 200 territories were occupied but only 19 by breeding pairs, all on bogs of northern Finland. At least 50 pairs, mainly north of latitude 66° N, in 1985 (Lindberg, Schel and Wikman, 1988). 100 pairs in 1990 (p. Koskimies *in litt* to EBD 1993).

Denmark:
Two to five pairs in 19th century. Last nesting attempt in 1972, but failed (Donark, in Wille, 1977). One pair in 1992 (H. H. Brask, pers. comm.).

Belgium:
In 1950–55, 15–20 pairs bred; in 1964 only 4 pairs; in 1971 one bird seen, subsequently believed extinct (Verheyen and Dambiermont, in Bijleveld, 1974).

Netherlands:
From 1900–79 bred 11 times, two ground nests and nine tree nests. In 1991 a pair bred successfully in a Carrion Crow nest on a building (Schepers *et al.*, 1992).

Luxembourg:
Bred in three valleys in 1940s, 3 pairs in 1960, extinct in 1965 (Morbach, Hulten and Wassenich, in Bijleveld, 1974).

West Germany: In 1950 estimated 400–430 pairs, of which 50 pairs were exclusively tree-nesters in the north-east (Mebs, 1969, 1988). Breeding performance became poor in early 1950s, and decline set in, with 305–315 pairs in 1955, 210–220 in 1960, 105–120 in 1965 and about 75 in 1968–69 (Mebs, Kuhk and Bezzel, in Glutz *et al.* 1971). Only 40 pairs remained in 1975, but thereafter numbers increased again, with 140 occupied eyries in 1985 and expanding annually. The tree-nesting population became extinct quite early in the decline (Mebs, 1988).

East Germany: A pre-1940 estimate of 300–500 pairs, with still 140–150 active tree-nest territories in 1950. There was decline to a total 85 pairs in 1960, 36 in 1965 and 24 in 1970. Virtual extinction followed some time between 1974–79, and although the species was nesting again in 1980, only 5 pairs were known in 1985 (Kleinstäuber and Kirmse, 1988).

France: Monneret (1988) has doubled the previous estimate of pre-1950 population to 900–1000 pairs, including Corsica (100 pairs). The bulk (c. 700 pairs) were in the Jura, Alps and Pyrenees. Decline began in the north-west (60–65 pairs) before 1955, and was complete by 1963. Small numbers lingered in the Vosges and Burgundy areas, but the southern mountains still had 150–180 pairs by 1970. The decline halted around 1970, and within a few years clear signs of recovery appeared, leading steadily to the healthy position of 570–660 pairs for the whole country in 1985.

Switzerland: Fifty known haunts 1951–65, declining from 20+ pairs before 1960 to 16 in 1961, 10 in 1965, 9 in 1967 and 1 in 1970 (H. Herren, in Bijleveld, 1974). The revision by Juillard (1988) gives the earlier population as 150–200 pairs, and reports an increase in the Swiss Jura from 1 pair in 1971 to more than 50 in 1985; with nearly 100 pairs in the whole country. 120–150 pairs in 1990 (O. Biber *in litt* to EBD 1993).

Austria: Sparse in 1950, but at least 50 pairs. Decline during 1950s and 60s and only 5–8 pairs in 1977 (Bauer, in Cramp and Simmons, 1980). 80–100 pairs in 1990 (A. Ranner *in litt* to EBD 1993, citing Gamauf, 1991).

Spain: A widely distributed population of at least several hundred pairs in mid-1960s was stable or showed only slight decline by 1971 (Bernis, in Bijleveld, 1974). Still 2000 pairs in 1975 but decreasing (Garzon, in Chancellor, 1977). A survey reported by Heredia *et al.* (1988) revealed 1628–1751 pairs, as a conservative estimate. Symptoms of decline in 1970–80 were noted, but the population now appears stable.

Italy: A reassessment by Allavena (1988) gives a relatively healthy and stable population of 430–550 pairs, 67% of which are in Sicily, Sardinia and the smaller islands. It is unclear whether there was any decline contemporary with that in other parts of Europe.

Czechoslovakia: In Moravia 10 pairs in 1955, 1 in 1970. Disappeared from Bohemia around end of 1950s. Still in small numbers and declining (>10 pairs?) in 1965. At least 2 pairs in 1969 (various authors, in Bijleveld, 1974). Hudec (1988) gave 1–4 pairs as the fluctuating level in 1975–85.

Poland: At least 180 pairs, probably many more, in 1935, mostly in trees. Decline since mid-1950s and probably at least 50 pairs left in 1960s, perhaps only 15 pairs in 1971 (Glutz *et al.* 1971; Sokolowski, in Bijleveld, 1974). Possibly up to five pairs in 1990 (M. Gromadski *in litt* to EBD 1993).

Greece: 100–250 pairs in 1990 (J. Catsadorakis *in litt* to EBD 1993).

Croatia: 150–200 pairs in 1990 (G. Susic *in litt* to EBD 1993).

Soviet Union: There is little recent information on any USSR populations. Fischer (1967) estimated 450 pairs in the forest zone and 400–500 pairs in the tundra zone of European Russia in earlier years, but this was said by Galushin to be decreasing (Cramp and Simmons, 1980). In Estonia, 40 pairs in 1947–57 had dropped to less than 10 in the mid-1960s and to evident extinction by 1972 (Kumari, in Bijleveld, 1974). Extinct in Latvia and Lithuania (Cramp and Simmons, 1980).

During the last 100 years the Peregrine seems to have been a sparse breeder in Albania, Andorra, Bulgaria, Hungary, Romania, Portugal, Cyprus and Malta. Present status is uncertain, though the limited data available suggest a tendency to decline in at least some of these countries, and the only suggestion of a substantial reservoir is in Turkey, with 100–500 pairs (Cramp and Simmons, 1980).

Although relatively little work has been done on pesticides and Peregrines over much of continental Europe, informed opinion in most countries where there was decline accepts that the organochlorines were responsible. The general synchrony of the declines in different countries, the similarity of the effects (including eggshell thinning and reduced breeding performance), the closeness of the correlation between falcon distribution/movements and predictable exposure to agricultural chemicals, and the scattered analytical evidence of DDE and dieldrin residues in the species, all add up to support the view that there is a strong cause–effect relationship here too. More direct human impact has been an important factor in local decline, but when allowance has been made for this, it is quite inadequate as a total explanation of the scale and rate of decrease across almost the whole of Europe. Recovery again matches restrictions placed on organochlorine pesticides in most European countries. Newton (1988) has summarised the population changes and organochlorine evidence for Europe as a whole.

In the New World the Peregrine has declined variably. North America probably held between 7000 and 10,000 breeding pairs before 1940 (Kiff, 1988). The breeding population of the eastern United States, conservatively estimated at around 350 pairs before 1942, began to show symptoms of incipient decline in 1947, had decreased strongly by the mid-1950s and was virtually extinct by 1964 (Hickey, 1942, 1969). This is the best documented population. At the Madison Peregrine Conference in 1965 it was clear that Peregrine populations in other parts of the United States and south-eastern Canada had undergone serious decline, and by 1970 the large populations of the *anatum* and *tundrius* races in the taiga and tundra regions of North America were declared to be in dire trouble, with numerous territory desertions and abundant breeding failures. In 1975, a mammoth survey of Peregrine breeding grounds over a large part of North America was undertaken by a big team of field surveyors and the results were worrying indeed (Fyfe, Temple and Cade, 1976). The *anatum* race of Peregrine persisted as a sparse and scattered breeder in western regions from Baja California and northern Mexico, through the mountain systems and canyons of New Mexico, Arizona, Colorado, Utah, Wyoming, Idaho, Nevada, Montana, California and Oregon; and in the coastal ranges of the last two states and Washington. In 1975, only 62 occupied haunts were found plus another 39 possibly occupied out of 557 known breeding localities in the whole of this vast territory, and only 18 broods were known.

In Canada breeding Peregrines were still apparently absent in 1975 from Alberta, Ontario, the Maritime Provinces and southern Labrador, which formerly held at least 46 pairs. Good numbers of Peale's Falcon remained in the Queen Charlottes and the Aleutians in 1975 (105+ occupied haunts out of a known total of 162+, but with the possibility of nearly another 400 pairs in remote and unvisited islands of the Aleutian chain. In the taiga and tundra regions of Alaska and northern Canada the former size of the Peregrine population is unknown, but this huge wilderness country must have held considerable numbers of the bird, even though it was apparently not regularly distributed. Fyfe (1969) estimated a former population of 7500 pairs in northern Canada. The 1975 survey checked 349 known taiga territories, in northern Alberta, the Mackenzie District, the Yukon Territory and Alaska: 97 were occupied, another 50+ were possibly occupied, and 35 + broods were reared. In the Arctic tundra regions of western Greenland, northern Quebec, the Arctic Islands, the North West Territories and Alaska, 184 known localities produced 60 pairs, nine possibles and 34+ broods.

Much careful work established that these remaining populations of the *anatum* and *tundrius* races of the North American Peregrine were sufficiently contaminated by DDE residues to account for a rate of reproductive failure which reduced productivity to around or below the critical replacement level. Peakall *et al.* (1975) tentatively concluded that 15–20 ppm DDE in the egg was the critical level for hatching failure in the Peregrine, and found that during 1968–73 DDE residues in Alaskan Peregrine eggs were well above this level, at 20–70 ppm. Eggshell thinning was regarded as the main intermediary factor in the high rate of breeding failure of falcons still breeding in North America. Samples of eggs of Aleutian Peale's Falcon contained lower DDE levels, in the range 3–5 ppm, and their shell thinning level of 8% was regarded as insufficient to cause a rate of egg-breaking and breeding failure which would lead to population decline; whereas 12–13% thinning and 17 ppm DDE in Queen Charlotte *pealei* eggs approached the critical levels for a downward trend (White and Nelson, in Fyfe, Temple and Cade, 1976).

The relatively sedentary habits of the *pealei* race protected this population, whereas the strongly migratory *tundrius* falcons move far south to Central and northern South America, there to acquire considerable loads of DDE in the developing agricultural parts of these regions. Their prey populations also collect considerable residue loads in their wintering and passage haunts and carry these back to the northern wilderness regions in spring. Heavy restrictions on DDT use in the United States and Canada since the early 1970s have, however, borne fruit, and the 1985 Peregrine conference brought welcome news of recovery through parts of North America. In Alaska, where the taiga *anatum* race had declined by 55% and the tundra *tundrius* race by 65% in the early 1970s, numbers began to increase again in the late 1970s and were still doing so at the last reported surveys, in 1987 (Ambrose *et al.*, 1988). There was also dramatic recovery on the Yukon and Porcupine Rivers in the Yukon Territory, though earlier groups on the North Slope and Southern Lakes were extinct in 1984 (Mossop, 1988). It was less clear whether decline had occurred in other parts of the Canadian Arctic, but stable and healthy or increasing populations were reported in 1985 for Ungava Bay, Quebec (Bird and Weaver, 1988) and the Northwest Territories (Bromley, 1988; Bromley and Matthews, 1988). Peale's Falcon was found to have increased in the Queen Charlotte Islands, while the previously stable Aleutians population remained so. Another important Arctic Peregrine population, in south and west Greenland, estimated at 400–500 pairs, was stable and reproducing remarkably well after recovery from minor decline during 1965–75 (Mattox and Seegar, 1988; Falk and Moller, 1988).

The northern Peregrine populations can thus be regarded as once more being in a normal and flourishing state overall. Indeed, Cade *et al.* (1988) estimate, from trapping rates of banded migratory Peregrines on passage, that between 5000 and 10,000 pairs nest north of latitude 55°N, and that the number has been increasing since 1975.

In the western United States south of Canada, the recent picture has been variable, from regions with marked recovery to those with none, but without any clear geographical pattern. In many areas, assessment has been hindered by the lack of any previous survey information, both for pre-1940 years and for the main period of decline 1940–70. Recovery has been strongest in Colorado, Utah, the northern coastal ranges and central coast of California, Arizona, southern Baja California and the Gulf of California. Less certain increase has occurred in Washington, Oregon, the Sierra Nevada, Texas and northern Mexico; while Peregrines are still few or absent in Idaho, Montana, Wyoming, northern and southern coastal California and the Channel Islands, and northern Baja California. The western region of the United States held at least 443 pairs in 1989 (The Peregrine Fund *Annual Report*, 1989). There is concern that DDE levels in eggs and eggshell thinning in many regions are still critically high for successful reproduction. Where recovery has occurred, it has often been slow, even though aided by eyrie manipulation (double-clutching and fostering of chicks hatched in captivity) and numerous releases of captive-bred adults.

The Peregrine Fund reported that, in 1991, at least 30 pairs of Peregrines (22 of them nesting) were located in the Midwest and Great Lakes region, while the eastern States held no fewer than 91 territorial pairs, of which 51 were successful (Cade, 1991). This recovery from extinction represented the successful results of the huge captive breeding and release programme pioneered by the Fund and its Founding Chairman and Director, Tom Cade, at Cornell University and later Boise, Idaho. In south-east Canada, at least 20 pairs are again breeding, as another response to numerous captive bred releases there (Cade, 1991).

The former population of around 1500 pairs of *Falco peregrinus anatum* south of Alaska is now evidently restored to around 40% of its former size. The hope and expectation is that, as environmental contamination by DDT/DDE gradually declines, the breeding nuclei will gradually build up numbers to levels limited only by the food supply and availability of suitable nesting places. And since many falcons are now habituated to man-made structures, including city buildings, the scope for increase is considerable. The greater Philadelphia and New York City areas had seven and ten pairs in 1991. The overall situation in North America is thus propitious.

Other regions

In South America Peregrines breed widely in western regions from Ecuador to Tierra del Fuego, and may well prove to be more widespread as survey extends. The estimated population of at least 1000 pairs appears to be stable and healthy (McNutt *et al.*, 1988).

Cade (1979) noted that there was little information about Peregrines in Asia, though declines were reported from some parts of Siberia (e.g. the Yamal Peninsula; Galushin, in Chancellor, 1977) and indicated indirectly by other evidence, including a high level of eggshell thinning locally (Peakall and Kiff, 1979), and a reduction in the migration stream of Peregrines passing through the Middle East (J. Mavrogordato). Almost a decade later, Cade *et al.* (1988) reported that the situation is still obscure, though one estimate is for several thousand pairs nesting in the former Soviet Union east of the Ural Mountains. Southern Asiatic and

Indian races have apparently declined, but few data are available, and Cade describes occurrence of the Peregrine in China as the greatest enigma of all in Asian distribution. Japanese ornithologists have said that the species has decreased in the islands of Japan from several hundred pairs to only 54–68 pairs known since 1982.

In Australia, Olsen and Olsen (1988) report a large and generally healthy population estimated at 4500 pairs, widely distributed wherever there are suitable cliffs. Local declines, of up to 20%, were apparent in some of the most heavily agricultural districts, in Tasmania and Victoria, and were closely correlated with levels of DDE contamination and eggshell thinning. Recovery has taken place in most of the affected districts. Large sections of the Australian population had little contact with pesticides and remained unaffected.

Only in a few parts of the world have Peregrines so far been shown to be free of organochlorine residues, e.g. in certain of the Indonesian islands and some desert regions of Australia. While there may be a number of other remote populations which are virtually free from contact with these substances, *Falco peregrinus* is rightly regarded as an endangered species on the global scale.

SOME REFLECTIONS

The anxiety of the early 1960s, that the Peregrine in Britain and Ireland was possibly heading for extinction, now seems a distant memory. While there remains a slight concern, that numbers in a few districts are still below normal, the overall position is that our Peregrine population has never been in better state. While complacency is always dangerous, this appears to be one of the few conservation successes of the post-war period, relieving the general sense of environmental deterioration that has caused such serious losses of wildlife and habitat during the last half century. Part of this success story is attributable to good luck and part to hard work. The good luck was simply the fact that, at the height of the crash, the Peregrines in some regions were less exposed to pestical contamination than in others. It was especially the mountain ranges of the Scottish Highlands which held a viable segment of the Peregrine population – a region sufficiently large, remote and productive for considerable numbers of the bird to live throughout the year in an almost pesticide-free environment. If it had not been for this chance of nature in providing ecological sanctuary, our Peregrine could have gone the way of the species in Fennoscandia or the eastern United States: reduced to very small numbers or totally extinct.

The hard work part of the story was spread over some years. There were the dedicated efforts of field ecologists and laboratory scientists, painstakingly collecting and sifting the evidence, and then building it into a sound and convincing case. Two major landmarks stand out in the development of the scientific offensive on the growing problem of pesticide effects on wildlife in general, and on raptor populations in particular – for in Britain serious declines in numbers of Sparrowhawks, Kestrels, Barn Owls and in breeding success of Golden Eagles were also reported (Prestt, 1965). In July 1965, Norman Moore convened at Monks Wood Experimental Station an international symposium which brought together for the first time scientists from many parts of the World who were working on various aspects of this rapidly developing subject. The resulting

synthesis gave perspective to the problems and served to convince participants of the paramount importance of the role of the persistent organochlorine insecticides (Moore, 1966). In September 1965, Joseph J. Hickey convened a World conference on the Peregrine Falcon in the University of Wisconsin, bringing together American and European Peregrine enthusiasts to discuss the evidence for the possible causes of the apparent decline in the species in many parts of the globe. This was by far the most exciting scientific meeting I have ever attended, with a clear goal, and I believe it had a tremendous effect in stimulating various lines of work on the conservation of the Peregrine. The fruits of this symposium were published as *Peregrine Falcon Populations. Their biology and decline*, edited by J. J. Hickey (1969).

The scientific campaign would have achieved little without a great deal of exacting committee work in which a few people patiently presented the evidence and argued the issues over and over again with a largely unsympathetic and, at times, hostile majority. In Britain, the brunt of this wearisome task of convincing the unwilling fell on Norman Moore, formerly head of the Toxic Chemicals and Wildlife Section of Monks Wood Experimental Station. The successful outcome, in the form of progressive restrictions and phasing out of the most harmful compounds is a tribute to Norman's skills of diplomacy and persuasion, and to his scientific authority.

It was not an easy time. Some of us had our first experience of scientists playing politics, and we learned how vicious a vested interest under pressure can be. It was clearly in many people's interests, one way or another, to believe that the wildlife conservationists were talking nonsense, and they left no stone unturned in trying to establish this. Every new paper with more evidence was dissected and gone over minutely, to see what flaws could be found. Some of the toughest opposition came, not surprisingly, from the agrochemical industry's own scientists, but certain members of the Government's agricultural establishment were well to the fore. Tactics at times resembled those of the courtroom rather than the scientific debating chamber and 'smear technique' was openly used. There were tedious arguments about the nature of proof and the validity of circumstantial evidence. The attempts to deny effects of pesticides on wild raptors descended now and then into obscurantism. When the evidence for eggshell thinning was first presented, one Ministry of Agriculture scientist declared it to be an artefact, caused by the weeding out of thinner shelled eggs in collections, through differential breakage with the passage of time! And a senior official of the Department of Agriculture for Scotland refused permission for his analyst staff to join with me in authorship of a paper presenting the results of egg residue analysis they had made.

One can have a fair argument over differences in viewpoint, on whether wildlife is being treated as more important than agriculture, whether banning dieldrin and DDT in Britain could cost human lives in the Third World, and so on. This is all good, honest stuff, and one can respect a straight opponent, or agreement to differ at the end of the day. What is not acceptable is when paid apologists resort to deliberate special pleading, rhetoric and debating tricks, and when some scientists feel such moral indignation or need to defend personal attitudes and positions on such issues that they allow themselves to do the same. Some of the pesticide protagonists actually said that because it was 'only wildlife' set against pressing human needs, the acceptable level of proof of cause and effect had to be of an altogether higher order than in a more neutral scientific issue. The validity of a scientific hypothesis or argument is quite unrelated to its relevance to human affairs and value judgements. Not that the other side showed on the whole any great desire to establish the real truth of the matter. They were much more concerned to find evidence to support their own case, and their unhelpful attitudes, delaying tactics and covering up of unpalatable facts made it that much harder for the truth to be found. It was a close-run thing and the Peregrine could easily have been brought to the edge of extinction if action had not been taken in 1962.

It is only fair to say that the nature conservation side had a wild fringe given to making irresponsible statements, which embarrassed those trying to establish the facts. In the end the accumulating weight of hard, irrefutable evidence and the total lack of any convincing counter-evidence slowly silenced the pesticide apologists and brought reluctant concessions by way of reducing the wildlife hazards. There are still mutterings from people, including eminent scientists, who will never be convinced, and continue to deny the evidence. There is nothing to stop scientists taking irrational views if they so wish, but they destroy their own credibility with the rest of the scientific community. The consensus of informed opinion accepts the case as proven, and that is what matters. Nowadays, the Government's Pesticide Safety Precautions Scheme (PSPS), which has to clear new products and new uses against information provided by manufacturers on their effects, provides a crucial defence against a recurrence of such problems. Though it can never give a cast-iron screen against new wildlife hazards, there has so far been a considerable measure of success. Had the PSPS existed before the introduction of the organochlorine insecticides there might never have been a problem of the magnitude of the one that had to be faced. It must, however, be said that the Government's Advisory Committee on Pesticides, which operates the PSPS, works behind closed doors in an atmosphere of great secrecy. To most scientists this is unnecessary and to citizens in general is unacceptable because it is so far removed from the 'open-government' approach to such matters which we were promised. It is now 22 years since the Committee last published a report on its work.

Over most of the western World, governments have accepted the evidence of environmental hazards posed by the organochlorine pesticides, and either banned them outright or phased them out. The EC has instituted a mandatory ban to be upheld by member states. The good results of this action are reflected in the trend to recovery of Peregrine populations in almost every country where decline was reported. Yet, in Europe outside Britain and Ireland, only France, West Germany and Switzerland report substantial increases. There are, moreover, still large areas of the world where the Peregrine situation remains unclear – in European Russia, Africa, most of Asia and South America. The organochlorine insecticides still find a ready market in the undeveloped countries, where the scale of human casualties of pesticide poisoning generally is an indication of the lax standards of control. Previous evidence has shown that organochlorine and other pesticide use in Latin America posed serious contamination risks for many migratory North American Peregrines and prey species wintering there. There are worries that many bird species, in different countries, are being adversely affected.

While we may take heart from what has been achieved, the pesticide story is far from ended, as a global issue.

CHAPTER 14

Other enemies

It should be abundantly clear that Man is enemy in chief of Peregrines in most parts of the World, and the few bird predators have been mentioned in Chapter 12. The remaining enemies are the other carnivorous mammals and, more importantly, the agents of sickness and disease.

MAMMAL PREDATORS

The cliff-nesting habit is likely to be an adaptation against various ground predators besides Man. In Britain the ranks of such species have been thinned by extinction, and the fox is probably now potentially the most serious vertebrate enemy. The occasional taking by foxes of young Ravens from the more accessible crag nests has suggested that these mammals could be predators on Peregrines, at least while the young falcons were still in the eyrie. Yet it was not until 1979 that I heard of a definite instance of such predation. At a Pennine eyrie, Paul Burnham found that an eyass which had fallen from the eyrie to the ground below was taken one night by a fox, though the other youngster flew successfully. In 1983, T. Pickford found a brood of young Peregrines evidently eaten by a fox at a Lakeland eyrie. Foxes would normally have little chance of raiding even the more accessible cliff eyries because one or other parent, usually the female, is nearly always on guard nearby, both day and night. The aggressiveness of nesting Peregrines towards dogs suggests that they would not hesitate to attack a fox, and Cade has seen such attacks in Alaska. In Devon, I. Waldren watched a tiercel and three fledged eyasses stoop repeatedly at a fox which appeared on the cliff-top above their eyrie, just missing its head. They kept up this performance until the animal retreated to 400 m. The commensal association between ground-nesting Peregrines and other birds in Siberia is an indication that Arctic foxes give the eyries a wide berth.

The more nimble pine marten, polecat and feral mink might have more success in raiding a cliff eyrie by means of a quick dash and then hiding, though they would stand even less chance than a fox if the Peregrine caught them in the open. Pine martens have been regarded as significant predators at Peregrine eyries in continental Europe, especially Germany, and efforts made locally to deter them (M. Everett). Even the stoat and weasel, which are to be seen at times about Peregrine crags and are known to predate Merlin nests occasionally, might attack an unguarded brood. The wildcat would also be a potential enemy in the Scottish Highlands. There are no records of any of these mammals predating Peregrines or their eyries, and the risks would seem to be quite small.

In North America there is a larger contingent of ground predators which might attack Peregrines. Raccoons have been suspected of predating eyries locally (e.g. in Hickey, 1969) but the evidence is uncertain. Beebe (1960) has pointed out that the introduction of such ground predators as raccoons or rats to islands with large seabird colonies could affect Peregrines indirectly, through reducing their food supply. Nelson (1990) suggests that such effects, by rats, may have been a factor in the Peregrine decline on Langara Island. More powerful carnivorous mammals such as wolverine, wolf and lynx would seem to pose a bigger threat to the more easily accessible Peregrine eyries, though tropical Africa presumably musters the biggest line-up of potential predators. Altogether, though, there is no evidence anywhere in the World that mammals other than Man are a significant factor in the population biology of the species.

PARASITES AND DISEASE

Peregrines, as predators feeding on an extremely wide range of prey species, must be exposed to contact with a large number of parasites and pathogens. The Madison Peregrine conference was at some pains to examine the possibility that epidemic disease could account for some of the declines in falcon populations then reported (Hickey, 1969). Distinguished pathologists and parasitologists who also had a keen interest in raptors discoursed on the various infections and organisms known to occur in Peregrines, both wild and captive, and examined the likelihood that any of these could have produced the kind of mortality and sub-lethal effects indicated by the observed population changes. The main problem in such an issue is to determine how far infestations and diseases which are known to cause deaths of individual birds could also be responsible for deaths on a massive scale. It is the difference between 'normal' death rate and epidemic mortality. Any bird carries organisms which are potentially capable of causing illness or even death and, apart from direct trauma, infectious or parasitic disease is usually the commonest cause of death in wild birds (Jennings, 1961). Moreover, a bird which is weakened by some other factor, such as cold, starvation, poison or injury may become more prone to a sickness which actually kills it. It is thus not sufficient to establish that Peregrines have died of a range of infections or parasitic diseases; an enhanced scale and rate of death have also to be shown before the importance of such conditions as population factors can be asserted.

At Madison, Trainer (1969) listed trichomoniasis, aspergillosis, coccidiosis and heart filaria as infectious diseases known in captive Peregrines, and trichomoniasis, botulism, myiasis (fly maggot infestation) and filaria in wild falcons. He also pointed out that a number of diseases could produce a range of symptoms, from varying degree of reproductive impairment and ill-health to actual death, corresponding closely to those observed in declining Peregrine populations. Stabler (1969) discussed the possibility that trichomoniasis, well-known to falconers as 'frounce' and a scourge of captive hawks, could have been involved in Peregrine declines. This disease is caused by a protozoan parasite *Trichomonas gallinae* living in the mouth, throat and crop of an infected bird and causing, in virulent strains, extensive lesions which may block the passages or produce an excess of toxins. Pigeons are the normal host of this organism, but Stabler concluded that because of the predominant occurrence of non-virulent strains, which normally produce immunity in the host bird against virulent strains, there is little risk of trichomoniasis causing more than low level mortality in the Peregrine. The Madison conference conclusion was that the case had not been made for implicating disease as the cause of collapse of Peregrine populations and breeding performance across two continents (Hickey, 1969).

Even for the diseases which might seem more likely to be possible causes of decline, and which produce symptoms parallel to those observed in a pesticidally-induced decline, there is no evidence of infections on the scale which would have to occur, if this were the real cause of a population decline. Botulism is a long-standing and recurrent epidemic disease amongst some waterfowl populations, and while some raptor species are said to have died from it, and Peregrines are known to have eaten infected ducks in some places, there is just no evidence to suggest that it could have been responsible for more than local and small-scale deaths in this falcon. Recurrent epidemics of Newcastle disease (fowl pest) in wild birds have also been suggested as possible causes of raptor declines.

Ian Prestt, who studied the population status of the smaller British raptors, was concerned to elucidate the part played by disease in mortality. His study involved close consultation with specialists in avian diseases and the post-mortem examination of several hundred raptor specimens, but no evidence to suggest an unusually high incidence of any particular lethal infection was found. It so happened that the appearance of Newcastle disease and infectious bronchitis in Britain in 1947 coincided with the onset of eggshell thinning – and various diseases are known to produce shell thinning. Infectious bronchitis is unknown in wild birds, but Greenwood (1977) states that Newcastle disease was recorded sporadically in birds of prey and then more frequently in 1970–72 when there were serious outbreaks of this disease amongst poultry in Britain. Greenwood mentions work which showed that there was a highly virulent and infective strain of virus and that Kestrels and Barn Owls were most susceptible, though no species was completely resistant. Populations of these species had declined in parts of lowland and especially eastern England by 1965 (Prestt, 1965), and there was no indication that disease caused any noticeable change in the situation in either species in 1970–72.

Greenwood also discusses two diseases, avian pox and herpesvirus hepatitis, which occur in non-raptor species in Britain, and have infected raptors abroad. In such instances he suggests that risks of infection from importation of captive raptors should be minimised by still stricter quarantine regulations. He also suggests that, since the virus causing 'louping-ill' in sheep has been isolated in Red Grouse in Scotland, this disease might be another hazard to Peregrines here. Tuberculosis is known in a number of British raptor species, and Peregrines are quite likely to be exposed to this disease, as also to pseudotuberculosis, salmonellosis, listeriosis, aspergillosis and erysipelas (Greenwood).

Greenwood has further discussed the circumstances under which disease can affect wild raptor populations, and the conditions under which the impact on numbers would be likely to be most serious. He believes that the known mortality survey figures in wild birds, of 10–25% of deaths attributable to infectious disease or parasitism and another 10–25% to other organic disease, may be less than the true incidence of such conditions in the wild. While, as he suggests, a great deal more pathological determination, especially of virus infections, is needed to establish the true state of affairs, this will only be ecologically meaningful if it is paralleled by a fairly close monitoring of mortality rates in the populations of the same species. Wild birds have to die of something, and if other factors such as pesticide poisoning or the traumas of direct persecution diminished, it would be quite likely that disease-induced death would increase as a major alternative mortality factor. Sub-lethal effects attributable to toxic chemicals might also undergo substitution by 'inapparent' disease, leading to reduced fertility, egg hatchability, growth and lifespan. In birds which die from 'natural causes', disease is likely to be at least a contributory factor to death in a majority of individuals. Conservationists are thus more worried by disease when this becomes a major additive cause of death or when, from a position as major mortality factor, it causes a substantial increase in actual death rate.

Nelson (1970) has suggested that the tendency of Peregrines to switch between alternative nest sites in different years is an adaptation which reduces the risk of parasite and micro-organism infection. A befouled eyrie with litter of prey remains after a brood has flown is a veritable incubation ground for parasitic and disease organisms, and must indeed provide a fair risk of infection to a bird which returned the following spring. Chapman (1924) also suggested that Ravens used alternative sites to allow at least a year's cleansing of the old eyries by the elements. It is perhaps best not to take this idea too far, since the same eyrie is very often used by Peregrines (and Ravens) for at least two years running, and in the cool, wet British winter quite a lot of cleansing of an eyrie ledge can occur. Except in very sheltered sites, droppings usually disappear within a few weeks. The habit of the young in defaecating outwards from the eyrie ledge and of the parents in removing prey remains could be regarded as sanitary devices, yet they are variably developed among individuals.

The role of disease in Peregrine ecology is at present little understood, and has been eclipsed by the preoccupation with pesticide problems. It is such a highly specialised field that knowledge is likely to grow but slowly, and one hopes that people with the necessary expertise and facilities will give the subject more attention.

I am grateful to Professor John Cooper for the following additional statement, and a list of relevant organisms and conditions (Table 31).

DISEASES IN THE PEREGRINE

By Professor John Cooper, Sokoine University of Agriculture, Tanzania

In its broadest sense 'disease' means any 'impairment of normal physiological function affecting all or part of an organism' and therefore includes nutritional disorders, developmental abnormalities, poisoning and other causes of ill-health as well as conditions caused by living organisms such as viruses, bacteria, fungi and parasites.

Most information on diseases of Peregrines comes from studies on captive birds, but these are of value in providing information on the diseases to which the species is susceptible. Captivity also offers opportunities for controlled studies on these conditions – for example, host/parasite relations – which may be relevant to free-living Peregrines. Other information has been gleaned from investigation of Peregrines found sick or injured (Greenwood, 1977; Cooper, 1978) and these help to throw light on factors that may contribute to morbidity (ill-health) or mortality (death) in the wild. There has, however, been remarkably little study of apparently normal Peregrines, and relevant work has tended to be part of larger surveys (e.g. on bacteria), with little or no attempt to relate the findings to population status.

Non-infectious diseases have been reported in many captive Peregrines and include nutritional deficiencies such as osteodystrophy, visceral gout, fractures, luxations and various types of poisoning (Cooper, 1978; Cooper and Greenwood, 1981). Non-infectious conditions should not be overlooked in any analysis: apart from their possible role *per se* in morbidity and mortality they may predispose a bird to infectious disease. Developmental abnormalities occasionally occur both in captivity and in the wild.

Many infectious diseases have been reported from captive Peregrines and a few described in birds living in the wild. It is important to distinguish, however, between 'infection' and 'disease'. A Peregrine can be *infected* with an organism such as the bacterium *Salmonella*, and perhaps be excreting it in its faeces, but may exhibit no clinical signs. 'Disease' on the other hand, implies that the Peregrine is not only harbouring the organism but is also showing evidence of ill-health. Under certain circumstances an 'infection' may develop into a 'disease' for example, if the Peregrine is stressed or the number of organisms to which it is exposed become excessive. Thus, as studies on other captive falcons have shown, small numbers of *Capillaria* worms can be tolerated without any obvious ill-effects while large numbers are likely to cause diarrhoea and dysentery, sometimes culminating in death.

The Madison Peregrine conference looked into the possibility that infectious disease might account for some of the decline in falcon populations then reported (Hickey, 1969). The scientists involved in the debate were not, however, able unequivocally to implicate any of the many conditions known to kill captive Peregrines in the decline of free-living populations. Subsequent conferences on diseases in birds of prey – for example, the International Symposium in London in 1980 (Cooper and Greenwood, 1981) and its successor in Minnesota in 1987 (Redig *et al.*, 1993) – began to focus on the possible role of infectious agents and disease not in *killing* birds of prey, but in having an adverse effect on aspects such as egg production or growth rate, and thus influencing populations in more subtle ways, through 'a reduction in fitness'. It is not only the diseases with epizootic (epidemic) potential that must be evaluated when considering the role of infectious organisms in population dynamics but also those that are present much of the time (enzootic) which may be having a less obvious effect.

While much of the recent work on avian parasites has involved species such as grouse rather than Peregrines, it is relevant to the present discussion. Current thinking is that a parasite may be at a selective advantage if it successfully transmits its offspring to other hosts, even if it kills itself and its host in the process. Parasites are often density-dependent and as such may regulate host populations.

It is not sufficient to consider only those conditions that might under certain circumstances cause disease and death on a large scale. *Any* organism that can loosely be termed a 'parasite' – whether 'macro' (such as a worm) or 'micro' (such as a virus) needs careful evaluation. With this in mind, some examples of organisms and diseases reported from captive or wild Peregrines are listed in Table 31, together with brief notes on their effects.

A particularly encouraging feature has been the tendency in Europe, North America and elsewhere, for those interested in the role of toxic chemicals to work much more closely with veterinary pathologists and parasitologists so that dead Peregrines and other birds of prey are investigated fully. In time, this multidisciplinary approach will undoubtedly yield information which will help us to understand better what part infectious and non-infectious diseases might play, both on their own and in combination with other factors, in the population biology of the Peregrine.

CHAPTER 15

Appearance, form and geographical variation

Brown and Amadon (1968), Hickey and Anderson (1969) and White and Boyce (1988) have given an account of the different races of *Falco peregrinus*, while Cramp and Simmons (1980) have dealt with those of the Western Palaearctic. I do not intend to go into any depth over taxonomy and distribution, nor to describe plumages and other morphological or anatomical features in detail. This information may be found in the works just mentioned, and I shall give only a condensed treatment here, based on the nominate race *peregrinus* and indicating some of the geographical/ecological divergence which has taken place from this.

THE NOMINATE FORM

Size (mm)

Adult: Sexual size dimorphism is especially pronounced, as follows:
  Male: Wing 290–325, wing span 785–890, tail 130–160; bill to tail 400–450, tarsus 45–49.
  Female: wing 345–370, wing span 930–1000, tail 163–185, bill to tail 450–490, tarsus 51–56.
Juvenile:
  Male: Wing 305–325, tail 147–159
  Female: Wing 350–375, tail 173–190

Females are on average about 15% larger than males and juveniles are slightly but significantly larger than adults (Cramp and Simmons, 1980). Females have relatively larger and more powerful feet and talons than males.

Weight   (g)

Adult:
  Male: 580–770, av. 680
  Female: 925–1300, av. 1125

The size difference is usually fairly obvious when a pair are flying together, but if they are at varying distances it may be much less clear. The female is a bulkier looking bird with a fractionally heavier flight, but now and then a small female mates with a large male and I have seen pairs in which the two sexes were difficult to identify even when close together. I share Dick Treleaven's wonder at the ornithologists who can tell at a glance whether a single Peregrine is male or female. As he says, outline, and especially shape of the wings, depend on how the bird is flying, and this depends on factors such as wind. Treleaven mentions an interesting observation by the late D. M. Reid Henry, that the eyes of the two sexes are exactly the same size, so that those of the male appear relatively larger.

Wing-loading

The Peregrine is a powerful bird, heavy for its size and with long, fairly broad but pointed wings, and a relatively broad, short tail (compared with other falcons). Brown and Amadon have discussed the effect of wing-loading (ratio of total weight to wing surface area) on flight in raptors. They comment that since wing-loading tends to increase with size, it must vary somewhat within *Falco peregrinus*, as between males of the smallest race and females of the largest race. Their one figure, 0.63 g/cm^2, for a male Peregrine of 813 g was double those of smaller falcons in the range 145–282 g. I would suggest that a more meaningful measure of wing-loading would be one that discounted the effect of increasing size (attributable to the fact that area increases as the square, while volume (= weight) increases as the cube). Otherwise there seems likely to be an anomaly in that female Peregrines would have higher wing-loading than males, which would contradict the general point that high wing-loading goes with greater agility in flight. Cade (1982) has since given figures of 0.52–0.91 g/cm^2 for Peregrines, and confirms that wing-loading measured in this way is usually higher in females than males, for a range of raptor species.

In general, Brown and Amadon are correct in pointing out that low wing-loading is associated with the slower type of raptor flight in which gliding and soaring are important (the harriers, eagles, buzzards and vultures) and high wing-loading with the rapid, flapping and manoeuvrable type of flight (the falcons and accipiters). Peregrines are, nevertheless, much given to soaring and have a steep and rapid rate of climb in an up-current. They are also capable of long migrations, and can evidently make crossings of the major oceans.

Adult plumage

The upper parts vary from dark slate to dove-grey tinged with blue, the rump being the palest and bluest area, and the outer wings and head the darkest. The mantle, back and wing coverts are faintly barred transversely with darker slate and have paler edges, while the rump and upper tail coverts are more strongly barred, and the markings on the primaries, secondaries and tail feathers form broad horizontal bands. The upper part of the head is dark slate, with this colour extending as a still blacker broad moustache from the base of the bill to below the eye. The size and shape of the moustache varies greatly between individuals and is a means of identification, though often only reliably so in photographs. Some falcons have a complete hood of black-brown, but there is typically a paler forehead, above the base of the bill.

The under parts are white or cream, though the actual shade is variable, the chest usually tending to a warm buff or even salmon-pink or pale rufous tint, especially in the female, whereas the males are whiter. Some birds are grey-fronted and Walpole-Bond (1938) and Nethersole-Thompson (1931) each commented that Sussex coast Peregrines tended towards dirty-grey on the chest. Perhaps this was noticeable against a background of chalk cliff. The upper middle part of the breast is marked with vertical ticks, then spots, wedges, crescents and arrowheads of dark slate which quickly change to the horizontal bars of the lower breast, underwing and undertail coverts, flank and thigh feathers. The auxiliaries and underwing coverts are especially heavily barred. Apart from the facial moustache and chest colour, the main individual variations in Peregrine plumage are in the heaviness of the horizontal barring on the front, and the distance this extends upwards towards the throat. Females tend to be more heavily barred than males. All the large wing feathers, the primaries and secondaries, have heavy transverse bars of dark slate, and this shows up especially in the underside view (see p. 156). The tips of the outer primaries show slight emargination. The tail feathers are paler, with more conspicuous barring on the underside.

Juvenile

The plumage differs from that of the adult in that there is an overall brownness, and although on the upper parts this is very dark and dull and merges into slate colour, the characteristic tendency to blueness in the adult is mostly lacking. The frontal plumage is altogether darker, with the light colour a distinct buff or dirty white and the smaller body feathers more heavily marked with brown to red-brown in a different pattern: those of the upper chest are usually vertically streaked and this changes on the lower chest and flanks to broader, wedge, diamond or pear-shaped marks which may cover the whole feather except for a conspicuous pale edge. The facial moustache is less distinct and horizontal barring limited to broad banding of the larger wing and tail feathers and their coverts. There is a conspicuous cream-coloured terminal band to the tail which is much reduced and barely noticeable in the adult.

Colour tone of the darker plumage in Peregrines is highly dependent upon lighting conditions. In dull light an adult can sometimes appear as brown as a juvenile when seen from some angles, while from above in bright sunlight the same bird can look as grey-blue as a Rock Dove. For this reason I tend to be chary of accepting every record of breeding juveniles. Treleaven (1977) has pointed out that unfledged eyasses often have a distinct, bluish, grape-like sheen to their plumage, but that this fades when they begin bathing. He also suggests that the browner colour of the young provides especially good camouflage when they crouch flat on a ledge.

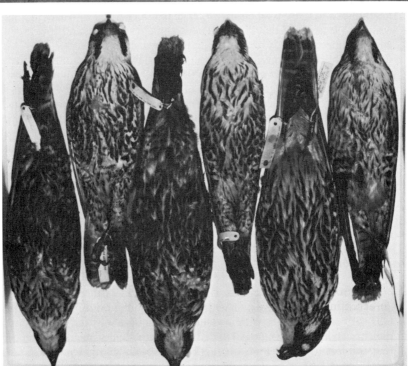

Cabinet skins of British Peregrines, showing plumage variations and sex differences. Above: Adult birds; males upper row, females lower row. Below: Immature birds; males upper row, females lower row (photos: D. A. Ratcliffe), courtesy British Museum (Natural History). The upper photograph is smaller in scale than the lower.

Although Peregrines are fond of bathing in water and do so frequently, they appear to be disadvantaged, especially in hunting, by prolonged heavy rain (Frederick II, 1250; Baker, 1967). Beebe (1960) has commented that Peale's Falcon, living in the excessively humid climate of the Queen Charlotte Islands, has a powder down on the feathers, in both young and adults, which appears to waterproof the feathers against the drenching rains and damp mists of the region. He found that, in captivity, other forms of Peregrine and other species of falcon lacked this ability to shed moisture and eventually became wet, bedraggled and dispirited if shelter was lacking; whereas Peale's Falcons did not absorb water and remained lively. The powder down gives a glaucous appearance to the juveniles. Kennedy (1970) has given a detailed discussion of the effects of rain on birds, and indicates that flight impairment could be an important factor in the Peregrine.

Moult

There is a good deal of variation in time of first moult by the juveniles: it begins in some in the first March of life and in others it is still incomplete by December (Witherby *et al.*, 1939). Most young birds probably moult in April–June, i.e. at age 10–12 months. Juveniles which pair and even breed (always with an adult partner) are often in transitional plumage, with a mixture of dark brown and slate grey. Ernest Blezard saw an eyrie with three eggs at which the juvenile female had cast two opposite primaries on the ledge. The adult plumage is assumed at the first moult and there is so far no evidence that it changes with age, though some writers have asserted that the tendency to blueness increases. Birds breeding in adult plumage can thus be of any age from two years upwards.

Adult breeding Peregrines do not usually begin to moult until nesting is well advanced or actually over, i.e. during May–July in Britain, though most incubating birds usually leave a scatter of down and small body-feathers in the nest-scrape. Some individuals begin earlier, in April, while others do not start until late summer or even autumn. Moult usually begins with the primaries and takes 18–26 weeks to complete (see Cramp and Simmons, 1980, for details).

In common with other raptors, Peregrine tail and wing feathers sometimes show 'hunger traces' – horizontal marks across the shaft representing points of weakness where the feathers can easily snap off. Falconers are on the look-out for these in their birds and repair breakages by 'imping' (attaching an equivalent portion of new feather by a pin), but they may be more frequent in captive than wild birds, often as a result of a period of starvation when eyasses are first removed from the nest.

Bare parts

In the nestling the iris is black, and the cere and feet pale grey. Juveniles have a dark brown iris, a blue-grey bill with darker tip, and the cere, eye ring and feet are blue-grey to blue-green, with the feet sometimes greenish-yellow. Adults have a dark brown iris, a slate blue bill tipped black on the upper mandible, and cere, eye ring and feet usually yellow, the feet being especially bright yellow (Cramp and Simmons, 1980) or occasionally almost orange (Treleaven). Treleaven (1977) notes that the feet of young birds can vary in colour from blue-grey through greenish yellow to pale butter yellow, and believes these variations are connected with diet. The talons are black.

OTHER RACES

The other races of *Falco peregrinus* vary in number according to taxonomic viewpoint. Dementiev (1951) recognised 22 races, but Brown and Amadon (1968) reduced the number of subspecies to 18, by deleting *F. p. germanicus*,

An early Peregrine portrait, c. 1910; Isles of Scilly, south-west England
(photo: Francis Heatherley)

arabicus, caucasicus, brevirostris and *pleskei*, but adding two more, *F. p. submelanogenys* (S.W. Australia) and *F. p. madens* (Cape Verde Islands), and treating *F.
kreyenborgi* as a separate species. *F. kreyenborgi* from the southern Patagonia and
Tierra del Fuego region has since been regarded as a pale colour phase of *F. p.
cassini* (Ellis and Garat, 1983). There remains disagreement over whether the
Old World desert forms, the Barbary Falcon *F. p. pelegrinoides* and Red-naped
Shaheen *F. p. babylonicus* should be regarded as separate species. In the latest
taxonomic revision, White and Boyce (1988) accept the Brown and Amadon
treatment, but add *F. p. tundrius* which has become distinguished as the Arctic
tundra Peregrine of North America and Greenland. Nineteen subspecies are
thus currently recognised (see Fig. 22).

The various races of Peregrine seem to conform to Bergmann's Rule in that the
low latitude forms in the hotter climates tend to be smaller and the high latitude
forms in the colder climates tend to be larger. Those around the coastal north
Pacific regions are the largest of all, while the desert forms are the smallest,
especially in Africa. Peregrines are pale coloured in dry climates and dark in humid
climates, and those of hot, dry climates tend to rufous colour, with the Barbary
Falcon and Red-naped Shaheen pale and distinctly red-brown on the nape. The
Mediterranean *F. p. brookei* is intermediate between these and the typical
European race. The formerly widespread United States form *F. p. anatum* is a
generally darker, more heavily barred form than the nominate race of central and
northern Europe. Peale's Falcon *F. p. pealei* of the north-east Pacific islands is
probably the largest race and one of the darkest, while the Arctic forms in both the
New and Old Worlds, *F. p. tundrius* and *F. p. calidus* are very white underneath. The
race in the south-west Pacific islands *F. p. ernesti* is another very dark, heavily
barred form. In some of the dark Peregrines the 'moustache' effect is extended into
large cheek patches which give a black-headed appearance to these birds. Brown
and Amadon (1968) should be consulted for descriptions and colour illustrations
of the various races, and White and Boyce (1988) for a learned essay on the
taxonomic problems of this species.

Ecological divergence

Although the habits of only a few races of Peregrines have so far been reported
in the literature, there appears to be a general and striking similarity in breeding
biology between the forms studied. Perhaps the most notable difference is in the
degree to which the migratory habit is developed, largely in response to the
behaviour of the prey populations. This is discussed in Chapter 9, and is most
marked in Peregrine populations of various races north of about 55°, or perhaps
at lower latitudes in continental regions with intensely cold winters. More local
movements also occur in other latitudes according to largely climatically
determined movements of the main prey species.

Adaptation to different climatic regimes has produced a number of physiological adjustments. Fischer (1967) has surmised that the length of the period
between courtship/nest site selection and laying is contracted in the strongly
migratory Peregrines. He showed that actual laying time is strongly dependent
upon latitude/temperature and that clutches are completed as follows: in the
Mediterranean region (Spain and Sicily) around the end of February to the

F. p. pealei   F. p. peregrinus   F. p. calidus

F. p. brookei   F. p. cassini   F. p. babylonicus

beginning of March; in the lowlands of central Europe (S. Germany, Switzerland) around early to mid-March, but in the higher Alps and Jura not until a month later; in north and east Germany in early April; in Britain and southern and central Sweden between 9 and 15 April; in the central European parts of Russia during late April or early May; and in the taiga and tundra regions of the Arctic at the end of May or in early June. The latitudinal range of Peregrines appears to involve a parallel gradient of conditioning to change in daylength, and to achieve successful captive breeding, it has been important to adjust photoperiod to the regime appropriate to the region of origin of each pair.

The Peregrine is everywhere largely a bird feeder, though it takes a small proportion of mammals, mainly ground-dwellers, but locally bats. Cade (1960) reviewed Peregrine predation on lemmings reported in various parts of the Arctic and concluded that the species is an opportunist feeder on these rodents and not a lemming predator such as the Snowy Owl or Pomarine Jaeger (Skua), which are highly dependent on lemmings, as regards both numbers and reproductive performance. Court (1986) later found local adaptation to lemming prey in a tundra population of Peregrines in northern Canada. Hickey (1969) has concluded that wherever it is found, the domestic pigeon is the favourite prey of Peregrines: in Britain, France, Belgium, Holland, Germany, Sweden, Spain, the eastern United States (formerly), parts of Australia, and in cities the World over. Only in regions where there are few or no pigeons is the Peregrine forced to concentrate on other prey. In the Boreal and Arctic regions inland, prey consists mainly of duck, waders, grouse, gulls (including skuas and terns) and passerines (e.g. Cade, 1960, for Alaska; Hautola and Sulkava, 1977, for Finland; Schej, 1977, for Norway).

One of the most interesting ecological divergences in any race of Peregrine is the apparent feeding specialisation of *F. p. pealei* on certain seabirds even when a

*Female Peale's Falcon, snared near the eyrie for banding (ringing) studies; Amchitka,
Aleutian Islands, 2 June 1970 (photo: Clayton M. White)*

variety of other bird forms is available (Beebe, 1960; Nelson, 1970). This has
been commented upon in various places (e.g. p. 118) and appears to break the
rule that the Peregrine is a catholic bird feeder in most parts of its global range.
The adaptation to small auks and petrels allows Peale's Falcon to capitalise on the
huge abundance of these prey species within parts of its limited range and to
achieve the highest breeding density yet known in any race of *Falco peregrinus*; yet
it also renders it vulnerable to collapse in food supply, as seems to have happened
in the place of highest density, with resulting decline in falcon numbers (Langara
Island; Nelson 1970). Curiously, this largest form of Peregrine on average takes
some of the smallest prey.

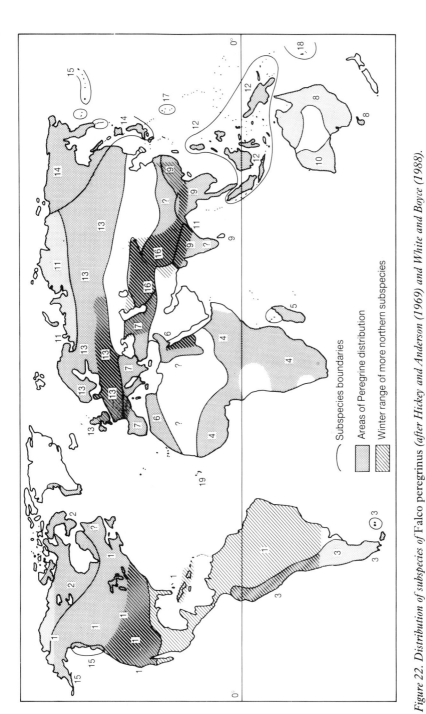

Figure 22. Distribution of subspecies of Falco peregrinus *(after Hickey and Anderson (1969) and White and Boyce (1988).*

NOTES: 1 *anatum*, 2 *tundrius*, 3 *cassini*, 4 *minor*, 5 *radama*, 6 *pelegrinoides*, 7 *brookei*, 8 *macropus*, 9 *pergrinator*, 10 *submelanogenys*, 11 *calidus*, 12 *ernesti*, 13 *peregrinus*, 14 *japonensis*, 15 *pealei*, 16 *babylonicus*, 17 *furuitii*, 18 *nesiotes*, 19 *madens*.

The Peregrine is primarily a cliff-nester in virtually all parts of its World range, and the local departures from this habit are intriguing. In particular, the quite wide region of tree-nesting in northern Europe around the Baltic seems not to expand, yet it has been an apparently successful adaptation. Tree-nesting is strangely local in North America and Australia, too, as though it has not quite 'caught on' there. True ground nesting is evidently quite widespread in Siberia, but rare in Arctic North America, and the fascinating habit of breeding on the hummocks and ridges between the pools of patterned bogs in the Boreal forest region is far more restricted than the occurrence of the habitat itself. One suspects that incidence of ground nesting in raptors may be linked with level of mammal predation, but the connection is not obvious in this instance. These could be evolutionary developments which have not yet proceeded very far or are perhaps held in check by arresting factors not yet understood.

Dust bathing

CHAPTER 16

Conservation and the future

In recent years a great concern has developed over the possible extinction of quite a large number of wild creatures and wild plants, including some of the most spectacular remaining members of the world fauna. In virtually every case, the threat to survival stems from some aspect of man's growing domination of the globe. Man is increasingly competing with wildlife by exploiting the productive capacity of land and water to the limit for his own ends, so that the maximum amounts of energy and nutrients are channelled into crop species, and less and less are left for wild plants and animals. Often the damage is caused by destruction of habitat for agriculture, 'tree-farming' modern forestry, or some form of urban–technological development. Sometimes it results from the removal of species seen as competitors with man, which are labelled as pests and subjected to campaigns of control or eradication. In some instances it is exploitation of wild animals themselves as a crop which directly threatens their existence. In yet another direction it is both the deliberate and the incidental outpouring of a galaxy of chemical substances, both naturally occurring and man-made, but all in some degree harmful when in excess, which results in destruction of wildlife and degradation of habitat. We now face the threat of change in global climate through atmospheric pollution.

The birds of prey and other vertebrate predators are, in a sense, key species in their particular ecosystems. Because they stand at the top of the pyramid of numbers and represent the terminal focus of energy in a wildlife community, they are likely to be sensitive to any important changes that may occur in the whole system of inorganic habitat and living organisms. In particular, these predators can be expected to respond to any environmental changes which are sufficiently powerful and pervasive to impinge on their prey populations as a whole. The birds of prey may thus be the most sensitive indicators of changes in their ecosystems. This has been the case with the Peregrine and pollution. During the last three decades the species has acquired a new symbolism, not only as one of the Earth's wild creatures most threatened by 'progress' but also as an ecological barometer which has pointed so clearly to the enormous implications of uncontrolled release of toxic chemicals for impact on the global environment. The Peregrine–pesticide issue was in the forefront of the new wave of concern for the environment. In the pollution field alone this concern has led to the rapid growth of a huge new area of research and a literature so vast that even specialists have difficulty in keeping up to date.

The Peregrine's particular 'indicator value' in this context may be partly the result of the chance that it appears, with other raptors, to be especially sensitive to the organochlorine insecticides, but it is also partly an expression of its special ecological position. Nor is the species alone in this respect, either. Several other raptors in Britain showed reduction in breeding performance and/or numbers, attributable to the same cause: the Kestrel, Sparrowhawk, Barn Owl, Golden Eagle and Merlin. Along with the Peregrine, these species – except the last – have recovered well from the adverse effects of pesticides. The present position of our raptor populations is, indeed, one of the few success stories in nature conservation in this country. After the gloomy predictions of extinction made in 1963–64, the Peregrine has pulled back strongly and beaten all expectations.

The synthetic pesticides and perhaps to a lesser extent the industrial pollutants so reduced the Peregrine populations of Europe and North America that *Falco peregrinus* was declared one of the World's endangered species and added to Appendix 1 of the Convention on International Trade in Endangered Species of Wild Fauna and Flora. There has, happily, also been a considerable recovery of Peregrine populations in mainland Europe south of the Baltic, and in parts of North America. While the Peregrine can still be regarded as endangered in certain regions, such as Fennoscandia and perhaps the Islands of Japan, the designation 'threatened' would now be more appropriate over some other parts of its World range. This would recognise that the species is extremely vulnerable to spread of the damaging effects of environmental pollutants, as agricultural intensification and urban–industrial development continue to expand over the undeveloped regions of the World.

The problem for this and other raptors is much larger than one of pollution alone, and amounts to expansion of all aspects of human impact on environment. Although I dislike having to use such an analogy, it seems to me that nature conservation is comparable to being on the weaker side in a long-drawn-out war, in which the other side has overwhelmingly superior forces and must eventually and inevitably win. Certain positions may be held and even small readvances made locally, but on the whole the line of the defenders is gradually beaten back. While the other side's overall plan of campaign is obvious enough, it may be difficult to know where the next attack will occur and in what strength. In this situation, the defenders' strategy must be one for minimising losses overall and maintaining maximum tactical flexibility to repel new advances. So it is with nature conservation. Having won a particular battle, we have to shift the weight of our defence or counter-attack to another part of the front where pressure is heavier, but we can never assume safely that there will be no renewal of attack at the site of recent victory.

What hazards for the Peregrine lie ahead? There could be more pesticide or other toxic chemical problems ahead; with new substances, at least, if not with the old ones. The intensification of land use, especially through modern methods of farming and forestry, will do nothing to help the Peregrine and could, foreseeably, reduce its food resource. Other human activities may impinge more adversely on the bird than at present. Yet I, for one, would not have the confidence to say that we can predict all the eventualities for threat. I prefer to see a lesson in the fact that the last and most serious threat to the Peregrine was largely unforeseen. Some perceptive biologists were alarmed quite early on at the prospect of widespread and indiscriminate use of new synthetic pesticides (e.g. Vogt, 1948), but the dangers of secondary poisoning were not fully appreciated for some time, and who could have foreseen that DDT, a compound with relatively low avian and mammalian toxicity, could have caused eggshell thinning in many species of birds and around a large part of the world? This particular effect and its cause were not recognised until 20 years after they first appeared.

A certain wariness over the future and what it could bring may be wise. If toxic chemical problems can be contained, the Peregrine would seem nevertheless to be one of the most secure of our rarer birds in Britain. It has proved to be a resilient species and its nesting places are on the whole the least threatened of all habitats in the face of environmental exploitation. The Peregrine's choice of food is sufficiently catholic to buffer its population against all but the most pervasive of adverse influences which may impinge on other birds, though the future status of the domestic pigeon, the Red Grouse, and the rocky coast seabirds are especially significant to its prospects.

The effect of future changes in human activity on food supply is potentially the most serious factor for the British peregrine population. Kleinstäuber (1969) mentions that during World War II and the early post-war years, scarcity of feed caused German pigeon keepers to reduce their flocks to a minimum, with the result that free-flying domestic pigeons were hardly to be seen in the countryside. He suggested that the resulting food shortage for some pairs of Peregrines could have had an adverse effect, at least on reproduction. If any dire economic circumstances or other changes substantially reduced the number of domestic pigeons at large in Britain, we could indeed look for a considerable reduction in breeding performance and numbers of Peregrines, at least in the more southerly districts where the pigeon is the principal prey. Such a situation seems unlikely at the moment, though, since the recent trend has been towards an increase in pigeon racing.

It is possible that agricultural intensification could have reduced food supply for Peregrines in a few parts of Britain. In particular, the intensive cultivation of the South Downs after 1940 might explain the failure of the Peregrine during 1946–55 to recover its former high breeding density on the Sussex coast.

However, on the whole, breeding falcons in this country are unlikely to be influenced by any changes in abundance of prey populations which may have occurred in the mainly arable lowlands, for so few of them ever bred in these districts. The widespread improvements in the marginal lands of both coastal and upland districts of the north and west have reduced wader populations, and an effect on Peregrines would be possible where pigeons are in short supply.

Large-scale coniferous afforestation of moorland and hill has not yet affected Peregrine numbers or breeding success. However, if new forests continue to expand open-endedly in the Highlands, a measurable effect would be predictable. Afforestation is increasingly affecting those parts of the Scottish Highlands where the domestic pigeon is little available to Peregrines and where the falcon depends largely on birds living within its hunting range. Under these circumstances the planting of large tracts of open moorland, especially grouse ground, will necessarily reduce Peregrine food supply, probably to the level where some pairs stop breeding or drop out altogether.

The future of the Red Grouse is important for the Peregrine, especially in Scotland. Apart from afforestation, increase in sheep or red deer stocks, in combination with indiscriminate moor-burning, has caused a great retreat in the area of heather moorland in many parts of the British uplands, and the process continues. The Red Grouse declines rapidly as heather and bilberry, its main food plants, diminish, and it has lost a great deal of ground during the last hundred years. Only in the western Highlands has this so far been important for Peregrines, since domestic pigeons are freely available in most other affected districts.

The future of the seabirds on which falcons principally feed in some coastal localities is closely tied up with oil-spill hazards at sea. This is in a sense a slightly academic issue at the moment, since so few of the major seabird colonies have breeding Peregrines just now. If the marine pollutant hypothesis is true, there could in fact be an incongruous position whereby a decline in seabirds might even benefit coastal Peregrines by reducing contamination risks. Whatever the case, the fate of these great seafowl concentrations will depend on the success or otherwise of the measures taken to prevent or contain oil-spills, especially in the area of the North Sea oilfields and the associated tanker routes and terminals.

The grounding of the tanker *Braer* and spillage of its entire cargo of 85,000 tons of North Sea crude oil near the southern tip of Shetland, in January 1993, has changed risk into reality. It will be some time before the total biological impact of this misfortune becomes clear, but there is a certain irony that it should happen in an area where Peregrines appear to be at their lowest ebb in Britain through other forms of marine pollution.

The major human impact problems discussed above well illustrate that conservation of the Peregrine in Britain has to rely especially on broad measures affecting the countryside as a whole, rather than on the more localised approach of protecting specific areas under nature reserve or other special status. The pesticide problem is a perfect example of an important widely pervasive influence affecting a large part of Britain and making local land designations irrelevant to the safeguarding of birds such as this. Moreover, raptors such as the Peregrine require such large areas for breeding and feeding that even the largest nature reserve could hold only a few pairs. Nevertheless, it is both fitting and desirable that such a spectacular and ecologically important species should be represented on such reserves if they are truly to include examples of the most intact and characteristic ecosystems (biotopes) in this country.

The National Nature Reserves set up by the Nature Conservancy Council, held at least 30 breeding pairs of Peregrines in 1991. And within the key sites of national importance to nature conservation identified in *A Nature Conservation Review* (Ratcliffe, 1977), there are another 157 currently occupied and 47 vacant Peregrine territories. These key sites are all scheduled as Sites of Special Scientific Interest though this designation does not confer statutory protection. The reserves of the Royal Society for the Protection of Birds hold at least 24 pairs at present, but among the major corporate landowners, the Forestry Commission and the National Trust probably have the largest numbers of Peregrines on their properties.

As a species which tolerates a good deal of casual disturbance by humans, Peregrines are probably little troubled on the whole by the increasing invasion of many coastal and inland haunts by recreation seekers. A few small crags and tors are too disturbed by walkers and climbers for the birds to settle, and there are problems on some bigger cliffs much frequented by rock climbers. Some of the expanding hill roads have been driven uncomfortably close to certain resting places, facilitating access and increasing disturbance. As well as this, the new sports of hang- and para-gliding have caused occasional desertion of nests by both Peregrines and Ravens in northern England. Yet, overall, the problems of recreational disturbance are not serious.

The general measures adopted in Britain for regulating and restricting the use of pesticides depended on voluntary arrangements, but became mandatory through European Community regulations. The Nature Conservancy Council's statutory functions and powers have been transferred to the three successor bodies in England, Wales and Scotland, and the Joint Nature Conservation Committee, but legislation affects the Peregrine mainly through the Wildlife and Countryside Act 1981, which give the species special protection against deliberate human interference, including disturbance at the nest. Killing the bird or taking its eggs are allowed only for scientific purposes and under licence, and taking for falconry is subject to discretionary licensing, now seldom exercised. The law protecting Peregrines has been flouted freely, nevertheless, though things have become tougher for transgressors. I have discussed some of these issues in Chapter 1 and will simply sum up future prospects here.

With the recovery in Peregrine population, the problem of predation on homing pigeons has surfaced again. The wheel has almost turned full circle since 1960, with renewed angry protests from fanciers and demands for at least local 'control' of falcon numbers, plus a certain amount of surreptitious destruction of nests and birds. One source of outcry has grown into an hysterical campaign against birds of prey in general, with propaganda so far 'over the top' as to destroy its credibility. This is an issue unlikely to go away, and will exercise the judgement and resolve of the conservation bodies. Peregrine enthusiasts will continue to point out that this is still numerically a rare bird, and that its recovery shows this country to be honouring its international obligations to wildlife conservation.

An increasing number of game-preserving landowners, shooting tenants, syndicates and estate staff strongly support the bird protection laws and look after any Peregrines on their ground. Those shooters and their employees who show contempt for these measures and thereby cast a cloud over the rest will have to recognise that the public will no longer tolerate the kind of arrogance which was summed up in the words of a harrier-killing keeper on the Durham moors – 'We make the law up here.' And blatant double standards are just not acceptable. The raptor-killing landowners and keepers are zealous indeed in invoking the law to protect their game against human predators, and they should pay equal respect to the law which Parliament in its same wisdom has seen fit to pass to protect birds of prey as another part of the national heritage of wild nature.

The view of some game biologists that Hen Harriers, Golden Eagles and Peregrines cause appreciable reduction in grouse shooting bags has led some shooters to press for legal control of these species. We also hear much of the arguments that grouse moors are splendid habitats for other wildlife (i.e. 'leave us alone, we are doing a good job'); and that if they cannot be made to pay their way, afforestation will have to take over as the more viable land use. Grouse moors may be better than most sheepwalks, but they are not ideal wildlife habitats, for the precise reason that the larger predators are often so poorly represented. We should remember also that the option of going over to forestry is one almost entirely conditional on the fact that the taxpayer carries the bulk of the costs. The continuing widespread and wholly illegal destruction of raptors on and around so many grouse moors is likely to be another burning conservation issue into the foreseeable future. The embarrassment of some public figures over the conviction of their estate staff has had a salutary effect, and the moves to make landowners accountable for actions performed in their interest by their employees must reinforce this. However, surreptitious destruction is very difficult to detect, let alone stop, and in the end only a change of attitude will make much difference. Only when those keepers and their employers who detest Peregrines can take a more sportsmanlike view of a fellow hunter is there likely to be much hope for this bird on some moors.

Egg collecting may have been a fine sport and hobby once, and it may have helped to fire the youthful enthusiasms of many serious ornithologists still living. But it has had its day, and is an activity no longer consonant with the prevailing attitude to wildlife today. While I believe that the damage attributed to egg collecting has often been greatly over-rated, it does have an unfortunate tendency to focus on the rarer species and may have helped to prevent some of these from expanding their British range. But for the existence of large private collections, the thin eggshell story would have taken longer to unravel and the change could never have been dated so neatly. However, that is in the past, and it is to the future that we should look now. If scientific material of this kind is needed then it should be acquired in a legitimate and carefully planned way and not left to chance and haphazard taking.

Above all, egg collecting is an essentially selfish activity which sometimes spoils many other people's enjoyment and can be a complete nuisance to those engaged in serious study of breeding biology of an uncommon or local species. One of the least pleasant aspects of egg-collecting is that it has been a fruitful outlet for a few people whose twisted psychology gives them the urge to score off others. Nor is there great credit in the behaviour of those who could not resist the urge to collect large series of clutches of uncommon species for the simple pleasure of possessing beautiful objects, or to satisfy the trophy-hunter's instinct. Many of them neither knew nor cared whether they were having an adverse effect on the population. Those who were aware that more or less the same number of Peregrines attempted to breed every year argued that their activities were having no effect, but this situation depended on there being enough eyries elsewhere which were not looted. Some argued that their robberies saved the birds from being destroyed by keepers or pigeon fanciers. It was also argued that the systematic 'farming' of Peregrine clutches in some districts prevented the pigeon predation issue from becoming a worse problem, by reducing the food demands of whole falcon populations. Yet no amount of special pleading will remove the fact that the Peregrine is a relatively rare bird, and that the law is the law. The self-righteousness which 'scientific' purpose can generate led to a particularly squalid episode involving law-bending by an eminent scientist and his suppliers of material, which included Peregrine eggs. This cast a final cloud over British oology which had been striving hard for a respectable modern image.

There is no excuse for the private acquisition of either cabinet skins or mounted specimens of Peregrines. The larger museums in Britain have extensive series of skins sufficient to satisfy most taxonomic purposes, and Peregrines found dead continue to supply any further scientific needs for tissues or specimens. Taxidermy has declined greatly, and its remaining practitioners are strictly regulated under licence. The sale of mounted Schedule 1 birds is not allowed, and those in possession of illegally acquired specimens are liable to prosecution. As with eggshells, there continues to be a black market, with evident overseas connections, in cabinet skins and mounted specimens of rare birds, and it is a problem over which the authorities rightly maintain vigilance.

Falconers are understandably hurt at being mentioned alongside egg and skin collectors, for they are devoted to the living bird and see their sport as being on an altogether higher plane. Falconry today is accepted as a legitimate activity accommodated within the law. The problem, as discussed on pp. 29–30, is that while the Peregrine is still the favourite hawk, we have democracy and not oligarchy today, and so demand far exceeds the allowable supply. The official licensing authorities have issued very few permits for taking Peregrines from the wild in recent years, but there is nevertheless a large number of birds in captivity. Captive breeding of this and other raptors has become popular though, partly to reduce the way in which it was being used as a cover for illegal taking from the wild, it is now a legal requirement for all captive birds of prey, and changes in their ownership, to be registered. Sealed rings are placed on the birds' legs, and registered owners can be inspected at any time. This appears to have reduced the illegal trade in Peregrines, and captive breeding has increasingly supplied the demand. The wild population continues to be raided, even so, and within the last few years several continental falconers or their agents have been caught in Britain with batches of Peregrine eggs in incubators. Falconry still has a wide enough following overseas, especially in the Middle East, to ensure an international black market in birds; and despite the use of captive breeding, Britain and Ireland appear to be regarded as major sources of supply.

The need to tighten the law protecting Peregrines and other rare birds has resulted from the behaviour of an irresponsible minority who care nothing for the wishes of the rest of society. While the various kinds of direct molestation of wild falcons may altogether amount only to an insignificant population effect, compared with the indirect aspects of human impact previously discussed, they could easily get out of hand if no prohibitions existed. The robbery of young Peregrines was assuming alarming proportions by 1977, and remedial action was highly desirable. Deliberate interference could so easily and rapidly become serious that it would be too risky to allow any relaxations which would otherwise seem desirable.

There is little doubt of the good results of the clampdown on robberies. More young falcons are now reared annually in districts such as Lakeland and the Southern Uplands than anyone can remember ever being fledged in any year before the 'crash'. This is a fine achievement, and no one with the welfare of the Peregrine at heart would wish a return to the old days. For the freedom of that time led to the wholesale looting of nests. It was an age of exploitation with little thought for conservation, and there has been a major shift in attitudes since then. Those who have abused the lack of restraints in the past have brought upon everyone a loss of freedom through the need to protect eyries against intrusion. The gadgetry of modern surveillance has now been brought to bear on the problem, and certain eyries are now protected by 24 hour guards, electronic eyes and alarm circuits, time-lapse cameras, and invisible markers on eggs and young. Would-be raiders stand a fair chance of walking into a veritable hornet's nest, or of receiving an unexpected visit from the police after they have returned home.

I count myself fortunate to have grown up at a time when there were fewer restrictions on my personal freedom. Fifteen-year-old youths with a burning desire to climb to Peregrine eyries will find considerable curbs on their enthusiasms nowadays. The law has been invoked to restrain such instincts, and 'intentional disturbance' is now subject to the same penalties as the actual robbing of nests. This measure has occasionally been applied with mistaken zeal, and has clearly not prevented much of the intrusion by those intending harm, though it may have deterred some. The photography of this and other Schedule 1 birds at the nest is also strictly regulated by a permit system.

I personally regret that it has become increasingly difficult for the average person to see nesting Peregrines on close terms without becoming involved in form-filling, licence-carrying, reporting and, sometimes, close supervision of actual field activities. Can all this policing and bureaucracy ever be relaxed? It seems more likely to become worse. It is not just that there will continue to be so many heedless, selfish people who will, if uncontrolled, bring harm to the bird. The great dilemma of nature conservation is that the presence of too many people, however well-intentioned, can produce such concentrated disturbance that they begin to destroy the things they love. And so the distant view, through binoculars or telescope, is all that most people are likely to be allowed of Peregrines at the eyrie and, indeed, this is as much as many of them want.

Peregrine enthusiasts have long been inclined towards secrecy in defence of their falcons. Tim Sharrock, in compiling the Peregrine map in *The Atlas of Breeding Birds in Britain and Ireland* (1976), responded to concern felt by local ornithologists for their lately returned falcons by displacing 22 dots by one 10 km square, and by indicating all records for south-west England and the Republic of Ireland by a larger conventional displacement. In some districts where there has been recent recovery, some Peregrine enthusiasts are extremely reluctant to divulge locality information at all, lest this 'leaks' to eyrie raiders. This attitude is understandable but is now limiting understanding of the total national picture of

population behaviour. This would be ironical as well as unfortunate, for it was only by presenting the truth about the Peregrine situation, based on the freely given records of earlier surveyors, that measures were implemented to save the species. The happy position that many present-day Peregrine enthusiasts are able to witness, in the recovery of their local populations, owes much to the willingness with which a previous generation handed over their secret information when the bird really was in trouble. The whereabouts of most occupied nesting places are usually well enough known to the ill-intentioned, who spend a great deal of time doing their own checking and making enquiry amongst local people.

Conservation of the Peregrine is inseparable from people's interest in and attitudes about the bird. It has enemies and detractors as well as admirers and supporters. Even within the ranks of those who are for the Peregrine, differing standpoint produces a considerable degree of conflict, as between those who wish to exploit the bird in some way and those who wish simply to watch, admire and learn. Even the latter group keep a wary eye on each other. The Peregrine is a quite strongly political bird. Many years ago, Joe Hickey said, 'No other North American bird is surrounded by so much jealousy and suspicion,' and his remark has echoed around the World. Peregrine watchers very readily develop near-proprietorial feelings about 'their' particular birds and can show territorial behaviour almost matching that of the bird itself. Actual conservation measures thus have to take account not only of the Peregrine itself, but also of people and especially their emotions. With so much variation in viewpoint, it is not an easy task.

Captive breeding of Peregrines was pioneered as a conservation measure in the United States by professional ornithologists who were also falconers. Tom

Cade developed raptor breeding as a major activity of the Cornell Laboratory of Ornithology. The technique rapidly found favour, and captive breeding of raptors has become widely practised during the last 25 years in the United States, Canada and Europe, including Britain. Captive breeding was seen as the only hope of restoring the totally extinct eastern North American *anatum* form of the Peregrine. The idea was to breed up a stock of birds which could be released in areas where organochlorine pesticide levels had become low enough to allow a reasonable prospect of survival, pairing and successful breeding. Since 1974 well over 3000 captive bred young Peregrines have been hacked to the wild in North America, the bulk of them by the Cornell team, who set up an independent organisation *The Peregrine Fund*, in 1970. This costly and long-term project was a test of commitment and confidence, but has proved enormously successful and vindicated the vision of those concerned. By 1991 at least 120 territories were occupied in the eastern United States, with 73 successful pairs producing 165 fledged young. Many of the nests were on buildings, towers and bridges, though some were on natural cliffs. In Canada, a parallel captive programme was established under the leadership of Richard Fyfe, and resulted in the release of around 1000 young Peregrines. At least 20 pairs were breeding in south-east Canada by 1991. Roughly one-third of the former Peregrine population that existed in the eastern region of North America, prior to its extinction by pesticides, has thus been restored through captive breeding and reintroduction (Cade, 1991).

I believe that the Peregrine recovery programmes in North America represent one of the most positive and far-sighted wildlife conservation projects yet attempted anywhere in the World. A great deal of scientific insight into Peregrine biology has also been gained in the process. There seems also a good case for using captive breeding as a means of restoring Peregrine populations in those European countries where the species is almost or quite extinct, though it will be wasted effort unless there has been amelioration in the pesticide situation which caused decline. In Britain the Peregrine has made such good recovery that there is no case for using captive breeding for this purpose and its main validity here is to make unnecessary the taking of falcons from the wild population for falconry.

Research on the Peregrine in Britain should continue, for the advancement of knowledge in its own right and in support of conservation measures. Appropriate people will have to be permitted to visit nesting places to check eyries and to contribute to the surveillance of population status that is so crucial. Monitoring of pesticide residue levels must continue, particularly through collection and analysis of addled eggs. It is also important to maintain the programme of protection work, including the marking of eggs and young in some areas. Enthusiastic ringer-climbers have helped to boost the annual total of ringed falcons to a really useful level which is paying large dividends in information on movements and rate of population turn-over, and this work should continue. From a conservation viewpoint it will be important to be able to detect any significant changes in cause of death which may be concealed within a constant overall mortality rate, through substitution of one factor for another. This would be a warning sign for incipient population decline.

Some people believe that there should be more positive attempts at management to produce increase even within a healthy population (e.g. Hickey, 1942).

The Peregrine recovery work in North America has shown that habituation of captive-bred or reared eyasses to new types of nest site is a real possibility. In Britain and Ireland it looks as though the adaptation to nesting on buildings and other structures could 'take off' of its own accord. Some Peregrine enthusiasts are keen to speed the process by providing nest trays on buildings where Peregrines are seen but evidently cannot find suitable nesting sites, or on other structures in likely areas. It has also been suggested that tree nesting might be encouraged by artificial manipulation, including release of captive young from such sites. Given the present situation, of a still expanding population which has already increased far beyond any previously known level in many districts, such efforts to boost numbers still further carry certain risks. In particular, they could inflame an already delicate situation over the problem of Peregrines and domestic pigeons. While eyries on town buildings have considerable potential in educational and public relations value, the matter of deliberate intervention to encourage such nesting would seem to call for careful evaluation and due consultation.

As things stand, the Peregrine situation in Britain and Ireland is a conservation success story, and one of the few campaign outcomes in which we can take satisfaction. Yet questions remain. Do we continue to worry that the population of northern and western Scottish coastal areas appears chronically depressed and unlikely to recover, and accept that this regional shortfall is more than compensated by the large increases farther south? If the problem there really is marine pollution, is it unrealistic to believe that something can be done to reduce it; or should we take this as the best available evidence that marine pollution is causing biological damage, and use it as a stick with which to beat the Government for its failure to clean up the seas? How much more monitoring and ecological research is necessary to support conservation of the Peregrine – or is it now time to switch scarce resources into effort on more urgent and deserving cases? The RSPB and BTO have evidently made up their minds on this point already, by reducing their inputs to Peregrine work.

The warfare analogy supports the view that wildlife conservation has to be an essentially pragmatic business. We cannot dwell too long on the few scenes of success, but have to move on to tackle the urgent and critical problems that demand attention elsewhere. But neither can we afford to be complacent about the Peregrine. Now that the organochlorine pesticide problems are largely overcome, and direct human depredations are much reduced, its future prospects may be brighter than those for much of our wildlife. It is a species whose wide spectrum adaptations in food and breeding habitat have allowed it to buck the trend shown by some of its associates. The Golden Eagle, Merlin and Raven are showing a slow drift downwards in numbers, whereas the Peregrine has not yet reached its ceiling. Yet, if conservation experience elsewhere in the World has any message, it is surely that nothing is safe, anywhere.

It would thus be rash to imagine that the Peregrine is now secure, because there are no foreseeable threats. The country's socio-economic problems dictate that development and growth will continue to be political objectives that override any needs of wildlife conservation whenever the two are in collision – as they are all the time. The Peregrine is a species too entangled with human affairs to remain untouched by the further onslaughts on our natural environment that surely lie ahead. If, as has so often been said, it is a key species that acts as a barometer of ecosystem health, then its fortunes should be a matter of widespread concern. More particularly, those to whom the Peregrine is a source of inspiration and wonder have a special duty of vigilance, and a willingness to do battle with the future philistines who care nothing for the beauty of wild nature. It will be their responsibility to ensure that it survives, not just for its aesthetic, scientific and other value, but in its own right as one of the most spectacular inhabitants of our planet.

APPENDIX 1

Plant species in the text

Alder *Alnus glutinosa*
Ash *Fraxinus excelsior*
Aspen *Populus tremula*
Beech *Fagus sylvatica*
Birch *Betula verrucosa, B. pubescens*
Hazel *Corylus avellana*
Hornbeam *Carpinus betulus*
Larch *Larix kaempferi*
Lodgepole pine *Pinus contorta*
Oak *Quercus robur, Q. petraea*
Rowan *Sorbus aucuparia*
Scots pine *Pinus sylvestris*
Sitka spruce *Picea sitchensis*
Small-leaved lime *Tilia cordata*
Willow *Salix* spp.
Wych elm *Ulmus glabra*

MEDIUM SHRUBS

Blackthorn *Prunus spinosa*
Bramble *Rubus fruticosus* agg.
Gorse *Ulex europaeus, U. gallii*
Juniper *Juniperus communis*

DWARF SHRUBS

Bearberry *Arctostaphylos uva-ursi*
Bell heather *Erica cinerea*
Bilberry *Vaccinium myrtillus*
Cowberry *V. vitis-idaea*
Cross-leaved heath *Erica tetralix*
Crowberry *Empetrum nigrum,*
   E. hermaphroditum
Dwarf birch *Betula nana*
Heather (ling) *Calluna vulgaris*
Ivy *Hedera helix*
Mountain avens *Dryas octopetala*

FERNS

Bracken *Pteridium aquilinum*
Broad Buckler Fern *Dryopteris dilatata*
Polypody *Polypodium vulgare*

GRASSES AND ALLIES

Bent *Agrostis canina, A. tenuis, A. stolonifera*
Cotton grass *Eriophorum vaginatum,*
   E. angustifolium
Deer sedge *Trichophorum cespitosum*
Great woodrush *Luzula sylvatica*
Heath rush *Juncus squarrosus*
Mat grass *Nardus stricta*
Purple moor grass *Molinia caerulea*
Red fescue *Festuca rubra*
Sheep's fescue *F. ovina, F. vivipara*
Sweet vernal grass *Anthoxanthum odoratum*
Wavy hair grass *Deschampsia flexuosa*

OTHER HERBS

Bluebell *Endymion non-scriptus*
Cloudberry *Rubus chamaemorus*
Foxglove *Digitalis purpurea*
Golden-rod *Solidago virgaurea*
Red campion *Silene dioica*
Rosebay willow-herb *Chamaenerion angustifolium*
Scentless mayweed *Matricaria maritima*
Scurvy grass *Cochlearia officinalis*
Sea campion *Silene maritima*
Sea plantain *Plantago maritima*
Thrift (Sea pink) *Armeria maritima*
Sorrel *Rumex acetosa*
Wall pennywort *Umbilicus rupestris*
Woodsage *Teucrium scorodonia*

OTHER

Prickly pear *Opuntia* sp.
Bog moss *Sphagnum* spp.

Nomenclature follows the *Flora of the British Isles*, by A. R. Clapham, T. G. Tutin and E. F. Warburg, second edition, 1962.

APPENDIX 2

Bird species in the text

American Kestrel *Falco sparverius*
Ancient Murrelet *Synthliboramphus antiquus*
Arctic Skua *Stercorarius parasiticus*
Arctic Tern *Sterna paradisaea*
Asiatic Golden Plover *Pluvialis dominica fulva*
Barbary Falcon *Falco peregrinus pelegrinoides*
Bald Eagle *Haliaeetus leucocephalus*
Bar-tailed Godwit *Limosa lapponica*
Barn Owl *Tyto alba*
Barnacle Goose *Branta leucopsis*
Blackbird *Turdus merula*
Black Grouse *Lyrurus tetrix*
Black Guillemot *Cepphus grylle*
Black-headed Gull *Larus ridibundus*
Black-tailed Godwit *Limosa limosa*
Black Stork *Ciconia nigra*
Black Tern *Chlidonias niger*
Black-throated Diver *Gavia arctica*
Blue Tit *Parus caeruleus*
Brambling *Fringilla montifrigilla*
Brent Goose *Branta bernicla*
Broad-winged Hawk *Buteo platypterus*
Brown Pelican *Pelecanus occidentalis*
Bullfinch *Pyrrhula pyrrhula*
Bushchat *Saxicola* sp.
Buzzard *Buteo buteo*
Canada Goose *Branta canadensis*
Capercaillie *Tetrao urogallus*
Carrion Crow *Corvus corone corone*
Cassin Auklet *Ptychoramphus aleutica*
Chaffinch *Fringilla coelebs*
Chough *Pyrrhocorax pyrrhocorax*
Coal Tit *Parus ater*
Collared Dove *Streptopelia decaocto*
Common Gull *Larus canus*
Common Sandpiper *Actitis hypoleucos*
Common Scoter *Melanitta nigra*
Common Tern *Sterna hirundo*
Coot *Fulica atra*
Cormorant *Phalacrocorax carbo*
Corn Bunting *Miliaria calandra*
Corncrake *Crex crex*
Crane *Grus grus*
Crested Tit *Parus cristatus*

Crossbill *Loxia curvirostra*
Cuckoo *Cuculus canorus*
Curlew *Numenius arquata*
Dartford Warbler *Sylvia undata*
Dipper *Cinclus cinclus*
Domestic Fowl *Gallus domesticus*
Domestic Pigeon *Columba livia*
Dotterel *Eudromias morinellus*
Dunlin *Calidris alpina*
Dunnock *Prunella modularis*
Eagle Owl *Bubo bubo*
Eider *Somateria mollissima*
Eleonora's Falcon *Falco eleonorae*
Fieldfare *Turdus pilaris*
Fulmar *Fulmarus glacialis*
Gannet *Sula bassana*
Glaucous Gull *Larus hyperboreus*
Goldcrest *Regulus regulus*
Golden Eagle *Aquila chrysaetos*
Goldeneye *Bucephala clangula*
Goldfinch *Carduelis carduelis*
Golden Plover *Pluvialis apricaria*
Goosander *Mergus merganser*
Goshawk *Accipiter gentilis*
Great Black-backed Gull *Larus marinus*
Great Horned Owl *Bubo virginianus*
Great Spotted Woodpecker *Dendrocopos major*
Great Tit *Parus major*
Greenfinch *Chloris chloris*
Greenshank *Tringa nebularia*
Green Woodpecker *Picus viridis*
Greylag Goose *Anser anser*
Grey Plover *Pluvialis squatarola*
Grey Wagtail *Motacilla cinerea*
Guillemot *Uria aalge*
Gyr Falcon *Falco rusticolus*
Hawfinch *Coccothraustes coccothraustes*
Hen Harrier *Circus cyaneus*
Herring Gull *Larus argentatus*
Heron *Ardea cinerea*
Hobby *Falco subbuteo*
Honey Buzzard *Pernis apivorus*
Hooded Crow *Corvus corone cornix*
House Martin *Delichon urbica*
House Sparrow *Passer domesticus*
Jackdaw *Corvus monedula*

Jay *Garrulus glandarius*
Kestrel *Falco tinnunculus*
Kingfisher *Alcedo atthis*
Kittiwake *Rissa tridactyla*
Knot *Calidris canutus*
Lanner Falcon *Falco biarmicus*
Lapland Bunting *Calcarius lapponicus*
Lapwing *Vanellus vanellus*
Lesser Black-backed Gull *Larus fuscus*
Linnet *Carduelis cannabina*
Little Auk *Alle alle*
Little Owl *Athene noctua*
Little Ringed Plover *Charadrius dubius*
Long-eared Owl *Asio otus*
Long-tailed Skua *Stercorarius longicaudus*
Magpie *Pica pica*
Mallard *Anas platyrhynchos*
Manx Shearwater *Puffinus puffinus*
Marsh Hawk (Hen Harrier) *Circus cyaneus*
Meadow Pipit *Anthus pratensis*
Merlin *Falco columbarius*
Mistle Thrush *Turdus viscivorus*
Moorhen *Gallinula chloropus*
Nightjar *Caprimulgus europaeus*
North American Black Duck *Anas rubripes*
North American Ring Dove *Streptopelia risoria*
Osprey *Pandion haliaetus*
Oystercatcher *Haematopus ostralegus*
Partridge *Perdix perdix*
Peale's Falcon *Falco peregrinus pealei*
Peregrine *Falco peregrinus*
Pheasant *Phasianus colchicus*
Pied Wagtail *Motacilla alba*
Pomarine Jaeger (Skua) *Stercorarius pomarinus*
Prairie Falcon *Falco mexicanus*
Ptarmigan *Lagopus mutus*
Puffin *Fratercula arctica*
Purple Sandpiper *Calidris maritima*
Quail *Coturnix coturnix*
Raven *Corvus corax*
Razorbill *Alca torda*
Red-backed Shrike *Lanius collurio*
Red-breasted Goose *Branta ruficollis*
Red-breasted Merganser *Mergus serrator*
Red Grouse *Lagopus lagopus*
Red Kite *Milvus milvus*
Red-legged Partridge *Alectoris rufa*
Red-naped Shaheen *Falco peregrinus babylonicus*
Redshank *Tringa totanus*
Redstart *Phoenicurus phoenicurus*

Red-throated Diver *Gavia stellata*
Redwing *Turdus iliacus*
Reed Bunting *Emberiza schoeniclus*
Ring Ouzel *Turdus torquatus*
Ringed Plover *Charadrius hiaticula*
Robin *Erithacus rubecula*
Rock Dove *Columba livia*
Rock Pipit *Anthus spinoletta*
Rook *Corvus frugilegus*
Roseate Tern *Sterna dougallii*
Rough-legged Buzzard *Buteo lagopus*
Saker Falcon *Falco cherrug*
Sanderling *Calidris alba*
Sand Martin *Riparia riparia*
Shag *Phalacrocorax aristotelis*
Short-eared Owl *Asio flammeus*
Skylark *Alauda arvensis*
Siskin *Carduelis spinus*
Snipe *Gallinago gallinago*
Snow Bunting *Plectrophenax nivalis*
Snowy Owl *Nyctea scandiaca*
Song Thrush *Turdus philomelos*
Sparrowhawk *Accipiter nisus*
Starling *Sturnus vulgaris*
Stock Dove *Columba oenas*
Stonechat *Saxicola torquata*
Stone Curlew *Burhinus oedicnemus*
Storm Petrel *Hydrobates pelagicus*
Swallow *Hirundo rustica*
Swift *Apus apus*
Teal *Anas crecca*
Treecreeper *Certhia familiaris*
Turnstone *Arenaria interpres*
Turtle Dove *Streptopelia turtur*
Twite *Carduelis flavirostris*
Water Rail *Rallus aquaticus*
Wedge-tailed Eagle *Aquila audax*
Wheatear *Oenanthe oenanthe*
Whimbrel *Numenius phaeopus*
Whinchat *Saxicola rubetra*
White-tailed Eagle *Haliaeetus albicilla*
Wigeon *Anas penelope*
Willow Warbler *Phylloscopus trochilus*
Woodcock *Scolopax rusticola*
Woodlark *Lullula arborea*
Wood Pigeon *Columba palumbus*
Wood Sandpiper *Tringa glareola*
Wren *Troglodytes troglodytes*
Yellowhammer *Emberiza citrinella*

APPENDIX 3

Vertebrate non-avian species in the text

MAMMALS

Extinct
Mammoth *Mammuthus primigenius*
Woolly rhinoceros *Coelodonta antiquitatis*
Giant elk *Megaloceros giganteus*
Horse (virtually extinct in the wild) *Equus caballus*

Britain
Brown hare *Lepus europaeus*
Brown rat *Rattus norvegicus*
Fox *Vulpes vulpes*
Mink (introduced) *Mustela vison*
Mountain hare *Lepus timidus*
Pine marten *Martes martes*
Polecat *Mustela putorius*
Rabbit *Oryctolagus cuniculus*
Red deer *Cervus elaphus*
Reindeer (re-introduced) *Rangifer tarandus*
Short-tailed field vole *Microtus agrestis*
Stoat *Mustela erminea*
Water vole *Arvicola amphibius*
Weasel *Mustela nivalis*
Wild Cat *Felis silvestris*

Other Countries
Arctic fox *Alopex lagopus*
Arctic lemming *Dicrostonyx torquatus*
Bison *Bison priscus*
Brown bear *Ursus arctos*
Elk *Alces alces*
Jack rabbit *Lepus townsendii*
Lion *Panthera leo*
Lynx *Lynx lynx*
Musk ox *Ovibos moschatus*
Norway lemming *Lemmus lemmus*
Northern vole *Microtus oeconomus*
Raccoon *Procyon lotor*
Richardson's ground squirrel *Citellus richardsonii*
Spotted hyaena *Crocuta crocuta*
Varying hare *Lepus timidus*
Wolf *Canis lupus*
Wolverine *Gulo luscus*
Yellow-bellied marmot *Marmota flaviventris*

AMPHIBIA

Frog *Rana temporaria*
Toad *Bufo bufo*

REPTILES

Adder *Vipera berus*

FISH

Brown trout *Salmo trutta*

APPENDIX 4

Calls of the Peregrine

I have followed the terminology of Cramp and Simmons (1980), who have summarised the numerous descriptions of calls for various races of the Peregrine. The most detailed descriptions, and the only published sonagrams of Peregrine calls, are those of Wrege and Cade (1977), who found that most calls are used in numerous contexts, and communicate intensity of motivation rather than show association with particular behaviour. I have indicated some of the behaviour contexts of calls in the text, mainly in Chapters 7 and 8.

ADULTS

1. Cacking-call

This is the most familiar call, consisting of a single harsh note repeated rapidly in staccato and monotonous fashion, giving a chattering scream. It has more usually been rendered by British observers as 'kek–kek–kek . . .' or 'hek–ek–ek . . .'; and 'cack–cack–cack . . .' or 'kak–kak–kak . . .' is the preferred American version. Monneret (1974) commented on the regularity of delivery, with an interval of 0·5 second between syllables. Attempts have been made to differentiate the notes given by the sexes, the higher pitch of the male's voice tending towards a 'kaik–kaik–kaik . . .'. There are, however, considerable individual variations in this call in both sexes, in pitch, frequency and other finer qualities only revealed by the sonagram.

This is an aggressive call, given in response to disturbance, whether by other Peregrines or potential predators, including man, and is given when at rest as well as on the wing. It is thus often described as the alarm call, and is most often heard when falcons with eggs or young are disturbed by humans. It is also given in territorial threat and in attacks on intruders.

2. Wailing-call

This is variously rendered as a long-drawn, shrill and whining 'kee–arrk' repeated slowly (Walpole-Bond, 1938); a 'kaa–aa–ack kaa–aa–ack' rising in pitch (Herbert and Herbert, 1965); "eeyaik eeyaik" (Cade, 1960); 'waayk', 'waik', 'waaik' or 'wayee' (Nelson and Campbell, 1973; Weaver and Cade, 1973, in Cramp and Simmons, 1980). To my ears it sounds more like 'yee–errk yee–errk. . .' with the second syllable emphasised more strongly and on a slightly ascending scale.

Nelson and Campbell suggest that this call is used between the sexes in various contexts to indicate 'I want something', whether food, copulation, or turn at incubation. It is commonly used as a food call, both by the female in urging the perched male to hunt, and by the male to warn her of his approach. Cade has taken the still wider view that the Wailing-call signals motivation for a change of state. The Wailing-call is most frequently heard during the courtship period, and often changes to the Creaking-call during various displays. It can also change into the Cacking-call if an antagonistic situation develops. Wailing-calls are often given by birds which have lost eggs or young, though this may signify a renewal of courtship prior to a re-nesting attempt. Captive Peregrines which falconers term 'screamers' are prone to give the wailing-call whenever their owner approaches, and its significance is probably then mainly as a food-call.

3. Whining-call

This is distinguished by Wrege and Cade (1977) and is sharper and more incisive than the Wail though closely related in both physical structure and function. Cade suggests that it conveys greater persistence in motivation, and believes that the food-begging call is a Whine in its most typical form, rather than the Wail.

4. Creaking-call

This is the note likened by Hagar (1938) to the creaking of a rusty hinge and rendered by him as 'wi–chew' repeated several times in rapid succession, with the first syllable markedly lengthened and emphasised. Others have described this call as 'quat–yak' (Nethersole-Thompson, 1931), 'kleechip' (♂) and 'kleechup' (♀) (Cade, 1960), 'eechup' (Herbert and Herbert, 1965), 'eechip' (Nelson and Campbell, 1973), 'iiitchep' or 'iiitsick' (Monneret, 1974). It is a variable call and while, typically, both syllables are sharp, clipped and equally accented, it may be reduced to a monosyllabic 'chuck'. Wrege and Cade (1977) have noted a more complete three syllable form 'ku–ee–chip'.

The Creaking-call is nearly always given by one Peregrine to another, usually as an exchange between partners. It is, with the wailing-call, one of the two important calls of the courtship period, used by a male to attract a female and as an appeasement note during displays, and especially during copulation and incubation change-overs. It is also occasionally given by a defending Peregrine against an intruding falcon, and its aggressive content is denoted by the observation that it is invariably followed by a close attack on the intruder.

5. Chupping-call

This note is a clipped 'chup' or 'yapp', repeated several times, and similar to the second syllable of the Creaking-call; there is also a resemblance to the clucking of a domestic hen (Herbert and Herbert, 1965). Monneret (1974) described a Jackdaw-like 'yack' which seems to represent the same call. It merges into a quieter 'peeping' (Wrege and Cade, 1977). This is mainly a parental call, usually by the female, when feeding the young, and so is one of the less familiar calls of the Peregrine.

6. Chittering-call

This is mentioned but not specifically described by Wrege and Cade (1977), though it may be the call given by Walpole-Bond (1938) as 'hek–herrech–kerrech' and likened to a call of the Kestrel. It is given by both sexes in captivity, but especially by the male during aggressive interactions between the pair and during pre-copulatory behaviour and copulation (Wrege and Cade, 1977). It was also heard in the wild from a male when delivering food to the female for the young (Cade, 1960).

7. Other calls

Walpole-Bond (1938) mentions a single grunting 'ugh' given by a Peregrine surprised at close quarters.

YOUNG

Young Peregrines give several of the adults' calls, though less strongly and at a higher pitch. Monneret (1974) found that unhatched chicks cheeped in the egg up to 48 hours before hatching, and during hatching he heard a sharp 'yack' note. The small nestlings have a soft food call, sounding as a chitter or cheeping, and a treble whine when the parent approaches with food (Nelson, 1970; Herbert and Herbert, 1965). Monneret found that the young gave the 'yack' call resembling the adult wailing-call 'waaik–waaik . . .', which Cade noted was audible at well over one km on a calm day. Older nestlings disturbed by a man will hiss, especially when they have thrown themselves on their backs in defensive posture. Feathered nestlings sometimes give the 'cack–cack' alarm call, echoing that of their demonstrating parents, when the eyrie is visited.

APPENDIX 5

Some English names of the Peregrine

Great-footed Hawk	North America	J. J. Audubon
Duck Hawk	North America	formerly the accepted name but Swainson said name was also used in N. England
Hunting Hawk	Mainly England	
Game Hawk	Mainly England	
Blue Hawk	Mainly Scotland and N. England	
Blue Sleeves	Central Scotland but usually applied to Hen Harrier	
Gled or Glead	Widespread, usually applied to the Red Kite	
Blue-backed Falcon	N. England	
Grey Falcon	Yorkshire, England	T. Pennant
Perry Hawk	Yorkshire, England	T. Nelson
Stone Falcon	Usually applied to Merlin	
Rock Eagle	Lancashire	Whitaker

BIBLIOGRAPHY

ABRAHAM, G. D. 1919. *On Alpine Heights and British Crags*. Methuen, London.

ALBERTUS MAGNUS, 1262–80. *De Falconibus Asturibus et Accipitribus*. In *De Animalibus*. First edition composed at Cologne.

ALERSTAM, T. 1987. Radar observations of the stoop of the Peregrine Falcon *Falco peregrinus* and the Goshawk *Accipiter gentilis*. *Ibis* 129, 267–73.

ALLAVENA, S. 1988. Status and conservation problems of the Peregrine Falcon in Italy. Chapter 24 in *Peregrine Falcon Populations. Their management and recovery*, ed. T. J. Cade, J. H. Enderson, C. G. Thelander & C. M. White. The Peregrine Fund, Inc., Boise, Idaho.

AMADON, D. 1975. Why are female birds of prey larger than males? *Raptor Res.* 9(1/2), 1–11.

AMBROSE, R. E. RITCHIE, R. J., WHITE, C. M., SCHEMPF, P. F., SWEM, T & DITTRICK, R. 1988. Changes in the status of Peregrine Falcon populations in Alaska. Chapter 11 in *Peregrine Falcon Populations. Their management and recovery*, ed. T. J. Cade, J. H. Enderson, C. G. Thelander & C. M. White. The Peregrine Fund, Inc., Boise, Idaho.

ANDERSON, D. W. & HICKEY, J. J. 1972. Eggshell changes in certain North American birds. *Proc. XV International Ornithological Congress*. E. J. Brill, Leiden. Pp. 514–40.

ASHFORD, W. J. 1928. Peregrine Falcon nesting on the ground in Hampshire. *Brit. Birds* 22, 190–1.

BAKER, J. A. 1967. *The Peregrine*. Collins, London.

BANNERMAN, D. A. 1956. Peregrine Falcon, in *The Birds of the British Isles*, Vol. 5. Oliver & Boyd, Edinburgh and London.

BATTEN, H. M. 1923. *Inland Birds*. Hutchinson, London.

BAXTER, E. V. & RINTOUL, L. J. 1953. *The Birds of Scotland: Their history, distribution and migration*. 2 vols. Oliver & Boyd, Edinburgh.

BEEBE, F. L. 1960. The marine Peregrines of the north-west Pacific coast. *Condor*, 62, 145–89.

BENT, A. C. Life histories of North American birds of prey. Part 2: Orders Falconiformes and Strigiformes. *Bull. U.S. Nat. Mus.* 170, 42–70.

BIJLEVELD, M. 1974. *Birds of Prey in Europe*. Macmillan, London.

BIRD, D. M. & WEAVER, J. D. 1988. Peregrine Falcon populations in Ungava Bay, Quebec, 1980–1985. Chapter 6 in *Peregrine Falcon Populations. Their management and recovery*, ed. T. J. Cade, J. H. Enderson, C. G. Thelander & C. M. White. The Peregrine Fund, Inc., Boise, Idaho.

BLEZARD, E., GARNETT, M., GRAHAM, R. & JOHNSTON, T. L. 1943. The birds of Lakeland. *Trans. Carlisle Nat. Hist. Soc.* Vol. 6.

BOGAN, J. A. & MITCHELL, J. 1973. Continuing dangers to Peregrines from dieldrin. *Brit. Birds* 66, 437–439.

BOLAM, G. 1912. *The Birds of Northumberland and the Eastern Borders*. Blair, Alnwick.

BOLAM, G. 1913. *Wildlife in Wales*. Frank Palmer, London.

BOLAM, G. 1932. A catalogue of the birds of Northumberland. *Trans. Nat. Hist. Soc. Northumb. and Durham (NS)* 8, 71–2.

BOND, R. M. 1946. The Peregrine population of western North America. *Condor* 48, 101–16.

BRAMWELL, D. 1959–60. Some research into bird distribution in Britain during the late-glacial and post-glacial periods. *Bird Report, 1959–60, of the Merseyside Naturalists' Association*.

BROMLEY, R. G. 1988. Status of Peregrine Falcons in the Kitikmeot, Baffin and Keewatin Region, Northwest Territories, 1982–1985. Chapter 7 in *Peregrine Falcon Populations. Their management and recovery*, ed. T. J. Cade, J. H. Enderson, C. G. Thelander & C. M. White. The Peregrine Fund, Inc., Boise, Idaho.

BROMLEY, R. G. & MATTHEWS, S. B. 1988. Status of the Peregrine Falcon in the Mackenzie River Valley, Northwest Territories, 1969–1985. Chapter 8 in *Peregrine Falcon Populations. Their management and recovery*. ed. T. J. Cade, J. H. Enderson, C. G. Thelander & C. M. White. The Peregrine Fund, Inc., Boise, Idaho.

BROUN, M. 1948. *Hawks Aloft: the story of Hawk Mountain*. Kutztown Pub., Kutztown, Pa.

BROWN, L. H. 1976. *British Birds of Prey*. New Naturalist Series, Collins, London.

BROWN, L. H. & AMADON, D. 1968. *Eagles, Hawks and Falcons of the World*. 2 Vols. Country Life Books, Feltham.

BROWN, L. H. & WATSON, A. 1964. The Golden Eagle in relation to its food supply. *Ibis* 106, 78–100.

BROWN, R. H. 1929, 1934. The food of certain birds of prey. *Brit. Birds* 23, 269–70; 28, 257–58

BROWN, R. H. 1974. *Lakeland Birdlife 1920–1970*. Charles Thurnam, Carlisle.

BUCKLEY, T. E. & HARVIE-BROWN, J. A. 1891. *A Vertebrate Fauna of the Orkney Isles*, David Douglas, Edinburgh.

BURNHAM, W. A. & MATTOX, W. G. 1984. Biology of the Peregrine and Gyrfalcon in Greenland. *Meddelelser om Gronland* 14, 1–30.

BUTURLIN, S. 1933. Au sujet de la nuisibilité de certains oiseaux. *Le Gerfaut* 23, 18–22.

CADE, T. J. 1960. Ecology of the Peregrine and Gyrfalcon populations in Alaska. *University of California publications in Zoology*, 63(3), 151–290.

CADE, T. J. 1979. A perspective for the review of the status of *Falco peregrinus* on the list of endangered species. Pp. 1–7, Unpubl. memorandum. Cornell University.

CADE, T. J. 1980. Review of *Population Ecology of Raptors*, by Ian Newton. *J. Wildlife Manage.* 44, 969–72.

CADE, T. J. 1982. *The Falcons of the World*. Comstock/Cornell Univ. Press, Ithaca, New York.

CADE, T. J. 1991. Production and release: eastern Peregrine recovery. *Peregrine Fund Newsletter*, No. 21, 4.

CADE, T. J. & DAGUE, P. R. 1979. *The Peregrine Fund Newsletter* No. 7, Fall 1979. Cornell Univ. Laboratory of Ornithology.

CADE, T. J., LINCER, J. L., WHITE, C. M., ROSENEAU, D. G. & SWARTZ, L. G. 1971. DDE residues and eggshell changes in Alaskan falcons and hawks. *Science*. 172, 955–7.

CADE, T. J., ENDERSON, J. H. THELANDER, C. G. & WHITE, C. M. (eds) 1988. *Peregrine Falcon Populations. Their management and recovery*. The Peregrine Fund, Inc., Boise, Idaho.

CAMPBELL, R. W., PAUL, M. A. & RODWAY, M. S. 1978. Tree-nesting Peregrine Falcons in British Columbia. *Condor* 80, 500–1.

CHANCELLOR, R. 1977. *Report of Proceedings. World Conference on Birds of Prey, Vienna 1975*. International Council for Bird Preservation.

CHAPMAN, A. 1924. *The Borders and Beyond*. Gurney & Jackson, London.

CLARKE, A. 1977. Contamination of Peregrine Falcons with Fulmar stomach oil. *J. Zool., Lond.* 181, 11–20.

COCHRAN, W. W. & APPLEGATE, R. D. 1986. Speed of flapping flight of Merlins and Peregrine Falcons. *The Condor* 88, 397–8.

COOKE, A. S. 1973. Shell thinning in avian eggs by environmental pollutants. *Environ. Pollut.* 4, 85–152.

COOKE, A. S. 1975. Pesticides and eggshell formation. *Symp. Zool. Soc. Lond.* 35, 339–61.

COOKE, A. S. 1979. Changes in eggshell characteristics of the Sparrowhawk (*Accipiter nisus*) and Peregrine (*Falco peregrinus*) associated with exposure to environmental pollutants during recent decades. *J. Zool., Lond.* 187, 245–263.

COOKE, A. S., BELL, A. A. & HAAS, M. B. 1982. *Predatory Birds, Pesticides and Pollution*. Institute of Terrestrial Ecology, Cambridge.

COOPER, J. E. 1978. *Veterinary Aspects of Captive Birds of Prey*. Standfast Press, Gloucester.

COOPER, J. E. & GREENWOOD, A. G. (eds) 1981. *Recent Advances in the Study of Raptor Diseases*. Chiron Publications, Keighley.

COOPER, J. E. & PETTY, S. J. 1988. Trichomoniasis in free-living goshawks (*Accipiter gentilis gentilis*) from Great Britain. *J. Wildl. Dis.* 24, 80–7.

COURT, G. S. 1986. Some aspects of the reproductive biology of tundra Peregrine Falcons. M.Sc. thesis, University of Alberta, Edmonton, Alberta.

CRAIGHEAD, J. J. & CRAIGHEAD, F. C. 1956. *Hawks, Owls and Wildlife*. Stackpole Company and Wildlife Management Institute, Harrisburg, Pa.

CRAMP, S. & CONDER, P. J. 1961. The deaths of birds and mammals connected with toxic chemicals in the first half of 1960. *Report no. 1 of the BTO–RSPB Committee on Toxic Chemicals*. RSPB, Sandy.

CRAMP, S. & SIMMONS, K. E. L. (eds) 1980. *The Birds of the Western Palearctic*, Vol. 2. Oxford Univ. Press, Oxford.

CRAMP, S., CONDER, P. J. & ASH, J. S. 1962. Deaths of birds and mammals from toxic chemicals, January–June 1961. RSPB, Sandy.

CRAMP, S., BOURNE, W. R. P. & SAUNDERS, D. 1974. *The Seabirds of Britain and Ireland.* Collins, London.

DARLING, F. F. 1955. *West Highland Survey: An essay in human ecology.* Oxford.

DEMENTIEV, G. P. 1951. The Peregrine Falcon in the U.S.S.R. Pp. 80–100 in *The Birds of the Soviet Union*, Vol. 1, ed. G. P. Dementiev and N. A. Gladkov. Soviet Science, Moscow (in Russian).

DENNIS, R. H. 1970. The oiling of large raptors by Fulmars. *Scot. Birds* 6, 198–99.

DEPPE, H. J. 1972. Einige Verhaltensbeobachtungen in einem Doppelhorst von Seeadler (*Haliaetus albicilla*) und Wanderfalke (*Falco peregrinus*) in Mecklenburg. *J. Orn.* 113, 440–4.

DUNLOP, E. B. 1912. Natural history of the Peregrine Falcon. *Trans. Carlisle Nat. Hist. Soc.* 2, 89–93.

D'URBAN, W. S. M. & MATHEW, M. A. 1895. *The Birds of Devon.* R. H. Porter, London.

ELLIS, D. H. & GARAT, C. P. (1983). The Pallid Falcon *Falco kreyenborgi* is a color phase of the Austral Peregrine Falcon (*Falco peregrinus cassini*). *The Auk* 100, 269–71.

ELLIS, P. M. & OKILL, J. D. in press. The population and productivity of the Peregrine *Falco peregrinus* in Shetland, 1961–1991. *Scottish Birds*.

ENDERSON, J. H. 1969. Peregrine and Prairie Falcon life-tables based on band-recovery data. Pp. 505–508 in *Peregrine Falcon Populations. Their biology and decline*, ed. J. J. Hickey. Univ. of Wisconsin Press, Madison and London.

ENDERSON, J. H. & KIRVEN, M. N. 1983. Flights of nesting Peregrine Falcons recorded by telemetry. *Raptor Res.* 17, 33–7.

ENDERSON, J. H., TEMPLE, S. A. & SWARTZ, L. G. 1972. Time-lapse photographic records of nesting Peregrine Falcons. *Living Bird* 11, 113–28.

EUTERMOSER, G. 1961. Erläuterungen zur Krähenstatistik. *Deutscher Falkenorden* 6, 49–50.

EVANS, A. H. 1911. *A Fauna of the Tweed Area.* David Douglas, Edinburgh.

EVANS, A. H. & BUCKLEY, T. E. 1899. *A Fauna of the Shetland Isles.* David Douglas, Edinburgh.

EVANS, H. ap. 1960. *Falconry for You.* London.

FALK, K. & MOLLER, S. 1988. Status of the Peregrine Falcon in South Greenland: population density and reproduction. Chapter 5 in *Peregrine Falcon Populations. Their management and recovery*, ed. T. J. Cade, J. H. Enderson, C. G. Thelander & C. M. White. The Peregrine Fund, Inc., Boise, Idaho.

FERGUSON-LEES, I. J. 1951. The Peregrine population of Britain, Parts I & II. *Bird Notes* 24, 200–5; 309–14.

FERGUSON-LEES, I. J. 1957. The rarer birds of prey. Their present status in the British Isles. Peregrine. *Brit. Birds* 50, 149–55.

FISCHER, W. 1967. *Der Wanderfalk.* A. Ziemsen Verlag, Wittenberg Lutherstadt.

FISHER, J. 1952. *The Fulmar.* New Naturalist Monographs. Collins, London.

FISHER, J. 1966. *The Shell Bird Book.* Ebury Press and Michael Joseph, London.

FORESTRY COMMISSION 1978. *The Wood Production Outlook in Great Britain. A review*, Edinburgh.

FORMON, A. 1969. Contribution à l'étude d'une population de Faucons pèlerins dans l'est de la France. *Nos Oiseaux* 30, 109–39.

FORREST, H. E. 1907. *The Vertebrate Fauna of North Wales.* Witherby, London.

FOX, G. A. 1979. A simple method of predicting DDE contamination and reproductive success of populations of DDE-sensitive species. *J. Appl. Ecol.* 16, 737–41.

FOWLER, M. E., SCHULZ, T., ARDANS, A., REYNOLDS, B. AND BEHYMER, D. (1990). Chlamydiosis in captive raptors. *Avian Dis.* 34, 657–62.

FREDERICK II, EMPEROR 1248–50. *De Arte Venandi cum Avibus* Original MS, first printed in 1560 at Geneva (see Harting 1891), translated by Wood, C. A. and Fyfe, F. M. (1943) as the *Art of Falconry*, Stanford Univ. Press, California.

FROST, R. A. 1978. *Birds of Derbyshire.* Moorland Publishing, Hartington.

FYFE, R. 1969. The Peregrine Falcon in Northern Canada. Pp. 101–114 in *Peregrine Falcon Populations: Their biology and decline*, ed. J. J. Hickey. Univ. Wisconsin Press. Madison and London.

FYFE, R. W. 1988. The Canadian Peregrine Falcon Recovery Program, 1967–1985. Ch. 56 in *Peregrine Falcon Populations. Their Management and Recovery*, ed T. J. Cade, J. H. Enderson, C. G. Thelander and C. M. White. The Peregrine Fund Inc., Boise, Idaho.

FYFE, R. W., TEMPLE, S. A., & CADE, T. J. 1976. The 1975 North American Peregrine Falcon survey. *Canad. Field Nat.*, 90, 228–73.

FURR, P. M., COOPER, J. E. & TAYLOR-ROBINSON, D. 1977. Isolation of mycoplasmas from three falcons (*Falco* spp.), *Vet. Record* 100, 72–3.

GEMAUF, A. 1991. Birds of prey in Austria: populations, threats, laws. *Monographien des Unweltbundesantes Band*, 29: Vienna (In German).

GIBBONS, D. in press. *The New Atlas of Breeding Birds in Britain and Ireland*. T & A. D. Poyser, London.

GIBSON, J. A. 1953. The status of the Peregrine on the Clyde Islands. *Glasgow West Scotl. Bird Bull.*, 2, 53.

GILBERT, H. A. 1927. Notes on the nesting habits of the Peregrine Falcon. *Brit. Birds* 21, 26–30.

GILBERT, H. A. & BROOK, A. 1931. *Watchings and Wanderings Among Birds*. Arrowsmith, London.

GILBERTSON, M. 1969. The distribution of the Peregrine Falcon in Northern Ireland, *Irish Nat. J.*, 16, 131–3.

GJERSHAUG, J. O., THINGSTAD, P. G., ELDØY, S. & BYRKJELAND, S. (eds.) *Norsk Fugleatlas* (in preparation).

GLADSTONE, H. 1910. *The birds of Dumfriesshire*. Witherby, London.

GLUTZ VON BLOTZHEIM, U. N., BAUER, K. M., & BEZZEL, E. 1971. *Handbuch der Vögel Mitteleuropas*. Vol. 4. Akademische Verlagsgesellschaft, Frankfurt am Main.

GORDON, S. 1938. *Wild Birds in Britain*. Batsford, London.

GRAHAM, H. D. 1852–70. *The Birds of Iona and Mull*, ed. J. A. Harvie-Brown, 1890. David Douglas, Edinburgh.

GRAHAM, D. L. & HALLIWELL, W. H. 1986. Viral diseases of birds of prey. In *Zoo and Wild Animal Medicine*, ed. M. E. Fowler. W. B. Saunders, Philadelphia.

GRAY, R. 1871. *The Birds of the West of Scotland, Including the Outer Hebrides*. Glasgow.

GREENWOOD, A. 1977. The role of disease in the ecology of British raptors. *Bird Study* 24, 259–65.

GROUNDWATER, W. 1974. *Birds and Mammals of Orkney*. Kirkwall Press, Orkney.

GURNEY, J. H. 1921. *Early Annals of Ornithology*. London.

HAGAR, J. A. 1969. History of the Massachusetts Peregrine Falcon population. Pp. 123–31 in *Peregrine Falcon Populations. Their biology and decline*, ed. J. J. Hickey. Univ. Wisconsin Press, Madison and London.

HALL, G. H. 1955. *Great moments in action. The story of the Sun Life Falcons*. Mercury Press, Montreal.

HALLIWELL, W. H. & GRAHAM, D. L. 1986. Bacterial diseases of birds of prey. In *Zoo and Wild Animal Medicine*, ed. M. E. Fowler. W. B. Saunders, Philadelphia.

HANTGE, E. 1968. Zum Beuteerwerb unserer Wander-falcen. *Orn. Mitt.* 20, 211–17.

HARDEY J. 1981. Prey taken by Peregrines in the Grampian Region. *Gramp. Ring. Group Rep.* 3, 30–5.

HARRISON, J. M. 1953. *The Birds of Kent*. 2 Vols. Witherby, London.

HARTING, J. E. 1883. *Essays on Sport and Natural History*. Horace Cox, London.

HARTING, J. E. 1891. *Bibliotheca Accipitraria. A catalogue of books ancient and modern relating to falconry*. Bernard Quaritch, London.

HARVIE-BROWN, J. A. 1906. *A Fauna of the Tay Basin and Strathmore*. David Douglas, Edinburgh.

HARVIE-BROWN, J. A. & BUCKLEY, T. E. 1887. *A Vertebrate Fauna of Sutherland, Caithness and West Cromarty*. David Douglas, Edinburgh.

HARVIE-BROWN, J. A. & BUCKLEY, T. E. 1888. *A Fauna of the Outer Hebrides*. David Douglas, Edinburgh.

HARVIE-BROWN, J. A. & BUCKLEY, T. E. 1892. *A Fauna of Argyll and the Inner Hebrides*. David Douglas, Edinburgh.

HARVIE-BROWN, J. A. & BUCKLEY, T. E. 1895. *A Fauna of the Moray Basin*. David Douglas, Edinburgh.

HARVIE-BROWN, J. A. & MACPHERSON, H. A. 1904. *A Fauna of the north-west Highlands and Skye*. David Douglas, Edinburgh.

HAUTOLA, K. & SULKAVA, S. 1977. Näringsval hos finska pilgrimsfalkar. Pp. 43–8. in *Pilgrimsfalk*. Report from a Peregrine conference held at Grimsö Wildlife Research Station, Sweden, 1–2 April 1977, ed. Peter Lindberg. Swedish Society for the Conservation of Nature, Stockholm.

HAVILAND, M. D. 1926. *Forest, Steppe and Tundra: Studies in animal environment*. Cambridge Univ. Press.

HEATHCOTE, A., GRIFFIN, D. & SALMON, H. M. 1967. The Birds of Glamorgan. *Trans. Cardiff Nat. Soc.* Vol. 94.

HEATHERLEY, F. 1913. *The Peregrine Falcon at the Eyrie*. George Newnes, London.

HERBERT, R. A. & HERBERT, K. G. S. 1965. Behaviour of Peregrine Falcons in the New York City Region. *Auk* 82, 62–96.

HEREDIA, B., HIRALDO, F., GONZALES, L. M. & GONZALES, J. L. 1988. Status, ecology and conservation of the Peregrine Falcon in Spain. Chapter 25 in *Peregrine Falcon Populations. Their management and recovery*, ed. T. J. Cade, J. H. Enderson, C. G. Thelander & C. M. White. The Peregrine Fund, Inc., Boise, Idaho.

HICKEY, J. J. 1942. Eastern population of the Duck Hawk. *Auk* 59(2), 176–204.

HICKEY, J. J. (ed.) 1969. *Peregrine Falcon Populations. Their biology and decline*. Univ. Wisconsin Press, Madison and London.

HICKEY, J. J. & ANDERSON, D. W. 1968. Chlorinated hydrocarbons and eggshell changes in raptorial and fish-eating birds. *Science*, 162, 271–3.

HICKEY, J. J. & ANDERSON, D. W. 1969. The Peregrine Falcon: life history and population literature. Pp. 3–42 in *Peregrine Falcon Populations. Their biology and decline*, ed. J. J. Hickey. Univ. Wisconsin Press, Madison and London.

HOLDEN, B. 1973. Unpublished report to the Irish Wildbird Conservancy on Peregrine Surveys in the Republic of Ireland 1967–73.

HOWARD, H. E. 1920. *Territory in Bird Life*. John Murray, London.

HUDEC, K. 1988. Status of the Peregrine Falcon in the Ceskomoravska Vrchovina Highlands and other parts of Czechoslovakia. Chapter 21 in *Peregrine Falcon Populations. Their management and recovery*, ed. T. J. Cade, J. H. Enderson, C. G. Thelander & C. M. White. The Peregrine Fund, Inc., Boise, Idaho.

HUDSON, P. J. 1992. *Grouse in Space and Time. The Population Biology of a Managed Gamebird*. Game Conservancy Limited, Fordingbridge.

HUNT, W. G. 1988. The natural regulation of Peregrine Falcon populations. Chapter 63 in *Peregrine Falcon Populations. Their management and recovery*, ed. T. J. Cade, J. H. Enderson, C. G. Thelander & C. M. White. The Peregrine Fund, Inc., Boise, Idaho.

HUNTER, R. E., CRAWFORD, J. A. & AMBROSE, R. E. 1988. Prey selection by Peregrine Falcons during the nestling stage. *J. Wildl. Mgmt* 52, 730–6.

HUSTLER, K. 1983. Breeding biology of the Peregrine Falcon in Zimbabwe. *Ostrich* 54, 161–71.

HUTCHINSON, C. D., 1989. *Birds in Ireland*. Poyser, Calton.

INGRAM, G. C. S. & SALMON, H. M. 1929. Notes on the nesting habits of the Peregrine Falcon (2). *Brit. Birds* 22, 198–202.

INGRAM, G. C. S. & SALMON, H. M. 1936. Birds of Glamorgan. *Glamorgan County History* 1, 212–21.

INGRAM, G. C. S. & SALMON, H. M. 1957. The Birds of Brecknock. *Brycheiniog* 3, 181–259.

JEFFERIES D. J. 1973. The effects of organochlorine insecticides and their metabolites on breeding birds. *J. Reprod. Fert., Suppl.* 19, 337–52.

JEFFERIES, D. J. & PRESTT, I. 1966. Post-mortems of Peregrines and Lanners with particular reference to organochlorine residues. *Brit. Birds*, 59, 49–64.

JENKINS D., WATSON, A. & MILLER, G. R. 1963. Population studies on Red Grouse, *Lagopus lagopus scoticus*. (Lathe.), in north-east Scotland. *J. Anim. Ecol.* 32, 317–76.

JENKINS, D., WATSON, A & MILLER, G. R. 1964. Predation and Red Grouse populations. *J. Appl. Ecol.* 1, 183–95.

JENNINGS A. R. 1961. An analysis of 1000 deaths in wild birds. *Bird Study* 8, 25–31.

JUILLARD, M. 1988. Recolonization of the Swiss Jura Mountains by the Peregrine Falcon. Chapter 22 in *Peregrine Falcon Populations. Their management and recovery*, ed. T. J. Cade, J. H. Enderson, C. G. Thelander & C. M. White. The Peregrine Fund., Inc., Boise, Idaho.

KEARTON, R, 1909. *With Nature and a Camera*. Cassell, London.

KENNEDY, R. J. 1970. Direct effects of rain on birds: a review. *Brit. Birds* 63, 401–14.

KIFF, L. F. 1988. Changes in the status of the Peregrine in North America: an overview. Commentary, pp. 123–39 in *Peregrine Falcon Populations. Their Management and Recovery*, ed. T. J. Cade, J. H. Enderson, C. G. Thelander and C. M. White. The Peregrine Fund Inc., Boise, Idaho.

KIRKPATRICK, C. E. & TREXLER-MYREN, V. P. 1986. A survey of free-living falconiform birds for *Salmonella*. *J. Am. Vet. Med. Assoc.* 189, 997–8.

KLEINSTÄUBER, K. 1969. The status of cliff-nesting Peregrines in the German Democratic Republic. Chapter 17 in *Peregrine Falcon Populations. Their Biology and Decline*, ed. J. J. Hickey. University of Wisconsin Press, Madison and London.

KLEINSTÄUBER, G. & KIRMSE, W. 1988. Status of the Peregrine Falcon in East Germany, 1965–1985. Chapter 20 in *Peregrine Falcon Populations. Their management and recovery*, ed. T. J. Cade, J. H. Enderson, C. G. Thelander & C. M. White. The Peregrine Fund, Inc., Boise, Idaho.

KORPIMAKI, E. 1986. Reversed size dimorphism in birds of prey, especially in Tengmalm's Owl *Aegolius funereus*: a test of the 'starvation hypothesis'. *Ornis Scand.* 17, 326–32.

KRETSCHMAR, A. A. 1965. Zur Brutbiologie der Rothalsgans, *Branta ruficollis* (Pallas) in West Taimyr. *J. Ornith.* 106, 440–5.

KRETSCHMAR, A. A. & LEONOVICH, V. V. 1967. [Distribution and biology of the Red-breasted Goose in the breeding season.] *Problemy Severa* 11, 229–34 (In Russian).

KUMARI, E. 1974. Past and present of the Peregrine Falcon in Estonia. Pp. 230–52, in *Estonian Wetlands and their Life*, ed. E. Kumari. Estonian contribution to IBP, No. 7 Acad. Sci. Estonian S.S.R.

KUYT, E. 1967. Two banding returns for Golden Eagle and Peregrine Falcon. *Bird-Banding* 38, 78–9.

LACK, P. 1986. *The Atlas of Wintering Birds in Britain and Ireland*. Poyser, Calton.

LEHNER, P. N. & EGBERT, A. 1969. Dieldrin and eggshell thickness in ducks. *Nature* 224, 1218–19.

LINCER, J. L. 1975. DDE-induced eggshell-thinning in the American Kestrel: a comparison of the field situation and laboratory results. *J. Appl. Ecol.* 12, 781–93.

LINDBERG, P. 1975. *Pilgrimsfalken i Sverige*. Svenska Naturskyddsföreningen, Stockholm.

LINDBERG, P. 1977. Ringmarkning av pilgrimsfalk i Sverige. Pp. 39–42 in *Pilgrimsfalk*. Report from a Peregrine conference held at Grimsö Wildlife Research Station, Sweden, 1–2 April 1977, ed. Peter Lindberg. Swedish Society for the Conservation of Nature. Stockholm.

LINDBERG, P. 1986. The Peregrine Falcom *Falco peregrinus* Project. *Faunaoch Flora* 81, 171–2 (in Swedish).

LINDBERG, P. & ODSJO, T. 1983. Mercury levels in feathers of Peregrine Falcon *Falco peregrinus* compared with total mercury content in some of its prey species in Sweden. *Environ. Pollut. (Ser. B)* 5, 297–318.

LINDBERGT, P., SCHEI, P. J. & WIKMAN, M. 1988. The Peregrine Falcon in Fennoscandia. Chapter 18 in *Peregrine Falcon Populations. Their management and recovery*, ed. T. J. Cade, J. H. Enderson, C. G. Thelander & C. M. White. The Peregrine Fund, Inc., Boise, Idaho.

LINDQUIST, T. 1963. Peregrines and homing pigeons. *Brit. Birds* 56, 149–51.

LINKOLA, P. & SUOMINEN, T. 1969. Population trends in Finnish Peregrines. Pp. 183–92, in *Peregrine Falcon Populations. Their biology and decline*, ed. J. J. Hickey. Univ. Wisconsin Press, Madison and London.

LOCKIE, J. D. 1955. The breeding habits and food of Short-eared Owls after a vole plague. *Bird Study* 2, 53–69.

LOCKLEY, R. M. 1949. *The Birds of Pembrokeshire*. West Wales Field Society, Cardiff.

LUMEIJ, J. T. & VAN NIE, G. J. 1982. Tuberculosis in raptorial birds. Review of the literature and suggestions for clinical diagnosis and vaccination. *Tijdschr. Diergeneesk* 107, 573–9.

MACGILLIVRAY, W. 1840. *A history of British Birds*, Vol. III. London.

MCGRATH, D. 1987. The Peregrine Falcon in south-east Ireland, 1981–1986. *Irish Birds* 3, 377–86.

MACINTYRE, D. 1914. Flights by wild falcons in Kintyre. *Chambers Journal*, 11 July 1914.

MACINTYRE, D. 1960. *Nature Notes of a Highland Gamekeeper*. Seeley Service, London.

MCKELVIE, C. L. 1973. Distribution and breeding success of the Peregrine Falcon in Northern Ireland, 1970–73. *Hawk Trust Ann. Rep.* 1973, 20–7.

MACKENZIE, O. 1924. *A Hundred Years in the Highlands*. London.

MACNALLY, L. 1979. Peregrine apparently killed by Golden Eagle. *Scot. Birds* 10, 234.

MCNUTT, J. W., ELLIS, D. H., GARAT, C. P., ROUNDY, T. B., VASINA, W. G. & WHITE, C. M. 1988. Distribution and status of the Peregrine Falcon in South America. Chapter 26 in *Peregrine Falcon Populations. Their Management and Recovery*, ed. T. J. Cade, J. H. Enderson, C. G. Thelander and C. M. White. The Peregrine Fund, Inc., Boise, Idaho.

MACPHERSON, H. A. 1892. *The Vertebrate Fauna of Lakeland*. David Douglas, Edinburgh.

MACPHERSON, H. A. & DUCKWORTH, W. 1886. *The Birds of Cumberland*. Charles Thurnam, Carlisle.

MCVEAN, D. N. & LOCKIE, J. D. 1969. *Ecology and Land Use in Upland Scotland*. Edinburgh.

MCWILLIAM, J. M. 1927. *The Birds of the Island of Bute*. Witherby, London.

MARQUISS, M. NEWTON, I & RATCLIFFE, D. A. 1978. The decline of the Raven, *Corvus corax*, in relation to afforestation in southern Scotland and northern England. *J. Appl. Ecol.* 15, 129–44.

MARTIN, A. P. 1980. A study of a pair of breeding Peregrine Falcons (*Falco peregrinus peregrinus*) during part of the nestling period. Unpublished B.Sc. dissertation, Dept Zoology, Univ. Durham.

MATTOX, W. G. & SEEGAR, W. S. 1988. The Greenland Peregrine Falcon survey, 1972–85, with emphasis on recent population status. Chapter 4 in *Peregrine Falcon Populations. Their management and recovery*, ed. T. J. Cade, J. H. Enderson, C. G. Thelander & C. M. White. The Peregrine Fund, Inc., Boise, Idaho.

MEAD, C. J. 1969. Ringed Peregrines in Great Britain. Pp. 385–390, in *Peregrine Falcon Populations. Their biology and decline*, ed. J. J. Hickey. Univ. Wisconsin Press, Madison and London.

MEAD, C. J. 1973. Movements of British raptors. *Bird Study* 20, 259–286.

MEARNS, R. 1982. Winter occupation of breeding territories and winter diet of Peregrines in south Scotland. *Ornis Scand.* 13, 79–83.

MEARNS, R. 1983a. The diet of the Peregrine *Falco peregrinus* in south Scotland during the breeding season. *Bird Study* 30, 81–90.

MEARNS, R. 1983b. Breeding Peregrines oiled by Fulmars. *Bird Study* 30, 243–4.

MEARNS, R. 1984. Winter sightings of Peregrines at Caerlaverock. *Scot. Birds* 13, 73–7.

MEARNS, R. & NEWTON, I. 1984. Turnover and dispersal in a Peregrine *Falco peregrinus* population. *Ibis* 126, 347–55.

MEARNS, R. & NEWTON, I. 1988. Factors affecting breeding success of Peregrines in south Scotland. *J. Anim. Ecol.* 57, 903–16.

MEBS, T. 1969. Peregrine Falcon population trends in West Germany. Pp. 193–207, in *Peregrine Falcon Populations. Their biology and decline*, ed. J. J. Hickey. Univ. Wisconsin Press, Madison and London.

MEBS, T. 1971. Todesursachen und mortalitätsraten beim Wanderfalken (*Falco peregrinus*) nach den Wiederfunden deutscher und finnischer Ringvögel. *Die Vögelwarte* 26, 98–105.

MEBS, T. 1988. The return of the Peregrine Falcon in West Germany. Chapter 19 in *Peregrine Falcon Populations. Their management and recovery*, ed. T. J. Cade, J. H. Enderson, C. G. Thelander & C. M. White. The Peregrine Fund, Inc., Boise, Idaho.

MEINERTZHAGEN, R. 1959. *Pirates and Predators: The piratical and predatory habits of birds.* Oliver & Boyd, Edinburgh and London.

METEOROLOGICAL OFFICE. 1952. *Climatological Atlas of the British Isles.* HMSO, London.

MICHELL, E. B. 1900. *The Art and Practice of Hawking.* Methuen, London.

MITCHELL, F. S. 1892. *Birds of Lancashire.* Gurney & Jackson, London.

MITCHELL, J. 1973. Peregrine Falcon and Wood pigeons. *Glasgow Naturalist* 19, 62.

MONNERET, R.-J. 1974. *Répertoire comportemental du Faucon pèlerin. Falco peregrinus* Hypothése explicative des Manifestations Adversives. *Alauda* 42, 407–28.

MONNERET, R.-J. 1988. Changes in the Peregrine Falcon populations of France. Chapter 23 in *Peregrine Falcon Populations. Their management and recovery,* ed. T. J. Cade, J. H. Enderson, C. G. Thelander & C. M. White. The Peregrine Fund, Inc., Boise, Idaho.

MONTAGU, G. 1813. *Supplement to the Ornithological Dictionary of British Birds.* Exeter.

MOORE, N. W. 1957. The Buzzard in Britain. *Brit. Birds* 50, 173–97.

MOORE, N. W. (ed.) 1966. Pesticides in the environment and their effects on wildlife. Proc. of an Advanced Study Institute sponsored by the North Atlantic Treaty Organisation, 1–14 July 1965. Monks Wood Experimental Station, England.

MOORE, N., KELLY, P. & LANG, F. 1992. Quarry-nesting by Peregrine Falcons in Ireland. *Irish Birds* 4, 519–24.

MOORE, R. 1969. *The Birds of Devon.* David & Charles, Newton Abbot.

MORIARTY, F. 1975. *Pollutants and Animals. A factual perspective.* George Allen & Unwin, London.

MOSSOP, D. 1988. Current status of Peregrine Falcons in Yukon, Canada. Chapter 9 in *Peregrine Falcon Populations. Their management and recovery,* ed. T. J. Cade, J. H. Enderson, C. G. Thelander & C. M. White. The Peregrine Fund, Inc., Boise, Idaho.

MUELLER, H. C. 1971. Oddity and specific searching image more important than conspicuousness in prey selection. *Nature* 233, 345–6.

NAUMOV, S. P. 1931. Mammals and birds of the Gyda Peninsula, north-eastern Siberia. *Trudy Polyrn. Komm. Akad. Nauk. SSSR.* 4 (in Russian).

NELSON, M. W. 1969. The status of the Peregrine in the Northwest. Pp. 61–72, in *Peregrine Falcon Populations. Their biology and decline,* ed. J. J. Hickey. Univ. Wisconsin Press. Madison and London.

NELSON, R. W. 1970. Some aspects of the breeding behaviour of Peregrine Falcons on Langara Island, B.C. Unpubl. M.S. Thesis, Dept Biology, Univ. Calgary, Alberta.

NELSON, R. W. 1973. Behavioural ecology of coastal Peregrines, Langara Island, B.C. Unpubl. report to B.C. Fish and Wildlife Branch, Canadian Wildlife Service. Dept Biology, Univ. Calgary, Alberta.

NELSON, R. W. 1977. Behavioral ecology of coastal Peregrines (*Falco peregrinus pealei*). Ph.D. Dissertation, Univ. Calgary, Calgary, Alberta.

NELSON, R. W. 1988. Do large natural broods increase mortality of parent Peregrine Falcons? Chapter 69 in *Peregrine Falcon Populations. Their management and recovery,* ed. T. J. Cade, J. H. Enderson, C. G. Thelander & C. M. White. The Peregrine Fund, Inc., Boise, Idaho.

NELSON, R. W. 1990. Status of the Peregrine Falcon, *Falco peregrinus pealei,* on Langara Island, Queen Charlotte Islands, British Columbia, 1968–1989. *Canad. Field Nat.* 104, 193–9.

NELSON, R. W. & CAMPBELL, J. A. 1973. Breeding and behaviour of Arctic Peregrines in captivity. *Hawk Chalk* 12, 39–54.

NELSON, R. W. & MYRES, M. T. 1975. Changes in the Peregrine population and its seabird prey at Langara Island, British Columbia. *Raptor Res,* 3, 13–31.

NELSON, R. W. & MYRES, M. T. 1976. Declines in Peregrine Falcons and their seabird prey at Langara Island, British Columbia. *Condor* 78, 281–93.

NELSON, T. H. 1907. *The Birds of Yorkshire.* 2 Vols. A. Brown, London.

NETHERSOLE-THOMPSON, D. 1931. Observations on the Peregrine Falcon. *Ool. Rec.* 11, 73–80.

NETHERSOLE-THOMPSON, D. 1973. *The Dotterel.* Collins, London.

NETHERSOLE-THOMPSON, D. & WATSON, A. 1981. *The Cairngorms.* The Melven Press, Perth.

NEWTON, I. 1979. *Population Ecology of Raptors.* T. & A. D. Poyser, Berkhamsted.

NEWTON, I. 1988. Changes in the status of the Peregrine Falcon in Europe: an overview. Commentary on pp. 227–34 in *Peregrine Falcon Populations. Their management and recovery*, ed. T. J. Cade, J. H. Enderson, C. G. Thelander & C. M. White. The Peregrine Fund, Inc., Boise, Idaho.

NEWTON, I. 1988. Population regulation in Peregrines: an overview. Commentary on pp. 761–70 in *Peregrine Falcon Populations. Their management and recovery*, ed. T. J. Cade, J. H. Enderson, C. G. Thelander & C. M. White. The Peregrine Fund, Inc., Boise, Idaho.

NEWTON, I. & BOGAN, J. A. 1978. The role of different organochlorine compounds in the breeding of British Sparrowhawks. *J. Appl. Ecol.* 15, 105–16.

NEWTON, I. & HAAS, M. B. 1988. Pollutants in Merlin eggs and their effects on breeding. *Brit. Birds*, 81, 258–69.

NEWTON, I. & MEARNS, R. 1988. Population ecology of Peregrines in South Scotland. Chapter 62 in *Peregrine Falcon Populations. Their management and recovery*, ed. T. J. Cade, J. H. Enderson, C. G. Thelander & C. M. White. The Peregrine Fund, Inc., Boise, Idaho.

NEWTON, I., BOGAN, J. A. & HAAS, M. B. 1989. Organochlorines and mercury in the eggs of British Peregrines *Falco peregrinus. Ibis* 131, 355–76.

NICHOLSON, C. F. 1986. *Peregrine: Symonds Yat Rock, Gloucestershire, 1986*. Royal Society for the Protection of Birds, Droitwich.

NORRISS, D. W. & WILSON, H. J. 1983. Survey of the Peregrine *Falco peregrinus* population in the Republic of Ireland in 1981. *Bird Study* 30, 91–101.

NORRIS, D. W. in press. The 1991 survey and weather impacts on the Peregrine Falcon *Falco peregrinus* breeding population in the Republic of Ireland. *Bird Study*.

NORRISS, D., WILSON, H. J. & BROWNE, D. 1982. The breeding population of the Peregrine in Ireland in 1981. *Irish Birds* 2, 145–52.

NYGÅRD, T. 1983. Pesticide residues and shell thinning in eggs of Peregrines in Norway. *Ornis Scand.* 14, 161–6.

ODSJÖ, T. & LINDBERG, P. 1977. Reduction of eggshell thickness of Peregrine in Sweden. Pp. 59–60, in *Pilgrimsfalk*. Report from a Peregrine conference held at Grimsö Wildlife Research Station, Sweden, 1–2 April 1977. Ed. Peter Lindberg. Swedish Society for the Conservation of Nature, Stockholm.

OLENDORFF, R. R. & KOCHERT, M. N. 1977. Land management for the conservation of birds of prey. *Proc. ICBP World Conf. on Birds of Prey*. Vienna 1975, pp. 294–307.

OLSEN, P. D. 1982. Ecogeographic and temporal variation in the eggs and nests of the Peregrine, *Falco peregrinus* (Aves: Falconidae), in Australia. *Aust. Wildl. Res.* 9, 277–91.

OLSEN, P. D. & OLSEN, J. 1979. Eggshell thinning in the Peregrine *Falco peregrinus* in Australia. *Aust. Wildl. Res.* 6, 217–26.

OLSEN, P. D. & OLSEN, J. 1987. Sexual size dimorphism in raptors: intrasexual competition in the larger sex for a scarce breeding resource, the smaller sex. *Emu* 87, 59–62.

OLSEN, P. D. & OLSEN, J. 1988. Population trends, distribution and status of the Peregrine Falcon in Australia. Chapter 28 in *Peregrine Falcon Populations. Their management and recovery*, ed. T. J. Cade, J. H. Enderson, C. G. Thelander & C. M. White. The Peregrine Fund, Inc., Boise, Idaho.

OLSSON, V. 1958. Dispersal, migration, longevity and death causes of *Strix aluco, Buteo buteo, Ardea cinerea* and *Larus argentatus*: a study based on recoveries of birds ringed in Fenno-Scandia. *Acta Vertebratica* 1, 85–189.

ORTON, D. A. 1975. The speed of a Peregrine's dive. *The Field* 25 Sept, 588–90.

ORTON, K. J. P. 1925. Bird life in the mountains. Chapter VIII in *The Mountains of Snowdonia*, ed. H. R. Carr and G. A. Lister. Crosby Lockwood, London.

OSMAN, C. 1963. End of the Peregrine problem. *The Racing Pigeon*, 198–9.

OSMAN, C. 1970–71. The Peregrine Falcon. Pt. I. History of Attacks. Pt. II. The problem solves itself. *Racing Pigeon Pictorial*, 1, 263–265, 285; 2, 157–9.

PALMER, E. M. & BALLANCE, D. K. 1968. *The Birds of Somerset*. London.

PARKER, A. 1979. Peregrines at a Welsh coastal eyrie. *Brit. Birds* 72, 104–14.

PATON, W. & PIKE, O. G. 1929. *The Birds of Ayrshire*. Witherby, London.

PEAKALL, D. B. 1976. The Peregrine (*Falco peregrinus*) and pesticides. *Canad. Field Nat.*, 3, 301–7.

PEAKALL, D. B. & KIFF, L. F. 1979. Eggshell thinning and DDE residue levels among Peregrine Falcons *Falco peregrinus*: a global perspective. *Ibis* 121, 200–4.

PEAKALL, D. B., CADE, T. J., WHITE, C. M. & HAUGH, J. R. 1975. Organochlorine residues in Alaskan Peregrines. *Pesticide Monitor. J.*, 8, 255–60.

PEAKALL, D. B., REYNOLDS, L. M. & FRENCH, M. C. 1976. DDE in eggs of the Peregrine Falcon. *Bird Study* 23, 183–6.

PEARSALL, W. H. 1950. *Mountains and Moorlands*. New Naturalist Series, Collins, London.

PEREGRINE FUND ANNUAL REPORT. 1989. World Center for Birds of Prey, Boise, Idaho.

PETTIFOR, R. A. 1983. Territorial behaviour of Kestrels in arable fenland. *Brit. Birds* 76, 206–14.

PICOZZI, N. & WEIR, D. 1974. Breeding biology of the Buzzard in Speyside. *Brit. Birds* 67, 199–210.

POPHAM, H. L. 1897. Notes of birds observed on the Yenisei River, Siberia, in 1895. *Ibis*, 7th series, 3, 89–108.

PRESTT, I. 1965. An enquiry into the recent breeding status of some of the smaller birds of prey and crows in Britain. *Bird Study* 12, 196–221.

PRUETT-JONES, S. G., WHITE, C. M. & DEVINE, W. R. 1981. Breeding of the Peregrine Falcon in Victoria, Australia. *Emu* 80, 253–69.

PRUETT-JONES, S. G., WHITE, C. M. & EMISON, W. B. 1981. Eggshell thinning and organochlorine residues in eggs and prey of Peregrine Falcons from Victoria, Australia. *Emu* 80, 288–91.

RATCLIFFE, D. A. 1958. Broken eggs in Peregrine eyries. *Brit. Birds* 51, 23–6.

RATCLIFFE, D. A. 1962. Breeding density in the peregrine *Falco peregrinus* and Raven *Corvus corax*. *Ibis* 104, 13–39.

RATCLIFFE, D. A. 1963. The status of the Peregrine in Great Britain. *Bird Study* 10, 56–90.

RATCLIFFE, D. A. 1967. Decrease in eggshell weight in certain birds of prey. *Nature* 215, 208–10.

RATCLIFFE, D. A. 1969. Population trends of the Peregrine Falcon in Great Britain. Pp. 239–69, in *Peregrine Falcon Populations. Their biology and decline*, ed. J. J. Hickey. Univ. Wisconsin Press, Madison and London.

RATCLIFFE, D. A. 1970. Changes attributable to pesticides in egg breakage frequency and eggshell thickness in some British birds. *J. Appl. Ecol.* 7, 67–115.

RATCLIFFE, D. A. 1972. The peregrine population of Great Britain in 1971. *Bird Study* 19, 117–156.

RATCLIFFE, D. A. 1973. Studies of the recent breeding success of the Peregrine *Falco peregrinus*. *J. Reprod. Fert.*, Suppl. 19, 377–89.

RATCLIFFE, D. A. (ed.) 1977. *A Nature Conservation Review*. 2 Vols. Cambridge Univ. Press, Cambridge.

RATCLIFFE, D. A. 1984a. The Peregrine breeding population of the United Kingdom in 1981. *Bird Study* 31, 1–18.

RATCLIFFE, D. A. 1984b. Tree-nesting by Peregrines in Britain and Ireland. *Bird Study* 31, 232–3.

RATCLIFFE, D. A. 1988a. The Peregrine population of Great Britain and Ireland, 1965–1985. Chapter 17 in *Peregrine Falcon Populations. Their management and recovery*, ed. T. J. Cade, J. H. Enderson, C. G. Thelander & C. M. White. The Peregrine Fund, Inc., Boise, Idaho.

RATCLIFFE, D. A. 1988b. Human impacts on the environment in relation to the history and biological future of the Peregrine. Chapter 77 in *Peregrine Falcon Populations. Their management and recovery*, ed. T. J. Cade, J. H. Enderson, C. G. Thelander & C. M. White. The Peregrine Fund, Inc., Boise, Idaho.

RAWNSLEY, H. D. 1899, *Life and nature at the English Lakes*. James MacLehose, Glasgow.

REDIG, P. T. 1981. Aspergillosis in raptors. In *Recent Advances in the Study of Raptor Diseases*, ed. J. E. Cooper & A. G. Greenwood. Chiron Publications, Keighley.

REDIG, P. T. 1986. Mycotic infections of birds of prey. In *Zoo and Wild Animal Medicine*, ed. M. E. Fowler. W. B. Saunders, Philadelphia.

REDIG, P. T., COOPER, J. E. & HUNTER, B. (eds) 1993. *Raptor Biomedicine*. Univ. Minnesota Press, Minnesota.

REMPLE, J. D. 1981. Avian malaria with comments on other haemosporidia in large falcons. In *Recent Advances in the Study of Raptor Diseases*, ed. J. E. Cooper & A. G. Greenwood. Chiron Publications, Keighley.

RINTOUL, L. J. & BAXTER, E. V. 1935. *A Vertebrate Fauna of Forth*. London.

RISEBROUGH, R. W. & PEAKALL, D. B. 1988. The relative importance of the several organochlorines in the decline of Peregrine Falcon populations. Commentary, pp. 449–68 in *Peregrine Falcon Populations. Their Management and Recovery*, ed. T. J. Cade, J. H. Enderson, C. G. Thelander and C. M. White. The Peregrine Fund, Inc., Boise, Idaho.

RITCHIE, J. 1920. *The Influence of Man on Animal Life in Scotland*. Cambridge Univ. Press, Cambridge.

RODRIGUEZ, F. 1972. The Peregrine Falcon: ace of bird hunters. Pp. 94–119 (Chapter 60) in *World of Wildlife*, Vol. 5, Orbis Publishing, London.

ROGERS, W. & LEATHERWOOD, S. 1981. Observations of feeding at sea by a Peregrine Falcon and an Osprey. *Condor* 83, 89–90.

ROYAL SOCIETY FOR THE PROTECTION OF BIRDS. 1980. *Silent Death. The destruction of birds and mammals through the deliberate misuse of poisons in Britain*. RSPB, Sandy.

ROYAL SOCIETY FOR THE PROTECTION OF BIRDS & NATURE CONSERVANCY COUNCIL. 1991. *Death by Design. The persecution of birds of prey and owls in the UK 1979–89*. RSPB and NCC, Sandy and Peterborough.

ROTHSCHILD, M. & CLAY, T. 1952. *Fleas, Flukes and Cuckoos*. New Naturalist Series. Collins, London.

RUDEBECK, G. 1951. The choice of prey and modes of hunting of predatory birds with special reference to their selective effect. *Oikos* 3, 200–31.

RYVES, B. H. 1948. *Bird Life in Cornwall*, Collins, London.

SALMINEN, P. & WIKMAN, M. 1977. Pilgrimsfalkens populationstrend och status i Finland. Pp. 25–30 in *Pilgrimsfalk*. Report from a Peregrine conference held at Grimsö Wildlife Research Station, Sweden, 1–2 April 1977. Ed. Peter Lindberg. Swedish Society for the Conservation of Nature. Stockholm.

SAUROLA, P. 1977. Ringmärkning av Pilgrimsfalk i Finland. Pp. 33–8 in *Pilgrimsfalk*. Report from a Peregrine conference held at Grimsö Wildlife Research Station, Sweden 1–2 April 1977. Ed. Peter Lindberg. Swedish Society for the Conservation of Nature, Stockholm.

SAXBY, H. L. 1874. *The Birds of Shetland*. Maclachan & Stewart, Edinburgh.

SCHANTZ, T. VON & NILSSON, I. N. 1981. The reversed size dimorphism in birds of prey: a new hypothesis. *Oikos*, 36, 129–32.

SCHEJ, P. J. 1977. Prosjekt Falk – resultater og erfaringer fra 1976. Pp. 17–23 in *Pilgrimsfalk*. Report from a Peregrine conference held at Grimsö Wildlife Research Station, Sweden, 1–2 April 1977. Ed. Peter Lindberg. Swedish Society for the Conservation of Nature, Stockholm.

SCHEPERS, F., VAN ASSELDONK, E. & LINSEN, F. 1992. Terugkeer van de Slechtvalk *Falco peregrinus* als broedvogel in Nederland? *Limosa*, 65, 28–9.

SCHILLING, F., VON, BOTTCHER, M. & WALTER, G. 1981. Probleme des Zeckenbefalls bei Nestlingen des Wanderfalken. *Journal für Ornithologie*, 112, 359–67.

SEEBOHM, H. 1880. *Siberia in Europe*. John Murray, London.

SERVICE, R. 1903. The diurnal and nocturnal raptorial birds of the Solway area. *Trans. Dumfries Galloway Nat. Hist. Antiq. Soc.* 17, 327.

SHARROCK, J. T. R. (ed. for British Trust for Ornithology and Irish Wildbird Conservancy) 1976. *The Atlas of Breeding Birds in Britain and Ireland*. T. & A. D. Poyser, Berkhamsted.

SHEAIL, J. 1976. *Nature in Trust. The history of nature conservation in Britain*. Blackie, Glasgow and London.

SNOW, D. W. 1968. Movements and mortality of British Kestrels. *Bird Study* 15, 65–83.

SPEEDY, T. 1920. *A Natural History of Sport in Scotland with Rod and Gun*. William Blackwood, Edinburgh and London.

STABLER, R. M. 1969. *Trichomonas gallinae* as a factor in the decline of the Peregrine Falcon. Pp. 435–8, in *Peregrine Falcon Populations. Their biology and decline*. ed. J. J. Hickey. Univ. Wisconsin Press, Madison and London.

STEVENSON, H. 1866. *The Birds of Norfolk*, vol. I.

STOVIN, G. H. T. 1964. *Breeding Better Pigeons.* Faber & Faber, London.

STUART, A. J. 1977. The vertebrates of the last cold stage in Britain and Ireland. *Phil. Trans. R. Soc. Lond. B.* 280, 295–312.

SYKES, G. P., MURPHY, C. & HARDASWICK., V. 1981. *Salmonella* infection in a captive peregrine falcon. *J. Am. Vet. Med. Assoc.* 179, 1269–71.

TABKEN, H. D. 1972. Die Erhaltung des Wanderfalken, vom Blickpunk der Salmonellosen und im Vergleich zur Pestizidliteratun gesehen. Inaugural Dissertation, Hannover Veterinary School.

TAYLOR, J. C. & BLACKMORE, D. K. 1961. A short note on the heavy mortality in foxes during the winter 1959–60. *Vet. Rec.* 73, 232–3.

TEMPLE LANG, J. 1968. Peregrine Falcon Survey 1967–68. *Irish Bird Rep.*, 16, 3–4.

TEMPLE LANG, J. 1969–72. Unpublished reports on Peregrine surveys in the Republic of Ireland to the Irish Wildbird Conservancy.

TERRASSE, J.-F. & TERRASSE, M. Y. 1969. The status of the Peregrine Falcon in France in 1965. Pp. 225–30, in *Peregrine Falcon Populations. Their biology and decline,* ed. J. J. Hickey. Univ. Wisconsin Press. Madison and London.

THESIGER, W. 1959. *Arabian Sands.* Longmans, London.

TICEHURST, N. F. 1909. *A History of the Birds of Kent.* London.

TRAINER, D. O. 1969. Diseases in raptors, a review of the literature. Pp. 425–34, in *Peregrine Falcon Populations. Their biology and decline,* ed. J. J. Hickey. Univ. Wisconsin Press, Madison and London.

TRELEAVEN, R. B. 1961. Notes on the Peregrine in Cornwall, *Brit. Birds* 54, 136–142.

TRELEAVEN, R. B. 1977. *Peregrine. The private life of the Peregrine Falcon.* Headline Publications, Penzance.

TRELEAVEN, R. B. 1980a. Note on the hunting behaviour of the Peregrine. *Brit. Birds.*

TRELEAVEN, R. B. 1980b. High and low intensity hunting in raptors. *Z. Tierpsychol.* 54, 339–54.

TRISTAM, H. B. 1905. *Birds, in Victoria County History of Durham,* James Street, London.

TUCK, G. S. 1970. Landbirds onboard on the ocean routes. *Sea Swallow* 20, 36–8.

TUCK, L. M. 1960. *The Murres.* Canadian Wildlife Service, Ottawa.

TURBERVILE, G. 1575. *The Booke of Faulconrie or Hawking.* London.

TURNER, L. M. 1886. *Contributions to the Natural History of Alaska.* Govt. Print. Off., Washington.

TYLER, C. 1966. A study of the eggshells of the Falconiformes. *J. Zool., Lond* 150, 413–25.

TYLER, S. J. & ORMEROD, S. J. 1990. Mammals taken by Peregrines in Mid Wales. *Welsh Bird Report,* 57.

USPENSKI, S. M. 1966. Verbreitung und Okologie der Rothalsgans. *Falke* 13, 83–5.

USSHER, R. J. & WARREN, R. 1900. *The Birds of Ireland.* Gurney & Jackson, London.

UTTENDÖRFER, O. 1939. *Die Ernährung der deutschen Raubvögel und Eulen.* Neudamm.

UTTENDÖRFER, O. 1952 *Neue Ergebnisse über die Ernährung der Greifvögel und Eulen.* Eugen Ulmer, Stuttgart.

VENABLES, L. S. V. & VENABLES, U. M. 1955. *Birds and Mammals of Shetland.* Oliver & Boyd, Edinburgh.

VILLAGE, A. 1990. *The Kestrel* T. & A. D. Poyser, London.

VOGT, W. 1948. *The Road to Survival.* Gollancz, London.

VON SCHANTZ, T. & NILSSON, I. N. 1980. The reversed size dimorphism in birds of prey: a new hypothesis. *Oikos* 36, 129–32.

WALKER, W., MATTOX, W. G. & RISEBROUGH, R. W. 1973. Pollutant and shell thickness determinations of Peregrine eggs from West Greenland. *Arctic* 26, 256–7.

WALLACE, J. 1693. *A description of the Isles of Orkney.* Edinburgh.

WALPOLE-BOND, J. 1914. *Field Studies of Some Rarer British Birds.* Witherby, London.

WALPOLE-BOND, J. 1938. *A History of Sussex Birds.* 3 Vols. Witherby, London.

WALTER, H. 1979. *Eleonora's Falcon; adaptations to prey and habitat in a social raptor.* Univ. Chicago Press, Chicago and London.

WARD, F. P. 1986. Parasites and their treatment in birds of prey. In *Zoo and Wild Animal Medicine,* ed. M. E. Fowler. W. B. Saunders, Philadelphia.

WATSON, J. 1888. The ornithology of Skiddaw, Scafell and Helvellyn. *Naturalist*, 161.

WEIR, D. N. 1977. The Peregrine in N.E. Scotland in relation to food and to pesticides. Pp. 56–8 in *Pilgrimsfalk*. Report from a Peregrine conference held at Grimsö Wildlife Research Station, Sweden, 1–2 April 1977, ed. Peter Lindberg. Swedish Society for the Conservation of Nature, Stockholm.

WEIR, D. N. 1978. Wild Peregrines and Grouse. *Falconer* 7, 98–102.

WEIR, D. 1979. Brown trout among food remains in a Peregrine's nest. *Bird Study* 26, 200.

WHITE, C. M. 1975. Studies on Peregrine Falcons in the Aleutian Islands. *Raptor Res. Rep.* no. 3, 33–50.

WHITE, C. M. & CADE, T. J. 1971. Cliff-nesting raptors and Ravens along the Colville River in Arctic Alaska. *The Living Bird*, Tenth Annual, Cornell Laboratory of Ornithology.

WHITE, C. M. & BOYCE, D. A. 1988. An overview of Peregrine Falcon subspecies. Chapter 76 in *Peregrine Falcon Populations. Their management and recovery*. ed. T. J. Cade, J. H. Enderson, C. G. Thelander and C. M. White. The Peregrine Fund Inc., Boise, Idaho.

WHITE, G. 1789. *The Natural History of Selborne*. Edition of 1901 by Grant Allen. Bodley Head, London.

WHITNEY, L. F. 1961. *Keep your Pigeons Flying*. London.

WILLE, F. 1977. Pilgrimsfalken i Danmark. P. 31 in *Pilgrimsfalk*. Report from a Peregrine conference held at Grimsö Wildlife Research Station, Sweden, 1–2 April 1977, ed. Peter Lindberg. Swedish Society for the Conservation of Nature, Stockholm.

WITHERBY, H. F., JOURDAIN, F. C. R., TICEHURST, N. F. & TUCKER, B. W. 1939. *The Handbook of British Birds*, Vol. III. Witherby, London.

WOODFORD, M. H. 1960. *A Manual of Falconry*. London.

WREGE, P. H. & CADE, T. J. 1977. Courtship behavior of large falcons in captivity. *Raptor Res.* 11, 1–27.

YOUNG, H. F. 1969. Hypotheses on Peregrine population dynamics. Pp. 513–518 in *Peregrine Falcon Populations. Their biology and decline*, ed. J. J. Hickey. Univ. Wisconsin Press, Madison and London.

ZUCKERMAN, S. 1955. Toxic chemicals in agriculture, risks to wildlife. Report to the Minister of Agriculture, Fisheries and Food and to the Secretary of State for Scotland of the working party on precautionary measures against toxic chemicals used in agriculture. HMSO, London.

Table 1   405

TABLE 1: *Distribution and numbers of Peregrine nesting places in Britain*

County	Number of recorded territories		Estimated average number of breeding pairs 1930–39		Number of breeding territories occupied 1991	
	Coast	Inland	Coast	Inland	Coast	Inland
ENGLAND						
Kent	9		9		1	
Sussex	13	2	10		2	
Isle of Wight	5		4		3	
Dorset	18		16		9	
Devon	38	9	30		37	9
Cornwall	41	3	36		40	3
Somerset	9	5	6	2	5	4
Gloucester		3		1		3
Hereford		1				1
Wiltshire		1				
Shropshire		2				2
Stafford		2				1
Derbyshire		5		1		5
Cheshire		3				3
Yorkshire	5	28	2	7	3	26
Durham		4				1
Lancashire		25		2		23
Westmorland		40		12		36
Cumberland	3	46	1	17	2	44
Northumberland	1	16		5		14
Isle of Man	18	4	11		18	2
Total	160	199	125	47	120	177
WALES						
Monmouth	1	8		3	1	7
Glamorgan	7	19	6	4	4	17
Carmarthen	3	11	2	2	3	11
Pembroke	39	3	30		33	3
Cardigan	13	14	8	5	11	12
Brecon		17		8		16
Radnor		14		7		12
Montgomery		23		7		22
Merioneth		41		20		40
Denbigh		18		3		18
Caernarvon	14	32	11	14	13	26
Anglesey	11	3	5		9	2
Flint		2				2
Total	88	205	62	73	74	188

continued overleaf

TABLE 1 (*continued*)

County	Number of recorded territories		Estimated average number of breeding pairs 1930–39		Number of breeding territories occupied 1991	
	Coast	Inland	Coast	Inland	Coast	Inland
SCOTLAND						
Dumfries		27		10		26
Roxburgh		3				3
Peebles		10		2		10
Selkirk		1				1
Berwick	4	3	4		3	1
E Lothian	4	1	1		1	1
Midlothian		4				3
Kirkcudbright	7	27	5	12	6	27
Wigtown	20	1	12		18	1
Ayr	7	22	4	6	6	19
Lanark		3				3
Clackmannan		2		1		2
Fife	2	2			1	2
Kinross		3				3
Bute	11	6	6	4	8*	5*
Stirling		15		3		14
Dunbarton		8		2		7
Perth		93		45		75
Argyll	62	41	45	40	50	29
Inverness	43	70	30	65	27*	56*
Angus	2	29	2	10	1	29
Kincardine	3	?	3	2	3	?
Aberdeen	6	53	4	10	6	53
Banff	4	?	4	5	4	?
Moray	1	4	1	2		3
Nairn		1				1
Ross & Cromarty	18	42	18	30	13*	27*
Sutherland	25	45	23	35	13*	32*
Caithness	16	4	12		10*	3*
Orkney	32	2	25		23	
Shetland	30		30		5	
Total	297	522	229	284	198	436
GB total	545	926	416	404	392	801

NOTES:

* = Includes an estimate for territories not visited, based on recent history of occupation and sample results.

1. Relationship of counties to regions and districts of Tables 2–6 is indicated in Chapter 4.

2. Number of recorded territories and 1991 occupations for Kincardine and Banff are included in Aberdeen figures.

Table 2   407

TABLE 2: *Peregrine population level and breeding performance in 1961 compared with 1930–39*

	1	2	3		4		5		6		7	8
Region/district	Number of territories visited 1961	Estimated av. no. of pairs 1930–39	Number of territories occupied	%	No. of pairs producing eggs	%	No. of pairs hatching eggs	%	No. of pairs rearing young	%	Est. av. total no. of pairs 1930–39	Est. total no. occupied terr. in 1961
SE England	24	21	7	33	2	10	2	10	2	10	23	7
SW England	42	38	13	34	4	11	3	8	1	3	91	20
Wales coastal	28	21	7	33	1	5	1	5	1	5	62	18
Wales inland	62	53	21	40	10	19	7	13	7	13	73	28
N Eng coastal	10	9	3	25	1	11	–	–	–	–	14	4
N Eng inland	46	34	27	79	14	41	6	18	5	15	44	31
S Scot coastal	18	12	5	42	3	25	1	8	1	8	26	7
S Scot inland	23	20	19	95	8	40	5	25	5	25	30	29
S & E Highland fringe inland	22	21	20	95	7	33	3	14	1	5	69	66
S & E Highland west coast	18	18	17	94	11	61	9	50	8	44	40	37
S & E Highland east coast	5	5	4	80	1	20	1	20	1	20	14	7
S & E Highland centre inland	39	37	36	97	25	68	18	49	12	32	83	80
N & W Highland west coast	29	28	25	89	19	68	17	61	16	57	82	73
N & W Highland east coast	34	33	32	97	21	64	16	48	15	45	69	67
N & W Highland inland	31	30	24	80	13	43	7	23	7	23	100	80
GB Total	431	380	260	68	140	37	96	25	82	22	820	554

TABLE 3: *Peregrine population level and breeding performance in 1962 compared with 1930–39*

	1	2	3		4		5		6		7	8
Region/district	Number of territories visited 1962	Estimated av. no. of pairs 1930–39	Number of territories occupied	%	No. of pairs producing eggs	%	No. of pairs hatching eggs	%	No. of pairs rearing young	%	Est. av. total no. of pairs 1930–39	Est. total no. occupied terr. in 1962
SE England	27	24	1	4	—	—	—	—	—	—	23	1
SW England	46	36	5	14	2	6	2	6	2	6	91	10
Wales coastal	37	33	6	17	—	—	—	—	—	—	62	9
Wales inland	51	42	13	31	4	10	3	7	3	7	73	21
N Eng coastal	16	14	6	43	3	21	2	14	2	14	14	6
N Eng inland	38	31	16	52	8	26	2	6	1	3	44	21
S Scot coastal	17	15	3	20	1	7	1	7	1	7	26	5
S Scot inland	25	23	20	87	6	26	2	9	1	4	30	25
S & E Highland fringe inland	29	27	19	70	10	37	6	22	1	4	69	48
S & E Highland west coast	18	16	12	75	8	50	8	50	6	38	40	29
S & E Highland east coast	4	4	3	75	1	25	1	25	1	25	14	11
S & E Highland centre inland	38	37	34	92	26	70	23	62	17	46	83	76
N & W Highland west coast	49	45	32	71	17	38	17	38	15	33	82	58
N & W Highland east coast	52	48	46	96	22	46	18	38	17	35	69	66
N & W Highland inland	41	37	26	70	15	41	14	38	10	27	100	70
GB Total	488	432	242	56	123	28	99	23	77	18	820	456

Table 4   409

TABLE 4: *Peregrine population level and breeding performance in 1971 compared with 1930-39*

Region/district	Number of territories visited 1971	Estimated av. no. of pairs 1930-39	Number of territories occupied	%	No. of pairs producing eggs	%	No. of pairs hatching eggs	%	No. of pairs rearing young	%	Est. av. total no. of pairs 1930-39	Est. total no. occupied terr. in 1971
	1	2	3		4		5		6		7	8
SE England	27	24	–	–	–	–	–	–	–	–	23	0
SW England	64	52	10	19	5	10	5	10	4	8	91	15
Wales coastal	70	61	12	20	2	3	2	3	2	3	62	12
Wales inland	71	57	14	25	6	11	3	5	3	5	73	18
N Eng coastal	20	16	2	13	–	–	–	–	–	–	14	2
N Eng inland	54	39	29	74	17	44	14	36	13	33	44	32
S Scot coastal	24	20	9	45	4	20	2	10	2	10	26	11
S Scot inland	36	30	29	97	19	63	10	33	9	30	30	29
S & E Highland fringe inland	46	41	35	85	26	63	22	54	22	54	69	59
S & E Highland west coast	35	31	25	81	14	45	13	42	13	42	40	31
S & E Highland east coast	13	11	1	9	–	–	–	–	–	–	14	1
S & E Highland centre inland	76	70	66	94	43	61	37	56	36	51	83	76
N & W Highland west coast	71	67	41	61	21	31	19	28	19	28	82	48
N & W Highland east coast	61	58	25	43	11	19	8	14	8	14	69	27
N & W Highland inland	57	52	44	85	29	56	24	46	22	42	100	84
GB Total	725	629	342	54	197	31	159	25	153	24	820	445

TABLE 5: *Peregrine population level and breeding performance in 1981 compared with 1930–39*

Region/district	Number of territories visited 1981	Estimated av. no. of pairs 1930–39	Number of territories occupied	%	No. of pairs producing eggs	%	No. of pairs hatching eggs	%	No. of pairs rearing young	%	Est. av. total no. of pairs 1930–39	Est. total no. occupied terr. in 1981
	1	2	3		4		5		6		7	8
SE England	27	23	–	–	–	–	–	–	–	–	23	0
SW England	86	80	43	54	30	38	29	36	28	35	91	49
Wales coastal	76	62	44	71	27	44	25	40	24	39	62	44
Wales inland	100	73	81	111	51	70	43	59	39	53	73	81
N Eng coastal	17	12	12	100	8	67	8	67	7	58	14	12
N Eng inland	88	44	76	173	61	139	32	73	23	52	44	76
S Scot coastal	32	26	22	85	10	38	6	23	4	15	26	22
S Scot inland	53	30	45	150	35	117	23	77	16	53	30	45
S & E Highland fringe inland	86	69	76	110	58	84	48	70	46	67	69	76
S & E Highland west coast	42	31	38	123	23	74	17	55	17	55	40	45
S & E Highland east coast	14	14	5	36	3	21	3	21	2	14	14	5
S & E Highland centre inland	114	80	108	135	81	101	60	75	50	63	83	112
N & W Highland west coast	95	78	52	67	25	32	23	29	21	27	82	55
N & W Highland east coast	83	69	54	78	23	33	12	17	11	16	69	54
N & W Highland inland	96	85	74	87	59	61	48	56	47	55	100	75
GB Total	1009	776	730	94	494	64	377	49	335	43	820	751

Table 6   411

TABLE 6: *Peregrine population level and breeding performance in 1991 compared with 1930–39*

	1	2	3		4		5		6		7	8
Region/district	Number of territories visited 1991	Estimated av. no. of pairs 1930–39	Number of territories occupied	%	No. of pairs producing eggs	%	No. of pairs hatching eggs	%	No. of pairs rearing young	%	Est. av. total no. of pairs 1930–39	Est. total no. occupied terr. in 1991
SE England	27	23	6	26	5	22	5	22	5	22	23	6
SW England coastal	100	86	91	106	60	70	56	65	55	64	91	91
SW England inland	19	3	19	633	13	433	13	433	13	433	3	19
Wales coastal	87	62	74	119	55	85	39	63	39	63	62	74
Wales inland	206	73	188	258	146	200	108	148	99	136	73	188
Midlands	15	0	15	100	12	–	9	–	8	–	0	15
N Eng coastal	28	14	23	164	13	93	12	86	12	86	14	23
N Eng inland	155	44	143	325	125	284	101	230	96	218	44	143
S Scot coastal	39	26	34	131	24	92	17	65	17	65	26	34
S Scot inland	96	30	95	313	80	267	51	170	47	157	30	95
S & E Highland fringe inland	115	69	94	136	78	113	62	90	58	84	69	102
S & E Highland west coast	42	31	37	119	19	61	17	55	17	55	40	53
S & E Highland east coast	17	14	14	100	12	86	8	57	8	57	14	14
S & E Highland centre inland	165	71	145	204	120	169	92	130	89	125	83	157
N & W Highland west coast	82	70	44	63	25	30	22	26	19	21	82	67
N & W Highland east coast	72	65	34	52	15	25	13	21	12	20	69	39
N & W Highland inland	88	78	57	73	41	53	32	41	27	35	100	73
GB Total	1353	759	1113	147	843	111	657	87	621	82	820	1193

NOTES (to Tables 2–6):
1. Regions and districts are as shown in the map (Fig. 1).
2. Figures in column 2 are derived from knowledge of regularity of occupation of territories actually visited (column 1) in the particular year.
3. Percentages in columns 3–6 are derived as a proportion of figures in column 2 (= 100%). This gives a better impression of the regional scale of decrease in numbers and breeding performance than if columns 4–6 are expressed as proportions of column 3.
4. Figures in column 7 coincide with those in the middle two columns of Table 1.
5. Where figures in column 8 are larger than those in column 3, an estimate has been added for occupation of territories not visited, based on known occupation rate for each region.

TABLE 7: *Number of single Peregrines occupying breeding territories*

1	2	3	4		5		6		7
		Estimated 1930–39	Number of single		Number of occupied		Number of actual &		Estimated total GB
	Number of	population of	Peregrines		territories		notional pairs		population in
Year	territories visited	territories visited	Peregrines	% of col. 5	territories	% of col. 3	notional pairs	% of col. 3	territorial pairs
1961	431	380	51	20	260	68	235	62	508
1962	488	432	50	21	242	56	217	50	410
1971	725	629	66	19	342	54	309	49	402
1981	1009	776	79	11	730	94	691	89	730
1991	1353	759	47	4	1113	147	1090	144	1170

NOTES:
Strictly, breeding populations should be expressed as number of breeding pairs rather than number of occupied territories, since some of these are held by apparently single Peregrines. This table attempts to apply this correction by converting the numbers of single birds into notional 'pairs'. The resulting adjustments reduce the totals between columns 5 and 6 but give a more accurate basis for comparing populations in different years. The decline in proportion of single birds as recovery has proceeded is noteworthy. Figures in column 7 are derived by applying percentages in column 6 to the base-line population of 820 pairs, but those for 1991 are compiled from region-by-region estimates.

Table 8   413

TABLE 8: Prey taken by Peregrines in different districts of Great Britain

Species	Mean weight (g)	1 Lakeland 1904-1919	2 Lakeland 1928/9-1934	3 Lakeland 1923-1969	4 Lakeland 1945-1977	5 Lakeland 1961-1962	6 Snowdonia 1950-1957, 1971; 1978-79	7 Southern U'plands 1923-69	8 Southern U'plands 1946-1974	9 Southern U'plands 1974-1975	10 Highlands (inland) 1961-1972	11 Highlands (inland) 1961-1962, 1974	12 Highlands (inland) 1964-1975	13 Highlands (coastal, few seabirds) 1961-62, 1971	14 Highlands (coastal, seabird colonies) 1961-62, 1971
Manx Shearwater	400												1		
Fulmar	747													3	22
Mallard	1010						1	1	1		3	1	1		
Teal	261							1		1		2	4		
Wigeon	691								1	2		1			
Goosander	1358														
Red-breasted Merganser	1350		1					1					1		
Buzzard	982	1													
Sparrowhawk	193	1													
Peregrine	926	1													
Merlin	130														
Kestrel	208									1		1			
Red Grouse	637	8	18	24	5	10	2	9	40	39	1	2	3	4	3
Ptarmigan	500										49	37	111	2	
Black Grouse	1187								1		15	3	27		
Partridge	389	2							2	3	1	1			
Pheasant	1075	1							1						
Corncrake	140													1	
Oystercatcher	524	9					2	2	12	17	10	3	1	4	4
Lapwing	214		2	9		6	1	2		3	13	5	13	3	12
Ringed Plover	80					1									
Dotterel	130												1		
Golden Plover	193	1		6	3	8		3	11	18	19	14	24	4	3
Snipe	106		14	15	10	5		6	5	27	10	1	35	1	3
Woodcock	267	1		1		2	1	1	5	1	1		5	2	
Curlew	704	4	3	5		2	1	1	1	1	11	3	4		3
Whimbrel	550									4	3	1		1	
Common Sandpiper	66										1		2		
Wood Sandpiper	90												1		
Redshank	150	2	2	8	4	6	1	1	6	16	3	1	4	2	6

continued overleaf

TABLE 8 (continued)

Species	Mean weight (g)	1 Lakeland 1904–1919	2 Lakeland 1928-9–1934	3 Lakeland 1923–1969	4 Lakeland 1945–1977	5 Lakeland 1961–1962	6 Snowdonia 1950–1957, 1971 1978–79	7 Southern U'lands 1923–69	8 Southern U'lands 1946–1974	9 Southern U'lands 1974–1975	10 Highlands (inland) 1961–1972	11 Highlands (inland) 1961–1962, 1974	12 Highlands (inland) 1964–1975	13 Highlands (coastal) tern seabirds 1961–62, 1971	14 Highlands (coastal) seabird colonies 1961–62, 1971
Greenshank	200									3		1	7		
Dunlin	55								2			2	2		
Knot	100					3			1				1	1	
Sanderling	100					1								1	
Purple Sandpiper	100														
Turnstone	100													1	
Great Black-backed Gull	1470								2			1		1	
Lesser Black-backed Gull	1020													2	1
Herring Gull	1020										1			4	10
Common Gull	410		2		1			2			5	1	3	3	
Black-headed Gull	266	1		2		1			3	23	9	4	28	1	
Kittiwake	385										3			9	23
Common Tern	122	1		1								3	1		
Arctic Tern	122						1								
Razorbill	625										1				7
Guillemot	600														12
Black Guillemot	400														19
Puffin	375								3				1		5
Auk species	500											2		2	62
Stock Dove	296			4	2		1				1				6
Rock Dove	300													24	
Domestic Pigeon	425	37	91	110	97	62	64	55	195	416	50	24	100	} 24	} 61
Wood Pigeon	480	3	19	1		12		4	5	6	5	2	13		
Collared Dove	200						1						1	2	
Cuckoo	110	1		2		2			1	4	5	7	6	1	
Barn Owl	291					1			1						
Little Owl	173					1									
Tawny Owl	427					1									
Long-eared Owl	300												1		
Short-eared Owl	300														

Table 8 (continued)   *415*

Species	Total													
Swift	40												1	
Green Woodpecker	186						1		1			2		
Greater Spotted Woodpecker	78	1								1		1		
Wryneck	80													
Skylark	37	1	3	8	11		12	4			11	2		1
House Martin	17	1	4	1	1	4			1			1		
Carrion Crow	572	1				4	20	21	12	4	} 3	1		2
Hooded Crow							1	4		11			1	10
Rook	482	1	5	6	4	3	1	1	4			9		
Jackdaw	245	2	2	3			1	7						
Magpie	231						1	1	1			1		
Jay	167	1			1				1					
Chough	240									1				
Blue Tit	11													
Coal Tit	10													
Treecreeper	9													
Dipper	64					1		1	1					
Mistle Thrush	118	9	2	20	2	1	1	11	5	3	4	2		1
Fieldfare	112	2	1	2	24	1	26	16	9		12	1		1
Song Thrush	80	36		8	2	1	9	4	8	1	6	5		2
Redwing	67	1			4	1	4	3	1		2			
Unidentified Thrush	80				29						20			
Ring Ouzel	90	2	6	1	4	2	1	7	5	2	11			1
Blackbird	92	2	12	9	69	7	30	24	12	13	4	4		1
Wheatear	27				1		3	2	3		1	1		1
Stonechat	15							1						
Robin	19			1	19			1						
Meadow Pipit	20	7	2	2		1	7	25	8	1	11			
Pied Wagtail	22	2				1	1	1						
Grey Wagtail	17	1						1			1			
Starling	77	21	24	21	7	52	6	37	57	13	7	14	7	16
Hawfinch	52	1												
Greenfinch	27	6	2	1	5			1	2					
Goldfinch	16													
Siskin	15	2									2			

continued overleaf

TABLE 8 (continued)

Species	Mean weight (g)	1 Lakeland 1904-1919	2 Lakeland 1928/9-1934	3 Lakeland 1923-1969	4 Lakeland 1945-1977	5 Lakeland 1961-1962	6 Snowdonia 1950-1957, 1971 1978-79	7 Southern Uplands 1923-69	8 Southern Uplands 1946-1974	9 Southern Uplands 1974-1975	10 Highlands (inland) 1961-1972	11 Highlands (inland) 1961-1962, 1974	12 Highlands (inland) 1964-1975	13 Highlands (coastal) jura seabirds) 1961-62, 1971	14 Highlands (coastal) seabird colonies) 1961-62, 1971
Linnet	18									1					
Bullfinch	22					2				3	2				
Crossbill	30										1				
Chaffinch	22	3			1	7	2	2	3	5	10	1	7		
Brambling	22										1				
Reed Bunting	19								1		2	1			
Snow Bunting	30		2												
House Sparrow	29					5									
Domestic chicken	300	6													
Rabbit	300		2						1	1	1			1	
Brown hare (leveret)	300									1					
Mountain hare (leveret)	300												1		
Water vole	100		3												
Field Vole	50	1							1						
Total number of prey individuals		143	241	300	182	407	92	113	446	778	329	177	526	100	296
Total number of prey species		35	24	29	18	41	20	21	38	43	46	39	50	33	26

NOTES:
1. Data were collected as follows:
   1. E. B. Dunlop and J. F. Peters
   2. R. H. Brown
   3. E. Blezard
   4. D. A. Ratcliffe
   5. F. Parr
   6. D. A. Ratcliffe
   7. E. Blezard
   8. D. A. Ratcliffe
   9. R. Roxburgh and R. Mearns
   10. D. A. Ratcliffe
   11. F. Parr, J. Hardey
   12. D. Weir
   13. D. A. Ratcliffe, K. D. Smith, J. Morgan
   14. K. D. Smith, E. Balfour, R. D. Lowe

2. Data are for breeding Peregrines during March-July, and are based mainly on pluckings or other remains of prey found at or near eyries.
3. Weights of prey species were provided by R. Spencer and give estimates appropriate to birds in breeding condition.
4. The following additional species have been reported taken as prey in Britain: Storm Petrel, Heron, Common Scoter, Goldeneye, Shelduck, Barnacle Goose, Brent Goose, Red-legged Partridge, Water Rail, Moorhen, Coot, Little Ringed Plover, Grey Plover, Black-tailed Godwit, Bar-tailed Godwit, Stone Curlew, Arctic Skua, Long-tailed Skua, Black Tern, Roseate Tern, Turtle Dove, Nightjar, Kingfisher, Woodlark, Swallow, Sand Martin, Raven, Great Tit, Whinchat, Redstart, Willow Warbler, Goldcrest, Dunnock, Rock Pipit, Twite, Yellowhammer, Corn Bunting.

TABLE 9: *Use of nests of other species*

	Ledge (no nest)	Raven	Buzzard	Golden Eagle	Carrion Crow	Total
North Wales	28	3	–	–	–	31
Northern England	56	21	–	–	–	77
Southern Scotland	104	60	4	–	1	69
Highlands	58	18	1	1	–	78
Great Britain Total	246	102	5	1	1	355

NOTE:
The data are limited to my own field records.

TABLE 10: *Altitude of Peregrine inland nesting cliffs in Britain*
(a) Records up to 1979, (b) new records after 1979.

District m		0–107	107–213	213–320	320–427	427–534	534–640	640+
Wales	(a)	1	7	13	42	31	10	8
	(b)	7	24	27	34	19	2	2
Northern England	(a)	–	6	21	27	39	17	3
	(b)	13	9	20	33	17	6	1
Southern Uplands	(a)	–	1	12	29	17	9	1
	(b)	5	10	13	21	10	1	–
Southern Highlands fringe	(a)	–	6	22	23	17	10	4
	(b)	1	13	23	14	12	5	1
Central Highlands	(a)	1	2	2	15	31	18	11
	(b)	2	4	8	21	17	9	9
North-east Highlands	(a)	3	11	9	13	2	–	–
	(b)	4	7	8	2	2	1	–
North-west Highlands	(a)	3	23	20	13	1	–	–
	(b)	2	3	6	3	2	–	–

NOTES:
Figures are numbers of cliffs (including alternatives) in each altitude class. Good cliffs at altitudes above 640 m (2100 ft) are available to Peregrines only in Snowdonia. Lakeland and the Scottish Highlands. Altitudinal descent in choice of breeding cliffs is most marked between the more continental central Highlands and the oceanic north-west Highlands.
Not all post-1979 records for the Central Highlands are available.

TABLE 11: *Vertical height of Peregrine inland nesting cliffs in Britain*

District	*m*	*0–11*	*11–20*	*20–30*	*30–44*	*44–60*	*60–75*	*75–90*	*90 +*
South Wales			2	8	6	4	1	1	
North Wales		1	4	3	16	8	7	4	14
Pennines		2	17	7	4	1			
Lakeland			1	7	16	13	7	9	14
Cheviots		4	10	3	1		1		
Southern Uplands		6	28	13	10	3	3	3	3
Southern Highland fringe			3	8	19	7	6	3	7
Central Highlands			7	7	15	15	5	4	8
North & West Highlands			6	7	16	8	7	6	6
Total		13	78	63	93	59	37	30	52

NOTES:
The above figures refer only to those cliffs for which I have been able to make a reasonable estimate of height, and so are far less than the total for Great Britain. Alternative cliffs are counted separately.

TABLE 12: *Aspect of Peregrine inland nesting cliffs in Britain*

District	*N*	*NE*	*E*	*SE*	*S*	*SW*	*W*	*NW*
South Wales	13	11	11	4	12	7	14	5
North Wales	11	26	24	13	9	7	14	16
Pennines	4	11	8	5	5	10	11	11
Lakeland	9	28	32	10	4	4	7	11
Cheviots	6	1	4	1	–	–	3	7
Southern Uplands	15	18	16	22	21	11	6	3
Southern Highland fringe	14	32	29	16	24	14	14	12
Central Highlands	15	11	21	28	11	5	12	18
North and west Highlands	16	18	11	13	25	14	10	16
Total	103	156	156	112	111	72	91	99

NOTES:
Alternative nesting cliffs are scored individually in the lists. This is not the complete list; many records of ravine nesting places do not report aspect, and this can vary by 180° when both sides of a ravine are used, as often happens.

TABLE 13: *Date of laying of first egg in different regions of Britain*

Region	Period	No. of clutches	Date of first egg	Mean alt. m	Mean temp* for Feb (°C)
SE England	1905–49	126	1/2 Apr	60	5·0
SW England	1913–56	20	3 Apr	60	5·8
Wales	1912–57	53	7/8 Apr	335	3·1
NW England	1903–77	113	8 Apr	425	1·7
S Scotland	1946–79	131	8 Apr	365	1·7
C & E Highlands	1949–71	20	9 Apr	395	0·8

(No data are available for other parts of the Highlands)
*Corrected for altitude.

TABLE 14: *Laying date in relation to altitude*

Altitude m	210–320	320–410	410–500	500–610
No. of records	57	60	59	44
Average date (April days)	6·6	8·2	8·7	9·6

TABLE 15: *Size, weight and thickness index of Peregrine eggshells in Britain and Ireland*

District	Period	No. of clutches	Average length (mm)	Average breadth (mm)	Length × breadth (mm²)	Average weight (g)	Standard error	% decrease in weight	Av. index of shell thickness	Standard error	% decrease in shell index
S E England	1841–1940	22	51·9	40·4	2097	3·84	±0·07	0·0	1·83	±0·03	0·0
	1947–49	2	50·2	41·4	2078	3·41	±0·04	11·2	1·64	±0·06	10·4
S W England	1875–1946	64	51·9	41·0	2128	3·94	±0·05	0·0	1·84	±0·02	0·0
	1948–59	20	51·0	40·8	2081	3·10	±0·06	21·3	1·49	±0·02	19·0
Wales coastal	1868–1941	76	51·6	41·2	2126	3·75	±0·04	0·0	1·76	±0·01	0·0
	1947–54	3	50·6	40·4	2044	3·28	±0·06	12·5	1·61	±0·04	8·5
Wales inland	1884–1946	80	51·2	40·3	2063	3·75	±0·04	0·0	1·82	±0·01	0·0
	1947–57	25	52·1	41·8	2178	3·22	±0·09	14·1	1·48	±0·04	18·7
	1977–79	7*	50·3	40·4	2032	3·37	±0·20	10·1	1·65	±0·06	9·3
N England	1898–1946	118	51·0	40·2	2050	3·77	±0·03	0·0	1·85	±0·01	0·0
	1947–71	36	51·7	40·7	2104	3·09	±0·06	18·0	1·47	±0·02	20·5
	1972–79	17*	51·8	40·4	2092	3·47	±0·11	8·0	1·70	±0·06	8·1
S Scotland	1898–1946	15	51·6	40·4	2085	3·78	±0·05	0·0	1·81	±0·02	0·0
	1947–71	52	51·5	40·9	2106	3·17	±0·05	16·1	1·50	±0·02	17·1
	1972–78	64*	51·7	41·1	2125	3·61	±0·05	5·0	1·70	±0·02	6·1
S & E Highlands fringe	1901–27	4	51·2	40·5	2074	3·77	±0·25	0·0	1·81	±0·07	0·0
	1967–71	8*	49·7	40·2	1998	3·19	±0·13	15·4	1·59	±0·05	12·2
	1972–78	17*	50·2	40·5	2033	3·33	±0·12	13·2	1·63	±0·05	9·9
S & E Highlands centre	1852–1932	12	52·8	40·9	2160	3·83	±0·12	0·0	1·80	±0·05	0·0
	1949–71	20*	51·9	40·8	2118	3·72	±0·11	2·9	1·76	±0·05	2·2
	1974–78	16*	51·5	41·2	2122	3·77	±0·09	1·6	1·78	±0·05	1·1

Table 15 (continued)   421

Region	Period									
N & W Highlands	1848–1925	30	51·6	41·2	2126	3·85	±0·07	0·0	1·83	±0·03	0·0
	1956–71	8*	51·0	41·0	2091	3·43	±0·21	10·9	1·64	±0·08	10·4
	1972–78	9*	51·5	41·0	2112	3·39	±0·13	13·6	1·61	±0·06	12·0
Ireland	1865–1946	47	51·8	41·1	2129	3·85	±0·05	0·0	1·81	±0·02	0·0
	1953	1	50·2	40·7	2043	3·00		22·1	1·47		18·8
All regions	pre-1947	468	51·5	40·7	2095	3·80		0·0	1·82		0·0
	1947–71	175	51·5	40·9	2106	3·23		15·0	1·53		16·0
	1972–79	130*	51·4	40·9	2102	3·55		6·6	1·69		7·0

NOTES:

1. *Mostly single, addled eggs taken under licence; otherwise data are for the means of clutches, mostly of 3–4 eggs.
2. With a sample size of less than 50 clutches, random variations in any attribute are relatively large.
3. There are no significant differences in size of eggs between regions.
4. In pre-1947 eggs, shell weight shows less variation than shell thickness index. This is probably because the index introduces but does not measure two other variables: egg shape, which determines the total area of shell; and shell density, which affects relative weight of the shell.
5. The only significant regional difference in shell thickness index for pre-1947 eggs is for coastal Wales; this is not understood, but nearly all the clutches in the sample were from Pembrokeshire and taken by the same collector (J. H. Howells).
6. The shell thickness index for 1947–71 eggs for the whole of Britain and Ireland is 1·82, slightly less than the previously published figure of 1·84 (Ratcliffe, 1970). The new figure is based on a much larger total sample of eggs, supplied partly by other workers. It includes not only the series from coastal Wales with a lower value, but also an unknown number of incubated clutches. My original (1970) sample excluded heavily incubated eggs, because in these there is slight loss of shell weight resulting from withdrawal of calcium carbonate by the developing embryo, and from detachment of the shell membranes which are then usually removed when the egg is blown.
7. In addled eggs shell membranes usually become detached and are removed when the egg is blown. This could result in a very slight decrease in eggshell weight and hence a downwards bias in shell thickness index, compared with a sample of fresh eggs. Such a bias would affect only those samples marked with an asterisk.
8. Eggshells of other races of Peregrine may be either larger or smaller than those of *F. peregrinus* in Britain, so that normal weight and thickness will also be different, e.g. North American and Australian eggs are larger and heavier, with thicker shells.

Addendum: Newton *et al.* (1989) give data for shell thickness index of 175 Peregrine eggs, from widely distributed coastal and inland localities in England, Wales and Scotland, during 1981–86; these give a mean index of 1·73 (5% below the pre-1947 level).

TABLE 16: *Eggshell thinning in different regions of the World*

Region	% thinning	Period	Authors
Alaska	19–24	1952–64	Anderson and Hickey 1972
Alaska	17–25	1967–71	Peakall *et al.* 1975
Aleutian Islands	8	1969–73	Peakall *et al.* 1975
Canadian Arctic	15	1947–69	Anderson and Hickey 1972
British Columbia	0–6	1947–66	Anderson and Hickey 1972
Queen Charlottes	12–13	1968–72	Nelson, in Fyfe *et al.* 1976
United States (excl. Alaska)	10–26	1947–52	Anderson and Hickey 1972
Greenland	14	1972	Walker, Mattox and Risebrough 1973
Siberia	25	1961–66	Peakall and Kiff 1979
Norway	19–23	1947–79	Nygård 1983
Sweden	18	1948–76	Odsjö and Lindberg 1977
Finland	17	1970–76	Odsjö and Lindberg 1977
Morocco	14	1958	Peakall and Kiff 1979
Southern Africa	15	1969–75	Peakall and Kiff 1979
Australia	0–24	1949–73	Peakall and Kiff 1979
Australia	3–15	1947–77	Olsen and Olsen 1979
Australia (Victoria)	20	1975–77	Pruett-Jones, White and Emison 1981
Indonesia (Celebes)	0	1949–54	Peakall and Kiff 1979

TABLE 17: *Clutch sizes of Peregrines in different regions of Britain*

Region	Period	Number of clutches	Number of eggs				Mean
			2	3	4	5	
S W England	1924–1946	13		4	9		3·69
Wales	1914–1953	55	4	18	31	2	3·56
	1975–1979	33	1	14	18		3·52
	1980–1991	99	7	45	47		3·40
N England	1905–1968	65	1	20	43	1	3·68
	1972–1979	76	1	25	48	2	3·67
	1980–1991	440	21	207	203	9	3·45
S Scotland	1946–1969	56	3	16	37		3·61
	1970–1979	146	4	54	86	2	3·59
	1980–1991	467	36	207	218	6	3·42
S & E Highlands fringe	1962–1979	49	1	14	30	4	3·76
	1980–1991	112	9	55	48		3·35
S & E Highlands centre	1961–1979	79	4	24	50	1	3·61
	1980–1991	141	8	65	66	2	3·44
N & W Highlands	1961–1979	50		16	34		3·68
	1980–1991	39		21	18		3·46
GB total	up to 1979	622	19	205	386	12	3·63
	1980–1991	1298	81	600	600	17	3·43

NOTES:

These are records of clutches seen in the eyrie and believed to be complete (i.e. they do not include clutches in collections). Clutches with evidence of egg depletion, notably the presence of recent shell fragments, are omitted, except when the original number of eggs was certain. There are no non-collector data for SE England, but see Chapter 8 for discussion of clutch size in Sussex.

Median clutch size decreased during 1980–1991 compared with the previous time-periods in all regions for which there were data. The significance of the changes was examined by Sue Holt, using the Mann–Whitney *U*-test, with the following results:

Wales: $n = 132$, $U = 1775·5$, $p = 0·401$
N England: $n = 516$, $U = 19810·0$, $p = 0·004$
S Scotland: $n = 613$, $U = 38805·0$, $p = 0·005$

S & E Highlands fringe: $n = 161$, $U = 3603·5$, $p < 0·001$
S & E Highlands centre: $n = 220$, $U = 6428·0$, $p = 0·033$
N & W Highlands: $n = 89$, $U = 1188·0$, $p = 0·039$

Table 18   423

TABLE 18: *Fledged brood size of the Peregrine in Britain*

Region	Period	No of broods	Number of young in brood					Mean brood size
			1	*2*	*3*	*4*	*5*	
South East England	1905–1933	18	–	1	6	11	–	3·56
South West England	1914–1946	22	3	7	9	3	–	2·54
	1980–1985	44	4	16	18	5	1	2·61
	1986–1991	129	23	55	42	9		2·29
Wales	1896–1946	60	8	21	23	8	–	2·52
	1961–1965	11	1	9	1	–	–	2·00
	1966–1970	13	3	4	5	1	–	2·31
	1971–1975	42	9	19	11	3	–	2·19
	1976–1979	107	17	43	38	9	–	2·36
	1980–1985	212	42	94	61	15	–	2·23
	1986–1991	121	31	59	25	6	–	2·05
Northern England	1904–1946	47	5	17	14	11	–	2·66
	1947–1960	25	7	7	7	4	–	2·32
	1961–1965	18	6	9	2	1	–	1·89
	1966–1970	34	9	14	8	3	–	2·15
	1971–1975	64	15	22	18	9	–	2·33
	1976–1979	86	18	24	33	11	–	2·43
	1980–1985	248	49	76	75	48	–	2·49
	1986–1991	346	64	112	127	43	–	2·43
Southern Scotland	1912–1939	8	1	3	3	1	–	2·50
	1961–1965	19	8	7	4	–	–	1·79
	1966–1970	41	20	14	7	–	–	1·68
	1971–1975	62	21	25	12	4	–	1·98
	1976–1979	91	22	28	29	12	–	2·34
	1980–1985	144	23	53	47	21	–	2·46
	1986–1991	241	55	89	74	23	–	2·27
Southern Highland fringe	1961–1965	17	5	5	7	–	–	2·12
	1966–1970	32	11	15	5	1	–	1·88
	1971–1975	78	18	31	20	9	–	2·26
	1976–1979	86	15	48	20	3	–	2·13
	1980–1985	178	35	64	58	21	–	2·37
	1986–1991	190	47	67	63	13	–	2·15
Central Highlands	1961–1965	61	10	27	19	5	–	2·31
	1966–1970	62	8	25	23	6	–	2·44
	1971–1975	95	18	28	39	10	–	2·43
	1976–1979	110	23	46	28	12	1	2·29
	1980–1985	132	21	60	38	13	–	2·33
	1986–1991	133	38	45	42	8	–	2·15

continued overleaf

TABLE 18 (*continued*)

Region	Period	No of broods	Number of young in brood					Mean brood size
			1	2	3	4	5	
North and west	1961–1965	20	4	11	5	–	–	2·05
Highlands inland	1966–1970	–	–	–	–	–	–	
	1971–1975	43	8	20	6	9	–	2·37
	1976–1979	56	13	22	18	3	–	2·20
	1980–1985	75	15	29	25	6	–	2·29
	1986–1991	30	8	9	10	3	–	2·27
North and west	1961–1965	53	21	20	12	–	–	1·83
Highlands coastal	1966–1970	19	7	5	6	1	–	2·05
	1971–1975	23	8	10	5	–	–	1·87
	1976–1979	21	8	8	3	2	–	1·95
	1980–1985	44	7	25	9	3	–	2·18
	1986–1991	28	9	13	6	–	–	1·89
GB total	1896–1946	93*	11	34	32	16	–	2·57
	1961–1965	199	55	88	50	6	–	2·04
	1966–1970	201	58	77	54	12	–	2·10
	1971–1975	407	97	155	111	44	–	2·25
	1976–1979	555	116	219	169	52	1	2·28
	1980–1985	1077	196	417	331	132	1	2·37
	1986–1991	1218	275	449	389	105	–	2·26

NOTES:
1. *Excluding south-east England, because of suspected upwards bias.
2. Data are mainly for broods seen on the wing, but include those of young more than 4 weeks old still in the nest. Broods of this age taken by falconers are included.
3. The numbers of broods listed are sometimes smaller than the numbers of fledged broods given in Table 19, because the latter include broods of unknown size.
4. The following statistical analysis was made by Sue Holt:
   (a) To test whether there was a change in medium brood size in the time periods between 1961 and 1985, Spearman rank-order correlation was used, testing each region separately:
   Wales: $n = 385$, $Rs = -0.016$, $z = -0.31$, $p = 0.7566$
   N. England: $n = 450$, $Rs = 0.120$, $z = -2.54$, $p = 0.0110$
   S. Scotland: $n = 357$, $Rs = 0.277$, $z = 5.23$, $p = 0.0001$
   S. Highland fringe: $n = 391$, $Rs = 0.128$, $z = 2.53$, $p = 0.0118$
   Central Highlands: $n = 460$, $Rs = -0.036$, $z = -0.77$, $p = 0.4412$
   N. & W. Highlands, coastal: $n = 160$, $Rs = 0.143$, $z = 1.80$, $p = 0.0718$
   N. & W. Highlands, inland: $n = 194$, $Rs = 0.043$, $z = 0.60$, $p = 0.5486$
   (b) To test whether median brood size changed between the 1980–85 and 1986–91 periods; Mann–Whitney U tests were used, testing each region separately:
   S. W. England: $n = 173$, $U = 3387.5$, $p = 0.042$
   Wales: $n = 333$, $U = 14360.5$, $p = 0.052$
   N. England: $n = 594$, $U = 4426.5$, $p = 0.503$
   S. Scotland: $n = 385$, $U = 19232.5$, $p = 0.062$
   S. Highland fringe: $n = 368$, $U = 18267.0$, $p = 0.162$
   Central Highlands: $n = 265$, $U = 9658.0$, $p = 0.137$
   N. & W. Highlands, coastal: $n = 72$, $U = 728.0$, $p = 0.156$
   N. & W. Highlands, inland: $n = 105$, $U = 1143.5$, $p = 0.890$

Table 19   425

TABLE 19: *Breeding performance of Peregrines in different regions of Britain 1961–91*

Regions	Period	No. of occupied territories	Only one bird present	Pair present no nest	Eggs laid but failed to hatch	Eggs hatched	Young died or disappeared	Young known to be robbed	Broods of young reared	Breeding success % pairs rearing young	Brood size, av. no. Young per successful pair	Productivity, av. no. Young per territory holding pair
		3	4	5	6	7	8	9	10	11	12	13
South-west England	1980–85	105	5	13	18	68	2	–	66	64	2·61	1·67
	1986–91	197	6	23	35	133	5	–	128	66	2·29	1·51
Wales	1961–65	76	22	34	5	15	1	1	15	23	2·00	0·46
	1966–70	58	19	22	2	15	–	1	13	27	2·31	0·62
	1971–75	95	17	22	5	51	0	2	49	56	2·19	1·23
	1976–79	221	20	49	23	129	8	5	124	59	2·36	1·39
	1980–85	469	26	95	64	284	8	14	262	57	2·23	1·27
	1986–91	262	9	45	44	164	2	8	154	60	2·05	1·22
Northern England	1961–65	99	19	30	26	24	2	–	22	24	1·89	0·45
	1966–70	93	13	23	13	44	3	1	40	46	2·15	0·99
	1971–75	138	13	33	19	73	8	4	61	46	2·33	1·07
	1976–79	160	4	26	33	97	10	8	79	50	2·43	1·22
	1980–85	511	13	72	125	301	15	25	261	52	2·49	1·29
	1986–91	622	23	83	130	386	12	19	355	58	2·43	1·41
Southern Scotland	1961–65	103	29	21	20	23	1	–	22	25	1·79	0·45
	1966–70	120	18	18	41	43	2	1	41	37	1·68	0·62
	1971–75	166	22	33	35	76	12	2	62	40	1·98	0·79
	1976–79	144	10	7	26	101	9	5	87	63	2·34	1·47
	1980–85	360	21	60	77	202	15	14	173	49	2·46	1·21
	1986–91	525	23	71	152	279	7	25	247	48	2·27	1·09
Southern Highland fringe	1961–65	101	20	23	8	50	5	3	42	46	2·12	0·97
	1966–70	93	11	24	1	57	2	1	54	61	1·88	1·15
	1971–75	162	25	29	11	97	3	3	91	61	2·26	1·38
	1976–79	158	15	32	22	89	1	2	86	57	2·13	1·21
	1980–85	344	38	56	49	201	6	4	191	59	2·37	1·39
	1986–91	392	49	72	52	219	6	3	210	57	2·15	1·23

continued overleaf

TABLE 19 (*continued*)

1 Regions	2 Period	3 No. of occupied territories	4 Only one bird present	5 Pair present no nest	6 Eggs laid but failed to hatch	7 Eggs hatched	8 Young died or disappeared	9 Young known to be robbed	10 Broods of young reared	11 Breeding success % pairs rearing young	12 Brood size, av. no. young per successful pair	13 Productivity, av. no. Young per territory holding pair
Central Highlands	1961–65	141	9	28	13	91	1	12	78	57	2·31	1·32
	1966–70	163	15	36	19	93	0	4	89	57	2·44	1·39
	1971–75	230	17	64	18	131	3	5	123	55	2·43	1·34
	1976–79	186	6	23	27	130	5	15	110	60	2·29	1·37
	1980–85	297	22	56	53	166	16	5	145	51	2·33	1·18
	1986–91	227	4	39	38	144	3	–	141	63	2·15	1·35
North and west Highlands inland	1961–65	64	9	14	8	33	1	–	33	55	2·05	1·13
	1966–70	23	5	5	1	12	–	–	12	57	–	–
	1971–75	79	10	14	9	46	2	–	44	60	2·37	1·42
	1976–79	113	12	9	21	71	4	3	64	60	2·20	1·32
	1980–85	175	13	24	27	111	1	6	104	62	2·29	1·41
	1986–91	57	4	12	9	32	2	3	27	49	2·27	1·11
North and west Highlands coastal	1961–65	197	35	50	19	93	1	2	90	50	1·83	0·92
	1966–70	105	32	21	13	39	–	–	39	44	2·05	0·90
	1971–75	89	28	15	6	40	1	–	39	52	1·87	0·97
	1976–79	68	19	13	8	28	–	1	28	47	1·95	0·92
	1980–85	154	47	30	21	56	3	1	52	40	2·18	0·87
	1986–91	80	23	21	4	32	1	–	31	45	1·89	0·85

NOTES:
1. Data for south-east England are too few to be worth including.
2. Figures in column 3 are for the samples of territories reported during each period, and are the totals of columns 4–7.
3. Figures in columns 4 and 5 include instances where eggs could have been laid, but breeding apparently failed.
4. Figures in column 6 include both 'natural' failures and robberies. Robbed clutches followed by successful repeats are not included in column 6.
5. Breeding success (column 11) is derived by expressing number of broods reared (column 10) as a percentage of number of territory-holding pairs (column 3 minus half the number in column 4, to convert single birds into pairs).
6. Productivity (column 13) is mean brood size (column 12) multiplied by breeding success (column 11).

TABLE 20: *Ringing totals of Peregrines, within Britain and Ireland by decades*

Decade	Nestlings	Full-grown
1921–30	30	
1931–40	54	
1941–50	40	2
1951–60	41	3
1961–70	89	
1971–80	1170	40
1981–90	3052	21
1921–90	4476	66

Table prepared by C. J. Mead.

TABLE 21: *Time of recovery of Peregrines moving 200 km or more*

Age at recovery	Jul	Aug	Sept	Oct	Nov	Dec	Jan	Feb	Mar	Apr	May	Jun	Total
1st Year	–	–	–	–	1	3	2	–	–	1	1	–	8
All older	–	4	2	2	–	2	1	–	2	2	2	–	17
Total	–	4	2	2	1	5	3	–	2	3	3	–	25

Table prepared by C. J. Mead.

TABLE 22: *Distances of Peregrine ringing recoveries, according to age*

| Age at recovery | Distance travelled from ringing site (km) | | | | | | | |
| | Males | | | | Females | | | |
	<50	50–99	100–199	>199	<50	50–99	100–199	>199
1st Year								
July–Dec	22	6	1	–	17	6	4	–
Jan–June	12	7	3	–	10	4	4	–
All older								
July–Dec	5	6	4	2	5	3	4	4
Jan–June	17	7	1	–	8	6	14	2
Totals	56	26	9	2	40	19	26	6
	Unsexed				All birds			
1st Year								
July–Dec	27	12	12	4	66	24	17	4
Jan–June	16	7	7	4	38	18	14	4
All older								
July–Dec	13	8	6	4	23	17	14	10
Jan–June	25	18	6	5	50	31	21	7
	81	45	31	17	177	90	66	25

Table prepared by C. J. Mead.

TABLE 23: *Distances of Peregrine ringing recoveries, according to region*

Ringing region	Males				Females			
	<50	*50–99*	*100–199*	*>199*	*<50*	*50–99*	*100–199*	*>199*
Highland	13	6	–	–	12	3	7	1
S Scotland	11	7	5	2	8	7	7	3
N England	23	9	2	–	10	8	8	1
Wales & SW	4	3	–	–	5	–	–	–
Ireland	5	1	2	–	5	1	4	1
Total	56	26	9	2	40	19	26	5
	Unsexed				*All birds*			
Highland	32	15	12	5	57	24	19	6
S Scotland	10	8	7	2	29	22	19	7
N England	14	7	7	7	47	24	17	8
Wales & SW	12	5	1	2	21	8	1	2
Ireland	13	10	4	1	23	12	10	2
Total	81	45	31	17	177	90	66	25

Distance travelled from ringing site (km)

Table prepared by C. J. Mead.

Table 24   429

TABLE 24: *Close nesting in Peregrines in Britain and Ireland*

County/Country	Locality	No. of pairs	Source
Kent	Folkestone – Hope Point	9 pairs in 17·5 km of seacliff regularly during 1920–40	G. Took
Sussex	Rottingdean – Newhaven	2–4 pairs in 8 km of seacliff	J. Walpole-Bond and
	Seaford Head – Beachy Head	6–8 pairs in 11 km of seacliff during 1905–45. Beachy Head usually had 3, occasionally 4 pairs in 3·0 km of cliff during 1905–45	D. Nethersole-Thompson
Dorset	St Albans Head – Ringstead Bay	10–12 pairs in 29 km of seacliff during 1920–39, with occasionally 2 pairs 1·0 km apart	L. Green and D. Humphrey
Devon	Lundy Island	Usually 2 pairs on 420 ha island	G. Blaine and R. Mitchell
South-west England	Atlantic coast	11 pairs in 32·6 km of seacliff in 1991	R. B. Treleaven
Pembrokeshire	Ramsey Island	Said once to have had 2 pairs, 1·8 km apart on island of c. 250 ha	
	Skomer Island	Said once to have had 3 pairs, on island of c. 300 ha, pre-1940	J. H. Howell
Central Wales hills		Cluster of 8 pairs, average nearest neighbour distance 2·8 km and average area 18·6 km² (5·4 pairs/ 100 km²) in 1991	I. Williams and RSPB
Mountains of Snowdonia		Cluster of 10 pairs, average nearest neighbour distance 2·9 km and average area 17 km² (5·9 pairs/100 km²) in 1991	I. Williams and RSPB
Lake District mountains		Cluster of 16 pairs, average nearest neighbour distance 2·5 km and average area 11·7 km² (8·5 pairs/100 km²) in 1991	G. Horne, P. Stott, T. Pickford, C. Smith, P. Marsden and G. Fryer
Eastern Southern Upland hills		Cluster of 6 pairs, average nearest neighbour distance 2·9 km and average area 16·2 km² (6·2 pairs/ 100 km²) in 1991	G. Carse
Western Southern Upland hills		Cluster of 7 pairs, average nearest neighbour distance 3·3 km and average area 19·7 km² (5·1 pairs/ 100 km²) in 1991	R. Roxburgh

continued overleaf

TABLE 24 (continued)

County/Country	Locality	No. of pairs	Source
Hills near Glasgow		Cluster of 6 pairs, average nearest neighbour distance 2·7 km and average area 13·6 km² (7·4 pairs/100 km²) in 1991	J. Mitchell
Ayrshire	Ailsa Craig	2 pairs ?1 km apart on island of 105 ha in 1634–5	W. Brereton
Buteshire	Holy Island, Arran	2 pairs on island of c. 250 ha in 1947 and 1949	J. A. Gibson
Sutherland	Handa Island	Formerly 2 pairs only 1·7 km apart on 320 ha island	J. Fisher
Inverness-shire	St Kilda	Formerly at least 4 pairs in island group of 852 ha. 2 pairs 2·0 km apart on Oiseval and Dun in 1934	R. Gray, K. Muir, D. Lack and J. Harrison
Orkney	North Hoy	4 pairs in 6·5 km of seacliff in 1957–62 2 pairs in 1·0 km apart in 1963	E. Balfour / D. A. Ratcliffe
Shetland	Fair Isle	2–3 pairs on island of c. 700 ha, 5·2 km in length up to 1899	E. V. Baxter and L. J. Rintoul
	Noss	2 pairs on island of c. 313 ha around 1830–40	R. Dunn
Northern Ireland	Rathlin Island	8 pairs on island of 1359 ha, with an L-shaped length of 12·5 km and an average width of 1–2 km in 1991	RSPB
Republic of Ireland	Waterford Coast	12 pairs spaced 2·02 km apart on suitable continuous cliff sections in 1991	D. McGrath, D. W. Norriss

Table 25   431

TABLE 25: *Peregrine breeding density in different districts of Britain*

District	Habitat	Date	Earlier period			1991		
			No. of pairs	Mean nearest neighbour distance (km)	Mean nest territory size (km²)	No. of pairs	Mean nearest neighbour distance (km)	Mean nest territory size (km²)
South-east England (Kent, Sussex)	Coastal	1910–40	21	2·1	—	Only 2 pairs present		
South-west England (Dorset)	Coastal	1930–40	18	2·9	—	6	5·6	still increasing
(Cornwall, Devon, Somerset)		1930–40	45	5·3	—	39	4·1	—
Wales (Glamorgan, Pembroke, Cardigan, Caernarvon)	Coastal	1930–40	50	5·1	—	62	4·7	—
Wales (Caernarvon, Merioneth)	Inland	1950–57	18	5·5	55	35	3·9	25·9
North-west England (Isle of Man)	Coastal	1930–39	11	5·1	—	18	4·3	—
North-west England (Cumberland, Westmorland, N. Lancs)	Inland	1900–60	28	5·5	48·6	65	3·6	21·4
South-west Scotland (Kirkcudbright, Wigtown, Ayr)	Coastal	1950–60	15	5·3	—	23	4·3	—
South-west Scotland (Kirkcudbright, Ayr)	Inland	1946–60 1971–79	14	5·4	54·6	23	4·0	27·3
South & east Highland west coast (Bute, Argyll)	Coastal	1971–79	15	6·1	—	26	5·6	—

continued overleaf

TABLE 25 (continued)

District	Habitat	Date	Earlier period			1991		
			No. of pairs	Mean nearest neighbour distance (km)	Mean nest territory size (km²)	No. of pairs	Mean nearest neighbour distance (km)	Mean nest territory size (km²)
South & east Highland fringe (Arran, Stirling, Dumbarton, Perth, Argyll)	Inland	1971–79	44	6·4	65.7	56	5·2	52·1
Central Highlands (Perth, Inverness, Aberdeen, Angus)	Inland	1961–79	67	7·2	90·1	103	6·1	75·0
North-west and North-east Highlands (Sutherland, Caithness)	Coastal	1950–70	36	6·2	–		No change	
North & west Highlands (Inverness, Ross, Sutherland)	Inland	1971–79	49	9·0	192·0	44	8·0	119·0
North & east Highlands (Inverness, Ross, Sutherland)	Inland	1971–79	30	5·8	69·6	25	5·4	57·2
Orkney	Coastal	1959–63	31	5·8	–		No change	
Shetland	Coastal	1950–55	21	7·4	–		Breeding ceased	

NOTES:

1. The numbers of pairs refer to areas where I judged that availability of suitable cliffs was not a limiting factor, and are thus different from the totals for the same districts given elsewhere. Few inland pairs for Argyll are included, because of irregular spacing. Number of pairs for 1991 is sometimes less than for the earlier period, either because the area of uniform distribution has changed, or because areas were not completely surveyed.

2. The methods used for measuring nearest neighbour distances and size of breeding districts are described in Chapter 10. Coastal populations usually have a linear distribution so that only spacing distances can be given.

Table 26   433

TABLE 26: *Mortality of Peregrines in various countries*

Country	Mortality of young (0–1 year old) %	Mortality of adults (1–6 years old) %	Critical productivity (young per pair)
Sweden (Lindberg, 1977)	59	32	2·3
North America (Enderson, 1969)	70	25	2·3
Germany (Mebs, 1971)	56	28	1·8
Finland (Mebs, 1971)	71	19	1·6

Data from Lindberg 1977. The figures refer to declining populations during the height of the pesticide problems.

TABLE 27: Life-table for Peregrines ringed as nestling in Britain and Ireland up to the 1990 breeding season

Years	Total	Age in (years)																	Totals
		0	1	2	3	4	5	6	7	8	9	10	11	12	13	14	15	16	
To 1950	118	4	4	1		2		1	1	1									14
1951–70	138	2		2		2	2			1	1							1	11
1971	24	1											1						2
1972	10	1											1						2
1973	34	1	1					1											3
1974	67	1	1	1	2												1		6
1975	90	6	2	3								1							12
1976	133	3	6	2	2	1		2											16
1977	185	11	2	3							2	1							19
1978	197	7	3	4	2			3	2	5	1			1					28
1979	204	9	4	1	2	2	1	1	2	2	1	1							26
1980	226	12	5	2	2	1	3				2								27
1981	231	7	5	4	2	2		1	1		2								24
1982	262	10	5	1				2	1										19
1983	191	4	2	1	3	2		1											13
1984	381	18	3	4	2		2	1											30
1985	311	11	4	4	1	1	1												22
1986	294	10	6	1		2		1											20
1987	375	10	4	2	1	2													19
1988	334	6	4	1	3														14
1989	351	13	2																15
1990	322	14																	14

NOTES:
1. Year (or years) of ringing are given with the total of nestlings recorded as being ringed during the year (or period). Age 0 are birds recovered up to end of March of second calendar year of life – subsequent years (1–16) cover a full year from April to March inclusive.
2. Table prepared by C. J. Mead.

TABLE 28: *Recovery rates for Peregrines in three age-classes*

| | Age–class | | | | | | | | |
| | First year | | | Second year | | | Third year | | |
Recovery period	No. ringed	No. found	%	No. ringed	No. found	%	No. ringed	No. found	%
1976–78	515	21	4·08	408	10	2·45	290	5	1·72
1979–81	616	28	4·24	627	12	1·91	686	8	1·17
1982–84	834	32	3·84	684	12	1·75	719	6	0·83
1985–87	980	31	3·16	986	13	1·32	883	9	1·02
1988–90	1007	33	3·28	1060	10	0·94	1003	7	0·70
Decrease from 1976–78 to 1988–90		1·07%			1·44%			0·88%	

NOTES:
1. Decreases are calculated from fitted regressions which are significant at, respectively, $p < 0.05$, $p < 0.01$ and $p < 0.10$.
2. Number ringed moves backwards one year for each annual increment of age-class, e.g. third-year birds recovered in 1988–90 are compared with numbers ringed in 1986–88.
3. Table prepared by C. J. Mead.

TABLE 29: *Organochlorine residues in livers of Peregrines in Britain*

Date	Location	Age/sex	Analyst	HEOD	Heptachlor expoxide	DDE	PCBs
6.63	Lundy Island, Devon (C)	Ad. ♂	GC	4·0	1·5	70·0	NA
8.64	Strath Carron Easter Ross	Ad. ♀	GC	0·6	0·2	6·3	NA
9.64	Biggar Lanarkshire	Juv. ♂	GC	1·9	0·1	7·3	NA
3.65	Newquay Cornwall (C)	Ad. ♀	MW	2·2	3·0	50·0	NA
2.65	Netherlands (captive)		JK	9·3	–	60·0	NA
3.66	Braemar Aberdeenshire	Juv. ♂	GC	0·3	–	0·4	NA
8.66	Fair Isle Shetland (C)	Ad. ♀	GC	0·7	–	9·0	NA
4.69	Fair Isle Shetland (C)	♂	GC	1·9	–	22·0	25·0
3.71	Auchinleck Ayrshire	Ad. ♂	GC	2·0	0·2	30·0	9·0
4.71	Dunblane Stirlingshire	Ad. ♂	MW	9·2	–	5·0	6·2
5.71	Dunnet Head Caithness (C)	Ad. ♀	GC	3·0	1·6	50·0	200·0
11.71	Northam Devon	Ad. ♀	MW	2·0	–	26·8	4·7

continued overleaf

TABLE 29 (*continued*)

Date	Location	Age/sex	Analyst	HEOD	Heptachlor epoxide	DDE	PCBs
12.71	Isle of Lewis Outer Hebrides (C)	♂	MW	2·1	–	23·1	59·4
12.71	Holkham Norfolk (C)	♂	MW	7·0	–	6·6	17·4
2.73	Keswick Cumberland	♂	MW	9·6	–	5·9	3·7
7.73	John o'Groats (C) Caithness	Ad. ♀	GC	1·5	–	16·0	100·0
2.73	Strathendrick Stirlingshire	Ad. ♂*	JAB	17·3	–	5·3	3·4
4.73	Strathendrick Stirlingshire	Ad. ♀*	JAB	43·9	–	8·9	4·8
1.74	Balbeggie Perthshire	Juv. ♀	MW	13·5	–	2·1	–
1.74	Kinlochewe Ross-shire	Juv. ♂	GC	0·1	–	0·1	–
6.75	Lerwick (C) Shetland	Ad. ♀	MW	1·0	0·3	10·0	40·0

*Believed to be the partners of a breeding pair.

NOTES:
1. Residues were determined by gas-liquid chromatography and are expressed as parts per million (wet weight).
2. Analysts and laboratories:
   GC   D. C. Holmes and J. O'G. Tatton, Laboratory of the Government Chemist, Department of Industry, London.
   MW   C. H. Walker and M. C. French, Monks Wood Experimental Station, The Nature Conservancy and, from 1974, the Institute of Terrestrial Ecology.
   JAB   Dr J. A. Bogan, Department of Veterinary Pharmacology, University of Glasgow.
   JK   Dr J. Koeman, University of Utrecht, Netherlands.
3. Sources: Jefferies and Prestt (1966); Ratcliffe (1972); Bogan and Mitchell (1973); Cooke, Bell and Haas (1982).
4. Most of these Peregrines were found dead, dying or in poor condition (dying soon afterwards). Several had marked physical injuries and those of 5·71, 7·73 and 6·75 were badly oiled by Fulmars, Jefferies and Prestt (1966) suggested that a combined dieldrin and heptachlor epoxide level of 5·0–9·0 ppm in the liver of Peregrines could represent a lethal dose, but Cooke *et al.* (1982) believe that 10 ppm of HEOD (dieldrin) in the liver is the more generally accepted lethal level for many bird species. Heptachlor epoxide has a similar avian toxicity to HEOD, but DDE is much less poisonous, and only liver levels of over 100 ppm are regarded as indicating poisoning by DDT type compounds (Cooke *et al.*, 1982). While only 6 of the 20 Peregrines analysed have cyclodiene residues high enough to be strongly implicated as cause of death, it is possible that lower contamination levels by these and other compounds could produce impairment of body functions which might in turn lead to conditions directly responsible for death. Only 4 birds had residue levels that could be regarded as insignificant. The sample of 20 birds was sent to Monks Wood by chance finders, but may be biassed towards poisoned birds because Peregrines illegally killed were not sent. Nevertheless, an enhancement of mortality by only 25% through poisoning could have serious effects for the Peregrine population (see Chapter 11).
5. The specimens analysed by the Government Chemist and Monks Wood were part of the pesticide – wildlife studies conducted by the Toxic Chemicals and Wildlife Section of the former Nature Conservancy, and continued since 1974 by the Institute of Terrestrial Ecology (to which Monks Wood Experimental Station now belongs) under contract to the Nature Conservancy Council.
6. C = Coastal location.

Table 30   *437*

TABLE 30: *Organochlorine residues in the eggs of Peregrines in Britain*

NORTHERN ENGLAND

Year	Analyst	Location	HEOD	Heptachlor epoxide	DDE	PCBs
1963	EC	Westmorland	0·7	2·9	15·8	NA
	EC	Cumberland	0·4	0·7	10·0	NA
	EC	Cumberland	1·1	4·1	30·8	NA
1965	GC	Cumberland	0·6	0·8	25·0	NA
	GC	Westmorland	0·8	1·0	24·0	NA
1966	GC	Westmorland	2·6	0·5	23·0	NA
1968	GC	Cumberland	1·0	–	16·0	NA
1969	GC	Westmorland	0·3	–	8·0	< 1·0
	GC	Cumberland	0·4	–	5·0	6·0
1971	GC	Cumberland	0·1	–	3·0	2·0
	GC	Cumberland	0·4	–	3·0	< 1·0
	GC	Cumberland	0·6	–	13·0	2·0
	GC	Westmorland	0·7	–	3·0	1·0
1972	GC	Yorkshire	0·7	–	2·0	2·0
1973	GC	Cumberland	1·2	–	2·0	–
	GC	Westmorland	1·5	–	1·0	–
	GC	Westmorland	2·0	–	2·0	–
	GC	Westmorland	0·5	–	0·5	–
1974	GC	Cumberland	0·4	–	3·0	1·0
	JAB	Cumberland	2·0	–	2·6	2·1
	JAB	Cumberland	1·6	–	2·2	1·9
1975	GC	Cumberland	0·6	–	1·0	–
	GC	Cumberland	0·7	–	3·5	7·1
1976	JAB	Cumberland	1·9	–	4·8	4·3
	JAB	Cumberland	0·9	–	1·1	3·5
1978	JAB	Westmorland	0·2	–	2·0	1·8
	JAB	Westmorland	0·3	–	6·7	4·3
	JAB	Cumberland	1·2	–	6·3	2·3

WALES

Year	Analyst	Location	HEOD	Heptachlor epoxide	DDE	PCBs
1977	GC	Dyfed	0·3	–	2·5	2·0
	GC	Clwyd	2·0	–	5·5	2·0
	GC	Gwynedd	1·0	–	2·5	4·0
	GC	Gwynedd	2·0	–	3·0	8·0
	GC	Powys	0·5	–	2·0	2·0
	GC	Powys	0·3	–	1·2	1·0
	GC	Powys	0·3	–	1·4	2·0

continued overleaf

SOUTHERN SCOTLAND

Year	Analyst	Location	HEOD	Heptachlor epoxide	DDE	PCBs
1963	EC	Dumfriesshire	0·1	0·1	2·6	NA
	EC	Peebles-shire	0·4	0·6	4·4	NA
	EC	{ Peebles-shire	0·5	0·6	21·2	NA
	EC	{ Peebles-shire	0·3	0·5	23·2	NA
	EC	Kirkcudbrightshire	0·7	0·4	14·1	NA
	EC	Kirkcudbrightshire	0·1	0·4	9·0	NA
1964	GC	{ Dumfriesshire	1·3	0·2	4·7	NA
	GC	{ Dumfriesshire	1·8	0·7	7·3	NA
	GC	Kirkcudbrightshire	0·1	0·1	10·8	NA
	GC	Peebles-shire	0·8	0·4	12·0	NA
1965	GC	Kirkcudbrightshire	0·5	4·3	22·3	NA
	GC	Dumfriesshire	0·5	0·2	10·2	NA
	GC	Peebles-shire	0·5	0·2	18·1	NA
1966	GC	{ Kirkcudbrightshire	0·3	1·0	22·0	NA
	GC	{ Kirkcudbrightshire	0·6	1·0	22·0	NA
	GC	Kirkcudbrightshire	0·2	0·1	13·0	NA
1967	GC	{ Kirkcudbrightshire	0·2	0·4	16·0	1·0
	GC	{ Kirkcudbrightshire	0·3	0·3	15·0	1·0
	GC	Kirkcudbrightshire	0·1	trace	6·3	1·0
	GC	Peebles-shire	0·4	0·2	11·0	1·0
1968	GC	{ Kirkcudbrightshire	0·1	–	8·6	0·6
	GC	{ Kirkcudbrightshire	0·2	0.2	15.0	–
	GC	Kirkcudbrightshire	1·4	–	33·0	1·0
	GC	⌠ Dumfriesshire	0·4	–	14·0	1·0
	GC	⟨ Dumfriesshire	0·4	–	11·0	< 1·0
	GC	⌡ Dumfriesshire	0·3	–	11·0	6·0
	GC	Peebles-shire	0·9	–	9·0	1·0
	GC	Kirkcudbrightshire	0·2	–	4·7	–
1969	GC	⌠ Dumfriesshire	0·2	–	11·0	1·0
	GC	⟨ Dumfriesshire	0·1	–	11·0	< 1·0
	GC	⟨ Dumfriesshire	0·2	–	13·0	1·0
	GC	⌡ Dumfriesshire	0·3	0·1	6·5	< 1·0
	GC	Peebles-shire	0·3	–	16·0	2·0
	GC	Kirkcudbrightshire	0·3	–	10·0	1·0
1970	GC	Kirkcudbrightshire	0·1	–	3·0	< 1·0
	GC	Dumfriesshire	0·1	–	3·8	< 1·0
	GC	Dumfriesshire	0·7	–	5·0	< 1·0
	GC	Peebles-shire	0·2	–	4·0	1·0
1971	GC	Dumfriesshire	5·0	–	5·0	3·0
	GC	Peebles-shire	0·5	–	6·0	3·0
1972	GC	Kirkcudbrightshire	0·6	0·1	7·0	30·0
	GC	Kirkcudbrightshire	0·5	–	3·0	1·0
	GC	Dumfriesshire	0·8	trace	6·0	3·0
	GC	Dumfriesshire	3·0	–	6·0	1·0

Table 30 (continued) **439**

SOUTHERN SCOTLAND (*cont.*)

Year	Analyst	Location	HEOD	Heptachlor epoxide	DDE	PCBs
1973	GC	Dumfriesshire	6·0	–	5·0	1·0
	GC	⎰ Dumfriesshire	5·0	–	2·0	< 1·0
	GC	⎱ Dumfriesshire	3·0	–	1·2	< 1·0
	GC	⎧ Kirkcudbrightshire	0·4	–	2·0	< 1·0
	GC	⎪ Kirkcudbrightshire	0·3	–	1·3	< 1·0
	GC	⎨ Kirkcudbrightshire	0·2	–	1·5	< 1·0
	GC	⎪ Kirkcudbrightshire	0·4	–	2·0	< 1·0
	GC	⎩ Kirkcudbrightshire	0·3	–	1·7	< 1·0
		Wigtownshire (C)	4·0	–	21·0	4·0
1974	JAB	Ayrshire	5·0	–	3·9	1·6
	JAB	Kirkcudbrightshire	1·3	–	19·1	1·2
	JAB	Kirkcudbrightshire	1·0	–	14·5	1·7
	JAB	Kirkcudbrightshire	0·4	–	2·8	0·7
	JAB	Kirkcudbrightshire	2·2	–	5·4	5·7
1975	JAB	Kirkcudbrightshire	1·9	–	4·1	1·5
	JAB	⎰ Kirkcudbrightshire	0·2	–	2·3	1·6
	JAB	⎱ Kirkcudbrightshire	0·3	–	3·4	2·4
	JAB	⎧ Kirkcudbrightshire	1·6	–	3·6	1·7
	JAB	⎨ Kirkcudbrightshire	1·6	–	3·7	1·7
	JAB	⎩ Kirkcudbrightshire	2·0	–	5·1	2·3
	JAB	Kirkcudbrightshire	0·6	–	3·4	3·0
	JAB	⎰ Kirkcudbrightshire	2·8	–	3·1	2·4
	JAB	⎱ Kirkcudbrightshire	2·7	–	3·4	2·4
	JAB	Kirkcudbrightshire	0·7	–	3·3	4·4
	JAB	Kirkcudbrightshire	1·6	–	11·0	6·1
	JAB	⎰ Kirkcudbrightshire	0·6	–	3·0	2·8
	JAB	⎱ Kirkcudbrightshire	1·1	–	3·6	3·4
	JAB	Ayrshire	0·7	–	3·7	2·2
	JAB	Dumfriesshire	2·2	–	2·5	1·4
	JAB	⎰ Dumfriesshire	2·6	–	5·9	3·2
	JAB	⎱ Dumfriesshire	0·8	–	3·5	2·2
	JAB	⎰ Dumfriesshire	0·4	–	1·8	2·2
	JAB	⎱ Dumfriesshire	0·4	–	1·7	2·2
	JAB	Dumfriesshire	1·7	–	1·5	2·7
1976	JAB	Ayrshire	4·3	–	5·0	6·5
	JAB	Ayrshire	9·4	–	3·4	8·0
	JAB	⎰ Dumfriesshire	4·9	–	4·0	2·6
	JAB	⎱ Dumfriesshire	7·0	–	3·3	3·7
	JAB	Dumfriesshire	5·4	–	5·5	3·2
	JAB	Dumfriesshire	2·2	–	3·1	8·3
	JAB	Kirkcudbrightshire	3·0	–	4·8	6·2
	JAB	Kirkcudbrightshire	1·9	–	6·5	3·4
	JAB	Kirkcudbrightshire	0·9	–	7·1	6·6
	JAB	Kirkcudbrightshire	1·6	–	3·4	9·4
	JAB	Kirkcudbrightshire	1·3	–	1·8	7·5
	JAB	Peebles-shire	2·0	–	4·4	4·1
1977	JAB	Dumfriesshire	1·1	–	4·6	5·7
	JAB	Dumfriesshire	2·1	–	8·4	9·8
	JAB	Dumfriesshire	2·9	–	7·3	11·0

continued overleaf

SOUTHERN SCOTLAND (*cont.*)

Year	Analyst	Location	HEOD	Heptachlor epoxide	DDE	PCBs
	JAB	Peebles-shire	0·1	–	0·8	NA
	JAB	Ayrshire	0·3	–	1·7	6·2
	JAB	Kirkcudbrightshire	0·5	–	4·0	5·0
	JAB	Kirkcudbrightshire	0·1	–	8·7	4·4
	JAB	Wigtownshire (C)	0·8	–	9·2	38·3
1978	JAB	Ayrshire	0·1	–	1·9	2·1
	JAB	Wigtownshire (C)	0·5	–	12·0	71·9
	JAB	Dumfriesshire	0·3	–	6·8	3·6
	JAB	Dumfriesshire	0·2	–	2·0	1·1
	JAB	Dumfriesshire	0·2	–	7·4	9·0
	JAB	Dumfriesshire	0·6	–	1·9	1·7
	JAB	Dumfriesshire	trace	–	0·1	0·3

SOUTHERN HIGHLAND FRINGE

Year	Analyst	Location	HEOD	Heptachlor epoxide	DDE	PCBs
1961	GC	Perthshire	1·1	0·6	2·6	NA
1967	GC	Argyll	0·7	0·2	18·0	4·0
1968	GC	Argyll	0·3	–	3·0	<1·0
	GC	Argyll	0·2	–	14·0	2·0
1970	GC	Stirlingshire	0·6	–	3·4	4·0
1971	GC	Perthshire	0·1	–	0·1	–
	GC	Buteshire	3·0	–	6·0	3·0
	GC	Argyll	0·1	–	2·1	1·0
	GC	Perthshire	2·0	–	4·0	3·0
1974	JAB	Argyll (C)	1·7	–	8·6	67·4
1975	JAB	Stirlingshire	0·7	–	2·4	9·8
	JAB	Stirlingshire	3·7	–	1·8	2·6
1976	JAB	Stirlingshire	0·3	–	0·2	1·4
	JAB	Perthshire	0·1	–	0·5	2·4
	JAB	⌠ Perthshire	2·2	–	2·5	2·4
	JAB	⌞ Perthshire	2·7	–	2·8	3·9
1977	JAB	Stirlingshire	0·5	–	4·1	7·2
	JAB	Stirlingshire	0·4	–	2·2	5·2
	JAB	Stirlingshire	0·2	–	1·1	10·8
	JAB	Perthshire	0·3	–	0·6	3·4
	JAB	Perthshire	0·9	–	4·6	7·7
1978	JAB	Perthshire	0·2	–	5·2	4·7
	JAB	Perthshire	<0·1	–	0·4	0·8
	JAB	⌠ Argyll (C)	0·1	–	0·9	4·8
	JAB	⎸ Argyll (C)	0·3	–	1·9	10·0
	JAB	⎨ Argyll (C)	0·7	–	10·2	57·4
	JAB	⎸ Argyll (C)	0·6	–	8·4	43·5
	JAB	⌞ Argyll (C)	1·3	–	6·7	94·2

Table 30 (continued)   *441*

CENTRAL HIGHLANDS

Year	Analyst	Location	HEOD	Heptachlor epoxide	DDE	PCBs
1963	EC	Inverness-shire	0·5	0·2	6·9	NA
	GC	Angus	0·6	1·9	5·4	NA
1966	GC	Inverness-shire	0·1	trace	3·6	NA
	GC	Inverness-shire	0·3	trace	2·8	NA
	GC	Angus	1·6	1·2	7·8	NA
1967	GC	Aberdeenshire	0·1	trace	10·0	2·0
	GC	Aberdeenshire	0·3	0·1	4·1	3·0
	GC	Banffshire	0·1	trace	1·3	1·0
	GC	Perthshire	0·2	–	2·4	1·0
	GC	Inverness-shire	trace	trace	1·0	1·0
	GC	Inverness-shire	0·2	trace	2.4	2·6
1968	GC	Inverness-shire	0·1	–	0·8	< 1·0
	GC	{ Inverness-shire	–	–	trace	–
	GC	{ Inverness-shire	trace	–	0·2	–
	GC	Inverness-shire	0·2	–	1·0	–
1969	GC	Inverness-shire	0·2	–	2·6	3·0
	GC	Inverness-shire	0·4	–	1·3	1·0
	GC	Inverness-shire	0·2	–	1·0	–
	GC	Inverness-shire	trace	–	4·0	1·0
	GC	Angus	–	–	0·6	–
1970	GC	Aberdeenshire	–	–	5·0	3·0
	GC	Aberdeenshire	0·1	–	3·0	< 1·0
		Fifeshire	0·1	–	3·8	< 1·0
1971	GC	Inverness-shire	0·7	–	1·0	5·0
	GC	Inverness-shire	0·2	–	4·0	2·0
	GC	Inverness-shire	trace	–	0·7	1·0
	GC	Inverness-shire	0·1	–	0·6	1·0
1972	GC	Inverness-shire	trace	–	0·8	1·0
1974	GC	Inverness-shire	–	–	0·4	–
	JAB	{ Aberdeenshire	0·5	–	4·6	5·0
	JAB	{ Aberdeenshire	trace	–	2·4	2·3
	JAB	Aberdeenshire	0·1	–	2·0	2·2
	JAB	Perthshire	0·3	–	2·5	3·4
1975	JAB	Inverness-shire	0·2	–	1·7	2·2
	JAB	Inverness-shire	0·1	–	3·4	12·8
	JAB	Inverness-shire	0·1	–	1·6	2·9
	JAB	{ Banffshire	0·1	–	0·8	1·4
	JAB	{ Banffshire	0·1	–	0·7	1·1
1976	JAB	Perthshire	0·5	–	5·0	8·9
1978	JAB	{ Perthshire	trace	–	0·7	2·4
	JAB	{ Perthshire	trace	–	1·1	3·6

NORTHERN AND WESTERN HIGHLANDS

Year	Analyst	Location	HEOD	Heptachlor epoxide	DDE	PCBs
1967	GC	Wester Ross	–	–	6·0	13·0
1969	GC	Wester Ross	–	–	0·7	–

continued overleaf

NORTHERN AND WESTERN HIGHLANDS

Year	Analyst	Location	HEOD	Heptachlor epoxide	DDE	PCBs
1971	GC	Wester Ross	0·2	–	2·4	3·0
	GC	Wester Ross (C)	0·3	–	4·0	10·0
	GC	Orkney (C)	0·1	–	2·1	3·0
	GC	Sutherland (C)	0·2	–	4·0	7·0
	GC	{ Sutherland (C)	–	–	0·4	1·0
	GC	{ Sutherland (C)	–	–	0·7	1·0
1972	GC	Wester Ross	trace	–	2·0	5·0
1973	GC	Sutherland (C)	trace	–	4·0	20·0
	GC	Sutherland (C)	–	–	1·2	3·0
	GC	Caithness (C)	1·0	–	1·8	8·0
	GC	Caithness (C)	0·5	–	6·0	15·0
	GC	{ Wester Ross	trace	–	0·9	6·0
	GC	{ Wester Ross	trace	–	0·9	6·0
	GC	{ Wester Ross	–	–	0·4	1·0
	GC	{ Wester Ross (C)	0·1	–	0·5	1·0
1976	JAB	Wester Ross	trace	–	0·6	3·0

NOTES:

1. Residues were determined by gas-liquid chromatography and are expressed in parts per million in wet weight of total egg contents.
2. Analysts and laboratories:
   GC D. C. Holmes and J. O'G. Tatton.
   Laboratory of the Government Chemist, Department of Industry, London.
   JAB Dr J. A. Bogan, Department of Veterinary Pharmacology, University of Glasgow.
   EC Dr G. Hamilton, East Craigs Laboratory, Agricultural Scientific Services, Department of Agriculture and Fisheries for Scotland, Edinburgh.
3. DDE is pp' DDE, the principal metabolite of the insecticide DDT in avian tissues. Most of the DDT ingested by the Peregrine's prey species has been already metabolised to DDE.
4. HEOD is the active ingredient in the insecticide dieldrin and a metabolite of the active ingredient in the insecticide aldrin in avian tissues.
5. Heptachlor epoxide is the metabolite of the insecticide heptachlor in avian tissues.
6. PCBs are the complex of polychlorinated biphenyls.
7. NA = Not analysed (PCBs in all eggs before 1967).
8. Eggs from the same clutch are bracketed together.
9. Egg residue analyses show clearly the decreasing contamination of Peregrines by DDT/DDE after about 1966.
10. Egg residue analyses provide no evidence of decreasing contamination of Peregrines by HEOD since 1963. Egg analysis did not begin in earnest until 1963, by which time the most important restrictions on the use of dieldrin had already begun to take effect. No eggs were ever analysed from the districts hardest hit by the crash (southern England and Wales) and the few Welsh eggs for 1977 were examined when recovery was far advanced. Studies of other birds, especially aquatic species, such as the Heron and Shag, nevertheless pointed to a general decline in environmental contamination by dieldrin in Britain by around 1967. A local upsurge of HEOD residues in 1975–76 is believed to reflect the using-up of dieldrin stocks when the final restrictions on use of this insecticide on cereals were announced.
11. The highest level of HEOD found in a British Peregrin egg is 9·4 ppm, and levels above 6·0 ppm are rare. In the bird itself, a liver concentration of 10 ppm is regarded as potentially lethal. It is likely that, before HEOD reaches a lethal tissue level, Peregrines will cease breeding, so that egg analysis will exclude the more heavily contaminated individuals which continue to occupy territories without producing eggs. Egg analysis is thus of limited value for monitoring contamination of a bird popularion when highly toxic residues are involved.
12. Heptachlor, one of the other widely used and highly toxic cyclodiene insecticides during 1956–65, has virtually disappeared from use.
13. The specimens analysed by the Government Chemist and Monks Wood were part of the pesticide –wildlife studies conducted by the Toxic Chemicals and Wildlife Section of the former Nature Conservancy, and continued since 1974 by the Institute of Terrestrial Ecology (to which Monks Wood Experimental Station now belongs) under contract to the Nature Conservancy Council.

Table 31   443

TABLE 31: *Examples of infections and diseases of the Peregrine*

Organism	Reported effect on Peregrines	References
Ticks *Ixodes arboricola*	Local morbidity and mortality in feee-living nestlings	Schilling *et al.* (1981)
Lice (e.g. *Colpocephalum* spp.)	Occasional morbidity only	Cooper (1978)
Flies (e.g. *Lucilia, Calliphora*)	Occasional infestation of wounds, sometimes fatal	Cooper (1978)
Hippoboscids (e.g. *Ornithomyia avicularia*)	Occasional anaemia, transmission of blood parasites	Cooper (1978)
Mites (e.g. *Ornithonyssus sylviarum*)	Local morbidity and mortality	Cooper (1978)
Nematodes *Serratospiculum* spp.	Occasional mortality: depend for life cycle on presence of intermediate host	Jefferies and Prestt (1966)
Other species e.g. *Capillaria, Ascaridia*	Occasional morbidity and mortality in captivity, sometimes in wild	Ward (1986)
Protozoa *Trichomonas gallinae* ('frounce')	Mortality of young captive birds (no records traced from free-living Peregrines)	Cooper and Petty (1988) Stabler (1969)
Plasmodium relictum ('avian malaria')	Depression and lethargy in capitive birds; role in free-living Peregrines unclear	Remple (1981)
Coccidia	Morbidity and mortality in captivity	Cooper (1978)
Bacteria *Salmonella* spp.	Mortality of captive birds; apparently asymptomatic carriage by other birds; various species of *Salmonella* have been identified in eyries in Germany and may contribute to morbidity or mortality	Sykes *et al.* (1981) Kirkpatrick and Trexler-Myren (1986) Tabken (1972)
Escherichia coli	Occasional morbidity and mortality of captive Peregrines; possible reduction of hatchability in both captive and free-living birds	Cooper (1978)
Mycobacterium avium (avian tuberculosis)	Mortality of captive birds	Lumeij and van Nie (1962)
Mycoplasmata Species uncertain	Isolated but role unclear	Furr *et al.* (1977)

continued overleaf

TABLE 31 (*continued*)

Organism	Reported effect on Peregrines	References
Chlamydia psittaci ('Psittacosis')	Reports of clinical disease rare but organism may be widespread and possibly significant	Fowler *et al.* (1990)
Fungi *Aspergillus fumigatus*	Common cause of mortality in captivity and probably also a frequent terminal condition in free-living birds	Redig (1981)
Candida albicans ('thrush')	Occasional morbidity and mortality of captive Peregrines; role in free-living birds unclear	Redig (1986)
Viruses Avian pox	Morbidity, occasionally mortality, in captive and free-living birds	Cooper (1978)
Falcon Herpesvirus	Mortality in captive birds; role in free-living birds unclear	Graham and Halliwell (1986)
Paramyxovirus ('Newcastle disease')	Morbidity and mortality in captive birds; role in wild not clear	Graham and Halliwell (1986)
Bacterial toxins Botulism	Mortality in free-living birds, usually in association with disease in waterfowl	Halliwell and Graham (1986)

In this table a clear distinction is not always made between effects reported in free-living (wild) as opposed to captive birds. Where necessary the original references should be consulted.
Table prepared by Professor John Cooper.

Index

Scientific equivalents to English names of plants, birds and other vertebrates are given in Appendices 1–3.